D0982603

NEWSWEEK CONDENSED BOOKS

As told to ROBERT SPECHT

_____

DAVID NIVEN

_____

JOHN BAXTER and THOMAS ATKINS

_____

GOLDA MEIR

_____

TISHA
THE STORY OF A YOUNG TEACHER
IN THE ALASKA WILDERNESS

BRING ON THE EMPTY HORSES

THE FIRE CAME BY
THE RIDDLE OF THE
GREAT SIBERIAN EXPLOSION

MY LIFE

NEWSWEEK BOOKS, New York

The original editions of the books in this volume
are published and copyrighted as follows:

*Tisha, The Story of a Young Teacher
in the Alaska Wilderness*
Published by St. Martin's Press
Copyright © 1976 by Robert Specht

Bring on the Empty Horses
Published by G.P. Putnam's Sons
Copyright © 1975 by David Niven

The Fire Came By
Published by Doubleday & Company, Inc.
Copyright © 1976 by John Baxter and Thomas Atkins

My Life
Published by G. P. Putnam's Sons
Copyright © 1975 by Golda Meir

CONTENTS

TISHA

THE STORY OF A YOUNG TEACHER
IN THE ALASKA WILDERNESS

A condensation of the book as told to

ROBERT SPECHT

*"Tisha," as she appears today, holding a copy
of the book that tells the story of her life.*

I arrived in the Forty Mile country of Alaska back in 1927, when I was a prim and proper young lady of nineteen. I'd always been thrilled with the idea of living on a frontier, so when I was offered the job of teaching school in a gold-mining settlement called Chicken, up near the Yukon Territory, I accepted right away.

Green as goose grass and full of lofty ideals, off I went, thinking of myself as a lamp unto the wilderness. The last thing I expected was that the residents of Chicken weren't going to think of me in that way at all.

All that was forty-eight years ago, yet I can still remember how excited I was on the day I set off for Chicken by pack train. It was the final leg of a long journey, and the pack train left from a village called Eagle. . . .

September 4, 1927

CHAPTER 1

Even though it was barely eight o'clock and the sun had just come up, practically the whole town of Eagle had turned out to see the pack train off. Counting the Indians, who'd come down from their fish camp for the dance the previous night, there must have been close to a hundred people gathered around—miners in hip-length boots, old sourdoughs in battered Stetsons, even women and children. I was excited, but I was scared too.

I wasn't afraid of the ninety-mile trip, it was the horse I'd be riding for the next four days that was scaring me. I'd last been on a horse eight years before, when I was living with my grandmother on her farm. I was only eleven then, and Tom was a pretty big horse, but he was so gentle that you could almost curl up on his broad back and go to sleep and you wouldn't fall off. This one was mean.

Blossom was so huge that even if I stood on my toes I wouldn't have been able to see over the saddle, and he was scared and wild-looking. After he caught the sleeve of my jacket once, I made sure to hold the reins close to the bit and keep him at arm's length. But everytime I thought he'd settled down, he'd jerk his head up and nearly pull my arm out of its socket.

". . . And if you have any problems at all," Mrs. Rooney was saying, "write to me and I'll be glad to give you any advice I can." She fingered the cameo brooch on the front of her dress. "And remember what I said—spare the rod and spoil the child. Show those kids right off that you're the teacher and you won't have a bit of trouble."

"I will."

"If you have to smack a couple of them do it."

Somebody went over to Mr. Strong's stable and started to close the doors. I caught a glimpse of the big sled that was in there: a couple of months from now, after the first heavy snowfall, Mr. Strong would be bringing my trunk out on it.

The doors slammed shut and the odor of hay and manure drifted over. And then Mr. Strong was beside us, clearing his throat. Even though it was sunny and comfortable, he was wearing a mackinaw. It was open, and I could see the top button of his long underwear under his flannel shirt.

He was a tall, stoop-shouldered man, and he had such a courtly way about him that if he wore a beard he'd have made me think of Don Quixote. When I'd first met him yesterday his manners had seemed so out of place in this rough country that I thought he was joking and almost laughed. I was glad I didn't, though, because he acted that way with almost everyone. I'd been waiting over two days for this pack train to come in, but when I'd asked him if he could take me to Chicken all he'd said was, "Yes, madam, I can."

"Will you be going soon?" I'd asked him.

"Yes, madam. My pack train leaves for Chicken on the fourth, the fourteenth and the twenty-fourth of each month. I shall, therefore, be leaving tomorrow. Eight a.m. sharp."

"I'd like to go," I'd told him.

"The rent for your horse will be ten dollars per day. That will include your meals along the way and your lodgings. The journey will take four days. I hope that will be satisfactory," Mr. Strong said.

I'd told him it would be fine and that was that.

"If you are ready, madam," he said to me now, "I shall assist you to mount."

I grabbed the saddle horn and he boosted me up. Once I was in the saddle the ground looked pretty far down. Blossom started to dance around and a few people laughed. I thought they were laughing at the trouble I was having trying to get him to stand still, but as soon as he settled down I saw they were laughing at my legs. The saddle was so big and wide that they stuck out like wings.

Mr. Strong shortened the stirrups until I could get my feet into them, but I was still spread out pretty wide.

"When we stop over at my camp in Liberty tonight," he said to me, "I will have a smaller saddle for you." He looked at my clothes skeptically. "Are you sure, madam, you will not reconsider my offer of the coat?" A little earlier, when he saw how I was dressed, he had offered to lend me a coat, saying that the weather was very changeable. But I'd told him I didn't think I'd need it.

"I'm really very comfortable," I said now. "I mean it's such a lovely day."

If I was back in the States I'd have felt ridiculous, but here in Alaska nobody cared how you dressed. I was wearing the jacket of my pink Easter suit, a pair of boy's corduroy knickers I'd bought for the ride, cotton stockings and some old sport brogues. I knew that the flowered hat I'd bought in Portland the past summer would end up crushed if it was put on the pack animals with my other things, so I wore that too. My ensemble was completed by a nickel-plated revolver that a fellow had given me at the dance last night.

Mr. Strong started for the front of the pack train and I looked around. Aside from Mr. Strong's stable and the stables of a couple of other freighters, the schoolhouse was the only other building here at the edge of town. Mrs. Rooney had showed me the inside of it and I was looking forward to teaching in it when I took over from her next year. Made of squared-off logs, it was good and sturdy. I only hoped the schoolhouse I was heading for now would be nice.

Farther up the line of pack animals a few men were rechecking some of the loads, but most people were just gathered around talking.

The Indians stood apart from the whites, and I wondered where they'd spent the night. There were about twenty-five of them, mostly men. Compared to the whites, who were laughing and joking about how much they'd drunk and danced, the Indian men were quiet, just watching what was going on. They looked so serious, all of them, that if I hadn't seen them having such a good time last night, I'd have thought they were angry or resentful. But they were just different from the whites. When they didn't have anything to say they didn't say anything.

I felt kind of sorry for the Indian women, especially the girls. Most of them had changed to moccasins, but a few still had on high heels and bright shawls. In the crisp morning air they looked out of place, their silk stockings full of runs and their makeup all smeared. For all the attention the white men paid them now they might just as well have not existed. It hadn't been that way at the dance. The white men had been pretty free with them then—a little too free. The Indian women hadn't minded it, or the Indian men either, but the white women hadn't liked it at all. Only one or two of the white women had even danced with the Indian men. The rest looked down their noses at them or, like Mrs. Rooney, disliked them outright. "Dark faces all packed full of bones," she complained to me, "you never know what they're thinking."

"Cabaret" Jackson's hatchet face grinned up at me, his Adam's apple looking as though it was going to pop through his skin. One of his eyes was closed and there was some dried blood in his nostrils, but he'd cleaned himself up pretty well and he didn't look too bad.

"Hate to see you leavin' here," he said. "Don't suppose you'd change your mind about what I asked you last night?"

"Thanks, Cab, but I don't think so."

He was the one who'd given me the revolver, telling me that I shouldn't be going into the wilds without a little protection. Last night, before he got too drunk and had a fight, he'd proposed to me, promising he'd give me everything under the sun. He'd been a real gentleman, but as soon as he got drunk he turned mean. In the fight he'd had, he'd beaten the other man bloody and got so wild he tried to bite the man's ear off. The whole thing had made me sick to my stomach.

"Well," he said, "I'll be mushin' out there to Chicken some time after the freeze-up, and I'll just try you again when I do." He grinned. "Take care, Teacher."

At the front of the line Mr. Strong had mounted up. Holding a coiled bullwhip, he wheeled his horse and slapped a few of the animals on the rump. To the accompaniment of whoops and hollers from the crowd, the pack train slowly moved out.

It was easy going for the first couple of miles, the wagon road gently curving through the forest, the only sounds the clatter of the pack animals' cowbells and the clop of their hooves. After a while my backside began to ache a little and I felt some stiffness in my shoulders, but I didn't mind. Blossom wasn't giving me any trouble and it was warm enough so I could open my jacket. It was hard for me to believe this was Alaska. Even though it was only the beginning of September, somehow I'd expected to find snow on the ground and cold weather. So far, it hadn't been much colder than it would·be back in Forest Grove, Oregon, where I'd come from.

The wagon road ended suddenly and turned into a trail that was barely wide enough for one horse to pass through at a time. Trees and buckbrush pressed in on each side. Branches and bushes tore at my jacket, and pulled the threads out. Now I realized why Mr. Strong had offered me the coat.

The farther we went the more uneven the trail became and I kept slipping and sliding all over the saddle. After a while I tried to stop Blossom so that I could get off, but no matter how hard I pulled on the reins he kept going. When I kept it up, he turned and tried to bite my foot.

An hour later we started down a canyon and without warning the sun disappeared and everything was gray and chill. A few minutes later big feathery snowflakes were drifting down and it was like being in the middle of winter. When I finally reached the bottom of the canyon, my teeth were chattering. My hands were so numb I couldn't move my fingers.

The pack train had stopped and so did Blossom. Mr. Strong came riding back, the olive-drab coat over his arm. Leaning over, he helped me on with the coat. "I believe you'll be more comfortable now," he said. "There are mittens in the pockets."

"Could we stop here for a while?"

"I'm afraid not, madam, I have U.S. mail to deliver and we have twenty-five miles to cover before nightfall. I must stay on schedule. We'll have a rest stop at Gravel Gulch."

"How far is that?"

"Seven or eight miles."

When Gravel Gulch came into view I hardly minded that Blossom speeded up, even though it hurt. It was only a few cabins nestled in a gulch, the slopes around them thick with willow and tamarack. Four men and a woman were waiting for us.

The men seemed a little shy when they saw me and went right to the pack animals instead of saying hello. The woman wasn't shy at all. Her name was Mrs. Ross. Short and fat, with jolly red cheeks, she was stuffed into a lumberjack shirt and a pair of Levis rolled up at the bottoms. She

came right up to me, took in my flowered hat and the apparition underneath it and said, "Good Lord, what'na hell happened to you?"

She wasn't expecting an answer and I didn't give her any. "One of you
galoots get this poor thing down from there," she said. A man came over
to me and lifted me out of the saddle as if I was a toy. When he set me
down my knees gave way, and the next thing I knew the woman was practically carrying me into the cabin.

She swabbed my arms and hands with a washcloth and then served up
a delicious lunch of hot bear soup, hot sourdough bread and moose pot
roast.

A half hour later we left Gravel Gulch. The country smoothed out into
gently sweeping hills, and I could sometimes see for hundreds of miles
in every direction. It was all so big that it made me feel as if something exciting was going to happen, yet so quiet and lonely I felt lost in it.

Darkness came slowly after a long twilight, but once the sun was down
it became cold fast. It was past eight o'clock when we reached Liberty,
where we all bedded down in an old sagging cabin.

CHAPTER 2

It was just starting to get light when we finished breakfast and were
ready to go. But this time when Mr. Strong cupped his hands to boost
me into the saddle I was too stiff to raise my foot. He had to lift me. He'd
found a smaller saddle for me as he'd promised, and it helped a lot at first
by not rubbing me where I was raw, but after a while it started new raw
places.

That day Mr. Strong became more friendly. I told him about how I'd
been teaching in Forest Grove Elementary in Oregon when the territorial
commissioner of education visited there last year. "He gave a lecture in
the auditorium about teaching here, and he made it sound so exciting
and adventurous that I made out an application. And here I am."

"Where were you brought up?"

"In Colorado. My father was in the mining business," I said. Somehow
it sounded better than saying he'd just been a coal miner.

"You seem a little young to be out on your own."

"I'm almost twenty," I said.

"You don't look it."

I knew he was going to say that. Just before I'd left Forest Grove I'd

14

gone into a barbershop and had my hair bobbed. I'd figured that since I was going to be teaching somewhere in the wilds, it would be easier to take care of it if it was short. Up to then people always took me for being older than I was, but from then on they kept telling me I looked like a kid.

"I mean no offense by that, madam," he said. "I was twelve when I left home and the experience hasn't hurt me yet."

"I was an old woman compared to you. I was sixteen when I left Colorado and started teaching in Forest Grove."

The two of us having left home early gave us something in common. He didn't stop calling me madam, but I could tell he felt kind of fatherly towards me. All the rest of that day, seeing how badly off I was, he helped me down and let me walk a little even when we weren't going down a steep hill. It meant that the whole pack train had to slow up and I really appreciated it.

From Steel Creek, where we spent the second night, the going was easier and I began to feel better.

All during the trip down the Yukon I'd kept wondering what it was that made this country so different from what I'd known so far. I'd thought it was the bigness, but it was also the rawness. Back in Oregon the trees billowed out fat and heavy even at this time of year. Here they were tattered, leaner and tougher—the tall spruce looking like huge giants ready for a scrap. Everything was that way, like the thick groves of willow that some animal had chewed half up, stripping the bark from them. They just kept on growing anyway, unkillable. Even the clouds seemed to move faster. The air was all charged up, as if something was going to happen.

I'd have thought that with all the noise the cowbells were making, we wouldn't see hide nor hair of any wild animals, but it was just the opposite. The noise made them curious, and every so often I'd look off and see something watching us. Once it was a whole bunch of foxes. They were frisking on a shelf when we came on them, two blues, a couple of blacks and one cross fox. They just stared at us as nervy as you please, then went right back to what they were doing.

Soon a settlement appeared in the distance—a line of about fifteen cabins set back from the banks of the Forty Mile River. A few small boats were pulled up on the bank and there were some food caches standing on poles in back of the cabins.

"An Indian village," Mr. Strong said. "We'll stop there."

I'd seen a couple of Indian villages from the riverboat coming down the Yukon, but never close up. Before that I hadn't even known there'd be Indians in Alaska. I thought there'd be Eskimos. This village looked so picturesque I couldn't wait to get there.

But when we drew near I was shocked. It was a shanty-town, worse than any of the worst sections I'd seen in all the coal towns I'd lived in. There might have been three or four decent-looking places, but the rest were hovels, sway-backed cabins and sagging shacks that were patched with everything the owners could get their hands on—tarpaper, rotting planks, scraps of galvanized iron, even old animal hides. Rusting tin cans, rags, paper, shreds of hide, bottles and fishbones littered the ground. There was no breeze blowing and the stench that hung over everything was nauseating.

As we rode in people stared at us from doorways. Many dogs, half starved and chained to stakes, snarled and leaped at us as we went by. They were jerked back and landed in their own dung. A few children kept pace with us, giving the horses plenty of room. Barefoot and in rags, noses running, they were having a good time. One little boy, with open running sores all over his head, tripped over one of the dogs and barely avoided being bitten. Another boy had the same kind of sores all over his neck. They were from tuberculosis, I found out later.

Mr. Strong seemed to know everybody, greeting a few people by their first name. " *Skooltrai* here?" he asked.

The woman nodded and at almost the same time the door to one house opened. An Indian and a white girl came out, and no two people could have looked more different than they did. Maybe it was because the girl was so beautiful, but I thought the Indian was one of the ugliest men I'd ever seen. He was tall and thin, the skin over his cheekbones drawn so tight that it glistened, and his eyes were small and set wide apart. His shirt was open at the throat and his neck looked as though somebody had once wound barbed wire around it, it was so covered with scars.

They were followed by a little boy. He must have been about eight years old and you could see he was part white. Like the other kids, he was as skinny as a rail.

"Good day, Miss Winters," Mr. Strong called to the girl. Up to then, he'd been smiling and friendly with everybody, but he didn't look friendly now. "This young lady is bound for Chicken," he went on, "and she needs a short rest. I would appreciate it if you would accommodate her."

The girl didn't act any friendlier to him than he did to her, but she came right over to me.

"I'm Cathy Winters," she said, after I was able to stand by myself.

"Thanks," I said. "I'm Anne Hobbs."

She indicated the tall Indian beside her. "This is Titus Paul."

I told him I was glad to meet him, but he didn't return the compliment.

Her place was less than half the size I'd thought it was from the outside, one dingy room with a cracked brown linoleum on the floor and a tiny bedroom. She helped me off with my coat and I plopped down on a battered couch.

She set about getting a basin and a washcloth and I just sat back and watched her move around. She had on a dress that was as beautiful as her figure, some kind of homespun embroidered with Indian designs around the hem and the half-length sleeves. It was tied with a leather thong at the waist.

The little boy came in then and put her mail on the counter.

"This is Chuck," Cathy said, taking a pitcher and dipping it in a barrel of water. "He'll be keeping you company the rest of the way. Chuck, I'd like you to meet Miss Hobbs."

"Please . . . to . . . meet you," he said gravely.

"I'm pleased to meet you too," I said.

She told him to run along and he went out, grateful to get away.

After I washed up, I felt a little better, and over a cup of coffee I found out why her place was so small. She was the schoolteacher here and these were her living quarters. The rest of the house was the schoolroom. I admired her. She didn't have much of a place, but she'd certainly made it comfortable. There were books all over and all kinds of Indian articles on the walls—a quiver full of arrows, bows, a couple of wooden ceremonial masks and dozens of other things.

"Are you here all alone?" I asked her.

"Sure." She must have realized what I was thinking because she said, "I know how you feel. I felt the same way when I first came. But there's nothing to be afraid of here. If you like, I'll show you around. You should walk a little anyway—get the kinks out."

Outside, Mr. Strong had untied a badly sagging load on one of the animals and laid the contents out on the ground. He and the Indians who'd ordered stuff were stooped around it. They had their money ready as he handed them their goods: a frying pan for one, kerosene lantern for another, canned milk, a teapot. The others just looked on.

The onlookers made way for Cathy and me when we came out, and Cathy introduced me to them in their own language. I caught the words "skooltrai" and "Chicken" as she explained who I was.

Cathy took me from one end of the village to the other. There wasn't much to see, but the more she showed me of it the worse I felt. I'd always thought of Indians who lived in the wilds as being strong, proud people able to live off the land, but here there were up to seven and eight people huddled in small one-room cabins. Through a couple of open doors I could see that except for some crude bunk beds, a stove and a few chairs and boxes, most of them were bare.

I couldn't understand it. "Why do they live this way?"

"It's not an easy question to answer. The main thing is not to judge what you see here by white standards. Most of these people didn't meet whites until about thirty or forty years ago. Up to then they were living in the Stone Age."

"What kind of Indians are they?" I asked her.

"Athapascans. That's the general designation for all the Indians up here. Then that's broken down into tribes. These people are Kutchins."

On the way back we passed a huge caldron boiling over an open fire. The odor from whatever was bubbling around in it was awful. An old crone, her spindly legs bowed so badly they looked like they were going to snap, was trying to get something out with a wooden spoon. But she was too short and couldn't reach over without almost falling in. Cathy said something to her in Indian, took the spoon and tin enamel plate from her and scooped out some pieces of salmon. When she handed it back the old woman took it gratefully. She had only a couple of teeth in her mouth and two lines of tobacco juice ran down each side of her chin.

"What's that cooking in there?" I said.

"Fish heads, animal guts, rice." The old woman sat down on the ground and began eating. "That's Lame Sarah. That little boy who's going along with you—Chuck—he's been living with her. Thank God he's getting out of here."

When we were ready to leave, the old woman and Chuck were standing by one of the mules, which had an old beat-up saddle on it. She hugged him to her, murmuring endearments. He was only half listening, though. His eyes were on the mule and he looked worried. It towered over him the way Blossom did over me, and I knew exactly what was on his mind.

"Up we go, Chuck," Cathy said to him. She tried to lift him into the saddle, but he pulled away from her. "No!" he yelled. Cathy kneeled down in front of him. "Chuck, if you want to see your mother you're going to have to ride that mule."

Mr. Strong came over and asked what the matter was.

"He's a little afraid to get on," I said.

"Is that right," he said. Without another word he grabbed the back of Chuck's mackinaw, lifted him bodily and plunked him down on the mule's back. "You stay put," he warned him, "savvy?"

Terrorized, Chuck didn't answer, but he looked as though he were about to cry.

"Do me a favor, Anne," Cathy said. She tossed her head in Mr. Strong's direction. "For all he cares, Chuck is just another piece of baggage—maybe less. Look after him, will you? He's hardly even gone further than a few miles out of this village and he'll be scared to death."

"I'll look after him."

The pack train moved out then, and Chuck made out all right as long as we stuck to the river bank. But a few seconds later his mule jumped over a dead tree and he went tumbling off. By the time I was able to get Blossom to stand still long enough to get off, Chuck had thrown up and was crying.

I led him over to the tree, sat down with him and put an arm around him.

Mr. Strong made his way back to us a few minutes later leading both Blossom and the mule.

"He fell off," I said.

Mr. Strong waited until he was able to stop crying, then he said, "Chuck, I think maybe you go back home, huh?"

Chuck looked stricken. "You no want me?"

"You fall off mule. No can ride. We ride far, sleep tonight long distance from here, ride tomorrow. Too tough for you."

"I ride," Chuck promised. "You take me I no fall down no more."

Mr. Strong raised a finger. "You fall once more you go home, savvy?"

Somehow we made it to the next rest stop. We had a half hour before we were to leave and I spent part of it showing Chuck how to ride the mule. By the time we were ready to go, he was having fun. "Giddap, mool," he said, and we were off.

Our next overnight stop was the O'Shaughnessy roadhouse. It was run by a pleasant Irishman with a thick accent. Since I was a woman he gave up his bedroom, and I shared his bed with his wife, a plump Indian woman who saw to it that Chuck was well fed and bedded down in a warm sleeping bag in our room. I tucked him in and was going out when he called to me. "Tisha . . . You talk me?"

He wanted company. He was scared being in a strange place. I sat down on the sleeping bag. "I bet you'll be glad to see your mother."

"Oh yiss," he said.

"She must be very nice."

"She beyoodeeful, Tisha—like you."

"I'll bet. Is your father in Chicken too?"

19

"Yiss."

"What kind of a man is he?"

"Big man," he said. "Got plenty guns, lotsa things. Got big glass eyes see far." He curled both his fists in front of hs eyes to make binoculars. "I no like him," he added.

"Why not?"

"He no like me and Et'el."

"Is Ethel your sister?"

"Mmm . . . You got nice school?" he asked drowsily.

"I don't know. I haven't seen it yet."

"You let me come?"

"Sure. Do you like school?"

"Like too much," he said enthusiastically. "School plenty warm. Big. Miss Wintuhs make good grub for kids. You make good grub you school?"

"I never have, but I probably could. What do you like to eat?"

He didn't answer. He'd fallen asleep.

CHAPTER 3

We were up at five the next morning, the fourth and last day of the journey, and on our way an hour after a hearty breakfast.

Right from the start Chuck was lively as a squirrel, riding that mule as though he'd done it all his life. In fact a couple of times he gave me a turn, slapping the mule to make him jog and pretty near falling off in the process.

Around noon, Mr. Strong stopped the pack train as we were making our way through a dense growth of cottonwood. The cowbells that had been clanking all the way down the line were quiet all of a sudden, and all I could hear were the merry waters of the meandering creek we'd been crossing and recrossing for a while.

"There it is, madam," Mr. Strong said. "That is Chicken."

I could barely make it out through the trees—a settlement about a mile away and a little below us. It was too far to really see what it was like.

"If you don't mind, Mr. Strong, I'd like to change my clothes."

"What is the matter with what you have on?"

"I'd feel more comfortable if I were more properly dressed."

He was nice about it, unpacked the suitcase I asked for and brought it to the edge of the creek, where I washed up.

After I finished I put the army coat back on and brought my suitcase back. I'd changed into a long black skirt, cotton stockings and white blouse. "You look quite nice, madam," Mr. Strong said gallantly.

I looked off at the settlement, my stomach doing flip-flops. This is it, I thought. I'm almost there. I'd come to a far place, just as my Grandmother Hobbs used to tell me I would. When I was a little girl back in Colorado I used to hate the ugly mining towns I lived in. I felt sure I'd be living in them forever, but Granny said no I wouldn't and she'd been right.

"You be a teacher, Annie," she used to tell me, "an' you can go anywhere in the world you want."

When I thought about her now I could see her as clearly as if she were right in front of me. She wasn't like anybody else in our whole family. The rest of us were light skinned and had blue or gray eyes like mine and we were all very serious most of the time. But not Granny. She was a full-blooded Kentuck Indian and her face had been brown and broad, with wonderful black eyes that usually sparkled and laughed. If it hadn't been for her I couldn't think of what might have happened to me.

My father had never cared anything about me, nor my mother either for that matter, but Granny had adored me. Every time my father lost his job or left the house I was sent to live with her, and I couldn't wait to get there. She had a little farm in Deepwater, Missouri, that had hardly any kind of a house on it at all, just a little ramshackle place in the backlands, but I thought it was wonderful. It made me smile just to think about it now.

"Madam?" Mr. Strong had finished checking the animals over and had mounted up again. "I asked you if you are ready."

"Yes," I said, "I am."

As we moved forward I thought of that last morning I'd spent with Granny. When it was close to train time a neighboring woman had ridden into the yard with a buckboard. Granny had gone as far as the main road with us, then we hugged each other good-bye. She'd felt like a strong little bird.

As the buckboard drove off and I turned around to see her waving to me I had to fight to hold in the tears. "Don't worry," the driver said, "you'll be back some day."

I hadn't answered her, not knowing how to explain that I wasn't crying because I was going away, but my grandmother had looked so small and alone as she stood in the middle of the road gently waving good-bye. I'd never seen her again after that. She'd died during the first year I'd been teaching. I hadn't found out about it until three weeks later.

"You'd best keep a tight rein on him, madam," Mr. Strong was saying. As soon as we'd broken into the open, the pack train speeded up and so did Blossom. I pulled back on the reins.

We'd descended into a small level valley. About a quarter of a mile ahead were maybe twenty-five or thirty buildings strung along the same side of the creek we were on.

"Is that all of it?"

"Just about."

I'd imagined it would be something like Eagle—a town—but from this distance it looked more like the Indian village we'd gone through. It couldn't have been built in a better place, though, set down snug on the valley floor. Low hills ringed the valley, rolling away from it into a blue haze of high mountain peaks. The creek was deep and narrow here, spilling down from the slope behind us. It got wider as it went, and right smack in the middle of the settlement a wooden bridge arched across it.

"What do you think of it?"

"It looks wonderful," I said.

It wasn't anything like the Indian village at all. The street between the creek and settlement was wide, with patches of late grass here and there, no tin cans, no trash. I could see vegetable gardens in a few backyards, along with dog kennels and stacks of corded wood. As soon as we neared the edge of the place the crowd started calling and waving.

The whole place was about three city blocks long, the post office right in the middle, opposite the wooden bridge. The first couple of cabins were in bad shape, one just a rotted skeleton, roof gone and weeds spilling out the door, the others all boarded up. As far as I could make out, a few others down the line weren't lived in either. The ones that were lived in, though, were solid and sturdy, with traps, harness, and washtubs hanging from posts and railings.

As we came to the edge of the crowd Chuck dismounted and ran to his mother—a slight dark Indian woman who had a little girl by the hand. From the quick glimpse I caught of her as she kneeled down to hug him she looked like a beauty.

I kept smiling and getting smiles in return. But what with everything else that had gone wrong on this famous trip, I should have known I wasn't going to make a dignified entrance. In dismounting I lost my footing and the next thing I knew I was sitting in the mud and everybody was staring down at me.

Two old men helped me up and fussed around trying to get some of the mud off me until they were pushed aside by a big burly woman.

"Awright, awright, for Chrissake. Leave 'er alone before you wind up killin' 'er. I'm Angela Barrett," she announced. "You're the new school-mom, I take it. What's yer moniker?"

I told her, and she led me over to another woman who was wearing a long navy blue coat buttoned up to the neck. She had a broken nose. "She's the new schoolmom, awright," Angela said to the woman.

"I'm Maggie Carew," the woman said. "What's your name, honey?"

"Anne Hobbs." My skirt was clinging in back of me and I could feel water trickling down my legs.

"Let's get you over to the schoolhouse."

When we stepped up onto the porch of the frame building, Angela Barrett moved to the closer of two doors. It was studded with mean-looking nails that stuck out about three inches. "This here's the schoolroom," she said, opening it. "The other door there's to your quarters. Watch out for them nails."

As I followed her in my heart sank. The room was big, but it was in a shambles. A few assorted tables and chairs were piled in one corner, and some boxes in yet another corner held old books and papers. Dust and dirt covered the buckled plank flooring. Light came in through windows fogged with smoke and grime.

The other room was neater, the same size as the schoolroom, but except for a brass bed that had no mattress, two chairs, and a big pot-bellied stove, it was empty.

"How do you like 'er?" Angela Barrett asked. She must have weighed two hundred pounds and she towered over me. I tried to think of something nice to say.

"It's a good big room."

"Glad you feel that way," Angela said. "You're the one's gonna be livin' in it."

"Do you think it will take much time to get it ready?"

"What do you mean ready?" Angela asked. "It's ready now."

Both women were staring at me as if there was something wrong with me. I was almost afraid to ask the next question. "Don't I have to have a mattress?" I said. "Or blankets, or a table?"

It took a moment before they seemed to realize that I had a point.

"Where'na hell'd it all go?" Angela said, as if she'd turned her back for a minute and somebody had snatched everything away. "It's your fault, Maggie, you're the school janitor. It's your responsibility."

"When there's no school there's no janitor," Maggie said tartly, "and there ain't been a school here in well over a year."

"What are we gonna do?" Angela said.

Maggie thought for a minute. "Come on," she said finally.

Angela and I followed her outside. "We got a problem that needs everybody's attention. This is Anne Hobbs, our new teacher," she said to the crowd, "and she needs some help. Some of you mutts have borrowed everything there is in the teacher's quarters. There's nothin' left in there and I mean nothin'. I ain't sayin' who took what, but it's got to be packed back here pronto. The poor girl's got an empty cabin."

"What do you need, Miss?" a tall good-looking man asked. He was trying on a heavy fleece-lined jacket he must have ordered.

"Just about everything."

"I've got a couple of good Hudson Bay blankets I can spare."

Angela Barrett snorted. "Leave it to Joe. Gives you a couple of blankets one day, tryin' to climb under 'em the next."

"How about the rest of you?" Maggie said.

After that the offers came thick and fast—a broom and pan, a rocking chair, a wash boiler and a dozen other items. One man said he'd taken the chifforobe and would return it. Everybody got into the spirit of the thing, telling me not to worry, they'd take care of me.

The men were as good as their word. While I kept busy cleaning and scrubbing up the place the rest of the day, everybody kept trooping in carrying things. Within a few hours I not only had a firm straw mattress for the bed, but also a blanket, a pillow, a table and some chairs. Someone even thought to bring a water barrel. My prize possession was a wood-burning cookstove. It took four men to carry it in, and it was a beauty. Black wrought iron with shining nickel-plated fittings, it had hardly been used. All I needed was a stovepipe and I could start cooking.

I didn't even have to clean the place alone. Five of my pupils showed up to help. The three Vaughn girls were first—Elvira, Evelyn and Eleanor. Then Maggie Carew's two children came over. While we were working the man who'd promised me the blankets rode up. "I'm Joe Temple," he said when he came in. The two blankets he'd brought were almost new. I offered to pay him for them, but he said forget it. "Use them for as long as you like."

He was good-looking and he knew it. He was too old for me—I figured he was about thirty-two or thirty-three—but I could have thought of half a dozen teachers in Forest Grove that would have taken to him right away. I'd unpacked all my dresses and hung them wherever I could find a nail. "I haven't been Outside in a couple of years," he said, looking at them, "but I thought they were wearing dresses shorter than that."

"They are. I guess I'm pretty conservative."

"Not all the time, I hope." I didn't know how to take that so I didn't say anything. "You'll have to let me take you out to dinner," he said.

"I didn't see any restaurant signs coming in."

"Right down the street—Maggie's roadhouse. She's the best cook in town."

"Maybe after I get settled."

"How about tomorrow night? I won't bite you."

"All right, you're on."

"See you around six," he said, going out. "I'll go over and tell Maggie now."

Maggie Carew came by a little before dark and sent the children home. "Place looks a lot better," she said.

"Thanks to you. I appreciate your helping me."

"Don't mention it. Joe Temple tells me you're comin' over the roadhouse with him tomorrow night. Fast worker, that one," she said admiringly.

"What does he do?"

"Mines, like everyone else. Damn good miner too. Got a college education to boot. Do 'im good to go out with a white woman for a change. You hungry?"

"Starved."

"Come on over the roadhouse when you're ready and I'll fix you some supper. On the house."

"Thanks, but Mr. Strong said he'll be coming back with some food and I was to wait for him."

As she went out I asked her what all the nails in the doors were for.

"Bear," she answered. "Last teacher here threw a fit when one came sniffin' at the door one day. I'd have'm hammered down if I was you. Kids might hurt themselves."

Alone, I sat down on the bed and looked the room over. It needed a lot of work. The walls were just rough planks with canvas stretched over them like wallpaper, and the canvas was peeling in places. But I didn't care. This was the first place I'd ever had to myself. Right now, with everything piled all over, it looked like a second hand store, but when I fixed it up it would look nicer even than Cathy Winters' place.

It was getting chilly, drafts coming in from the spaces around the molding. I went over to check the potbellied stove. Opening the door, I saw that the wood was just embers now. I tried to start it up again, but I didn't have any kindling. I felt lonely all of a sudden.

Then I heard footsteps outside. I knew they didn't belong to Mr. Strong. He'd gone to make some deliveries on some outlying creeks and I'd have heard his horses. Then there was a soft knock at the door.

Grabbing for my nickel-plated revolver, I stayed still, hoping whoever it was would go away. When the knock came a second time, I decided that whoever was out there could get in just by turning the doorknob anyway. "Come in," I said, "but be careful."

The chair I'd left in front of the door slid forward and I could just make out a dark man with thick black hair staring at me from the porch. As soon as he saw the gun he raised his hands. He was nervous, but he smiled. He was darker than a Spaniard, and his teeth looked deadly white.

"Did you come to see me?" I asked him.

He stayed at the threshold and kept his hands up. "My mother sent me over to see if you'd like to have supper with us."

As soon as he said that I realized how silly I was being.

"Can I put my hands down?"

I nodded yes.

"I'm sorry I scared you. My father said you came in with the pack train today, and my mother thought this being your first night, you wouldn't be set up to cook. She thought maybe you'd like to eat with us."

"Oh," I said again. "That's awfully nice of her, but I better not. Mr. Strong is coming back soon and he'll be bringing dinner with him."

He looked uncomfortable. "Do you live here in the settlement?" I asked him finally.

"No, a little further up Chicken Creek," he said.

I tried to think of something else to say, but for the life of me I couldn't.

"I guess I better be going." He said good-bye and closed the door before I could even think to ask him his name.

"That was young Fred Purdy," Mr. Strong said when he finally came back. He seemed pleased that I hadn't accepted the invitation. Later, as we were finishing the cold chicken he had brought, he smiled when I mentioned how I'd held the gun on Fred.

"You'd have been more than safe with him. Fred undoubtedly will never amount to anything, but he is a fine young fellow . . ."

"Why won't he ever amount to anything?"

"Couldn't you see? He's a half-breed. Mother's Eskimo, father's white."

"He seemed very nice."

"He is. Smart too. The whole family is as good as they come."

"Then why won't he ever amount to anything?"

He got up and began to collect the plates. "I told you," he said patiently, "he's a breed—a product of race mixture. That's what happens when you mix races. I've seen it all my life—seen it in the South, see it here. It's always the same—the offspring have to suffer."

He made it sound as if anybody who wasn't all white had some kind of a disease. It kind of disappointed me in him a little. I wondered what he'd think of me if he knew my grandmother had been Indian.

"What is Chuck's father like?" I asked him, changing the subject.

"Joe? Good miner, good trapper. You can bet your bottom dollar he regrets ever having involved himself with a native woman."

"Joe Temple is Chuck's father?"

"Why do you look surprised?"

"He's supposed to take me to dinner tomorrow night."

"Well, it's nothing for you to be concerned about. Mr. Temple is a gentleman and he will treat you like a lady."

"But he's married."

"No, he is not and I'm sure he thanks God for it."

Married or not, I still felt funny about going out with him.

Before Mr. Strong left I knew just about everything there was to know about everyone here. As far as the Purdys were concerned, he respected Mr. Purdy even though he felt he'd lowered himself by marrying an Eskimo woman. He advised me to act towards them the way he did himself—"the way you'd act towards anybody who abides by the law no matter what their color is . . . You know what I mean, just about the same way you'd act towards niggers."

CHAPTER 4

After Mr. Strong left I started to think about the things Lester Henderson had told me when he interviewed me in Juneau. He was the commissioner of education for the whole territory and when I told him I was worried because I'd never taught in a one-room schoolhouse, he'd told me not to be.

"It'll be much easier than you think," he'd gone on. "I doubt that you'll have many more than ten pupils, and I know you'll be able to handle them. What does concern me a little is your age. May I be frank with you?"

"Of course."

"You're just about one of the youngest teachers I've ever sent into the' bush. Ordinarily I'd place you here in Juneau first, or some other more well-populated place. The only reason I haven't is that it's not easy to find qualified people who will go into the bush. Does that surprise you?"

"Yes." I really was surprised. "When you lectured at my school I figured you'd be swamped with applications."

"Well I'm not. I hope that doesn't make you less enthusiastic."

"Not at all."

"Good. You see, I fought hard to get these territorial schools established. I believe that where there is even one child who needs schooling— not ten as the law says there must be—there should be a school for him. What I'm trying to say, Miss Hobbs, is that education is so important to me that despite my misgivings about sending a nineteen-year-old chee- chako into the bush country, I'm going to send you anyway."

"A cheechako is a greenhorn, isn't it?"

"The greenest. You've done some reading about Alaska, I see . . ." He paused, then went on. "Before you leave this office I'd like to give you a bit of advice. I have the feeling that you are a pretty tolerant young lady— young enough to be open to new ideas. Where you're going you'll find that most people are not. They have their own code and they don't take to anybody who tries to go against that code or change it. In short, I hope you're not going into this job with, well . . . shall I say missionary zeal?"

"I don't think so," I said, but I'd gotten all red. More than once I'd imagined the smiles on the faces of hardy backwoods parents as their chil- dren came home from my log-cabin school brimming over with the learn- ing I'd given them.

We talked a while longer and he shook my hand warmly before I left. "I want to hear from you," he said, "and I don't mean only in your regular monthly report. Write to me anytime you need help or advice. If there's anything I can do for you, let me know immediately."

He'd meant it, I knew, and it made me feel good even now. But now that I was here I was more worried than ever about being able to handle the job. Teaching in Forest Grove, there was a system, a time for study, for recess, for lunch, for auditorium, for everything. Here I didn't even have a register, or report cards. I wondered what I would do if I couldn't control the class.

The more I thought about it the worse I felt. All I had was a high- school education. I knew my subject matter pretty well, but suppose a couple of the children were smarter in some subjects than I was? I didn't even have a library I could go to. Suddenly the whole idea of coming here seemed like a mistake. I was going to fall on my face, I was sure of it.

The next morning Mr. Strong took me over to his store, a small log building about five cabins away.

The store was crowded with canvas parkas, snow shoes, animal traps, overalls and long underwear, furs and hanging slabs of bacon.

Looking the shelves over, I felt a lot better. There was everything here, even tins of butter. Inside of a few minutes, Mr. Strong and I had loaded up two sacks with canned goods, cereal, flour, sugar and other staples and then he gave me the key to the store, something he said he'd never done with anyone else. I was to take what I wanted as I needed it, and we'd settle up once a month. In return if anyone wanted anything while he was away I would give it out and keep a record of what was bought.

By mid-morning I was working in the schoolroom when I heard footsteps on the porch. It was Fred Purdy and what I thought at first were two younger sisters with him. Only one of them was his sister, though. The other was his mother. She was even smaller than Granny Hobbs, and cute. She was Eskimo for sure—round dark face, wide mouth and strong uneven teeth. She just seemed to light up when she saw me and I liked her right off.

"Ah, the teasher," she said. "I am so happy to meet you. I am Mrs. Purdy, and this is my daughter, Isabelle."

She put a hand out and it felt small and capable. "My son Frayd have tell me how pretty you are," she said after I introduced myself. "Before he say only lynx is pretty. Now I see for myself. Indeed, you are very lovely."

When I invited them in she complimented me on how much I'd done with the cabin.

"Indeed, Ahnne," Mrs. Purdy said, "there still is mush work to do in this place." She grew serious. "You cannot live here in such . . ."

Fred supplied the word. "Conditions."

"Conditions, yes. Thank you, Frayd."

"Do you really think it's so bad?"

"It is not terreebul, yet it is not good. There are many things to do here." She pointed to the baseboard where light was coming in. "This must be fixed or in winter you will freeze to the death." She reeled off all the other things that had to be fixed—sagging shelves, loose floorboards, crippled tables in the schoolroom.

"You will work here," she said to Fred, "and Father will do your chores at home."

Fred grinned. "Yes, boss."

Before they left Mrs. Purdy asked me when I'd like to come to supper and we made it for the next night.

A couple of hours later Fred came back driving a wagon that looked like a long thin buckboard. It had a load of boards on it and a big tool box.

We were soon gabbing about everything under the sun, from the Marines in Nicaragua to Lindbergh's trip across the Atlantic. I told him I was surprised he knew so much about what was going on in the world.

"One thing everybody does plenty of around here is read," he said. "There's not much else to do at night."

By noontime he'd connected a stovepipe to the cookstove and run it up through the roof. After we had a fire going in it I made lunch for the two of us—canned ham and sweet potatoes. "There has to be something else people do here at night besides read," I said while we were eating.

"Every other Friday night there's a dance. We've been having them at the roadhouse, but as soon as the schoolroom's in shape we'll have them there."

"When will the first one be?"

"You call it. You're the teacher."

We decided on a week from the following Friday.

While we worked people kept dropping by to lend me more things they thought I might need, a kettle, some spoons and knives, even an old encyclopedia. I told Fred that I knew people in Alaska were hospitable, but I hadn't expected it to be like this.

"Everybody wants to do what they can to make you stay," he said.

"Why should they think I won't?"

"For the same reason the teacher who was here last didn't. This is tough country, especially for a cheechako."

"When do I stop being a cheechako and become an Alaskan?"

"Maybe by the time the river goes out in the spring."

"What do you mean—maybe?"

"Well," he said, "some people never really become Alaskans. They never get to like it the way it is. They just tolerate it."

"You'll think I'll make it?"

"No reason why you shouldn't. Just make sure you've got good footgear and plenty of warm clothes—and take people's advice."

"When they give it to you, you mean. Up to now I keep finding things out hit and miss."

"That's the way it is. If somebody tells you something you have to listen the first time. They won't tell you twice. They'll let you find out for yourself."

We kept working all day and he didn't go home until a little before Joe showed up.

There wasn't anybody else in the roadhouse except for Maggie and her family, so Joe and I had the place to ourselves. The boiled moose tongue she made was delicious, and while we ate I found out that Joe had gone to Washington State University. He'd come to Alaska in 1920, right after he got out of the Army. After we finished eating, Maggie and her husband sat down with us while her two little boys sat at another table listening.

"Heard you dropped in for a visit with Cathy Winters," Maggie said. "Did you see that Indian buck she's living with?"

"I just saw him for a second," I said. "I wasn't there for very long."

"She's one a them communists," Maggie said, "—believes in free love an' all that. She won't be around much longer. Comes spring they'll send her Outside on the first water—kick 'er right up the Yukon. How's the Purdy kid comin' along fixin' your place up?"

"Fine. It won't look like the same place when he's done."

"He's a good kid for a half-breed," she said.

"Mr. Strong didn't seem to think too much of him, or his family for that matter."

"Mr. Strong's a little old-fashioned," Joe said to me. "The last I heard he was trying to get the town council in Eagle to pass a law saying the Indians had to be out of there by sundown."

"Who says that's a bad idea?" Mr. Carew asked. "I'm no crazier about siwashes than he is. Half-breeds either for that matter."

While we were talking Mr. Vaughn came in. After Mrs. Carew poured him a cup of coffee he just sat and listened for a while. Finally he asked me what kind of teaching I was going to do.

"I'll teach the best way I know how, I guess. Arithmetic and reading are important, but there are other things too. Literature and poetry. Civics, music."

"Sounds pretty fancy to me," Mr. Vaughn said.

"Hey, give her a chance, will you?" Joe said. "She hasn't even started yet."

"What's wrong with us being interested?" Mr. Vaughn said. "That's why we have a school board."

"I'm glad you are," I said. "Does the school board meet very often?"

"When we think it's necessary," Mr. Vaughn answered. "We'll let you know when we think we should have a meeting."

A little while later Joe walked me back to my place. It was so misty you could hardly see three cabins ahead.

"What's a sy-wash?" I asked him.

"Siwash? An Indian."

"That's what I thought. Is it an Indian word?"

"French. *Sauvage.* Savage. The old-timers weren't too finicky about their accent."

He came in with me and built up the fire in the stove. I thanked him for the supper.

"My pleasure," he said. "We'll have to get together again soon."

"I'll tell you the truth, Joe. I feel a little funny about going out with you."

"Why?" He saw I was embarrassed. "I see . . . Mary Angus?"

"I guess so."

"Don't let that worry you. We split the blanket a while back."

We dropped the subject and after a couple of minutes he left.

The next day while Fred and I were working I asked him about Joe and Mary.

"It's pretty much of an old story," he said. "Mary lived in the Indian village and Joe was doing some mining near by. They fell in love and took up housekeeping. They were like man and wife for a long time until they finally broke up about a year ago. Then a few months ago Mary came out to be with him. I don't think he really wanted her to, but she's still in love with him, so she did."

"Where does she live?"

"About a half-mile from here, on the way to my house."

Later on we stopped off at her cabin when Fred took me over to his house. He'd said it was just an old line shack, a place put up by a trapper to stay in overnight as he moved along his trapline, so I hadn't expected it to be much. But it was awful—an old weathered shack that looked as if one good wind would blow it right over. A stovepipe leaned out of the roof and a couple of broken window panes had rags stuffed in them.

Mary Angus was out in front sawing some wood, and when she turned around it was hard for me to believe she was the same woman I'd glimpsed a few days ago. Although she was probably in her mid-twenties, she was old and tired. Her face was pock-marked and there were dark circles under her eyes. She was flushed and perspiring from the work she'd been doing.

"I'm glad to meet you," I said. "Is Chuck around?"

"In cabin. He sick."

"Can I say hello to him?"

She gave Fred a questioning look and he nodded slightly. Later he told me that white people didn't usually go into Indians' cabins, at least not white women.

Inside, the odor was so bad I almost gagged. The floor was dirt, and Chuck was lying on some kind of fur robe, a couple of dirty blankets pulled over him. The small Yukon stove was going full blast and there was some gray stew bubbling in a coffee can on top of it. An oil lamp on a shelf gave off a faint yellow light. It was a nightmare, the smell from a slop jar so foul I had to breathe through my mouth. Chuck had a cold. I stooped down alongside him.

"How are you feeling?" I asked him.

"Bad sick," he murmured.

"You take care of yourself," I said. "I'll see you in school when you're better."

He didn't answer. He wasn't in any shape to be interested in me, school, or anything else. I went outside so furious at Joe Temple I wanted to scream.

"How can he let them live like that?" I asked Fred when we went on. "Can't he help them out at all?"

"He probably would if Mary would go back to the Indian village," Fred said.

"Couldn't he at least move her into one of those empty cabins in the settlement? A couple of them are ten times better than that shack."

"The people there don't want her."

"Fred, that's inhuman. Joe lived with that woman. Those are his children. It's all wrong."

"There's nothing anybody can do about it."

"There has to be."

"What Joe does is his business—his and Mary's. That's the way it is."

He didn't seem to want to talk about it, so I didn't say anything more, but I was a little disappointed in him for saying something like that.

His own house was beautiful, a big log cabin that was built on a knoll. A few outbuildings were around it, and telescoping out from the rear of it were a couple of smaller cabins.

It was a nice evening, with everybody talkative and good-humored—and a delicious dinner to boot. The only one who didn't have much to say was Fred's father. The only time he really said anything was when I asked him where he was from. "New England," he said. Then, as if he didn't want me to ask any more questions, he asked me where I was from. I told him, and that ended the conversation between us. Right after dinner he excused himself and went into the next room. For the rest of the evening I could see him through the curtained doorway, working on a crystal radio he was making.

CHAPTER 5

School was supposed to start at nine, but by a quarter to they were all outside, so with the oldest boy helping me, I ran the flag up to the top of the pole and then we all said the Pledge of Allegiance.

Once we were in the schoolroom I had stage fright. For a full minute the whole class stared at me silently and, completely tongue-tied, I stared back at them. The only sound was everybody's breathing and the squeak of the floorboards.

"How do you like the schoolroom?" I finally managed to croak.

"Real spiffy," Jimmy Carew said. He and his little brother and the Vaughn girls had seen it already, and so had Isabelle. Robert Merriweather and Joan Simpson hadn't. They all looked around, murmuring their approval. I was proud of it. Fred had done a wonderful job. All the tables were covered with oilcloth and he'd painted the place with some pale green paint we'd found in Mr. Strong's store.

"It smells good," Joan Simpson said. She was six years old, blue eyes, blond hair. I'd have to teach both her and Willard Carew to read.

After we decided which chairs and tables would be most comfortable for everybody and who would sit with whom, I asked them what they thought they were coming to school for.

"'Cause we have to." Jimmy answered. That brought a laugh.

"All right, that's one reason. How many want to?"

Everyone's hand went up.

"Wonderful. Why?"

"To learn readin', writin' and 'rithmetic," Eleanor Vaughn said. She and her twin looked exactly like their father, the same big teeth and stern frown.

"Nothing else? Anybody here know how to play the harmonica?"

"I do," Robert answered.

"Anybody want to learn?"

"Me," Jimmy said.

"All right, you'll learn."

"Here in school?"

"Certainly. That's what school's for—to learn what you want to learn."

"I'd like to learn sewing," Elvira Vaughn said.

"Me too," I said. "I'm terrible. Any good sewers here?"

Isabelle Purdy raised her hand.

"Think you can show Elivra how?"

"Sure," she said.

"That takes care of sewing. Anything else anybody wants to learn, they can learn it—as long as they keep up with their work. Maybe we can even learn a little bit about each other, like where we're all from."

The Purdys had come from Canada, we found out, the Carews from Pennsylvania. It gave me a chance to use one of the few teaching aids I had—a big map of the U.S. and Canada. It was my pride and joy and I wasn't about to pass the chance up.

Before we broke for lunch I gave my six older children a diagnostic arithmetic test and while they were taking it I kept Willard and Joan busy making cut-outs and pasting. One thing I could see was that I didn't have to worry about keeping their attention. Everything was new to them and they were hungry to learn.

Their big problem was reading. The only pupil who could read well was Isabelle Purdy. The rest of the class had trouble reading orally from a third-grade reader. The Vaughn twins were thirteen, but their sister Elvira, three years younger, could read better than they could.

When 3:30 came, school was over for the day.

Fred popped in a little while after they left and asked me how I thought I did. I told him I'd been scared at first, but now I felt pretty optimistic.

"The only thing I'm not sure of, though, is how to make one class out of them. I need some kind of a project they can all work on, something local. I'm going to take them on field trips, but I need something else."

"You could take them to see some of the old sourdoughs."

"You think they'd like that?"

"The kids? They'd love it. So would the old men."

"That's not a bad idea. The only thing I'd have to do is make sure I don't wind up getting lost."

He laughed. "Make a map."

I could have kissed him. "You just found my project for me."

I was just about to explain the idea to him when there was a knock at the door. It was Eleanor Vaughn. "I'm sorry to bother you, Teacher," she said, "but I lost a mitten. I thought maybe I left it in the schoolroom."

We took a look around, but it wasn't there.

I didn't think anything about it until later, when I remembered that her father had dropped in the night before. Fred had been with me then too. It could have been a coincidence, but I had the uncomfortable feeling it wasn't. I tried to remember how the twins had been dressed when they came to school. They lived only right next door, and after I thought about it I realized that all they'd had on were sweaters. Neither of them had worn mittens.

CHAPTER 6

The next day I told the class about the project I had in mind. "It's something we can all work on together," I said. "We're going to make a map of Chicken, using one whole wall for it. Everybody can draw a little picture of their own cabin and we'll put it up in the right place.

"But that's only part of the project," I said. "What we'll do is find out all about Chicken—its history and geography, what grows here, what's produced here, everything. After that we'll find out about other places."

By the time the first week was over I felt pretty good. But on Monday I was in trouble with the school board. Chuck showed up Monday morning about fifteen minutes before shcool. He was thinner than ever and his lips were chapped. His mackinaw was so small his wrists stuck out and his pants were so big the bottoms were ragged from scraping the ground.

We had the Pledge of Allegiance, then I introduced Chuck, gave him a seat and started everybody working. He did well with a first-grade reader and his arithmetic wasn't bad.

The class was restless that morning, too many of them preoccupied with giving each other looks about him. A couple of times he got hit by a spitball, but I couldn't see who did it.

During vocabulary with the older children I gave Evelyn Vaughn the word "intelligent" to put into a sentence.

"Siwashes aren't very intelligent," she recited. A few of the older kids giggled.

"Can you tell me what the world siwash means?" I asked her.

"Sure. It's a dirty low-down black Injun."

More giggles. I felt like throttling her. "There are certain words," I said, "which I don't want to hear in this class room. One of them is siwash."

"How about if I said *Indians* aren't very intelligent?"

"Do you really think that's true?"

"I sure do," she answered.

"All Indians?"

She nodded.

"How about people who are only part Indian?"

"You mean like half-breeds? I guess so," she said.

"I should tell you," I said, "that my own grandmother was an Indian. That makes me part Indian too. Do you think there's anything wrong with my intelligence?"

Eleanor shifted uncomfortably. "No."

"How come you don't look Indian then?" Jimmy asked.

36

"I guess I take after my grandfather. He was white."

"*That's* why you're smart enough to be a teacher."

"Not necessarily. My grandmother was a pretty smart woman."

Robert Merriweather hadn't said anything up to then. He raised his hand. "If your grandmother was an Indian," he said logically, "then your father was a half-breed."

"I guess that's right. But where I come from nobody cared about it. What people are doesn't matter, whether they're Indian or Irish or Negro or anything else—they're just people."

When school was over for the day, Chuck hung around for a few minutes. "You tell truth, Tisha?" he asked me. "You Indian?"

"I'm part Indian, yes."

"You make moccasin?"

"No. I don't know how to do that."

"Cut fish?"

"Not too well."

"Trap?"

"I'm afraid not."

He thought it all over. "Funny Indian," he murmured.

Elvira Vaughn knocked at my door right after supper that night. She was all embarrassed. "My father said to tell you that me and my sisters won't be coming to school tomorrow," she said.

"How come?"

"My father said you'd know why."

I didn't sleep too well that night, and the next morning the Vaughn girls didn't show up at all. And neither did Willard and Jimmy. At nine I went out and rang the bell for late call, but there was nobody in sight. The settlement was quiet.

I hadn't done anything wrong, but I still felt guilty. They were the ones who were wrong—Maggie and Angela and Mr. Vaughn. They had no right to keep Chuck or any other little kid out of the school just because they thought they were dirt. By suppertime I decided that I'd go over and talk to Maggie. The idea of going through another day and maybe more, with less than half a class was unbearable.

Maggie saved me the trouble, though. Just before six Jimmy knocked at the door. "My mother says is it all right if the school board comes over after supper?"

"Sure. You can tell her 7:30 would be fine."

They were grim. They turned me down when I offered them tea.

Mr. Vaughn cleared his throat. "We'd like to know on what grounds you've taken Joe Temple's half-breed into the school," he said.

"The same grounds on which I'd take any pupil in, Mr. Vaughn."

"He doesn't belong here. If you weren't a cheechako you'd know that. He belongs in the Indian village school."

"But he's not *in* the Indian village now."

"That has nothing to do with it. He shouldn't be in the same school with our children."

"I don't want to argue with you, but I don't see on what grounds you want to keep him out."

"According to the law," Mr. Vaughn said, "this school is open to, and I quote, 'white children and children of mixed blood who lead a civilized life.' You are aware of the law, I take it."

"Oh yes," I lied.

"Then there's your ground—'children of mixed blood *who lead a civilized life.*' That kid isn't civilized. None of those Indians from that village are."

"Isn't that your interpretation, Mr. Vaughn? Chuck can read, he can write, as far as I can see he's like any other little boy who—"

Maggie cut me off. "My kid says he can't even talk civilized."

"Besides that he's a bastard," Angela Barrett said.

"I just can't tell that little boy to get out of class for no good reason."

"You've been given the reason. We're not running a school for uncivilized siwashes and the law will back us up. Now are you going to tell him or do I have to do it myself?" Mr. Vaughn asked.

"I can't."

"Then I'll do it for you. We'd better take a vote on it to show we're doing it lawfully. I make a motion that the half-breed child known as Charles Temple be excluded from the school on the grounds that he does not lead a civilized life. How do you two vote?"

Maggie and Angela said aye.

"That settles it," Mr. Vaughn said. "If there's no further business, we can close this meeting."

Not as far as I was concerned. Without my even having to think about it I heard myself say, "It's too bad I had to come all the way out here for nothing."

"How's that?" Mr. Vaughn said.

"I'm going to have to close the school."

Mr. Vaughn's eyes narrowed. "What are you talking about?"

"I don't have enough of an enrollment," I said. I had to hold my hands tight in my lap, they were shaking so much.

"You got plenty enrollment," Maggie said.

"No I haven't," I said, trying to keep my voice even. It sounded to me as if I was squeaking. "Under the law there has to be ten pupils."

"You got my two boys, his three girls, the Merriweather kid, Simpson's little girl, and Isabelle and Lily Harrington."

"That only makes nine."

"Well, so what?" Maggie said. "That's just a technicality."

"I don't know anything about that," I said, "but this is my first teaching job in Alaska and I don't want to start out by breaking the law." My hands were sweating and my heart was pounding so loud I thought they could all hear it.

Maggie stared at me for a long moment as the point got home to her. "You telling us you'd pack up and git?"

"That's what I'd have to do, Mrs. Carew."

"You dirty little snotnose," Mr. Vaughn snarled. "How dare you give us an ultimatum?"

"Will somebody please tell me what's going on?" Angela yelled.

"We're being blackmailed, that's what's going on," Mr. Vaughn said. "We've got a second Catherine Winters here—another Indian lover. I heard you're part siwash," he said to me, "now I believe it. For my part you can just pack up and get the hell out of here right now. This meeting is adjourned." He walked out without saying another word.

Angela didn't say anything, but her expression spoke worlds. It was pure hate.

"Angela, you go on back to the roadhouse," Maggie said. "I'll be there in a few minutes."

When she was gone Maggie said, "You're expectin' to teach in Eagle next year I take it."

"Yes."

"If I was you I wouldn't—not if you keep that little half-breed in the class. They got a school board there too. If they don't want you they don't have to take you. They're not gonna like it when they hear about this."

"There's not much I can do about that."

She got up. "You got gall, I'll say that much for ya—more gall than a Government mule. You're a good kid and I like ya, but I'm gonna tell ya something and I'll tell ya right to your face—don't go too far or you won't be teachin' in Eagle or anywhere else in Alaska next year. People are goin' to be writin' to the Commissioner about this, more people than you think. You're a little too interested in siwashes for your own good."

She walked out without saying good-bye.

CHAPTER 7

The next morning I couldn't wait for the class to arrive, and when they all showed up, even the Vaughn girls, and when we sang that morning you could have heard my voice clear over to Steel Creek I was so glad.

But I found out right away what Maggie meant about people not looking the other way. People started to come by to reclaim the furnishings they'd so willing lent me only days before. First it was the wash boiler. Then about 11:30 an old sourdough who lived all alone on the other side of the creek came in and said would I mind letting him have the two chairs he'd loaned me. He was expecting company, he said. My dishes went next.

The one person who surprised me was Mrs. Purdy. "I think you have make mush trouble for yourself, Ahnne," she said when I was over at the house one night.

"Why, Mrs. Purdy?"

"Can you not see, Ahnne? He is ignorant. He is dirty and smells bad."

"That's simple," Fred said to me. "Tell him to take a bath."

"I've been thinking of it."

"Mary's got to pack water pretty far," Fred said, "but even if she didn't she wouldn't force him if he didn't want to. Indians are kind of easy on their kids."

"Think she'd mind if I gave him one?"

"Not at all. *He* would, though, I'd bet."

Mrs. Purdy shook her head. "Ahnne, you are young. You do not know what is in the heart of people here. *I* know. My children know. You must be careful."

Later on Fred walked me home. The ground was as hard as concrete and when I slipped on some leaves he grabbed me. When he let me go we were both a little self-conscious. We kept trying not to bump into each other all the rest of the way. When we reached the schoolhouse we were walking a couple of feet apart.

"Anything you need to have done in the classroom?" he asked me.

I told him I could use some cubbyholes for the kids to put their stuff in, and he said he'd come by some time in the next few days.

Chuck stayed.

How he was able to put up with the way the other kids treated him, I didn't know, but he stayed. They made life miserable for him. Once they even waylaid him after school and threw rocks at him, chasing him all the way home to his shack. When I mentioned it to Mr. Vaughn and Maggie Carew they said they couldn't do anything about it.

One afternoon, after Chuck had left the room, Mr. Vaughn dragged Chuck back in by the scruff of his neck. Chuck's pants were open and he was trying to hold them up and keep from tripping at the same time.

"Here's your star pupil," Mr. Vaughn said. "He's so civilized he doesn't know enough to use the privy. I caught him squatting out in back."

He walked out leaving Chuck standing in front of the class, his own waste all over his pants and the class laughing. I took Chuck into my quarters and cleaned him up as best I could, but he smelled awful—worse than he had before. I told him to stay in my quarters and when school was over I did what I should have done when he first came. I got all my pots out, filled them with water and put them on the stove. Then I took him over to the store with me. There we picked out a couple of good warm flannel shirts for him, two pairs of bib overalls and some socks. He loved them, but back in my quarters, when I told him he was going to have a bath before he could put them on his jaw dropped.

"Aw no, Tisha."

"You want those new clothes?"

"Yiss."

"You want to come to school?"

"Yiss."

"Then you're going to have to take a bath. "

In he went, and when he was finished and all dressed up he looked like a different boy. I let him see himself in the big piece of mirror I had. "Like yourself?" I'd given him a shampoo and combed his hair.

He smiled. "Look too much good."

When the kids saw him the next day they almost didn't recognize him. It didn't make them any friendlier to him, though. When they found out I'd given him a bath and got him some new clothes they called him teacher's pet. But he kept coming.

I had to admit that I was fond of him. I couldn't help it. There was just something about him that was so good and steady that it made me furious when the kids picked on him.

He dropped over to see me on Saturday and brought his little sister with him. She was a beautiful little thing, long black hair, delicate nose and big brown inquiring eyes.

"She name Et'el," Chuck said. He tried to get her to say hello to me, but she was too afraid. She hid in back of him.

Chuck brought her into the schoolroom and showed her some of his work, his leaf book, a couple of spelling papers and a picture of a moose he had drawn.

Before the two of them left I asked him where he liked it better—the Indian village or here.

"Indian village," he said. "Kids no play me here."

"I guess you'll just have to give it more time."

"I don' know, Tisha. I wait and wait and wait for them kids know me. They never know me."

"Sooner or later they will."

He sighed. "I hope maybe you be right. I wait too long I be old man."

CHAPTER 8

I guessed I was never so happy in my life as around that time. Everything just seemed the way I'd dreamed it would be—the settlement and all the country around hushed under a thick white blanket, the snow dry enough so you could walk around in moccasins and never get wet. Now I realized what the North was really like. It was made for winter, because winter was when everything went on. You could ski any place you wanted to and get there twice as fast and twice as easily as you could before there was snow. The whole country just opened right up. You could hear somebody talking on the trail half a mile away, or dropping a pan on the stove a mile from the settlement. It was so quiet and open and free that it was like being let out of prison. It put everybody in good spirits and they went around looking the way the country did—clean and fresh.

Came noon, after bolting their lunch, the kids were outside with sleds and skis. I learned how to ski in no time at all.

The one thing I would have liked to learn was ski-joring—holding onto a string of dogs and letting them pull you. Fred tried to teach me a couple of times, but the dogs kept pulling me off balance. Finally, on the second try, he told me he was going to work something out where that wouldn't happen. "You be ready next Saturday morning," he said when I asked him what it was. "I'll be by around ten."

Almost on the dot I heard him call my name, and when I opened the door he was out there on his own skis, waiting. "You ready?"

It wasn't that cold out, so I threw on a canvas parka with a warm sweater underneath. Then I saw what he'd done. He'd fitted an extra pair of straps on his own skis so I could stand behind him.

"You think it'll work?" I asked him.

"I don't know," he said. "I never tried it."

We didn't go too fast at first because the dogs weren't able to dig into the packed-down snow of the settlement. Once we were on the trail, though, we speeded up. Then Fred began to sing *Sweet Rosie O'Grady* to them and they began to pull like sixty. Everybody had a different way of making sled dogs pull. Some used a whip. Others, like Angela Barrett, yelled and cursed at them all the time. Fred sang to his.

I held onto his parka as tight as I could, his skis crunching under us. The dogs were thirty feet ahead, the full length of the lead rope. If they geed or hawed all of a sudden I knew I was going to be dumped.

After a while I was doing pretty well. I leaned into turns easily and could key my movements to Fred's, as if we were on a bicycle built for two. We must have gone half a mile before we ended up in a drift, laughing. We didn't bother to get up right away, just lay back where we fell. "You all right?" Fred asked.

I looked up at the blue sky. It was still early, but the sun was low, skimming the distant mountain tops and sending out long blue shadows from the trees.

I watched Fred while he straightened out the harness. He'd been out on the traplines the week before and he was brown as a coffee bean. I'd really liked being so close to him on the skis and I wondered if he felt the same thing about me. I had a feeling he did. Even if he did, though, he didn't show it. It was the way he always acted with me. Careful.

Fred got up now, brushed himself off and gave me a hand.

"When are you going to take me on that snow picnic?" He'd promised to a couple of times already.

"I was thinking we'd go in a couple of weeks."

"Why so long?"

"Have to go out on the trap line in a few days."

I was disappointed. He'd be gone for about a week. What was worse was that he hated everything about trapping. Most of the time the animal was still alive when he got to it. Hissing and snarling with fear, it had to be clubbed to death, then skinned before the carcass froze. The only reason he did it was because his family needed the money.

"I wish you didn't have to go," I said.

"Me too. I'm going to miss you."

"I feel the same way. I'll miss you too."

If that didn't let him know how much I liked him, then nothing would. He dropped the skis on the snow and I got all tensed up wondering if he was going to kiss me. I could tell he wanted to because he looked very serious. Suddenly I thought of what he'd said about going out on the trap line. "Fred, you're not going to miss the dance, are you?" The Friday night dance was only a few days away.

"Don't you worry, I won't."

"Wouldn't it be nice if we could have midnight supper together this time?"

Uncle Arthur Spratt always brought his gramophone to the dances and along about eleven o'clock the square dancing stopped and everybody danced to the scratchy records he put on. He always saved the *Home Sweet Home* waltz for last and nobody knew when he was going to play it. When he did, it was the signal for each man to run and grab the woman he wanted to take to the roadhouse for a midnight supper. I'd ended up with Mert Atwood one time and Joe Temple the other, but never with Fred. Uncle Arthur always made sure we were too far apart to get to each other.

"I'll keep an eye out," Fred said, "but I think the odds are against it. Wouldn't do for you to end up with a half-breed."

It was the first time he'd ever said anything like that.

"I know, but will you try anyway?"

"I have. I even know the label on that record is green, but Uncle Arthur's pretty cagey."

I'd stayed as close to him as I could without stepping on his feet, so if he wanted to kiss me he had all the chance in the world. He looked at me in that serious way again, his arms went around me, and then Fred's mouth was on mine. I felt gawky and nervous at first and my heart was pumping like a steam engine, then all of a sudden I was feeling warm and wonderful, as if this was where I'd always been headed. After he kissed me he held me away from him a little and the way he looked at me I knew he'd always cared for me more than he'd let on.

We found a place to sit down on a small shelf of rock right over a creek bottom. Fred cut some spruce boughs for us to sit on and we leaned back, me in the crook of his arm. It was a cozy spot and we snuggled together for warmth. After a while I said, "You think you shouldn't be kissing me?"

"Uh-huh."

"How come?"

"Anybody sees us you'll be in for trouble."

We started talking about what he wanted to do in the future. He'd worked for wages a few times and he hadn't liked it. What he wanted more than anything was to be on his own. He and his father had plans to buy a tractor. With it, he said, he'd be able to do ten times the mining they were doing with pick and shovel now.

"You just look out there," he said. "It's so big and beautiful it makes you feel wonderful just to be alive. I couldn't even think of living anyplace else."

We were still talking when all of a sudden a gust of cold air hit me. It was as if a giant box of dry ice had dropped on us. It took my breath away.

"We'd better get back," Fred said. "Temperature's starting to drop."

I couldn't understand what his hurry was. We weren't more than half an hour away from the settlement. Ten minutes later I realized what he meant, though. The ice fog became so thick that we had to depend on the dogs to stay on the trail. If I'd been alone I'd have been scared, but as long as I was with Fred I wasn't. All the way back I felt as if I were part of him, his body pressing against mine, lean and strong.

By the time we reached my quarters the thermometer outside read thirty-five below zero. When he'd called for me it had been zero.

The weather didn't keep anybody from coming to the dance, though. By the time it was 8:30 the schoolroom and my quarters were jam-packed and we were ready. Then with Fred on banjo, his mother on accordion and Ben Norvall playing the fiddle and calling, everybody stomped and swung their partners so hard the dirt kept jumping up between the floorboards. It got so hot we didn't even need the stove after a while.

As the evening wore on I kept looking over at Uncle Arthur whenever I could, hoping I'd spot that label. I saw him start to put it on once and so did Fred, but he took it off again when he saw us head for each other.

It was almost two o'clock before he slipped it on. I was talking with someone and the next thing I knew Joe Temple was tapping me on the shoulder and grinning down at me. I caught Fred's eye and we both kind of shrugged as if to say that's the way we knew it would be.

CHAPTER 9

Before the Saturday of the snow picnic Fred and I had planned Mrs. Purdy paid me a visit after school. When I opened the door I couldn't have been more surprised to see her. She smiled up at me from under a beautiful hat of otter fur that made her look as chic as a Paris model. She needed something from Mr. Strong's store, she said, but I had the feeling she wanted to talk with me in private.

Inside the store it was cold enough so that you couldn't smell the usual collection of musty odors. All she wanted, she said, was a can of peppercorns. As I was writing it down, she said, "You are going on snow picnic with my Frayd he tell me."

"On Saturday."

"He like you very mush, Ahnne," she said.

"I feel the same way about him."

"Please, Ahnne," she said slowly, "do not like him. It is not good . . . You savvy what I say?"

"Mrs. Purdy, do you think that Fred and I have done anything wrong?"

"No. I not say this. I say only that now there is mush trouble. Three days ago Mr. Strong come see me. He tell me Frayd like you too mush. People know, and it is very bad. When Frayd he come home I talk with him. He say it is true, and I weep. I am afraid. Ahnne. People will not talk with Frayd like before. Not talk with me, with my husband, and my Isabelle."

"Then maybe they're not your real friends, Mrs. Purdy."

She shook her head impatiently. "Ahnne. You are young, not understand. People here not like see white man, dark woman. Mush worse they not like see white woman, dark man. You like my Frayd too mush, Ahnne. Better to close book on that. Too many tears come your eyes, too many pains in your heart . . . I ask you—I tell Frayd you not like him anymore. Yes?"

"I'm sorry . . ."

She was angry, but it only lasted a few seconds.

"I say goodnight to you, Ahnne," she said, "but first I tell you something make me sad almost to cry. You must come my house no more."

She went out. I called to her, but she didn't turn around.

When Saturday morning came, Fred was outside with his sled almost on the dot of nine. It was still dark out—the sun wouldn't be up for a couple of hours yet—but it looked as if it was going to be clear.

As soon as I came out I saw that Pancake wasn't his lead dog this time. He'd put Pancake at wheel instead, directly in front of the sled, and harnessed all the malamutes up front with Shakespeare in the lead. Fred had taught me enough about sled dogs so I knew why. It had snowed again a few days before and the dogs would have to break trail part of the way. The heavier dogs like Pancake would be more likely to break through the snow and have tough going. The lighter malamutes would pack it down.

Shakespeare, the lead dog, was really anxious to show what he could do, and as soon as I was tucked in the sled we were off.

Once the hummock ice was behind us we moved along fast, and finally we reached the crest of a hill from where we could see West Fork joining the Forty Mile River. Ahead of us stretched endlessness.

We found a picnic spot at the base of a soaring face of rock, and Fred tied the dogs. In a little while, what with the fire and the bright ball of sun, it was warm enough for us to take off our parkas. I made some tea and we sat drinking out of tin cups.

"You think we'll ever get to go to the roadhouse with each other after the dance?" I asked him.

"No." He took my hand and held it in his own. "We shouldn't even be here, together like this."

"You don't have to worry about me."

"Well, I do. If I had any sense I wouldn't have taken you out here all alone."

"Do you want to go back?"

"No."

After we ate we took a walk out onto the river. It had frozen smooth in the center, but near the banks it was a mass of twisted shapes. On our way back to the sled we were moving through a thick tangle of buckbrush when all of a sudden the whole brush came alive and exploded with a flock of ptarmigan. In a moment they were gone.

When we got back to the sled I was all for building up the fire and staying there, but it was dark already and Fred said we should get back.

CHAPTER 10

Cabaret Jackson showed up for our Thanksgiving dance. He was all dolled up in his Saturday-night cowboy clothes, and just as loud and brassy as when I'd seen him in Eagle last. But he was such a good-natured grinning fool that I just had to like him.

"You must have struck it rich."

"I sure did," he said craftily. "What I got on that sled a mine's more precious than gold, grub or fire."

"What have you got?" I asked. I'd heard he was running liquor all over the Forty Mile.

"Never you mind," he said.

I saw his team the next day, kenneled in back of the roadhouse. They were a mean bunch, but they looked fast: lean in the flanks and heavy in the shoulders. If Cab had wanted to make money honestly with them he could have. There were always people who were willing to pay top dollar for a man who knew the country and had a good team of dogs—metallurgists or businessmen who wanted to be mushed into the interior for one reason or another. It made me feel kind of sorry for him. He just didn't want to do things the right way, or maybe he didn't know how. All he was interested in was wasting his time drinking and bragging about how he'd been in every cabaret and honky-tonk from Dawson to the Bering Sea.

The square dancing ended about ten o'clock, but we were still going to have midnight supper over at the roadhouse. I should have known something was going to happen when Uncle Arthur and a few other men started talking with Cab about how fast Fred's team was.

Cab buttonholed Fred and was all for having a race with him then and there.

"Thanks, Cab, but I'm not a racing man."

Cab had that stubborn look that said there was just one thing in his mind and he wasn't going to be talked out of it.

"Hell, I hear them's all Indian dogs you got anyway. Ain't worth the fish ya feed'm."

Fred walked away from him, but Cab was back at it again right after Fred and I danced a fox-trot. By this time his eyes were all bloodshot and he was getting mean. I was hoping that even if I didn't end up with Fred when the *Home Sweet Home* waltz went on, at least I wouldn't end up with Cab. He was willful when he was sober, drunk he was impossible. But when the *Home Sweet Home* waltz did go on I was flabbergasted: for the first time Fred was right beside me.

In the roadhouse Fred and I sat at the end of one of the long tables. There wasn't too much talk coming from where Cab was, just some murmuring, but there was something in the air, all right. Fred and I got up and he went to pay for our supper.

"Hey now, Teacher, you ain't leavin'. so early, are ya?" Cab yelled out.

"Sure am, Cab. I'm dead tired."

He got up from the table and made his way towards us. Fred brought my coat over and Cab tried to take it from him.

"It's all right, Cab," Fred told him. "I'll take her home."

"You will like hell," Cab said. "Let it go." Fred looked at me, but before he could decide what to do Cab shoved him. Fred let my coat go and fell against the counter.

"I don't want any fightin' in here," Maggie Carew said. "The two of you want to settle it, go on outside."

"That's fine with me," Cab said.

"Cab, I don't want to fight with you," Fred told him.

"Thought so," Mr. Vaughn said. "He's going to crawfish."

Fred was dead white around his mouth and he was all tightened up as he went over to get his parka where it was hanging on a hook, and took it down. Cab rushed over to him and gave him another shove that sent him flying into a whole bunch of men. They pushed him right back and Cab must have thought Fred was coming after him because his fist went out and he hit Fred in the mouth. It was just a glancing punch, but Fred's lip started to bleed and it kind of stunned him. That did it for everybody. Mr. Carew and another man grabbed Cab, two others grabbed Fred, and they hustled them both out the door.

I tried to follow Fred, but Angela Barrett grabbed me.

"Let me go, Mrs. Barrett."

"You just settle down," she said thickly, "or he won't be the only one to get the shit knocked out of 'im."

What happened next made everybody jump. There was a big explosion and I caught a flash of flame out of the corner of my eye and smelled the sharp odor of burnt powder.

Someone had fired a shotgun into the air and the noise brought everyone to their senses.

Cab was drunk, but he wasn't so drunk that those two barrels staring him in the face didn't sober him a little. He cursed, then he slouched back into the roadhouse and everybody else started moving back in too. I pulled away from Angela.

"C'mon, Fred." I took his arm.

All the way back to my quarters Fred was trembling so hard I thought he was going to fall down. Inside, he slumped into a chair. His chin was smeared with blood and his lip was a little puffy. I got a wet cloth and gave it to him. He went over to the mirror and dabbed the cut.

"I'm glad you're not hurt bad."

He almost smiled. "Me too. I just wish there was some way I could keep my mother from finding out about it."

"What'll you tell her?"

"Oh, that Cab just got drunk and took a poke at me. This is a mess," he said. "Anne . . ." He started to say something else, but then he just hugged me so tightly it took the breath out of me. Before he walked out, he stared at me in a way that gave me the most awful feeling, as if he'd pushed me away or shut me out. I wanted to call him back. But I didn't. I just stood there, looking at all the cabins strung along the snow.

"F red went over to Steel Creek," Isabelle told me Monday morning. I asked her what he'd gone for, but she said she didn't know.

His father showed up for the mail when Mr. Strong came into the settlement a few days later.

"How's everybody in the family?" I asked him while we were standing on line outside the post office.

"Fine," he said. "They all say hello."

"What did Fred go to Steel Creek for?" I asked him.

"See some people over there. He ought to be back in a few days."

I had the feeling he was holding something back and I wanted to ask him more about it, but I couldn't bring myself to pry any more.

There was a letter for me from Lester Henderson. He wrote me that he'd received the first monthly report I'd sent him at the beginning of October, and he was very satisfied with it. Then he went on to say that he'd received letters from a few people in Chicken.

. . . The general tone of them is that you are a good teacher and have high moral standards. I've received two letters from parents, however, who object to your association with a young man of mixed blood, Fred Purdy. I want you to know that I have the utmost faith in you and your abilities, and your personal life is your own. I do wish to advise you, however, to be as diplomatic as possible, especially if you wish to teach in Eagle next year. . . .

There was a letter from Cathy Winters too, inviting me up to the Indian village for a few days during Christmas vacation. She'd written to me right after the whole business about Chuck coming to school had happened and since then we'd written to each other a few more times. I wrote her that I'd love to come if I could arrange transportation. "If I can, I'll be there around Christmas day. That way I can come back with Mr. Strong when he comes through there on the 27th."

Those next five or six days just seemed to drag by. But then Fred came back from Steel Creek. I poured him coffee and put his cup down on the edge of the cookstove. Somehow I had a good idea what he was going to say, and I didn't turn around. I braced myself, waiting for it.

"I'm going back to Steel Creek. There's some guys doing some winter mining there and they can use another hand."

"How long will you be there?"

"Till June."

Till June. I'd be gone then.

"When are you going?"

"Tomorrow. I don't want to go, Anne, but I have to."

"Why?"

"I don't want to see you hurt."

"I can take care of myself."

"Not once these people turn against you, and that's what they're doing. Come spring you won't have a job in Eagle or anywhere else in Alaska. They can write letters to the commissioner that'd curl your hair."

"They already have. I'm not scared of them."

"I am. Not for me. For you. For you, for my mother and my sister."

I think I must have groaned then, I felt so awful. "Oh Fred . . ."

He was as miserable as I was. "Don't you see, Anne? There's nothing else I can do. I've thought it over and over. I can't do you anything but harm. I don't have a thing right now. I can't give you anything, I can't take care of you."

I moved over to him and my arms went around him. I knew he'd made up his mind and I kept trying to think of a way I could change it. Maybe he didn't know how much I loved him, I thought. Maybe if he did—if he really knew—he wouldn't be able to leave.

"Please, Fred," I asked him, "don't go. I love you so much."

"Anne, don't let's do it like this," he said, his voice hard. "I'm going."

That stopped me almost as if he'd slapped me. I was acting cheap. I let him go. He said something else before he went out and closed the door behind him, but I didn't listen. I heard him walk off the porch and move off around the back and I kept thinking it wasn't fair. I'd never loved anybody as much in my entire life as I loved him and now he was going away from me for the stupidest reason in the whole world. It wasn't until later that I realized what he'd said before he went out. He'd said, *I love you.*

CHAPTER 12

The next morning I was so bleary-eyed when I woke up it seemed as if I'd slept only a few minutes. The blankets were frozen to the wall, as usual. I tugged them free and lay back, glancing at the clock. 7:30. I dived back under the covers and tried to go back to sleep, but it was no use. It was fifty-four below zero.

After dressing I started to walk over to the Forty Mile River. I was feeling so sorry for myself that I went out on the ice hoping I'd find a spot thin enough to break through. All I managed to do was stay out so long that I wound up with frostbite. I didn't even know it until I got back and realized my toes were numb. The pain was agonizing before circulation came back, and I knew I'd never do anything like that again.

Finally it was time to leave for the Indian village. Cathy was as glad to see me as I was to see her. Neither of us had talked with a girl near our own age since the last time we saw each other. The first night we stayed up until almost three in the morning and she told me why she had come here. She was writing a thesis on the Athapascan Indians of the Forty Mile for her doctorate. She was on her second year here and would have liked to stay on for another. But a lot of white people had written letters to the Alaska Native Service about her, saying that she was "spoiling" the Indians, so she had a feeling this was going to be her last winter.

Titus Paul had lunch with us that afternoon, and from the way Cathy acted around him I could see she was pretty fond of him. I couldn't understand why, though. He was a tough customer. With that tight-skinned face of his and eyes that bored right through you, he reminded me of a lizard. The TB scars all over his neck didn't help either. He hardly said a word the whole time he was there.

Titus was sort of the unofficial head of the village, she told me, one of the few Indians the whites couldn't boss around.

"Honest to God, Cathy," I told her. "I don't know how you can bear to stay here."

"Somebody has to do it."

"I wouldn't."

"Oh yes you would. From what I hear you've stuck your neck out a few times already."

"That's different. What I can't see is doing things for people when they won't do anything for themselves."

"Anne, I told you when you first came through here," she said sharply, "that you couldn't judge these people by white standards."

"Cathy, you have to have *some* kind of standards. Can't they go out and just cut enough wood to keep warm, or put up meat for the winter?"

"They're doing the best they can. They just don't think about the future the way white people do. They did fine before the white man came along."

"That's what I'm trying to say. Now they have everything you can think of, so how come they just sit around and starve?"

"Because they're weak. Before the whites came these people were hunters. Their diet was almost all meat and that practically raw. They had the strength to go out and take some game. Now they eat the white man's grub—flour, sugar, canned goods, junk. And they drink his liquor . . ."

I dropped the subject, but I still didn't understand. But the next night, after the dance in the church, I got into a conversation with Ben Norvall that made me understand.

"Think of it this way," Ben said. "Before we came these people just drifted from place to place. Well, imagine living out there in all that wind and ice and the only thing between you and starvation whatever game you can take. Half the time they starved. Sometimes they'd go so long without eating they'd chew the rawhide off their snowshoes. They had a tough time of it even before the white man came.

"One day the white man turned up. And by God, here was the answer to a hunter's prayer. 'Behold!' that Indian said. 'Just look at the white critter, will you? Comes into this country out of nowhere and before you know it he's building himself cabins ten times bigger than ours. And grub? Great Spirit, look at it all! He's got it stacked in tin cans, in sacks, in boxes, shoots it without the least trouble.'

"So the Indian went to this white man and he said, 'Bud, I like your style. Want to live the way you do. How do I do it?'

"'Bring me furs,' the white man says, 'all kinds—lynx, muskrat and marten, black fox, red fox and wolf. I'll take 'em all.' 'Easy,' says the Indian. And he stopped hunting food and started hunting fur, started trading for axes and traps and guns, flour and tea.

"He stopped traveling from place to place and settled down where the white man was. For a while he didn't do too bad. Missionaries came around and taught 'im all about Jesus Christ, which was fine with him, because the one thing he wanted to know more about was the God that had made this white critter so rich and powerful.

"Well, for a good many years that Indian did real fine. Until the price of fur went down. Then for a while the white man hardly wanted any furs at all. That Indian was stuck. From living in one place and eating the white man's food, he'd gotten weak. Weak as he was, he picked up all the white man's diseases—influenza, whooping cough, TB. The only thing that made him feel good for awhile was liquor, so he drank that whenever he could get enough money to pay for it. But no matter how weak or sick he got, he still held onto the faith that'd kept him going when he was a hunter—'Something'll turn up. Somehow I'll make it through the winter.' And that's what keeps all these people in this village going even today—the faith that something's bound to turn up. And that's the awful part of it. This time it looks like it's not going to."

CHAPTER 13

When school opened again I could feel almost from the first day that something was different about me. I wasn't short with the children or anything like that—we still sang in the morning and had as much fun as before—but I made them work harder. They only had till June to get all the schooling they could, I figured, and they were going to get it.

I couldn't put my finger on what it was, but I felt different, all right—as if all my life I'd been trying to be what other people like my parents or Mr. Strong or all the people here in Chicken wanted me to be. Now I was going to be myself. I wasn't going to be hard to get along with, or go out of my way to say anything mean, but from now on people were going to have to take me for what I was.

A couple of weeks after school started I got a letter from Fred, in response to a letter I'd written him on New Year's Eve. He hadn't been trifling with my affections at all, he wrote. He cared for me more than he'd ever cared for anybody in his life.

I did what I thought was right, Anne. I didn't do it because I was scared of anybody. I can't tell you how much it turned me inside out to come here, but I did it because I love you so much that there was nothing else I *could* do. . . .

If I can take it, I'll be staying here until summer, so I won't be seeing you for a long time. Maybe never again. I don't know. . . . Come the summer you'll be going to Eagle to teach and then you'll probably forget all about me. And maybe that's the best thing.

I read the letter over and over, and every time I saw the words *if I can take it* I winced. Fred lived in a workshed all by himself when here he had the most beautiful home of anybody and a family that loved him. And it was all my fault. He hated working for wages, and on top of it he had to work with men who didn't even want him.

I wrote him a letter telling him I thought he should come back. "We don't have to see each other at all," I ended it.

In a way that was the most peculiar time I ever went through. I'd never felt more alone in my life, and yet at the same time I felt more whole than ever. I didn't seem to need anybody, as if there was a protective shell around me that made me so sure of myself I couldn't say or do anything wrong. I didn't know what it was, but I took everything in stride.

One night Maggie Carew invited me over to supper to celebrate. It was the first time she'd had me over in quite a while, and it meant she wanted to bury the hatchet. Now that Fred was gone she felt more kindly towards me, or maybe she was even feeling sorry for what had happened. I didn't know and I didn't care. I liked her. At least she was honest and straightforward. She'd been about the only one in the settlement that really said what she thought and she hadn't made any bones about it.

After supper she asked me if I was looking forward to teaching in Eagle next year.

"I don't know," I said. "I hear the school board has some doubts about me."

"Well, I oughtta have something to say about that," she said. "End of next spring we're movin' there. I bought the roadhouse right alongside the dock. I'll put in a good word for you—unless a course you got other plans."

"No, I don't," I said.

Came February I almost wondered if I wanted to teach anywhere in Alaska at all. The sky stayed so dark you couldn't tell whether it was day or night. For almost a week the temperature dropped to fifty and lower and stayed there. Even if there'd been no thermometer we'd have known how cold it was: all the moisture was sucked out of the air, leaving everybody thirsty all the time—no matter how much tea or water we drank we still felt dry.

People began to get as mean as the weather. With the holidays over everybody had cabin fever—aggravation from staying indoors day after day—and they started quarrels with each other over everything. Maybe if I hadn't had the class to keep me busy I'd have felt the same kind of aggravation. Sometimes I'd find myself getting annoyed over small things, but most of the time I was calm—as if I was waiting for something to happen.

When it did finally, it was a day I'd never forget.

It was just after the class came back from lunch. It was sixty below that day and the little children were using my bed again. I was beginning to think the bed was the most important article of furniture I had. Besides the kids using it when the floor was too cold, I had had to put the sack of potatoes in it because it was the only place we could be sure they wouldn't freeze.

We were tidying up in my quarters when I heard three distant rifle shots, one right after the other. We all knew what they meant. Someone was calling for help. After that there was no keeping the class in, so I let them all go.

"I think maybe come from Mary Angus," someone said.

Outside, even though I had a scarf over my face the first breath I took caught in my throat. A gray-black mist hung over everything, and the cold made it impossible to talk, so we trudged all the way in silence, moving fast enough to stay warm, slow enough to avoid perspiring.

The kids were playing outside the shack when we got there. A couple of them were riding in Mary's hand sled while Robert Merriweather pulled it and Jimmy pushed from behind yelling, "Mush!" As soon as they saw me they came running over.

"Mary's dead, Teacher!" Jimmy yelled.

"Dead as a doornail," Willard chimed in.

I pushed the door open. There were a lot of people inside, but only a sputtering candle for light so at first I could only make out Angela, the Carews and Joe Temple. "Close that goddamn door before this candle goes out!" I heard Angela yell.

Ben Norvall was in a corner with Chuck, the two of them bending down over what must have been Mary's body. Ben was covering her up with a wolf robe.

"What happened?" I asked Maggie.

"She musta hemorrhaged," Maggie said. "We're tryin' a decide what to do," she said to me. "Joe here's gonna get his sled and mush the body to our place. We'll keep it in the extra cache till Strong can tote it up to the Indian village, but we ain't figgered out what to do with the kids yet."

Now that my eyes had adjusted to the darkness I saw Ethel. She was sitting on a box, with nobody paying attention to her. She was wide-eyed and scared from all the commotion. I went over to her.

"How about it, Joe," Angela said. "You gonna take the kids?"

"I don't know anything about taking care of kids," he said.

"That's what they all say," Angela said. "They can make 'em, but they don't know how to take care of 'em."

Ben and Chuck got up from Mary's body. There was blood on the edge of the mattress and a big pool of it on the dirt floor that was all frozen and blackened. Chuck was in shock. I put an arm around him and he just let me hold him without making a sound. "This one had it the worst," Ben said, putting a hand on Ethel's head. "I was going by and didn't see any smoke coming from the chimney. Came in and she was sitting alongside Mary there." He patted her head. "If ol' Ben hadn't happened by," he said to her, "you'd be liable to have froze to death."

"Maybe she'd of been better off," Maggie said.

"That's sure as hell true," Angela said. "She certainly ain't got nothin' to look for'ard to in that Indian village."

Mr. Carew spoke up. "Unless we're gonna stand around here jawin' all day, let's decide what we do with the kids."

Chuck was limp against me. I put a hand on his shoulder.

Angela said, "I vote Joe takes 'em. Teach 'im a good lesson."

"That's not funny. I told you before I wouldn't know what to do with them."

"How about you, Maggie?" Angela asked. "You got the bunkhouse."

"I got my own to look after."

"I'll take them," I said to Joe.

"*You'll* take 'em!" Angela said.

"Yes."

"How are you going to take care of them and teach school too?" Mr. Vaughn asked.

"I can manage it."

"That's fine with me," Joe said, relieved. "Thanks, Anne."

"I don't think it's right," Mr. Vaughn said.

"I agree with 'im," Maggie said. "She's just a kid."

"Then why don't you take them?" Joe snapped at her.

She looked as if she was considering it and for a few seconds I held my breath. I wanted them. I wanted them badly.

"I got my own," she repeated.

"They're all yours," Joe said to me.

I picked up Ethel. Chuck stayed by my side.

Nobody made a move to get out of the way. They just stared at me as if I was some kind of a circus freak.

"Anybody else want them?" I said.

Nobody answered.

"Then if nobody minds, I'll take these children home."

CHAPTER 14

Ethel was quiet until we reached the door. Then she realized that I was taking her away and she began to scream. I could barely stop her from running back inside the shack. She was just too young to realize her mother was dead.

If it hadn't been for Ben Norvall I don't know how we'd have gotten her home. He went and got Mary's hand sled from the kids, then helped me tuck a blanket around Ethel and tie her into the sled. It was the only way we could get her out of there. She wouldn't even pay any attention to Chuck when he tried to talk to her.

At the house, Ethel ran straight under the table and sat there crying. And no sooner was Chuck inside than he started crying too, and then he wanted to know when his mother was going to wake up. I had to tell him that she wasn't going to, that she was dead. "Who take care me now?" he asked. He looked as though he was going to start crying again.

"I'm going to but I need your help," I said. "The first thing we have to do is explain to Ethel that she has nothing to be afraid of here. She doesn't understand what's happened. You're going to have to tell her. Can you do that?"

He went over to the table and kneeled beside his sister. She was still sniffling, but she listened to him. She let Chuck lead her out from under the table. My sense of smell had been frozen up to then, but it came back just as Ethel stood up. The worst odor in the world hit me. A bath was necessary.

After we had enough hot water in the washtub I took off Ethel's parka, but when I tried to take off her clothes she pulled away and began to cry. I asked Chuck what was wrong.

"She not like take off clothes," he said. "Nevuh take off."

"She has to have a bath."

Chuck explained to her in Indian, pointing to the washtub. She shook her head and dived under the bed. There was nothing else for it but to go after her, which we did. I got a bite on the hand before we dragged her out screaming to high heaven. I took off her clothes—knee-length moccasins, a light jacket, and a calico dress with another cotton dress underneath. Her undergarment had me stumped when I got to it. It was tight-fitting, like a union suit. It even had a drop seat, but there were no buttons up the front. The drop seat was brown, soggy and foul. I cut it off her, then lowered her into the tub.

Ethel kept struggling to get out, thrashing around and fighting so hard that I was almost ready to give up. Until suddenly Ethel just sat back, choking out sobs, all the fight gone out of her. She was a little scared when I added some hot water after about ten minutes, but it was only to look at me with soft liquid eyes, silently pleading with me not to hurt her.

After some supper I put the children in my bed and they soon fell into an exhausted sleep.

Outside a wind rose and little drafts of freezing air nipped in. I thought of Mary lying cold and alone in the dark cache. There was nobody to take care of Chuck and Ethel now, nobody at all. They were all by themselves. Back in the shack, when everybody had been standing around trying to decide what to do with them I'd wanted them right away. Maybe it was because nobody had ever wanted me either when I was a little kid— nobody except Granny. They needed somebody to take care of them, and I could do it. But the fact was, they were still Joe Temple's children and I'd have to talk to him before I could go ahead and keep them. If he said no, there wasn't anything I could do.

For the first few days Ethel never let Chuck out of her sight. Everything was new to her and she was scared, but otherwise she was about the most self-possessed little girl there ever was. She was timid, but she had every right to be. She couldn't understand a word of all the English flying around her head.

For a full week I kept putting off talking to Joe Temple about keeping Ethel and Chuck. I was shy about doing it. But finally, a couple of days before Mr. Strong was due in, I skied over to see Joe, who lived about a mile from the settlement on Stonehouse Creek.

The cup of coffee he handed me when I arrived felt nice and warm. Joe poured himself some coffee, and sat down.

"Joe—"

"Don't say a word. I want to see if I can guess what this visit is all about. You didn't come for my company, I'm sure of that. Or for supper—it's too late. I guess I give up."

"It's about Chuck and Ethel. Can I have them?"

"Are you serious?"

"Of course I am."

"Good enough. Take them. You know you're going to get people all riled up, though, don't you?"

"I guess so."

"Doesn't that suggest anything to you?"

"Like what?"

"You mean it doesn't seem peculiar to you when a young single girl decides that she's going to play mother, especially when she knows that everybody isn't exactly fond of the offspring she'll be playing it with."

"I'm not playing anything."

"Then why not avoid a whole mess and let those kids go to the Indian village where they belong?"

"Joe, you know what that Indian village is like. It's not a place for a dog, much less for children. Don't they mean anything to you at all?"

"No."

I got up and asked him to let me have my parka.

"I've got a couple more things to say," he went on. He took my parka down from the rack and handed it to me.

"You stepped on a lot of toes since you've been here and if you weren't as nice a kid as you are you wouldn't have gotten away with it. Or maybe it's just that you're a kid and so everybody looked the other way. If people don't like Indians they don't like Indians and that's their business. I've got nothing against Indians myself, but I'm not about to start lecturing other people on how to feel toward 'em, and that goes for half-breeds too. Fred Purdy did you the biggest favor in the world when he pulled out of here, only you don't have enough sense to see that. This is his home. He has to live in this country. He's not about to make it tough on himself by messing around with a white girl. He did the right thing by you. You ought to be grateful. Instead you have to go ahead and stick your foot right smack in people's faces again and take these kids. You're making a mistake."

He looked so smug and superior I felt like gnashing my teeth. "Joe, honestly, I'd really like to give you a punch. All you've told me so far is that you don't like the country and people around here don't like Indians. Well, if I want to like both of them that's my right—and I'm getting sick and tired of people looking at me as if I'm a nut because of it."

He smiled. "It hasn't stopped you so far. Go ahead, take the kids. Do what you like with them. Just remember they're still part savage."

"If they are it's probably the part they got from you."

When I got home Ethel was asleep, but Chuck was still up. I told him the news and he let out a yell and hugged me. "I know you make him say yes, Tisha, I know you make him say yes!" He was so excited he didn't fall asleep until after ten.

CHAPTER 15

On the days Mr. Strong came into the settlement I always let the class out about fifteen minutes before he arrived. This time I threw a sweater around my shoulders and also went out. The air was flying white and it was cooler than it usually was when it snowed.

Mr. Strong was standing up looking like a big bear, furred from head to toe, cracking his whip and urging the two horses on. There was somebody sitting up front alongside Mr. Strong. As soon as the sled stopped he jumped down and yelled at the men who were crowding forward. "Just hold on, all a you! Lemme get my wife and baby out."

It was Elmer Terwilliger, Maggie Carew's son-in-law from Eagle. He moved to the back of the sled where somebody was already pushing up the covering canvas from underneath. When he pulled it back, there was his wife Jeannette, swaddled in a cocoon of furs. She started to hand Elmer a little bundle wrapped in blankets, but Maggie was already alongside of him and said, "Give 'er to me!"

I got all my mail, then went back to my quarters with the children. There was a letter from Lester Henderson, and he didn't have very cheering news. "Your reports are thorough and your pupils seem to be making excellent progress," he wrote. "However, there may be some difficulty in my placing you in Eagle next year."

I knew what that meant. People had written to him about me, and the chances were that the school board in Eagle wouldn't want me teaching there. I tried not to let it bother me too much, but it did.

After supper, a party started up at the roadhouse. I had to go over to Mr. Strong's store to go over all the accounts with him and give him the cash I'd taken in.

I was hoping the store would be empty, but Mr. Vaughn and a couple of other men were sitting around the oil-drum stove when I walked in. Harry Dowles shifted his quid of chewing tobacco and asked me if I was coming over to the roadhouse.

"I don't think so," I said.

"Too bad." He spat into the big tin can sitting by the stove. "Fred Purdy's liable to show up."

Mr. Strong was leaning over the counter going over some figures. He looked up at me over his glasses. "Fred came in with me," he said.

"How come I didn't see him?"

"He jumped off at Stonehouse Creek and siwashed it from there."

Harry Dowles chuckled. While I went over the accounts with Mr. Strong I knew they were all giving each other know-it-all looks in back of me, but I just pretended I wasn't affected. I kept hoping they'd leave before I talked with Mr. Strong about Chuck and Ethel, but they stayed put. After we finished tallying up I was about to mention it, but Mr. Strong beat me to it.

"Too bad about Mary Angus," he said. "I'll be bringing the body back to the Indian village," Mr. Strong said. "I won't be paid for it, but it's my duty. It was commendable of you to look after the two youngsters."

"I didn't mind at all."

"You may bring them over here tonight if you wish. I can give them a couple of sleeping bags. Or if you don't mind I can pick them up before I leave tomorrow."

"You won't have to do either," I said. "They're going to stay with me."

He peered at me over his glasses again. "I don't understand."

"I'm going to keep them for a while. I don't think they ought to go back to the Indian village just yet."

Mr. Vaughn made a snorting noise and Harry Dowles spat. Mr. Strong frowned. "Madam, I'm sure your intentions are good, but those children belong among their own people."

"I already spoke with Joe Temple. He said it's all right with him."

"For how long do you intend to keep them?"

"For quite some time."

"Quite some time," Mr. Vaughn mimicked. "Jesus Christ." He got up without another word, took his parka from the wall and walked out. He'd be headed for the roadhouse to tell everybody.

"I'd suggest, madam, that you bring those two children here tonight."

"I've pretty well made up my mind."

"I would be doing you a service if I were to go over to your quarters right now and take them forcibly."

"I don't think you'd do something like that, Mr. Strong," I said. I was pretty upset by now, scared he'd do it. He shook his head a little and his mouth tightened up. "Goodnight, madam," he said finally.

I walked out shaking. I'd wanted to stop at the roadhouse and see Maggie's granddaughter, but with Mr. Vaughn inside spreading the good news about Chuck and Ethel, I wasn't about to.

After Chuck and Ethel were in bed I sat down to write to Mr. Henderson. I told him that if he could manage it I'd prefer to teach in Eagle, but that if he couldn't I'd take another school. I also wrote him about Chuck and Ethel, explaining who they were. "I'll be keeping them with me at least until June," I wrote, "and I have the feeling you'll be getting some letters about them from people."

While I was addressing the envelope there were quick footsteps on the porch and the door was flung open. I was scared out of my wits, thinking it was a bunch from the roadhouse come to take the kids, but it was Maggie Carew, fuming mad. She hadn't even bothered to put on a shawl. "Just what the hell are you up to now!" she yelled.

"The kids are asleep, Mrs. Carew."

I brought the lamp into the schoolroom and we closed the door behind us. "I don't want to hear any blabber. All I wanna hear is that those kids are goin' outta here. Look, I'm try'na tell you somethin' for your own good. You keep those kids and you're askin' for it. Goin' daffy over that half-breed was bad enough, but this takes the cake. Do you realize you're lousin' up your whole future?"

"I'm not worried about it."

"Well you better. You better worry about a lot of things from here on in. There's talk over to the roadhouse about some of them comin' over here and takin' those kids whether you like it or not."

That did it. I went into the cache and felt around for the nickel-plated revolver, my hand finally closing around the holster.

"What are you gonna do with that?" Maggie said when I marched back into the schoolroom.

"If I have to I'm going to use it." I took the revolver out of its holster. "You tell anybody at the roadhouse who has a mind to set foot in here and take those children from me that if they try to, so help me God I'll shoot 'em. I will shoot them dead."

"I'll tell 'em. But I'll tell you one thing too. Maybe you don't know it, but I been stickin' my neck out for you. Come spring I'm leavin' here for Eagle as you well know and buyin' the Adkins' roadhouse there. That Adkins woman is on the school board and she wrote me to find out if you were as crazy as she's been hearin'. Well, I wrote her back, sayin' you were a cheechako and didn't know the ropes, but that you were a damn good teacher and if she could swing it, to see that the school board didn't turn you down. Well, I'm gonna tell you here and now that I'm about to change my mind and tell her you're as crazy as a bedbug. Now are those kids leavin' here tomorrow or ain't they?"

"They're staying with me."

"Then I wash my hands of the whole thing. I'll tell you one more thing, young lady. This ain't over yet—not by a long shot."

CHAPTER 16

The next day, after school I heard footsteps on the porch. Somehow I had a feeling it was going to be Fred, and sure enough, it was. I'd kept preparing myself for when I'd be seeing him again, and I'd made up my mind to be level-headed and poised. As soon as he walked in, though, any poise I thought I'd have turned to mush.

We both started to say something at the same time, then told each other to go ahead. "I was just going to say," I said, "that I guess you heard about my taking Chuck and Ethel."

"Me and everybody else in the Forty Mile," he said.

"What did you think?"

"That is was just the kind of thing I'd expect you'd do."

Then I put my foot in it. "Why'd you come over?" I blurted out.

"I wanted to see you one more time," he said.

"You going away again?"

"No, but I came to say good-bye anyway."

"That's stupid." There I go again, I thought, saying exactly the wrong thing. "Why do we have to say good-bye? Can't we even be around each other, be friends?"

He shook his head as if he was tired. "The reason I went to Steel Creek was to take the pressure off you and my mother, but I realized I could do the same thing here. All I had to do was make sure you and I stayed away from each other. That way everybody'd be happy."

"Except you and me."

He shrugged, then he said, "Anne, if you ever need me for anything at all, I'll be here. That's what I came over to tell you."

"Thanks. Should we shake hands now or something?"

He just stared at me without saying anything for the longest time. "I didn't mean that," I said finally.

"I know. But I meant what I said."

He went past me and out the door.

A few days later, when it rained, Mrs. Purdy showed up for Isabelle. Like Fred, it just wasn't in her nature to stay mad at someone. We had a cup of tea before she took Isabelle home. She didn't pay any attention to Chuck and Ethel at all but she knew they were there.

"How long you take care them, Ahnne?" she asked me.

"They're with me to stay. I wouldn't give them up for the world."

She shook her head disapprovingly. "You are foolish. There are many people who do not like this, a fine white girl who is teacher ruin reputation with such children."

"Frankly, I think they've finally stopped caring one way or the other."

"This is not so. I tell you long time ago, Ahnne, you are verree important person in settlement." She waved a hand around the room. "Here children come school—my Isabelle, Vaughn girls, Carew children, others. All these people must be friendly with you—talk with you. People come here for dance. They must talk with you or not come. You have keys Mr. Strong's store. People come store must talk with you. If they tell you truth, no more can they come. Better not to tell truth, be friendly, talk. Yet inside"—she tapped her heart—"they very angry."

"I don't think there's anything I can do about it, Mrs. Purdy."

"Indeed, Ahnne, there is something make you happy, make everybody happy." She looked over at Chuck and Ethel, picked up a handful of air and threw it towards the door.

At the next dance I couldn't help thinking about what she'd said.

Elmer and Jeannette Terwilliger had come with the Carews and they brought the baby along. I didn't think I'd ever seen anything so tiny. Patricia was about two months old and just about perfect in every way. Maggie was holding the baby while her daughter and Elmer were dancing.

"Can I hold her?" I asked.

Maggie handed her over to me. She was sleeping and I rocked her a little. "Like to have one like that?"

"I sure would."

"You won't as long as you got those two," she said.

A few days later Jeannette and her husband started for Eagle, with Jeannette and the baby tucked into the Carews' sled. They had a fairly good string of dogs, but there was an awful lot on the sled for them to pull. Since Maggie would be closing the roadhouse, she was trying to move as many things to Eagle as she could. All told there must have been about six hundred pounds there.

Ben Norvall said they oughtn't to go with so much packed on the sled. "There's a storm comin' down," Ben said, "and you're liable to run right into it."

A few hours later Ben proved right. A really mean freeze came in so fast that you could hear the nails in the walls snapping as they contracted. Even after we built up the fire till the sides of the stove were red hot the schoolroom was hardly bearable. It was the wind that did it, sweeping down from the north and bringing sleet that drove against the windows so hard I thought they'd break.

When I was putting Chuck and Ethel to bed that night somebody knocked at the door. It was still sleeting out and I could hardly see beyond the edge of the porch. Hugging the wall so tight his Stetson was tipped down to his nose was Cab Jackson. It was too cold to do anything but invite him in and have him get the children all awake again.

"D'you come in from Eagle?" I asked.

"Nulato. Did a little business there. I'll be mushing over to Eagle when I leave here—tomorrow mornin' I reckon. Teacher," he said, "you mind if I tell you somethin'?"

"I'll have to hear it first."

"You're roonin' your whole career, people are sayin', an' they're right. The only thing stoppin' that school board in Eagle from givin' you your walkin' papers right now is old Strong. He's a-tellin' 'em to wait 'n see . . . And Teacher, I don't want you to lose that job. I got some pretty deep feelings about ya, as you do know by now."

"I appreciate it, Cab. I appreciate everything you're trying to tell me, but I know what I'm doing and I want to do it."

"No you don't, Teacher. You got a heart big as all outdoors and you're lettin' it rule out your good sense. I'm askin' you as one who is truly interested in your welfare and your good name—you just let me mush them two kids outta here and you'll wind up the happiest female in the Forty Mile. You will."

He got up and took his mackinaw down from the drying rack. Then he said something I thought was really touching. "I guess you think I'm kinda wild and not smart. And maybe I'm *not* too smart either. But I got deep feelin's for you, Teacher. I wanta do somethin' for you, in the worst way. I wanna be a help to you. You know what I mean?"

"I think so . . . I appreciate it."

"Good night."

When I went to sleep the wind was raging, blowing so hard that if the windows hadn't been frozen in place they'd have been rattling loud enough to keep us all awake. I woke in the middle of the night. It was warmer and it wasn't sleeting. Snow was falling softly.

The next day it was gloomy and foggy, so we didn't even go outside for recess. A little after school was over Harry Dowles knocked at the door and said he needed a couple of things from the store. Joan's mother hadn't come to pick her up yet and I didn't like the idea of leaving the children alone, so I offered to give him the key.

He said no thanks. "Wouldn't want to be accused of shoplifting. Only take a minute," he said.

I peeked into the schoolroom. The three of them were playing so well that I didn't see any harm in leaving them for a few minutes. I told Chuck to make sure the three of them stayed in the schoolroom, then I went out.

In Mr. Strong's store, Harry said he needed some blue thread. The color he wanted wasn't on the rack with all the other thread so I had to hunt through some boxes before I found it. Then he asked for a tin of tea and five pounds of sugar. After I weighed out the sugar, he looked around, scratching his head. "Somep'n else I wanted," he said.

I should have realized then and there something was wrong, but I didn't. I reeled off a bunch of things and he kept saying no, none of them was it. Finally I told him I had to get back and that made him all kinds of nervous.

Then from outside I heard Cab yell out "Yah-h-h—mush!" I didn't take particular note of it except to wonder why he was leaving so late.

"Well," Harry Dowles said then, "I guess I can't think of it. You go ahead and tally up." He put a hand on the counter and it was shaking. I looked at him and his eyes shifted away.

And then it came to me. My first instinct was to say I was wrong, that nobody would do a thing like that. But then I knew I was right. It was written all over Harry's face, and I felt sick.

I ran for the door, and then I was outside, running along the path to the schoolhouse. Cab's sled was speeding up the trail beside Chicken Creek, and he was cursing his dogs a blue streak, yelling for them to move faster. When the dogs swung to the left where the creek jogged, the sled was in full view for a few moments.

Chuck and Ethel were in it.

CHAPTER 17

Except for little Joan, who was standing on the porch of the schoolhouse shivering, the whole settlement could have been deserted. Inside my quarters I asked her what happened.

She was almost too bewildered to tell me. And frightened. "They just came in here, Teacher," she stammered, "a whole bunch of 'em. They came in and took Ethel and Chuck away—just took 'em. I was scared they were gonna take me away too."

She broke into tears. It took a few minutes before she could tell me who had done it.

"Mr. Vaughn. And Mrs. Barrett. And that man whose sled it is . . . Why did they do that, Teacher?"

She looked as though she was going to cry again. "There's nothing to be scared of," I told her. "They won't be back."

I gave her a cookie to munch on and I looked around. The bureau drawers were open. At least they'd taken some of the children's clothes.

After Joan's mother came to get her, I sat listening to how quiet it was. I had to think, figure out how to get Chuck and Ethel back.

My hands were sweating and cold. I went over to the stove to warm them. I hadn't felt so bad since Fred had walked out on me. My mind was going a mile a minute. I tried to think where Cab was now. He'd probably gotten to Stonehouse Creek already. From there . . .

An idea hit me and I put on a few pairs of socks under my moccasins, got my parka and went out. It only took me twenty minutes to get to Fred's house. He was around back in the stable, sitting down, working the treadle of the grindstone, sparks flying from the ax he was holding. He looked up, and as soon as I saw him I could feel everything I'd kept bottled up inside me start to spill over. I was able to blurt out, "Fred, they took Chuck and Ethel away from me," and then I was in his arms blubbering and carrying on.

"They didn't have any right to do that," he said. "They didn't have any right at all."

"Fred, will you help me? If we can get to Cab before he reaches the Indian village I'll be able to reason with him. I know he'll let me have them back if I can just talk to him."

I was asking a lot, I knew that, and I made up my mind that if he said no I wouldn't ask him again.

"You sure you want to go after him?" he said.

"I do."

He thought about it. Then he said, "Go on home. Put on your warmest clothes and pack some spares. I'll be by as soon as I can."

A half-hour later Fred came to my cabin. He had everything we'd need for a week, he said. "I don't know how long it'll take us to catch up with Cab, and if the trail is bad we may need everything we have."

"Somebody just mushed in to the roadhouse. Maybe you can ask him."

We went over together. The man was trying to wolf down a steak and answer Maggie Carew's questions about the Terwilligers at the same time.

"You didn't see a sign of them at all?" Maggie asked.

"Only sled I seen was Cabaret Jackson's, 'n' that was about two hours ago," the driver said.

Her husband was trying to calm her down. "Now, Maggie, they coulda hit some bad weather and holed up in any number of places."

"What's the trail like through Franklin?" Fred asked him.

"Drifted in," the driver answered. "Unless you got somethin' won't wait I'd advise you to stay put."

"You're goin' after Cab," Maggie said to Fred.

Fred nodded and Angela Barrett said, "I hope he kills ya."

"Shut up!" Maggie snapped at her. Maybe she'd have felt the same way as Angela if she wasn't so worried about Jeannette and Elmer, but she didn't give a hoot right now about anything or anyone but them. "Be on the lookout, will you, Fred?"

"I will," he said. "But I wouldn't be worried if I were you. Elmer knows this country. He wouldn't do anything foolish."

A few minutes later we were in the sled. The dogs dug in, then swung to the right, and we were off.

Once we left the tundra behind it was like moving along in a slow-motion dream, following a trail that wound ahead without any end, dipping across a creek, narrowing around a hill, then around still another hill when that was left behind. The dogs never let up, trotting along at a fast willing pace when we hit the flats, digging in almost as if they enjoyed it when the going was rough. Night came on fast and black and the northern lights billowed like curtains across the starlit sky.

We reached the base of the saddle three hours later, a long slope of white with nothing to mark it but the twin tracks of Cab's sled running up as far as we could see. We rode down a long slough to the river, then once we were on it we went like an express train, swinging around big drifts and patches of rough ice. Again Fred was able to ride the runners for long stretches and I hardly had to get out. The river widened, and we began to pass little islands.

It was three hours later that we pulled up by a small cabin buried up to the eaves. The owner had dug a path from the door and uncovered the window, but otherwise you'd have hardly known there was a cabin there at all. "You stay here," Fred said. "I hear this man isn't too friendly."

There was smoke coming from the stovepipe and a faint yellow light coming through the window. Inside, a dog growled threateningly when Fred knocked.

"Did another sled mush by here in the last few hours?" Fred asked the man.

". . . Yeah."

"How long ago?"

"Maybe three hours. Cab Jackson it was."

"Thanks." He came over to the sled. "He'd go on to the O'Shaughnessy roadhouse. Probably stay there overnight. I'm for pushing on if you can make it."

"I can make it," I said meekly.

Those eight miles took us almost four hours, and when the O'Shaughnessy roadhouse came into view a bundled-up figure came out the door. It was Mr. O'Shaughnessy.

"Inside with ye," he yelled over the wind when he saw I was a girl. "Oi'll help yer man put up the dogs."

I didn't need any urging. The heat of the place hit me with a lovely

warm sting and the quiet almost made me reel. Mr. O'Shaughnessy's Indian wife had already pushed the table close to the oil-drum heater.

I kept my voice low. "Is Cab Jackson here?"

Mrs. O'Shaughnessy shook her head. "He left here a half hour ago."

CHAPTER 18

No, ye'll not catch oop with *that* bludy rascal bafore he's ta the Indian
village," Mr. O'Shaughnessy said in his thick accent.

"You're sure that maybe he won't stop anywhere else?" I asked him.

"An' where would he be stoppin'?" He seemed surprised I'd even ask
such a thing. "There ain't nahthin' 'twixt here 'n there but one cabin."

"What made him go on?" I asked. "What's his hurry?".

"Because he's daft! 'It's an outra-a-a-geous hardship for the little tykes,'
I sez to 'im. Wud he listen? He wud not. 'Oi has a mission,' he sez."

I looked over at Fred. There were dark circles under his eyes. He'd
hardly spoken a word since we'd come in. "Suppose we went over The
Drop," he asked Mr. O'Shaughnessy. "You think we'd have a chance of
catching him then?"

"The Drop?" He crooked his head and made a grudging sound. "It's a
bad toime for takin' that pass."

"It would save us two hours."

"You moight catch him," he said to Fred, "if your sled holds together."

"You have some chain I can borrow?" Fred asked.

"All ye need," Mr. O'Shaughnessy said.

Fred glanced at me. He was tired. We both were. He looked away
quickly. "If you'll tell me where it is I'll go get it," he said, standing.

For as long as I lived I'd never forget those next six hours. Compared to
the trail we now took, traveling on the river had been a breeze. We sidled
up hills that grudged us the narrow paths that bordered them and kept
trying to edge the sled off. Twice, for stretches of a quarter of a mile, Fred
had to put on snowshoes and break trail across snow that would have
swallowed us up to the waist, while I stayed at the handle bars inching the
sled forward. Time and again we both had to push from behind as the
dogs labored to pull the sled up a steep bluff or the sharp bank of a creek.
Half-buried bushes caught in the runners and tore at our moccasins.

In a little while the trail eased and we pushed ahead up a winding creek.
"There it is!" Fred yelled, "Ptarmigan Drop!"

It was just one long cascade of snow and ice-covered rock that ended half a mile below at Ptarmigan Creek. Even on foot you'd have to slide down most of it.

Fred was already untying the dogs. We were almost finished rough-locking the runners with chain when Fred pointed to something way off. "Look."

All I saw was the long flat sweep of the river.

"It's Cab," he said.

Then I saw it—a faint speck darker than the gray around it. From this distance it looked as if it was barely moving.

"You're sure it's him?" I began to feel excited.

"It's him," Fred said. "He may be a little ahead of us when we hit the river, but not much."

We finished chaining the runners quickly, then Fred told me to start down with the dogs. "I'll catch up with you." .

I started down with all the dogs except Pancake, Fred's lead dog. Fred needed him to keep the sled pointed. All I had to do was keep my balance and practically slide down, the dogs nipping at each other and frisking around.

Twenty minutes later we were back on the sled again, and we caught a glimpse of Cab's sled going around a bend in the river. A few minutes later when we rounded it ourselves there he was no more than a quarter of a mile away. We kept narrowing his lead until Fred called out to him. "Cab!" The hills picked it up and echoed it: *Cab. Cab. Cab.*

He stopped his team and waited. I couldn't see Chuck or Ethel. I saw him take off a mitten and rub his eyes, trying to see who we were. As soon as he recognized us back went the mitten and he was off again.

Cab let out a blood-curdling screech. "Mush, you buzzards," he roared. "Yah-h-h!" At almost the same time Fred let out a yell of his own and our sled jumped forward. We flew across that snow with the wind behind us and the sled rocking like a cradle. I slid down until I could just barely see ahead. We were running almost neck and neck.

We caught up with him at Cross Creek.

Fred stopped the sled far enough away from him so the dogs couldn't get to each other, then he just stood for a couple of minutes trying to get his breath back. Cab was out of breath too. I got out of the sled and went over to Chuck and Ethel. They weren't any the worse for wear, but they were scared. Ethel put her arms out to me and I started to lift her out.

"Leave 'er be, Teacher," Cab said. "Sorry you came all this way, but I can't let you have 'em."

I tried to convince him that he was wrong. No matter what I said he shook his head. He was doing it for my own good.

"Let her have them, Cab," Fred said.

"I wouldn't butt in if I was you," Cab said.

"If Anne wants those kids it's her right to keep them."

"I'm takin' them where they belong," Cab said. He took off his mittens. "That's the way it's gonna be."

Fred went to the sled and made as if to lift Ethel out. He never got to touch her. Cab charged right into him and gave him a hefty shove that almost made him lose his balance.

Fred just stood there with his mittens bunched up in front of him as if he wasn't sure how you went about the whole thing. Then all of a sudden Cab hit Fred on the side of the jaw. Fred fell right down, stunned. He spat a chunk of blood out and there was a tooth in it. I started to go over to him, but Cab said, "Leave 'im be, Teacher."

Fred wiped his mouth and smeared blood all over his chin, then he looked down at his tooth. When he looked up again I hardly recognized him. It wasn't only the blood, it was something else, that same expression he'd had when he'd almost fought Cab back in Chicken. I'd seen him get it on the trail when we had tough going. There wasn't any fear in it. It was calculating and deadly. All of a sudden I knew that the last thing he was going to do was call it quits.

Chuck and Ethel were on each side of me, holding on to me for protection. Scared, they'd clambered out of the sled and come right over to me.

Fred didn't get up fast, but when he did it wasn't like a man getting up, it was like an animal that was using every muscle in its body even before it was on its feet. As he did it a sound came from deep inside him that I didn't know a human being could make. When I heard it I felt that something terrible was about to happen, felt it even before Cab got hit the first time. Cab didn't have a chance. One second he was standing there with his fists weaving in front of him and the next there was blood spurting out of his nose and he was backing off with Fred wanting to kill him. I don't know how many times Fred hit him before he just toppled over backwards and his head hit the ice with an awful sound. Then Fred pounced on him, pounding him as if he'd gone insane.

I kept trying to grab him and pull him off, but he didn't stop until Cab's head was lolling, his face smeared heavy with blood.

We sat him up against his sled and put his mittens on him, then Fred set about trying to wake him up. We bathed his face with snow. His nose was broken and one eye was almost closed. Even after he healed, he wouldn't be looking the way he had before the fight.

He didn't come to for almost ten minutes, and at first he couldn't remember what had happened. As soon as he could stand up he told Fred he truly admired him, that he hadn't any idea Fred could handle himself that way. I was really worried about his being able to make it as far as the Indian village and so was Fred, but Cab said he'd be all right.

Chuck and Ethel were all bedded down in our sled and we were ready to go.

Cab still looked in bad shape. He smiled at me. "Teacher, I'll tell you somethin' from the bottom of my heart. You're an Alaskan."

"Thanks, Cab."

And that's the way we parted.

CHAPTER 19

S starting out, we piled Chuck and Ethel into the sled and Fred and I took turns riding the runners and trotting alongside. We'd take the route Mr. Strong followed, Fred said, along the river. If the weather held we could make the O'Shaughnessy roadhouse in seven hours, stop there to sleep, then push on for Chicken. He didn't say what we'd do if the weather didn't hold and I didn't ask. It would have been an easy trip if it hadn't been for the wind and the fact that we'd been up for almost twenty-four hours.

We'd been traveling for almost an hour. It must have been around nine o'clock and the sun should have been coming up. Instead it was growing darker and the wind was getting worse, lifting drifted snow and hurling it at us like balls of smoke. I was trotting alongside the sled when all of a sudden a blast came along that banged at us so hard I was nearly bowled over. Even the sled rocked. Fred stopped it and the dogs immediately dropped on all fours and started curling up.

"We're in for it!" he yelled.

The snow drove at us like a wall. We couldn't even talk. The two of us got down behind the sled and sat, waiting the blast out.

"Is it over?" I said after it died down.

"It hasn't started," Fred said, getting up. "This is just a lull."

"What'll we do?"

"Keep our fingers crossed. There's a cabin we can head for. A couple of miles farther up. We can hole up there."

A few minutes later the wind was at us again. It wasn't strong enough to keep us from going on, but it was meaner and colder than ever. I began to feel thirsty, and I had to stop myself from eating some snow. In this kind of cold it would be the worst thing to do, sucking precious body heat and giving nothing in return. The temperature was dropping fast and evaporating every bit of moisture.

We swung around a small delta, and Fred headed the sled for a big cleft in the bank, a slough. "Cabin's about a quarter mile up!" he yelled.

It was a long quarter mile. The land leveled off a little, and finally Fred stopped. He and Chuck went off to look around. I had to marvel at how fast they could move on snowshoes. Using them exhausted me, but Fred and Chuck swept around on them without the slightest effort. Fred kept moving farther and farther away, looking for landmarks, anything that would give him a bearing on where we were.

The dogs had been lying down quietly, muzzles flecked white. Now, one after the other, they got to their feet, sniffing the air. Either the wind had shifted and they smelled something they hadn't smelled before, or something was around that hadn't been up to now.

Pancake uttered a low growl, the ruff around his neck bristling. The other dogs were doing the same thing, and some of them began to whine. I called to Fred and he came over.

"Whatever it is, we can't worry about it," Fred said as Chuck joined us. "We'll head over that way." He pointed to where a double line of straggling willow and birch marked the path of a creek. "It's got to be around here somewhere."

He and Chuck started off, and I mushed the sled after them. The dogs started to move up the slough, then stopped dead, and no matter how much Fred yelled at them they wouldn't move. Whatever was a little farther on had them too frightened to move.

"Stay here," Fred said to me and Chuck. He moved along the edge of the slough, then when he was almost out of sight I saw him stoop down and pick something up. He came back with it—a length of dog harness. It had been chewed. "There's what's left of a dog over there, just the skull, a few bones and some hair."

"Bear?" I asked him.

"Wolf," Chuck said.

Whatever Fred was thinking he kept to himself. He chained the dogs to a tree, then took his rifle out of the sled. "You stay here with the kids," he said to me. "I'm going to take a look around."

"Oh no. We're going with you."

We slogged after him. I knew that wolves didn't attack people—at least not people who were alive—but I still felt nervous. Before long we found the remains of another dog. There was something else too. Chuck found it snagged in a bush—a small length of polished hardwood with some webbing attached. It was part of a sled.

We went on a little farther until we all stopped at almost the same time. There a little above us was some kind of a ledge in the path of the slough, almost as though someone had built a curved platform across its banks. On it a pack of wolves circled around something. We were downwind from them, so they hadn't caught our scent, and with the wind blowing they hadn't heard us approach.

I counted seven of them. The smallest wasn't under a hundred fifty pounds. They looked like ghosts through the flying drift, all of them staring at something, milling around as if they didn't know how to get to it. And that was the weird part. There was nothing there, at least nothing I could see.

They saw us a few seconds later. The way they sized us up made my skin crawl. Fred took aim, and his rifle cracked. The biggest of them, which must have weighed close to two hundred pounds rolled down to the end of the ledge, then just disappeared. The rest of them took off.

Fred told us to stay where we were and made his way up along the border of the slough. He glanced over to where the wolf had disappeared below, then moved out onto the ledge. I still couldn't figure out what it was, an ice bridge across the banks or what.

Fred went down on his hands and knees and inched forward. He stopped at right about the place where the wolves had been peering down and I thought I heard him call out, say something to somebody.

"Fred, what is it?" I called to him.

He turned and waved me over. "Leave the kids there," he said.

I followed the same path he took. The ledge was bigger than I'd thought, bulging up a little towards the center. It wasn't solid either. There was a jagged hole almost in the middle of it. It was big, maybe four feet wide and three times as long.

Fred pushed himself back from the hole. "Take a look," he said, ". . . It's Jeannette and Elmer."

I crawled up to the edge of the hole and peered in. It was like a scene from another world. Underneath me was a huge domed ice cavern, and there in the darkness a dozen feet below, her face partially covered with a fur robe, her eyes boring into mine, lay Jeannette Terwilliger. I thought she was dead until her eyes blinked, and I saw the glint of tears in them.

She was lying on her side among the rocks of the slough bed, a fur robe wrapped around her. Beside her was the smashed sled. Elmer was a short distance away from her. All I could see were his legs. He'd crawled up the side of the slough, where he lay now, not moving. I couldn't tell if he was alive or dead.

In a split second I saw it all as it must have happened: the loaded sled moving across the innocent-looking snow, the domed roof of ice under it giving, shattering like an egg and the sled crashing to the ravine below.

"Jennie?" I managed to croak out. "We'll get you out."

"You stay here with Ethel," Fred said. "I'll take Chuck with me." He gave me his rifle. "Hold onto this. You probably won't need it, but keep it anyway."

"Where are you going?"

"To find that cabin. I know where it is now."

He and Chuck went off to get the sled and while the two of us huddled together, I kept thinking about the accident and how it had happened. Jennie and Elmer had probably done exactly what Fred and I had—hit bad weather and come up here looking for the same cabin. For some reason they hadn't seen that the ledge was false until it was too late. I wondered how long Jennie had been down there. It could have been as much as three days, three days of lying in a frozen dungeon with hardly the barest chance of being found, and the wolves circling around above. If it hadn't been for the wolves we'd never have gone to the spot at all. She and Elmer probably wouldn't have been found until spring, maybe not even then.

Over an hour must have passed before Fred came back with the sled. "We've found it!" he said. It was drifted in, just as he'd thought. He'd left Chuck to finish the job of clearing the door. He'd brought a strong slender birch trunk with him that he'd chopped down. Tying a rope around the center of it he went over to the ledge and placed it across the narrowest width of the hole. After he made sure the ice on each side would hold, he let himself down the rope. I watched from above.

He lifted the sled off of Jennie. Half of the load was still in it, the rest of it—picture frames, a gold scale, mining tools, traps—was scattered all over the ravine bed.

He made Jennie as comfortable as possible and put another robe over her before he looked around. The slough was flat at the bottom, the banks sloping up gently to where the ice met them. He picked up a mattock that had spilled from the sled and chopped a good-sized rock loose from the frozen ground.

76

"I'm going to try to dig out of here."

"Fred, what about the baby?"

"I think it's all right. It's under her parka."

"Can you hand it up to me?"

"Jennie's arm is broken. I don't want to touch her until we can get her out. . ." He moved out of sight and I heard him start chopping.

I went back to Ethel and we waited. She fell asleep again before Chuck came back. When he did I told him what Fred was doing and he went over to the hole, swung himself over the birch trunk and disappeared. I kept looking towards the spot where I thought Chuck and Fred would come out for so long my eyes started doing tricks on me. Then finally I saw a small hole appear. After that the snow began caving in like quicksand, and I roused Ethel. Chuck's head popped up and he levered himself out of the hole. "We digged out!" he yelled excitedly.

I lowered myself into the hole slowly. My feet touched the solid bank and I felt Fred grab me. Then I was below the ice and Fred helped me down the bank.

It was like a gloomy world where time had stood still. Overhead was a dome of ice that stretched across from one bank to the other and maybe thirty feet up and down the slough. Outside the wind was howling, but it was quiet in here, snow flakes drifting down through the opening above. Elmer was stretched out on the bank opposite, his head almost touching the ice above him. He was frozen, one hand still upraised. There was a hunting knife in it, and above him you could see where he'd tried to chop away at the ice.

I went over to Jennie.

"Jennie, do you want me to take the baby?" My voice bounced off the ice above.

She nodded. I pulled away at the furs that Fred had covered her with, and lifted up her parka. The baby was lying against her stomach. When I lifted the blanket from her face my heart sank. Her face was a sickly blue, her little body still. The barest wisp of vapor curled from her mouth. I put her inside my own parka and she felt cold next to me.

Fred picked up a man's shirt that lay in a pile of other clothes. "Rip that up," he said. "I'm going to set her arm."

He went after the sled with an ax until he had two lengths of wood for splints. After that he rolled Jennie on her back and eased the broken arm out of her parka. While he set her arm in the splint I walked up and down the slough bed, hoping I could jostle the baby into making even the smallest move. It didn't do any good, though. She lay stiff.

Fred kept working methodically and I marveled at how he could act so coolly. "How's the baby?" he asked.

"She's not moving."

"You'd better give her to Chuck," he said. "I'll need your help with Jennie."

I handed the baby over. "Hold her tight," I said. I could have saved my breath. He was eight years old, but if ever I'd seen a boy act twice his age it had been him.

Fred lifted Jennie's shoulders and I took her legs. Halfway up the bank one of them slipped out of my grasp. Her foot dropped onto a rock, making a horrible sound—as if it was a rock itself. I glanced up at Fred, cringing inside. His mouth set itself in a tight line. Only one thing could have made a sound like that—a foot that was frozen solid.

CHAPTER 20

We made a few trips back in to bring out food and things for the baby. There'd been some traps on the sled, and before we left, Fred brought five of them out and set them around the hole. We hoped they'd keep the wolves away from Elmer's body.

When we reached the cabin I wondered how Fred had found it at all. It squatted so low against a hill that I didn't even see it until we were practically on top of it.

Inside, the sloping ceiling was too low for Fred or me to stand up straight except by one wall, and there wasn't too much room to move around. It was shelter, though, and it was all we needed. There was oil in a dusty lamp. After Fred lit it we brought Jennie in and laid her on a rickety canvas cot, then Fred started a fire in the stove.

I took Patricia out from under my parka. Her face and hands were a sickly violet, and there wasn't anything I could do for her except sit by the stove and hold her.

After we stored our gear and filled some pots with snow, I started some stew thawing while Fred and Chuck went to work on Jennie. Fred filled a small washtub with snow, then took the moccasin and socks off her frozen leg. He put it into the washtub and began to bathe the leg with snow while Chuck bathed her face. Jennie moaned softly and moved her head. Some snow fell away from her face.

"How bad is she, Fred?"

"Her foot's frozen to the bone. The leg may be too, I can't tell."

"What can we do?"

"Get her to a doctor."

Outside the wind was blowing hard as ever, making the stovepipe hum. "How can we?"

"We have to. *I'll* have to . . . Even if she does get to a doctor she's going to lose her foot, maybe the whole leg."

"Where's the nearest one?"

"Dawson."

That was over a hundred and fifty miles.

"I could take her as far as Forty Mile," he said. "There's bound to be someone who could take her to Dawson from there."

Forty Mile was the first town across the Canadian border, a distance of ninety miles. I didn't see how he could make it, not as tired as he was. The weather outside was as mean as ever.

"When would you start out?" I asked him.

"After we eat and I get a few hours sleep. You'd have to manage here alone. Mr. Strong's due up the river in a day or two. I'll leave word at Steel Creek that you're here. With the weather like this, well, you'll be here a couple of days. Maybe more.

"You better get to sleep," I said.

I took Patricia out of my parka to look at her again. She was losing her blue color and her little hands were pink.

Fred laid out another sleeping bag and told me to wake him in three hours. He fell asleep almost as fast as the kids had. My watch had stopped, so I set it at twelve, then sat down on the edge of the cot. Jennie's face had begun to blister. Her foot was still in the washtub, the skin on her leg beginning to wrinkle. I leaned over, picked up some snow and bathed her leg. When my hand touched the flesh it made me shudder.

After a few minutes I felt sleepy and got up. I took the baby out and rocked her. She squirmed a little and there was a flash of pink tongue before she sucked it back in her mouth. Then she stopped and was still.

There was a small fruit crate lying by the stove with some kindling in it. I laid some newspapers on the bottom, then wrapped a blanket around Patricia and placed her in the crate. After that I put some more wood in the stove. I caught myself falling asleep, so for the next couple of hours I kept putting snow on my face and neck to stay awake.

A half hour before I was supposed to wake Fred, Jennie thrashed around, screaming in pain. Immediately Fred was on the other side of the cot, holding her in a firm grip, talking to her while she stared at us wild-eyed. She kept trying to talk, but her mouth was twisted and her words were just a babble of sound.

"Jennie, you're here with Anne and me," Fred kept repeating. "You're safe. You're safe, Jennie. Try to understand."

The wild look went out of her eyes. She stopped struggling and fell back in exhaustion. She realized where she was. Her eyes closed and tears of pain welled up from them.

"Patricia's here, Jennie," I said. ". . . She's sleeping. Do you want to hold her?"

She nodded.

I brought the baby and laid her in the crook of Jennie's arm. She raised her head to look at the baby for a moment, then slumped back and closed her eyes. She had her baby.

"Jennie," Fred said, "I have to get you to a doctor . . . you understand?" She nodded without opening her eyes. "Anne'll stay here with the baby and take care of her." She only made the barest movement.

While Fred made preparations to leave I warmed up a chunk of vegetable soup and fed the broth to Jennie, then we carried her out.

Then Fred was gone, the sled disappearing in a gray swirl. I turned back into the cabin.

After a while I knew I couldn't stay awake any longer. I'd kept walking back and forth with Patricia as long as I could, coaxing her to wake up. It wasn't doing any good. She'd move a little, open and close a tiny fist, and that was all. I put some more wood in the stove, then crawled into Fred's sleeping bag with her.

I didn't know how much later it was that I started to wake up, thinking there was an alarm ringing somewhere. Groggy, at first, it made me angry until I realized it wasn't an alarm at all. It was a baby crying.

Beside me, Patricia was spluttering in rage—the most wonderful sound I'd ever heard.

I looked at my watch. It said 8:30. That meant I'd slept almost five hours since Fred had gone. I wondered what the real time was, whether it was day or night. I'd lost track and there was no way to tell. Sleet was needling at the window. It was iced over and it looked to be night outside.

Chuck's head popped out of the sleeping blanket. He eased himself out of it, shivered, then slipped on his parka. He watched while I tried to get Patricia to take the bottle I'd prepared.

"Baby no hungry," he said.

"She is hungry, Chuck. That's why she's crying. She hasn't eaten in a couple of days. I don't know what to do."

I tried the nipple again, but she spat it out and started crying. Maybe she was too weak to hold onto the nipple. "Chuck, get me the first-aid kit."

There was a medicine dropper in it, and I pulled some milk up into the dropper and put it in her mouth. When I was almost ready to give up she began holding on to a few drops.

"She's taking it, Chuck."

I put her back in the fruit crate, then set about getting a meal ready. Then, with the dishes done the three of us sat on the cot while I fed Patricia again with the medicine dropper.

Time passed, and Patricia woke up every hour or so. I kept trying her with the nipple, until finally—it must have been almost a day later—she took it. She finished a whole bottle, then threw half of it back up, but she was getting stronger.

We had been there three days before I heard a familiar sound.

It was Mr. Strong's sled. Chuck let out a yell and ran down towards the river and disappeared. A few minutes later I heard him yelling and calling to Mr. Strong, the sound of the bells on the sled getting louder.

I put Patricia on the cot, then went out to wait until the two of them appeared, making their way up towards me, Chuck hopping and jumping like a sparrow, Mr. Strong clumping along after him. I was so happy to see him that I threw myself into his arms and almost knocked him over.

"Now, madam," he cajoled, "don't take on so. The situation is well in hand. We'll be out of here in no time."

He hadn't seen Fred, he said, but Fred had left word where I was at Steel Creek.

He stayed long enough to bring Elmer's body into the cabin, and there he left it covered with a blanket, the knife still clutched in Elmer's frozen hand. Then we started out.

Later on, a few days after we were back and school was open again, the one thing that stuck in my mind was the moment when the settlement came into view. Sure enough, everybody was waiting in front of the post office. I caught a flash of the surprised look on everybody's face as we went by—Mr. Vaughn's all displeased at seeing Chuck and Ethel, Angela Barrett's screwed up in anger. Mr. Strong halted the sled in front of the roadhouse and he'd already jumped down and was pulling the tarp back from us when everybody came running up.

Everybody was staring at me and the children, Mrs. Purdy startled, wondering where Fred was, nobody saying a word. I had Patricia beside me, all swaddled in a wolf robe with just an opening for her to breathe, so nobody saw her until I picked her up. As soon as Maggie Carew saw what I was holding the life seemed to drain out of her. I handed the baby down to her and she took her from me, her eyes asking the questions she couldn't bring herself to ask out loud.

Mr. Strong lifted me down from the sled and after that I hardly knew what was going on. Everybody was pressing forward, Mr. Carew asking me in a croaking voice where Jennie and Elmer were, Mrs. Purdy wanting to know about Fred, all the faces around me stunned, none of them angry anymore. Then Chuck and Ethel were beside me and Mr. Strong was herding the three of us into the roadhouse and trying to keep people back, telling them to give me a chance to get inside and warm up before they made me answer all their questions.

CHAPTER 21

For the whole first week I was back Maggie Carew made me and the children come over to the roadhouse for supper. She said that I'd been through an ordeal and that she wanted to make sure I had plenty of good hot food and didn't wear myself out. Her husband had left with Mr. Strong the next day, headed for Dawson, and she was all alone except for Patricia and the children. Having me there helped her feel better, she said, helped her feel closer to Jennie. She tried not to keep asking me if I thought Jennie would be all right, but she couldn't stop herself.

Even when Fred came back we didn't know much more. He pulled into the settlement in the early afternoon eight days later, and a few minutes later we were all in the roadhouse listening as he told us what had happened. He'd mushed Jennie as far as Forty Mile, where he ran into the man who carried the mail up and down the Yukon between White Horse and Eagle. They transferred Jennie to his sled and he'd mushed off with her to Dawson. There was a telegraph station at Forty Mile and they'd wired the authorities at Dawson that Percy was carrying an injured woman who was going to need treatment. "Before I left," Fred said, "Dawson wired back that there'd be a doctor waiting at the hospital."

It wasn't until the end of March, three weeks later, that Mr. Strong returned with the full story. Jennie's face wasn't going to be scarred, he said, but they'd had to amputate her foot to well above the ankle.

Maggie took it pretty hard, and it worked a big change in her. Not that she became soft, just a little more tolerant. I knew that deep down she still felt that I had no business having Chuck and Ethel with me, that I was making a mistake, but she didn't look at them anymore as if they carried the plague or something worse. She even had them come over to the roadhouse every so often to play with Jimmy and Willard. Everybody else who'd been mad at me kind of eased up a little too. Maggie had a lot to do with it, I was sure. She swung weight in the settlement, and when people saw her having me and the children come over to the roadhouse they started acting a little more sociable. Then one night when I went over to the roadhouse to pick up Chuck and Ethel, Maggie asked me a question that surprised me.

"You done anything about buying yourself a cabin in Eagle?" she asked me. "You gotta provide your own quarters."

"I know," I said, "but I still don't know if I'll be teaching there."

"What makes you think you won't?" she said.

"Well, nobody told me I *wouldn't*," I said, "but I didn't think the chances were too good."

Maggie's lip curled into that disgruntled sneer of hers. "I know everybody on that schoolboard," she said, "and if they got any objections I wanna hear about it . . . How much you want to pay for a cabin if they take ya? How big a one might you want?"

"Well . . . big enough so maybe Chuck and Ethel could have their own room."

"We'll find you one," Maggie said. "Far as I'm concerned a bird in the hand's worth two in the bush. We know what we got with you. Lord only knows what they're liable to send out from Juneau if we let'm."

Having Maggie on my side went a long way. Nobody came up to me and told me they thought any better of me than they had before. That wasn't people's way. It was just something I could feel, something in their manner. Like at the next dance we had.

When everybody came in they gave me a big hello or a howdy instead of just a grudging nod as they usually did, and one or two even made a point of admiring the map of Chicken on the wall. As big as it was, they'd never seemed to notice it before. Now they said they'd never seen anything like it, and how clever all the kids were to have made it.

The only thing that didn't change at all was the way things were between Fred and me. I didn't see him again for almost three weeks after he got back, and then only when he came in to pick up some hardware he'd ordered from Mr. Strong. He'd made up his mind he was going to stay away from me for my sake and that was that.

Sure enough, came mid-April Mr. Strong brought me the news that I'd been accepted to teach at Eagle. I was happy about it. Yet at the same time I wasn't. Chuck and Ethel were worrying me. Ever since I'd brought them back to Chicken we hadn't been getting along.

I had to keep after them all the time—to dress neatly, to be clean, to help me keep my quarters in order and to mind their manners around people. I wasn't doing it just to be bossy. It was for their own good. Even though the uproar over them had died down, most people still looked at them differently.

Stupidly, I felt that any criticism of them was criticism of me and I decided I wasn't going to give people a chance to criticize. I really kept after them. At the same time I nearly worked myself to death ironing dresses for Ethel, scrubbing, washing, and keeping my quarters neat so that people would have a good impression when they came. I was especially tough with Chuck, always reminding him to hang up his clothes, to mind his manners, speak correctly, be good.

The two of them kept fighting me on everything, or at least that's the way it seemed. Ethel started eating half the time with her hands and getting food all over her. One time she got up on a chair, pulled down some of her newly-ironed dresses from the wall and stomped all over them. Chuck changed too. I had to force him to wash up all the time and getting him to take a bath was a major battle. He became lazy in his schoolwork and surly around the house.

Something had to give, and it did. They both ran away.

We tramped through the wet woods, yelling and calling, but there was no sign of them. Around midnight everybody went home, telling me not to worry. It was the beginning of May, the nights were short and kind of dusky-daylight. I stayed out until past two before I gave up and went home to change out of wet footgear and go looking again.

I couldn't think about sleep. Over and over I imagined them lying at the bottom of a cliff, or swept away by a swollen creek, or attacked by a bear. I had a cup of tea and I forced myself to sit down and try to think calmly where they might have gone. The first thought that occurred to me was that they might have headed for the Indian village. A couple of times when I'd bawled Chuck out he'd threatened to. If they were headed there it might take all day to catch up with them.

The sun was nudging in the window, tinging everything with gold. I looked around the room, and noticed that Chuck's rifle was gone. And his parka. The last time I'd seen him he'd been wearing his mackinaw, which meant he must have taken the parka out some time before he left. The more I looked around the more I noticed things missing: a few of Ethel's dresses, a dress suit I'd bought for Chuck, a couple of blankets, two pillow cases. There was only a little bread left in the breadbox, and I knew there should have been two loaves. Chuck must have been removing things bit by bit over the last few days and caching them somewhere. They'd taken too many things with them to carry all at once, especially if they were going to the Indian village. If they were anywhere it was someplace in the vicinity. And if I was right there was only one place where they could have gone. I ran out.

The spicy odor of willow buds was in the air when I reached the trail that led down to Mary Angus' shack. I pushed the door open and there they were, the two of them lying on a bed of spruce boughs, sleeping together under a couple of blankets.

I bent over them and stared at them a long time before I woke Chuck up. They were beautiful. I remembered them living here with their mother. They'd been cold and hungry more often than not, but that hadn't mattered to them because they'd had *her*, the one person in the world they'd loved and trusted, the one person who knew and understood them. Here in this shack she'd touched them and held them. Not me. Her. They hadn't asked for me. Even though I was the only one in the world who cared anything about them, they hadn't asked me to take them. I was a stranger. So they'd run away from me and come back to where there was nothing but a memory of someone who'd held them close, spoke to them softly and loved them the way Granny Hobbs had loved me.

"Chuck . . ."

He woke up slowly. I watched his eyes, wanting to see what would be in them when he was aware of me, whether he'd be looking at a stranger or at someone who cared for him. What I saw hurt.

"What you want, Tisha?" It was a simple question, no more than that.

"I came to take you home," I said.

He shook his head. "No."

"You can't stay here."

"I stay for a while. Hunt. Get meat. Then I go Indian village. I go live with Indian mudda."

He meant Lame Sarah, the old woman he'd lived with in the Indian village. "I guess that means you don't want to live with me anymore."

"No more."

"Why?"

"I hate you, Tisha," he said simply. "You not nice me."

Ethel woke up, innocent and beautiful as the morning. She stared at me the way he had.

"Am I angry at you all the time?"

"Alla time. Alla time angry me, angry Et'el too."

"Does Ethel hate me as much as you do?"

"More. Say you white devil-woman. Make scare her. She no more live with you too. We live with Indian mudda. She like us."

"Chuck, I love you. You and Ethel."

"Tisha, you tell one very big lie."

"I'm not lying at all. I mean it."

"Oh, no. You hate me, say I bad boy. Alla time bad boy." He was getting aggravated.

"Is that what I do?"

"Foreva! All day long you say, 'Chuck, you bad boy, you make floor dirty. Oh, Chuck, you bad boy, you make mud all over clothes. Chuck, you do not have good manners, dirty, make table dirty, make big mess, make everything dirty.' Tisha, " he spluttered, "soon you tell me I make whole world dirty!" I didn't want to cry, but what he said next cut the ground from under me.

"Once upon a time, Tisha, you be nice to me. You be so nice I love you truly." He shook his head. "No now. Now you shame me. Shame way I talk. Shame everything me. You no love me, Tisha. You hate me."

He said it so simply and honestly that I burst into tears, ashamed of myself. Then we talked. He told me how much I'd picked on him and tried to get him to do things in the past month that were too tough, and the longer we talked the more I realized he was right. I'd been ashamed of him, and of Ethel too. In class I gave everybody extra help but him. At lunchtime I asked nobody else to mind their manners but him. It didn't matter why I'd done it. I'd been wrong. Instead of hugs and pats for the things he'd accomplished I'd given him criticism for the things he hadn't.

In the end he and Ethel came home with me, and I promised him things would be different.

CHAPTER 22

After that I stopped trying to make Chuck and Ethel into model children. They tested me a few times. They spilled things, splashed water from the barrel and insisted on wearing the same clothes for too long, wanting to see what I'd do. When I didn't pay any attention to it they stopped by themselves. In fact, about a week after they ran away, when I was dumping some of my own clothes in the wash boiler, Ethel came up to me with a little blue dress that was her favorite.

"What do you want me to do with it?" I asked her.

"Do." She pointed to the wash boiler.

"Wash? You want me to wash it?"

"Yiss," she said. "Watch."

It was just around then, in mid-May, that spring came. Tender shoots of grass sprinkled the hills and wild canaries flashed through trees haloed in green. I started taking the class on field trips again and we even started our own garden. I wouldn't be around when it came up, but it was fun just the same.

At the end of May we held the last dance.

Everybody kept asking me if there was anything wrong with me, wanting to know if I was having a good time. I was, but I couldn't help feeling sad. In a few days I'd be leaving, yet when I looked around the room it seemed to me as if it was only yesterday that I'd arrived. In less than a year I'd lived a whole lifetime here.

With Fred playing the banjo during most of the square dances, I only got to dance with him once. If it was up to me we wouldn't have left each other's side. On this night of all nights especially I wanted to be with him as much as possible. Even after Uncle Arthur wound up his gramophone and the round dancing started we didn't get to dance together that much. Since I was going away, Uncle Arthur and Joe and some of the other men insisted I had to dance with them at least once. I didn't mind it early on, but as it started to get late and there was more and more chance that Uncle Arthur would play *Home Sweet Home,* I began to get nervous.

I'd just danced with Jake Harrington when Fred ambled over to me. He had a big smile on his face.

"You look like the cat that ate the canary," I told him.

"Funny you should say that. I was just licking my chops."

"Over what?"

"Over the supper you and I are going to have."

Uncle Arthur had already put the next record on and was lowering the needle. The *Home Sweet Home* waltz began to play. Then I saw that there were a whole bunch of people smiling at the two of us. Uncle Arthur gave me a little wink. "We had it all arranged," Fred said.

His arm slipped around my waist, and like the first time we danced that waltz together the walls of the schoolroom moved right back and everybody disappeared. I was so far away in my mind that not until the record was over and everybody began to clap did I realize that no one else had danced. All of them had stopped to watch Fred and me.

It was almost two in the morning and everybody was just about done eating when a couple of chords sounded on the piano. Maggie Carew came out carrying a huge chocolate cake with a candle in the center. She set it down in front of me. "Good Luck" was written on it in icing. I was too surprised to say a word, even more so when Uncle Arthur walked over with a beautifully wrapped box and handed it to me. "We passed the hat around and got this for ya," he said. "A little token of our appreciation."

Inside the box was about the most expensive camera you could buy, all black leather and nickel plate. Everybody clapped and yelled for me to make a speech.

"I wish I could," I said, "but I'm not very good at making speeches. All I can say is, thanks—I appreciate it."

"No more than we appreciate you, Teacher," Ben Norvall said. "There isn't a soul in this room that doesn't think you're a fine honest girl and a true-blue Alaskan to boot."

It was almost three when Fred and I left and went for a walk.

As soon as we were out of sight of the settlement Fred took my hand. We talked a little about Eagle and what it would be like living there with Chuck and Ethel. He said he wanted to come and see me after the freeze-up. We sat down on a grassy creek bank to scoop up a drink. The water was cold and sweet, dyed clear amber from roots and dried hillside moss.

"I guess you're relieved," I said, lying back. The ground was warm.

"About what?"

"That I'm going."

"Why should I be?"

"You won't have me chasing after you anymore."

"You didn't do that," he said.

"Yes, I did. I'm doing it right now. I'll be leaving in a few days, so what does it matter? It's the truth." He didn't like hearing that, but I didn't care. I didn't have a bit of shame left in me and I was glad of it. He could be a gentleman if he wanted. I was sick of being a lady. "I've been chasing after you almost from the time we met."

That made him squirm. "Anne, if I could give you a home, if I had money enough to take care of you, I'd ask you to marry me right now."

I felt like shaking him, doing anything to make him realize I didn't care how much he had or how little, that all I wanted was him. There was no point to it, though. We'd been through all this before, so I just stared at him long enough until he couldn't do anything else but kiss me.

When I finally opened my eyes and looked into his I loved what I saw.

"I want to say something to you," I told him.

He waited while I got it all straight in my mind, and I said, "I don't know what it is you think you have to have before you want to keep company with me, but you just remember this, I love you. I won't be chasing after you anymore because we're going to be far away from each other, but some day, when you get ready, you better come and marry me. Because I'm never going to marry anybody else. I mean that, Fred Purdy. If you don't marry me some day I'm going to be an old maid."

"No you won't," he said.

"Is that a promise?"

"That's a promise."

"You better not break it."

"You better not break your promise either," he said.

A little while later we started to walk back arm in arm, stopping every so often to linger and embrace. We went on that way until we came in sight of the settlement, then we let each other go.

September 16, 1975

Fred and I didn't get married until over ten years later, on September 4, 1938. By that time Chuck had graduated from high school, Ethel had entered it, and I'd adopted three more children.

It was worth all the waiting, though. We had a grand life together. Fred mined in the summer, and in the winter sometimes we stayed home, sometimes we packed up the family and went Outside. One winter, maybe the finest we ever spent, we took on the job as teacher and custodian in an Indian village. As for children, Fred loved them as much as I did, so we went ahead and adopted four more.

I'm 67 years old now. Fred passed away ten years ago, and although I've since gotten over the sharp pain of losing him, I still miss him badly at times. Mostly when there's a gentle rain falling. I think of it falling so quietly all over the hills, soaking into the ground to bring out new life, and it's hard for me to accept that I'm never going to see him again or hear that wonderful laugh of his. It's as hard as trying to imagine springtime without the sound of birds.

Anne Hobbs Purdy
Chicken, Alaska

BRING ON THE EMPTY HORSES

A condensation of the book by

DAVID NIVEN

David Niven accepting an Oscar for his 1958 role in Separate Tables.

CHAPTER 1

THE PLAYPEN

When Gertrude Stein returned to New York after a short sojourn in Hollywood, somebody asked her, "What is it like—out there?"

To which, with little delay and the minimum of careful thought, the sage replied, "There *is* no 'there'—there."

To try to describe to the reader the self-styled "Glamour Capital of the World," it seems best to do so as it appeared just before the outbreak of World War II, because although this book describes some events between 1935 and 1960, that particular upheaval caused the number of inhabitants and automobiles in Los Angeles to double. Up until then there had been plenty of room and fresh air for everyone—one square mile for every four persons, to be precise—very little industry, the worst transportation system of any major U.S. city and clear blue skies without a hint of smog.

There were four ways to approach Los Angeles from the East Coast: (1) by automobile, which took ten days of fast driving and entailed facing red dirt roads across large tracts of Arizona and New Mexico with no prospect of a motel at the end of the day; (2) by train, leaving New York on the 20th Century Limited at 6 P.M. and standing respectfully aside while famous movie stars smiled for the New York papers as they were escorted by railroad officials along a red carpet to their sleeping compartments; on arrival at Chicago the following morning, the sleeping cars were shunted around the marshaling yards and by noon were tacked on to the rear of the Santa Fe Chief (steam locomotives until 1939), which two days later puffed to a stop at the Union Station, Los Angeles, where the famous movie stars perched on piles of matching baggage and smiled for the Los Angeles papers; (3) by plane, which was not for the fainthearted—a minimum of eighteen cramped and often nerve-racking hours flying in unpressurized and largely unheated twin-engined machines at low altitudes through sometimes appalling weather with the nasty possibility of thudding into either the Allegheny or Rocky mountains at one end of the trip—or (4), as I did it, by sea, an endless voyage of fluctuating comfort in a "dry" ship via Cuba and the Panama Canal.

The whole Los Angeles area was subject to frequent earth tremors, accounted for by an ill-advised proximity to the San Andreas Fault, and on the very day of my arrival in San Pedro I had noted from the deck of SS *President Pierce* that people at dockside beneath a swaying water tower were scurrying about looking nervously upward, wondering which way it would fall. It didn't, as it happened, and the next morning the Chamber of Commerce routinely reassured us that there had been no cause for alarm, but it was perhaps an early warning that I was heading for the breeding ground of stresses and strains.

The "film folk," I discovered, unwound at their favorite playgrounds, the beaches, the mountains at Arrowhead and Big Bear and the desert at Palm Springs—a tiny colony in the middle of Indian-owned land which boasted a main street and two hotels. Santa Anita Racecourse was also very popular with them, and there were various country clubs which dispensed golf, tennis, and an extraordinary degree of segregation. Not one had a black member, and several refused to have Jewish members, prompting the Jewish community to start their own country club and to take in no Gentiles. (They also found oil in satisfactory quantities beneath their fairways, which provided them with a splendid opportunity for nose thumbing.) But the topper was the prestigious Los Angeles Country Club which adamantly refused to have anything to do with *anyone* in the motion-picture industry irrespective of race, creed, or color.

Everything in Southern California seemed to me to be an enlargement—the bronzed and sun-bleached girls and boys of the beaches were representatives of a master race bred in freedom, sunshine, and clean air—but if the robins were the size of pigeons and the butterflies had the proportions of bombers, the diminutive honey-hunting hummingbirds brought things back into perspective as they whizzed about with their tiny waistcoats of turquoise, vermilion, and gold flashing in the sunlight.

The relaxed villagelike atmosphere of Beverly Hills was very catching, and at the hub of the movie social wheel in the Brown Derby restaurant, the men wore loafers, open-neck shirts, and sports jackets, while the girls, lately liberated by Marlene Dietrich's earthshaking appearance in a man's suit, appeared enthusiastically in slacks, and the waitresses were pretty, would-be actresses in varying stages of disenchantment.

The two tennis clubs most highly regarded by the movie colony were the Beverly Hills and the Westside. The Beverly Hills was by far the better club, and the tennis there was of a much higher standard, with Fred Perry giving points and taking on all comers, but I myself joined the Westside because the committee had wisely decided that beautiful girls were a more digestible ingredient than perspiring professionals. I will never forget a fancy dress party on the premises at which at young lawyer named Fred Bautzer arrived, on his face a grin so wide he looked like a Hammond organ and on his arm, aged seventeen, ridiculously beautiful, and dressed as Bopeep, Lana Turner.

In the late thirties the twice-weekly program presented by most theaters consisted of a newsreel, a cartoon, a short, the second feature, and the first feature. The whole show lasted for a bum-numbing four hours, but as a result, Hollywood was booming, with Metro-Goldwyn-Mayer, one of the seven major studios, boasting that it alone turned out one feature film each week.

Edmund Lowe was famous for many films, but chiefly for the one he made in partnership with Victor McLaglen, and he and his secretary befriended me soon after my arrival in Hollywood because she decided that I looked like her employer. She had noticed this resemblance because I had been standing outside the main gate of Paramount Studios watching for the stars in their fancy automobiles and had stood out, apparently, from the curious throng of sightseers and out-of-work extras, because in my mouth had been a large cork. This cork and the likeness to Edmund Lowe had so intrigued the lady that she had ordered the chauffeur to return and bring me before her master. Eddie Lowe was a friendly, smiling man; he explained that he was looking for a double and asked me if I would be interested in the job. I thanked him and told him that I was hoping to become an actor myself and did not mention that I thought he looked like my father.

"Why the cork?" he asked. I explained that E. E. Clive, an elderly character actor from the theater who had cornered the film market in butler and judge roles, had lately given me a valuable hint on how to increase the resonance of my voice which he had decided was negligible.

"Get a long cork, my boy," he had ordered, " out of a hock bottle preferably—thought I doubt if many people drink hock in this backwater—shove it lengthwise between your teeth, and when you have nothing better to do, repeat the Lord's Prayer half a dozen times. It'll work wonders."

Under Eddie Lowe's sponsorship I spent days wandering about the back lot and also the main studio at the heart of the Dream Factory, where for some reason the buildings, parking lot and streets were uniformly white or pale yellow, thus extracting the maximum amount of glare from the cloudless California sky. Twenty or thirty towering, hangarlike sound stages clustered together dominated the center, surrounded by the fire department, the generator turbines, the electrical grid, the transportation, construction, carpenter and plasterer departments, cameras and electrical stores, wardrobe departments, legal departments, acres of dismantled sets and furniture repositories, tailoring and dressmaking shops, and ever-widening circles of photographic studios, painters' stores, cutting rooms, makeup, hairdressing, and sound departments, projection rooms and theaters, rehearsal halls, orchestra recording theaters, accommodation for set designers and set dressers, the story department, accounting offices, publicity offices, casting offices, fan mail departments, greenhouses, restaurants, a hospital, a gymnasium, and a shoeshine parlor.

An outer circle was rather stately by comparison, and green lawns softened the overpowering glare of the buildings, the barnlike dressing rooms allotted to the swarming extras and the double-decker rabbit warrens which housed the small-part actors. Shaded by trees, connected by paths, and sourrounded by flowering shrubs, the bungalow dressing rooms of the stars gave an outward impression of an enclave of peace and tranquillity, but inside, as I was to learn, their walls bore the scars of countless exhibitions of temperament, noisy moments of triumph, and far too many lonely heartbreaks.

I was also to learn that writers got drunk, actors became paranoid, actresses pregnant, and directors uncontrollable. Crises were a way of life in the Dream Factories, but by some extraordinary mixture of efficiency, compromising, exuberance, gambling, shrewdness, experience, strongarm tactics, psychology, blackmail, kindness, integrity, good luck, and a firm belief that "the show must go on," the pictures came rolling off the end of the production lines.

The star system was the logical answer to the first question asked by investors when it was hinted that they might put money into a film or by moviegoers when it was suggested that they should buy tickets to see the finished product.

"Who's in it?" they would cry.

The studios expended immense sums providing attractive answers to this question by signing established stars to long-term contracts and by discovering and developing young unknowns to take their places later.

Once a studio was convinced that performers had "caught on" with the public, great care was taken to maintain their popularity by presenting them only in roles and vehicles in which their special talents and attractions would be displayed to the maximum advantage. On the other hand, when a studio became disenchanted and convinced that a star's popularity was waning, a wide variety of maneuvers were employed to bring their mutual contract to a speedy conclusion. The easiest way, of course, was to mobilize the forces of the actor's own congenital insecurity and give him an inferior part to play. The actor would fluff up his feathers of hurt pride and "refuse to be seen in such a crappy role." The studio then, piously referring to the wording of the long-term agreement between the actor and itself, would suspend the actor's contract for the duration of the picture and instruct its publicity department to leak the news to the world that their hero was a man who refused to honor his obligations. Certainly if an actor refused to perform, he could not expect to be paid, but the monstrous thing was that even if the studio handed an actor a bad part *truly* believing it to be a good one, and he turned it down, not only was he suspended for the duration of the filming of the picture (probably at least four months), but he was also suspended for an additional 50 percent of that time *as a punishment* . . . and the entire period of six months was added to the end of the contract.

Some of us gave twelve or fourteen sulfurous years of our short actor's lives working off a seven-year contract which had originally been conceived in mutual admiration and respect.

After one important actress had the guts to take her case against Warner Brothers all the way to the Supreme Court, a ruling was handed down that no contract with an employee could be extended without the employee's consent, and every contract actor in Hollywood blessed Olivia de Havilland . . . but after her courageous stand, she was seldom offered a role in a Hollywood picture.

When a film was completed, the next trick was to sell it to the public, and studios allocated millions of dollars to their publicity departments to this end. In the earliest days circus-type ballyhoo had been employed, and the first recorded press agent, Harry Reichenbach, was in fact lured away to the "moving pictures" from Barnum and Bailey's Circus. The first film he was hired to publicize was *The Return of Tarzan*. His method was effective. He booked into a smart New York hotel just across from the theater where the picture was opening, and a wooden crate was delivered to his room. He then called room service and ordered fifteen pounds of raw meat to be served for his luncheon. The waiter on arrival let out a piercing yell and dropped the meat—wearing a napkin, a large lion was sitting at the table. The waiter sued, and the headlines blossomed.

Francis X. Bushman was nervous about the possible non-renewal of his contract, so he hired Reichenbach to impress his studio by underlining his popularity.

Reichenbach made Bushman walk with him from Grand Central Station all across New York City to the studio office. By the time he arrived the easily identifiable figure of Bushman was being followed by enthusiastic thousands, traffic was jammed, and the studio heads witnessed a most impressive chaos from their windows. What they had not noticed was Reichenbach walking immediately behind Bushman and dribbling several hundred dollars' worth of nickels and dimes through a hole in his overcoat pocket.

Publicity departments went through their most difficult period when the studio heads decided that their stars should represent the sum total of all the virtues: They should not drink, swear, or, above all, copulate, and they must be presented to the public as the All-American Boy or the Girl Next Door. Self-inflicted dents in the facades of these paragons had, therefore, to be papered over without delay, so close contacts were forged with the police departments of Los Angeles, Beverly Hills, and the San Fernando Valley, and over the years only a thin trickle of the normal output of nightclub brawls, drunk drivings, scandals, accidents, assaults, attempted suicides, and rapes were reported in the press.

For each production a unit publicist was ordered to remain on the set from the first day of shooting in case anything newsworthy took place; in addition, in the main office, were specialists for the trade papers, general news specialists, magazine specialists, radio specialists, and legmen whose only job was to service the top columnists throughout the country, and all the while the still photographers dutifully pumped out reams of cheesecake, home layouts, and fashion layouts. Publicity campaigns for personalities and individual pictures were not always mounted with the meticulous planning of D Day, and occasionally they misfired.

Warner's, with misguided zeal, tried to show its top "tough guy," Edward G. Robinson, out of character and persuaded the iron man to be photographed in a bubble bath, but it quickly had to mount a second campaign to nullify the first because whispers became widespread that Eddie Robinson was a "fairy."

A quite extraordinary rapport existed between many stars and the publicity chiefs of their studios—the sort of understanding that soldiers develop for one another when experiences have been shared—and many stars, who had been nursed through marriages, divorces, disasters, scandals, tremendous triumphs, and dreadful inflations, found themselves disproportionately dependent on the counsels of these men. A risky situation, when one considered the number of cupboards that were clanking with skeletons, and, with puritanism rampant across the country, how fatal to careers it could have been if there had been a misuse of the keys, but there was a flamboyant honor among the publicity men, and I never heard of one of them breaking his vows of silence.

Hollywood was a village, and the studios were the families. Everyone knew everyone else's business, weaknesses, kinky leanings, and good points. We were all in the same boat, involved in the early years of a terribly exciting experiment; it was an international community, and there was the maximum of camaraderie and the minimum of bitchiness. At all studios, employees from the most glamorous stars to the lowliest riveters on the heavy construction gangs felt that they were members of a team, gloried in the success of their "hit" pictures, and occasionally indulged in college humor at the expense of their rivals. "In case of an AIR RAID" —they chalked up on the main entrance at Paramount—"go directly to RKO . . . *they* haven't had a hit in years."

Hollywood was hardly a nursery for intellectuals, it was a hotbed of false values, it harbored an unattractive percentage of small-time crooks and con artists, and the chances of being successful there were minimal, but it was fascinating, and IF YOU WERE LUCKY, it was fun. And anyway, it was better than working.

CHAPTER 2

THE KING

A blond sunburned fuzz covered his muscular forearms, and his pot-belly hung over the top of his pants. Gross, pig-eyed and rude, Chet Liebert was a loathsome human being but he had one great asset—a 45-foot spear-fishing boat named *König*. He also had an undeniable talent in his chosen profession, and by the other charter boat skippers working out of Balboa, California, he was grudgingly acknowledged to be the most successful. They had no option but to bestow this accolade on him because every year he caught more broadbill and marlin swordfish than they did.

In an effort to keep deckhands, he paid generously, and this attracted me to him like a moth to a flame. As a $2.50 a day Hollywood extra, who worked only spasmodically, I was in no position to be choosy, so I swallowed the heavy insults and eagerly grabbed the $6 a day he gave me for ten hours of dangerous, dirty, and backbreaking work as a deckhand, spotter, spearman, hauler, gutter, and swabber.

When we were out spearing the giant broadbill swordfish for sale in the market, I took those six bucks, but I also gratefully pocketed the generous tips that were slipped into my hand when *König* was chartered by private individuals in the more exciting and less exacting pursuit with rod and reel of the blue and white marlin.

"Okay, so you're late," said Liebert when I showed up for work at five o'clock one morning. "Get her cleaned up from top to bottom, gut a dozen flying fish, and check two sets of gear and the teasers—make sure the head is spotless too, goddammit, because we've a charter today and the guy is bringing a broad with him. They'll be here at six thirty, and they'll need breakfast, so see that the coffee's ready, and stand by with ham and eggs and all the crap. They're picture people," he added, "so keep your goddamned trap shut about being a lousy phony actor, and get on with the job."

By six o'clock on a still and cloudless morning *König*, as ordered, was swabbed down, mopped, dried, and polished, and by the time a large open Packard turned onto the quay, the aroma of good coffee was rising from the galley.

"Okay, now go over and fetch their gear, and don't get movie-struck," he added.

When I approached the Packard, I saw what he meant—the girl was blond and willowy with a fresh, open, fun-loving face. She wore a blue reefer jacket and red slacks, and her yachting cap was tilted at a rather exotic angle over her right eye. I don't think I noticed what the large, muscular man was wearing—he was opening the trunk of the car, and his back was toward me—but when he turned around, smiled, and said, "Hi, it looks like a good day," I nearly fell into the harbor. The man was Clark Gable.

I relieved him of rods, various professional-looking tackle boxes, a large ice bucket, a bottle of scotch, and watched him stride purposefully toward *König*; the blonde held onto his arm.

"Okay, Chet, bait 'em up and let's go," he yelled happily as he leaped aboard.

We had a lucky day. Gable landed two big blue marlin and was once broken after an hour's struggle with a gigantic, leaping mako shark. We also found a school of hungry yellow tail tuna which were striking at everything in sight, and even the blonde amid shrieks of excitement landed a couple of twenty-pounders. She also became rather maudlin toward late afternoon when she hooked a dolphin on a white feather lure and decided that it was the soul of a dead sailor . . . the whiskey bottle was almost empty by then. She pawed Gable a great deal.

Six months later, in the spring of 1935, I landed something myself, a small contract with Samuel Goldwyn, the doors of Hollywood began to open, and I met Gable again. The iron man from Cadiz, Ohio, was looking rather trapped in white tie and tails, but the occasion demanded his discomfort. It was the Academy Awards presentation dinner—the annual handing out of the early Oscars. The year before he had won one himself for his performance in *It Happened One Night*, and his acceptance speech was the shortest on record, two words—"Thank you!"

He did not win this time, though his picture *Mutiny on the Bounty* came out on top. Excitement ran high among the 200 tribesmen and women who filled the private banqueting room downstairs at the Ambassador Hotel. A demure Bette Davis was proclaimed the winner for her performance in *Dangerous*, and Victor McLaglen (who, to everybody's delight, belched loudly when receiving his prize) was voted Best Actor for his portrayal in *The Informer.*

Gable was seated with a party from his studio—Irving Thalberg, the producer of *Mutiny on the Bounty*; Thalberg's wife, Norma Shearer; Jean Harlow; William Powell; Joan Crawford; and others. Ria, Gable's second wife, was also there, and I looked at her with interest. Several years older than her husband, she looked very calm and distinguished, and Gable was smiling across the table at her in the conspiratorial way happily married couples signal mutual boredom at dull parties. I was remembering with pleasure the unaffected charm and friendliness Gable had dispensed aboard *König* when, suddenly, he glanced directly at me. For a moment he looked puzzled; then my face must have clicked into place because he waved, smiled a friendly smile, and mimed the hooking of a big fish. I nodded and waved back, and after the presentations were over, he came to Goldwyn's table and shook my hand.

"Good to see you again," he said. "What are you doing here, trying to get Sam to go tuna fishing?"

I felt embarrassed at first telling it to the "King," as he was known throughout Hollywood, but bathed in the warmth of the great man's personality, I relaxed and explained that I had changed my job and had lately landed a contract with Goldwyn.

"Well, that's just *great*," he exploded. "I'm moving over to the Goldwyn lot for the next one, so I'll hope to see you around. We can forget about making pictures for a while and yak about steelhead—is that a deal?"

"Fine," I said, delighted at the prospect of seeing him again and not unaware of the soaring of my personal stock among my high-powered dinner companions.

Several weeks later Goldwyn gave me my first speaking part: the role of a sailor in *Barbary Coast*—it consisted of one line: Thrown out of the window of a waterfront brothel in San Francisco and sailing past the madam, I was called upon to say, "Orl right—I'm goin'!" Then as I lay facedown in several inches of mud, the two stars of the picture, Miriam Hopkins and Joel McCrea, accompanied by several donkeys and a posse of vigilantes, walked over the top of me.

Gable was by now working at the Goldwyn Studio making *The Call of the Wild*, and on the morning of my big moment he, the greatest star in the Hollywood firmament, took the time and the trouble to walk over to the back lot to wish good luck to an unknown beginner. He also insisted on stills being taken of the two of us, and the Goldwyn publicity department gleefully grabbed the golden opportunity to rub off a little of the "King's" glamour onto their nameless charge.

Several times I visited Gable while *The Call of the Wild* was being made, and I soon discovered that he had many other things to talk about besides fishing and hunting.

Certainly, more than anything, he enjoyed the great outdoors, and just as surely he felt uncomfortable at formal parties and despised the Hollywood hostesses and their "success lists."

"They only invite me because at the moment I'm on top of the heap," he said, "but when I fall on my ass, they'll just move someone else up a notch, and I'll go down to the bottom of the pile."

One January day we did more than talk about the big fighting seagoing rainbow trout of Oregon. His excited voice came over the telophone. "Hey! Let's go! . . . I've just been talking to some pals who have a fishing camp on the Rogue—the steelhead are running!"

"I don't have a rod," I said feebly.

"Forget it," he said. "I've got everything—I'll pick you up at noon, we'll spend the night in Frisco and be at Grants Pass tomorrow afternoon."

He was a fast and dedicated driver, and he made it clear that he could do without the small talk because it ruined his concentration. This was perfectly all right with me, and I sat back and reveled in the glories of two-thirds of California.

At Grants Pass, where we stayed overnight at the fishing lodge, we were joined in the cold dark of the following morning by the guide, who came with his wife to fetch us. A squat, unsmiling, flaccid-faced Indian who smelled heavily of spirits, he was, according to Clark, the best man on the river. He was also the worst driver in the neighborhood and in the semi-gloom of that freezing winter dawn, his dilapidated Chevy, unbalanced by trailing a heavy fishing skiff behind it, swung terrifyingly around icy mountain bends. Clark watched me averting my eyes from the roaring river several hundred feet below, noted my tight smiles and high-pitched polite conversation, and correctly diagnosed my condition as one of abject terror.

"Don't worry," he said. "He'll make up for it when he gets on the river, and his wife, thank God, drives us back." He indicated the almost totally round and equally smelly lady who was huddled, unspeaking and blanketed, beside her erratic husband.

As the sky began to lighten we slithered down a winding track and came to rest on a sandy beach between towering gray pine-topped cliffs. There we manhandled the skiff into the water, loaded it, and watched as the spherical wife took her husband's place behind the wheel and disappeared in a barrage of flying gravel up the almost perpendicular hillside, to meet us at dusk miles downriver.

Gable was wearing a heavy checkered mackinaw and his "lucky" long peaked cap. He had not bothered to shave, and a heavy black stubble was discernable in the growing light. It was bitterly cold.

"What are you giving us for breakfast, Chuck?" he asked the Indian.

"Small trout fried in butter," said the unsmiling one, "but you've got to catch 'em before I can cook 'em, don't you?"

"Sure thing." Gable grinned. "Let's get going."

The river was broad and sluggish where we put in, but the Indian knew the likely pools, and using a wet fly, we soon had half a dozen beautiful brook trout about eight inches long.

We pulled over to a sandbank, and while Gable and I collected dry driftwood, the guide, with a few quick flashes of his hunting knife, cleaned our catch.

You learn a lot about a man in four days of strenuous fishing and four nights of medium to heavy drinking. There was not a phony bone in Gable's body.

Clark had a moderate opinion of studio heads.

"They're bastards," he said flatly. "They encourage people to be larger than life, they'll give 'em anything, take any crap from them provided they'll interest the public and the public pays to see them, but the moment they slip—oh, brother! Look at the kids on our lot at Metro now, Garland, Taylor, Gardner, Rooney, great kids, all of 'em, and loaded with talent, but they'll probably ruin 'em all. Right now they can do anything they like, show up late, keep everyone waiting, go home when they want to, but God help them if the public stops coming—they'll pull the rug out from under 'em all over town."

I asked how it felt to be in the number one spot in the whole industry.

"Well"—he laughed—"as sure as hell there's only one place I can go from where they've got me now! So I just go along with Tracy's formula and hope for the best."

"Tracy's formula?"

"Sure. Get there on time, know the jokes, say them the best way you can, take the money, and go home at six o'clock."

Gable talked about Hollywood and everything connected with it, but he remained completely unimpressed by it. He certainly never took his success for granted.

"Look," he said, "so they call me the goddamn 'King' at the moment, but there are dozens of people warming up in the wings, and anyway I'm just out in front of a team, that's all. Metro has half a dozen people, top writers, whose only job is to find the best possible properties for me, things that I fit into with the least risk of falling on my ass . . . that way I remain valuable to them, and everyone's happy—for the moment."

"Don't ever let them kick you around," he warned. "They squeeze people dry and then drop them. When you start to fade, they put you into skid pictures so you'll turn them down and they can put you on suspension and get you off the payroll. Be tough with them if you get up there, because it's the only language they understand, and that's the only place where you can use it. Remember you're dealing with people who believe that a two-thousand-dollar-a-week writer is guaranteed to turn out better stuff than a guy who is only asking seven fifty.

"Most executives at the big studios have no guts. They're so busy holding onto their jobs they never stick their necks out. Know how Lubitsch found out the other day that he was no longer head of Paramount? From his goddam masseur, for chrissake! This guy had been rubbing down the studio brass, and they all told him what was happening, but nobody had the guts to tell Ernst to his face that he was through."

Gable never spoke much about his wives; he felt no urge to unburden his domestic problems on his friends, and he was strangely fatalistic when his marriages broke up, which they did with great regularity. He never went out of his way to make men friends. He reckoned that he was what he was, people could take him or leave him, and if they preferred to leave him, that was perfectly OK with him. Above all, unlike so many big stars, he felt no need to bolster his ego by surrounding himself with stooges and sycophants, so his circle of friends was small and independent.

It is difficult to paint a fascinating picture of a man whom nobody seemed to dislike. As David Selznick remarked during the filming of *Gone with the Wind*, "Oh, Gable has enemies all right—but they all like him!"

However, wherever there is competition there is jealousy, and where there is jealously the knockers will knock. So in Hollywood people occasionally nudged each other and said, "Gable only likes older women."

It was the understatement of the century—Gable loved *all* women: older, younger, blondes, brunettes, and redheads . . . he loved the lot.

True, his first wife, Josephine Dillon, happened to be twelve years his senior, and his second wife, Ria, five years more than that, but Carole Lombard, Sylvia Fairbanks, and Kay Williams, when they became numbers three, four and five, were all in the junior league.

It was said by the knockers that Josephine, who was a well-educated drama teacher, had "invented" Gable, and the same source of bitchery passed around the happy word that Ria had paid for him to have his teeth capped. Clark just laughed when he heard this. "My mom and dad invented me," he said, "and L. B. Mayer paid for my teeth."

Clark was not really stingy with money; he was "careful." With the whiskey bottle, however, he was always lavish, and for years I was amazed at the amount he could consume with no apparent effect.

Gable said that acting did not come naturally to him—"I worked like a son of a bitch to learn a few tricks, and I fight like a steer to avoid getting stuck with parts I can't play."

He never agreed that his breakthrough into the Hollywood big time was the glamorous rocket-propelled affair claimed by the MGM publicity department and always gave credit for it to two people: Lionel Barrymore and Joan Crawford.

Barrymore got him a test for the native boy in *Bird of Paradise*. Barrymore directed the test himself, and according to Gable, "They curled my hair; then they stripped me and gave me a G-string; a propman stuck a knife in my G-string, which scared hell out of me in case his hand slipped; then he stuck a goddamn hibiscus behind my ear and told me to creep through the bushes."

Irving Thalberg, the boy wonder of MGM, saw the result and told Barrymore, "You can't put him in a picture. Look at his ears . . . like a bat!"

Nevertheless, he was finally hired by MGM to play a milkman in a Constance Bennett picture, and a small contract followed, which brought in its wake the all-important contribution by Joan Crawford. She bullied and cajoled the studio till Gable was given a major part in *Dance, Fools, Dance*—a tough hard-boiled character. His success was instantaneous. The critics raved, and the movie audience found a new hero, and for what it's worth, both Crawford and Gable always vehemently denied that their friendship was anything but platonic.

I have hinted that Clark was a little close with a buck, but this was only in connection with things his honest Dutch-German blood persuaded him were extravagant or unnecessary. For instance, none of the many women in his life were ever seen festooned with goodies.

Divorce, however, was something else again. Gable never skimped on that, and to obtain his freedom from Josephine, Ria, and Sylvia, he, almost without arguing, was nearly wiped out financially three times in the process. Each time he was divorced, he issued the same hopeful statement: "I don't intend to marry again—ever" but each time he soon forgot what he had said.

One of the interim ladies to whom he was attached for a while observed, rather sourly, "Of course, Clark never really *married* anyone. A number of women married *him* . . . he just went along with the gag."

As I came to know him better, I became convinced that he would consider no marriage perfect without a son—he really longed for a family.

In the mid-thirties there was a rather snooty success-conscious club in Hollywood named the Mayfair, whose members attended dinner dances in the Beverly Wilshire Hotel. Norma Shearer, reigning queen of MGM, and her brilliant husband, Irving Thalberg, arranged a foursome there one Saturday night and invited me to bring the delectable Merle Oberon.

Everyone at the club got dressed up to the nines; white tie and tails for the men, and the women were told most particularly to wear white. Everyone in the film business knew that a splash of red on the screen immediately drew all eyes, and the dress designers, in those early days of Technicolor, invariably swathed their leading ladies in crimson or vermilion. There was, therefore, a gasp of indignation when our party made its entrance and it was seen by the local vestal virgins that alone in the room, Norma Shearer was wearing a bright-red dress.

Gable that night was escorting the fascinating Carole Lombard, who was renowned for her uninhibited observations, but a second gasp went up when she asked in a loud voice, "Who the fuck does Norma think she is? The house madam?"

Carole and Clark made a highly attractive couple. Carole had everything that Clark wanted in a woman. Supreme blond good looks, a sense of humor, lovely wild bursts of laughter, his own brand of down-to-earthness and, most important, his love of wild country, hunting, fishing, and the same determination to separate her public life from her private one. They were soon openly living together, a situation made a little tricky by the fact that Clark was still married to Ria.

Hollywood was going through a housecleaning phase at that time, and people shacking up together came in for some tart observations from various organizations, church groups, legions of decency, and so forth.

The number one fan magazine, *Photoplay*, brought this simmering criticism to a boil with an article entitled "Hollywood's Unmarried Husbands and Wives."

It is difficult to imagine in these permissive days that such a dreary piece of journalism could so easily have put the cat among the local pigeons, but the cluck-clucking of disapproval first heard in the Bible Belt of mid-America became a rising crescendo of threats to boxoffice receipts by the time it reached California, and the big studio brass soon hauled their emancipated stars onto the mat and bludgeoned them into reorganizing their nesting habits.

Clark and Carole, Constance Bennett and Gilbert Roland, George Raft and Virginia Pine, Robert Taylor and Barbara Stanwyck, Paulette Goddard and Charlie Chaplin were all mentioned in the article, and most of them bustled off to their priest, minister, or rabbi and toed the party line.

Ria Gable played a cool hand with good cards, and Clark paid a stiff price to become respectable, so stiff in fact that whenever thereafter he criticized Carole, she was apt to crack, "Well, what did you expect for a lousy half million, for chrissake—perfection?"

Apart from a few almost clandestine games of golf, I saw little of Clark once Carole entered his life; they were completely happy in each other's company and needed no stimulation from outsiders. I tried to organize a couple of all-male fishing safaris, but Clark made no bones about the reason for sidestepping my invitations. "The trouble is," he said, "Carole thinks you're a pain in the ass." I must have looked a little crestfallen because he laughed and softened the blow by adding, "As a matter of fact, she thinks anyone is a pain in the ass who might be a better fisherman, a better shot, or a bigger boozer than she is. Don't forget this is my third time up at bat, and one lesson I have learned about wives is that the first thing they want to do is get rid of all their husband's friends. It'll soon pass, but I'm not going to fight it."

In September 1939 they invited me out to the house for a farewell dinner. Clark and I sat in deep armchairs in the paneled den, and Carole sat on the floor at Clark's knee. We ate and drank, and the conversation was perhaps a trifle stilted because I was off to the war, and as none of us knew what the hell I was letting myself in for, we talked of other things. They were so happy and evidently had so much together that I wondered aloud if there could be anything else they had their eyes on. Carole looked up into Clark's face.

"I'll tell you what Pappy wants," she said quietly, "and I just hope to Christ I can give it to him. . . . He wants a kid."

"Yeah, that's right," said Clark, stroking her hair. "I'd give my right arm for a son."

There was a semi-embarrassed silence till Carole let out one of her famous yelps of laughter. "And he's sure as hell working on it!"

Shooting had just finished on *Gone with the Wind*, and Clark said he was delighted with the result. He had nothing but praise for Vivien Leigh—"She's going to be the biggest thing in this business when they see the picture."

David Selznick he admired enormously, but Selznick's penchant for bombarding him daily with memos about his performance left him unmoved—"I never read the goddamn things." He said, "All you can do is put your trust in the director and try to give him what he wants. If you start horsing around trying to please everyone, you wind up a nothing."

During our last evening together Carole had talked a little about Hitler. She really hated everything he stood for. Clark had been more phlegmatic—for him it all seemed like a famine in China, something one read about in the papers before one turned hurriedly to the sports page—but Carole was already arguing powerfully that the United States should get into the war. Later her sense of patriotism increased a thousand-fold, and the day after Pearl Harbor she wired President Roosevelt offering both her own and Gable's services in any way they could be useful. This hardly earthshaking but nevertheless helpful offer to a harassed chief of state was duly filed in some government office, and later their help was invited to go on a bond selling tour. Clark was stuck finishing a picture, so Carole went alone.

The tour started in Salt Lake City and wound south through Texas. The last stop was Fort Wayne, Indiana.

Carole booked a sleeper on the train for Los Angeles, but at the last second, anxious to get home, she changed her mind and caught a milk-run plane instead. Gable was delighted when she phoned him and made plans for her early return. Carole loved gags, so Clark dreamed up a surefire one. He borrowed a wax nude dummy from the studio, fixed it up with a long blond wig, and carefully arranged it in a suggestive pose in Carole's bed. Then he spruced up to go to the airport. Carole's plane had already taken off from Las Vegas, the last stop, about an hour before, and Clark was just getting into his car when a call came from the studio police department. Something had gone wrong with Carole's flight, they said; they had no other details, but Eddie Mannix, one of the vice-presidents of MGM and a close friend of Clark's, was on his way out to the house; a plane had been chartered to fly to Las Vegas.

A terrible chill settled on Clark. He waited for Mannix. On the way to the chartered plane Mannix told him the latest news. Someone had seen an explosion in the sky thirty miles from Las Vegas, and another pilot had reported a fire burning fiercely on Table Rock Mountain. Carole's plane was still unreported two hours later, when Gable and Mannix reached Las Vegas and a search party with packhorses had been readied to make the ascent to the summit. Mannix talked Gable out of going with the searchers.

"It could be a false alarm, Clark," he said. "How will she feel if she arrives home and you're not there to meet her?"

Clark remained at the foot of the mountain, and Mannix went up with the climbers. After hours of toiling through deep snow the charred and smoking debris of the plane was found scattered over a large area. Mannix was able to identify Carole chiefly by a pair of earrings which he had helped Clark choose for her.

Clark did not delegate to anyone the making of the necessary heartbreaking arrangements. Ice-cold and monosyllabic, he supervised everything himself from the ordering of a hot meal for the exhausted search party on that dreadful night to the choosing of hymns for the funeral three days later. Then he went to the Rogue River, holed up at his favorite fishing camp, and for three weeks drank himself into a stupor.

MGM, with the soaring costs of an unfinished picture very much on their minds, dispatched mealymouthed emissaries to inquire as tactfully as possible when their star might be expected to report for work. Clark never saw them. He just roared through the locked door of his cabin, "I'll be back when I'm good and ready . . . now beat it."

Finally, he showed up unexpectedly at the Culver City lot. Outwardly he appeared unchanged. He kidded with old friends and dropped in to see acquaintances. Always on time, always knowing his lines and as always, the professional. Grief, like everything else, was very private to Clark.

The day his picture was finished he enlisted, asked to be trained as an air gunner and to be posted overseas. Clark did several bombing missions over Germany, and one flak-shredded plane he was in nearly disintegrated over the Ruhr. No false hero, he said he was scared stiff the whole time.

With the end of the war in sight Clark was released from the service.

GABLE'S BACK AND GARSON'S GOT HIM screamed the billboards all over the world. Clark was being relaunched by MGM in a dreary potboiler with, as costar, someone not among his most favorite leading ladies.

He lived at his Encino ranch, the thirty-acre spread in the San Fernando Valley where he had so far spent his happiest days. Carole's room was a shrine, and nothing was allowed to be touched—her clothes, photographs, perfume bottles, all remained exactly as she had left them—but the sprawling white brick-and-frame house did not become a mini-monastery. Far from it—its steps were polished by the expectant arrival and disappointed departure of a steady stream of carbon copies of Carole Lombard: beautiful blond ladies of the utmost attraction and sophistication whom he entertained, "used," perhaps, and in several cases, sent away broken-hearted, actresses, society ladies, cover girls and secretaries.

They all did their best to fill Carole's shoes. They laughed with him, drank with him, and even apprehensively donned blue jeans and safari jackets and went duck hunting with him, but when each in turn failed to measure up, Martin, his faithful majordomo, would lower the electrically controlled boom at the end of the driveway and Clark would seek lonely comfort in his favorite whiskey.

When I returned to Hollywood after the war, Clark seemed to be withdrawing more and more into his shell. I think the arrival of my wife Primmie and myself, with our two little boys, provided him with a tiny port in his personal storm. At any rate, hardly a day went by when he did not drop in at the appalling Moorish prison of a house which we had rented in Beverly Hills, loaded with goodies for the children and playing with them for hours; and he found great peace and comfort in the calm serenity of Primmie.

We had been installed in the Moorish prison only six weeks when Clark called early one morning.

"Come on, kid," he said. "I've got it all fixed. We'll drive up to Pebble Beach and play golf for a few days. I've got a bungalow for you two at the country club, and I've got permission for us to fish in the reservoir up in the forest . . . that's elk country in there . . . maybe we'll show Primmie an old-fashioned California elk."

We took off, and Primmie's eyes were like saucers as we drove north through green rolling hills to Santa Barbara through the Alisal Ranch and San Luis Obispo, then along the coast road below W. R. Hearst's castle at San Simeon, through Big Sur, and along the high winding scenic route to Monterey with the tumultuous and incongruously named Pacific crashing against the rocks far below.

We played a lot of golf, stayed up much too late, caught very few fish, saw no elk, and laughed all the time. Clark was at his best, completely relaxed and reveling in showing Primmie such a spectacular section of his beloved California. During the weekend Primmie wrote to her father in England saying she had never been so happy in her life. Two days after we returned to Beverly Hills, as the result of an accident, she died.

I don't know how people can get through periods of great tragedy without friends to cushion and comfort them. To be alone in the world when disaster strikes must be an unbearable refinement of the torture, and I will forever bless those who helped me over the initial shock, but there comes a time when friends have to get on with their own lives and you have to face the problem alone—this is the worst part.

During that long period of utter despair Clark was endlessly thoughtful and helpful, and he checked up constantly to see if I was all right. Without my realizing it, he was drawing on his own awful experience to steer me through mine, and for the next eighteen months I saw a great deal of him, being one of the small handful whose voice on the intercom at the electrically controlled ranch gate was instantly greeted by Martin with "Why, drive right on up—Mr. Clark is right here."

Martin adored Clark and always had his best interests at heart, but sometimes his anxiety over his employer's well-being got the better of his judgment. Once I drove "right on up" with a particularly attractive companion who happened to be a happily married lady from San Francisco, and Martin decided that she was just his master's type, so he slipped a Mickey Finn into my drink and drove me home semiconscious.

Women adored Clark, but although he loved them and their beauty and gaiety, he was never a womanizer in the crude sense of the word.

"Hell," he said, "If I'd jumped on all the dames I'm supposed to have jumped on, I'd never have had time to go fishing."

If he ever discussed any of the aspiring beauties who visited the ranch, it was only in a generous, laughing, and flattering way—very unlike the broadsides he reserved for the new guard at MGM. L. B. Mayer, whom he had disliked but respected, had been replaced by others whom he disliked and despised. He also seemed to have lost interest in making pictures, a normal reaction among actors who had been away fighting a war; it seemed so childish for a fully grown man to put on makeup and spend the day playing charades.

He drank more than before and gained weight, which worried him. To counteract this tendency, he lapped down Dexedrine, which was supposed to make him lose his appetite. All it did, however, was make his head shake alarmingly.

I went away to Europe for six months to make a film, and when I returned, Clark seemed slightly perked up. He was even issuing occasionally from the ranch and being seen in public with a couple of his favorite dates, a sweet, gentle blond actress who lived near him in the Valley— Virginia Grey—and Anita Colby, a top cover girl from New York who was so beautiful she was known all over the United States as the Face.

He also seemed to take heart from the fact that, with great good luck, I myself, after two years, had again found great happiness and had remarried while in Europe. He approved mightily of Hjördis and was the first guest we invited to our house in Pacific Palisades.

Clark made no bones about it—he was longing to be married again— but when a man of fifty is looking around desperately hoping to fill a void, he is usually not seeing too clearly.

Sylvia Fairbanks, the widow of the inimitable Douglas, fascinated Clark from the moment he met her, and because of her ravishing blond beauty, her outspokenness, and her impeccable sense of humor, she seemed to him to be out of the same mold as Carole. There is no question—he rushed it. A few weeks after he had met Sylvia they called us from Santa Barbara in a haze of champagne (not his favorite drink incidentally).

"Guess what?" yelled Clark. "We've done it! We're married!"

As usual, Clark had kept his mouth shut about his love affairs, and it would have been grossly unfair, in the unlikely event that he had asked my advice, if I had by a single word tried to reverse the trend, but I had known both of them for many years, and I would certainly have marked them down as a high-risk combination.

Clark was a selfish man; Sylvia was a selfish woman . . . so far a standoff. Clark was a man's man, but Sylvia was a man's woman . . . a red light. Clark lived for the open air, blood sports, the big country, and large dogs. Sylvia was devoted to the great indoors, to her milky white skin, her flawless complexion, loathed the thought of animals being slaughtered, was happiest among the chattering chic of café society and owned a Chihuahua the size of a mouse named Minnie.

Possible friction points could perhaps have been welded into a great happiness by their mutual devotion to laughter had it not been for a further divergence: Clark was close with a buck, while Sylvia adored spending money.

Three weeks after they were married Clark was looking grim. Sylvia had blithely revamped Carole's room at the ranch and invited some smart friends from the East to come out and stay in it.

The King, with the expression of a man with a dead fish for a tiepin, was occasionally seen carrying Minnie, and when he returned from Long Island and Nassau, whither Sylvia had dragged him to meet some of the "beautiful people" of the day, it was obvious that a gross miscalculation had been made. After seventeen months of marriage Sylvia, claiming she had been locked out of the ranch upon returning from a second and this time solitary trip East, retained the great criminal lawyer Jerry Giesler to take care of her side of the divorce proceedings, only to discover that Clark had no intention of being wiped out for a third time by the California laws on community property and had taken certain evasive action. He had arranged for his contract to be suspended by MGM and had created a legal residence in Nevada, whence he moved everything he owned except the walls and roof of the ranch.

True to form, Gable kept his mouth shut about how much this latest and shortest idyll had cost him, but once the settlement had been made, his sense of humor returned, and he took a certain delight in displaying to his friends his Christmas card from Sylvia: "THANKS A MILLION." Then he issued his customary statement—"I don't intend to marry again *ever*"—and took off for Africa to make *Mogambo* with Ava Gardner and Grace Kelly.

When he returned from Africa, he spent a few months touring around Europe in a sports car; the passenger seat was seldom empty. I was filming in England and Italy, so Hjördis and I were treated to previews of the selected passengers, and inevitably the ones in whom he seemed most interested were all outwardly Lombardesque.

Mogambo was released and was a big hit, the most successful picture Clark had made since MGM wanted him to sign a new long-term contract, but the King was tiring. He was sick of the studio, the people who were running it, and the petty politics in which they indulged. So after fifty-four pictures and twenty-three years, he left MGM, never to return. He was oddly vitriolic about the company that had found him and built him up. Of course, he too had had a sizable hand in his own success, but surprisingly for such a down-to-earth man he fell into the actor's trap of thinking he had done it all by himself, and nothing would ever persuade him to make another picture at the studio. MGM, in turn, fell into the usual studio trap—they thought they could "buy" him back, and the more vehemently he refused to return, the higher went their offers. They finally gave up when they learned of his instructions to his agent: "See how high you can get those sons of bitches to go; then tell 'em to take their money and their studio and shove it up their ass."

His choice of pictures after leaving MGM was not inspired; in his mid-fifties even the King was finding it difficult to land good roles. A realist, he tried not to look over his shoulder, but he knew only too well that the Young Pretenders were breathing down his neck. A long love affair with scotch was also beginning to show. He was becoming heavy and bloated, but above all, he was lonely, and his dream of a happy marriage and perhaps a son was fading rapidly. There was a discernible air of quiet desperation about him, but he kept his own counsel, retained his humor, and soldiered on.

The sun when least expected came out for Clark at the age of fifty-five. One day he ran across someone he had seen only a couple of times in the past ten years, Kay Williams. Kay was his type in looks, blond, beautiful, and with periwinkle-blue eyes, but she also possessed something which attracted him even more, something which Carole had had in abundance. She was gutsy; she didn't kowtow to anyone; she was prepared to give as good as she got.

She had a couple of other things too that he liked the look of as soon as he saw them—a little boy of four and a girl of three.

"The kids'll screw it up for Kay," sniffed one of Clark's ex-girl-friends to me. "The son of a bitch might go for her if she had dogs instead."

Kay had been divorced three times, was now in her mid-thirties, and had decided that her acting career would never amount to much, so she was ready with a wealth of experience to settle down and make the right man happy. His friends knew it was serious when Clark disappeared from view, the boom was lowered at the ranch, and he no longer showed up at gun clubs and golf courses. A year later the two of them surfaced to get married in northern California.

Kay was perfect for Clark, and she set out intelligently to make him happy and content. Instead of sweeping the memories of Carole under the rug, she encouraged them. She became a good shot and an excellent fisherwoman, played golf with him and, if she didn't actually go drink for drink with him, usually contrived to have a glass in her hand at the same time he did.

Soon after they were married, Kay became pregnant, and Clark was ecstatic with joy, but after eleven weeks, she lost the baby, and he doubted if his longing for a son could ever be fulfilled. Kay's two children adored Clark, and he was a redoubtable stepfather but—

Every picture was a job to Clark; the complete professional, he gave full value to work at hand. He was always on time, always word-perfect, always prepared to do his utmost to give the director what he wanted. Engrossed as he was in his marriage, he did jobs as they came along, but his popularity remained enormous, and in spite of the rather mediocre material he selected, on the edge of sixty he seemed indestructible.

Early in 1960 he finshed making *It Started in Naples*. The shooting of this nonsense had been mostly on the island of Capri, and bored by the smallness of the place and by the endless attentions of the paparazzi sent swarming over from the mainland by his leading lady's producer husband, he took heavily to the pasta and red vino. By the time he returned to the ranch he was thirty pounds overweight, but he couldn't have cared less and even talked blithely of retiring. Then one day a script arrived on his desk that really fascinated him. The screenplay of *The Misfits* had been written by America's number one playwright—Arthur Miller. John Huston was to direct, and for costars he would have Marilyn Monroe and Montgomery Clift. The role was perfect for Gable, the best he had been offered in years, and in a high state of excitement he and Kay took off for the desert, where he promised himself he would get into top shape before shooting started. He played golf every day, watched his diet, and cut right down on the booze; the professional was getting down to his fighting weight for a special job. In July 1960 he reported to the location near Reno, Nevada. He was the picture of health and vitality and looking forward eagerly to the start of the film.

There was a delay. Monroe called from Los Angeles to say she was unwell and could not come up for several days. Shooting was postponed, but any annoyance or letdown that Clark might have felt was quickly eliminated when a radiant Kay arrived with the best possible news from her doctor: She was pregnant again. That was a lovely day for Clark. Everything at last seemed to be perfect.

John Huston was not too happy with Arthur Miller's script—the first screenplay Miller had tackled incidentally—but the annoyances or rewrites and script conferences paled into insignificance with the arrival of Monroe and Clift. Marilyn had acquired a reputation for unprofessionalism and had a nasty habit of showing up late for work. She had become a mass of inhibitions, terrors, and indecisions, and the poor doomed girl was headed for a breakdown. Montgomery Clift a few months previously when leaving the hilltop home of Elizabeth Taylor and Michael Wilding had smashed through the guardrail on the twisting mountain road, and when he had been extricated from the wreck, many bones were broken and his face was terribly disfigured. Plastic surgery had done miracles, but the shock and the necessary pain-killing drugs had changed him terribly. Now he was subject to fits of the blackest depression, and he, too, frequently found it unbearble to show up on the set.

On the Reno location Miller kept rewriting the script and Huston kept rewriting the rewrites; then either Monroe of Clift would be hours late—sometimes they never turned up at all—and every day Clark was there on time ready to start work, and every day the sun climbed relentlessly in the cloudless sky. By eight o'clock it was 100 in the shade, by miday over 130, and every afternoon the hot desert wind covered everything and everybody with a thick alkali dust from the dried-up lake bed.

Out of pure boredom, Clark insisted on doing some stunts that would normally have been done by a double. Anything was better than sitting day after day in the baking desert just waiting, but roping a wild mustang in searing heat and being dragged along the desert floor at 30 mph behind a truck are not sensible pastimes for a man of sixty. Huston tried to dissuade him, and Kay was appalled when she nightly doctored his cuts and rope burns, but he persisted, and never once did he say a word against the others. He understood their problems and felt desperately sorry for Arthur Miller, who was married to Monroe and must have been bearing the brunt of all her difficulties behind the scenes.

At long last and weeks over schedule, the picture was finished. Clark saw a rough cut, and although he seldom discussed his work, he told one and all that it was the best thing he had done since *Gone with the Wind*; then he forgot about the past miserable months and sat back and waited contentedly but impatiently for the birth of his child.

Early one morning Kay woke to find Clark standing by the bed half dressed, his face chalky white. "I've a terrible pain," he said simply.

The doctor was called and immediately sent for an ambulance. It was a massive heart attack. Kay moved into the hospital with him, and he improved steadily over the next nine days.

On the tenth day he looked like a new man, relaxed and happy. Kay says that he asked her to stand sideways against the light so that he could see her silhouette. Laughing happily, he used the doctor's stethoscope to hear the heartbeat of the little boy he longed for so much but would never see. During the night he was struck down a second time.

CHAPTER 3
HEDDA AND LOUELLA

At every Hollywood breakfast table or office desk the day used to start with an avid perusal of the columns of Louella Parsons and Hedda Hopper. The fact that many had paid their press agents large sums of money to make up lies and exaggerations and then plant these items with Louella and Hedda detracted nothing from the pleasure they got from seeing this nonsense in the morning papers—they even believed it when they saw it.

Louella, short, dumpy, and dowdy, with large brown eyes and a carefully cultivated vagueness of smile and manner, was a Catholic, married three times, first to a real estate man, secondly to a riverboat captain, and thirdly to a doctor who specialized in venereal diseases. From the earliest days she had been a newspaperwoman and during her Hollywood reign was one of the star reporters of the W. R. Hearst publishing empire. Her flagship was the Los Angeles *Examiner.*

Hedda, who came on the scene later, was tall, thin, and elegant, with large blue eyes and a brisk, staccato way of demanding replies rather than asking questions. Of Quaker stock, she had been married only once to a four-times-divorced stage actor twenty-seven years her senior, whom she herself had divorced when she caught him cheating on her at the age of sixty-three. An ex-chorus girl, she graduated to small parts on Broadway and in films and was a washed-up middle-aged Hollywood character actress when she took to journalism as a last resort. Her flagship was the other local morning paper, the Los Angeles *Times.*

They were an unlikely couple, but they had one thing in common— they loathed each other.

Hollywood folklore insisted that Louella held her job with W. R. Hearst because she knew literally where the body was buried. In 1924 Hearst had organized a trip aboard his yacht *Oneida.* Among others on board were Louella and the producer Thomas Ince. Far out in the Pacific, so the story went, Hearst entered the cabin of his mistress, Marion Davies, and found her thrashing around naked beneath a similarly unclothed Ince. An altercation followed, during which Hearst shot Ince. He then carried the body on deck and dumped it over the side. Louella, who was dozing unseen in a deck chair, was supposed to have heard the splash and reached the rail just in time to see the dead producer bobbing past, and Hearst was supposed to have told Louella to keep her mouth shut, in exchange for which she was promised a job for life.

The two major flaws in that story were, first, that Ince left the yacht in San Diego suffering from indigestion and took the train to Los Angeles, where he died two days later of a heart attack, and secondly, that Louella Parsons was never a member of the yachting party. The truth of her beginnings with Hearst was that she was a very good reporter who appreciated the excitement that was being generated by the infant film industry and Hearst knew a good reporter when he saw one.

Hedda's emergence as a newspaperwoman came some ten years after the beginning of Louella's reign as the undisputed queen of the Hollywood scene. In 1935 Hedda was in trouble. She was fifty years old and a very bad actress. She was a striking-looking woman, however, who spent every cent on her clothes, sparkling company too, always equipped with the latest juicy pieces of information, but she was hardly ever offered a part in films. She somehow kept going, doing anything that came along, from modeling middle-aged fashions to a stint with Elizabeth Arden.

A champion of hers at that time was Louella Parsons, who frequently mentioned her activities in her column and introduced her to W. R. Hearst and Marion Davies. It was at the Hearst ranch at San Simeon that a fellow guest, Mrs. Eleanor Paterson, the publisher of the Washington *Times-Herald*, became so captivated by Hedda's brittle and spicy observations about Hollywood that she invited her to write a weekly newsletter, and Hedda's first step toward becoming Louella's archrival was taken.

Once it was available for syndication, the number of newspapers subscribing to Hedda's column was far from spectacular until lightning struck in 1937—she was bought by the Los Angeles *Times*. Now she was read by everybody in the motion-picture industry, and overnight sources of information were opened to her that had remained firmly closed when her output was only being glanced at in remote corners of the country. As news and gossip flooded in on Hedda from hundreds of press agents and private individuals, her column received a blood transfusion and improved immeasurably. Within a very short time it was syndicated in as many newspapers all over the world as that of an increasingly resentful Louella.

The arrival on the Hollywood scene of a second queen who had to be pandered to, pacified, or prodded posed some very tricky questions for the publicity-hungry citizens. How to plant a story with one while still keeping the amiability of the other? How to arrange a private showing of a new film for one without offending the other? And above all, how to give the story of an impending marriage or divorce to one without incurring the implacable wrath of the other? It seems incredible, but in a town with a herd instinct and a concentration of insecurity, it needed only one of these ladies to hint that an actor or actress was "box-office poison" for contracts to be terminated and studio doors to be slammed. Discretion was, indeed, the better part of valor, and the great majority of us played a humiliating game of subterfuge and flattery, having long since decided that it was far less troublesome to have them with us than against us. If they were susceptible to flattery, they were also very astute, and it was fatal to try to get by with an untruth—for that there was no forgiveness.

Hedda should have been the easier to deal with. Having been so long a frustrated actress herself, she understood, but she was unpredictable and ruthless in her championship of causes and in her attacks. With her private list of "pinkos," she made Senator McCarthy sound like a choirboy.

Louella was a much softer touch, easily humored by a bunch of roses, but also erratic because she was apt to listen to the last voice before her deadline, and many of her scoops were a long way off target as a result. On one occasion she announced that Sigmund Freud, "one of the greatest psychoanalysts alive," was being brought over from Europe by director Edmund Goulding as the technical adviser on Bette Davis' picture *Dark Victory*. This posed a difficult logistical problem because Freud had been dead for several months.

When conducting interviews for her big Sunday full-page story, Louella, in her comfortable house on Maple Drive, invariably set the oldest of tongue-loosening traps—she plied her subject with glasses the size of umbrella stands, filled to the brim with whiskey or gin—but often she trapped herself by keeping the subject company and her notes became illegible.

Hedda used the same technique and plied her subjects with booze, but she shrewdly sipped tonic water herself. She always swore that her short marriage was the only sexual foray of her life; she certainly had a long procession of admirers, but she stoutly maintained that she had preserved her near virginity against overwhelming odds, and probably because of this puritan outlook, she attacked ferociously those she suspected of any extracurricular activities. She infuriated Joseph Cotten and greatly disturbed his wife, Lenore, when she printed heavy hints that Joe had been caught by the Malibu Beach patrol in the back seat of his car bestride the teenage Deanna Durbin. Joe Cotten, the epitome of the Southern gentleman from Virginia, warned Hedda that if she added one more line on the subject, he would "kick her up the ass"! Sure enough Hedda went into action again a few days later, and the next time Cotten saw Hedda's behind entering a smart Hollywood party, he lined up on the target and let her have it.

The two ladies were made of very durable material. Producing an interesting column every day and a feature story on Sunday entailed an immense amount of hard work and very long hours. True they employed legmen and legwomen, who scurried about on their behalf digging for gossip, but all the openings and major social events they attended themselves. They also manned the telephones for hours each day, sifting pieces of information and tracking down stories. Each nurtured an army of part-time informants who worked in restaurants, agents' offices, beauty parlors, brothels, studios, and hospitals, and no picture started shooting without its complement of potential spies eager to remain in the good books of Hedda and Louella.

Both had their favorites, and these were the happy recipients of glowing praise for their good looks, talent, kindness, and cooking, but when they fell from grace, retribution was horrible—and millions were informed that they could do nothing right. Sometimes, however, because of the good ladies' antipathy one toward the other, pedestals broken by one would be pieced together by the other, and life for the fallen idol would go on much as it had before.

Jealousy might have been the reason Hedda failed to appreciate great creative talent, but Louella had no excuse for joining her in scoffing openly at such giants as Garbo, Hepburn, Olivier, and Brando, and out of the ranks of the supertalented, each chose a target for real venom. For Louella it was Orson Welles; for Hedda—Charlie Chaplin.

When she discovered that *Citizen Kane* was modeled on her boss, W. R. Hearst, and Marion Davies, Louella screamed in print like a wounded peahen and flailed away at Welles on every occasion, accusing him of avoiding war service, stealing Rita Hayworth away from brave Victor Mature (who was in the Coast Guard), and dodging taxes by moving to Europe. She pilloried RKO Pictures, which had financed the film, and, backed by the power of the Hearst press, campaigned so effectively to have the picture destroyed before it was shown to the public that the heads of the industry got together and offered RKO $3,000,000 for the negative. Fortunately, the offer was spurned, but Welles was only infrequently invited to display his talent in Hollywood thereafter.

Hedda's stream of bile played for years upon Chaplin. She hounded him in print because of his avowedly liberal politics and for the fact that after making a fortune in the United States, he was still, forty years later, a British subject, and, having been herself married to a man twenty-seven years her senior, for some reason she nearly went up in flames when she heard that Eugene O'Neill's eighteen-year-old daughter, Oona, was planning to marry Chaplin, who was thirty-six years off the pace. When she published a string of stern warnings and dire prognostications, harping always on Chaplin's suspected preference for young girls, Chaplin ignored Hedda completely and went ahead with his wedding plans.

Louella and Hedda were not averse to a little "payola." Louella had earlier conned important stars into appearing on her radio show, *Hollywood Hotel.* Hedda had been less successful with her program, *Hedda Hopper's Hollywood,* but later made a successful transition with it to television, where she "persuaded" the biggest names in movieland to appear with her. This program stole a lot of viewers away from the Great Stoneface (Ed Sullivan), appearing at the same time on a rival network, and Sullivan complained bitterly that he was paying full salary to the performers on his show whereas Hedda was paying nothing to the lineup she had announced for hers—Gary Cooper, Judy Garland, Joan Crawford, Bette Davis, Lucille Ball, and Charlton Heston.

Some of Louella's payoffs were subtle: She persuaded Twentieth Century-Fox to buy the film rights to her unfilmable autobiography and made it quite clear to producers that whenever her husband, Dr. Harry "Dockie" Martin, was hired as "technical adviser" on their films, they would not lack for publicity.

Louella and Dockie were a devoted couple, and evenings at their home were relaxed and unpretentious. The conversation was strictly movie shop. At Hedda's, evenings were gayer, brighter and, because of Hedda's friends and interests outside Hollywood, more cosmopolitan and much more stimulating.

She was a sparkling hostess, chic, gay, witty, and acid. She used a great variety of four-letter words and enjoyed hearing her two poodles sing to her piano playing. Hedda always stated that she would make up for her late arrival in competition with Louella "by outlasting the old bag." By the mid-forties both ladies were nearing seventy, and some heavy bets were laid in movieland as to which one would run out of steam first, but seemingly indestructible, they continued to work punishing hours, and their columns were still widely read despite a certain erosion of readers. The old stars who had played the publicity game with Louella and Hedda were fading fast, and the new ones—Brando, Holden, Newman, and Dean—and the young producers and directors found it old-fashioned and unnecessary to bother about them. But if Hedda and Louella recognized this, they gave no sign of it except, sensing perhaps that they were entering the last few furlongs, each redoubled her efforts to outdo the other, and oneupwomanship became the order of their day.

The super love goddess Rita Hayworth decided to take her first trip abroad and asked my advice on a trip around Europe. Knowing how shy and gentle she was, and respecting her longing to avoid the goldfish bowl of publicity, I worked out a complicated itinerary for her, starting with a small Swedish liner to Gothenburg, quiet country hotels and mountain villages all the way south, and ending up in an oasis of Mediterranean calm, the Hotel La Reserve in Beaulieu-sur-Mer.

Rita departed with a girlfriend and the works of Jean-Paul Sartre. Everything went beautifully according to plan, and after three leisurely and peaceful weeks, she arrived radiantly relaxed at La Reserve. The champion charmer of Europe, Prince Ali Khan, saw her walk in, and a new chapter was added to Hollywood history.

It was indeed a romantic match, and Hedda and Louella spent frustrating weeks angling for invitations to the wedding. The ceremony was to be held at L'Horizon, the Ali's pink villa near Cannes. The Ali had no intention whatever of having a Hollywood-style wedding, and all newspaper reporters received a blank refusal to their requests for inclusion on the guest list.

Hedda and Louella could not believe that this treatment of the press included them, and they were particularly irked that with their immense power, their supplications received the same cold shoulder as that turned toward the reporter from Nice *Matin.* Poor gentle Rita with her inbred Hollywood fear of Hedda and Louella needed all the Ali's Olympian calm when threatening and ominous calls came from Beverly Hills, but she held her ground, and neither was invited to the wedding. Both ladies, however, goaded by their powerful employers, headed for the south of France, hoping for a last-minute breakthrough.

At last, an embittered Parisian newshawk broke the deadlock. He unearthed a Provençal law from Napoleonic times which stated that no wedding could be held in private if one citizen objected. Dozens of citizens—reporters from all over France—signed the objection, and the local mayor announced that the wedding must be held in public at the *mairie.* But both Hedda and Louella, after all their efforts, had to swallow their pride and join a cast of thousands hoping to catch a glimpse of the pair.

When Louella reached the age of eighty-one, she was still writing her column, but the flagship of her syndication fleet was foundering, and one day it sank without a trace. The Los Angeles *Examiner* ceased publication, leaving the Los Angeles *Times* as the sole morning newspaper in the city. Louella retired, and the stripling seventy-six-year-old Hedda had realized her wish—"to outlast the old bag."

She continued writing her column till the age of eighty-one, when illness incapacitated her, but she went down firing broadsides from her deathbed. "I hear that son of a bitch Chaplin is trying to get back into the country," she told all and sundry. "We've *got* to stop him!"

CHAPTER 4

ERROL

Errol Flynn and I started together in Hollywood at exactly the same time.

The great thing about Errol was you always knew exactly where you stood with him because he *always* let you down. He let himself down, too, from time to time, but that was his prerogative and he thoroughly enjoyed causing turmoil for himself and his friends.

When he started off in the Hollywood studios, the flacks went to work on us. I was publicized as the"son of a famous Scottish general" (in actual fact, my father had been killed in 1915 with the rank of second lieutenant), and Flynn was widely reported to be "as Irish as the potato and coming straight from a successful career with the Abbey Players." By some inscrutable logic, Warner Brothers decided that Errol would be more palatable to the American public as an Irish potato than as himself—an Australian brought up in Tasmania and New Guinea.

I first met Errol in Lili Damita's bungalow at the Garden of Allah in the summer of 1935.

Lili was a beautiful hourglass-shaped creature who epitomized the sexy French cover girls of *La Vie Parisienne,* but she was also one of those insecure ladies who feel the necessity to be surrounded by devout homosexuals, and as her usual coterie was around her that night, for a while both Flynn and I thought the other was a fag.

After sniffing suspiciously, we got this sorted out, and a tour of the dives off Hollywood Boulevard became the logical outcome of the evening. Flynn had that day completed his first part under his contract with Warner Brothers, playing a corpse on a marble slab in *The Case of the Curious Bride,* so we had much to celebrate, and during our foray he unburdened himself of his obsession with Lili. Their love affair blossomed quickly thereafter, and they were soon permanently bedded down in a house in the Hollywood Hills.

"Tiger Lil," as Errol called her, taught him a great deal about living and living it up, but a quick marriage in Arizona did nothing to dispel her pathological possessiveness, and in the next few months, during a spate of Herculean battles, Flynn drifted away from her. The truces between the battles became shorter and shorter, and one day Flynn called me and asked if I would like to set up a bachelor establishment with him. "Let's move in together, sport," he said. "I can't take that dame's self-centered stupidity for another day."

We rented 601 North Linden Drive, Beverly Hills, from Rosalind Russell, chartered a nice understanding black housekeeper, and pooled the expenses.

Flynn was collecting rather more from his contract with Warner Brothers than I was receiving from Samuel Goldwyn, so he forked out more in rent and insisted that he had prior claim to the largest bedroom, the one that housed the double bed. Flynn was fairly tight about money matters, so although on state occasions I was allowed to borrow his room, it was only in consideration of a readjustment to our financial arrangement.

One winter's evening I came back from work, and as I turned my car into the driveway, I perceived a sinister figure, his hat pulled down over his eyes and with the collar of his camel's-hair overcoat turned up; he was lurking in the bushes by the kitchen door. Never the bravest of men, I let myself in hurriedly by the front door and went looking for reinforcements in the formidable shape of Flynn. I discovered that he was not yet back from his studio, so I took a hefty nip from the whiskey bottle ever present on our hall table and went out to deal with the intruder. I stalked him successfully and grabbed him from behind. He turned out to be the highly erudite and popular producer Walter Wanger. He was in a very nervous condition. Wanger was very much in love with the gorgeous Joan Bennett, and in matters pertaining to her, he suffered from a very low threshold of jealousy. As I released him, he blurted out that he knew that his loved one was upstairs in the big double bed with Flynn. I was able with truth to tell him that Flynn was not in the house, but I withheld the information that in the living room awaiting Flynn's arrival was Joan.

Wanger, mollified, left, and Joan, rather precipitately, left soon after.

Flynn was lucky that day because a short time later Jennings Lang, an agent, also raised Wanger's possessive instincts to a high level and one evening in the parking lot in front of the offices of the Music Corporation of America, Walter produced a revolver from the pocket of his camel's-hair overcoat, took careful aim, and shot Jennings Lang in the testicles.

In those prewar days, Errol was a strange mixture. A great athlete of immense charm and evident physical beauty, he stood, legs apart, arms folded defiantly and crowing lustily atop the Hollywood dung heap, but he suffered, I think, from a deep inferiority complex—he also bit his nails. Women loved him passionately, but he treated them like toys to be discarded without warning for new models, and for his men friends he really preferred those who would give him the least competition in any department.

Humility was a word unknown to Errol. He became a big star overnight with his first Hollywood superproduction, *Captain Blood,* but it never crossed his mind that others—the producer, the director, the writers, the technicans, and above all, the publicity department—might have had a hand in his success. It all went straight to his head, and by the time I joined him in his second superproduction, *The Charge of the Light Brigade,* he was cordially disliked by most of his fellow workers.

Mike Curtiz was the director of *The Charge* and his Hungarian-oriented English was a source of joy to us all.

High on a rostrum he decided that the right moment had come to order the arrival on the scene of a hundred head of riderless chargers. "Okay," he yelled into the megaphone. "Bring on the empty horses!"

Flynn and I doubled up with laughter. "You lousy bums," Curtiz shouted, "you and your stinking language . . . you think I know fuck nothing . . . well, let me tell you—I know FUCK ALL!"

Toward the end of the picture Errol and I were placed in a large basket atop an elephant; for some obscure reason Warner Brothers had decided to twist history and to let the Light Brigade charge across the North-West Frontier of India instead of the Russian Crimea. The script-writers had been ordered to insert a tiger hunt into the proceedings to warm things up, and we were shooting this sequence at the studio instead of in open country. This proved just as well because the elephant, driven mad by the arc lights, and by Mike Curtiz's megaphone, went beserk and dashed madly all over the back lot trying to scrape off the basket with us inside it against trees, archways, and the side of the fire station.

Studio workers scattered like chaff as we trampled and trumpeted our way toward the main entrance, and only the astute closing of the gates by the studio police stopped us from careering out into the traffic of Pico Boulevard and heading for the Punjab. It was an unattractive interlude.

When the charge itself was shot, one man was killed and many more were hurt, but the wretched horses suffered most. Curtiz ordered the use of the "running W," a tripping wire attacked to a foreleg. This the stunt riders would pull when they arrived a full gallop at the spot he had indicated and a ghastly fall would ensue. Many horses broke legs or backs and had to be destroyed. Flynn led a campaign to have this cruelty stopped, but the studio circumvented his efforts and completed the carnage by sending a second unit down to Mexico, where the laws against maltreating animals were minimal.

By the end of *The Charge* Flynn sensed that Jack Warner was building him up to be the top box-office star of the studio, and he recokoned he could begin to throw his weight about. It started in the usual way with demands for a more lucrative contract, for a larger dressing room and all the trimmings, but as the years went by, Jack Warner found he was reaping the whirlwind he had sown. Flynn's pictures brought in millions, but he made a habit of breaking down the door of Warner's office when he was kept waiting for an appointment. Their contractual battles became legendary. It was a love-hate relationship, and there was admiration on both sides, but in the end King Jack ridded his court of his "turbulent priest."

After *The Charge* with the proceeds of a greatly increased contract, Flynn had bought himself a 65-foot ketch, which he named *Sirocco*. He'd read somewhere that a man named D'Arcy Rutherford had invented a new sport in the south of France—water skiing—and he showed me pictures of Rutherford skimming along behind a speedboat off Eden Roc.

"Look, sport," said Flynn, we've *got* to try that," and he designed a pair of very painful, heavy wooden skis which the studio carpenters knocked together for us. The following weekend we tried them out off Catalina Island—they worked. There is no record to prove it, but I am pretty sure that on that day in the mid-thirties, Flynn and I introduced water skiing to California and maybe even to the United States.

Be that as it may, on that memorable weekend, Ronald Colman aboard his *Dragoon* was anchored in a nearby cove a couple of miles away from *Sirocco* in Avalon Bay, and we decided to give Colman and his guests an exhibition of our newfound sport. Flynn was driving the speedboat when we arrived, and my girlfriend for the weekend was sitting beside him. I was slapping merrily along on the heavy boards astern. After we had suitably impressed the customers aboard *Dragoon*, Flynn pulled a typical "friend-discomfiter," and instead of stopping or turning back toward Avalon, he headed out into the open sea. By now I was getting very tired indeed. I signaled to him to stop, and about half a mile from *Dragoon* he obligingly did so. I sank gratefully into the blue water and waited to be picked up. As the boat came near me, Flynn pulled in the towrope. "So long sport," he called. "Why don't you drop in on Colman for a nice cup of tea? Betty and I are going back to *Sirocco* to take a nap." Betty, I noticed with some annoyance, seemed to be putting up only token resistance to this infamous suggestion, and with a roar of laughter, Flynn swept away, leaving me to face a long swim in mid-Pacific. However, it was a lovely afternoon, there was no adverse current, the sea was warm and oily calm, and when I wanted to rest, I had only to use the skis to support me. So I took my time, paddling gently along, rather enjoying my languorous journey.

About half the distance to *Dragoon* was covered when I got a nasty feeling that I was no longer alone. About ten yards on my right was a very large shark, its greasy black dorsal fin undulating above the surface as it moved effortlessly through the water.

Panic gripped me. I stopped swimming and tried to push the skis beneath my body for protection. With the uncoordination of fear I let go of one of them, which drifted toward the shark. The brute immediately flicked its giant tail and changed course to investigate. Some half-wit once said that you can frighten sharks away by splashing violently and making a noise . . . it's nonsense. . . . I splashed and shouted like a maniac, but my shark just came closer to find out what all the fuss was about. With one ski now beneath me, I hoped protecting my underbelly et cetera from being ripped away, I paddled slowly, gibbering with terror, toward Colman's yacht.

The shark in increasingly close attendance accompanied me the whole way. I prayed that he would remain on the surface, and I never took my eyes off his fin. Periodically, I yelled "Shark!" and "Help!" at the top of my lungs.

At long last I saw field glasses pointing in my direction and stopped paddling when Colman and a sailor jumped into the tender and started up the motor. Only when they were right on top of him did the shark lose interest in me. Then, with a mighty swirling convulsion, he slid into the depths below.

Aboard *Dragoon* a much-needed tumbler of brandy was pressed into my hand while I borrowed somebody's hand mirror to see if my hair had turned white, and when Flynn came over later to pick me up, I had a few words with him. He hooted with laughter. "Jesus!" he roared. "I wish I'd seen *that!*"

I never quite understood Errol's hero worship of John Barrymore. Still of blazing talent and unquestioned, if somewhat blurred, profile, Barrymore seemed to go out of his way to shock and be coarse. He was also conspicuously unclean and smelled highly on many occasions.

He had an abiding love of the theater and treated filmmaking as a financially necessary evil. Watching him work, I was amazed at the carefully arranged phalanx of boards, some stationary, some held aloft by moving stagehands, and all bearing the lines John Barrymore was required to speak during the scene at hand.

Painstaking rehearsals went into the placing and progress of these boards to enable the great man to move freely about during the playing of a scene without giving a hint that he was reading the whole thing.

Like boys who go to complicated lengths to cheat in exams, it would probably have been less time-consuming and nerve-racking to have learned the lesson in the first place, but Barrymore was adamant and had a stock answer when anyone dared to make such an observation.

"My memory is full of beauty—Hamlet's soliloquy, the Queen Mab speech, the fifteen-minute monologue by King Magnus in *The Apple Cart,* and most of the Sonnets . . . do you expect me to clutter all that up with *this* horseshit?"

Errol had sporadic reconciliations with "Tiger Lil" during his tenancy of 601 North Linden, but they amounted to little and did not seem to interfere with the main trend of his activities—a big turnover was the thing, with the accent on youth. One afternoon he said, "Come on, sport, I'm going to show you the best-looking girls in LA." We headed down Sunset Boulevard, and I thought he was taking me to the theater of *Earl Carroll's Vanities* which boasted an illuminated sign over the stage door: THROUGH THESE PORTALS PASS THE MOST BEAUTIFUL GIRLS IN THE WORLD.

He glanced at his watch. "They should be coming out any minute now," he said, and stopped the car. We were directly opposite the Hollywood High School.

Out came the girls, and they were indeed an eye-catching lot with their golden California suntans, long coltlike legs, and high, provocative breasts. All were made up, and many clutching their schoolbooks to their curves looked eighteen or nineteen. Flynn sighed and shook his head.

"Jail bait," he said. "San Quentin Quail. What a waste!"

A patrol car pulled up behind us, and a cop got out. "You fellows waitin' for someone?" he asked.

"No, Officer," said Flynn, "we are just admiring the scenery."

"Beat it," said the cop.

Early in 1939 Errol surprised me by informing me that his marriage was patched up "for keeps." "There's a whole new deal coming up with Lil," he said. "I'm going home."

601 North Linden was disbanded, and we went our separate ways.

During the inevitable wrangle over the "damages" we had done to Rosalind Russell's house during our long tenancy, tightfisted Flynn, who had been stupid enough to sign the lease, met his match. Our landlady had counted every piece in the woodshed when we moved in, and although we had constantly replenished her fuel supplies, in addition to other damage, we were asked to pay for thirty-seven small logs.

The following year we made *Dawn Patrol* together at Warner Brothers. Edmund Goulding directed, and it was a most happy assignment except that I could not help noticing that Flynn had really got the "star" bit between his teeth and was beginning to behave outrageously to the people who employed him and even toward some of those who worked with him.

In September, 1939, Hitler invaded Poland. I decided to go and fight; Flynn decided to stay—it was as simple as that.

During my absence a lot of things happened to Errol. Britain and Australia were at war with Germany and Italy, but he had no intention of being called to the colors. He felt no loyalty to Britain, and little to Australia; the United States had given him his big chance, so he took out American citizenship. Then the Japanese bombed Pearl Harbor, and young Americans started flocking to the recruiting offices. Errol hesitated, but he was confronted by "Tiger Lil" with a baby boy, Sean, in one hand and, in the other, one of the most punitive settlements ever handed down by the notoriously tough California divorce courts. But working on in Hollywood, Errol misguidedly accepted a series of war films in which he played highly heroic roles: *Dive Bomber, Edge of Darkness,* and *Objective Burma* to name a few. The press reacted angrily to his efforts, particularly in beleaguered England, where Zec, in the 4,000,000-circulation *Daily Mirror,* depicted Flynn in a half page cartoon, dressed in battle dress, seated in a studio chair with his name stenciled on the back and in his hands the script of *Objective Burma.* On the studio grass beneath his chair was a multitude of tiny crosses and, beneath the jungle trees, stood the ghostly form of a soldier. The caption read: "Excuse me, Mr. Flynn, but you're sitting on some graves."

Errol retreated to a mountaintop. High up on Mulholland Drive he built a luxurious one-floor bachelor pad. It had a Finnish sauna bath and a battlefield for a bed with a mirror on the ceiling. It had glorious views of the San Fernando Valley below and some stables in which highly illegal cockfights were staged on Sunday evenings, but apart from the inevitable girls, it became, according to Flynn, "the mecca of pimps, bums, gamblers, process servers, and phonies." It also became a refuge for the great John Barrymore, whose end was visibly drawing near. For a while he lived up there with Errol, but there was general relief in the household when he left and the frame of the living-room window could be re-varnished because during his visit Barrymore had made it a nightly habit to urinate out of it in the hopes, he said, of spraying Warner Brothers Studios in the Valley below.

Late in 1942 high jinks aboard *Sirocco* boomeranged on Errol, and he was arrested on four charges of statutory rape.

In the state of California statutory rape meant that a male had fornicated with a female below the age of eighteen. The fact that the lady in question had long since been deflowered and, far from withholding her consent, had entered enthusiastically into the proceedings made no difference, and conviction carried a sentence of five years. Looking back on many weekends aboard *Sirocco,* I could not remember any "crew members" flashing their birth certificates as they trooped expectantly up the gangplank.

It seemed obvious that Flynn was being framed, and young America was aroused. William F. Buckley, Jr., then at prep school, told me later that he had joined A.B.C.D.E.F., American Boys Club for the Defense of Errol Flynn. The accusing girls, Betty Hansen and Peggy Satterlee, had always looked like sophisticated well-upholstered twenty-two-year-olds, but for the trial the prosecution ordered them to take off their make-up, do their hair in pigtails, wear bobby socks, and carry schoolbooks.

It didn't work. The jury, confronted by the masterful tactics of Jerry Geisler, saw through the camouflage and pegged the girls for what they really were. Errol was acquitted, but the stigma of rape was attached to him. He never shook it off, and for years he gritted his teeth when hailed with cries of "In like Flynn!"

The long trial over, Errol married again—a quiet, pretty girl, with an uptilted nose, Norah Eddington—but by now he was so dependent on his bachelor life on Mulholland Drive that his new wife lived in a little house in Hollywood and never became the chatelaine of his mansion on the mountain. In 1945 Norah gave birth to a baby girl, but she and Flynn continued to live apart.

Errol was stuck with making a lot of Westerns, which he hated doing, but they made money for the studio and amid renewed sounds of strife he bowed to Jack Warner's directive and walked through his roles with haughty disdain. He also discovered vodka in a big way and proceeded to drink it as though it were going out of style. At seven o'clock in the morning he was gulping it down in the makeup chair—mixed fifty-fifty with 7-Up.

It was not a happy man I found upon my return to Hollywood at the beginning of 1946.

At left, the author as König's
deck hand, hoisting a prize catch;
relaxing at poolside above is the
"King," Clark Gable, whom
Niven met on the chartered boat.

The handsome Errol Flynn, one
of Niven's earliest friends in
Hollywood, on the deck of his
beloved yacht Sirocco.

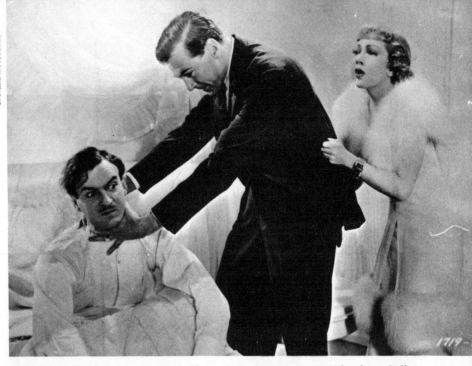

Above, Niven is about to be strangled by an irate Gary Cooper as Claudette Colbert looks on; a scene from Lubitsch's Bluebeard's Eighth Wife; *below left, Ronald Colman; below, Douglas Fairbanks and Sylvia visit* The Prisoner of Zenda *set; bottom, close friend Fred Astaire displays his catch on a Mexican cruise.*

ABOVE AND RIGHT: DAVID NIVEN

"Who is your dentist?" Niven prepares to ask Olivia de Havilland in Raffles; *below, arriving at the White Ball, Niven, Merle Oberon, Norma Shearer, Irving Thalberg.*

Another Hollywood yachtsman, Humphrey Bogart, at the helm of Santana; he
and Lauren Bacall were among Niven's closest friends. Below, Hedda Hopper in a
typically flamboyant headdress, eavesdrops on her archrival, Louella Parsons.

Miraculously, Errol still looked in good physical shape and gave the outward impression of being the same, insulated with charmingly cynical self-sufficiency, but there was something infinitely sad about him, something missing, and behind his eyes there was a shield—I could no longer see into his face.

With pride he showed me the spread on Mulholland Drive and, having discarded *Sirocco* as a bad dream, with loving care introduced me to every inch of his new "wife" *Zaca*—a 120-foot schooner which he had found in San Francisco. She was a dream, and he had spent a small fortune refitting her.

"And let me show you the house flag," he said as he unfurled a symbolic crowing rooster. "A rampant cock, sport, get it? That's what I am to the world today—goddammit—a phallic symbol."

He didn't smile as he said it.

Because of the implications, Errol tried hard to get away from making sex-symbol pictures, but they made money, and the studios kept him churning them out till the pointed fingers and the snide "rapist" cracks so depressed him that he drank more and more and even contemplated suicide, on one occasion sitting up all night with a bottle of vodka in one hand and a loaded revolver in the other.

Occasionally and unexpectedly during this low period Errol came down from his mountaintop to see us, and I would arrive home from work to find him playing with my little boys or helping my wife get supper. His tremendous charm enveloped us all like a tent, and he in his turn seemed to extract a certain peace from the closeness of our family. "This is the life, sport," he would say. "You've really got it made."

Norah had a second baby, and Flynn made a stab at family life for himself. He suggested that she move into Mulholland with their children, but the invitation came too late, and they were divorced. Errol, more restless than ever, then took *Zaca* through the Panama Canal and headed for the Caribbean where he fell in love with Jamaica and looked for a while like settling down, but he pulled up the anchor, set sail for the Mediterranean, and tried his hand at a new role—as international playboy in competition with Rubirosa and Freddie McEvoy.

He gambled, drank, fought, and became the target for every freeloader and trollop between Malaga and Taranto. He seemed to have lost all interest in making films, and although he still had a contract to make several more with Warner's, he never ran out of excuses for not returning to do so. But the schooner, with her large crew and complement of guests, was costing Flynn a fortune, and it finally dawned on him that if he didn't make films, he didn't get paid.

Good luck, which Errol was beginning to believe had deserted him forever, appeared out of the blue in the shape of a lovely and calm young actress from New York—Patrice Wymore. She became an island of peace
and common sense in the middle of his sea of false values, and eighteen
months after his divorce from Norah, Errol and Patrice were married.

Patrice persuaded Errol to return to Hollywood and work out his contract, but when they arrived there, she was appalled by the inroads that
had been made into his capital by lawyers, courts, wives, mistresses, ali-
monies, and, of course, the hangers-on, so when Errol went back on the
payroll, she persuaded him to grab the weekly checks and buy land on Jamaica—the island of his dreams.

This advice Errol took, and by the time his contract was finally terminated (in the course of one last convulsion with Jack Warner) he was
the owner of more than 5,000 acres, but he still had not cleared up his astronomical debts. Convinced that his career and earning power were
over, he had no intention of doing so, and as Patrice had produced a
baby, the three of them took off in a hurry for Europe to live on *Zaca*.
"Let Tiger Lil and the whole goddamned lot of them come after me and
try to collect," said Errol. "I'm sick of being taken."

First stop was Rome, where Errol put up half a million dollars—all the
cash he could raise—as a half share in the costs of a picture, *William
Tell*, but his Italian partners walked out, the picture collapsed halfway
through, and Flynn found himself more in debt than ever. He cabled an
SOS to his business manager in Hollywood, Al Blum, and discovered that
his trusted adviser had just died—a blow not softened when he learned
that in the last few weeks Blum had used the power of attorney Flynn had
conferred on him to make some very peculiar financial arrangements
which had effectively scraped the bottom of Errol's barrel. He also
learned that "Tiger Lil" had taken possession of Mulholland Drive.

For four years after the demise of *William Tell*, Flynn was a floating,
boozing bum. He made some trips to Jamaica to try to keep hold of his
land and was able to convince the banks there that its value had increased. He also made a couple of disastrous films in England for which
he was happy to be paid a fraction of his former salary.

Most of the time *Zaca* remained tied up in the minor ports of the Mediterranean while her owner caroused and brawled, intent, apparently, on
his own self-destruction. Vodka and other stimulants made terrible inroads into his health, his looks were fading fast, and with one exception,
Hollywood washed its hands of Errol Flynn. Sitting in his beautiful house

above Beverly Hills, surrounded by a most enviable collection of paintings, was a quiet, almost professorial man named Sam Jaffe—a highly successful agent. He had not forgotten Errol Flynn, and he had a hunch. He packed, left for Europe, and tracked Flynn down in Majorca.

He cajoled Flynn, and he appealed to his pride, and the loyal Patrice helped him. Flynn pulled himself together and before long was back in Hollywood, making a picture, *Istanbul*. He was not playing a beautiful young sex symbol anymore. He was playing himself, a middle-aged rake with the remains of elegance stamped on a face that had been lived in, and he loved doing it. After *Istanbul*, his old antagonist Jack Warner offered him the part of John Barrymore in *Too Much Too Soon*. Drawing heavily on his personal experience of the man, he turned in a performance that delighted critics and public alike. Next came *The Roots of Heaven*—another role from the same mold to be shot in Africa with John Huston directing and $4,000,000 being spent on the production.

In 1958 I met Errol by chance in London. Ten years had passed since I had last seen him, and it was a joyful reunion. We lunched, largely on Pouilly Fumé, at a little place in Soho, and I cannot pretend that I was not shocked by the physical change; he had been doing himself grave damage, the face was puffy and blotchy, and the hand that had once held the bow of Robin Hood could not have put the arrow through the Taj Mahal at ten paces, but there was an internal calm and a genuineness about him that I had never seen before.

He brought me up to date about all his wives—he had just separated from Patrice, and he talked wistfully of how hard she had tried to help him and how impossible he must have been to live with. He told me with pride of his children, especially of Sean, and when he spoke of Jamaica, he positively glowed.

We filled our glasses and sat in that wonderful silence that old friends can afford.

After a while I said, "I see you've still got a couple of lawsuits going and all the usual tax problems. You seem very relaxed about everything—how do you do it?"

"I've discovered a great book, and I read it all the time—it's full of good stuff," said Errol.

I looked at him inquiringly.

"If I tell you what it is, sport, I'll knock your goddamned teeth down your throat if you laugh."

"I promise," I said.

"It's the Bible," said Flynn.

CHAPTER 5

TWO QUEENS

The big radio shows carried tremendous publicity value in the 30s and movie producers were delighted when their stars were offered the exposure. Some shows were popular with the top film performers; they lined up happily to be heard on the important dramatic offerings or even as guest stars on comedy programs with Bergen, Crosby, Benny, or Hope, being well aware that exposure to the listening millions in well-written and well-produced material could do their film careers nothing but good. Some, like Constance Bennett, were a trifle condescending in their attitude toward what they considered the poor relation of the entertainment world, and this was a hazard for which I had been ill prepared when my first boss, Samuel Goldwyn, gave the electrifying news that he had lent me to the *Shell Hour* to play opposite the most highly paid film star in the world in selected love scenes from Pirandello.

Constance Bennet I had long worshiped from afar. She seemed to me the quintessence of a movie queen. She radiated glamour from her exalted position in the Hollywood firmament, and everything about her shone! Her burnished head, her iridescent skin, her jewels, her famous smile, her lovely long legs, and the highly publicized fact that she pulled down thirty thousand bucks a week. If Marlene Dietrich possessed a Cadillac the length of a subway train, driven by a chauffeur named Briggs who had a mink collar on his uniform in winter and a brace of revolvers on his hips, and Jeanette MacDonald was ferried about in her conveyance by a smart gentleman who shared the front seat with a large gray and white sheepdog, then Constance Bennett was out of place in anything but her Rolls-Royce, a shiny black beauty of a phaeton, with *her* chauffeur sitting outside in all weather while she sat behind in a velvet-lined compartment decorated on the outside with yellow wickerwork. I was excited at the thought of what the next few days had in store for me, but the Shell people were overwhelmed to have such a glamour queen on their program, and their awe of her seemed to inhibit them from giving her precise calls to rehearsal.

"Here's her home number, Dave," said the director ten days before the fatal Saturday. "Why don't you give her a call, then go over to her place and kick it around together before we start full rehearsals Tuesday?"

Over the first weekend I familiarized myself with the scenes, and on Monday, about midday, I dutifully called Constance Bennett's house.

"Miss Bennett does not awaken before three o'clock," said a butler. "Kindly leave a message and your phone number with her secretary." He switched me over. I explained to the secretary the reason for my call. She was sympathetic but unimpressed.

"Well, there's plenty of time, isn't there? . . . The show's not till Saturday, and it's only radio! . . . We'll call you later."

I hung around my boxlike apartment for the rest of Monday, but nothing happened. On Tuesday morning early the director called me.

"How's it been goin', kid?" he asked, and from the anxiety in his voice, I knew that he too had enjoyed little contact with his star.

"Jesus!" he shrieked when I told him. "The first rehearsal's at two o'clock."

Later he called back and said that it had been canceled for that day but that he had arranged an appointment for me at Constance Bennett's house on the morrow.

"And you'd better be there," he snarled as though I were responsible for the nonevent so far.

As ordered, I reported at a most attractive house on Carolwood Drive at eleven o'clock on Wednesday morning. The butler showed me into a library, where I read magazines till two o'clock. At three I heard a car leave, and the butler brought me a tuna fish sandwich and a glass of beer.

"Miss Bennett has fittings at the studio," he said. "She said she was sorry to miss you and to come back tomorrow at the same time."

"I'd like to speak to the secretary," I said.

"She's gone too," said the butler. "Coffee?"

On Thursday morning about ten o'clock the secretary called. "Sorry to disappoint you," she said. "Miss Bennett can't make it today, after all, but you have an invitation to lunch tomorrow, two thirty and bring a tennis racket." She hung up.

Nobody called from the *Shell Hour,* so I decided they must have been keeping themselves abreast of events.

I awoke on Friday morning in a highly nervous condition. One did not fool around with Pirandello, even if one was reading it, and certainly not in front of 20,000,000 people. The dress rehearsal with full orchestra and effects was scheduled to begin the following morning at ten o'clock, and the show itself would be broadcast at five that evening. Much depended on my forthcoming luncheon date with the star.

I arrived on the dot of two thirty to find a couple of dozen people already sampling various beverages on the patio. The secretary introduced herself and presented me to others. It was a friendly and extroverted group, and I was able to relax. The talk was mostly about a poker game the night before at which, I gathered, my hostess had been the big winner. Good-humored threats of revenge were being issued, but La Bennett did not hear them—she was sleeping peacefully upstairs. After luncheon her resident and permanent "beau," the romantic-looking Mexican actor Gilbert Roland, took me by the arm. "Let's get some exercise, amigo," he said, and led me down to the tennis court.

We played singles and doubles till the light began to go. As it faded, I remembered Pirandello, and my nerves started twanging anew. I enlisted Gilbert Roland's sympathetic help. "I'll talk to her," he promised.

Up at the house people were arriving for cocktails, and a poker game was already under way. At the table I noticed Myron Selznick, the top agent in Hollywood, Joseph Schenck, the head of Twentieth Century-Fox, and Irving Berlin. Constance Bennett was also there. I had seldom seen a more beautiful human being: straight, shiny, very blond hair, pencil-thin brows over big, blue, intelligent eyes, a finely chiseled face with high cheekbones, and a rather determined jaw. Her skin was creamy white, and her beautifully slim body was encased in and encrusted by the latest in fashion and the most expensive jewelry.

Gilbert chose a lull in the action and bent over her. She let out a peal of delicious laughter, waved gaily at me, and turned her concentration once more to the business in hand.

"She says," said Gilbert, "why don't you go home and change. It's a buffet supper, and she's running *The Good Earth* afterward. She'd be delighted to have you join us."

"My God," I croaked, "what about tomorrow? . . . We've got to do that show!"

"You only have to *read* it, amigo," said Gilbert, "but I'm sure she'll find time to run it through with you during the evening."

By the time I returned an hour later forty or fifty people had converged on Carolwood Drive and presupper convivality was in full swing. The poker game was still in progress in the cardroom, and from the totally engrossed expressions of the players I judged it unlikely that much rehearsing of tomorrow's radio show would be taking place. The buffet supper came and went. *The Good Earth* with two good Jewish actors, Paul Muni and Luise Rainer, looking determinedly Chinese while swatting away at swarms of MGM's home made locusts, was dutifully applauded, and around two o'clock in the morning the party began to thin out. I checked on the situation in the cardroom—it was unchanged, and the sight of discarded ties and jackets, plus the presence of plates of sandwiches and the monumental size of the pots, made it obvious that it would remain that way for some time to come.

At four o'clock I went home, none too relieved by Gilbert's latest piece of information: "She can't quit now because she was such a big winner last night. . . . She says she'll be ready at nine o'clock in the morning, so you be here then. . . . You can drive down with her and run it through a couple of times down at the studio before the rehearsal. . . . Don't worry, amigo, it's only radio!"

I couldn't sleep and had visions of a promising career going up in smoke, so I worked till dawn on the scenes determined by now to embark upon a policy of *sauve-qui-peut.*

Sharp at nine, eyes blinking in the blinding California sun and shaking with black coffee and Benzedrine, I rang the doorbell at Carolwood Drive. A housemaid looked surprised. "I've an appointment with Miss Bennett," I said.

The girl motioned me toward the still heavily curtained library redolent with the smell of after-party staleness. I couldn't believe my eyes. In the cardroom beyond, I beheld the poker game still going full blast; the players, with the exception of Constance Bennett, haggard and blue of jowl.

The hostess saw me and announced, "Last hand, fellows, I have to go to work."

Soon it was over, and an hour later I found myself seated in the Rolls-Royce phaeton beside an incredibly beautiful and apparently well-rested Constance Bennett. She must have been made of different stuff because with her unlined face and clear blue eyes she looked as though she had awakened from a dreamless sleep of at least ten hours.

During the twenty-minute drive to Vine Street, she filled me in on the outcome of the marathon game. "Poor Myron," she said, "I think he really will quit now. . . . He lost almost a hundred thousand bucks, but you can't mix martinis and cold hands . . . not with that group, you can't. He was that much ahead at one time, but at the end he blew it."

At the radio studio everyone was determinedly trying to look as though he was not at panic station. We were at least two hours late for dress rehearsal, but such was the awe in which my glamorous partner was held by the executives of the *Shell Hour* that they welcomed her as though she had come to inaugurate a new wing of the building. Waiting, too, were several hundred of her fans, screaming her name and begging her to spare them a smile, pleading for autographs and apparently undismayed by the fact that they were kept at a respectful distance from their idol, having been herded into a prisoner of war cage of high wire netting.

The director fawned on her and immediately acceded to her request that for the next half hour she and I should be left undisturbed in her dressing room so that she could "check a few things in the script."

Constance Bennett was completely composed as she took her first look at Pirandello's lines which she would be delivering later in the day to the expectant millions. Totally absorbed, she read for a few minutes then stopped and frowned. In silence she leafed ahead through the rustle-proof pages; then she threw them in the wastebasket.

"I'm not going to do this shit," she announced.

The producer and director were summoned; so too was the advertising agency man. She would not tackle Pirandello, she said, under any circumstances. A dew of sweat stood out on the assembled group. "But, Miss Bennett, it's almost one o'clock, and we go on the air at five," pleaded the director.

"Too bad," she answered.

"The orchestra has been rehearsing since eight this morning," murmured the producer.

"They get paid," said the star.

"Shell will cancel the account," groaned the man from the advertising agency.

"Screw Shell," said Miss Bennett.

For half an hour the men pleaded and cajoled but at one o'clock with air time a scant four hours away, the men agreed that she could instead play a couple of scenes from the picture she had just finished at Twentieth Century-Fox. Quite apart from the hideous spot into which this last-minute switch now put me (a situation nobody even mentioned), there was the question of obtaining the permission of Twentieth Century-Fox.

"You go ahead with that," said C. Bennett loftily. "Just call Darryl Zanuck; we'll go on back to the house and grab a bite to eat while we read through the scenes together. I have some scripts up there. You'd better send someone to pick one up so you can find out what it's all about. . . . Let's go," she said to me over her shoulder and headed for the door. As we departed, I saw the director conversing with the orchestra leader; their faces were a very odd color.

Constance B. smiled charmingly at her caged fans on her way to the Rolls-Royce, and on the long drive back to Carolwood Drive she remained cool and confident. She patted my wet hand. "Don't be nervous," she said. "These are great scenes, you'll love them."

Around two o'clock I was given a hamburger which turned into a bicycle in my stomach, and between bites I read the scenes. They were light and airy and, compared to Pirandello, much easier to play. I felt a little less apprehensive of my impending ordeal, but my optimism was short-lived when the *Shell Hour* spoke to Constance Bennett. They were desperate: Nobody at Twentieth Century-Fox could give the necessary permission; Zanuck was on his way to Santa Anita Racecourse, and even if they could locate him there, it would be too late. Schenck was at his home, and no one would give out his private number.

"Leave it to me," said the star. She glanced at the clock; it was almost three o'clock. Already the lines would have formed outside the radio station. She couldn't find her phone book, and the secretary was off for the day. Several calls later the secretary was tracked down, loudly relaxed at a liquid brunch in Santa Monica, but the whereabouts of the book were wrung out of her. It made no difference. Schenck, according to someone at his house, had given strict instructions not to be awakened till four o'clock. "He got home real late," said a soft black voice. "I know that, goddammit," said La Bennett loudly. "C'mon, let's go."

"Where?" I asked, panic rising.

"To Joe's place," said La Bennett. "I'll wake the son of a bitch up."

The chauffeur of the Rolls, spurred on now by a far less relaxed employer, catapulted the phaeton with smoking tires through Holmby Hills, but to no avail. We arrived to a head-on confrontation between a big film star and the stone-faced entourage of a big producer. His butler, the gardener, and a private detective lurking in the bushes all made it crystal clear that they had not the slightest intention of waking their boss before the appointed hour.

The big star wheedled, threatened and ranted. "But he was still in my house at nine o'clock this morning," she yelled, stamping a pretty foot.

They were unmoved. "Sorry, Miss Bennett . . . orders is orders!"

Finally, she gave up. "Let's go," she growled. "Back to the studio."

The Saturday afternoon traffic by now was bumper to bumper, and every light seemed to be red. Down in Hollywood an expectant audience of hundreds was settling itself, twittering with excitement at the prospect of seeing its own Constance Bennett, and millions all over the country were gathering around their radio sets to hear her voice. "We'll stop at Schwab's Drugstore," she said. "You go call those creeps at Shell and tell 'em it's Parendillo or whatever the hell his name is."

From a pay booth I called the *Shell Hour*, and a noise like boiling water issued from our producer, but I promised that I would indeed "get the bitch down there in fifteen minutes."

By the time we had run the gauntlet of the swollen number of her fans behind the wire netting (and I had to admire her—she smilingly took her time and even signed a few grubby slips of paper poked at her through the holes) it was less than half an hour before air time, and she was swept off to her flower-filled dressing room, where she nonchalantly changed her makeup and put on a stunning silver lamé dress. I sat bolt upright on a wooden chair, alone in a corner of the stage, avoiding the hostile glances of the orchestra, and with trembling fingers and unseeing eyes pretended to be working on my script.

At a quarter to five the curtain rose, and the announcer warmed up the studio audience with a few nervous jokes, explained to them how much their applause would contribute to the listeners' pleasure, extolled the beauty, brilliance, and dedication of our hardworking star and introduced the orchestra leader and the director.

Five minutes before air time the announcer remembered me and told the audience that the young man playing opposite Miss Bennett came from the Abbey Players in Dublin—a lie which aroused little response.

Thunderous applause and gasps of admiration then greeted the appearance of the star. She smiled beautifully and calmly settled herself on a chair next to mine and crossed her impeccable silken legs. After what seemed an eternity, the red sign ON THE AIR flashed; a fanfare, and the announcer began extolling the smiling efficiency of the Shell station attendants, the unequaled excellence of their product, and the cleanliness of their lavatories. Another fanfare, followed by an introduction of the main event, and Constance Bennett and I were alone on the stage, facing each other and twenty million Americans over the top of the microphone.

I didn't feel anything very much: I was numb with terror. I had to speak first; the director signaled frantically to me to begin. I stared back at him like a dog watching a snake; then I looked across at my partner, hoping that miraculously some of her superhuman calm might rub off on me. What I saw made me relax completely. She was human, after all—she was pale green and shaking like an aspen.

GARBO

In our itchy fustian trousers and jackets of the same material stained at the armpits with salty sweat rings and redolent of a hundred earlier occupants, we extras working on a Marie Dressler potboiler were making the most of our short lunch break on the MGM back lot, stretched out on the grass and foraging dispiritedly among the unappetizing contents of small cardboard boxes provided for our refreshment.

A dusty road separated the well-tended campus lawns on which we sprawled from the fronts of a row of prim New England clapboard houses. They had no interiors and no backs.

"Here she comes!" somebody announced in an excited whisper, and the message spread with the rapidity of a forest fire among the half hundred depressed citizenry.

"Who?" I asked my neighbor, a large Mexican lady of uncertain cleanliness who, I had noticed, when pinned against her in a doorway earlier in the day, had a cluster of blackheads between her bosoms.

"Garbo!" she replied, rising to her feet. "Every day at lunch time she takes her exercises."

The road at its nearest point to us was fifty yards away, and the extras, with one exception, making no move to close the gap, stood respectfully and watched in fascinated silence as a slim figure wearing dark glasses, a baggy sort of track suit, and a large floppy hat strode purposefully past. Upon the hardened, cynical faces of those long exposed to every great star in the business were looks of wonderment and awe. Suddenly the spell was broken. A young boy broke from the ranks, and brandishing a pencil and a grubby piece of paper, he ran across the grass toward the dusty road. "Miss Garbo!" he called.

The trim figure missed a beat and stiffened perceptibly; then she accelerated by lengthening her stride; as the cantering youth closed the gap, she broke first into a trot, and finally, as he gained upon her, she opened the throttle and, leaving him pounding along in her wake, disappeared at a graceful gallop toward the sanctuary of the main studio and her dressing room. She had never looked around, but she had the radar system of a bat when it came to avoiding contact with a stranger.

The studio was filled with stories of her determination to preserve her privacy. She liked to work always with the same crew and demanded that the redoubtable Bill Daniels photograph all her pictures. A great professional, she seemed perfectly at ease among others working on the same film, but as Bill said, "She could sniff an outsider a mile away, and if anyone, no matter who, came on the set to get a peek at her, she'd sense it even with a coupla hundred extras around and she'd just go and sit in her dressing room till they'd been put out."

Stories of her elusiveness were legion, and much enjoyment was extracted from the names, "Gussie Berger" and "Harriet Brown," under which she booked hotels and travel arrangements. The great Garbo quote "I want to be alone" was propably never uttered by her, but there was no question that she was a loner—painfully shy with people she did not know and preferring her own company to that of most people. "Making a film with Garbo," said Robert Montgomery, another star at MGM, "does not constitute an introduction." Garbo had an icy look in her eyes when anyone sought to impose upon her, as, according to studio gossip, Groucho Marx discovered one day. He saw a well-known figure approaching in slacks and floppy hat, waylaid her, bent down in his famous crouch, and peeked up under the brim. Two prisms of pure Baltic blue stared down at him, and he backed away, muttering, "Pardon me, ma'am. I thought you were a guy I knew in Pittsburgh."

When the talkies came in, there were many casualties among the great silent stars, but none suffered a more dramatic and humiliating decline than John Gilbert. The established number one male box-office attraction of the MGM Studios was wrecked upon the rocks of his first talking film, mistakenly titled *His Glorious Night*. Gilbert did not have a voice of great resonance, he had a light, pleasant voice, but somehow it did not suit the dark, flashing eyes and gleaming white teeth of the great screen lover, in addition to which sound in its infancy was unreliable in the lower registers and poor John Gilbert's first squeaky declarations of passionate love brought down the house. He was allotted no more roles by the studio where he had reigned supreme for so long, and stories abounded that the studio heads were trying to break his very expensive contract by trapping him with whores or getting him drunk in public and then invoking the morals clause whereby an actor undertook not to bring himself into disrepute with the public. In fact, the poor man was so desperately humiliated and unhappy that he refused to be seen in public, but his drinking bouts in private became legendary.

Garbo and Gilbert, some years before the debacle of *His Glorious Night,* had embarked on a highly publicized love affair. Too highly publicized perhaps for Garbo's taste because at the very moment when Gilbert thought that all was set for a wedding and a honeymoon in the South Pacific aboard a yacht specially and romantically outfitted for the occasion, Garbo had taken to her heels. Gilbert, thereafter, married twice, elsewhere, but both marriages fell apart, and with his career in tatters he was badly in need of a friend.

Garbo at the height of her popularity was preparing to make *Queen Christina,* and Laurence Olivier with great fanfare was brought over from England to play opposite her, but for some never fully explained reason, the studio decided at the last minute that he was wrong for the part and sent him home again. To see such a glorious opportunity blown away before his eyes and before the eyes of the world must have been a body blow to a young actor as yet unknown outside his own country, but Olivier, blessed with a massive talent and a highly justified faith in himself, returned later to Hollywood to take his pick of the best roles of all the studios. MGM, in the meanwhile, received a body blow of its own when Garbo informed it that she would make *Queen Christina* only with . . . John Gilbert.

The picture was a triumph for Garbo, but Gilbert's performance failed to rekindle the flame with his fans, and he sank back once more into despondency. Around this time (1935) Ronald Colman, who had befriended me, took me frequently to Gilbert's house to play tennis. The house, which was later purchased by David Selznick when he married Jennifer Jones and completely modernized and rejuvenated, was in Gilbert's day a somber place, a rambling Spanish-style structure at the end of a long, winding and highly dangerous mountain road with only the flimsiest of barriers at hairpin bends to save one from terrifying drops.

The gloom of the place was intensified by curtains permanently drawn against the light. When Gilbert showed up to play, the tennis was desultory, but the conversation, bonhomie, and refreshment were abundant. In his mid-thirties he was a man of sparkling good looks, but his good humor and laughter seemed dredged up with great effort. Often he did not appear at all, and Colman and I would take a swim in his sad leaf-filled pool. Once or twice I caught a glimpse of a beautiful face watching us from a window, and on one occasion, as we were climbing into Colman's car, a figure in a man's shirt, slacks and a big floppy hat approached from the scrub-covered hills and, with head down, hurried past us into the house.

I was afforded one more mini-glimpse of the famous recluse when Edmund Goulding, the director, invited me for a weekend at his desert retreat above Palm Springs. I arrived hot and dusty after a long drive, and Goulding pointed the way to his swimming pool in the palm trees below. "Go and cool off," he ordered.

As I neared the pool, it became apparent that standing in the shallow end was a naked female figure. As this incident took place in the mid-thirties, the reader will understand that I retreated to the house and asked my host for a clarification of the situation.

"Oh," he said, "it's only Garbo. She's staying somewhere down there and uses the pool when she feels like it."

I hastened once more down the garden path, but I was too late. All that remained was the disturbed surface of the water.

Garbo was finally dethroned as a working actress but remained inviolate as the most mysterious personality in Hollywood's history.

Her dethronement was sudden and remarkable because she apparently went down without a struggle. It could have happened to anyone—and frequently did. She chose the wrong film. Certainly in her position she could have refused it, but because it was wartime, she had agreed to do the sort of picture that was cheering people up—a farce.

Nothing in show business is more horrendous than a farce when it is not funny, and *Two-Faced Woman* was a four-star, fur-lined, oceangoing disaster. It also contained a surprising quota of "dirty" dialogue, was banned by the Legion of Decency, and roasted by the press with one eminent reviewer referring to Garbo's appearance as "embarrassing—like seeing Sarah Bernhardt swatted with a bladder."

The actors have always been the principal targets when shows flop, and they accept this as an occupational hazard—the producers rarely get blamed—but Garbo, instead of sweeping *Two-Faced Woman* under the rug of her memory, drawing comfort from an unassailable record of success, and being more selective in future, just stopped making films. It was an extraordinary abdication and rocked Hollywood to its foundations.

About five years after Garbo's retirement I purchased an old house in Pacific Palisades with "all mod cons, views, ocean and mts." It had been built by Vicki Baum, the author of the best-seller *Grand Hotel*, which had been made into a hit film starring Garbo. A neighbor of ours there was a rarity—a Hollywood hermit.

Richard Haydn first made his name imitating fish. "I was standing on a street corner as happy as could be, minding my p's and q's, when a large man tied a horse and cart to me. I uttered a cry. A passing fish-monger said 'Why! that is the mating call of the Goo Boo or Blushing Fish!' I was *amazed.*"

One evening Hjördis and I were sitting on our terrace when Richard Haydn materialized. His eyeglasses glinted mischievously.

"I've brought someone who says she spent some of her happiest days in this house," he announced. "She would like to see it again if it's not too inconvenient."

Birds of a feather had evidently flocked together because behind Richard stood Garbo.

I don't remember what she wore on that occasion because I was so stunned by the beauty of her face. She was utterly unaffected and completely easy and relaxed with a spontaneous and highly infectious laugh. My wife, being Swedish, took over the tour of the house, and by the time they came back the two of them were jabbering away like two Scandinavian conspirators. Garbo told us about our house during the Vicki Baum days—it must have been a fascinating place, a rendezvous for Leopold Stokowski and a host of European writers and artists.

During the years to come Garbo often came to see us. She reminded me of a child living in her own secret world, and with childish directness she came and went as she wished, swam when she felt like it or, when she missed the rains of her native land, walked about under the lawn sprinklers. But no amount of pleading on behalf of our Swedish cook could coax an autograph out of her. "I never give autographs or answer letters," she said firmly.

Garbo was in our house one summer evening when the time came for Hjördis and me to leave for a large cocktail party which we had promised to attend. We explained the situation to our visitor, who asked who was giving it, how many would be there, and so on. As it was to be at the home of a close friend who was celebrating the end of a long suspension by his studio, we were able to supply the answers and to hazard a guess that about a hundred people would be on hand.

"May I come too?" Garbo asked suddenly.

The party, when we arrived, was in full and boisterous swing, and when Garbo walked into the garden chockablock with young filmmakers, the effect was magical. They just could not believe their eyes. For a while she was left in a clear space, chatting happily with people she had worked with, but gradually as the throng pressed ever closer in its enthusiasm, her eyes took on the look of a hunted fawn, and suddenly she was gone.

Garbo's visits to California became rarer, but the myth remained as deeply entrenched as ever. The newspapers showed pictures of her fleeing from their photographers in European cities and printed reports of her aimlessly and alone walking the New York streets or haggling over the price of carrots and small antiques, and her apartment was reputed to contain a priceless collection of Impressionists stacked on the floor and all facing the wall. At the end of the period covered in this book we found ourselves in a house in the south of France. To our joy we discovered that Garbo was installed in a house on a neighboring promontory, the guest of a Russian-born New Yorker—George Schlee.

The property was ideal for her, isolated and perched high upon jagged rocks far from prying eyes. In calm weather she could descend some steps into the blue Mediterranean, and when it was rough, she could take her beloved exercises in the pool. Schlee was the ideal companion for Garbo, a cosmopolitan of immense knowledge, charm, kindness, and understanding. She seemed completely happy in his company and, after the passing of several years, more beautiful than ever. One day, when they were at our place, we laid out food and wine in the garden on an old table among the olive trees, but an unseasonable rainstorm arrived just as we were about to sit down to luncheon. "Help me carry everything into the house!" I ordered, grabbing something light.

"Nonsense," said Garbo firmly. "We put it all under the table and eat it there."

People who have climbed a cliff and are resting peacefully on the summit have been known to glance casually down into the void below and for the first time realize to their horror that they suffer from vertigo. With knees of jelly, pounding hearts, and spinning heads, they then inch their way down and never climb again.

I often wondered if something of the sort had overtaken Garbo at the pinnacle of her career, so seeing her before me, carefree and happy, munching away contentedly with the rain cascading off the table, I decided it might be a propitious moment to try to find out.

"Why *did* you give up the movies?" I asked.

She considered her answer so carefully that I wondered if she had decided to ignore my personal question. At last, almost to herself, she said, "I had made enough faces."

CHAPTER 6

SUMMIT DRIVE

RONALD COLMAN

In Beverly Hills, Summit Drive was well named but not for topographical reasons. It was a short street winding up a valley from Benedict Canyon. There were only six estates on the ridges on either side of this valley, but in prewar days in these six houses, hidden by magnificent specimens of sycamore, pine, eucalyptus, jacaranda, chestnut, and oak, reposed some of the crown jewels of Hollywood.

Up Summit Drive, the largest estate of all was at the bottom on the right, a rather untidy, comfortable, secluded, rambling hideaway belonging to one of the Hollywood pioneers—Harold Lloyd.

On the ridge opposite his estate was a more imposing structure—a large "stockbroker Tudor" edifice complete with beams, eaves, sloping roofs, ivy, and mullioned windows. From the stately wrought-iron gates at the entrance, a winding driveway led to the house past beautifully manicured lawns flanked, not by orange trees, brightly colored hibiscus, oleanders, or trumpet flowers, but by dark foreign-looking yew hedges. Waiting somberly dressed, at the top of the drive would be a diminutive general factotum named Tommy. "Mr. Colman," he would intone reverently, "is in the library. Pray follow me."

Ronald Colman, if not a recluse, had a mania for preserving his privacy—understandable really when one remembers that on any given day, hundreds of fans would be cruising, goggle-eyed, around Beverly Hills in limousines, jalopies, or buses equipped with loudspeakers, clutching in their hands the maps they had purchased for $1 from beery ladies parked beneath beach umbrellas at the city limits: "Maps of the Movie Stars' Homes."

Colman, a quiet man, was English. He had been recruited from an obscure position on Broadway when, panicking at the sudden event of talking pictures, Hollywood had convinced itself that none of the "silent" stars could talk. The choice of Colman as a standard-bearer was fortunate because he was indeed the possessor of a matchless speaking voice, plus darkly handsome good looks, massive charm, and great acting ability.

He lived alone, surrounded by a beautiful collection of Chippendale and Sheraton furniture; only English painters of the eighteenth and nineteenth centuries graced the walls, and the rooms were comfortable in a leathery sort of way. The place was masculine to a fault and screamed out for a lady of the house. Ronnie, under heavy camouflage in the late thirties, was laying the foundations of just that. Having lately tottered away, mentally bruised, from a most unhappy marriage, followed by an extremely painful divorce, he was highly nervous of any further entanglements, but egged on by his close circle of men friends, he was hesitantly chipping away at his mental barriers. The chipping soon passed the stage of wishful thinking, and working at night, he knocked a large hole in the wall bounding the back garden of his estate. Tommy produced some hinges, cement, and a heavy oak door, and the beautiful actress Benita Hume, who lived in a small Spanish-style house immediately behind Colman's kitchen garden, was able to come and go in the greatest secrecy.

This delightful intrigue by Hollywood's most eligible bachelor ended, as his friends always hoped it would, with the gate being removed, the wall being bricked up again, and Benita moving into the manor house as the second Mrs. Ronald Colman.

The misogynist Colman slowly thawed out under the warmth, gaiety, and humor of Benita. The small coterie of his old-time friends was enlarged, a daughter, Juliet, was born, and the house was filled with flowers and laughter, but if the flowers were usually stocks, roses or chrysanthemums, the mirth too remained predominantly British.

Colman was never part of the "British Colony" as personified by the Hollywood Cricket Club, Ernest Torrance's Sunday afternoon tea parties, and the tournaments on C. Aubrey Smith's croquet lawn. But his old American friends, William Powell, Richard Barthelmess, and the cowboy star Tim McCoy, found themselves outnumbered by the Nigel Bruces, the Basil Rathbones, and Herbert Marshall with a bewildering succession of wives and mistresses.

Christmas dinner at the Colmans' was a permanent fixture. On went the dinner jackets, down went the turkey, plum pudding, and champagne, and out poured the speeches.

After dinner the women withdrew, and over port and brandy, the older reminisced while the younger ones, Brian Aherne, George Sanders, Douglas Fairbanks, Jr., and myself, remained respectfully silent because mostly they talked about the Great War: Colman had been gassed in it, Rathbone had won the Military Cross, Nigel Bruce had absorbed eleven machine-gun bullets in his behind, and Herbert Marshall had lost a leg.

Before his second marriage Ronnie had invested large sums to protect his beloved privacy. First, he bought the San Ysidro Ranch in the hills above Montecito 100 miles north of Los Angeles. This was no cattle-raising spread; it consisted of several hundred acres of gently sloping land. Immensely tall eucalyptus trees framed the property, on which were groves of oranges, avocados, and lemons, and hidden among these were twenty or thirty white-painted frame bungalows with private gardens and verandas. There was a main dining room and bar, tennis courts, stables, a swimming pool, and a stunning view of the mountains and ocean. It was a Mecca of calm to which the same clientele returned faithfully each year at the same time like the swallows to Capistrano. A hundred years before, Robert Louis Stevenson had loved the place, and the little cottage in which he wrote many of his works was preserved with pride. Later Galsworthy wrote much of *The Forsyte Saga* in the same cottage, and John F. Kennedy spent some of his honeymoon there.

Ronnie's second investment in peace and quiet was a box of oil paints and an easel, a less costly extravagance than his third—an 85-foot copper-bottomed ketch, *Dragoon*. No sailor himself but cosseted by Tommy and an excellent crew, he liked at sundown to sit at the wheel with his yachting cap at a rakish angle, a large whiskey and soda in his hand, and fulminate against Samuel Goldwyn, for whom he had worked for years and at whose hands he vowed he had suffered unimaginable injustices. Apart from Goldwyn, I never heard Ronnie say an unkind word about anyone.

I had first met Colman in the pre-stockbroker-Tudor period, when he lived a hermitlike existence in a cul-de-sac above Hollywood Boulevard, Mound Street. I was still an extra.

I was taken there by Alvin Weingand to make up a four at tennis. After that I was invited back often, but *only* for tennis. Tommy each time would meet me at the gate, escort me through the back garden to the court, and escort me out again at the end of the game.

The players were always the same—Weingand, Colman's agent Bill Hawkes, Clive Brook, Warner Baxter, Colman, and myself. I was much the youngest, so usually I was teamed with Colman, who had, I noticed, rather flat feet; he left most of the running to me. When he finally became convinced that his inner self would not be imposed on by me, I was no longer escorted by Tommy to the gate at the end of a game—I was invited inside for a drink, and a lasting friendship slowly developed.

In all the years I knew him he was only interested in one woman— Benita. His favorite film leading lady had been lovely Alice Terry, a blithe and free spirit whose weakness was eating cream cakes.

Her studio remonstrated with her about this. "You can't do that and remain a star," they told her.

"All right," she replied. "I shall make a million dollars as fast as I can; then I'll retire and eat cream cakes." According to Ronnie, she did just that. She no longer read the scripts the studio sent her.

"Just tell me two things," she said. "Do I have to get wet or ride a horse?" If they said no, she would agree to make the film.

The last Ronnie heard of her, she had made her $1,000,000, had retired to the San Fernando Valley, and was up to her armpits in cream cakes, as happy as a clam.

Ronnie tried hard to further my fledgling career and when he was about to make *Lost Horizon* with Frank Capra, he did all he could to persuade Capra to cast me in the role of his younger brother. Capra reacted kindly to the suggestion but, after meeting me, was only moderately impressed. He did, however, say that he might give me a test the following week.

For six days I never moved more than a few feet from the phone, but it never rang. On the seventh day I concluded sadly that my chances were slim and decided to go fishing. Before I left, I took a small precaution in case by some miracle Frank Capra still might call and asked a girlfriend to stay in the house for me. If Capra rang, she promised to drive north of Malibu and to wave a sheet from the cliffs of Point Dume (pronounced DOOM—and for me it very nearly was).

The all-day boat from Malibu Pier pulled out on the dot of seven o'clock. It was a beautiful still morning with the sun just rising above the sea mist, not a ripple on the surface, just a long, lazy swell.

The fishermen were a jolly cross section of locals from Las Tunas, Santa Monica, and Venice, retired businessmen, carpenters, garage mechanics, house painters, and the like on their day off, with a sprinkling of college kids stealing a day away from their classrooms. We started fishing about three miles offshore, and while the live bait was being chummed overboard to attract the big fish, several fishermen, with a conspicuous lack of husbandry, started munching the contents of their lunch boxes, and beer cans were being opened freely even at that early hour. All in all, it promised to be a good day.

Suddenly, the water all around the boat erupted as a school of yellowtail tuna found the sardines and anchovies. The fishermen, with eager cries, flung aside their sandwiches and started overhead casting, with gleaming silver spoons—a dangerous time, that early first excitement, when the inexperienced caster frequently hooked somebody's ear with his backswing, but that morning no ears and a lot of fish were caught, and everyone was happy.

By noon the schools of big fish had completed their feeding, and we moved in toward the kelp beds off Point Dume, to tackle the bass and halibut. The sun was beating down, and the swells were heavier. A few fishermen changed color and became strangely silent. Such had been my total absorption that I was halfway through my lunch before I remembered my arrangement with the girlfriend and the sheet signal.

I alerted Jack, the captain, and he made a comic announcement, asking everyone to keep an eye open for a flapping sheet.

"How the hell are you going to get ashore, Dave?" he asked.

"I'll swim," I said blithely. "It's only a couple of hundred yards."

"More like five," said Jack doubtfully, "and don't forget that kelp . . . it can really hold you . . . that swell's real heavy."

Half an hour later a cry went up: "The sheet, Dave! . . . the sheet!"

My heart nearly stopped beating. There, far away on a bluff, stood a leggy blonde waving frantically.

A test with Frank Capra! For an important role in one of the biggest pictures to be made that year! Hurriedly, I stripped down to my underpants, and to the encouraging yells of "Attaboy, Dave!" and "Good luck, kid," I dived over the side and headed for stardom.

The kelp beds which form an unbroken chain along hundreds of miles of California coastline are about 200 yards in diameter; the great golden-brown slimy weed branches out to cover the surface, and the thick, weaving roots go down to the ocean floor a hundred feet or more below. Kelp feels very unpleasant to the naked body and has to be navigated carefully from open patch to open patch. It is not advisable to fight or panic, or one becomes entangled.

In the middle of the clearing, I was resting, floating on my back before tackling the next slippery barriers, when I thought of the sharks. Suddenly, about six feet away from me there was a swirling commotion, and a black shiny head with two huge eyes and a bristling mustache shot out of the water. When my heart restarted, I saw it was a baby seal, and it wanted to play. It swam all around me and under me and stayed with me all the way to the clear water on the beach side of the kelp beds. In fact, its presence gave me courage because by now I had heard the ominous sound of heavy surf—big oily swells rising and falling several feet in water a hundred feet deep are transformed into a series of giant foaming rollers when they arrive at a sloping shore.

From the tops of swells I obtained momentary glimpses of the girl and two men scrambling down a cliff path. I paddled on, but I still had quite a way to go. I was tired after my long struggle through the kelp. I was growing cold, too, and my fingers were curling up toward my palms. I began to wonder if I had made a horrible mistake.

Looking landward from the top of one swell, I could see a dozen more, and the farthest ones were curving out of sight away from me. Plumes of spray from their crests were flung back by an offshore breeze. For a few minutes, listening to the alarming pounding of the surf, I rested beyond the broken water, conserving my strength. I had decided to ease my way in, then swim fast with the last unbroken swell. This would carry me ten or twenty yards shoreward. The next one would break, and I would body-surf with it in the approved style, sliding, head down, from the crest. This, I guessed, would take me safely to the beach.

I guessed wrong.

Suddenly a mountainous surge gathered beneath me, and I found myself propelled forward in a crest of foam. I struggled, head high, for a lungful of air and somehow got into my surfing position. I was whizzing beachward at an alarming rate. Feeling myself sliding down the far side, I raised my head again for another much need gulp of oxygen and beheld a horrifying sight: Beneath me, about fifteen feet below, was nothing but sand liberally sprinkled with stones and small rocks. I had picked up the surfer's nightmare—a big shore breaker. The giant wave flung me onto the hard, unyielding foreshore. Tons of water crashed down on top of me, turned me over and over, and ripped me out again along the ocean floor. My mouth and nose were full of sand and water. The breath had been knocked out of my body. I was inside a giant washing machine. I tried to swim to the surface, but everything was dark brown. I didn't know which way up I was. Somehow, with bursting lungs, I found myself on the surface. I was picked up by another roller and flung once more shoreward. Providentially, this wave broke behind me and bore me along, rolling me over and over like a log almost to the high-water mark.

The girl and the men dragged me up among the stinking decayed seaweed, where someone turned me face down and pressed the water out of my lungs. Then I was sick. My chest had been almost stripped of skin.

The girl drove me home, anointed me with iodine, and bandaged me. Then I called Frank Capra's office at Columbia Studios. Capra had gone for the day, but his secretary was still there.

"Oh, you shouldn't have bothered to rush back from your fishing," she said, "Mr. Capra just wanted to tell you that he will not be making your test because he has cast John Howard in the part."

DAVID SELZNICK
AND *The Prisoner Of Zenda*

Colman was not put off by Capra's indifference, though he was full of misgivings when I landed a small contract with Samuel Goldwyn, and when he was preparing for his next picture, *The Prisoner of Zenda,* he walked across Summit Drive and talked about me to the producer, David O. Selznick.

Selznick lived fifty yards away in a white, brightly decorated, rambling one-story house; a belt of towering trees marked the boundary between his property and that of Harold Lloyd. The gardens were full of color, and the place was equipped with the inevitable pool and tennis court. There was no front gate; one turned off Summit Drive into a circular driveway.

Selznick was a huge giant panda of a man, standing about six feet two and permanently struggling with a weight problem. He wore thick glasses and had thick, curly hair. He chain-smoked incessantly, had a broken nose, a wild sense of humor, a great deal of kindness, a weakness for dry martinis and terry-cloth bathrobes, and a completely nonexistent sense of punctuality.

Not even his friends, and he had hundreds of them, could have called him handsome, but such was his charm that it never crossed one's mind that he was anything else. Selznick was married to dark, flashing-eyed

Irene, the daughter of the all-powerful chief of Metro-Goldwyn-Mayer, the foxy, mercurial and frequently vindictive Louis B. Mayer.

Selznick's courting of Irene must have been a nail-biting period. When it came to the affairs of his daughters Irene and Edith, Mayer made Papa Barrett look like Winnie-the-Pooh. His ambitions for Edith were shaken to the core when she announced her intention of marrying quiet, witty Billy Goetz, who had just lost his job as an assistant studio supervisor, and when the young couple asked for an unobtrusive wedding, Mayer nearly blew a gasket. After endless arguing, they reluctantly agreed to what he thought was more fitting to *his* station, an overproduced publicity-oriented bash at the Biltmore Hotel. But as a reward he presented them with a hefty chunk of stock in a new film company which he was largely financing—Twentieth Century-Fox.

If he swallowed with difficulty the marriage of Edith to Bill Goetz, he found the possibility of a match between Irene and David Selznick totally indigestible. "That schnook, that bum" he called David, "that son of a Selznick." David's father, Louis, had been a partner of Mayer's in earlier days, a partner, according to Hollywood legend, who had been unloaded and destroyed by massive jiggery pokery. This belief was certainly held by David and his brother, Myron, a powerful agent, both of whom had sworn to get even on their father's behalf.

Myron was often successful at this and, by manipulating his stable of sought-after stars, was able, from time to time, to give his father's old enemy a right royal financial screwing. David, of course, did not fall in love with Irene in order to do his bit in the Selznick-Mayer war, but he did cause the enemy great anguish. Mayer did all he could to dissuade Irene from the enterprise, and his house shook with emotional scenes, but Irene was unmoved, and finally he gave his consent.

Mayer genuinely admired David's success as head of production at RKO Studios, and once he realized he had lost the battle for Irene, his search for good potential manpower overcame his personal distate, and he offered David a comparable job at MGM plus, as an inducement, the same amount of stock in Twentieth Century-Fox that he had lately given to the other newlyweds. Selznick spurned the stock offer, took the job, quickly turned out a string of great successes, and then announced that he was leaving MGM to form his own production company.

L. B. Mayer did everything in his considerable power to hold Selznick, but David was wary of his aforementioned vindictiveness, stuck to his guns, left MGM, and even won the final jackpot. In a bewildering series of plots and counterplots, he maneuvered Mayer into lending him Clark

Gable, the biggest box-office star at MGM, for *Gone with the Wind*.

Colman's good words on my behalf fell on receptive ears, and one Sunday I received an invitation from Irene Selznick to come play tennis. I arrived at two thirty to find David Selznick in the hall, wrapped in a terry-cloth robe, consuming a plate of smoked salmon, cottage cheese, and pumpernickel.

"Like some breakfast?" he asked cheerfully.

I had just finished lunch, but I thought it might be diplomatic, so I accepted.

"Ronnie Colman talked to me about you," he went on between mouthfuls. "He thought you could play Fritz von Tarlenheim . . . I'll kick it around with John Cromwell tomorrow—he's going to direct—but don't raise your hopes too high because I'm aiming for an all-star cast. I've signed Madeleine Carroll to play Princess Flavia opposite Ronnie, Mary Astor will play Madam de Mauban, Raymond Massey I'm negotiating with for Black Michael, and I may bring Doug Fairbanks, Junior, over from Europe, if he can tear himself away from Gertie Lawrence, to do Rupert of Hentzau. Dear old C. Aubrey Smith wants to play Colonel Zapt, which will be great, so that leaves Fritz."

He stared at me for a long time over the top of a cup of coffee, and I sat there thinking about the last two times I had seen him—lying flat on his back, having been knocked cold at Hollywood parties. Both David and his brother, Myron, compounded their weakness for dry martinis by having very short fuses when arguments started, and they were continually getting into fights which they lost. Chronically bad performers in the noble art, they were further handicapped by very short sight, so the locals when challenged by one of them had a way of bringing matters to a speedy conclusion by first flicking off their eyeglasses and then delivering a quick one-two punch. The crash of falling Selznicks was frequently heard around midnight in Hollywood high society.

"It might work out," said Selznick suddenly. "Let's go down to the court and see who's there." I followed him past rows of bookcases and out into the garden.

Some good tennis was being played by a men's four and some spectacular ladies were watching, including Marlene Dietrich, Paulette Goddard, and Claudette Colbert.

David and Irene Selznick introduced me around and made me feel completely at home. Never for one moment during that long day was I allowed to feel out of it in the presence of an endless procession of the mighty and the talented of Hollywood. I was pressed to stay for drinks and then for a buffet supper and a movie and, like many before me, fell completely under the spell of David Oliver Selznick.

When he bade me good-night, my heart jumped. "Good night, Fritz," he said. "I'll talk to Cromwell tomorrow. Maybe we'll make a test."

All went well. A test was made, and during a game of gin rummy, probably as part of the stakes, Selznick acquired my services from my boss, Samuel Goldwyn.

The Prisoner of Zenda, the classic story of intrigue and high adventure in Ruritania, was an ideal film subject. Donald Ogden Stewart and John Balderston turned out a masterful screenplay full of duels, chases, coronations, and ballroom spectacles.

Selznick assembled the cast he had hoped for, and for four months a great time was had by all. Usually when one makes a film, it is a little like being too long on an ocean voyage. At the end of the trip, total strangers who have been thrown together for several weeks part, swearing eternal allegiance to each other, but never doing much about it. *Zenda* was different. Everyone became friends and remained so.

Colman was the leader and very much the star—a most serious and dedicated performer who was never his easygoing self until the end of the day when Tommy would come and lead me to the star bungalow to join him in his ritual six o'clock "beaker."

Madeleine Carroll was a porcelain beauty of great sweetness and fun, and Mary Astor, who looked like a beautiful and highly shockable nun, had a sweet expression and a tiny turned-up nose and made everyone feel she was in desperate need of protection. In point of fact, she was by her own admission happiest and at her best in bed. She was also, it turned out, highly indiscreet and confided all in her private journal, starting each revealing daily entry "Dear Diary . . . ."

"Dear Diary" right in the middle of the picture caused a major reshuffling of the shooting schedule because it was stolen and turned up as prime evidence in a sensational divorce case, and Mary had to testify.

If "Dear Diary" caused a stir among the *Zenda* company, it was nothing to the upheavals and near heart attacks it perpetrated throughout the upper echelons of the film colony. Mary, it appeared, had been a very busy girl indeed, and her partners had gleefully been awarded marks in "Dear Diary" for performance, stamina, et cetera.

After being absent for days in a blaze of scandal and being laid bare (to coin a phrase) for all to see, Mary returned to the set of *Zenda,* looking just as sweet and demure as ever, and everyone, as usual, desperately wanted to protect her.

C. Aubrey Smith was over seventy when *Zenda* was made, six feet four, ramrod straight, alert and vigorous. Never did he forget a line or misunderstand a piece of direction. Unfailingly courteous, kind and helpful, he was beloved by all.

His great, craggy face was frequently creased by worry because he loved England very deeply, and as it was early in 1937, he had little faith in the way Neville Chamberlain was coping with the Rome-Berlin Axis and Germany's anti-Comintern Pact with Japan. Refusing to read the "local rags," the Los Angeles *Times* or the *Examiner,* trusting only the London *Times* to keep him up to date, and with airmail across the Atlantic almost nonexistent, Aubrey was usually eight to ten days behind a crisis. Nobody spoiled his fun by telling him the news, so it was almost two weeks after it had happened that the old man flung down his morning paper and boomed across the set, "The bloody feller's done it!"

"Who, sir? What, sir?" we chorused.

"That whippersnapper Hitler! He's marched into Austria!"

John Cromwell, the director, was highly respected and highly efficient, but he was a little low on humor, which created certain hazards for Raymond Massey and Doug, Jr., two of the most inveterate gigglers in the business.

The scene at the state ball was most important. Colman, masquerading as the king, was proposing to Princess Flavia in a small anteroom. Outside, a courtier was eavesdropping. At the end of the long intimate love scene this courtier, a large fat man with a mauve face, had to hurry to Fairbanks, Massey, and myself, waiting in our resplendent uniforms at the bottom of a long flight of steps at the entrance to the castle. On arrival he had to say two words: "Good news!"

It was what is known as a production shot, designed to give richness, size, and color to the film by showing the maximum number of people in their magnificent costumes and the most advantageous views of the extravagant sets.

The famous Chinese cameraman James Wong Howe had excelled himself, and by a "marshaling yard's" arrangement of tracks and overhead trolleys, his cameras were able, all in one flowing movement, to witness the love scene, then follow the mauve-faced courtier through several anterooms filled with beautifully gowned ladies and bemedaled gentlemen across a giant white marble multipillared patio, around a lily pond on which cruised haughty black swans, thence up a flight of ornate stairs into the candlelit main ballroom, where 300 couples of the handsomest and most glamorous extras were executing a carefully rehearsed waltz.

Past the minstrel's gallery the mauve courtier hurried, on through the kitchens and vestibules, followed everywhere by a battery of wondering eyes—what would his message be?

Finally, the big moment came. Satin-breeched flunkies flung open the huge main doors, and as the tension mounted, he ponderously descended 120 steps to our little group waiting at the bottom.

"Good news!" he said loudly, and we reeled back. It was bad news for us—he had a breath like a buzzard.

When the courtier tramped back to his starting position for the next run-through, we dared not look at one another. Fairbanks, I sensed, was beginning to vibrate, and out of the corner of my eye, I could see that Ray Massey was making a great production of polishing his monocle.

We suffered through half a dozen more rehearsals and six more broadsides from "Halitosis Harry." By the time John Cromwell was satisfied and ordered the first take we realized we were doomed. A sort of schoolboy hysteria had gripped us, and although we still avoided one another's eyes, we knew we could never get through the scene.

"Let's pretend it's drains," I whispered.

We could hear the love scene being played in the distance, and with dread we followed the sounds of the courtier's slow progress toward us. The orchestra in the ballroom fell silent as he approached the end of his journey so that his two golden words could be recorded for posterity.

The doors above us were flung open, and our tormentor, relieved to be at the end of his complicated trip, descended smugly toward us.

"Good news!" he said.

We greeted his announcement with gales of pent-up laughter.

"Cut! What the hell's going on?" demanded a furious Cromwell, rushing up, but the more angry he became, the more uncontrollable became our mirth.

Fairbanks behaved in a most craven manner. "Ask Mr. Massey what's wrong," he blurted out, tears streaming down his face. "He's the oldest."

Ray's suggestion didn't help at all. "Gee, Mr. Cromwell, perhaps it would give us a kind of springboard if the gentleman *whispered* the line."

The whisper brought us a whif of pure phosgene.

In the end Cromwell rearranged his shooting schedule so that our reactions to the fateful "news" could be photographed the following day when, as he succintly put it, "You bastards will have had a whole night to calm down."

Hollywood always felt that the leading characters of costume pictures should be seen riding prancing, frothing, and often unmanageable steeds, so when we came to the shooting of the coronation procession, I had a few words with the head wrangler, some currency changed hands, and I was mounted on a nice quiet old mare. Unfortunately, she was in heat. Trotting through the cheering citizens beside the golden coach bearing Ronnie and Madeleine, resplendent in cuirass and silver helmet topped by a golden eagle, I was blissfully unaware of danger gathering like a storm astern of me. Ray was riding a large black stallion.

A high-pitched whinnying rose above the screams of hurriedly departing townsfolk, and about six feet of easily identifiable stallion equipment passed me like a torpedo. I turned in my saddle to find thrashing hooves and gnashing teeth all around me. Far above, I saw Ray's horrified face. Not wanting to go down with the ship, I hurriedly disembarked by flinging myself to the ground, leaving my mare to her happy fate and Ray to a ringside seat. For a while it looked as if he were on a rocking horse.

Selznick's *Prisoner of Zenda* was a triumphant success, critically and financially, and a testament to what happens when a producer infuses all those around him with loyalty, enthusiasm, and joy in their work.

DOUGLAS FAIRBANKS

At the top of Summit Drive stood Pickfair, a walled estate that had long been the focal point of all that meant Hollywood.

The home of the two biggest stars of silent pictures, Douglas Fairbanks and Mary Pickford, Pickfair had hosted the most ostentatious parties and royal entertainments of the great dawning of Hollywood.

The "King of the Silent Films," the most popular male star in the world, hero of such muscular, exciting, and intentionally amusing spectacles as *The Three Musketeers, Robin Hood, The Mark of Zorro, The Black Pirate,* and *The Thief of Bagdad,* had married "America's Sweetheart"—a Hollywood bonanza!

Fairbanks had a hold on the filmgoers of the world, young and old, that has never to this day been equaled. Mary Pickford, too, "Little Mary of the Golden Curls," had her own immense and devoted following. The marriage had ended in divorce the year before I arrived in Hollywood, and the Pickfair I saw was a sad, overfurnished, and melancholy place of memories and closed doors. Mary was a wan and gallant little hostess, relying more and more on the companionship of a serious curly-haired young actor-singer whom she subsequently married—Buddy Rogers.

Fairbanks was far from wan and sad. He was being comforted by the glorious, willowy, lemon-meringue blond Lady Ashley.

Sylvia Hawkes had been a chorus girl and small-part actress till she met dull good-looking Lord Ashley. Before long, she met the far from dull, but equally good-looking, Sir Tim Birking, a rich racing motorist, but a year after her divorce from Lord Ashley she upset the books by marrying Fairbanks.

When he departed from Pickfair, Fairbanks moved down to a Santa Monica Beach house with Sylvia.

Doug in his mid-fifties still had the figure of a young athlete, and he paid constant attention to keeping it that way. He took a sunbath daily in a small green canvas compartment in the garden, burning himself the color of chewing tobacco. He was curiously coy in the presence of the friends he invited to join him there, always covering his private parts with his two cupped hands.

Chuck Lewis, his personal trainer, was always in attendance, giving massages and organizing workouts, steam baths, tennis, golf, or long-distance swims. Doug enjoyed hugely displaying his acrobatic talents and watching those half his age trying to catch up with him. I nearly killed myself jumping off his high diving board onto the low springboard alongside, which he had assured me would give me a "real tremendous bounce." It did. I missed the water altogether and landed in some petunias below the drawing-room window. While we disported ourselves in the business end of the pool, Sylvia, ever careful of her famous creamy white skin, paddled about in the shallow end beneath a huge floppy hat. Douglas was an overgrown schoolboy reveling in practical jokes, simple and elaborate.

The simple ones ranged from giving people exploding cigars, lighting orange flash papers, playing ostentatiously with a twenty-pound cannonball, exchanging it unseen for a rubber replica, yelling "catch," and tossing it to some poor unsuspecting wretch, to disappearing beneath the dinner table on serious evenings, crawling on hands and knees, and gently opening the fly of a pompous man sitting between two equally haughty ladies at the far end.

The elaborate ones turned sometimes into expensive productions. He announced in the trade papers that Dr. Hans Strassmann, the head of the German film company UFA, was coming out to visit him. Then he arranged for a "professional insulter"—a small bald actor named Vince Barnett—to board the Santa Fe Chief at San Bernardino, the last stop before Los Angeles.

Barnett, in Tyrolean hat and green cloak, made a triumphant entry into the film capital, and Fairbanks welcomed him at Union Station with red carpet, photographers, and a large crowd. The next night Fairbanks gave a white-tie dinner, and everyone was in the know except Samuel Goldwyn. At the end of the meal, cigars were lit and speeches of welcome were made. The last guest called on was the unfortunate Goldwyn. When Barnett rose to reply, with a heavy German accent, he thanked all the speakers but said that he was a little surprised that Goldwyn had been invited to meet him because he considered him to be the least talented filmmaker in the United States. He went on to say that Goldwyn was famous for stealing actors like Gary Cooper away from other studios, that everyone in Berlin knew that the only reason he had brought the Russian actress Anna Sten out to Hollywood was "because he wanted to get into her bloomers."

Poor Goldwyn was slow to catch on, and it took Fairbanks a long, long time to put matters right.

Fairbanks was a low handicap golfer, an excellent tennis player, and a top-class performer with saber, épée, or foil. His film duels were high spots in all his productions, and his daring stunts, as a matter of pride, he did himself, scorning the use of doubles.

One was really spectacular: Escaping from the heavies from a high balcony in *Robin Hood,* with both hands he plunged his sword into an eighty-foot-high velvet curtain and whizzed down to safety. He repeated this stunt in *The Black Pirate:* Trapped in the highest crosstrees, he slid down a billowing mainsail and arrived safely on deck, leaving his adversaries in the rigging.

Plagued by questions on how his hands and wrists could possibly have been strong enough to keep the sword at exactly the right angle, he one day divulged to us that on the other side of the curtain and sail the swords had been bolted into a board—but it was still a very dangerous descent.

Doug's prowess and ability aboard movie ships did not extend to his seamanship in real life. One Fourth of July he and Sylvia chartered a motor cruiser and invited a small group to sail with them to Catalina. The idea was to anchor on arrival alongside Cecil B. DeMille's sleek white three-masted schooner. Our captain had an ominous name—Jake Puke.

Except for the deckhand who really had been prostrated by seasickness, the four-hour trip to the island had been uneventful, and without difficulty, we located DeMille's schooner. Nearby was a large circular mooring buoy, and Captain Puke decided to attach his boat to the ring on top of it. With DeMille's smartly dressed guests applauding our arrival, we rammed this buoy at considerable speed because when Captain Puke rang down to the engine room for "full astern," the engineer was on deck picking his teeth and contemplating DeMille's yacht.

Finally, we maneuvered into position for someone to jump down onto the buoy and secure us. "Now," yelled Captain Puke.

"I'll go," said Fairbanks bravely. "Quick, David, up to the sharp end!"

I followed him to the bow, where he grabbed a rope I was holding and, with his famous grace and feline agility, leaped down onto the pitching buoy. Further applause greeted this effort, but it was premature because the rope turned out to be attached to nothing on our boat, and when the engineer at last obeyed Captain Puke's unnautical command to "BACK UP . . . YOU SON OF A BITCH!" we pulled away, leaving our host stranded. I fetched him later in the dinghy.

Such heady stuff was it for an unknown young actor to be accepted by one of the Hollywood giants that it was some time before I realized that beneath all his gaiety, flamboyance, and love of youth, Fairbanks lived with a great sadness. He fought off the advancing years valiantly and perhaps a little desperately, but the afternoon light was already softening the contours of a career that had long been illuminated more brightly than any other in the history of the movies, and it was with a rather sad smile he bade me one day bend down and look at myself in the mirror top of a coffee table. The blood ran into my cheeks and under my eyes, and I found myself staring at a warthog.

"That's what you'll look like when you're fifty!" He laughed.

Still acclaimed, applauded, and stopping traffic wherever he went, even in the remotest parts of the world, he accepted the adulation with a flashing smile, but it must have been a knife in his guts to know that, at an age when his contemporaries in other walks of life were just reaching their zenith, he had already been turned out to grass.

CHARLES CHAPLIN

On the same side of Summit Drive as Pickfair and Ronald Colman's house sprawled an estate of about the same acreage as that of Harold Lloyd. . . . It also was owned by a founding father of Hollywood—Charles Spencer Chaplin.

It boasted stands of beautiful trees, green lawns sloping down to a swimming pool and, of course, a tennis court. The house was large, cluttered, of yellow-ocher color and Victorian design: high french windows giving on to the gardens retrieved it from being supersuburbia. Few people were invited there, not because Charlie Chaplin shunned all contact with the Hollywood he had done more than any other to change from a citrus-growing community into one of the biggest industries in the United States. Rather, it was for two very basic reasons: The greatest public entertainer in the world had only a sketchy idea of how to entertain in private, and he was also allergic to laying out large sums of money for food and drink to be guzzled by those he reckoned to be passengers and non-contributors. He enjoyed going out, however, to selected houses, and nothing made him happier than playing the elder statesman, sitting in a chair after dinner, with the faithful at his feet, while he held forth with gestures and sublime caricature.

Not the greatest listener in private life, Chaplin was a great advocate of it as an essential part of the actor's equipment. One night Doug Fairbanks ran a film after dinner at the beach house, and in it was one of my earliest efforts. When it was over, the others made the insincere but flattering noises so dear to an actor's heart, but Chaplin sat still, saying nothing.

Finally, I plucked up courage to ask him what he thought.

"Don't just stand around like most actors waiting for your turn to speak," he said flatly. "Learn to listen."

The uncompromising directness of this excellent advice was typical of Chaplin. The folk hero of millions in every land, the tattered courageous little tramp who loved flowers and children and raised two rude fingers at the Establishment, he was in himself an extremely opinionated man with a highly developed sense of his own place in history. He loved being asked for advice and gave it freely.

Beside Fairbanks' pool one day, the playwright Charles MacArthur, who had lately been lured from Broadway to write a screenplay, was bemoaning the fact that he was finding it difficult to write visual jokes.

"What's the problem?" asked Chaplin.

"How, for example, could I make a fat lady, walking down Fifth Avenue, slip on a banana peel and still get a laugh? It's been done a million times," said MacArthur. "What's the best way to get the laugh? Do I show first the banana peel, then the fat lady approaching; then she slips? Or do I show the fat lady first, then the banana peel, and then she slips?"

"Neither," said Chaplin without a moment's hesitation. "You show the fat lady approaching; then you show the banana peel; then you show the fat lady and the banana peel together; then she steps over the banana peel and disappears down a manhole."

Chaplin was devoted to Douglas Fairbanks and never wearied of telling that it was Fairbanks' business antennae which had sensed the fact that with Mary Pickford the three biggest stars in the business were overpricing themselves so heavily that producers, seeing little profit from their pictures, would soon be unwilling to employ any of them.

"It's simple," Fairbanks had said. "We cut out the producers; then we make our own pictures and employ ourselves."

The result had been the highly profitable United Artists Company.

I recounted to Chaplin some of the experiences I had endured in the "meat Market," the loathsome practice of some directors when casting the smaller parts of their films, calling twenty or thirty "possibilities" to the sound stage and making each in turn play a key scene *in front* of the remainder, finally dismissing all except one.

Chaplin told me that this embarrassing and unfair system was a legacy from Broadway and that it had not changed since he had come to New York in 1913 with Fred Karno's *A Night in an English Music Hall* (another member of that small troupe had been Stan Laurel, later of Laurel and Hardy). Chaplin was interviewed by William Gillette, a great actor-manager of that time, who was casting for *King Henry V,* and twelve nervous young actors were lined up on the stage, hoping for the microscopic part of Williams, one of the English soldiers.

Gillette, an intimidating figure draped in a long black coat with a fur collar, addressed the group.

"Gentlemen," he intoned, giving full range to his famous voice, "I shall approach each of you in turn and say, 'The dauphin is dead!' Your reply will be one word, 'Dead!' He who makes the most of that one word will play the part of Williams."

The group of young hopefuls shuffled nervously about. At the farthest end of the line in a black suit with a high white stiff collar stood Chaplin—by several inches the shortest.

"The dauphin is dead!" boomed Gillette at the first actor, but the young man was so terrified he just managed to roll his eyes and emit a pitiful squeak: "Dead?"

He was dismissed. "The dauphin is dead!" roared Gillette, but the next actor decided that an English soldier would be delighted at the news. "Dead?" he asked, smiling happily as though his stock in the Union Pacific Railroad had risen twenty points. He too was dismissed.

As the line was thinned out and an impatient Gillette drew inexorably nearer, Chaplin became increasingly nervous. Eight actors had been dismissed with ignominy, taking with them every inflection and every nuance with which he he had hoped to embellish the word "Dead." Three more dismissals followed in quick succession, and the diminutive Chaplin found himself alone on the stage confronted by the towering figure of the now exasperated actor-manager.

Gillette looked down with distaste upon the sole survivor. "The dauphin is dead!" he yelled.

Chaplin's mind went blank.

He shook his head mournfully from side to side, then clicked his tongue loudly on the roof of his mouth. "Tch! tch! tch! tch!" he went.

Gillette slowly raised his arm, pointed scornfully to the exit, and Chaplin disappeared alone and with dignity into the sunset.

Feeling himself pilloried too long in the American press for not taking out his U.S. citizenship, for his leftist political views, for his former love affairs with young actresses, and finally for his marriage to the teenaged daughter of Eugene O'Neill, Chaplin folded his tents and one night silently stole away to live peacefully in Vevey, a small, sleepy town on the shores of Lake Geneva.

Reclining in a hospital bed into which Chaplin had inadvertently put me, I read of his sudden departure and was amazed because a few hours before I had been playing tennis with him on Summit Drive.

A highly organized man, as his military-style withdrawal demonstrated, he liked his tennis games neatly arranged. With a clearly defined preference for winning, he had given me as a partner for the afternoon's sport Tim Durant, a slow-moving elderly man, later famous as the galloping grandfather courageously flogging also-rans around the Grand National Steeplechase. As his own partner Chaplin had invited none other than Big Bill Tilden, unquestionably the greatest tennis player the world had ever seen.

Tilden served first to me, and because of his great height, the ball came out of the sun. I never saw it—but I *heard* it as it went by and became embedded in the wire netting behind me.

Durant fared no better, and Chaplin looked smug.

"Thirty-love," he crowed.

For the next serve to me, Tilden decided to be kinder and instead of acing me with another bullet, he uncorked a delivery that had so much spin on it that the ball was egg-shaped as it floated over the net. When it hit the ground, it shot straight up in the air above my head. With visions of smashing the Great Tilden's top-secret delivery, I leaped in the air and flailed at it.

I thought I had received a blow with an ax behind my leg, and I fell to the ground writhing in excruciating agony. I had not pulled a tendon; I had snapped my entire calf muscle clean in half.

Tilden was galvanized into action. He leaped the net. "I know what it is," he said. "Quick, somebody, get adhesive tape!"

Chaplin disappeared toward the house, and with hindsight, I suppose he must have done some unpacking. At any rate, the most appalling pain I have ever experienced was relieved when he reappeared.

"I'm going to tape your heel up as high as it will go," said Tilden. "That'll point the toes down and make the muscle go slack. It'll help the pain; then we'll put you in the hospital."

He did as he promised; then he and Durant carried me to his car and drove me away. My final view of Chaplin, with his last day's tennis in California ruined, was of a small, white-flanneled figure disconsolately hitting balls against the green canvas of the backing.

Within a few hours, Hollywood's one true genius was gone forever to the land of peace, understanding, milk chocolate, and all those lovely snowcapped tax benefits.

CHAPTER 7

BOGIE

Humphrey Bogart was born in December, 1899, which, up to a point, was perfectly all right with him. The thing he deeply resented about it was that it happened on Christmas Day. "Got gypped out of a proper birthday, goddammit."

Bogie's father, a well-to-do New York physician, was incessantly nagged by his wife. Bogie too enjoyed needling people, and he practiced it from an early age.

His famous lisp was caused by a badly performed operation on his lower lip in which a splinter of wood had become embedded. I asked him how the piece of wood had got into his lip in the first place. "Accident as a kid." He shrugged. The Warner Brothers publicity department improved upon this and announced that it was a "shrapnel wound suffered in combat during World War I."

Bogie endured a well-to-do eastern seaboard upbringing, attended Andover, and headed for Yale. He didn't make it there, much to his mother's annoyance. She told him he was a failure and ordered him to go get himself a job. He complied, the next day enlisted in the U.S. Navy, and at seventeen and a half aboard the troop carrier *Leviathan* did indeed see service in the closing months of World War I.

After two years he was honorably discharged from the Navy and for the next eighteen months was employed as a runner for a Wall Street brokerage house. He didn't run fast enough apparently and resented openly the financial Establishment which employed him, so to the accompaniment of catcalls from his mother and with very little encouragement from his father, he drifted little by little into the theater.

First, he became stage manager to William Brady, the father of a school friend, who was producing plays in Brooklyn, and later he played his first part for the same suburban impresario in a play called *Swiftly*. Opposite him was a young actress, Frances Howard, who left the production to become the wife of my own future boss—Samuel Goldwyn.

Bogie caught on in a small way and, by the age of twenty-six, was regularly employed in New York and the suburbs as a sleek juvenile lead complete with white tie, tails, and occasionally a tennis racket. These being the Roaring Twenties, he also set about making a name for himself in the speakeasies of Prohibition, where he took happily to the use of scotch. Although never at any time was he near alcoholism, Bogie maintained from then on an awe-inspiring level of consumption—he enjoyed it; he liked the taste of it; he approved mightily of its effect upon him—but he never allowed it to interfere with his work.

Bogie married a successful young actress named Helen Menken. The marriage fell apart after eighteen months, with Bogie blaming himself for putting his career before the possibilities of a happy home life—a lesson which remained unlearned because one year later he married another successful young actress, Mary Phillips, and promptly departed for Hollywood, where he had been offered a small contract.

The fulfilling of this long engagement 3,000 miles away from his new wife did nothing to help his new marriage or to further the career which he still found all-important, and on his return to New York he was only routinely surprised when Mary Phillips informed him that she had fallen in love with a New York-based actor, Roland Young.

The depths of the Depression coincided with Bogie's return to Broadway, and work for actors was scarce to nonexistent, but against this somber background Bogie and Mary made a brave stab at putting together the Humpty-Dumpty of their partnership. They moved into peeling, crumbling lodgings on the East Side and for a while were supported solely by Bogie's prowess at chess; he played for 50 cents a game in sleazy Sixth Avenue dives.

To be thirty-four years old, an unemployed married actor, small in stature, short on presence, with a pronounced lisp and little professional experience, must have been daunting even for Bogie, but he gamely plodded off on his rounds of agencies and producers' offices, and in 1934, a few weeks after the death of his bankrupt father, Bogie struck theatrical oil. Arthur Hopkins was casting *The Petrified Forest* by Robert Sherwood, and Bogie was given a chance to read the part of the sentimental killer, Duke Mantee. He shaved off most of his thick thatch of hair and delivered his lines with a snarl made even more menacing by his lisp.

Neither Hopkins nor Sherwood was impressed, and from the darkness of the stalls Bogie heard the dreaded "Thank you very much, don't call us, we'll call you." As Bogie slunk from the stage, renewed whispering broke out. Leslie Howard, the star of the play, had been sitting quietly in the back row. Now he moved forward and urgently begged the others to reconsider. He was convinced that Bogie was ideal for the part. Bogie read again, Sherwood agreed with Howard, and finally, Hopkins nodded his assent.

The play was a huge success, and Bogie made a personal success of enormous proportions. He was signed with Leslie Howard to make the picture for Warner Brothers at the end of the Broadway run, but when he and Mary in high excitement arrived in Hollywood, all set to knock the film world for a loop, he learned to his stunned dismay that the studio had decided to pay him off and put one of their biggest contract stars into the role of Duke Mantee—Edward G. Robinson.

Bogie had no intention of meekly swallowing this, his first taste of big studio duplicity, so he fired off an SOS to Leslie Howard in England. Howard reacted immediately and unleashed a return salvo at Warner Brothers: "It's either with Bogart or without me."

Bogart it was, and film history continued smoothly on its way. He never forgot, never ceased to acknowledge the helping hand he had received when he had most needed it and, as a gesture of his gratitude, named his second child, a girl, Leslie.

The brothers Warner, never renowned for the delicacy and foresight with which they handled their contract players, decided that they had hatched a golden egg, so Bogie was treated like a battery hen and in the next four years was forced to pump out no less than twenty-nine gangster films, in each of which he played a carbon copy of Duke Mantee; this nearly finished his career and completely ruined his marriage. Seeing nothing of her husband except glimpses of a zombie who worked punishing hours on Warner's production line, Mary took off for New York to do a play. Bogie was sad to see her go but consoled himself with an undulating blonde of conspicuous cleavage named Mayo Methot. Mayo was a hard case, a drinker who went refill by refill with Bogie, but unlike him, she was unable to handle it, and by the time Mary divorced Bogie Mayo was well on her way to alcoholism. In 1938 Mayo and Bogie married, and at a famously liquid reception the Russian actor Mischa Auer appeared from behind the giant wedding cake and danced before the befuddled guests stark naked.

Bogie settled down for the third time to married life, but his latest partnership soon developed into the toughest situation he had ever had to handle.

I witnessed some of it. I had met Bogie the year when he had been lent by Warner Brothers to Samuel Goldwyn to make *Dead End,* and one day we drank lunch together at the Formosa Café across the street, but we did not like each other very much. I found his aggressively tough and needling manner rather tiresome, and he obviously marked me down as a prissy Englishman. We parted with expressions of mutual respect and a determination from then on to avoid each other like the plague.

The next time I came face to face with Bogie he was underneath a table in the Restaurant La Maze on the Sunset Strip. This was a favorite hangout of the younger Hollywood group because it boasted the best music in town and the manager made a welcome specialty of keeping it off limits to the prying eyes of the columnists, possibly because the place also catered to the Mickey Cohen gangster element of Los Angeles, and indeed there had lately been a full-scale killing on the premises.

Bogie, like all movie mobsters since the beginning of films, was plagued by drunks who would lurch up to him in public, trying to pick a fight in order to impress others with how they had "taken care of the tough guy." Bogie was adept at avoiding all forms of physical combat. It was not that he was cowardly; it was just that he was quite small—a bantam-weight— who had not the faintest intention of being knocked around by people twice his size. His love of the needle, however, sometimes ended in dangerous brinkmanship.

That night at La Maze Bogie was confronted by a large man with a flushed face wearing an open-neck shirt turned down outside his jacket.

I was sitting in a corner with the "Oomph Girl," Ann Sheridan. Bogie with Mayo was a few tables away. We couldn't hear the confrontation, but we could see that the scene was developing along traditional lines. The large man was bending over their table and poking Bogie in the chest with a forefinger. Bogie was smiling insults, Mayo was rising like a ruffled hen turkey from her seat, and waiters were circling warily around, taking up action stations to isolate or eliminate the impending conflict.

Suddenly all hell broke loose. Bogie threw a full glass of scotch into his aggressor's eyes, and at the same moment Mayo hit the man on the head with a shoe. I caught a momentary glimpse of flinty-eyed characters rising purposefully from the table whence the large man had come and of a solid phalanx of waiters converging on the battle area. Cries of rage and alarm rose on all sides, and the air became thick with flying bottles, plates, glasses, left hooks, and food.

"Quick," screamed the Oomph Girl. "Under the table."

This was a suggestion with which I was only too happy to comply, but for some technical reason, it was impossible to get beneath our own table, so we threw ourselves to the floor and crawled on hands and knees to a larger sanctuary a few yards away.

We had not been installed there for more than a few seconds before Bogie came padding in on all fours; he was laughing like hell.

"What's going on up there?" I asked.

"Everything's OK," he chortled. "Mayo's handling it . . . I wish I'd brought a fork, though—I might be able to jab the bastard in the leg."

Mayo did indeed handle it. The attacker and his party were ousted, and the evening dusted itself off and returned to normal.

After that night Bogie nicknamed Mayo Sluggy, and she lived up to it. The skirmishes between the "Battling Bogarts," as the Hollywood press corps christened them, were noisy in the extreme, and complaining neighbors insisted that they were nonstop. Jealousy on the part of Mayo seemed to be the spark that ignited the flames—jealousy mixed with booze, a lethal cocktail, with Bogie playing his role of "stirrer." He and Mayo would drink: then her jealousy, generally of his current leading lady, would come to the boil, and Bogie would gleefully go into action, goading her till the bottles started whizzing past his head. It must have been a most exhausting period for him, and it was certainly dangerous, because on one occasion Mayo slashed her wrists, on another she set fire to their house, and on a third she stabbed him in the back with a carving knife. "Only went in a little way," he said as he was being stitched up.

The "Battling Bogarts" were still at it hammer and tongs in September, 1939, when, in a moment of military lunacy, I departed for Europe. I did not see Bogie again till I returned in 1946, but a mutual friend, writer John McClain, serving with the American navy, had kept me up to date.

Bogie, he told me, had widened the area of conflict and had decided to take on Jack Warner at the same time as he was conducting his running battles with Mayo. He had realized that he must get away from his gangster screen image because he saw clearly that with the wartime carnage being fully reported, the "Mob" in action had become tame stuff indeed, so he refused to work at all and was suspended. After much resistance from Warner, John Huston was allowed to put Bogie into *The Maltese Falcon,* a picture regarded at the studio with undisguised apprehension. With the success of this picture a new career opened up for Bogie, and in *Casablanca* he played a romantic soldier of fortune opposite Ingrid Bergman. He became the pet of the Warner Brothers lot, and a beaming Jack Warner told him he could have the pick of all the scripts.

As Bogie's film popularity soared, so his home life deteriorated. Mayo became a confirmed alcoholic; her looks and figure collapsed, and she made an increasing number of hideous scenes in public, but Bogie, trying nobly to keep the ship afloat, would never hear a word against her.

"She's an actress," he would say with menacing quiet, "a goddamn good one, but she's not working much at the moment, which is tough on her . . . understand?"

When Mayo heard this, she was apt to scream out that Bogie was "a Four-F coward and a phony," but somehow he got through the battle-scarred nights and still arrived on time for work early the next morning.

It couldn't last at that pace, of course, and when in 1944 Bogie made *To Have and Have Not,* he fell head over heels in love with his nineteen year-old leading lady, an ex-theater usherette and cover girl, Lauren Bacall. Mayo's antennae picked up the message early, she scented battle and sailed into the studio, and Bogie's next love scene was interrupted by the strident voice of his wife inquiring how he was getting along with "that poor child half your age."

Betty Bacall was equally in love with Bogie, but all she could do was suffer and pray that Bogie could work things out so that he would be free to marry her. Bogie gave his marriage to Mayo another try to see if he could forget Betty, but it didn't work. Poor Mayo—her jealousy made her ugly, and her ugliness made her drink, and a guilt-ridden Bogie ducked her flying bottles and pretended not to hear her abuse, but even he was not made of steel, and his nerves finally cracked under the strain.

One morning in the studio makeup department, a girl was washing Boggie's hair. His chin was cupped sleepily in the aluminum bowl, and the hairdresser was proudly giving him the benefit of her best friction rub. Suddenly the poor creature stared aghast into the basin; then she let out a piercing shriek and fainted dead away. The entire growth of hair on the head of the most valuable star in her studio had come away in her hands. It grew back in time as his nerves recovered, but Bogie never again had the same luxurious thatch. From then on it always looked to me as though the cat had been at it.

Divorce became inevitable, and Mayo, a classic Hollywood casualty, departed for her Oregon birthplace, and there six years later, as the tragic decline accelerated, she died all alone in a motel.

When Betty and Bogie married in the Ohio home of Louis Bromfield, there was exactly twenty-five years' difference in their ages. This sparked off some spicy observations about "old folks' homes" on the part of Betty's father, and the Hollywood smart money went on an early breakup. The locals, over the years, had been afforded ample opportunity to study Bogie's form, but they underestimated Betty, who was an unknown starter. In spite of her extreme youth, she had a mountain of common sense and the guts to put it to work. She never kowtowed to Bogie, she never nagged him, and above all, she truly admired him as a man and as an actor. For his part he adored her and was proud of her looks, her honesty, and her spirit. He cut back conspicuously on his whiskey consumption because "Betty doesn't go for it too much, and it's no fun drinking alone." Her explanation was probably nearer the mark: "Bogie drank a lot because he was unhappy. Now he's happy."

This then was the couple that John McClain took me to visit when we both returned to Hollywood in 1946. Nobody likes being dropped in on, especially when tired after a long day's work, but Betty had arranged a surprise party for Bogie on his forty-seventh birthday—a potentially dangerous tactic.

When Bogie walked in and discovered thirty people hiding in cupboards, seated on toilets or under beds, he became loudly abusive, and it seemed that no amount of singing "Happy Birthday" could soften his attitude. Betty finally won the day by playing it his way. "All right then, you son of a bitch," she yelled. "You stay here alone, and we'll all go out for dinner."

He bared his teeth in the famous wolf grin and snarled, "Okay, you bastards—you're welcome." The party went on till dawn.

Bogie bought a sailing boat from Dick Powell, the 65-foot ketch *Santana,* and next to Betty, she became the most important thing in his life. He was a first-class sailor, an ocean racer of repute, and his love of the sea was deep, almost mystical. Betty was smart enough not to be jealous of this other love and realized that he derived much peace and strength from his weekend voyages. Occasionally she went along, but mostly she encouraged him to go alone with Pete, his Danish crewman, and a couple of pals.

During his forty-seventh birthday party, Bogie learned that I, too, had sailed all my life, and his face softened. "There's hope for you yet," he growled. "Come to the island next weekend."

I enjoyed the trip immensely, but I subsequently discovered that while I had been reveling in being told to take the helm or put up a spinnaker, I had, in fact, been under Bogie's microscope. His theory was simple—if a man could handle a boat in rough weather or be a good shipmate in days of calm, he should be awarded one star like a reliable restaurant in the *Guide Michelin.* If in addition, he proved to have interests, experience, and curiosity outside the small world of filmmaking and enjoyed a game of chess, he might receive a higher rating. I never learned my own classification, but imperceptibly almost, our understanding prospered from then on, and one day I looked up to find Bogie and Betty among my closest friends.

This was flattering because Bogie did not really like actors as a breed, and apart from Tracy, Sinatra, and Peter Lorre, he usually kept his distance, much preferring the company of writers such as Huston, Bromfield, Nunnally Johnson, Mark Hellinger and Alistair Cooke.

On the many, many subsequent trips I had aboard *Santana,* I grew to realize what a very special man Betty had married. Things to Bogie were either black or white; he had little patience with the grays. To sort people out quickly, he used the shock technique. Early on in an acquaintanceship he would say or do something completely outrageous, and the reaction of the other person told Bogie most of what he wanted to know. People in movie theaters saw him as the personification of the tough and the sardonic, and up to a point they were not far from wrong. He gamely presented the same façade in real life, but my own theory was that he worked to maintain it and had a difficult time covering up the fact that he was really kind, generous, highly intelligent, and deeply sentimental. Animals loved him, too—the best sign of all.

I think he had a horror of being unmasked, and being very publicity-conscious, he gradually eliminated nearly all contact with the press, preferring, if he had anything to say, to give it to one man who wrote a column in the New York *Herald Tribune*—Joe Hyams. Other people would then pick it up.

Joe was an intelligent and respected newspaperman, and he kept Bogie's image alive in exactly the colors Bogie wanted. Whether he was taken in by Bogie or whether his personal friendship impeded him in his reporting of some of the subtler shadings of his subject, it was hard to decide, but he certainly played the game according to Bogie's rules.

Bogie set himself up as a noncomformist, and this was no act. He really intended to do his own thing and despised those who pandered to the Hollywood code of good behavior.

"I'm not one of the boys next door. I leave that to all those good-looking bastards with their button-down shirts."

And he would go on his merry way, tilting at the windmills of convention, arriving at nightclubs with giant panda dolls, arguing with all and sundry, championing left-wing causes, and making heavily quoted statements about the unreliability of people who never drank.

Once sitting on the deck of *Santana* in a quiet cove off Catalina Island, eating delicious lobsters caught in his illicit trap (his publicity incidentally stated that he never fished because he loved animals too much), I heckled him about his obvious determination to bend the rules.

"You're very clean about your own house," I said. "Why do you make such a point of going out to dinner unshaven and wearing a stinking old tweed jacket when you've been asked to arrive in a tuxedo?"

"The point I'm making," he said, "is that if I choose to show up unshaven and stinking, it's nobody's goddamned business but mine, and nobody gets hurt but me."

"Working on the Bogart image?" I asked.

"How far can you swim, you jerk," he countered, "because it's sixty miles from here to Santa Monica!"

Bogie one day was reminiscing on how great a part luck had played in his early days at Warner Brothers; he reminded me yet again that he had played *The Petrified Forest* only because of Leslie Howard's determination and added that he had got *The Maltese Falcon* only because George Raft had turned it down and *High Sierra* had come his way because Paul Muni had huffily refused it on the grounds that it had first been offered to George Raft. "But that's the way the piss pot cracks," he said.

I couldn't resist it, as I had been husbanding the dangerous morsel for years. "Now I'll tell you how you got an Oscar for *The African Queen* in 1951," I said.

"Please do," said Bogie with chilling calm.

"Because Bette Davis turned it down!" I announced smuggly.

When the explosion died away, I told him more.

C. S. Forester wrote the story in 1935, and Warner Brothers bought it for Bette Davis. In 1938 their producer, Henry Blanke, borrowed me from Samuel Goldwyn to play the Cockney "river rat" opposite her. The deal was signed, and bemused by my glorious opportunity, I had spent four weeks polishing up a Cockney accent. I even grew a beard which made me look like a diseased yak, but at the last minute, Bette Davis fell out with Blanke and told him she refused to be photographed out of doors (a likely story), so the picture was canceled and the property sold to Twentieth Century-Fox, where twelve years later John Huston unearthed it.

When I finished, I waited for the Bogie bombshell. It never came. He put a consoling arm around my shoulders and said very thoughtfully, "Kid . . . I think you would have stunk up the screen in that part."

Sitting long evenings below decks in *Santana,* I was constantly amazed at the simplicity of Bogie's character; he just could not be bothered to camouflage his weaknesses. Although right at the top of his profession, he also possessed the actor's Achilles' heel—he was jealous and showed it.

The actor he admired most was Spencer Tracy. They were highly professional performers, and both despised the "stars" who were not. Bogie wanted to make a picture, *The Desperate Hours,* and the "dream casting" was to play Spencer and Bogie in the two tailor-made roles. Both were longing to do it, and both wanted badly to play with the other. Again and again, they met and got all steamed up about the prospect, but each time it mysteriously collapsed, the reason being that the moment they parted they quickly contacted their respective managers—neither of them would take second billing. They never worked together.

If he was childish about billing, which is something the public is blissfully unconscious of, he was also overly quick to react to the threat of "new faces."

"Why the hell don't they lift some of the old ones? All those bastards at the studios are trying to do is find fifty-dollar-a-week Gables, Coopers, and Bogarts." And he was positively vituperative about the Method acting of the New York Group Theater and the Actors Studio—the "scratch-your-ass-and-belch school" he called them. Actually Bogie and Tracy, the down-to-earth-no-frills actors par excellence, had been performing naturally for years in just the way the pupils of these schools were now learning to do. Bogie had no time for people who took their talent for granted or for actors who denigrated or downgraded their own profession; he admired the ones who worked hard to improve what they had been given.

Being married to Bogie even for someone with the understanding and intelligence of Betty could have been no smooth ride. For a start he was as set in his ways as a streetcar and had an utter disregard for personal comfort. Betty was soon champing at the bit to break out of his small gloomy canyon house with its disturbing memories. For a long time her pleas for more elbowroom fell on deaf ears—"you were raised in one room in the Bronx, for chrissake, and there's nothing wrong with *you.*"

But finally he forked out a down payment on a beautiful tennis-courted and pooled house in the high-tax-bracket area of Holmby Hills. Bogie felt he was being conned into joining the Establishment, which he whole-heartedly despised, and *Santana* for a while rocked with resentment, but Betty smiled like a big cat and smoothed him down and became pregnant a second time, and he grew to be obsessively proud of his new acquisition. He never dressed the part of a Holmby Hills squire and forever slopped about the place attired in a grisly selection of antiquated moccasins, sweaters, windbreakers, and dungarees—usually with a battered yachting cap on his head; dogs and cats everywhere.

Betty was the perfect mate for Bogie, and as they were both completely honest with each other and utterly straightforward in their approach to life, the friction points were few and far between. Occasionally there would be an almighty explosion, but it never lasted long, and with the air cleaned, life went on more smoothly than ever. Betty gave as good as she got, but she also understood his need for male companionship, and she appreciated his longing for arguments, though she was never too happy when his extreme needling tactics were used to provoke them. She never was just a decoration in her husband's home, though Bogie loved her to be beautiful and admired her looks, her taste, and her talent. He was, above all, proud of the fact that he had a partner with whom he could share everything good or bad. He never looked at another woman.

John Huston was always a joy to Bogart, probably his favorite compan-ion and certainly his favorite director. Bogie could never measure up in-tellectually, but Huston stretched him to the utmost, and some classic discussions developed.

Director Huston got the most out of Bogie as an actor, and if they worked perfectly as a team and together turned out some classics—*The Maltese Falcon, The Treasure of Sierra Madre, The African Queen,* and *Beat the Devil* among others—the leg pulling was also mutually satisfac-tory. Huston was waiting to hear the news about his induction into Spe-cial Services with the Army during World War II. The word came by phone when he was in the middle of directing Bogie in a small building. His escape had been carefully rehearsed—whom he shot, whom he knifed, and through which window he would jump, et cetera.

Huston never said a word about the receipt of his call-up, he just tripled the number of Japanese around the building, boarded it up with the hero inside, and left for Europe. A hastily summoned takeover director found a note on the door: "I'm in the Army—Bogie will know how to get out."

I don't remember when I first noticed Bogie's cough, probably sharing sleeping quarters with him aboard *Santana.* I expect I thought it was just a smoker's cough because he used up a great number of cigarettes—

"coffin nails" he called them. But the cough slowly got worse, and Betty prevailed on him to see a doctor. The doctor made some tests and then called Bogie in to tell him the news—it was as bad as a man could hear.

There followed an eight-hour operation, and the slow slide began. "I've got it licked if I can put on some weight," he said. But as the weeks went by, he lost weight steadily. His eyes became enormous in his pitifully gaunt face, but his courage shone out of them.

At the funeral service on January 17, 1957, his friends were determined that his departure should be dignified and purged of all Hollywood gloss and bad taste, and we unceremoniously bundled outside into the sunshine several newsmen who attempted to enter the church with concealed cameras.

John Huston was always the closest to Bogie, so it was right and fitting that he should write and speak a few words of farewell at the service. No one could have done it better, and he has most graciously given me permission to remember some of them here.

"Bogie's hospitality went far beyond food and drink. He fed a guest's spirit as well as his body, plied him with goodwill until he became drunk in the heart as well as in the legs.

"This tradition of wonderful hospitality continued on to the last hour he was able to sit upright. Let me tell you at what effort it was extended through the last days. He would lie on his couch upstairs at five o'clock, when he would be shaved and groomed in gray flannels and scarlet smoking jacket. Then, as he was no longer able to walk, his emaciated body would be lifted into a wheelchair and pushed to a dumb-waiter on the second-floor landing. The top of the dumbwaiter had been removed to give him headroom. His nurses would help him in, and sitting on a little stool, he would be lowered down to the kitchen, where another transfer would be made, and again by wheelchair he'd be transported through the house into the library and his chair. And there he would be, sherry glass in one hand and cigarette in the other at five thirty when the guests would start to arrive. They were limited now to those who had known him best and longest, and they stayed, two and three at a time, for a half hour or so until about eight o'clock, which was the time for him to go back upstairs by the same route he had descended.

"No one who sat in his presence during the final weeks would ever forget. It was a unique display of sheer animal courage. After the first visit—it took that to get over the initial shock of his appearance—one quickened to the grandeur of it, expanded, and felt strangely elated, proud to be there, proud to be his friend, the friend of such a brave man. . . ."

CHAPTER 8

THE ACE

Europeans, particularly the British, have a loathsome habit of arriving on American doorsteps bearing "letters of introduction," and upon receipt of these missives, Americans have an endearing habit of asking no questions and opening wide the doors of their boundless hospitality.

I had such a letter to Fred Astaire, from a slight acquaintance in England—Lord Graves (the only titled bookmaker to be found taking bets on the rails)—and I decided to present it one evening in 1935 after a hot game of tennis. I wandered over to the Astaire house, but I forgot to put my shirt on.

I rang the bell.

After a while the door opened and a doll-like, ravishingly beautiful redhead stared at me cooly. She looked about fifteen.

"Is Mr. Astaire home?" I inquired.

"Who wants him?" she asked, raising eyebrows at my attire and sniffing slightly.

"Well, he won't know who I am, but I have a letter here."

"Who's it from?"

"Er, a bookmaker . . . Tommy Graves is the name."

"Your name?"

"No, the bookmaker's name."

The redhead looked at me with distaste, held out a slim hand for the letter, and started to close the door.

"I've met Mr. Astaire's sister," I added hastily, but as the words came out, I knew they were rash because under cross-examination I was bound to be exposed as having once been taken backstage for two minutes to her London dressing room when Adele Astaire was the toast of the town in *Stop Flirting.*

"Stay here," commanded the redhead icily.

From inside I heard her calling, "Fwed, Fwed, come quickly! . . . There's a perfectly *dwedful* man at the door without a shirt . . . he says he knows your sister and has a letter from a bookie called Gwaves."

From these unpromising beginnings, a friendship grew which perhaps meant more to me than any other in Hollywood.

Fred and Phyllis blended together with an almost uncanny smoothness, though the mixture had been potentially an unreliable one: the highly bred New York society girl with no interest whatever in the theater or theater people and the dedicated professional entertainer born in

Omaha, Nebraska, the son of a small-time brewer, an Austrian immigrant. Fred had been a vaudeville performer at the age of five, doing a touring act with his sister. They had worked hard, and their talents had not gone unappreciated for long. Soon Fred and Adele had taken both Broadway and London by storm, and when Fred met Phyllis at a Long Island luncheon given by Mrs. Vanderbilt, the Astaires' musical *The Bandwagon* was the hottest ticket on Broadway.

Fred immediately fell in love with the slim, steady-eyed girl who could not pronounce her *r*'s, but it took him two agonizing years to persuade her that marriage to an actor would not necessarily mean entering a den of iniquity.

RKO Studios offered Fred a contract, his first picture to be *Flying Down to Rio,* and he decided to take a flyer in the movies.

Would Phyllis give up her Long Island summers and winters in North Carolina and take a flyer, too?

"Yes, I will," said Phyllis to Fred's unbounded joy, and after a one-day honeymoon, the newlyweds flew to Hollywood.

Before Fred started work on *Flying Down to Rio,* in typical Hollywood style, his studio bosses decided first to lay off the bet they had made by lending him out at an exorbitant fee elsewhere, thereby securing his services free for themselves. Fred found himself reporting to MGM and ordered to do a couple of dances with Joan Crawford in *Dancing Lady.*

In Fred's own words, "I didn't have much to do so I just did as I was told, but when I saw myself on the screen . . . gosh! I looked like a *knife.*"

Fred was just about to start filming *Flying Down to Rio* when that "perfectly dwedful man without a shirt" came banging on his door. He had actually started the rehearsals of his one number with the star, Dolores Del Rio, but he had already spotted that his best opportunity in the picture would be in the "Carioca," a subsidiary dance number which he considered the best thing Vincent Youmans had ever written.

A full-time worrier, Fred was very concerned about who would be his partner for this big opportunity. When he heard the name, he was overjoyed. Ginger Roger was an old friend and an excellent dancer whom Fred, a year before, had been called in to help when she was having choreographic troubles in her own Broadway show.

As partners they caught fire in the "Carioca," and the rest is movie history, but Fred always swore that he "never realized we were starting something."

As their smash hits piled up—*Gay Divorcee, Roberta, Top Hat, Swing*

Time, Shall We Dance, and many, many others—Fred and Ginger together became the top box-office attraction in the world, but Fred remained mystified by his success. "I'm just a hoofer," he said. Phyllis stayed outwardly aloof but inwardly glorying in his success.

"You go ahead, Fwed, and make the money . . . I'll look after it for you." She did too, quite brilliantly, spurning the local business managers with their get-rich-quick schemes of golf courses in Mexico, oil drilling in Mozambique and Black Angus herds on windswept Colorado escarpments. She talked quietly to friends in New York, made minute entries in ledgers the size of Ping-Pong tables, and enabled the family to live in comfort for the rest of their days.

Self-effacing Phyllis only infrequently visited the studio to watch Fred working, and there was a widely believed rumor that she forbade him to kiss Ginger. This was, of course, complete fabrication. Ginger and Fred had a mutual distaste for slowing things up with what Fred described as "long, mushy love scenes," but the rumors provoked a counterattack, and in *The Barkleys of Broadway,* they took a deep breath and were glued together in the longest and most unrelenting kiss so far recorded on film.

Fred invited me to RKO Studios to watch the filming of his "Cheek to Cheek" number in *Top Hat,* and Phyllis came with me. Fred spent a minimum of two months meticulously preparing his dance routines for each picture; then, on shooting days, he would run the pertinent number through for the camera, lighting, and sound experts, put on his costume, turn up the playback of the music, and usually have it "in the can" at the first take—the supreme professional. People begged for a chance to be present on those historic shooting days.

Phyllis settled herself down unobtrusively to watch Ginger and Fred do their long run-through on the vast sound stage. Ginger rehearsed in slacks, and when she appeared for the first take, she looked ravishing in a dress composed almost entirely of red feathers.

"She looks like a wooster," Phyllis giggled.

It transpired that the dress was only just ready in time owing to some sartorial hitch in the wardrobe department. The playback blared forth, and the dance started. Slowly, one at a time at first, the feathers parted company with the parent garment. Then, as Fred whirled Ginger faster and faster about the gleaming set, more and more flew off. It became reminiscent of a pillow fight at school, but they pressed bravely on with the number, and by the end Ginger looked ready for the spit.

Altercations broke out between the director, the cameraman and the wardrobe mistress. Phyllis pulled my sleeve.

"Let's get out of here," she said, "Fwed will be so embawassed."

Summit Drive appealed to the Astaires, not because of its glittering inhabitants, but because of Phyllis' bird-dog nose for good business. They occupied two houses on that illustrious street in fairly quick succession. Phyllis invested in some choice acreage just below Pickfair, on the Colman ridge. She divided this land in two and on one half built a nice, comfortable, easy-to-run family house complete with swimming pool and tennis court.

Fred remonstrated about the court. "I don't like tennis; everybody beats me," he complained.

"David and I will play on it," said Phyllis smugly, "and anyway, this house is not for us . . . it's for sale."

She then put the house on the market, sold it at a succulent profit to William Wyler, the director of *Wuthering Heights, The Best Years of Our Lives, Ben Hur,* and many other movie milestones, and built a second and bigger one on the other half of the land.

Peter Potter, the child of a brief former marriage of Phyllis,' was a three-year-old when Fred and Phyllis married. He was joined, very early on, by two enchanting Astaire children, Fred, Jr., and Ava, and it was impossible to find a more devoted family. Fred and Phyllis had everything in common, love of their three children, a longing for a peaceful life, a loathing of Hollywood parties and "chichi," and a fascination with horses and horseracing. This last resulted in the purchase of a ranch at Chatsworth in the San Fernando Valley and the accumulation, by judicious buying and breeding, of a very handy string of racehorses.

One, Triplicate, bought as a three-year-old for $6,000, a beautiful animal with a coat of beaten bronze, went on to earn well over $250,000 in prize money, capturing, en route, the Hollywood Gold Cup and the San Juan Capistrano Stakes. Other horses they owned did well too, including one oddly named The Fag.

The ranch became the center of their lives. It was always spick-and-span, as I can witness, having been frequently bullied into painting and repainting what seemed like miles of white paddock fencing. Fred, one of the few people in the world about whom it could be claimed that he would never hurt a fly, in point of fact loathed the insects because they annoyed his beloved horses. He invested in electric "fly crematoriums" for stables; any flies landing on their seductive surfaces were instantly incinerated.

Fred loved gadgets. He began losing his hair early, and although philosophical about it, referring to "my high intellectual forehead," he fought a permanent battle to try to maintain the status quo: hence the purchase of an electric hair restorer, a strange, throbbing rubber cap containing elaborate coils and impulses. He must have misread the directions and assembled it incorrectly because on opening night it went into reverse and yanked out a large proportion of what he had left.

Fred dreaded "social" dancing, and Ava swore that the most embarrassing night of her life was at a debutantes' ball. There was a father-daughter dance, and according to his daughter, Fred, the focal point of all eyes, "tripped all over me." Above all, he dreaded lugging around a dance floor some eager matron or starry-eyed teenager who would breathe, "Gee, I just can't believe I'm dancing with the *great* Fred Astaire!" But an inhibited and self-conscious social dancer, he would occasionally "take off" in private. Coming home one night in 1950 and hearing loud canned music booming out of my house, I found Fred leaping from staircase to bookcase, to sofa, to floor, using my golf clubs as swords for a sword dance and Hjördis for a partner and, all the time, beating an incredible tattoo with his winged feet.

Since Fred was established as a dedicated worrier, it was inevitable, after a string of ten consecutive box-office smashes, that he would become convinced that he was due for a slump. The interest of audiences toward all musicals had indeed started, slowly, to erode all over the world, and as his last two pictures with Ginger had been merely "great successes" instead of "sensational hits," he talked so persuasively to his costar that she too decided that they might indeed have done enough together and agreed to a "trial separation."

Ginger chose to do a straight comedy, *Bachelor Mother,* with a new, young leading man—David Niven—and Fred took a whole year off to enjoy himself.

Ginger bloomed in her success as a straight actress, but poor Phyllis, instead of spending twelve months of hard-earned relaxation with her husband, found herself cooped up with a hand-wringing wreck who was convinced that he was permanently unemployed, could no longer hit a golf ball, spot a winner, or get a job. But the scene changed unexpectedly. Musicals became the perfect antidote to the grimness of the latest intercontinental lunacy—World War II. Suddenly they were back with a rush, and Fred, with a variety of sparkling partners (of whom Rita Hayworth was his favorite), found himself back on top of the tree.

With the war over, Fred was immediately consumed with renewed doubts about continuing dancing and even went so far as to officially announce his retirement. Photographs were flashed to a horrified public of

Fred performing his "last dance," but "Somebody Up There" had no intention of letting Fred off the hook that easily and allowing him to spend the rest of his life with racehorses and mashie niblicks, so he sneakily arranged for poor Gene Kelly in the middle of rehearsals for *Easter Parade* to break a leg.

An SOS went out to Fred, and much to everyone's delight, including Gene's, Fred Astaire's "retirement" ended overnight.

Apart from his soaring talent, this kind, generous, and gentle man had three children who adored him and whose adoration he had earned by being unfailingly understanding and helpful during their growing-up problems, their early careers and marriage. He had a home where he felt safe and at peace; he had his racehorses and had earned and kept money enough to minimize all the everyday problems. Above all, he had Phyllis, the vibrant, vital little auburn beauty he worshiped with all his heart. Theirs was the prototype of a gloriously happy marriage. But Fred, the worrier, deep down felt that his luck was too great, and that it was all too perfect, that something was *bound* to ruin it all, and, one day at Belmont Park Ráces, Phyllis, who had never known a day's illness, asked to be taken home. "I feel dizzy," she said.

The next day she felt fine, and Fred thought no more about it till a few weeks later, this time at Santa Anita Races, she said in a quiet voice, "I feel faint—please take me home." Fred went cold, and at his insistence Phyllis visited a doctor who ordered a series of X-rays, the result of which was an emergency operation.

On a hot afternoon I sat with Fred in a small waiting room at St. John's Hospital, Santa Monica, during her five hours of surgery. Finally, relieved doctors came in and told him the good news. "Looks like we've got it all," they beamed, but their optimism was short-lived. Complications set in, and at 4 A.M. back she went into the operating room, and there was little hope of survival. Fred was numb, but friends can do nothing to help on these occasions—all they can do is stick around in case they are needed and try somehow to share the awesome helplessness.

As the cool, flower-scented California dawn broke, Fred was told that a miracle had happened. Phyllis had come through once more. Frail, waif-like Phyllis was made of stainless steel. She endured weeks of X-ray treatments, put on weight, and even joked about her past ordeal.

"The only time I thought I was in trouble was just before I went in for the second time . . . a lot of nuns came into my woom, knelt down, and started pwaying."

Two months of euphoric remission ended abruptly with further emergency surgery, and Fred's own words will postscript his lost happiness: "She lapsed into a coma for several weeks. I *knew* she would snap out of it. She didn't. She looked like a beautiful child. She never lost her sweet facial expression. Phyllis . . . slipped away from us."

CHAPTER 9

LONG SHOTS AND CLOSE-UPS

CARY

It is very easy to write about Cary Grant's pedigree as an actor, to enthuse over the way he comported himself as a great star, and to be amazed at the extraordinary composure he displayed on the screen—appearing utterly relaxed and therefore, like a magnet, drawing the eye of the beholder—but it is another thing altogether to try to describe Cary, the private individual, because he was a will-o'-the-wisp.

Enthusiasm was a most important ingredient in Cary's makeup, and it shone out of that side of his character which he presented to his friends; the other side was as mysterious as the dark side of the moon. Cary's enthusiasm made him search for perfection in all things, particularly in the three that meant most to him: filmmaking; physical fitness; and women.

He found it without too much difficulty in the first two categories, becoming a perfectionist in his work and a living monument to bodily health, but in the third group he struck a few snags. He passed rapidly through his marriages to Virginia Cherrill, Barbara Hutton, and Betsy Drake and filled in the lonely gaps between them by falling in and out of love with most of his leading ladies, which, as his output of films was prodigious, underlined the excellence of his physical condition.

"The trick," he said, "is to be relaxed. If you can attain true relaxation, you can make love forever." This was heady advice, but it seemed odd coming from the mouth of one who freely admitted that from the age of twelve when he had run away from school to join an acrobatic troupe, he had been searching for peace within himself. When I say Cary attacked his amours with enthusiasm, I don't mean to conjure up a picture of him in an executioner's outfit, advancing purposefully with a rawhide whip; he was gentle and thoughtful, and they all loved him dearly. But he went headfirst into the affrays, throwing caution to the winds and quite convinced, in his boundless enthusiasm, that each romance was the one for which he had been put into the world.

He showed great resilience when things didn't work out, his recipe being "to stay within the pattern" and to try again with another lady of much the same physical appearance as the last. When he met the earthy Sophia Loren during the shooting of her first Hollywood picture, Cary took unto himself the role of "patron" and taught her carefully how to pick the most rewarding path through the Hollywood jungle. He often proclaimed that while doing this, he had fallen in love with her, but if so, he got over it with typical alacrity when Sophia, not the least ambitious of actresses, suddenly announced that she was marrying her portly producer, Carlo Ponti. Upon receipt of this news Cary allowed no grass to grow under his feet. He "followed the pattern" and was off like a flash in a gypsy caravan with a younger and more voluptuous edition of Sophia—a bouncing lady called Luba, a Yugoslav basketball player.

The first day that Cary, the perfectionist, walked into my house, he went immediately into high gear. He pursed his lips; made clucking noises, and set about straightening the pictures. Through the years to come he made generous efforts to straighten out my private life by warning me of the quirks and peculiarities of various ladies, by giving me complicated advice on how to play a part in a film I was making with him, by telling me which stocks to buy when I could not afford a phone call to a broker, and by promising that he could cure my liking for scotch by hypnotizing me. These offers of help were spontaneous and genuine, and if they did not noticeably improve my shortcomings, they did at least help me perceive that if Cary spent a great deal of his time worrying about himself, he spent much more worrying about others.

His was a restless soul. He changed houses the way most of us changed agents—without a backward glance—and long before computers went into general release, Cary had one in his own brain. A brilliant businessman himself, he was fascinated by the very rich and the ultrasuccessful and was in his element in the company of Howard Hughes, Onassis, Kirkorian, Hearst, and assorted tycoons.

His perfectionist urge with regard to his own body was nothing short of mystical. He invariably looked, moved, and behaved like a man fifteen or twenty years his junior. "I just *think* myself thin—and it happens," he was fond of saying, but he conveniently forgot his frugal eating, his daily workouts, and his appointments with the masseur.

Early one morning at his Palm Springs hideaway (he was passing through his Desert Period at the time), I heard loud commands followed by hideous grunts and splashing. Cary was taking lessons in how to swim the crawl. "Why lessons?" I asked sleepily from my bedroom window.

"You swim the crawl beautifully—I've seen you do it for years."

"I want to do it *perfectly*," he gurgled, and plowed on.

During the same period Cary, who had seldom thrown a leg over a horse, invested in a white stallion and a beautifully cut riding outfit of black Levi's, discreetly decorated with small silver stars, and within an incredibly short space of time he was a Valkyrie, galloping about the dunes with great panache and perfect control.

Anyone as silhouette-conscious as Cary was bound, sooner or later, to go through a health food period, and some of us suffered stoically through his Days of the Carrot. A vast clanking machine was installed in his kitchen, shaped like the mouth of a great white shark.

"Today we'll have nothing but carrot juice," Cary announced, and emptied a couple of sacks of roots into its gaping maw. Fearful throbbings and crunchings followed us into the garden, where we were given a pre-luncheon cocktail of buttermilk, wheat germ, and molasses. When the sinister sounds died down, we reentered the house to find that the machine had gone berserk and had redecorated the kitchen from top to bottom; walls, windows, ceiling, and linoleum flooring were covered with a fibrous yellow paste.

Cary's exercises in hypnotism were less messy, and he certainly cured himself of smoking by saying over and over for weeks, "Your fingers are yellow, your breath smells, and you only smoke because you are insecure." He also claimed that he had cured a nasty slash on his back collected in a film duel by applying oxygen to the affected area and commanding his lungs to dissolve the useless tissues. This so impressed us that before long we were lying like stranded tuna on his drawingroom carpet, waiting for him to bring us around.

Later Cary, to whom the unknown was an irresistible challenge, promptly registered himself with a Dr. Mortimer Hartman whose series of treatments included doses of LSD. He spent many weeks contentedly munching LSD, listening to music, and baring his soul. Apparently, it was a most salutary experience, sometimes joyful, sometimes shattering, but he persevered until he could announce to his spellbound friends, who were half envious and half horrified by what he had willingly subjected himself to, that he was a totally new man, cleansed and purged of all inhibitions, with a subconscious which could no longer cause problems.

"All actors long to be loved," he said. "That's why we become actors . . . but I don't give a damn anymore. . . . I'm self sufficient *at last!*"

It seemed to the rest of us a most hazardous trip for Cary to have taken to find out what we could have told him anyway: that he had always been self-sufficient, that he had always been loved, and that he would continue to give a damn about himself—and particularly about others.

GEORGE

If Cary Grant was an optimist then George Sanders was the opposite, and he genuinely harbored all the cynicism he so joyfully displayed.

Russian-born George, a giant grizzly of a man, had a face, even in his twenties, which looked as though he had rented it on a long lease and had lived in it so long he didn't want to move out. He was a highly under-valued actor probably because he didn't give a damn whether or not his efforts were appreciated. "I don't ask questions," he said. "I just take their money and use it for things that *really* interest me."

As early as 1937, when we were working on a John Ford picture togeth-er, he said, "I will have had enough of this earth by the time I am sixty-five After that I shall be having my bottom wiped by nurses and being pushed around in a wheelchair. I won't be able to enjoy a woman any-more, so I shall commit suicide."

I don't remember George's ever taking any exercise. He would show up immaculately dressed and watch the rest of us playing tennis or would sit comfortably near the eighteenth green till we finished playing golf and would throw up his hands in horror at any suggestion that he might like to take a walk along the beach.

His reaction to war service was one of instant repulsion, and he never modified it. "The stupidest thing young men can do is to throw away their youth, as Thomas Carlyle said, 'With clenched teeth and hell fire eyes hacking one another's flesh.' They'll never get me to do it." And they nev-er did. "I shall keep ahead of the sheriff," he announced. "Luckily I hold three passports—Russian, American, and British. I shall play one off against the other till they either give up or order me to do something. Then I shall immediately become a Quaker, and if they tell me to drive an ambulance, I shall crash so many learning how to drive that they'll send me home."

George did, however, try to make a tongue-in-cheek contribution to World War II. In 1943 he forwarded to Washington a detailed suggestion for the organization and administration of an infantry battalion equipped with roller skates. He enclosed a graph of gradients and the estimated at-tack speeds of troops along main roads. To me, in England, around the same time, he sent an envelope "To be forwarded instantly to Winston Churchill." It contained the specification of an attachment to be clamped to the nose cone of RAF bombs. Earthbound, he claimed, they would sound the German all-clear and the ensuing disaster among those issuing from their shelters would add "a gratifying bonus in casualties."

George suffered bouts of black oppression which his friends dismissed as "another of his Russian moods," but when they were on him, he was inconsolable. He was a loner and would often disappear for days on end into his beautifully equipped workshop; several strange but very clever inventions awaited patents as a result.

Women were fascinated by George, and before Zsa Zsa Gabor decided to become a caricature of her real self, the two of them made a fascinating couple. She enjoyed and encouraged his peculiar outlook on life and his sometimes outrageous utterances; he was fascinated by her very great beauty and her vivacity. No mean hand with an acid quip herself, Zsa Zsa once told me that she and Conrad Hilton, her millionaire ex-husband, "only had one thing in common . . . *his* money."

When Zsa Zsa "left" George, she somehow contrived to stay on in their Bel Air home facing the fifteenth fairway of the Country Club and took in as a houseguest "the Great Parisian lover" himself—Porfirio Rubirosa. If this infuriated George, he gave little sign of it, but it certainly awakened him to the very grave financial dangers of the California divorce laws.

"This is no time to behave like a gentleman," said George. "I am a cad and shall react like one."

On a misty evening in late December with the surrounding hills twinkling with half a hundred illuminated Christmas trees, George left his car near the fifteenth green and set off up the fairway. He was accompanied by his lawyer and a man with a big black camera. The lawyer and the photographer carried a ladder. George carried a brick.

The plan was simple. The french windows of the master bedroom, in which George was convinced action sooner or later would be taking place, overlooked the golf course. The french windows opened onto a veranda. Bedroom and veranda were on the second floor—hence the ladder. Once inside the room, George had every reason to believe he would find his wife in bed with Rubirosa—hence the camera. But, George reasoned, the french windows might well be locked—hence the brick.

The lawyer, with the caution of his ilk, was worried that police might intercept their cortege and ask embarrassing questions. "Certainly," he said, "there's not a reason on earth why a householder shouldn't enter his house by ladder if he so desires, but a brick could be construed as an offensive weapon. . . . I'm worried about that brick."

The operation, according to George, went without a hitch. When the signs were that the big double bed above was working overtime, the ladder was placed in position and the assault was mounted, but Zsa Zsa, an unwitting fifth columnist, had forgotten to lock the windows, and the brick became redundant.

Zsa Zsa and Rubirosa, their eyes wide with apprehension and dazzled by flashbulbs, were photographed clutching the sheets to their chins; then, like two plump partridges, they broke from the undergrowth and scuttled for the bathroom.

George and his henchmen waited, but the culprits, in a sudden burst of modesty, refused to come out again because there was only one towel. At last matters were arranged, dressing gowns were permitted, and the whole party descended the stairs in an embarrassed silence. Hesitant farewells were being made when Zsa Zsa, with a flash of great style said, "Oh, George darling, I almost forgot, I have a gift for you under the tree!"

To which George could not resist replying, "And I have a gift for *you*," and he handed her the brick.

The calmest time of George Sanders' life was during his marriage to Benita, Ronald Colman's beautiful widow.

The most understanding and generous-hearted of women, Benita encouraged George's inventions and eccentric ways and applauded his excellent screen performances. But George was not a man endowed with optimism and hope, and when Benita died, he became daily more cynical and disillusioned, and at the age of sixty-five, he did what he had always promised he would do: He took his own life.

ERNST LUBITSCH

Ernst Lubitsch was a pixie. There were three or four master directors in Hollywood in the thirties and forties, men for whom the biggest stars in the world tripped over each other in their anxiety to be invited to work. Ernst Lubitsch was the master's master. For a big established star to perform for Lubitsch was the sign that a career had reached its zenith, and for a beginner to be cast in a Lubtisch picture was notification that a new career was off to the most promising of starts.

One day in 1936 the "producers' producer" called me in to his office. I had lately been signed by him to a long-term beginners' contract, and I held him in such awe that if he had said, "I have cast you as a performing dog," I would have rushed out and taken barking and hoop-jumping lessons. The great Samuel Goldwyn looked at me unsmilingly out of his small, deepset eyes. "You are a very lucky young man," he said.

I nodded in agreement.

"But you don't know it," he added.

I nodded again.

"I have just loaned you to Ernst Lubitsch for *Bluebeard's Eighth Wife*. Report to Paramount Studios tomorrow. Keep your ears open and your mouth shut, and put yourself in Ernst's hands—they're the best in Hollywood."

Tottering on legs made rubbery by my unbelievable good fortune, I made my way to the office of Reeves Espy, the calm and considerate right hand of the volcanic Mr. Goldwyn.

"This is a real break for you," said Espy. "I've read the script—it's written by Billy Wilder and Charlie Brackett—it's marvelous, and your part is *great!*"

"What is it?" I asked breathlessly.

"Secretary to Mr. Brandon," said Espy.

"Who's Mr. Brandon?"

"Gary Cooper," said Espy, "and you're also in love with his girl."

"Who's his girl?"

"Claudette Colbert—and they both get to beat you up. . . . It's a very sympathetic role."

What a bonanza! An unknown beginner to be directed by Lubitsch, in a script by Wilder and Brackett, and to play with Paramount's two superstars, Gary Cooper and Claudette Colbert, and to be beaten up by both of them!

The next morning, shining like a new pin, I checked in at the Paramount lot, was handed the key to a dressing room and given a script.

"Read it right away, David," advised the casting director, "then about eleven go over to Ernst's office—he wants to meet you and talk to you about wardrobe et cetera."

By eleven o'clock I was in poor shape. The part was indeed beautifully written, but I was quite convinced that I could never play it.

Lubitsch was a very tiny man, with a heavy German accent, straight black hair slicked down, twinkling black eyes, and a cigar out of all proportion to the ensemble. When I walked into his office, he was in shirtsleeves with heavy suspenders supporting his pants. He rose from behind his desk and greeted me with both hands outstretched and a slice of blatantly overdone flattery.

"This is indeed a pleasure." He beamed. "We are so lucky to get you for this part! Now before we sit down," he said, "would you mind dropping your trousers?"

"I beg your pardon?" I said nervously.

Gales of laughter swept over the little man. "Don't worry." He chortled. "I have a very beautiful wife! But I have to see your legs, because your opening scene is on the beach with Claudette. If you have strong legs, there will be no problem, but if you have twigs like mine, we'll have to rework the scene so you can wear slacks."

I dropped my pants, and he pronounced himself satisfied. "Good"—he nodded—"like a Bavarian bullock."

Then he sat me down on a sofa and proceeded to act out all my scenes, giggling and hugging himself as he explained the visual business he was intending to incorporate into them, and the more he gesticulated and pranced about, the more convinced did I become that I did not have the equipment or the training to deliver to him that which he obviously thought was his for the asking.

Finally, sensing that I was holding something back, Lubitsch asked me what was the matter.

"I don't think I can do it, Mr. Lubitsch," I mumbled.

He looked at me, and his eyes shone with merriment. "Do I frighten you?" he asked.

"No, sir," I said, "but I'm terrified of Gary Cooper and Claudette Colbert. . . ."

He jumped up and hooted with laughter.

"Do you know something?" He chortled. "Claudette is frightened of Coop because of his natural acting, and Coop is frightened of Claudette because she's so expert and this is his first comedy, and both of them are scared out of their wits by the small-part players Edward Everett Horton, Franklin Pangborn and Herman Bing, because they are supposed to be scene stealers . . . but d'you know who is the most frightened of all? . . . Me!"

He put his arm around my waist (because he could not reach my shoulders) and led me to the door.

"Everyone will be nervous on the first day," he said, "even the electricians in case they set fire to the studio, but we're all going to be together for many weeks, and I promise you it'll be fun. Now run along to wardrobe and makeup, they have some fittings and tests set up for you. . . . Drop in to see me anytime. . . . We don't start for two weeks— you're a member of the family now!"

I couldn't wait to start.

When Ernst Lubitsch described us as his family, it was no understatement, and we all had complete respect for the father figure. I never once heard him raise his voice, and he loved to be given suggestions, listened patiently to them, and then patiently explained why they wouldn't work.

Billy Wilder, the future master director, was constantly on the set, and there was obviously a great rapport between him and Lubitsch: he may even then have set his sights on directing, because he was unfailingly understanding and appreciative with the actors, a nice change from many writers who winced painfully as their golden words fell from the performer's mouths.

Lubitsch took infinite pains with everyone, especially with me, the novice, and for several days before I started work, he ordered me to be on the set so that I could get to know everyone and feel at home.

"I don't know what I'm going to do about Gary." He chuckled. "He's just *too* relaxed!"

Cooper had ambled onto the set in a crumpled flannel suit.

"Just look at him!" said Lubitsch. "It's the first time he's played a comedy, and we had that business-tycoon suit made by Eddie Schmidt, but he still thinks he's a cowhand. Where've you been, Gary?" he asked conversationally.

"I just grabbed me a little shut-eye on that pile of straw back there on Stage Six," drawled the tall man from Montana.

Lubitsch sent for Slim, Cooper's gangling stand-in, and Cracker, his small devoted dresser from Georgia.

"Now you two!" He giggled. "Coop is playing a business tycoon on holiday in Cannes, France, his wardrobe is very elegant, and he has to be stopped going to sleep in it every time he finishes a scene, so get him out of that suit and into pajamas, then have it pressed *again!*"

Gary Cooper was no poseur—he was exactly what he seemed, a charming, slow-talking, gentle country boy who loved animals and open air and avoided problems—but he was also a phenomenal natural actor with spectacular good looks and a great sense of timing. I was fascinated by the way he "thought" on the screen, and during a lull when we were shooting a scene together, I asked him about this.

"You have such great concentration," I said. "How do you do it?"

Coop looked genuinely startled. "Concentration?" he said slowly. "Bullshit! I'm just tryin' to remember what the hell I have to say next!"

My first big scene was indeed on the beach with Claudette Colbert— outside the Carlton Hotel, Cannes. It was simulated by dumping a few truckloads of sand inside Stage 4, and gaudy umbrellas above bronzed extras completed the illusion. The scene was a long one, and the comedy content was delicate. Claudette and "Bullock Legs" were in swimsuits, and the sun arcs blazed down from on high. Claudette, the soul of enchanting fun and a most generous performer, did all she could to calm my twittering nerves, but she made things a little difficult for the cameraman because, convinced that it was her best side, she insisted that she be photographed only on the left side of her face. Many stars harbored the same beliefs and specified in their contracts which one could be presented to the camera.

Lubitsch perched himself atop a small stepladder at the side of the camera, the inevitable howitzer-type cigar in his mouth. He rehearsed us carefully and finally said, "Let's shoot it!" Very conscious of the fifty or so bronzed extras (all would-be stars), I was about as relaxed as a bulldozer, but Claudette patted my knee and whispered, "It's going to be great." We started the comedy scene, and I noticed that Lubitsch was crying.

"Cut!" he sobbed helplessly at the end. "That was *wonderful!* You made me laugh so much I nearly choked! . . . Now, just a couple of little suggestions. . . ."

We absorbed them eagerly, and he clambered back up his stepladder. "Action!" he commanded. Again we played the scene, and again Lubitsch wept.

"Wonderful! Wonderful! *How* you made me laugh! . . . Now just a couple of little suggestions. . . ."

We probably played the scene a dozen times, each time our efforts were saluted by paroxysms of mirth from the master director, and each time he managed to blurt out "a couple of little suggestions" before climbing back onto his perch. By the time we had performed the scene to his complete satisfaction we had, of course, like many before us, given performances of "pure Lubitsch," and as Claudette pointed out, "And why not? . . . He's better than any of us!"

JOHN HUSTON

All the directors had their little idiosyncrasies. Lubitsch had his cigar and his stepladder. John Ford sat beneath the camera chewing the corner of a grubby white handkerchief. Michael Curtiz strode about wearing breeches and riding boots and brandishing a fly whisk. William Wyler liked to make anything up to forty takes and then print the first. Otto Preminger seemed to enjoy working in an atmosphere of tension, and generated it by screaming loudly at people.

Of the master directors (Ford and Wyler were also on everybody's list) the most relaxed, with his poet's heart and misleading broken boxer's face, was John Huston. "Let's just kick it around, kids," he would say to his actors, and from their first natural and tentative playing and thereafter through many rehearsals, he would build up a scene piece by piece till he was satisfied; then he would invite the cameraman to watch a run-through. "That's it," Huston would say. "Now go ahead and light it." While that was being done, he would wash all problems from his mind by settling down with a box of panatelas and a good book.

I first met John in 1939 when he was a scriptwriter at the Samuel Gold-wyn Studios; his father, Walter, a monumental actor, was playing the name part in the film of *Dodsworth,* directed by William Wyler. I was playing a small part in the picture, and John was constantly on the set. In spite of his many great directorial successes there, John never fully settled for the Hollywood way of life and found his ultimate happiness with a home in Southern Ireland, leaping fearlessly over jagged stone walls as Master of the Galway Blazers Fox Hounds. He once made a tentative stab at living in Hollywood and moved into a house near Clark Gable's in the San Fernando Valley. It was a revolutionary structure consisting almost entirely of glass with some necessary beams and supports of redwood. John lived inside this bizzare cage with an extremely beautiful wife and a very ugly monkey. History does not relate where the monkey came from, but John persuaded delicious Evelyn Keyes to join him during a long din-ner at Romanoff's Restaurant. They flew that night to Las Vegas to get married after Mike Romanoff had first bustled off to his house and re-trieved a wedding ring which had fallen off somebody's finger into his swimming pool. Evelyn was a highly intelligent girl, and for a while great happiness reigned, interrupted admittedly by the gibberings and shrieks of the monkey.

Only those involved can ever know what tensions have pulled apart a marriage, and John maintained a gentlemanly silence when he and Eve-lyn finally called it quits. Evelyn, too, had nothing but the deepest affec-tion and respect for John, and they remained firm friends. Evelyn en-joyed relating the final scene before they went their separate ways:

EVELYN: John, darling, I'm sorry. One of us has to go. . . . It's the monkey or me.
JOHN: (after long pause) Honey . . . it's you!

During World War II John Huston headed a particularly gallant photo-graphic unit and became a familiar figure among front-line troops at Monte Cassino and other Italian battlefields, puffing away at his panatelas and calmly photographing the moments of maximum danger.

The war over, John returned to the United States and was there when I arrived aboard the *Queen Mary* with 15,000 joyful fighting men, mostly of the 101st Airborne Division. We were welcomed by several bands and a posse of beautiful Powers models, whose cover-girl smiles froze on their faces when the returning warriors released several hundred fully inflated condoms from the boat deck far above their heads. During drinks that evening at Jack and Charlie's, I reconstructed for John's benefit the spectacle of coveys of flying French letters eddying about the clifflike sides of the giant Cunarder, and he was moved to quote the observation of a Parisienne countess of the eighteenth century upon her first view of one of those well-intentioned envelopes: "A battlement against enjoyment, and a fishnet against infection."

The conversation having taken such a soldierly turn, I was not surprised to hear John say, "While we've been away, they've opened the greatest whorehouse right here in New York, better than anything in Rome or Paris—what d'you say we go take a look at it?"

I shook my head like a bishop finding a fly button in the collection. "No, thanks—I'm a happily married man these days."

"Oh, come on!" said Huston. "You don't have to *do* anything. . . . Just come and case the joint, then we'll take the madam out for dinner—she's a lot of laughs."

I was hungry, so after John had made a phone call, we set off. The house on Park Avenue had a most imposing façade. John pressed the bell, and a saucy-looking maid opened the door and took our coats. "Good evening, Mr. Huston." She smiled. "May I get you a drink while you're waiting?" Huston ordered a scotch, and I did the same. The maid served us the drinks in an attractively decorated drawing room, and John pointed casually to a Monet on the wall.

"Of course this is a clip joint on a big scale," he explained. "The madam has the greatest girls in New York, all shapes and colors, and anything goes, but boy, does she charge for it!"

"I'll bet," I said, "but even so—a Monet!"

"Well," said Huston, lighting up one of his smokes, "she has some old guy for herself who collects paintings, and she screws an occasional Impressionist out of the poor bastard—she had a dandy Braque right over her bed . . . it leaves marks on the wall as it swings!"

After a while the madam, very petite, beautifully dressed, and bejeweled, descended the stairs and walked into the room. John rose, kissed her hand, and introduced me.

"I'm so glad you could join us," she said in a charming voice. "John is an old friend, and he's told me so much about you."

"Well," I said, "I don't really want any action tonight, I just came to take a look at the place. . . . Where are the girls . . . all upstairs banging their brains out?"

The madam looked mystified, and Huston, like a canary-swallowing cat, smugly broke the news to me that she was in fact Nin Ryan, the most elegant society hostess in New York City.

John, the director, was famous for being easy and thoughtful with his actors; as a writer he was famous for being easy and thoughtful with his directors, and as an actor (he was an excellent performer when the spirit moved him) he was the soul of discretion in his relationships with one and all. A paragon of all virtues so it seemed, but when the smoke of his panatelas cleared away, it was invariably found that John had quietly achieved whatever he had been striving for, no matter which hat he had been wearing. He even ended up with Jack Warner of Warner Brothers eating out of his hand.

THE FIRE CAME BY

THE RIDDLE OF THE
GREAT SIBERIAN EXPLOSION

A condensation of the book by

JOHN BAXTER and

THOMAS ATKINS

The fire came by and destroyed the forest, the reindeer, and the store-houses. Afterward, when the Tungus went in search of the herd, they found only charred reindeer carcasses.

> Witness to the Siberian
> explosion of 1908

I was sitting on my porch facing north when suddenly, to the northwest, there appeared a great flash of light. There was so much heat that . . . my shirt was almost burned off my back. I saw a huge fireball that covered an enormous part of the sky . . . Afterward it became dark and at the same time I felt an explosion that threw me several feet from the porch. I lost consciousness. . . .

> Witness forty miles away from
> Siberian explosion

After the terrible flash—which, Father Kleinsorge later realized, remind-ed him of something he had read as a boy about a large meteor colliding with the earth—he had time (since he was 1,400 yards from the center) for one thought: A bomb has fallen directly on us. Then, for a few sec-onds or minutes, he went out of his mind.

> Survivor of Hiroshima
> explosion, 1945,
> from John Hersey's *Hiroshima*

TITLE PAGE: *Five miles from the mysterious Siberian blast's epicenter, large trees on a hillside have been scorched and flattened by the heat and shock wave of the explosion.* AMERICAN MUSEUM OF NATURAL HISTORY

CHAPTER 1

THE EXPLOSION

High above the Indian Ocean, a huge object hurtling from space pierces the earth's atmospheric shell. In the almost airless upper altitudes, there is no sound, barely any friction; unimpeded, it races toward the earth.

In a long sloping trajectory, it rockets northwards at supersonic velocity across the Asian mainland, high over the Himalayan peaks. Drawn lower by gravity, it hits the thicker strata of the globe's atmosphere. Intense frictional heat begins to build up.

It first flashes into the sight of a man over western China in the dawn of June 30, 1908. Caravans winding through the Gobi Desert halt and look in awe at a fireball blazing across the sky. It disappears over the border of Mongolia. Plunging into the denser air layers, it glows with the heat of 5,000 degrees Fahrenheit, brighter even than the thin morning sun.

In central Russia, a deafening roar terrifies the inhabitants of small towns and villages, the only settlements in this remote and deserted area. A powerful ballistic wave pushed before the descending object strikes the ground. Trees are leveled, nomad huts blown down, men and animals scattered like specks of dust.

At 7:17 A.M. the Central Siberian Plateau near the Stony Tunguska River, a sparsely populated, desolate region of peat bogs and pine forests, shudders under the impact of a cataclysmic explosion.

The detonation is of such violent force that the seismographic center at Irkutsk, 550 miles to the south, registers tremors of earthquake proportions. Vibrations travel 3,000 miles through the ground to other stations in Moscow and in the capital of the tsarist empire, St. Petersburg; and the earthquake observatory at Jena, Germany, 3,240 miles away, records strong seismic shocks. Even as far away as Washington and Java seismographs are activated by the immense blast.

Instantly, a gigantic "pillar of fire" flares up into the clear blue sky, ascending to such height that the blinding column is visible above the horizon to startled Siberians in towns several hundred miles away; then the air is wracked by a series of thunderous claps that can be heard for more than 500 miles. The noise is so great that some herdsmen closer to the blast are deafened; others are thrown into a state of dazed shock that renders them speechless.

Simultaneously with the brilliant fire in the sky, a searing thermal current sweeps across the hilly taiga, or northern woods, scorching the tall conifers and igniting fires that will continue to burn for days. Stunned citizens 40 miles away in the trading post of Vanavara shield their faces from the fierce heat draft. Seconds later, a shock wave generated by the blast rips through the small village, gouging up pieces of sod, collapsing ceilings, shattering windows, and flinging people into the air.

At a distance of 375 miles to the south-southwest, hurricanelike gusts rattle doors, windows, and lamps in Kansk, a station town on the newly completed Trans-Siberian Railway. Within minutes two additional waves of shock strike the town. People working nearby on rafts are hurled into the river, while farther south, horses stumble and fall to the ground.

Near Kansk, aboard the Trans-Siberian Express, passengers are frightened by loud bursts of noise and almost jolted out of their seats. The train is jarred and shakes wildly on its tracks. As the startled engineer sees the rails ahead vibrating, he quickly brings the train to a screeching halt.

As the dark masses of thick clouds rise to an altitude of more than 12 miles above the Tunguska region, the entire area is showered by an ominous "black rain," the result of sudden air condensation and the fountain of dirt particles and debris sucked up into the swirling vortex of the explosion. Intermittent rumblings of thunder, resembling heavy artillery, reverberate throughout central Russia.

Far across the continent to the west, in St. Petersburg, no one hears of the blast, nor will anybody hear of it for many years. The record of seismic shocks, when they are noticed, will at first be mistaken for earthquake tremors. In 1908 most Russians have their minds on other problems, for their country is gripped by social unrest and political tension that eventually will erupt in the Revolution.

In 1908, across the Pacific in the United States, where Theodore Roosevelt is serving the final year of his second term as President, few people pay attention to the upheavals occurring in the Tsar's distant country. No word of the Siberian explosion has yet reached the United States. Instead, Americans are watching the appearance of new machines that soon will revolutionize transportation, communication, and warfare throughout the world. Henry Ford has just released his Model T, the first mass-produced automobile. The United States War Department, after dropping his initial letter in the "crank" file, finally decides to give inventor Orville Wright a contract to build the first military airplane.

Around the world, scientists armed with the latest inventions of nineteenth-century technology are struggling to interpret the universe to the newly born twentieth century. Astronomers, observing the solar system and our galaxy through increasingly powerful telescopes, have gathered fresh and often puzzling information about the behavior of remote stars and other cosmic phenomena. In 1908 the cosmos is still regarded as basically stable and unchanging; its "edge" is thought to be the Milky Way, which has not yet been fully mapped.

Meteorological instruments, though still relatively primitive, are used to explore the intricate relationship between solar flares and the earth's magnetic fields, but without a solid understanding of nuclear physics such readings cannot be fully analyzed. At this time Robert Millikan is doing his ground-breaking work on X-rays; Albert Einstein will soon radically change scientific notions of space, time, and matter with his general relativity theory. The Nobel Prize in chemistry for 1908 is awarded to Ernest Rutherford for his pioneer studies of radioactivity; he will shortly formulate his atomic nucleus idea that is to become one of the fundamental concepts of modern physics.

The year 1908, in retrospect, seems to be a time of strange and inexplicable events, a period when people claim to see peculiar moving lights at night or captains report "magnetic clouds" descending on their ships. "Alien airships" are seen racing at fantastic speeds over the United States and Europe. That summer a "200-foot-long sea serpent" rises from the Gulf of Mexico off the Yucatan Peninsula and is described in great detail by passengers on a steamship. Scientists watching the sky in 1908 are prepared for new occurrences, yet poorly equipped to identify or interpret them—particularly one as unprecedented and complex as the event near the Stony Tunguska River.

Though news of the explosion has not appeared in the American or European press and scientists in the West as yet know nothing of the event, newspapers during the summer of 1908 are full of speculation about the unusual meteorological phenomena and magnetic disturbances that follow the devastating blast. A report from Berlin in the New York *Times* of July 3 attempts to explain the bizarre colors seen recently in the Northern Lights:

Remarkable lights were observed in the northern heavens on Tuesday and Wednesday nights, the bright diffused white and yellow illumination continuing through the night until it disappears at dawn. Director Archenbold of the Treptow Observatory says that because of the phenomenon's particular brilliancy he thinks it may be connected with important changes in the sun's surface, causing electrical discharges. Director Archenbold, however, mentions a somewhat similar phenomenon in 1883, which was directly traceable to an outbreak of the Krakatoa volcano in the Strait of Sundy [Sunda]. Reports from Copenhagen and Königsberg told of the same great lights being visible in these cities, and it is presumed that they were visible throughout Northern Europe.

But the 1883 eruption in the East Indies is similar only in its vast size and strength; the 1908 Siberian explosion is not volcanic, and the time scale and physical characteristics of the phenomena resulting from the event are utterly different—and ultimately far more frightening and mysterious—than those that followed Krakatoa.

Unusual atmospheric charges prompt speculation in England the evening after the explosion. "There was a slight, but plainly marked, disturbance of the magnets on Tuesday night," states an editorial in the *Times* of London; but this magnetic interference is at first mistakenly associated with "disturbances in the sun's prominences" rather than with the Siberian catastrophe, which has not been reported in British newspapers at the time.

Within five hours of the blast, turbulent air waves travel west beyond the North Sea, causing strong oscillations at meteorological stations in England. During a span of twenty minutes, sudden fluctuations in atmospheric pressure are detected by recently invented self-recording barographs at six stations between Cambridge, 50 miles north of London, and Petersfield, 55 miles south. Baffled weather researchers assume that a large atmospheric disturbance has occurred somewhere in the world; but not until two decades later, after the first news of the devastation in the Tunguska region finally reaches the English press, do they discover that their 1908 barographic records correspond with the astonishing Russian explosion of that same year and that its air waves circled the globe twice.

But perhaps even more striking than the unexplained effects on the earth's magnetic fields and the powerful air waves associated with the blast is the appearance at high altitudes of massive luminous "silvery clouds" blanketing Siberia and northern Europe. The light is so intense during the next few nights that in some places it is possible to take photographs at midnight and ships can be seen clearly for miles out at sea. A Russian scientist describes the glowing clouds as lit up by "some kind of yellowish-green light that sometimes changed to a rosy hue."

Extraordinary dust clouds and eerie nocturnal displays, moreover, are observed for weeks across the Continent as far south as Spain. According to the London *Times* of July 4, 1908, "The remarkable ruddy glows which have been seen on many nights lately have attracted much attention, and have been seen over an area extending as far as Berlin." The cause is assigned to "some condition of the atmosphere," such as occurred after Krakatoa, although, "no volcanic outburst of abnormal violence has been reported lately."

In the London suburbs citizens are drawn into the streets to view the frightening cosmic phenomenon. A woman in Huntingdon, north of London, alarmed by the vivid night lights, writes to the London *Times* that shortly after midnight on July 1 the sky was so bright that "it was possible to read large print indoors, and the hands of the clock in my room were quite distinct. An hour later, at about 1:30 A.M., the room was quite light as if it had been day; the light in the sky was then more dispersed and was a fainter yellow." She concludes, "I have never at any time seen anything the least like this in England, and it would be interesting if anyone would explain the cause of so unusual a sight."

But no satisfactory explanation is offered to the woman's question. The silence about the nature of the incredible nightly spectacles seen over Europe and the riddle of the great Siberian explosion is not broken for more than a decade.

CHAPTER 2

AN ENORMOUS SILENCE

Human history is marked indelibly with the destruction caused by great explosions.

In about 1500 B.C. most of the island of Thera in the Aegean, 70 miles north of Crete, disappeared in a blast which reduced a fertile kingdom to little more than a splintered shell. Today, one can see the crescent rim of the dead volcano and two blackened, still-active islets in the center of a

16-mile-wide lagoon where once stood an important center of Aegean culture. Sheer cliffs plunging a thousand feet into the dark water, their sides striped with the brilliant colors of blistered rock, attest to the force of the blast. Tidal waves from the explosion swept across 70 miles of sea to Crete, rolling over the palaces and temples, crushing the fragile frescoes and pillared colonnades of a society among the most enlightened in the world.

No similar catastrophe affected history until A.D. 62, when an earthquake caused by the eruption of Vesuvius toppled much of the towns of Pompeii and Herculaneum near Naples. Many of the houses had not been re-built seventeen years later when, on August 24, A.D. 79, Vesuvius erupted once more; in two days, both towns were inundated with hot ash, small stones, and lava as deep in some places as 23 feet. In Herculaneum, water mixed with this debris to create an impermeable plasterlike covering which has been gradually cleared by archaeologists in the last three centuries to reveal, frozen in time, the life of a busy Roman town.

The Vesuvius blast was dwarfed by what experts generally agreed to be the greatest natural explosion of modern times, the destruction of the volcanic island of Krakatoa between Java and Sumatra. Krakatoa, which had erupted intermittently for centuries, shuddered into life again in May of 1883. More eruptions were felt during June and August. On the early afternoon of August 26, the volcano began to explode, eventually discharging a 17-mile-high cloud of dark ash; and at 10 A.M. on the following morning the whole island was shaken by a cataclysmic blast. Ash fountained 50 miles into the sky. Air waves from the explosion registered all over the world, and the sound was heard 2,200 miles away in Australia. Five cubic miles of rock disappeared, some falling back as stones and ash on the surrounding islands and clogging the waters so badly that nearby ships were unable to move through the debris.

Tidal waves more than a hundred feet high smashed into the Java and Sumatra coasts, killing 36,000 people; the same waves registered on the coasts of South America and Hawaii. For several days, darkness masked the area around the volcano. Thrown into the higher atmosphere by the enormous force of the blast, tons of dust were carried around the world a number of times by the high-velocity winds—55 to 110 miles per hour—of the stratosphere between 12 and 25 miles above the earth. The dust so saturated the upper air that sunsets all over the world carried a noticeable bloody tinge for more than a year, and interference with solar radiation lowered the world temperature 0.5 degrees Fahrenheit for many years.

For all their enormous size, destructive capability, and long-term effects, none of these explosions could surpass the sheer force of the Tunguska blast in 1908. Its size, as registered on seismographs and barographs in Europe, deserves comparison only with the greater man-made explosions of the atomic age; even the Hiroshima blast and the nuclear tests of the early 1950s are dwarfed by it. Authorities in the U.S.S.R., Britain, and the U.S.A. agree that the estimated energy output of the Siberian blast—10^{23} ergs—would be comparable only with the explosion of the heaviest hydrogen bombs.

Today, the failure at the time to investigate the Tunguska explosion seems at first incredible; a cataclysm greater than any the world had ever known went without serious inquiry or comment for thirteen years and even then was discovered only by the most remarkable series of coincidental events and the stubborn efforts of one man. But, for numerous reasons, the vast silence of 1908 to 1921 is understandable.

Most catastrophes in human history have gone, by modern standards of communication, largely unrecorded; and the fact that the Tunguska explosion went unexplored for such a long period is not unusual. Chiefly because they were volcanic, the explosions of Thera, Vesuvius, and Krakatoa happen to be exceptionally well documented.

Volcanoes attract attention. In general, they herald their major eruptions with a fanfare of minor tremors, emissions of smoke, and showers of ash and leave behind, as in the case of all three major explosions, a wealth of geological evidence which, even on the island of Thera, can still be read thousands of years later. In addition, because volcanic ash provides the basis for rich and fertile soil, most volcanoes are surrounded by thriving communities and thus a generous corps of observers.

Meteorite explosions, among which the Tunguska blast was initially categorized, have proved less easy to document. Without giving any of the warning signs shown by a volcano, meteorites come rushing in at cosmic velocity—as fast as 25 miles per second—and, should they happen to reach the earth, it is often in a remote area; examples of meteorites injuring people or property in populated areas are extremely rare. Evidence of their trajectory and impact is often confused or inaccurate; and if they fell in the distant past, records may be dim or totally non-existent. The collisions which created the huge craters in Arizona and Quebec occurred from ten to fifty thousand years ago, and the actual impact holes remain as the primary evidence.

In the case of the Tunguska blast, its discovery and documentation were complicated by the nature of the terrain where the event occurred.

The very name "Siberia" derives from a Tartar word meaning "sleeping land." The vast central region lying east of the Yenisei River was, and still is in many ways, one of the most remote places on the face of the earth. Had the area been picked out as the location for such an event, it could not have been more secret.

For most Russians at the turn of the century Siberia remained an area as foreign and distant as the moon. Besides the local farmers and fishermen, many of its inhabitants were political prisoners or their descendants; generations of dissidents had been shipped to centers like Irkutsk and Krasnoyarsk, forced to slave in the mines and forests, then had been abandoned there with no choice but to settle and farm.

Though it covers a vast area, larger than Alaska, central Siberia has a relatively sparse population of only a few hundred thousand. Its migrating tribesmen, the Tungus, traversed only the areas best for trapping, so huge sections of the taiga were still unexplored. Distances here were given in terms of "summer" or "winter," those for winter being much shorter, since the snow enabled sleds to cross areas impassable during the brief thaw. Roads in the European sense were unknown; the trappers followed tracks worn by generations of foxes and hares and seldom imitated the foolish foreigners who, searching for Siberia's enormous gold and mineral wealth, struck out into the wilderness. In such places, distance and time had little relevance, as investigators found when they tried to piece together eyewitness reports of the 1908 event—another factor contributing to the silence that surrounded the explosion.

Within central Siberia, the region of the Podkamennaya Tunguska, or Stony Tunguska, River is even more impenetrable. One of the many streams that drain north into the huge Yenisei, which in turn feeds the Arctic Ocean, the Stony Tunguska rises in a mountainous wilderness of rolling taiga spotted with huge swamps. The taiga in this region is no ordinary woodland but, as Yuri Semyonov points out in his study of Siberia, a "vast and sinister" primeval forest in which "the weak and imprudent often perish" in its trackless depths and pathless bogs where "everything below is decayed and rotten, and everything above withered, where only the corpses of the huge trunks slowly moulder away in the brackish water."

Its chief inhabitants, the nomadic Tungus, survived mainly on their reindeer herds and on hunting bear, fox, and sable for their pelts. The few trading posts, situated along the riverbanks, were tiny and primitive. The Tunguska blast occurred during the height of the short summer, when the soil of the taiga melts to a swampy slush and the air is infested with ferocious Siberian mosquitos.

In addition to its remoteness and inhospitable climate, central Siberia had an atmosphere of ancient mystery and an accumulation of inexplicable phenomena. For centuries, the country around the Stony Tunguska had been gathering its share of strange stories and legends: weird species of fish existing in the depths of Lake Baikal, giant subterranean rats living beneath the ground, monstrous mammals encased in icy tombs. The explosion of 1908, just one more in a series of curiosities, must have seemed to some natives, and later to people in Moscow and St. Petersburg, hardly worth the trouble of comment.

To the southeast of the Tunguska region lies Lake Baikal, one of the most unusual bodies of water in the world. Lying across a fault in the earth's crust, the Lake Baikal area has been riven by earthquakes for millennia; the large number of shocks in the late nineteenth century obviously influenced scientists at first to class the 1908 explosion as seismic. Baikal is the largest body of fresh water in the world, a mile deep in some places, and harboring some of the oddest creatures known to science; of the 1,800 plants and animals in its waters, a thousand exist nowhere else on earth. Seals and fish normally found only in salt water live comfortably there, hundreds of miles from the nearest ocean; and Baikal is the only home of fish like the *golomyanka,* which lives at depths that can crush a steel tube.

Subterranean horrors loomed large in the mythology of the Tungus, who explained the frequent earth tremors in their region as signs of herds of giant rats that burrowed constantly under the earth, making tunnels in which their tramping feet set up the rumblings of earthquakes. Travelers to the Tungus region were inclined to explain away the legend of the giant earthquake rats as sheer fantasy until an 1846 surveying expedition discovered the remains of mammoths in an area on the Lena River. The early discovery of these bodies, which rotted too quickly to be saved, led to a rash of similar excavations and to an explanation of the old legend of the giant rats. Many mammoth bodies were found when riverbanks crumbled or landslips revealed frozen ground. With its tusks jutting out of the bank or its huge hairy feet exposed it probably looked uncannily as if some huge burrowing animal had been frozen in the act of tearing its way out of the earth.

In northern and large parts of central Siberia the underlying earth remains frozen at minus 4 degrees Centigrade for the entire year. Except for a few feet of the upper surface which softens in the summer thaw, the ground in much of central Siberia is as hard as concrete, a mixture of soil, rock, and water called *merzlota,* or permafrost, that has remained unchanged for millennia. Prehistoric animals like the mammoth, which fell into bogs or small streams in the thaw, were quickly covered in snow and buried still further by landslips or sedimentation. Captured by the permafrost, they remained much the same as when they died, the bacteria of decay numbed by the constant cold.

Because of its bleakly cold climate and eternal frost, Siberia is one of the few places in the world where the effects of the 1908 explosion would remain unchanged for such a long time. Most of the scars of its dreadful firestorm did not heal quickly but were preserved, almost as if in a deep freeze.

In addition to causing a firestorm, the blast in the Tunguska region had radiated enough heat in a few seconds to melt the permafrost stratum to a great depth, causing swelling of large rivers and flooding. Before the early 1920s only a few of the bolder Tungus, at great risk to themselves it was later learned, had dared to enter this scarred region to see the damage. Indifference, misinformation, and falsely preconceived ideas, as well as the remoteness of the region, had helped to prevent any serious scientific investigation until then; but the official Soviet research body, the Academy of Sciences, was soon to take the first steps that would begin to change this situation.

CHAPTER 3

THE FIRST EXPEDITION

The search for an answer to the Tunguska mystery began in what was for Russia a period of total disorder.

In October of 1917, during World War I, revolution had broken out. Shortly afterward, Russia withdrew from the war and the revolutionary government signed a separate peace with Germany. The Western Allies, concerned that Russia might become a German satellite, sent an expeditionary force into northwest Russia; the Japanese landed a force on the Pacific coast of Siberia; and Admiral Alexander Kolchak's White Army was engaged in a bloody war of resistance to the Red Army in central Siberia. For three years much of Siberia was a battleground, littered with corpses.

Split by civil war and threatened by foreign powers, the Soviet government had little time for scientific inquiry; it was not until 1921, with Kolchak executed, the Japanese and other foreign forces expelled, and order restored, that expeditions once again ventured into the interior of Russia and Siberia.

One of the first trips was mounted by the Academy of Sciences. Before the Trans-Siberian Railway was built the vast distances of Russia had hampered exploration. Now, with the war over and the railway back in operation, most areas of the remote back country were opened up; the Soviet government chose to exploit the situation by sending out not a prospecting or map-making team but one charged with tracking down and locating the many meteorite falls which had been recorded in Russia during and after the war years.

The government's incentive may have been financial. In the United States, a mining exploration company had begun work at Meteor Crater (also known as Barringer Crater) near Winslow, Arizona, to exploit the largest meteoritic mass known to have hit the earth. Analyzing samples of the meteoritic material, the company's engineers found it to be 93 per cent iron and 6.4 per cent nickel; but, more interestingly, mixed with these relatively common metals were traces of precious platinum and iridium which alone might have made the lode worth mining, had the deposit been less deeply buried.

Although the American group failed in its attempts to mine Meteor Crater, news of the operation obviously reached Russia; and the economically reeling Soviet government may have seen its meteorites as a source of quick profit. One of the members of a later expedition to the Siberian site, when the blast was still widely considered to be the result of a meteorite, was quoted as estimating enthusiastically that they might discover a metal mass worth a fortune in the Tunguska region.

The man placed in charge of the Soviet Academy's first special meteorite expedition was a remarkable thirty-eight-year-old scientist named Leonid A. Kulik, who was then doing research at the Mineralogical Museum at Petrograd (as St. Petersburg had been renamed in 1914). Born in 1883 in Tartu in Estonia, he had studied at the St. Petersburg Forestry Institute and in the physics and mathematics department of Kazan University. While working in the Urals as a forestry officer, Kulik met his scientific mentor V. I. Vernadsky, leader of an expedition searching for mineral deposits, and subsequently became extremely interested in mineralogy.

Vernadsky described him as a "lover of minerals and nature" who was "constantly taking pictures." He predicted that Kulik would follow in the footsteps of other great scientific researchers. E. L. Krinov, a noted Soviet scientist and meteorite authority, called Kulik "a vibrant, cultured man around whom young people flocked" and an outspoken individual who was not afraid to voice his opinions when he was convinced he was right. Vernadsky arranged to have Kulik transferred from the Forestry Department to his own expedition; and eventually Kulik went to work for the Mineralogical Museum of the Academy of Sciences in St. Petersburg.

When World War I broke out in 1914, Kulik was drafted and fought briefly in the Russian Army. He happened to be on a scientific expedition in the Urals and was trapped behind the lines when the civil war erupted. He then went to the Siberian city of Tomsk, where he taught mineralogy. After returning to Petrograd in 1920, he resumed his work at the Mineralogical Museum and devoted much of his time to the acquisition and study of meteorites, a relatively new discipline in which he rapidly established himself as a leading figure. With a single-minded intensity that had characterized all of his earlier work, he studied the literature available about meteorites and attempted to add to the national collection housed at the museum. It was a specialization that soon was to set him, almost by accident, on the track of the Siberian explosion; and yet, at the same time, Kulik's concern with meteorites was to mislead him by encouraging a false conclusion about the nature of the blast.

A "meteorite" in its strictest modern definition refers to any solid, natural extraterrestrial object—usually stone or iron—that strikes the earth. Until a few hundred years ago the word "meteor," from the Greek term meaning "something raised up," was the root used in words describing all phenomena associated with the air, such as lightning, clouds, snow, or rain. The present science of meteorology, or weather conditions, still retains this connotation. During the Rennaissance, for instance, man's concept of meteors reflected his picture of himself as existing on a planet located at the center of a fixed universe, in accordance with Ptolemaic cosmology.

Between the middle of the sixteenth century and the middle of the seventeenth, the earth-centered Ptolemaic cosmology had received a death sentence from the startling findings of astronomers like Copernicus, Galileo, and Kepler; and consequently men began to look with fresh eyes at the sky. Yet there was still much confusion and ignorance about cosmic phenomena such as meteorites. Aristotle had believed they were fiery exhalations of the atmosphere; later astronomers thought they might somehow be connected with lightning. In the eighteenth century the notion that meteorites were literally "stones from space" was greeted with skepticism, despite the evidence of numerous ancient records as well as current observations to support this fact. This extraterrestrial theory was at first totally dismissed by the prestigious Academie Française, and Thomas Jefferson scoffed at a report stating that stones had fallen from the sky in 1807 onto the soil of Connecticut.

When Leonid Kulik began his study of meteorites a century later, it was clear that we live on what Harvey H. Nininger, of the Colorado Museum of Natural History, was later to call a "stone-pelted planet," bombarded daily by millions of pieces of cosmic debris from asteroids or comets; most of these fragments are so small that they do not survive the superheated plunge through our upper atmosphere and evaporate as bright "shooting stars" or "meteor showers." The identification of the gigantic Meteor Crater in Arizona by geologist Daniel M. Barringer provided concrete proof that in our past the earth had been hit by immense meteorites.

In 1921, while preparing for his expedition to locate meteorites which had fallen in the Soviet Union, Kulik received a description of a strange event that aroused his curiosity. Another investigator passed along to Kulik a page from an old St. Petersburg calendar, containing on the back a reprinted Siberian newspaper account of the fall of a meteorite. Kulik had never before heard of this fall, and he read the story with great interest.

About 8 A.M., in the middle of June 1908 . . . a huge meteorite is said to have fallen in Tomsk several sagenes [a sagene is 7 feet] from the railway line near Fili-monovo junction and less than 11 versts [a verst is two thirds of a mile] from Kansk. Its fall was accompanied by a frightful roar and a deafening crash, which was heard more than forty versts away. The passengers of a train approaching the junction at the time were struck by the unusual noise. The driver stopped the train and the passengers poured out to examine the fallen object, but they were unable to study the meteorite closely because it was red hot. Later, when it had cooled, various men from the junction and engineers from the railway examined it, and probably dug round it. According to these people, the meteorite was almost entirely buried in the ground, and only the top of it protruded. It was a stone block, whitish in color, and as much as 6 cubic sagenes in size.

Most of this odd report turned out to be sheer fantasy; only the detail about the train stopping near Kansk was accurate. Yet for Kulik it marked the beginning of an obsession that was to last for the rest of his life. Believing that he might have stumbled on to the discovery of a large meteorite not known to scientists, he began searching through other Siberian newspapers for further stories of the fall. He soon found buried in these papers numerous accounts of a phenomenal event that had occurred in 1908, though the details were often confusing and ambiguous.

A newspaper published in Irkutsk, 550 miles from the explosion, related that on a morning in June of 1908, in a village north of Kirensk, peasants saw "a body shining very brightly (too bright to look at with the naked eye) with a bluish-white light. It moved vertically downwards for about ten minutes. The body was in the form of 'a pipe,' i.e., cylindrical." The paper further stated that after the bright object fell, "a huge cloud of black smoke was formed" and a crash as if from "gunfire" was heard. "All the buildings shook," the report went on, "and at the same time a forked tongue of flame broke through the cloud."

Kulik must have been both elated and somewhat puzzled. Meteorites were usually observed at night, not in the early morning, and the "pipe" shape did not sound like a normal meteoritic object. The cloud of black smoke and the flame were also baffling, unless the fall had set the taiga on fire. But this was unlikely at the height of summer when, as every Russian knew, much of the area was an impassable swamp.

Becoming increasingly fascinated and perplexed by each new revelation, Kulik pored through the musty newspapers, now more than twelve years old. An extraordinary story was unfolding in bits and pieces. An enormous "fiery object" had been seen over villages and towns throughout the Yenisei River province; some described it as moving almost horizontally from the south, and almost everybody had felt strong earth tremors and heard loud explosions. A Tomsk newspaper suggested that the event had been an earthquake, followed by "a subterranean crash and a roar as from distant firing. Doors, windows, and lamps were all shaken. Five to seven minutes later a second crash followed, louder than the first, accompanied by a similar roar and followed by yet another crash."

If it had been a meteorite, Kulik was sure that it must have been gigantic—greater than any that had ever fallen before in Russia and perhaps in the world, in order to have caused tremors like an earthquake. But where exactly had it fallen? According to the fragmentary newspaper reports, the phenomena of the fall had been observed over an area extending more than 500 miles.

One of the most specific and dramatic accounts came from a Krasnoyarsk paper in 1908, which stated that in several villages along the Angara River, in the heart of the taiga, people saw "a heavenly body of fiery appearance cut across the sky from south to north . . . when the flying object touched the horizon a huge flame shot up that cut the sky in two. . . . The glow was so strong that it was reflected in rooms whose windows faced north. . . . On the island opposite the village, horses began to whinny and cows to low and run wildly about. One had the impression everything would be swallowed up in the abyss."

The unexpectedness and magnitude of the event seemed to have created a sense of superstitious dread among frightened villagers throughout central Siberia; after days of absorbing the newspaper reports, which tended to corroborate one another on many basic details, Kulik was not surprised that some Siberians had thought "the abyss" had opened that morning in 1908. What was surprising to him was the fact that this remarkable event had not yet been studied by any scientists—a mistake he intended to remedy on his upcoming expedition.

In a preliminary report outlining what he had learned thus far, Kulik listed the event as the "Filimonovo meteorite," since according to the first story he had read on the back of the calendar page, a train engineer had stopped at the Filimonovo junction after seeing the meteorite. At the station town of Kansk he expected to find witnessess who might clarify what had really happened and help him begin the difficult task of locating the fall point.

For the 1921 expedition, which his friend Vernadsky had persuaded the Academy of Sciences to finance, Kulik was given a railway carriage on the Trans-Siberian Express. He and his researchers left Petrograd in September, traveled across the Urals into Siberia, then made stops in Omsk, Tomsk, Krasnoyarsk, and finally Kansk.

At Kansk, though he quickly found that he was nowhere near the site of the 1908 explosion, Kulik was able to check out the story about the event as experienced along the Trans-Siberian Railway; the station agent had felt a "strong vibration in the air" and heard a loud "rumbling sound," and a locomotive engineer had become so frightened by the ground tremors and noise that he had halted his train, fearing it might be derailed. Investigators had eventually arrived from Tomsk and Irkutsk but had found no sign of a meteorite. As a result of a questionnaire he circulated in Kansk and the surrounding districts, Kulik collected a large number of remarkably vivid personal recollections of the incredible luminous phenomena and the destruction that occurred early in the morning of June 30, 1908. From these eyewitness testimonies, Kulik decided that the firey object must have impacted farther north, near the basin of the Stony Tunguska River.

Despite the fact that many of the details he acquired conflicted with the traditional signs of such a fall, he was convinced that the object had been a meteorite. Seeking the elusive proof of this became in time a life's work. But for now, he and his team had to return to Petrograd, and the search would have to wait six years.

CHAPTER 4

THE TUNGUSKA EXPEDITION

A lmost immediately after arriving back in Petrograd, Kulik began thinking about the next and more important expedition into Siberia. Following his report to the Soviet Academy of Sciences on the inconclusive 1921 journey and during the next six years, he received further data from other investigators and additional eyewitness stories that made the explosion seem even more potent than he had imagined. These reports confirmed his belief that its epicenter, or fall point, lay north in the region of the Stony Tunguska; and he soon became convinced that a thorough survey of this area, preferably in the early spring when the weather would be at least tolerable, would uncover the true nature of the strange detonation and enable him to sort out fact from fiction in the numerous rumors circulating about the event.

Several other scientists who happened to be working in the Tunguska region gathered intriguing and sometimes frightening tales from the local inhabitants, the Tungus. S. V. Obruchev, a geologist conducting research along the Stony Tunguska River in the summer of 1924, encountered superstitious awe among the natives about the blast, which he presumed had been caused by the impact of a large meteorite. "In the eyes of the Tungusi people," he wrote, "the meteorite is apparently sacred, and they carefully conceal the place where it fell." As Kulik was later to discover on his second Siberian journey, many Tungus were afraid to talk about the explosion and some completely denied its existence. Others reluctantly admitted to Obruchev only that a huge area of "flattened forest" could be found by traveling three of four days northeast of Vanavara to a wild and almost inaccessible part of the country near the Chambé and Khushmo rivers. Another local report sent to Kulik stated that, according to the Tungus, at least a thousand reindeer had been killed and several nomadic villages had vanished during the explosion. "A violent wind" had leveled the taiga, said others, and "water broke from the earth."

One of the most striking accounts of the effect of the explosion came from Ilya Potapovich, a Tungus who later became the chief guide for the 1927 expedition. Ilya Potapovich's harrowing story about his brother's experiences was recorded in 1923 and sent to Kulik by a geologist named Sobolev, who was working near the area:

Fifteen years ago his [Ilya Potapovich's] brother, who was a Tungus and could speak little Russian, lived on the River Chambé. One day a terrible explosion occurred, the force of which was so great that the forest was flattened for many versts along both banks of the River Chambé. His brother's hut was flattened to the ground, its roof was carried away by the wind, and most of his reindeer fled in fright. The noise deafened his brother and the shock caused him to suffer a long illness. In the flattened forest at one spot a pit was formed from which a stream flowed into the River Chambé. The Tunguska road had previously crossed his place, but it was now abandoned because it was blocked, impassable, and moreover the place aroused terror among the Tungusi people. From the Podkamennaya Tunguska River to this place and back was a three-day journey by reindeer. As Ilya Potapovich told his story, he kept turning to his brother, who had endured all this. His brother grew animated, related something energetically in Tungusk language to Kartashov, striking the poles of his tent and the roof, and gesticulating in an attempt to show how his tent had been carried away.

According to the Tungus brother's widow, Akulina, who was questioned in 1926 by ethnographer I. M. Suslov, the entire family in the tent was thrown into open air and several knocked out by the explosion. The tent was approximately 25 miles southeast of the blast site. When Akulina and her husband woke up, Suslov reported, they saw "the forest blazing around them with many fallen trees. There was also a great noise."

As the eyewitness tales continued to pour in, it became apparent why the Tungus regarded the 1908 catastrophe as a divine punishment, the inexplicable wrath of a vengeful god. Suslov, who was studying the culture of the people of northern and central Siberia and had established a rapport with the Tungus, constantly encountered tribesmen with horrifying tales of destruction. At Strelka, a tiny trading post on the Chunya River, he met the Tungus Podyga's children who had been living in a tent by the Avarkita River at the time of the explosion. "A terrible storm, so great that it was difficult to stand upright in it, blew down the trees near their hut," Suslov was told. "In the distant north, a large cloud formed which they thought was smoke."

At Strelka Suslov talked with a group of about sixty Tungus who agreed not only that the 1908 catastrophe had "crushed" the taiga, killing their animals and injuring some of their people, but also that the blast had "brought with it a disease for the reindeer, specifically scabs, that had never appeared before the fire came."

The 1908 fireball's direction of flight and the probable location of the blast had been estimated in the mid-1920s by A.V. Voznesensky, former head of the Irkutsk Observatory. Using some of the recent information acquired by Kulik and Obruchev, as well as earlier seismic data from Irkutsk and other Russian stations and observations of acoustical phenomena throughout central Siberia, he attempted to trace the path of the body and determine its impact point. He found that the effects of the explosion had been seen and heard by people over an incredibly immense geographical area, one larger than France and Germany combined. The "fiery object" racing through the cloudless sky had been observed by thousands from the southern border of Siberia to the Tunguska region, while the noise of the explosion, the heavy claps, and rumblings "like thunder" were audible for a radius of 500 miles. From these reports and the seismic data, he was able to gauge the time of the blast at about 7:17 A.M. on June 30, 1908. The place of the fall, he determined, was in the territory north of Vanavara.

The detailed eyewitness testimony gathered by Obruchev and Suslov and the calculations of Voznesensky were helpful to Kulik in persuading the Soviet Academy—despite the fact that many of its members remained unconvinced that the earlier evidence indicated a meteorite—to authorize the first expedition to the Stony Tunguska River basin. Thus, in February 1927, Kulik departed from Leningrad (as Petrograd had been renamed in 1924) with a research assistant and traveled by Trans-Siberian Express to Kansk and then farther east to the remote station of Taishet.

In each of these small outposts he met more people who agreed on the northward direction of the "ball of fire" and who had heard the "prolonged thunder" of its explosion. In Kansk, 375 miles southwest of the Stony Tunguska area, persons in the streets had "felt a subterranean rumble." Inside, hanging objects were noticed to rock, china was smashed, and in one house the inside wooden shutters rattled." Other reports from the Kansk district told of boatmen being thrown into the river and horses knocked down by the force of the thunder and the ground tremors. At Taishet, about a hundred miles farther along the railway line, buildings and telegraph poles shook, doors banged in houses, and objects fell to the floor.

In March, after gathering supplies and equipment, Kulik and his assistant began their journey northward from Taishet toward the presumed fall point. They traveled by horse-drawn sled along the Angara River to Keshma, a small village where they purchased more food and supplies. The country soon became more rugged, split with creeks, gullies, and steep hillsides. The high latitude confused their compasses. Maps were inaccurate, where they existed at all. Finally, near the end of March, they arrived at Vanavara on the Stony Tunguska River. The last stop before proceeding into the vast taiga, the tiny settlement consisted only of a few houses, trading stores, and muddy streets. Kulik hired Ilya Potapovich, the Tungus, as his guide and with his assistance began questioning local residents about the explosion.

From several inhabitants of Vanavara Kulik obtained remarkable stories of the blast, particularly of the searing heat and the shock waves. On the morning of June 30, 1908, S. B. Semenov, a farmer, had been sitting on the open porch of his house, looking toward the north when suddenly he saw a "great flash of light" above the northwestern horizon. He wrote of the event:

There was so much heat that I was no longer able to remain where I was—my shirt almost burned off my back. I saw a huge fireball that covered an enormous part of the sky. I only had a moment to note the size of it. Afterward it became dark and at the same time I felt an explosion that threw me several feet from the porch. I lost consciousness for a few moments and when I came to I heard a noise that shook the whole house and nearly moved it off its foundation. The glass and the framing of the house shattered, and in the middle of the area where the hut stands a strip of ground split apart.

At the same time a neighbor, P. P. Kosolapov, who had been working outside by the window of the house, felt his ears burned as if by a "powerful heat." He put his hands over his ears and asked Semenov whether he had seen anything. "How could one help but see it?" Semenov replied. "I felt as though I had been seized by the heat." Kosolapov went inside the house when abruptly "there was a great clap of thunder and the sod poured from the ceiling, a door flew off the Russian stove, and a piece of window glass fell into the room."

Although Kulik had never heard of such heat phenomena associated with a meteorite fall, he believed that this could be accounted for by the meteorite's size and the release of energy in its collision with the earth. He was wrong, but at this time neither he nor any other scientists had sufficient knowledge to explain this type of radiant burning.

Like earlier investigators, Kulik also found that some Tungus preferred not to discuss the event. A few were openly hostile. Gradually he learned the details of a new religion that had sprung up among some inhabitants of the taiga since the explosion, one which made the Tungus unwilling to help anyone approach the fall site. The fiery body, they claimed, was a visitation from the god Ogdy (Fire), who had cursed the area by smashing the trees and killing all the animals. No man dared approach the fall site for fear of being cursed by Ogdy's fire. Tales circulated of herds of reindeer being slaughtered to placate the god and of rumors that Ogdy, enraged at invasions of his territory, would hold back the thaw if visitors disturbed him.

These stories only made Kulik more anxious to see the blast area for himself. On April 8, Kulik, his assistant, and Ilya Potapovich set out with pack horses along the winding path of the Stony Tunguska River. By the time they reached the hut of Okhchen, a friendly Tungus, on the Chambé River, all were exhausted, suffering from scurvy brought on by the lack of proper food and from infections caused by pestilential marsh over which they had to move. Kulik and his colleague had never endured such hardship, but the belief that they were almost at the end of their journey gave them the energy to keep going.

From Tungus they learned that they were close to the beginning of the devastated forest, the edge of the blast area. After resting for one night, they loaded their equipment onto reindeer and set off along the bank of the Chambé, then left the river and proceeded directly north. Within two days, they crossed the Makirta River which flows into the Chambé. It was April 13. At the edge of the Makirta the small party stared at an incredible sight: the first signs of the enormous force of the 1908 explosion.

CHAPTER 5

FALL POINT

"The results of even a cursory examination exceeded all the tales of the eyewitnesses and my wildest expectations," Kulik later wrote of his discoveries in the Tunguska region. Standing on the sloping bank of the Makirta River, the first scientist to view the actual physical effects of the explosion, he gazed in stunned amazement at the sight. Nothing he had heard could have prepared him for the immensity of the devastation.

For as far as Kulik could see, both upstream and down, the upper part of the riverbank was littered with the trunks of fallen birches and pines, apparently smashed down by the shock wave of the blast. The lower part of the bank where the forest still stood was cluttered with undergrowth that included more trunks and the decayed limbs of trees. Against the blanket of snow, the uprooted trees and broken branches were outlined in stark relief. Small knolls along the bank, Kulik later wrote, stood out "picturesquely against the sky and taiga, their almost treeless snow-capped tops stripped bare by the meteorite whirlwind of 1908."

The weary party marched northward through even greater devastation. The number of uprooted trees increased, their tops always pointing toward the south, the direction in which they had been heaved by the blast.

In some places entire stands of giant larches several hundred years old had been knocked down; the ground was littered with fallen, dead trunks, their roots torn from the earth, their foliage stripped away. Often the group had to hack its way through the entangled limbs.

Eventually the party reached an area where the dead trees bore, in Kulik's words, "traces of a continuous burn from above." Even the broken limbs of those trees still upright were charred at the break. The fact that every broken branch showed signs of fire indicated that the burns were not those of a forest fire but the result of a sudden, instantaneous scorching—a flash of intense heat that seared and charred everything. As they progressed deeper into the taiga, the signs of heat flash increased. Kulik thought the scorching might have been caused by a "hot, compressed-air pocket" pushed before a meteorite.

After several more days of travel, Kulik made his way up one of the taiga slopes. Atop the Khladni Ridge he could see the entire area for miles in all directions and, for the first time, gain an impression of the total extent of the destruction.

The view before him was astonishing. The ridges of all the lower surrounding hills were stripped bare. As far as the eye could see stretched enormous dark patches of scorched, flattened forest—trees uprooted and laid down at the same angle, their tops facing south or southeast, the dead trunks with their exposed roots pointing directly north. Only in some of the deeper protected valleys to the east and west had the forest survived. Looking due north from the ridge for 6 or 7 miles to the horizon, Kulik could see little remaining of the great taiga.

Eager to push on immediately toward the center of the blast area, which he assumed lay beyond the distant northern ridges, Kulik urged his guides, Ilya Potapovich and Okhchen, to lead him straight through the burned-out taiga. But the superstitious Tungus, obviously fearful of the punishment which could follow this invasion of accursed territory, refused to go on. Kulik could not induce them to go farther north, and he found himself forced, this close to his goal, to retrace his steps to Vanavara and recruit another group of guides.

On April 30, after finding new helpers, Kulik and his assistant left the trading post and traveled by sled for three days back to the Chambé River. Now painfully aware of the difficulty of marching through the ruined forest, he and the Tungus built rafts with which they worked their way up to the swollen, rapids-ridden Chambé and Khushmo rivers toward the area of destruction. Then, loading themselves up like pack animals, the party headed north on the last leg of what had become an epic journey. Not until May 20 did they finally arrive again at the area of devastation. This time Kulik was determined not to return until he had found the fall point.

In another week of arduous travel, during which they often had to cut their way through the entangled mass of fallen, charred trees, Kulik set up camp in a valley near the mouth of the Churgima River. He was now far beyond the Khladni Ridge from which he had first surveyed the region and within reach, he estimated, of the point where the huge meteorite had crashed to earth. To the north, beyond the ridges and hills stripped of trees lay, according to his guides, a large marshy basin called the Southern Swamp, which must be the site of the enormous crater he had come to expect. Using this camp as a base, Kulik made daily trips into the shattered forest, until finally he had circled the entire area.

It was now early June, more than three months since the start of Kulik's inadequately equipped expedition—one which would soon become among the most famous and controversial in the annals of modern scientific investigation. In Leningrad, some of his scientific colleagues, having heard nothing from him since the beginning of his trip, had begun to worry about his safety, fearing that he might have become lost or even died in the uncharted Siberian wilderness; a relief expedition to search for him was considered.

Completely absorbed in his mission, Kulik had no idea that his colleagues back in civilization were wondering whether he might be dead. He had already found and photographed enough real proof of a cataclysmic event to amaze and puzzle the Soviet scientific establishment for decades. His main difficulty as he roamed through the shattered forest around the Southern Swamp, which he now mentally dubbed the Great Cauldron, was in deciding just what the evidence indicated.

After having made his way around the entire rim of the frozen swamp, about which trees lay flattened radially like a vast fan, Kulik knew he had reached his goal. "There could be no doubt," he wrote, "I had circled the center of the fall!" He stood on the edge of the region that, according to Tungus lore, had been cursed by the fire god. Yet it was an area that did not agree with any he had ever seen, and of the vast meteorite crater he expected there was no sign at all.

His notes betray his confusion and a desperate attempt to cling to the meteorite hypothesis which had brought him to the site. A single observer on the ground, clambering over the tangled trunks of huge trees and cutting his way through dense undergrowth, he saw the fall point only in a series of phantasmagoric vistas, flashes which he recorded accurately but which would not be put into context until expeditions decades later, armed with helicopters and sophisticated recording equipment, created a detailed picture of the area.

In places, the taiga was leveled like that of the area surrounding the fall point. "The taiga," Kulik recorded, "both in the cauldron and outside it, has been practically destroyed by being completely flattened. It lies in roughly parallel rows of bare trunks without twigs and tops, their upper ends turned away from the center of the fall."

But in another part of the woods, Kulik was astonished to see upright trees gradually begin to appear among the tumbled debris. Near what he was convinced must be the epicenter of the fall, he found himself back once again in a standing forest. Stripped of bark and limbs, as dead as those which lay in thousands on the ground for miles around, a zone of trees in the cauldron was miraculously preserved.

Kulik could only speculate about some freak effect of the shock wave which had left an area of trees protected from the blast. He guessed it to be "some kind of node or region of rest due to the interference of air-waves," but the dead, upright forest remained one of the most inexplicable discoveries of the expedition.

Beyond the zone of standing trees, which seemed to Kulik to exist in a huge ring around the actual impact point, he found what they had traveled thousands of miles to see—the peat bog in which, he guessed, the vast meteoritic mass had landed. It resembled a scene of utter devastation. "The peat marshes of the region are deformed," Kulik wrote, "and the whole place bears evidence of an immense catastrophe." Several miles of swamp appeared to have been blasted and tortured into a landscape like the fantasy of a surrealist painter. "The solid ground," read one of Kulik's reports, "heaved outward from the spot in giant waves, like waves in water," and he supposed it "actually must have splashed outward in every direction." Beneath a thin layer of new moss and vegetation, the marshy region showed marks of "uniformly continuous scorching, unlike the traces of an ordinary conflagration." In the northwest and northeast sections of the burnt area, Kulik found dozens of "peculiar flat holes" ranging from several yards to dozens of yards in diameter and several yards in depth.

The single, huge impact crater that Voznesensky had predicted did not exist. The shallow holes that pitted the area, Kulik assumed, must mark the fall point of individual fragments of a meteorite. Most of the holes were overgrown with moss and a few were filled with frozen water, but nature's partial disguise did not obscure the fact that they were unlike any known meteorite impacts. Kulik first theorized that "with a fiery stream of hot gases and cold, solid bodies, the meteorite had struck the cauldron, with its hills, tundra, and swamp and, as a stream of water striking a flat surface splashes spray in all directions, the stream of hot gases with the swarm of bodies penetrated the earth and both directly and with explosive recoil wrought all this mighty havoc."

This initial dramatic explanation of the waves or folds in the earth and the craterlike holes scattered about the peat bogs of the Southern Swamp was to be questioned by his fellow scientists and put in serious doubt by the realities of other recorded meteorite falls. Kulik had no satisfactory explanation for the upright trees in the "telegraph forest," later to be revealed as an essential physical clue pointing to the Tunguska explosion's true nature. Soon he would be forced to re-examine his early theories, though he never completely surrendered his notion of the meteoric origin of the blast. On subsequent expeditions he continued to probe beneath the taiga for evidence of a meteorite, but always in vain.

The tiny group had brought no equipment to bore into the pits nor to take precise measurements of the region. They could do little more than make a hasty survey and draw a rough map of the locale. Because of the dangerous summer thaws, remaining longer in the wilderness would have been hazardous. Kulik turned his thoughts to home and presenting the evidence, contradictory and confusing as it was, to his fellow scientists.

CHAPTER 6

THE RIDDLE

To the surprise of his debunkers, Kulik returned from the grueling ordeal of the 1927 expedition in triumph—or at least what seemed like triumph at the time. The solid evidence he had acquired impressed the Soviet Academy of Sciences and quashed the skepticism and indifference with which many scientists had previously greeted stories of the strange superblast. A catastrophic explosion rumored to have occurred almost two decades ago in the remote forests of central Siberia became, because of Kulik's firsthand documentation, an undeniable and even somewhat overwhelming reality that quickly aroused the fascination of experts not only in Russia but around the globe.

As his accomplishments were publicized, Kulik's reputation gradually changed from that of a relatively obscure meteorite researcher to that of a pioneering figure of growing international prestige. In addition to extensive coverage in Russian and European newspapers, articles appeared in the New York *Times* and the London *Times* featuring the Tunguska expedition and quoting Kulik's descriptions of the "blasted" and "bombarded" impact site. The mysterious explosion also received considerable attention in popular astronomy and science magazines as well as serious scientific journals. As the event became internationally known, additional records of huge seismic shocks and air turbulence in 1908 were uncovered and sent from other countries to the Societ Academy.

For the next several years exploratory trips to the fall region, under Kulik's direction, became almost annual events. On the second Tunguska expedition, begun in April of 1928, Kulik was joined by cinematographer N. Strukov from Moscow. After arriving at the Southern Swamp, the group explored a wider area around the fall point and conducted a magnetic survey, hoping to detect traces of meteorite fragments imbedded in the peat. Although some Tungus had reported finding unusual bits of shiny metal "brighter than the blade of a knife and resembling in color a silver coin," Kulik's primitive magnetic instruments detected nothing. The team tried to dig into the large circular depressions, which he was sure were craters caused by the meteorite fragments, but the water and boggy soil made penetration almost impossible without boring and draining equipment.

A third and better-equipped expedition, departing in February of 1929 and remaining in the wilderness for eighteen months, also concentrated on studying the Southern Swamp, particularly the craterlike pits and the huge peat folds or ridges which Kulik believed were formed by "the enormous lateral pressure of the explosion gases which emanated from the meteorite." Despite elaborate trench digging, excavations, and boring with large hand drills to depths of 25 yards, no proof was found to support this notion. The possibility that the pits and ridges were simply natural formations of the central Siberian landscape, caused by the thawing of the permafrost beneath the peat, had occurred to other scientists, including E.L. Krinov, a colleague on the third expedition and early authority on the Tunguska blast. Krinov, who lost a toe to frostbite on this expedition, believed that Kulik might have been more successful had he not focused his attention almost exclusively on what he was convinced lay hidden beneath the marshy Southern Swamp and instead broadened his scope to the larger region of the windfallen taiga.

But for the next decade Kulik obstinately persisted in his conviction that under the swamp lay "crushed masses of . . . nickeliferous iron, individual pieces of which may have a weight of one or two hundred metric

Above, the area of peat bog known as the Southern Swamp, which Leonid Kulik (below, right) called the Great Cauldron. The explosion took place in the air, two to three miles directly above this point; in the foreground, the puzzling "telegraph pole" forest. Below, left, Tungus guide and blast eyewitness, Ilya Potapovich. Opposite, below, Kulik and a sled husky in that "telegraph pole" forest.

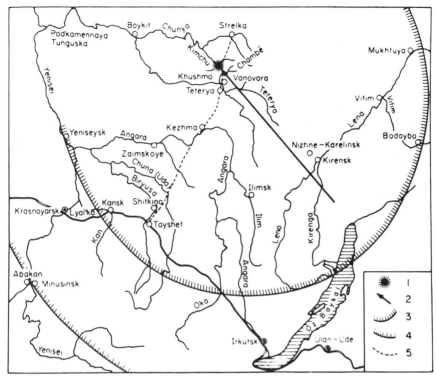

E. L. Krinov's map of the region between the Stony Tunguska and Lake Baikal, made after the 1929-30 expedition: (1) blast site; (2) proposed southeast to northwest flight path for the mysterious object that caused the blast; (3) extent of visual phenomena; (4) region over which blast was heard; (5) expedition route.

tons." The original meteorite, he estimated, probably weighed, before falling into the earth's atmosphere, "as much as several thousands of metric tons." A companion on the second expedition guessed that the value of the metal might be between 100 and 200 million dollars, chiefly for the iron and platinum. Following the 1928 trip to central Siberia, Kulik had given a lecture, accompanied by Strukov's motion picture of the Tunguska destruction, to a Moscow audience that, according to the New York *Times*, "shivered" as he outlined one of the more alarming implications of the event:

Astronomers and geologists know that this was an exceptional circumstance. But they know also that there is no reason whatever why a similar visitation should not fall at any moment upon a more populous region.

Thus, had this meteorite fallen in Central Belgium, there would have been no living creature left in the whole country. Had it fallen on New York, Philadelphia might have escaped with only its windows shattered, and New Haven and Boston escaped, too. But all life in the central area of the meteor's impact would have been blotted out instantaneously.

The position of the 1908 explosion raised another chilling question. Anyone glancing at a global map could see that Leningrad is on the same latitude as the Tunguska cataclysm. Had the event happened slightly later that morning and the earth rotated only a few more hours, would this huge city have been annihilated by a direct hit from the cosmic orbit?

In the United States, an astronomer at the Leander McCormick Observatory at the University of Virginia, Charles P. Oliver, writing in 1928 for *Scientific American*, labeled the Siberian explosion "the most astonishing phenomenon of its kind in scientific annals" and said of Kulik's report that "one has to admit that many accounts of events in old chronicles that have been laughed at as fabrications are far less miraculous than this one, of which we seem to have undoubted confirmation." The curator of meteorites at the Colorado Museum of Natural History, Harvey H. Nininger, urged his fellow astronomers and scientists to equip and send an American expedition to Russia in order to thoroughly evaluate the "unparalleled" Stony Tunguska event discovered but not explained by Kulik. Further delay could mean the loss of invaluable physical evidence which was fading with the years; a properly equipped group of scientific investigators would "secure what is yet available of the greatest message from the depths of space that has ever reached our planet."

While many researchers agreed about the unique opportunity presented by the Siberian event, Nininger was not able to gain financial support for an American expedition; and U.S. astronomers had to be content with reading about Kulik and the increasing number of other Soviets involved in the Tunguska research. Discussing with a British writer his lack of success, after three expeditions, in locating positive proof of a meteorite fall, Kulik pointed to the possibility that the pits in the Southern Swamp might be "the marks of a ricochet where the meteorites struck the earth a glancing blow and then flew off into space again, or perhaps vaporized on the spot." He also conceded that the meteorites might "have been connected with the comet Pons-Winnecke, or indeed they may have been the comet itself." But Kulik's inability to substantiate his speculations encouraged the advancement of other theories to account for the catastrophe.

In the early 1930s two astronomers, F.J.W. Whipple, head of the Kew Observatory in London, and the Russian I.S. Astapovich, concluded independently that the celestial missle that scarred the taiga in 1908 had not been a meteorite but a gaseous comet which had left no trace of itself after impact. The absence of positive impact craters or sizable meteoritic fragments at the scene of the explosion appeared at first to support this idea. The atmospheric phenomena following the blast could have been caused, Astapovich contended, by the dust tail of the "nucleus of a small comet" rushing toward earth and exploding with a kinetic energy force of at least "10^{21} ergs per second"—more powerful than hurricanes, volcanic eruptions, and the most severe natural catastrophes.

Although Astapovich came close in his estimate of the blast's tremendous release of kinetic energy—it was established in the 1960s by the Soviets to be as much as 10^{23} ergs, or the equivalent of about 30 million tons of TNT—the comet hypothesis turned out to be highly questionable.

Originally believed for thousands of years to be burning exhalations of the air portending great misfortune, comets are now known to be cosmic bodies pursuing elliptical orbits stretching out for billions of miles around the sun. Sometimes called "dirty snowballs," comets have nuclei composed chiefly of ice, frozen methane, and ammonia; their spectacular tails, which in the case of Halley's Comet had a length of more than 90 millions miles, are always pointed away from the sun, the source of the dusty tail's glow.

There is no record of a comet ever colliding with our planet nor any evidence that their tails cause any unusual atmospheric or magnetic phenomena such as occurred in 1908. The passage of the earth through the tail of Halley's Comet in 1910, for example, did not precipitate any striking sunsets or provoke any magnetic disturbances; its density was less than water or even air. As they near the sun, most comets have an extremely luminous and, as the Greeks described them, "long-haired" appearance. Any comet, even a small one, following an orbit that would bring it into collision with the earth would be visible to half the globe long before it touched the atmosphere; but the Tunguska object was sighted only in the final phase of its trajectory before it exploded.

By the end of the 1930s the riddle of the great Siberian explosion was still far from solved. The cause of the blast itself was still uncertain, despite the work of astronomers, geologists, meteorologists, seismologists, and chemists and the resources of the Soviet Academy; and many aspects of the destruction site, such as Kulik's bare "telegraph pole" forest around the Southern Swamp, remained inexplicable. Samples of soil from the fall point had been collected but not fully analyzed. Because Kulik had concentrated primarily on the central region and no expedition had yet explored the entire area of the uprooted trees, the precise borders of the destroyed taiga had not been carefully mapped out or examined. The exact shape of the explosion wave was not yet known, although Krinov had surmised from partial observations that it had an oval form.

In 1938–39 Kulik led his last expedition into the Tunguska region, principally for the purpose of taking aerial photographs of the destruction. By this time a road had been cleared through the taiga leading 40 miles from Vanavara to a camp site near the Southern Swamp, and a small air strip had been set up near the trading town. Although the photos finally obtained in the 1938–39 trip were not entirely satisfactory—they did not cover the whole area and were taken during the summer when the leafage partially hid the uprooted trees—they did verify the radial direction of the smashed forest and confirm the Southern Swamp as the absolute center of the explosion.

For Kulik and the other scientists who still clung to the meteorite explanation, the research of the late 1920s and 1930s led to an impasse. If the Southern Swamp was indeed the blast's epicenter, why were there no traces left of the enormous meteorite's existence? By the beginning of the 1940s Kulik's friend Krinov, in attempting to resolve this contradiction, saw the direction that future researchers must take to unravel the puzzling Siberian event:

Thus the careful investigation of the cauldron as a whole, and of the South Swamp in particular, does not give any grounds for concluding that this cauldron is the place where the meteorite fell. But the absence, anywhere in the immediate or more distant neighborhood of the cauldron; of other areas that might attract attention as the possible places of fall; the coincidence of the cauldron's co-ordinates with those of the epicentre of the seismic wave; and finally the radial forest devastation around the cauldron—all point convincingly to it as the site of the explosion. There is only one possible explanation that removes the contradiction, i.e., that the meteorite did not explode on the surface of the ground, but in the air at a certain height above the cauldron.

But the intriguing possibility that the blast may have taken place at a high altitude was not immediately investigated. All research on the Tunguska catastrophe was abruptly halted by the advent of a greater holocaust, World War II.

On July 5, 1941, at the beginning of the Nazi advance into Russia, Kulik joined the Moscow People's Militia, a volunteer home unit composed chiefly of older men like himself with little military training. In October, while taking part in a battle on the front line, Kulik was wounded in the leg and captured by the advancing German Army. Imprisoned in a Nazi camp at Spas-Demensk, in the Smolensk district, the fifty-eight-year-old scientist contracted typhus and died on April 24, 1942.

CHAPTER 7

THE ANSWER?

Almost as if Leonid Kulik's tragic death had been a signal, speculation on the cause of the Tunguska explosion took a new and unexpected turn after World War II.

As a scientist, Kulik had been chiefly an observer and collector rather than an experimenter; he had been more inclined to accumulate and catalogue the wonders of the natural world than to inquire into their nature. With the help of a network of largely amateur collectors, who recorded new meteorite falls, Kulik had increased and meticulously catalogued the National Collection of Meteorites; and in his years of research he had done as much as one man could to illuminate the Tunguska mystery. But the new generation of scientists had a different view and a vastly more sophisticated technology to apply to the problem.

Their development accelerated by the war, communications in particular had become infinitely easier, with the result that a technologist in the Soviet Union could read of the latest theories in world science and apply them to his own field. At international conferences and on research trips, scientists of all nations observed at first hand the work of foreign colleagues and visited sites that would indirectly have a profound effect on their own work. Without such visiting between experts and pooling of research, the Tunguska riddle may have remained unsolved forever. But, in fact, the late forties brought about a revived interest in the explosion and a radical change in the theories advanced to explain the event.

Except among hard-line adherents to Kulik's theory, the word "meteorite" was seldom heard; most scientists preferred to call the Tunguska object a "cosmic body" and to describe the fall simply as an "event," a "phenomenon," or, more popularly, a "catastrophe." Every such reference suggested the new trend of speculation on what had caused the cataclysm of 1908.

One man was in no doubt over the cause of the blast. His theories, carefully presented over the postwar years and backed up with his considerable prestige as an author and technician, were fundamentally to change the whole structure of the argument.

If one could have set a computer to choose a person to carry on Kulik's task in solving the Tunguska riddle, it is unlikely that anyone better could have been found than Aleksander Kazantsev. He had actually been born in Siberia—at Akmolinsk in 1906—and had studied at Tomsk and Omsk, cities in which speculation about the Tunguska event had a long history. Graduating from the Tomsk Technological Institute in 1930, Kazantsev, like Kulik, went to the Urals where he became head mechanic of the Beloretsky Metallurgical Plant.

Kazantsev's vivid imagination and technical skill quickly brought him to the attention of the Soviet authorities, and during the 1930s he was promoted to a post in one of Moscow's scientific research institutes. Kazantsev joined the Army when Russia was invaded in 1941 but, too valuable to be wasted in the infantry, was soon appointed head engineer of a defense complex, where he worked on the development of new weapons.

Not content with his career as a technologist, Kazantsev had, long before the war, mastered chess and became an important writer on the game. In 1936 he had also exhibited another side to his multifaceted talent by entering a national competition for science-fiction film scenarios. His entry took first prize but, when it was not made into a film, he reworked it as a novel, *The Burning Island*, which was highly successful in the Soviet Union. After the war, he became a full-time author.

Like most Siberians, Kazantsev was fascinated by the bleak landscape of arctic Russia. To him, however, it represented something more than a mere frontier. He grasped the alien nature of the tundra; Mars, he felt, must look very like this frozen, wind-swept waste. Throughout his arctic travels of the mid-forties the image of northern Siberia as that part of the earth's surface most like another planet became stronger in his mind. It was to be a central concept in the evolving controversy over the Tunguska explosion.

The other impetus for new speculation on the blast came from a location less geographically remote than Mars.

In August 1945, when the American atomic bomb burst 1,800 feet above Hiroshima, the world had its first demonstration of the havoc a nuclear blast could inflict on a city. Kazantsev was among the Russian scientists who evaluated the Hiroshima data and visited the city some time after the blast. For him, the journey through its desolation had the eerie quality of a dream dimly remembered: he saw sights that were strangely familiar, phenomena that he had encountered before. Hiroshima in many respects resembled photographs he had seen of the blasted area on the Stony Tunguska where an explosion had occurred in 1908.

The Japanese explosion, made up almost entirely of flash and concussion, agreed in many ways with the damage done to the Siberian taiga in 1908 and the evidence of the eyewitnesses. At Hiroshima, only a few hundred yards from the blast center, was a group of trees, charred and stripped of their leaves but still standing upright, like those on the Stony Tunguska. Elsewhere, houses had been flattened just as the giant Siberian larches were toppled. The mushroom cloud, the black rain which fell after the blast—all were similar to what had been seen in Siberia. Every new investigation, including the detection of signs of radiation on the site, supported his theory; no meteorite or comet had caused the 1908 blast. What had exploded there was atomic.

An atom bomb in 1908? The idea at first made little sense. But to Kazantsev, with his fascination with Mars, there was only one credible explanation. An alien space ship, traveling from Mars, had chosen Siberia as a location for its landing or, more likely, plunged there out of control before exploding in the air. Why had the Martians come to earth? Kazantsev believed they came in search of water for their dying planet, and he conjectured that they may have originally been headed for Lake Baikal, the earth's largest body of fresh water.

Shrewdly, Kazantsev chose a popular magazine to publish his thesis. In America, science fiction has long been accepted as a legitimate form for the presentation of scientific theories, though few scientists took advantage of its opportunities for free speculation. In Russia the tradition was stronger, and the technically oriented Soviet society of the postwar years encouraged the growth of many magazines which mixed science fiction with science fact. In 1946 Kazantsev used one of these publications, *Around the World*, to put forward his theory that the devastation on the

Tunguska was caused by a nuclear space ship from another world exploding high over the taiga.

From another author, such a speculation would have been greeted with derision, but when presented by the distinguished Kazantsev, with his honored war record and background as a technologist, it commanded respect. Always careful to offer it only as an interesting hypothesis in the form of popular science or as science fiction, Kazantsev developed his theory for the next ten years, finally presenting it in 1958 in its most elaborate form in the story-article "A Guest from the Cosmos," which was published in *Young Technician*, the monthly of the Communist Youth League.

"A Guest from the Cosmos" was set in a locale that, for Kazantsev, was familiar: the cabin of an arctic survey ship carrying a group of scientists into northern Siberia. This time, however, their purpose is to find a spot in the Arctic that approximates the climate of Mars and establish whether life can exist there. One of the scientists, Krymov, claims to know with certainty that there *are* Martians and that they have visited earth. Having been born a Tungus in the area of the Stony Tunguska, he was a boy when the great explosion of 1908 occurred. The event had far-reaching effects both on him and his family.

"My father went into the fallen taiga," Krymov explains, "and saw a huge column of water flowing out of the ground. A few days later he died in terrible pain as if he was on fire. But there was no trace of fire anywhere on his body. The old people of the tribe became terribly afraid. They forbade all of the people to go into the area of the fallen trees. They called it a cursed place. The shaman said that it was there that the god of fire and thunder, Ogdy, descended to the earth. All who go to that place are burned with an unseen fire."

Pressed to give his interpretation of the death, Krymov adds, "In the legend about the god Ogdy who burns with an unseen fire—what could this fire be that leaves no traces on the body? It could be nothing other than radioactivity, which begins to appear at a certain time after an atomic explosion."

To Krymov, only one explanation—that the object was a burning spaceship plunging out of control through the earth's atmosphere—could explain what they knew of the Tunguska catastrophe. "Apparently the travelers died en route from cosmic rays or from meteorite bombardment," he states. "As the uncontrolled ship approached the earth, it resembled a meteorite because it flew into the atmosphere without reducing its speed. The ship burned up from friction just as a meteorite would burn. Its outer shield was burned off, and its atomic fuel experienced conditions that made possible a chain reaction. Then an atomic explosion occurred and our cosmic guests died on the very day they were supposed to descend to earth."

Though some dismissed the idea, many members of Soviet scientific circles carefully studied Kazantsev's theories. Writing in *Knowledge Is Strength* in June 1959, Professor Felix Zigel, who taught aerodynamics at the Moscow Institute of Aviation, remarked that "at the present time, like it or not, A. N. Kazantsev's hypothesis is the only realistic one insofar as it explains the absence of a meteorite crater and the explosion of a cosmic body in the air." As for Kazantsev's standing as a fiction writer, Zigel said, "It is generally known that at times—nay, often—new ideas that proved to be most valuable to science were first expressed not by scientists, but by writers of scientific fantasy." Within the Soviet Union Kazantsev's work remained highly respected and the subject of furious debate.

As the Tunguska controversy raged on, a gradual polarization became apparent. One group of hard-line meteorite experts refused to admit that anything except a conventional meteorite could have wreaked the havoc in Siberia in 1908. A growing body of ingenious, often younger technologists agreed with Kazantsev that the blast had been atomic. The postwar scientific establishment had seen enough of the atomic age and considered enough of the new theories to know that today's impossibility was tomorrow's reality. Applying the newest techniques of cosmology, atomic physics, and chemistry to the available data, they set out to seek a final explanation of the mystery of 1908.

CHAPTER 8

THE FIRE CAME BY

Could the explosion of 1908 have been atomic?

Was the sudden, dazzling "flash of light" that seemed to split the morning sky over the Tunguska region the flash of a nuclear blast?

Was the painful heat experienced by witnesses 40 miles away the instantaneous thermal wave of this flash?

Could the blinding "pillar of fire" that surged upwards for miles have been an atomic fireball?

The "huge cloud of black smoke" that billowed over the entire area— was this an atomic mushroom cloud?

Was the strange disease that produced scabs on the reindeer the result of radiation burns?

These questions set Soviet scientists on a furious quest for new data that might provide the answers, as well as on a search through the mountain of evidence already accumulated by the many earlier expeditions investigating the meteorite theory. In their quest they looked for comparisons to the Alamogordo test and to the Hiroshima and Nagasaki bombs, three events of 1945 that marked the beginning of a terrifying new age.

The bombs heralded a new scale of destruction, excelling even the biblical promises of fire and brimstone; and among their many effects on the consciousness of man was to cause a re-evaluation of the Tunguska event. Before 1945 no frame of reference existed to explain a relatively small flying object capable of vast devastation. Hiroshima and Nagasaki provided it.

Nor was the atomic bomb merely a simpler way to make a bigger blast. The form of an atomic explosion differs materially from that created by a comparable quantity of chemical explosives. Scientists measured atomic blasts in kilotons, a unit equal to the energy output of one thousand tons of the explosive compound TNT, and later in megatons, one million tons of TNT. The Hiroshima bomb was described as the equivalent of 20 kilotons of TNT, but the comparison is misleading. A chemical explosive, such as TNT, detonates in a single massive expansion of energy, the shock wave smashing through structures, then quickly moving on. By contrast, an atomic blast builds through a chain of destruction which makes it results far more devastating. First comes the glare and heat of the thermal wave, bursting out at a temperature of 300,000° Centigrade. Next in an atomic blast comes the shock wave. In three seconds it travels nearly a mile, in eight seconds twice that distance.

The atomic bomb's primary shock wave is followed by a secondary wave as the first blast, reflected from the ground and from clouds or heavy air masses above the target, crushes down once more, distorting and flattening structures already severely damaged. This second, reinforced wave can be as much as six or eight times greater than the first primary shock.

Meanwhile, inside the atomic fireball, the upward rush of superheated air and the fury of atomic fission have created a vacuum which demands to be filled. Air is drawn into the rising globe of fire, tearing apart any buildings in its range not already collapsed, whipping debris, both inanimate and human, into the air. Set afire by the thermal wave, blazing material is sucked upwards, creating a self-feeding firestorm.

All these phenomena—the thermal wave, the primary and secondary shock waves, the vacuum damage, and final firestorm—left indelible marks in both the Hiroshima and the Siberian blasts.

Scientists examining the ruins of Hiroshima emphasized the overwhelming effect of heat and light on the city. After examining significant ashes and melted bits, they concluded that the bomb's heat on the ground at the center must have been 6,000° C.

Most survivors recalled the bombs as "a noiseless flash," others as "a sheet of sun." Few in Hiroshima heard the bomb's noise, but all saw the vast, blinding glare and felt the wave of heat, which were followed closely by the roar of the explosion and its shock.

Into the vacuum created by the fireball was sucked all the debris, the smashed timber, the inflammable detritus of the shattered city. It fountained upwards in the mushroom cloud, 40,000 feet high and visible more than 400 miles out to sea. An official eyewitness report of the blast noted that the cloud "was observed from a combat airplane 363 nautical miles away with the airplane at 25,000 feet. Observation was then limited by haze and not curvature of the earth."

The sudden, chance phenomena characteristic of an atomic blast, with its multiple shock waves and thermal wave, astonished the Japanese. Men were knocked flat while those next to them remained upright. Others were stripped of their clothes but otherwise unharmed. Unlike an earthquake, the tremors resulting from the blast did not persist; yet the damage to the city was far greater than could have been caused by any natural disaster. According to one report, "The total damaged area in Hiroshima . . . was 18 square miles."

Later observers were impressed by the area's relative freedom from radiation; though in an air burst the gamma ray output is intense, the effect does not persist. The air burst therefore ensured that Hiroshima would suffer less from radioactive fallout. The experimental bomb at Alamogordo, New Mexico, which had been exploded on a hundred-foot steel tower, left the proving ground dangerously "hot." Dust and debris weighing thousands of tons, as well as the vaporized remains of the tower and a nearby farmhouse, were sucked up into the fireball, then sent billowing 40,000 feet into the air, where the mass flattened out in the soon-to-be-familiar mushroom-shaped cloud. An important factor discovered at Alamogordo was that the presence of dirt and other particles in the atomic fireball also impaired its efficiency. Consequently, the decision was made that any bomb used against Japan would have to be air burst, thus guaranteeing the maximum possible damage from heat and concussion.

As terrifying as scientists found the New Mexico bomb's explosive damage, they were more in awe of the terrible effects of radiation and heat. Heading towards the bomb site only a few hours after the blast in Sherman tanks sheathed with lead, the observers found an area for which they had no basis of comparison. Speaking of one observer, Lansing Lamont wrote in *Day of Trinity*:

A half-mile away he saw what looked like a great jade blossom amid the coppery sands of the desert. Where the shot tower had once stood, a crater of green ceramic-like glass glistened in the sun. The fireball had sucked up the dirt, fused it virescent with its incredible heat, then dumped the congealing particles back on the explosion point.

Scientists named the green glass "trinitite," after the Alamogordo code name "Trinity." Similar tiny globules of glass, many containing fragments of melted metal, were found in the soil at the site of the Tunguska blast.

Above the Alamogordo test site towered what was to become the most feared and potent symbol of the atomic age, a mushroom-shaped cloud. After the explosion, the still-expanding ball of lighter gases and dust, superheated beyond any fire that occurs naturally, erupted into the thin upper atmosphere about five miles above the earth; instantly the ball of gas was surrounded by a violet glow as heat and radiation ionized the air, creating a more vivid version of the aurora sometimes seen in the higher latitudes where changed particles from the earth's magnetic belts are drawn to react with the atmosphere. Carried by the winds of the upper atmosphere, the glowing ionized air above the New Mexican desert traveled around the world creating, as did all later atomic explosions, atmospheric glows and odd, prolonged sunsets that faded within a few days as the air cooled and reverted to a more stable form.

American physicist Philip Morrison, one of the observers sent into Hiroshima thirty-one days after the blast, was astonished at the relative lack of damage to the city's Castle area, which must have been almost directly under the fireball. Morrison's guide lamented the fact that a tree planted by Hirohito's father had been burned black and leafless. Some water lilies in the moat of the Castle had turned black, too, the guide added, but he was happy to say that they had begun to grow again. "I wanted to make sure of that," Morrison said, "and I asked him to show me the lilies. They were growing all right!"

The fact that the lilies were still growing proved to Morrison that because the blast had been an air burst the area had not been as completely saturated in gamma radiation as Alamogordo had been, where all life had been obliterated. The growth of the Hiroshima lilies was found to be characteristic of the accelerated plant growth which often followed atomic explosions. Not only did the black, leafless yet upright trees around the Hiroshima Castle at ground zero resemble the zone of burned, standing trees on the Tunguska site but a similar acceleration of growth was discovered in plants and trees closest to the center of the destroyed region in Siberia.

Just as the Japanese survivors first saw a "blinding flash" or "sheet of sun" in the sky, the Siberian witnesses recalled that the 1908 fire which suddenly appeared over the Tunguska was "brighter than the sun." The eyewitness descriptions of the Siberian explosion, in fact, coincide remarkably well with those of Hiroshima survivors. According to one account of the morning, "a huge flame shot up that cut the sky in two." Others spoke of an enormous "tongue of flame" or "pillar of fire" that flared over the taiga, followed by a tall, billowing column of "black smoke"—images that fit the nuclear fireball and mushroom cloud.

As at Hiroshima, the brilliant flash in the sky was accompanied by terrible heat. Sitting on his porch in Vanavara, 40 miles from the explosion, S. B. Semenov saw a "huge fireball" that gave off such a fierce heat that he could hardly remain seated. The heat "seized" Semenov, nearly burning the shirt off his back. The shock wave, which immediately followed the flash and heat, "shook the whole house," damaging the ceiling and breaking windows. After the shock came the loud roar of the blast, like distant thunder.

In April of 1927 the Tungus Ilya Potapovich had informed Kulik that the "center of the firestorm" of the blast occurred at the pasture land of his relative Vasily Ilich, who had a herd of fifteen hundred reindeer. "In the same area he owned a number of storehouses where he kept clothes, household goods, reindeer harnesses," Kulik was told. "The fire cau.e by and destroyed the forest, the reindeer, and the storehouses. Afterward, when the Tungus went in search of the herd, they found only charred reindeer carcasses."

No later investigator, not even those most completely committed to the meteorite theory, ever discredited these eyewitness reports. Krinov was initially perplexed by Semenov's description of the blaze of heat that seized him, since this was not consistent with a meteorite impact, but later he had to acknowledge that "Semenov's report about the moment of explosion is of great interest. Apparently the 'heat' was a direct result of the radiant energy of the explosion. He also noticed that a 'hot wind' followed—apparently the explosive wave that had reached Vanavara."

Summing up the evidence of the flash and heat wave, Felix Zigel wrote in *Knowledge is Strength* in 1961 that in order for the explosion to have caused a sensation of burning 40 miles away in Vanavara, the energy must have been "not less than 0.6 calories per square centimeter." He pointed out that in the village of Keshma, 125 miles from the epicenter, "the flash of light from the explosion was so strong that it caused secondary shadows in rooms with northern exposures. . . . All these estimates are independent of one another and show one fact: the radiant energy of the Tunguska explosion comprised several tens of percent of the total energy. But this correlation between the parameters is characteristic only of nuclear explosions. A chemical explosion is excluded without a doubt— for a chemical explosion the ratio between these parameters is much less. Knowing the basic parameters of the Tunguska explosion, its temperature can be calculated. It turns out that the temperature was several tens of millions of degrees!"

Expeditions of the late 1950s and 1960s analyzed in detail the evidence of the burned forest. A. V. Zolotov, a prominent geophysicist who led 1959 and 1960 expeditions, remarked of the forest that "one observes an alternation of burned and unburned parts of the area and also an alternation of burned and unburned branches at the top of the same, completely burned tree." Zigel commented, "This means that the combustion of the trees was caused by light radiation from the explosion, and only in those places which were not in the shadow of leaves and branches, that is, it was a radiant burn."

H. K. P. Florensky, as violent an opponent of the atomic theory of the Tunguska explosion as Zolotov was its supporter, devoted much of his time on an expedition in 1961 trying to disprove Zolotov's theories, but the reports of the forestry experts he took with him agreed that "the 1908 fire flared up at several points" and that "the rounded shape of the fire site and the complete destruction by fire of the old forest over an extremely great area are outstanding features of the area; it differs in these respects from ordinary forest burn-out."

Florensky's various expeditions, in 1958, 1961, and 1962, also completed the work of establishing the exact point at which the object had exploded. Had it indeed, as Kazantsev suggested, been an air burst? Both G. Plekhanov, of the Tomsk Medical Institute, and Zolotov, measuring the so-called "telegraph pole forest" and noting the way certain hillsides seemed to have been protected from the blast while others were entirely flattened, had concluded that only one explanation fitted these phenomena—an air burst about two miles above the taiga.

What about the appearance and height of the other sign of an atomic blast—the mushroom-shaped cloud? I. S. Astapovich, correlating the results of eyewitness reports taken over a period in the area, had written in 1933 that "the explosion was observed from many points in the form of a vertical fountain," and he went on to list some of the extraordinarily consistent descriptions of what witnesses had seen. In Kirensk, it was "a fiery pillar . . . in the form of a spear," while to those at Nizhne-Ilimsk it "changed into a fiery pillar and disappeared in a moment." All witnesses agreed on observing the rising "dense cloud" or "a huge cloud of black smoke," even though their homes were scattered over hundreds of miles. Astapovich calculated that "both the pillar of the explosion and the 'black smoke' rose to a height considerably greater than 20 kilometers."

Twenty kilometers is about 66,000 feet. The Hiroshima cloud rose to between 40,000 and 50,000 feet. In a 1951 article containing further data on the Tunguska explosion, Astapovich concluded that "the cloud afterward was exactly like an atomic mushroom cloud."

Other eyewitnesses spoke of the "black rain" which fell following the Tunguska blast—a rain identical with that observed at Hiroshima. Astapovich also mentioned other phenomena associated with atomic explosions such as the atmospheric glow and strange sunsets seen for a few days after the 1908 explosion. These night displays persisted from June 30 to July 3 throughout Russia and Europe.

In 1960 Plekhanov, a major figure in the Tunguska investigation, compared these midnight lights with those following the American nuclear explosion at Bikini Atoll in 1958. He found that almost identical, though smaller, atmospheric and magnetic effects followed Bikini as were observed in 1908. In a 1966 report, Soviet investigators determined that the magnetic and barographic effects, as well as the zone of destruction of the Siberian blast, corresponded with the 1958 high-altitude nuclear tests conducted by the United States. If the Tunguska event had taken place since 1958, they contended, it would have been immediately apparent to the new sophisticated instruments at the Irkutsk Observatory that a high-altitude atomic explosion had occurred.

The earlier meteorite and comet theorists found no explanation for the seismic shocks registered around the world in 1908—shocks never before noted in the case of a cosmic body striking the earth, but very similar to those later recorded for atomic tests.

The most telling evidence for the atomic-blast theory is that of actual radiation damage to the area and to its flora and fauna. Much of the data collected by Tunguska observers and scientists on expeditions of the 1920s and 1930s, though little understood at the time, suggests that the Tunguska fall point was as much infected by gamma radiation as Hiroshima. In 1926, when the ethnographer I. M. Suslov questioned a gathering of 60 Tungus herdsmen at Strelka on their experience of the catastrophe, all agreed on the flare, the shock, and the resulting thunder—but also on an inexplicable aftereffect none had ever experienced before. The blast, Suslov said, "brought with it a disease for the reindeer, specifically scabs, that had never appeared before the fire came." Reports on the 1945 New Mexico tests record "gray patches" and blisters on the hides of cattle exposed to radiation.

After 1958, expeditions to the Tunguska region also noted genetic changes in the plants at the fall point since 1908. There was accelerated growth both in new trees and in those damaged by the explosion. In some cases, a fungus infection had spread over the dead wood, then been covered by the wild new growth. Examination of growth rings on living trees showed that around the period of the blast there was a noticeable increase in cell production; the rings were both wider and more pronounced. Trees which germinated after the explosion would normally have grown to about 23 to 26 feet in height by 1958; instead, they towered between 55 and 72 feet high. Some of those which survived the blast were now almost four times their expected girth.

Zolotov's 1959 expedition drew attention to these anomalies, and Florensky's 1961 party made detailed examinations. The latter's report stated that "the features of accelerated tree growth established in 1958 have been confirmed by a great volume of data and are peculiar to the central region of the impact area."

Finally, and most convincingly, a group from Tomsk led by Plekhanov in 1959 spent six weeks accumulating elaborate soil and plant samples. A particularly sensitive spectrometer was used to examine the radiation level of all the samples. Even though fall-out from Soviet H-bomb tests above the Arctic Circle in Siberia may have masked some radiation, the scientists found that "in the center of the catastrophe, radioactivity is one and a half to two times higher than along the 30 or 40 kilometers away from the center." As for the plants, it was true that the outer rings did show signs of radiation from later fallout, but within the inner rings, particularly in those surrounding the area of 1908, radioactive cesium 137 was found in quantities far above normal.

As the Tungus had reported, "the fire came by" in 1908. There could now be no doubt that this fire was atomic.

How big was this fire? Though the destructive power of the Hiroshima blast was awesome, the force of the Siberian explosion was far greater. In the Japanese city, wood was ignited by the blast at a distance of one mile, on the Tunguska plateau at a distance of 8 to 10 miles from the fall point. The destroyed area in Hiroshima totaled 18 square miles, that on the Tunguska 1,200 square miles. Japanese naval students felt a hot breeze from the Hiroshima blast 60 miles away, while 375 miles from the Tunguska blast, in Kansk—six times as far—a hurricanelike gust of air was experienced.

The atomic blast on the Tunguska was, at the very least, ten times more powerful than that at Hiroshima. But when one takes into account the greater altitude of the Siberian blast and the much larger total area of forest destruction, the possibility exists of an explosion a hundred times more massive—in the megaton range.

CHAPTER 9

ANTIMATTER OR BLACK HOLE?

The overwhelming evidence of an atomic explosion in Siberia in 1908 prompted some scientists to look to rarefied areas of theoretical physics and astronomy for a natural explanation. If such an explosion could not be accounted for by any ordinary cosmic object, they asked, then could a previously unknown, extremely dangerous form of extraterrestrial matter have penetrated our atmosphere, producing a detonation equal to 10^{23} ergs of nuclear energy and yet leaving no physical trace of itself? "It is clear that the Tungus cosmic body . . . could not have been a comet," wrote the geophysicist A. V. Zolotov, speaking for many of his fellow Soviet scientists. "Neither could it have been a normal ice, stone, or iron meteorite. The Tungus body obviously represents a new yet unknown, much more complicated phenomenon of nature than has been encountered up to this time."

Could the great blast have been caused, for instance, by a small body of antimatter? Or perhaps a so-called "black hole" was responsible for the massive destruction of the taiga? Modern theoreticians examined both these newly conjectured cosmic phenomena as possible solutions to the Siberian riddle.

Even before the first experiments partially confirming the existence of antimatter had been conducted with the powerful atom-smashing accelerators at Berkeley and other scientific institutes, its presence in space had been surmised in the 1930s by Nobel prize-winning physicist P. A. M. Dirac, and later imagined by science fiction writers. The premise of antimatter is simple and logical. Why, physicists ask, should there not be floating in free space atoms in which the electrical charges of the particles are reversed—atoms in which positively charged particles (positrons) revolve around a negatively charged nucleus, rather than negative particles revolving around a positive nucleus, as in normal terrene atoms? If a fragment of antimatter came into contact with a terrene object, both would be instantly and totally annihilated.

In the view of some physicists and astonomers, antimatter might offer a natural explanation for scores of inexplicable phenomena.

In deserts around the world, for example, large pieces of fused greenish-yellow glass have been discovered that are almost identical with those found at meteor fall points. Samples have been collected in Libya, Australia, and across central and southern Africa. But no trace has been found of the meteorites that might have created such deposits.

Along the coastal plain of South Carolina, and elsewhere on the eastern seaboard, are found thousands of shallow, egg-shaped depressions known as "Carolina bays." From the air these bays are often quite apparent. "Geomorphologists," the Encyclopaedia Britannica notes, "have discovered no satisfactory explanation for these curious natural features."

To the north in Virginia, at the heart of the Great Dismal Swamp, Lake Drummond lies in a hollow, shallow and egg-shaped, burned out of the peat which forms the swamp. Indians claim a "firebird" created the depression, and scientists have suggested a meteorite as the cause of the burned area, which extends down through the peat to the sandy floor of the lake, but no meteoritic object has been found there.

All these incidents were recorded in technical journals of meteor science as possible results of minute scraps of antimatter striking the earth. A small contraterrene meteor would create an explosion out of all proportion to its size, then vaporize, leaving no trace except possibly the enigmatic craters called Carolina bays or deposits of fused sand in the desert. It might also, some scientists pointed out, provide a plausible explanation for the events on the Stony Tunguska.

Initially put forward in a paper published in the February, 1941, edition of *Contributions of the Society for Research on Meteorites*, one of the most respected international journals of meteor science, the antimatter theory drew wide attention and some disagreement. Lincoln La Paz, author of the paper, then in the Department of Mathematics of Ohio State University and later a leading meteorite expert at various American universities as well as cotranslator into English of many papers by Leonid Kulik on the Tunguska phenomena, had anticipated the most common objection to the theory—that antimatter would explode on its first contact with the earth's atmosphere. Quoting physicist V. Rojansky's calculations, La Paz wrote that "an approximately cylindrical, contraterrene iron meteorite, falling with its axis vertical, will survive transit through the atmosphere . . . . If a contraterrene iron meteorite of a size comparable to those of the largest irons conjectured to have fallen should strike the earth, an extremely powerful explosion would result, since, in addition to the large store of heat energy resulting from the transformation of the kinetic energy of motion of the meteoric mass, a vast amount of energy would be liberated by its annihilation."

One result of this explosion would be the increase of radioactive carbon in the atmosphere. Estimating that the carbon-14 yield produced by the annihilation of even a small antirock might be comparable to the amount released in the atmosphere by later nuclear bomb tests, Willard Libby (the American chemist who had developed the carbon-14 dating technique) and the other scientists measured deposits in American tree rings and found that the amount of radiocarbon increased after 1908, though they admitted that there were "uncertainties" in such proof. But most Soviet scientists rejected the antimatter concept, arguing that contraterrene meteorites, even if they existed, could not explain the actual physical effects of the Tunguska blast.

The 1969 U. S. sponsored committee report on unidentified flying objects, prepared under the direction of the physicist Edward U. Condon, examined the theory and pointed out that an antimatter explosion "has measurable consequences. When matter and antimatter come into contact, they annihilate each other, and produce gamma rays, kaons, and pions. If an antimatter meteoroid were to collide with the atmosphere, negative pions would be produced. The nuclei of the surrounding air atoms would absorb the negative pions and release neutrons. Nitrogen nuclei would capture the neutrons and be turned into radioactive carbon 14. As carbon dioxide, the radiocarbon would be dispersed throughout the atmosphere and be absorbed by living organisms."

The same report continued, "The energy of the Tunguska bolide was estimated from a study of the destruction that occurred. The initial quantity of antimatter and the amount of radioactive carbon dioxide produced was then estimated. Sections of trees which grew in 1908 were analyzed for radiocarbon. The conclusion of several scientists is that the Tunguska meteor was probably not composed of antimatter."

But to other scientists in the West, largely unfamiliar with the vast amount of data accumulated by later Soviet researchers, antimatter provided one of the few adequate explanations of the Tunguska explosions. This theory, however, was soon rivaled by another even more bizarre suggestion—that the explosion was the result of a collision between the earth and a "black hole."

As early as 1939 J. Robert Oppenheimer, a leading figure in the Manhattan Project that constructed the first atomic bomb, had speculated about other states of matter created by the pressures and temperatures of a collapsing star.

Most average stars, including those the size of the sun, eventually fade, gutter, and die like a bonfire, the outer layers collapsing on the dying core until it becomes a dense, spinning ball of neutrons. Was the same true of enormous stars, many times the size of our sun, scattered through the universe? Oppenheimer believed that these larger stars would collapse in an entirely different and terrifying way. As the outer layers fell inwards, the whole sun would become so dense as to form a new kind of matter, popularly known as a "black hole." Even a speck of this matter might weigh millions of tons.

Such objects would distort the fabric of space, sucking in light rays so greedily that they themselves and even the space around them became invisible; in the presence of another star they would draw in gas and emit floods of hard radiation. One estimate in the 1970s placed the number of black holes in the universe as high as a billion, ranging from some larger than our sun to other black holes with diameters no larger than that of a dust speck.

As New York *Times* science editor Walter Sullivan has noted, "Nothing in the art of the medieval alchemist or the contemporary science-fiction writer is more bizarre than the concept of the black hole." In a re cent article he examined the notion that "a tiny 'black hole' hit Siberia, passing through the entire earth and emerging in the North Atlantic." This idea was proposed in 1973 by A. A. Jackson and Michael P. Ryan, scientists at the University of Texas, to explain the blast in the Tunguska region. If such compressed "mini" black holes exist, one might have struck the earth, creating an effect akin to a nuclear explosion, then passing through the planet like a bullet until it exited on the other side and continued its rampage through the universe.

Soviet experts on the Tunguska event examined these new theories, but ultimately rejected them on the basis that they did not match the actual evidence. The enormous body of eyewitness testimony, supplemented by the findings of various expeditions, eliminate the possibility either of a black hole or a contraterrene particle.

Neither the antimatter nor the black hole thesis could account for the slowly descending tube-shaped object streaming a fiery trail, the barrage of widely spaced explosions, the oddly shaped pattern of leveled trees, the sudden growth of vegetation after the blast, the clear evidence of an explosion above the taiga rather than on its surface, or the scores of other inconsistencies which had earlier discredited the meteorite and comet theories.

CHAPTER 10

THE CYLINDRICAL OBJECT

Is it possible that the flaming "cylindrical" object that exploded in mid-air over central Siberia in 1908 was, in fact, a spacecraft?

As the debate over the multimegaton blast continued through the sixties and into the seventies, an increasing number of authorities came to the opinion that the answer inevitably must be "yes"—partly because all natural explanations of the "cosmic body" seemed to wither under rigorous analysis but also because, as mankind entered the age of space technology, the idea began to appear more feasible. The belief that the object was artificial, moreover, gained new credence from findings based on the peculiar shape of the explosion and a study of particles found at the blast site, as well as some surprising recent calculations by aerodynamics experts about the flight path through the atmosphere.

The strangely irregular boundaries of the blast region had already been noted by E. L. Krinov during the third Tunguska expedition of 1929. "The area of uprooted forest," he observed, "has an oval form with the major axis situated in a direction from southeast toward northwest." The 1938 aerial photographs further verified this oval pattern; and K. P. Florensky's expeditions in 1958, 1961, and 1962 determined from extensive ground and air surveys that the 1,200 square miles of forest leveled by the explosion and the scattering of "cosmic dust" from the blast had a definite elliptical contour.

Following his expeditions in 1959 and 1960, in which he re-examined all of the physical evidence in the Tunguska region, A. V. Zolotov came up with an explanation that many other experts found acceptable: the blast had an unusual oval shape because the explosive material was encased in some type of "container." The structure of this container, like the thick paper cylinder of a large firecracker, caused the explosive charge to fan out elliptically as it burst. The Tunguska object, Zigel commented, "consisted of at least two parts: a substance capable of nuclear explosion and a nonexplosive shell."

But is there any concrete proof of such a nonexplosive container? Some analysts believed that at least partial proof had already been acquired by Kulik—in the soil samples brought back by his expeditions. In the late fifties, when these specimens were subjected to extreme magnification and careful laboratory testing, small particles of extraterrestrial matter were discovered. The Tunguska soil contained concentrations of spherical globules, a few millimeters or less in size, composed primarily of silicate and magnetite, a magnetized iron oxide.

If the spheres were not of terrestrial origin, were they simply the usual micrometeorite dust that falls daily across the entire surface of the planet or could they be fragments of the Tunguska object? In 1962 Florensky attempted to resolve these questions. Using a helicopter, his team charted the pattern of the explosion's scattering ellipse over a large area and then collected a wide range of samples for chemical analysis. As they had expected, thousands of "tiny brilliant spheres," many fused together, were found imbedded like pellets in the earth and trees. The pattern of their distribution, moreover, conformed to the elliptical blast wave.

Florensky, still defending the obsolete comet theory, maintained that they were molten cometary debris; but Zolotov and many others were certain that the fused particles could not possibly have come from any known comet or meteoritic body. This notion was strengthened when more detailed analysis of the spheres revealed small amounts of cobalt and nickel, as well as traces of copper and germanium. Kazantsev and those supporting his views argued that the discovery of these metallic elements offered further proof of an artificial craft. "Remember that the ship must have had electrical and technical instruments," Kazantsev elaborated, "also copper wires, and surely means of communication—semiconductors containing germanium." The exact source of the strange globules, however, has not been fully determined. It is possible to surmise, with a strong degree of probability, that they may indeed be the only existing remnants of the cylindrical object—the "nonexplosive shell" that housed the atomic fire.

Soon Felix Zigel and several other aerodynamics authorities, experienced in modern rocket technology and upper atmospheric trajectories, came forward with some astonishing assertions that ultimately tipped the scales in favor of a spacecraft. When A. Y. Manotskov, an airplane designer, mapped the passage of the Tunguska object through the air, his calculations agreed with Zolotov's findings that the object must have arrived at a velocity much slower than that of a natural cosmic body. Manotskov decided that the 1908 object had a far slower entry speed than meteorites and that, nearing the earth, it reduced its speed less than half a mile per second, which is comparable to the velocity of a high-altitude reconnaissance plane. A Soviet rocket specialist examined these estimates and concurred that the object had behaved in its entry and velocity like a supersonic craft.

What flight path did this craft follow through the earth's atmosphere? Did the object arrive from the southeast or the southwest? At first the problem appeared impossible to resolve, for eyewitness testimony and forest damage could be produced to support either direction. The object had been visible overhead as a "fiery body" to villages near Kansk, southwest of the blast, but it had also been seen in Kirensk and other towns lying to the southeast. Scores of separate, reliable observations made both flight paths seem equally feasible, though obviously the same object could not have appeared almost simultaneously in two different locations hundreds of miles apart.

Or could it? The problem of the different trajectories was eventually solved with a startling answer: *both* paths were accurate. The object had switched direction in its journey over Siberia!

The information acquired by the Florensky and Zolotov expeditions about the ballistic shock effect on the trees provides a strong basis, in some scientists' view, for an alteration of the object's line of flight. In the terminal phase of its descent, according to the most recent speculations, the object appears to have approached on an eastward course, then changed course westward over the region before exploding. The ballistic wave evidence, in fact, indicates that some type of flight correction was performed in the atmosphere.

The same opinion was reached by Felix Zigel, who as an aerodynamics professor at the Moscow Institute of Aviation has been involved in the training of many Soviet cosmonauts. His latest study of all the eyewitness and physical data convinced him that "before the blast the Tunguska body carried out a maneuver." No natural object is capable of such a feat. Thus Zigel, together with Soviet rocket and aviation experts, joined Kazantsev in believing that the remarkable cylindrical object causing an el-liptically shaped atomic blast in 1908 could only have been "an artificial flying craft from some other planet."

CHAPTER 11

A COSMIC VISITOR

The Siberian superblast is approaching its seventieth anniversary. The scientist who first explored the immense destruction site but could not elucidate it, Leonid Kulik, has been dead for more than three dec-ades; and most of the next generation of investigators who tried to make sense of the cataclysmic event are well into middle age or beyond. Alek-sander Kazantsev, first to suggest that the Tunguska object was an inter-planetary vehicle, lives in an apartment in Russia's capital. Not far from Kazantsev's home, a new generation of ambitious young researchers at Moscow University and the Academy of Sciences study the different theories about the event and sift through the factual evidence, hunting for the sure proof, the ultimate clue to the riddle that confounded their predecessors.

Despite all attempts to label the 1908 intruder from the cosmos with an indisputable identity, it remains after nearly seventy years one of the most intriguing mysteries of modern science. In 1960 Albert Parry, an expert on Russian technology, commented: "Looking for incontrovertible proof that the messenger from the sky of 1908 was a spaceship and not a mere chunk of stone and metal is fast becoming a favorite sport for many ad-venturous souls in Soviet Russia. Newer and newer expeditions are going into the Tungus wilds to try for replies to baffling points now raised not only by Kazantsev but also by Zigel and his other supporters rallying to his romantic cause."

But now, in the second decade of the space age, it is no longer regarded as merely "romantic" to seek proof of the explosion of an extraterrestrial vehicle over Siberia. Scientific attitudes toward the possibility of intelli-gent life existing on other planets have radically changed in the past ten years. "Should this [the spacecraft theory] be finally confirmed by inves-tigations now in progress," Zigel remarked, "the significance of the Tun-guska disaster would be inestimable." Many experts today concur with this opinion and feel that it is not based on a whimsical hope.

Yet it is not likely that positive confirmation will result from new expeditions to Siberia. Although specialists from the Soviet Union and many other nations undoubtedly will continue to travel to the blast region to examine the scorched and broken trees—despite the passage of years, the original physical appearance of the shattered taiga has to a surprising extent been preserved, thanks to the subarctic climate—it is doubtful whether any revelations of great consequence about the impact site will be announced in the future. By now the facts are in: all existing evidence of the June 30, 1908, phenomenon has been photographed, measured, and analyzed—if not explained.

The present situation therefore is that the nature of the explosion is understood but not the cause. Although the case is far from officially closed, the majority of investigators agree that the total weight of the evidence leads inescapably to the conclusion that the holocaust released over Siberia was a high-altitude nuclear explosion of approximately 30 megaton yield. Yet the mystery of the event is not erased or even diminished by such knowledge—instead, it is deepened. There remains the question, difficult and so far unanswerable by any known natural cause: how could an atomic blast occur in an age when mankind had only a limited grasp of nuclear physics and absolutely no atomic bomb capability?

An essential item of evidence necessary to the final determination of the cause is missing—possibly annihilated by the very atomic conflagration it may have caused. Scientists confronting the Tunguska mystery are faced with a tricky situation similar to that of detectives trying to solve a baffling crime in which the murder weapon is irretrievably lost.

But if the circumstantial evidence surrounding the case is sufficiently strong and detailed, the missing element of the puzzle may sometimes be deduced or inferred and the facts reconstructed from the shape of the remaining pieces. In attempting to deduce the identity of the enigmatic object of 1908, analysts must cope with unique, unprecedented evidence that is often startling and ambiguous. The most recent hypotheses—such as those regarding a contraterrene particle or a tiny black hole—take us to the outermost edge of our present knowledge of the cosmos into highly speculative, untested areas of astronomy and astrophysics where belief requires a leap of imagination or faith.

But all cosmic exploration, actual and theoretical, depends upon such leaps or imaginative journeys beyond the limits of the known. Exploding galaxies, pulsars, and quasi-stellar radio sources (quasars)—to name only a few discoveries of recent astrophysics—are all elements in a gradually unfolding picture of the complex universe that we inhabit. Without fully understanding or being able totally to prove these phenomena, modern astronomers nonetheless are using them to construct a new model or scheme of our universe.

The Siberian riddle, which has perplexed our technology for more than half a century, may yield its meaning when we are able to fit it into an imaginative scheme, an amplified cosmological perspective that allows us to transcend the existing analysis of facts. This cosmology will have to be logical and coherent, responsive to observable facts yet always looking beyond them and finally enabling us to understand them. Kazantsev was the first interpreter of the Siberian disaster to see the problem in these terms; based on his observations at Hiroshima and his ideas about space travel, he formulated an abstract cosmological context to account for evidence that appeared inexplicable. His speculations led to an overthrow of the existing attitude toward the event and to the eventual discovery of fresh facts that had always been here but which had not been seen until his theory made them visible.

But even Kazantsev had not been prepared to see far enough. Although he was proved to be correct about the atomic nature of the explosion and his spacecraft theory is now regarded by many as a possibility that cannot be lightly dismissed, his cosmology was definitely too narrow and restricted to explain the possible origin of the Tunguska object. His picture of our solar system has been outmoded by the revelations of our space technology, particularly by NASA and Soviet probes to our closest planets Mars and Venus. As intelligent beings, we seem to be alone in our solar system.

In 1973 one of NASA's probes, Pioneer 10, after sending back photographs of Jupiter, headed out of the solar system bearing an aluminum plaque with an engraved message designed for extraterrestrials. The probability of the existence of some form of higher extraterrestrial beings drastically increases if we look past our planetary system which circles an insignificant star on the corner of a vast galaxy containing an estimated one hundred billion stars of all shapes, sizes, and ages. Within our Milky Way galaxy there may be as many as a billion stable suns with their own planetary systems, a million of which may contain warm habitable planets with environments similar to the earth's. Surrounding our galaxy, a relatively modest cluster of stars, are billions of other galactic systems, new and old, thriving and expiring, stretching beyond our present powers of detection. This complex, interrelated metagalactic system, according to some theoretical astronomers and cosmologists, may be only one of billions of other metagalaxies in a universe extending or continuously evolving into infinity.

Can mankind be the sole creatures possessing the faculty of intelligence and the capabilities of a sophisticated technology in all of metagalactic space? Only a few decades ago, when Kazantsev proposed his theory of extraterrestrial visitors, this question was generally regarded as too fanciful for serious scientific investigation. The issue seemed a subject fit only for speculative writers. Today, after American and U.S.S.R. space probes have visited planets in our solar system and radio astronomy has radically reshaped our traditional concepts of the cosmos, there has been a revolutionary change of attitude among many scientists on the possibility of a higher extraterrestrial life existing in other solar systems.

A landmark study of the subject, *Intelligent Life in the Universe*, by the Soviet astrophysicist I. S. Shklovskii of the Sternberg Astronomical Institue in Moscow and the American exobiologist and astronomer Carl Sagan of Cornell University, authoritatively outlined the current state of scientific knowledge of the biological origins of living organisms on a planet such as the earth and convincingly demonstrated the possibility that the conditions necessary for the evolution of higher life forms may be present on countless planets scattered throughout the cosmos. While stressing the speculative nature of some of their ideas, the authors estimate that in the future not only interstellar communication but flight eventually will be achieved.

Yet Sagan, Shklovskii, and most other reputable scientists involved in this experimental search emphasize that what is meant by "extraterrestrial life" is most certainly not the incredibly humanoid "ancient astronauts" conjectured largely from Latin-American artifacts and legends by Erich von Däniken and other writers following his fallacious but popular reasoning in *Chariots of the Gods?* (1970); nor are real extraterrestrials likely to resemble the benevolent blond Venusians or little green Martians claimed to have been sighted by some UFO contactees. These fantasies about alien life reflect an unimaginative, egotistically anthropocentric cosmology in which all living creatures in the universe are merely duplications of us, mirrors of our features and fears.

A more rational, less self-centered cosmological viewpoint, rooted in scientific logic, will admit that extraterrestrials, if they exist, are not likely in any way biologically to resemble what we know on our small planet. "Life, even cellular life, may exist out yonder in the dark," comments naturalist Loren Eisely in his book *The Immense Journey*. "But high or low in nature, it will not wear the shape of man. That shape is the evolutionary product of a strange, long wandering through the attics of the forest roof, and so great are the chances of failure, that nothing precisely and identically human is likely ever to come that way again."

In our universe nothing is fixed or immutable. On a scale of time and space vastly greater than ours, gigantic spiral and elliptical galaxies wheel, burst, and cool in the midst of a cosmos characterized not by stillness and stability but by turbulent events and energetic change. Stars pulsate, flourish, and collapse; bathed in their energy, circling planetary worlds pursue their own peculiar, random destinies, while whatever creatures that happen to be living on their surfaces adopt their own unique evolutionary modes of survival.

Within this considerably expanded cosmological perspective, we can let our imaginations outrun direct observations while staying firmly rooted in current scientific knowledge. We have already accomplished the previously unimaginable—begun the exploration of our solar system. Our probe, Pioneer 10, is now moving beyond our solar system into interstellar space. Is it fanciful or unreasonable, then, to accept that on some distant planet a civilization may be engaged in similar experimental voyages of discovery, launching their own probes and spacecraft? Once we admit this possiblilty—accepted by many contemporary scientists—we can then picture the missing element in the puzzling explosion of 1908.

We can extend our imaginations far out into space and construct an image of the mysterious missile that blew up over the Siberian woods. The image will be necessarily speculative, for no absolute proof exists; yet it will be true to scientific plausibility and to the newly enlarged cosmological view. Let us look at the event with the perspective of almost seventy years of technological progress, weighing again the evidence and ordering it in a way that provides a credible—perhaps the most credible—explanation of one of the greatest explosions our world has ever known.

It is the morning of June 30, 1908.

High above the Indian Ocean, a huge object hurtling from space pierces the earth's atmospheric shell. In the almost airless upper altitudes, there is no sound, barely any friction; unimpeded, it races toward the planet.

The object is an extraterrestrial vehicle; its hull is cylindrical, its mass thousands of tons. Propelled by nuclear fire, the giant craft has come from the depths of interstellar space at a velocity close to the speed of light, then decelerated before orbiting into our planetary system.

Now, rocketing toward the earth, the vehicle is in a state of emergency. Within its propulsion chambers, a malfunction had occurred; the temperature is rapidly rising in the fuel core. Barriers that prevent critical mass, the density necessary for a lethal chain reaction, are overheating and melting.

Eighty miles above the surface, the craft's navigational system steers toward a narrow entry corridor—the same atmospheric passage that many decades later lunar flights from earth will hit for safe re-entry. The entry must be precise, to avoid burning up in the thicker atmosphere or ricocheting back out into the void.

Plunging through the corridor, the craft reduces its velocity. In seconds, as its protective shield strikes the denser air layers, frictional heat rises to 5,000 degrees Fahrenheit, forming a fiery cone of ionized molecules more dazzling than the sun. Within the flaming sheath, the spacecraft glows like a brilliant fireball.

Half of the rotating globe below is in darkness; the sky arching over the other half is cloudless and clear as a glass dome. In a long, sloping trajectory, the craft soars beyond the ocean basin across jagged mountain ridges, steep valleys, vast undulating plains. It navigates directly along a meridian toward the planet's northern horizon, the arctic regions.

A shock wave of highly compressed air is thrust far ahead of the vehicle. The heat shield disintegrates, streaming an incandescent trail of molten particles. Above the northern hemisphere, sensitive optical instruments in the craft register signs of life on the surface.

In central Siberia a deafening roar terrifies the inhabitants of small towns and villages, the only settlements in this remote and deserted area. A powerful ballistic wave pushed before the descending craft strikes the ground. Trees are leveled, nomad huts blown down, men and animals scattered like specks of dust.

At an altitude of 2 miles, the inhabitants of the luminous spacecraft make a course correction, steering westward over the empty wooded terrain of the Central Siberian Plateau.

The maneuver is their last act.

The barriers separating the fuel cells have melted. The nuclear material reaches a density that is supercritical, and in an instant a chain reaction is triggered.

A fraction of a second later, the spacecraft and its occupants are vaporized in a blinding flash of light.

A towering primordial fire, hotter than the interior of a star, splits the sky in two and sears the landscape below for more than 30 miles.

Then the great fire is gone, leaving behind only a massive column of black clouds that will remain for days in the atmosphere and a scarred, shattered taiga that will forever hide its secret.

MY LIFE

A condensation of the book by

GOLDA MEIR

CHAPTER 1

MY CHILDHOOD

In a way, I suppose that the little I recall of my early childhood in Russia, my first eight years, sums up my beginnings, what now are called the formative years. If so, it is sad that I have very few happy or even pleasant memories of this time. The isolated episodes that have stayed with me throughout the past seventy years have to do mostly with the terrible hardships my family suffered, with poverty, cold, hunger and fear, and I suppose my recollection of being frightened is the clearest of all my memories. I must have been very young, maybe only three and a half or four. We lived then on the first floor of a small house in Kiev, and I can still recall distinctly hearing about a pogrom that was to descend on us. I didn't know then, of course, what a pogrom was, but I knew it had something to do with being Jewish and with the rabble that used to surge through town, brandishing knives and huge sticks, screaming "Christ killers" as they looked for the Jews, and who were now going to do terrible things to me and to my family.

I can remember how I stood on the stairs that led to the second floor, where another Jewish family lived, holding hands with their little daughter and watching our fathers trying to barricade the entrance with boards of wood. That pogrom never materialized, but to this day I remember how scared I was and how angry that all my father could do to protect me was to nail a few planks together while we waited for the hooligans to come. And, above all, I remember being aware that this was happening to me because I was Jewish, which made me different from most of the other children in the yard. It was a feeling that I was to know again many times during my life—the fear, the frustration, the consciousness of being

261

different and the profound instinctive belief that if one wanted to survive, one had to take effective action about it personally.

Also, I remember all too clearly how poor we were. There was never enough of anything, not food, not warm clothing, not heat at home. I was always a little too cold outside and a little too empty inside. Even now, from that very distant past, I can summon up with no effort at all, almost intact, the picture of myself sitting in tears in the kitchen, watching my mother feed some of the gruel that rightfully belonged to me to my younger sister, Zipke. Gruel was a great luxury in our home in those days, and I bitterly resented having to share any of it, even with the baby. Years later I was to experience the dread of my own children's hunger and to learn for myself what it is like to have to decide which child is to receive more food, but, of course, in that kitchen in Kiev, I knew only that life was hard and that there was no justice anywhere. I am glad that no one told me then that my older sister, Sheyna, often fainted from hunger in school.

My parents were newcomers in Kiev. They had met and married in Pinsk, where my mother's family lived, and it was to Pinsk that we all returned within a few years—in 1903, when I was five. My mother was very proud of her romance with my father and told us about it often, but although I came to know the story by heart, I never tired of hearing it. My parents had married very unconventionally, without the benefit of a *shadchan,* the traditional matchmaker.

I don't know exactly how it happened that my father, who was born in the Ukraine, had to report for military duty in Pinsk, but it was there that my mother once saw him in the street. He was a tall, handsome young man, with whom she instantly fell in love and about whom she even dared to tell her parents. A matchmaker was called in eventually, but only for what might be termed the technical arrangements. What was even more impressive—in her and our eyes—was the fact that she managed to persuade her parents that love at first sight was enough, even though my father, who had been orphaned of his father, had no money at all and his family could claim very little distinction. There was one saving fact, however. He was not an ignoramus. In his very early teens, he had studied for a while in a yeshiva, a Jewish religious seminary, and he knew the Torah. My grandfather duly took this fact into account, although I have always suspected that he was also influenced by the fact that my mother had never been known to change her mind about anything substantive.

My parents were very different from each other: my father, Moshe Yitzhak Mabovitch, was a slender, delicately featured, fundamentally optimistic man, much given to believing in people—unless and until proved wrong—a trait that, on the whole, was to make his life a failure in wordly terms. In short, he was what you might call an innocent, the kind of man who would probably have been more successful if circumstances had ever been just slightly easier. Blume, my copper-haired mother, was pretty, energetic, bright and far more sophisticated and enterprising than my father, but, like him, a born optimist and very sociable. Despite everything, on Friday nights our house was always full of people, members of the family mostly. I remember swarms of cousins, second cousins, aunts and uncles. None of them was to survive the Holocaust, but they live on in my mind's eye, sitting around our kitchen table, drinking tea out of glasses and, on the Sabbath and holidays, singing for hours—and I remember my parents' sweet voices ringing out above the others.

It was not a particularly religious household. My parents, of course, observed Jewish tradition. They kept a kosher kitchen and celebrated all the Jewish holidays and festivals. But religion as such—to the extent that it can be separated from tradition for Jews—played very little role in our lives. I can't remember as a child ever having thought very much about God or praying to a personal deity, although when I was older—we were already in America—I sometimes argued about religion with my mother. I remember that once she wanted to prove to me that God existed. She said, "Why does it rain or snow, for instance?" So I explained what I had learned in school about rain, and then she said to me, *"Nu, Goldele, du bist aza chachome, mach du zol gein a reigen!"* (So, Goldele, if you're so clever, *you* make it rain!) Since no one had heard of cloud seeding in those days, I couldn't think of an answer. As for the Jews being a chosen people, I never quite accepted that. It seemed, and still seems to me, more reasonable to believe, not that God chose the Jews, but that the Jews were the first people that chose God, the first people in history to have done something truly revolutionary, and it was this choice that made them unique.

At any rate, we lived in this—as in other respects—in the way most Jews lived in the towns and villages of Eastern Europe. We went to *shul* (synagogue) on festivals and fast days, we blessed the Sabbath, and we kept two calendars: one Russian, the other relating to that far-off land from which we had been exiled 2,000 years before and whose seasons and ancient customs we still marked in Kiev and Pinsk.

My parents had moved to Kiev when Sheyna (who was nine years my senior) was still very small. My father wanted to better his situation, and although Kiev was beyond the Pale of Settlement and in that part of

Russia in which Jews were normally forbidden to live, he was an artisan, and as such, if he could prove that he was a skilled carpenter by passing the necessary examination, he might receive the precious permit to move to Kiev. So he made a perfect chess table, passed the test, and we packed our bags and left Pinsk, filled with hope. In Kiev Father found work for the government, making furniture for school libraries, and even got an advance. With this money, plus money my parents borrowed, he built a little carpentry shop of his own, and it seemed as though all would be well. But in the end the job fell through. Perhaps, as he said, it was because he was Jewish, and Kiev was noted for its anti-Semitism. At all events, very soon there was no job, no money and debts that had to be paid somehow. It was a crisis that was to recur throughout my childhood.

My father began desperately to look for work everywhere; he would be out all day and much of the night, and when he came home in the bitter dark of the Russian winter, there was rarely enough food in the house to make him a meal. Bread and salt herring had to do.

But my mother had other troubles. Four little boys and a girl all fell ill: two of them died before they were a year old, two of them went within one month. My mother mourned each one of her babies with a broken heart, but like most Jewish mothers of that generation, she accepted the will of God and drew no conclusions about child rearing from the row of little graves. Then, right after the last of the babies had died, a well-to-do family who lived near us offered my mother a job as wet nurse to their new baby. They made one condition: my parents and Sheyna were to move from their miserable, damp little room to a larger, lighter, airier one, and a nurse was to come teach my poor young mother the rudiments of child care, so it was thanks to this "foster child" that Sheyna's life improved and that I was born into relative order, cleanliness and health. Our benefactors saw to it that my mother always had enough to eat, and soon my parents had three children, Sheyna, Zipke and me.

In 1903, when I was about five, we went back to Pinsk. Father, never one to give up, had a new dream now. Never mind the failure of Kiev, he said. He would go to America, to the *goldene medina*—the "land of gold," as the Jews called it—and make his fortune there. Mother, Sheyna, Zipke (the new daughter) and I would wait for him in Pinsk. So he gathered up his few belongings again and left for the unknown continent, and we moved to my grandparents' house.

I don't know to what extent any of my grandparents influenced me, although in Pinsk I lived with my mother's parents for a long time. Certainly it is hard for me to believe that my father's father played any role at all in my life, since he died before my parents met. But somehow or other he became one of the personalities that people my childhood, and now, going back into the past, I feel he belongs to this story. He had been one of the thousands of "kidnapped" Jewish children of Russia, *shanghaied* into the czar's army to serve for twenty-five years. Ill-clothed, ill-fed, terrified children, more often than not they were under constant pressure to convert to Christianity. My Mabovitch grandfather had been snatched by the army when he was all of thirteen, the son of a highly religious family, brought up to observe the finest points of Orthodox Jewish tradition. He served in the Russian army for another thirteen years, and never once, despite threats, derision and often punishment, did he touch *treife* (non-kosher) food. All those years he kept himself alive on uncooked vegetables and bread. Though pressed hard to change his religion and often made to pay for his refusal by being forced to kneel for hours on a stone floor, he never gave in. When he was released and came back home, he was nonetheless haunted by the fear that inadvertently he might somehow have broken the Law. So to atone for the sin he may have committed, he slept for years on a bench in an unheated synagogue with only a stone at his head for a pillow. Little wonder that he died young.

Grandfather Mabovitch was not my only tenacious—or, to use a more fashionable word applied frequently to me by people who are not great admirers of mine, "intransigent"—relative. There was also my maternal great-grandmother, whom I never knew and for whom I was named. She was known for her will of iron and for her bossiness. No one in the family, so we were told, ever dared take a step without consulting her. For instance, it was my Bobbe Golde who was really responsible for the fact that my parents were allowed to marry each other. When my father came to Grandfather Naiditch to ask for my mother's hand in marriage, my grandfather shook his head unhappily and heaved great sighs at the idea that his darling Blume was to marry a mere carpenter, even if that carpenter could be described as a cabinetmaker. But my great-grandmother came to the rescue at once: "What matters most of all," she said firmly, "is whether or not he is *mensch*. If he is, then a carpenter too can become a merchant one day. . . ." My father was to remain a carpenter all his life, but thanks to Bobbe Golde's ruling, my grandfather gave his blessing to the marriage. Bobbe Golde lived to be ninety-four and one of the stories I remember most distinctly about her is that she always took salt instead of sugar in her tea because, she said, "I want to take the taste of the *Goless* (Diaspora) with me into the other world." Interestingly enough, so my parents told me, we bore a striking resemblance to each other.

265

They are all gone now, of course: they and their children and their children's children: they and their way of life. The *shtetl* of Eastern Europe has gone, too, destroyed in flames, its memory preserved accurately only in the Yiddish literature to which it gave birth and through which it expressed itself. That *shtetl,* reconstructed in novels and films, which has become known today in places my grandparents never even heard of, that gay, heartwarming, charming *shtetl* on whose roofs fiddlers eternally play sentimental music, has almost nothing to do with anything I remember, with the poverty-stricken, wretched little communities in which Jews eked out a living, comforting themselves with the hope that things would somehow be better one day and with their belief that there was a point to their misery.

They were God-fearing and brave people, most of them, but their lives, like my Mabovitch grandfather's, were essentially tragic. And I myself have never felt—not even for a minute—any nostalgia for the past into which I was born, though it deeply colored and affected' my life and my convictions, about the way in which all men, women and children, everywhere and whoever they are, are entitled to spend their lives—productively and free of humiliation—and, even more, about the way in which Jews, in particular, should live. I have often told my own children, and more recently my grandchildren, about life in the *shtetl* as I myself dimly remember it, and there is nothing that makes me happier than the certain knowledge that for them it is only a history lesson. A very important lesson about a very important part of their heritage, but not something with which they can ever really identify themselves because their lives were so totally different from the start.

Anyhow, Father spent three lonely difficult years in America. He had painfully scraped together the money to get there, and like many thousands of the Russian Jews who streamed into the *goldene medina* at the turn of the century, he had thought of America as the one place where he would surely make the fortune that would allow him to return home, to Russia, and to a new life there. Of course, it didn't work out like that—not for him or for the thousands like him—but the idea that he would come back to us made our three years without him easier to bear.

Although the Kiev of my birth is lost to me in the fog of time, I have retained some sort of inner image of Pinsk, perhaps because I have heard and read about it so much. Many of the people I was to meet in later life came originally from Pinsk or from the townlets that clustered around it, including the families of Chaim Weizmann and Moshe Sharett.

The town that I remember was filled with Jews. Pinsk was one of the most celebrated centers of Russian-Jewish life and at one time even had had a Jewish majority. It was built on two great rivers, the Pina and the Pripet—both of which flow into the Dnieper—and it was these rivers that supplied most of the Jews of Pinsk with their livelihoods. They fished, unloaded cargo, did porterage, broke the giant ice floes in winter and dragged the ice to huge storage cellars in the houses of the well-to-do, where they served to create cooling facilities all through the summer. At one time my grandfather, who was fairly well off compared to my parents, owned such a cellar to which neighbors brought their Sabbath and holiday dishes when it was very hot and from which they took ice for the sick. The richer Jews dealt in timber and in the salt trade, and Pinsk even had nail, plywood and match factories that were owned by Jews and, of course, gave employment to dozens of Jewish workers.

But I remember mostly the *Pinsker blotte,* as we called them at home, the swamps that seemed to me then like oceans of mud and that we were taught to avoid like the plague. In my memory those swamps are forever linked to my persistent terror of the Cossacks, to a winter night when I played with other children in a narrow lane near the forbidden *blotte* and then suddenly, as though out of nowhere, or maybe out of the swamps themselves, came the Cossacks on their horses, literally galloping over our crouching, shivering bodies. "Well," said my mother later, shivering and crying herself, "what did I tell you?"

Cossacks and the black, bottomless swamps, however, were not the only terrors Pinsk held for me. I can remember a row of big buildings on a street that led to the river and the monastery that stood opposite the buildings on a hill. In front of it, all day, sat or lay numbers of wild-haired, wild-eyed cripples who prayed aloud and begged for alms. I tried to avoid passing them, and when I had to, I closed my eyes and ran. But if Mother really wanted to frighten me, she knew that all she had to do was mention the beggars and I would abandon all defiance.

Still, not everything could have been so fearful. I was a child, and like all children, I played and sang and made up stories to tell the baby. With Sheyna's help, I learned to read and write and even do a little arithmetic, although I didn't start school in Pinsk, as I should have. "A golden child, they called you," my mother said. "Always busy with something." But what I was really busy doing in Pinsk, I suppose, was learning about life—again, chiefly from Sheyna.

Sheyna was fourteen when Father left for the States, a remarkable, intense, intelligent girl who became, and who remained, one of the great influences of my life—perhaps the greatest, apart from the man I married. By any standard, she was an unusual person, and for me she was a shining example, my dearest friend and my mentor. Even late in life, when we were both grown women, grandmothers, in fact, Sheyna was the one person whose praise and approval—when I won them, which was not easy—meant most to me. Sheyna, in fact, is part of the story of my life. She died in 1972; but I think of her constantly, and her children and grandchildren are as dear to me as my own.

In Pinsk, although we were so pitifully poor and Mother only barely managed (with my grandfather's help) to keep us going, Sheyna refused to go to work. The move back to Pinsk had been very hard on her. She had gone to a wonderful school in Kiev, and she was bent on studying, on acquiring knowledge and getting an education, not only so that she herself would have a fuller and better life, but, even more, so that she could help change and better the world. At fourteen, Sheyna was a revolutionary, an earnest, dedicated member of the Socialist-Zionist movement, and as such doubly dangerous in the eyes of police and liable to punishment. Not only were she and her friends "conspiring" to overthrow the all-powerful czar, but they also proclaimed their dream to bring into existence a Jewish socialist state in Palestine. In the Russia of the early twentieth century, even a fourteen- or fifteen-year-old schoolgirl who held such views would be arrested for subversive activity, and I still remember hearing the screams of young men and women being brutally beaten in the police station around the corner from where we lived.

My mother heard those screams, too, and daily begged Sheyna to have nothing to do with the movement; she could endanger herself and us and even Father in America! But Sheyna was very stubborn. It was not enough for her to want changes; she had to participate in bringing them about. Night after night, my mother kept herself awake until Sheyna came home from her mysterious meetings, while I lay in bed, taking it all in silently: Sheyna's devotion to the cause in which she believed so strongly; Mother's overwhelming anxiety; Father's (to me, inexplicable) absence; and the periodic and fearful sound of the hooves of Cossack horses outside.

On Saturdays, when Mother went off to the synagogue, Sheyna organized meetings at home. Even when Mother found out about them and pleaded with Sheyna not to imperil us, there was nothing she could do about these meetings except nervously walk up and down outside the house when she got back on Saturday morning, patrolling it like a sentry so that when a policeman approached, she could at least warn the young conspirators. But it wasn't only the idea that an ordinary policeman might swoop down at any moment and arrest Sheyna that so worried my poor mother. What really gnawed at her heart throughout all those months was the fear (always rampant in the Russia of those days) that one or another of Sheyna's friends might turn out to be an *agent provocateur.*

Of course, I was much too small to understand what the arguments and tears and door slammings were about, but I used to squeeze myself onto the flat top of our big coal stove (which was built into the wall) and sit there for hours on those Saturday mornings, listening to Sheyna and her friends and trying to make out what it was that they all were so excited about and why it made my mother cry so. Sometimes when I pretended to be engrossed in drawing or in copying the strangely shaped letters in the siddur (the Hebrew prayer book), which was one of the few books in our house, I tried to follow what Sheyna was fervently explaining to my mother, but all I gathered was that she was involved in a special kind of struggle that concerned not only the Russian people, but also, and more especially, the Jews.

A great deal has already been written—and much more will certainly be written in the future—about the Zionist movement, and most people by now have at least some notion of what the word "Zionism" means and that it has to do with the return of the Jewish people to the land of their forefathers—the Land of Israel, as it is called in Hebrew. But perhaps even today not everyone realizes that this remarkable movement sprang up spontaneously, and more or less simultaneously, in various parts of Europe toward the end of the nineteenth century. It was like a drama that was being enacted in different ways on different stages in different languages but that dealt with the same theme everywhere: that the so-called Jewish problem (of course, it was really a Christian problem) was basically the result of Jewish homelessness and that it could not, and would not be solved unless and until the Jews had a land of their own again. Obviously, this land could only be Zion, the land from which the Jews had been exiled 2,000 years before but which had remained the spiritual center of Jewry throughout the centuries and which, when I was a little girl in Pinsk and up to the end of World War I, was a desolate and neglected province of the Ottoman Empire called Palestine.

The first Jews who made the modern return to Zion came there as early as 1878 to found a pioneering village which they named Petach Tikva (the Gate of Hope). By 1882 small groups of Zionists from Russia who called themselves the Hovevei Zion (Lovers of Zion) had arrived in the country determined to reclaim the land, farm it and defend it. But in 1882 Theodor Herzl, who was to be the founder of the World Zionist Organization, was still quite unaware of what was happening to the Jews in Eastern Europe and of the existence of the Hovevei Zion. The successful and sophisticated Paris correspondent of the important Viennese newspaper the *Neue Freie Presse,* Herzl became interested in the fate of the Jews only in 1894, when he was assigned to cover the trial of French army officer Captain Alfred Dreyfus. Shocked by the injustice done to this Jewish officer—and by the open anti-Semitism of the French army—Herzl, too, came to believe that there was only one possible permanent solution to the situation of the Jews. His subsequent achievements and failures—the whole amazing story of his attempt to create a Jewish state—are part of the history learned by all Israeli schoolchidren and should be studied by anyone who wants to understand what Zionism is really all about.

Although my mother and Sheyna knew about Herzl, the first time I can remember hearing his name was when an aunt of mine (who lived in the same house as the Weizmann family and who was therefore often the bearer of important tidings, both good and bad) came in one day, her eyes brimming with tears, to tell my mother that the unthinkable had happened: Herzl was dead. I have never forgotten the stunned silence that greeted her announcement. As for Sheyna, she decided—typically—to wear only black clothes in mourning for Herzl from that afternoon in the summer of 1904 until we reached Milwaukee two long years later.

Although the yearning of the Jews for their own land was not the direct result of pogroms (the idea of the Jewish resettlement of Palestine had been urged by Jews and even some non-Jews long before the word "pogrom" became part of the vocabulary of European Jewry), the Russian pogroms of my childhood gave the idea immediacy, especially when it became clear to the Jews that the Russian government itself was using them as scapegoats in the regime's struggle to put down the revolutionary movement.

Most of the young Jewish revolutionaries in Pinsk, although united in their determination to press for an end to the czarist regime and in their immense enthusiasm for education as a tool with which to liberate Russia's exploited and oppressed masses, were divided at that point into two main groups. There were the members of the Bund (Union), who believed that the solution to the plight of the Jews in Russia and elsewhere would be found when socialism prevailed. Once the economic and social structure of the Jews was changed, said the Bundists, anti-Semitism would totally disappear. In that better, brighter, socialist world, the Jews could still, if they so desired, retain their cultural identity, go on speaking Yiddish, maintain whatever customs and traditions they chose, eat whatever food they wanted to eat. But there would be no reason at all for clinging to the obsolete idea of Jewish nationhood.

The Poalei Zion (Labor Zionists), like Sheyna, saw it all differently. They believed that the so-called Jewish problem had other roots, and its solution therefore had to be more far-reaching and radical than merely the righting of economic wrongs or social inequalities. In addition to the shared social ideal, they clung to a national ideal based on the concept of Jewish peoplehood and the reestablishment of Jewish independence. At the time, although both these movements were secret and illegal, ironically enough the bitterest enemies of Zionism were the Bundists, and most of the debates that whirled about my head whenever Sheyna and her friends got together in our house had to do with the conflict between the two groups.

It was around this time that Sheyna met Shamai Korngold, her husband-to-be, a strong, clever, gifted boy who had given up the great joy of studying and his burning interest in mathematics in order to join the revolutionary movement. A close-to-wordless romance blossomed between them, and Shamai also became and stayed part of my life. He was one of the leaders of the young Zionists, nicknamed Copernicus in the movement. Shamai was the only grandson of a well-known Torah scholar, in whose house he and his parents lived and on whom they were financially dependent. He visited us often, and I can remember his whispered conversations with Sheyna about the increased revolutionary ferment in town and the regiment of Cossacks that were on their way to subdue Pinsk with their flashing swords. It was from these conversations that I gathered that something frightful had happened to the Jews of Kishinev and that in Pinsk the Jews were planning to defend themselves with arms and home-made bombs.

In response to the worsening situation, Sheyna and Shamai did more than merely hold or attend conspiratorial meetings; they did their best to bring other young people into the movement, even, to his horror, the only daughter of our white-bearded *shochet*, the ultra-Orthodox ritual slaughterer from whom we rented the room in which we lived. Eventually, Mother's anxiety for Sheyna and Zipke and me became intolerable, and she began to write frantic letters to my father. It was out of the question, she wrote, for us to stay in Pinsk any longer. We must join him in America.

But like many things in life, this was far easier said than done. My father, who had by now moved from New York to Milwaukee, was barely making a living. He wrote back that he hoped to get a job working on the railway and soon he would have enough money for our tickets. We moved out of the *shochet's* house to a room in a bagel baker's flat. The bagels were baked at night, so the flat was always hot, and the baker gave my mother a job. Then, late in 1905, a letter came from Milwaukee. My father was working, so we could start getting ready to leave.

The preparations for our journey were long and complicated. It was not a simple matter then for a woman and three girls, two of them still very small, to travel all the way from Pinsk to Milwaukee by themselves. For my mother, relief must have been combined with new anxieties, and for Sheyna leaving Russia meant leaving Shamai and everything for which they had worked so hard and risked so much. I can remember only the hustle and bustle of those last weeks in Pinsk, the farewells from the family, the embraces and the tears. Going to America then was almost like going to the moon. Perhaps had my mother or aunts known that one day I would be back in Russia as a representative of a Jewish state—or that, as prime minister of Israel, I would one day welcome to that country hundreds upon hundreds of Russian Jews with embraces and tears—they might have cried less bitterly, although God knows the intervening years were to bring more than tears to the family we left behind.

Not many of the details of our voyage to Milwaukee in 1906 have remained in my memory, and most of what I think I remember is probably made up of stories my mother and Sheyna told to me. What I do recall is that we had to cross the border into Austrian Galicia secretly because, three years earlier, my father had helped a friend reach America by taking that man's wife and daughters with him on his papers and pretending that they were members of his family. So when our turn came to leave, we also had to pretend to be other people. Although we obediently memorized false names and details about our make-believe identities and Sheyna sternly drilled us all until we were letter-perfect—even Zipke—our actual crossing was effected by bribing the police with money mother had somehow managed to raise. In the confusion most of our "luggage" got lost—or perhaps it was stolen. Anyhow, I remember that early one icy spring morning we finally entered Galicia and the shack in which we waited for the train that would take us to the port. We lived in that unheated shack for two days, sleeping on the chilled floor, and I remember that Zipke cried most of the time until the train finally arrived and distracted her. Then we moved on past a series of unremembered stops, first to Vienna and then to Antwerp, where we spent another forty-eight hours in an immigration center, this time waiting for the ship that was to take us to America and to my father.

CHAPTER 2

A POLITICAL ADOLESCENCE

My father met us in Milwaukee, and he seemed changed: beardless, American-looking, in fact a stranger. He hadn't managed to find an apartment for us yet, so we moved, temporarily and not comfortably, into his one room in a house that belonged to a family of recently arrived Polish Jews. Milwaukee—even the small part of it that I saw during those first few days—overwhelmed me: new food, the baffling sounds of an entirely unfamiliar language, the confusion of getting used to a parent I had almost forgotten. It all gave me a feeling of unreality so strong that I can still remember standing in the street and wondering who and where I was.

I suppose that being together with his family again after so long was not easy for my father either. At any rate, even before we really had time to rest up from the journey or get to know him again, he did a most extraordinary thing: refusing to listen to any arguments, on the morning after our arrival, he determinedly marched all of us downtown on a shopping expedition. He was horrified, he said, by our appearance. We looked so dowdy and "Old World," particularly Sheyna in her matronly black dress. He insisted on buying us all new clothes, as though by dressing us differently he could turn us, within twenty-four hours, into three American-looking girls. His first purchase was for Sheyna—a frilly blouse and a straw hat with a broad brim covered in poppies, daisies and cornflowers. "Now you look like a human being," he said. "This is how we dress in America." Sheyna immediately burst into tears of rage and shame. "Maybe that's how you dress in America," she shouted, "but I am certainly not going to dress like that!" She absolutely refused to wear either the hat or the blouse, and I think perhaps that premature excursion downtown marked the start of what were to be years of tension between them.

Not only were their personalities very different, but for three long years Father had been receiving complaining letters from Mother about Sheyna and her selfish behavior, and in his heart of hearts he must have blamed Sheyna for his not having been able to go back to Russia again and the family's having to come to the States. Not that he was unhappy in Milwaukee. On the contrary, by the time we came he was already part of the immigrant life there. He was a member of a synagogue, he had joined a trade union (he was employed, off and on, in the workshops of the Milwaukee railroad), and he had accumulated a number of cronies. In his own eyes, he was on the way to becoming a full-fledged American Jew, and he liked it. The last thing in the world he wanted was a disobedient, sullen daughter who demanded the right to live and dress in Milwaukee as though it were Pinsk, and the argument that first morning in Schuster's Department Store was soon to develop into a far more serious conflict. But I was delighted by my pretty new clothes, by the soda pop and ice cream and by the excitement of being in a real skyscraper, the first five-story building I had ever seen. In general, I thought Milwaukee was wonderful. Everything looked so colorful and fresh, as though it had just been created, and I stood for hours staring at the traffic and the people. The automobile in which my father had fetched us from the train was the first I had ever ridden in, and I was fascinated by what seemed like the endless procession of cars, trolleys and shiny bicycles on the street.

We went for a walk, and I peered, unbelieving, into the interior of the drugstore with its papier-maché fisherman advertising cod-liver oil, the barbershop with its weird chairs and the cigar store with its wooden Indian. I remember enviously watching a little girl of my own age dressed up in her Sunday best, with puffed sleeves and high-button shoes, proudly wheeling a doll that reclined grandly on a pillow of its own, and marveling at the sight of the women in long white skirts and men in white shirts and neckties. It was all completely strange and unlike anything I had seen or known before, and I spent the first days in Milwaukee in a kind of trance.

Very soon we moved to a little apartment of our own on Walnut Street, in the city's poorer Jewish section. Today that part of Milwaukee is inhabited by blacks who are, for the most part, as poor as we were then. But in 1906 the clapboard houses with their pretty porches and steps looked like palaces to me. I even thought that our flat (which had no electricity and no bathroom) was the height of luxury. The apartment had two rooms, a tiny kitchenette, and a long corridor that led to what was its greatest attraction for my mother, though I must say not for anyone else: a vacant shop that she instantly decided to run. My father, whose feelings were undoubtedly hurt by her obvious lack of faith in his ability to support us and who was not about to give up his carpentry, announced at once that she could do whatever she wanted, but that he would have nothing to do with the shop. It became the bane of my life. It began as a dairy store and then developed into a grocery; but it never prospered, and it almost ruined the years I spent in Milwaukee.

Looking back at my mother's decision, I can only marvel at her determination. We hadn't been in Milwaukee for more than a week or two; she didn't know one word of English; she had no inkling at all of which products were likely to sell well; she had never run or even worked in a shop before. Nonetheless, probably because she was so terrified of our being as abjectly poor as we had been in Russia, she took this tremendous responsibility on herself without stopping to think through the consequences. Running the shop meant not only that she had to buy stock on credit (because obviously, we had no surplus cash), but also that she would have to get up at dawn everyday to buy whatever was needed at the market and then drag her purchases back home. Fortunately, the women in the neighborhood rallied around her. Many of them were new immigrants themselves, and their natural reaction was to assist another newcomer. They taught her a few English phrases, how to behave behind the counter, how to work the cash register and scales and to whom she could safely allow credit.

Like my father's ill-fated shopping trip, my mother's hasty decision about the shop was almost certainly part of my parent's reaction to finding themselves in such alien surroundings. Unfortunately, both these precipitous steps were to have a serious effect not only on Sheyna's life, but also on mine, although in very differing degrees. As far as I was concerned, my mother's enforced absence every morning meant that somebody had to mind the store while she was gone. Sheyna, like my father, refused to help out in any way. Her socialist principles, she declared, made it impossible. "I did not come to America to turn into a shopkeeper, into a social parasite," she declared. My parents were very angry with her, but characteristically, she did what her principles dictated: she found herself a job. Before we took it in, Sheyna was in a tailorshop making buttonholes by hand. It was difficult work, which she did badly and she hated, even though she was now entitled to consider herself a real member of the proletariat. After she had earned the grand total of thirty cents for three days' work, my father made her give up the job and help Mother. Still, she managed to get away from the shop whenever she could, and for months I had to stand behind the counter every morning until mother returned from the market. For an eight- or nine-year-old girl, this was not an easy chore.

I started school in a huge, fortresslike building on Fourth Street near Milwaukee's famous Schlitz beer factory, and I loved it. I can't remember how long it took me to learn English (at home, of course, we spoke Yiddish, and luckily, so did almost everyone else on Walnut Street), but I have no recollection of the language ever being a real problem for me, so I must have picked it up quickly. I made friends quickly, too. Two of those early first- or second-grade friends remained friends all my life, and both live in Israel now. One was Regina Hamburger (today Medzini), who lived on our street and who was to leave America when I did; the other was Sarah Feder, who became one of the leaders of Labor Zionism in the United States. Anyhow, coming late to class almost every day was awful, and I used to cry all the way to school. Once a policeman even came to the shop to explain to my mother about truancy. She listened attentively but barely understood anything he said, so I went on being late for school and sometimes never got there at all—an even greater disgrace. My mother—not that she had much alternative—didn't seem to be moved by my bitter resentment of the shop. "We have to live, don't we?" she claimed, and if my father and Sheyna—each for his and her own reasons—would not help, that didn't mean *I* was absolved of the task. "So it will take you a little longer to become a *rebbetzin* (a bluestocking)," she added. I never became a bluestocking, of course, but I learned a lot at that school.

Apart from the shop and being aware of Sheyna's evident misery about having to live at home—and having had to part from Shamai, who was still in Russia and whom she missed terribly—I think back on those five years in Milwaukee with great pleasure. There was so much to see and do and learn that the memory of Pinsk was almost erased. I didn't know or care about it then—or for some time to come—but it occurs to me now that both Wisconsin in general and Milwaukee in particular were blessed by extremely liberal administrations. Milwaukee was a city of immigrants and had a strong socialist tradition, a socialist mayor for many years and America's first socialist congressman, Victor Berger.

Of course, it would have been better if Mother hadn't had to work so hard, if Sheyna had got along with my parents more easily, if we had had just a little more money. But even as it was, even with my secret sorrow about and loathing for the store, those early years in Milwaukee were full and good years for me. But they were less so for Sheyna. Almost everything was going wrong for her: she found it extremely hard to adjust, to learn English, to make friends. She was inexplicably tired, even listless, much of the time, and the constant conflict at home didn't help—particularly my parents' rather clumsy attempts to find her a husband as though Shamai didn't exist. At eighteen, her life had suddenly narrowed itself down to almost nothing.

Then—it seemed like a miracle—she heard about an opening in a big men's clothing factory in Chicago and was taken on there. But for some reason that didn't work out either, and she started work as a seamstress in a smaller factory—a sweatshop really—for women's clothing, where she finally settled down. After a while, however, she was back in Milwaukee with a badly infected finger. Had she been less run-down, it would have undoubtedly healed faster, but as it was, she had to stay at home for several weeks. My parents were triumphant about her return; but I felt very sorry for her, and during those weeks when I helped take care of her, comb her hair and dress her, we grew closer.

One day Sheyna told me that she had received a letter from our aunt in Pinsk about Shamai. He had been arrested but had escaped from jail and was now on his way to New York. Thoughtfully our aunt enclosed his address, and Sheyna wrote to him at once. By the time she heard from him her finger was completely healed, she had found another job, and she was busily planning Shamai's arrival in Milwaukee.

Needless to say, I was delighted that her spirits had lifted at last. Perhaps now that Shamai was coming, Sheyna would always be happy, and perhaps the atmosphere at home would change. I couldn't remember much about Shamai, but I looked forward to his arrival with a heart almost as full as Sheyna's. Unfortunately my parents, especially my mother, greeted the news very differently. "Marry Shamai? But he has no prospects at all," my mother said. "He is a pauper, a greenhorn, a young man with no means and without a future." And—never mind the logic—at the same time he was too good for Sheyna; he came from a well-to-do family which would never give its approval. The match would be a disaster, however one looked at it.

As usual, Sheyna went ahead and did as she thought best. She rented a room for Shamai and summoned him to Milwaukee. He arrived depressed and unsure of himself, but Sheyna was confident that together they could overcome any and all obstacles. Eventually he got a job in a cigarette factory, and they set about learning English at night.

Then Sheyna fell ill, and this time it was serious: the diagnosis was TB. She would have to go to a sanatorium, and it was questionable whether she would ever be allowed to get married. Her entire world caved in. She gave up her job and her room and reluctantly came home again. My parents hid their worry for her under a storm of rebuke and nagging, and I did my childish and not very effective best to cheer up both Sheyna and Shamai and to intervene on their behalf with my mother and father whenever the tension seemed about to explode into a crisis.

Within a few weeks everything had changed: Sheyna left for the Jewish Hospital for Consumptives in Denver, Shamai left for Chicago and began forlornly to look for a job there, and I started saving up my meager lunch money for stamps that I sent to Sheyna so she could write to me. Once or twice I even "borrowed" stamp money from Mother's till; since there was no correspondence at all between Sheyna and my parents, I was her only link with the family—which I thought justified the crime.

I missed Sheyna terribly, but the years without her went by quickly. School absorbed me, and in the little time I had left over from the shop (and helping my mother at home and Zipke—who had now been re-named Clara by Mr. Finn, the school principal—with her lessons) I read and read. Every now and then Regina Hamburger and I got tickets (per-haps through the school) for a play or a movie. Those were very rare treats, and to this day I remember one of them distinctly—seeing *Uncle Tom's Cabin* and suffering through every moment of it with Uncle Tom and Eva. I can still recall jumping to my feet in the theater, literally be-side myself with hatred for Simon Legree. I think it must have been the first thing I ever saw on a stage, and I told my mother and Clara the story over and over again. It had a kind of special reality for all of us.

When I was fourteen, I finished elementary school. My marks were good, and I was chosen to be class valedictorian. The future seemed very bright and clear to me. Obviously I would go on to high school and then, perhaps, even become a teacher, which is what I most wanted to be. I thought—and still think today—that teaching is the noblest and the most satisfying profession of all.

My parents, however—as I ought to have understood but did not—had other plans for me. I think my father would have liked me to be educated, and at my Fourth Street graduation ceremony his eyes were moist. He understood, I believe, what was involved; but in a way his own life had de-feated him, and he was unable to be of much help to me. My mother, as usual and despite her disastrous relationship with Sheyna, knew exactly what I should do. Now that I had finished elementary school, spoke En-glish well and without an accent and had developed into what the neigh-bors said was a *dervaksene shein meydl* (a fine, upstanding girl), I could work in the shop full time and sooner or later—but better sooner—start thinking seriously about getting married, which, she reminded me, was forbidden to women teachers by state law.

If I insisted on acquiring a profession, she said, I could go to secretarial school and learn to become a shorthand typist. At least, I wouldn't re-main an old maid that way. My father nodded his head. "It doesn't pay to be too clever," he warned. "Men don't like smart girls." As Sheyna had done before me, I tried in every way I knew to change my parents' mind. In tears, I explained that nowadays an education was important, even for a married woman, and argued that in any case I had no intention of get-ting married for a long time. Besides, I sobbed, I would rather die than spend my life—or even part of it—hunched over a typewriter.

But neither my arguments nor my tears were of any avail. My parents were convinced that high school, for me at least, was an unwarranted luxury—not only unnecessary, but undesirable. From the distance of Denver, Sheyna (now convalescent and out of the sanatorium) encouraged me in my campaign, and so did Shamai, who had joined her there. As they wrote to me often, sending their letters to Regina's house so my parents wouldn't find out about the correspondence, I knew that Shamai had first washed dishes in the sanatorium and had then been taken on to work in a small dry-cleaning plant that served one of the big Denver hotels. In his spare time he was studying bookkeeping, and most important of all, in the face of repeated warnings from Sheyna's doctor, they were going to be married. "Better we should live less," Shamai had decided, "but live together." It was to be one of the happiest marriages I ever knew, and despite the doctor's grim prediction, it lasted forty-three years and resulted in three children.

My parents were very upset at first, especially my mother. "Another lunatic with grand ideas and not a cent in his pocket," she sniffed. *That* was a husband for Sheyna? That was a man who could support and take care of her? But Shamai not only loved Sheyna, but understood her. He never argued with her. When he was sure that he was right about something, he went ahead and did it, and Sheyna always knew when she was beaten. But when she wanted something and it was really important to her, Shamai never stood in her way. To me, the news of their marriage meant that Sheyna now had what she most needed and wanted—and that I at last had a brother.

In my secret letters to Denver I wrote in detail about the continuing fights over school that were making my life at home almost intolerable and were leading me to decide to become independent as soon as possible. That autumn, the autumn of 1912, I defiantly began my first term at Milwaukee's North Division High School and in the afternoons and on weekends worked at a variety of odd jobs, determined never again to ask my parents for money. But none of this helped; the disputes at home went on and on.

The last straw was my mother's attempt to find me a husband. She didn't want me to get married at once, of course, but she very much wanted to be sure not only that I would get married at what she considered a reasonable age, but that, unlike Sheyna, *I* at least would marry somebody substantial. Not rich—that was out of the question—but at least solid. In actual fact, she was already discreetly negotiating with a Mr. Goodstein, a pleasant, friendly, relatively well-to-do man in his early thirties, whom I knew because he used to come into the store now and then to chat for a while. Mr. Goodstein! But he was an old man! Twice my age! I sent a furious letter to poor Sheyna. The reply came from Denver by return mail. "No, you shouldn't stop school. You are too young to work; you have good chances to become something," Shamai wrote. And with perfect generosity: "My advice is that you should get ready and come to us. We are not rich either, but you will have good chances here to study, and we will do all we can for you." At the bottom of his letter, Sheyna wrote her own warming invitation: "You must come to us immediately." There would be enough of everything for all of us, she assured me. All together, we would manage. "First, you'll have all the opportunities to study; second, you'll have plenty to eat; third, you'll have the necessary clothes that a person ought to have."

I was very touched then by their letter, but reading it today, I am even more moved by the readiness of those two young people, still so far from being established themselves, to take me in and share whatever they had with me. That letter, written from Denver in November, 1912, was a turning point in my life because it was in Denver that my real education began and that I started to grow up. I suppose that if Sheyna and Shamai had not come to my rescue, I would have gone on fighting with my parents, crying at night and still somehow going to high school. I can't imagine that I would have agreed under any circumstances to stop studying and marry the probably much-maligned Mr. Goodstein; but Sheyna and Shamai's offer was like a lifeline, and I grabbed at it.

In the years that have passed since that November, I have also often thought of Sheyna's last letter to me before I joined her in Denver. "The main thing," she wrote, "is never to be excited. Always be calm and act coolly. This way of action will always bring you good results. Be brave."

Getting to Denver was not easy. I couldn't possibly expect my parents to agree to my leaving home and going to live with Sheyna. The only solution was not to tell them anything at all, simply to leave. It might not be the bravest course, but it would certainly be the most efficient. Sheyna and Shamai sent me some money for a railway ticket, and Regina and I planned my flight down to the last detail. The first problem to be solved was how to get together enough money to pay for the rest of my ticket. I borrowed some of it from Sarah, and Regina and I persuaded a number of new immigrants on the street into taking English lessons from us for ten cents an hour. When we had collected enough money, we set about plotting the details of my departure.

Regina was a marvelously devoted ally. What she proposed—and what

I very gladly accepted—was that since we lived above the store then, I should make a bundle of my clothes (just as well that it wouldn't be a very large bundle) and lower it in the evening before my departure to Regina, who would spirit it away to the railway station. Then, in the morning, instead of going to school, I could go right to the train.

When the fateful evening arrived, I sat in the kitchen with my parents as though it were just any ordinary night, but my heart was very heavy. While they drank tea and talked, I scribbled a note for them to read the next day. It was only a few words and not very well-chosen ones at that. "I am going to live with Sheyna, so that I can study," I wrote, adding that there was nothing for them to worry about and that I would write from Denver. It must have hurt them terribly to read that note the next morning, and if I were to write it today, I would do so only after much thought and with very great care. But I was under extreme pressure then and only fifteen. Before I went to sleep that night, I went over to Clara's bed and looked at her for a minute. I felt very guilty about leaving her without even saying good-bye, and I wondered what would happen to her now that both Sheyna and I were out of the house, as I thought, for good. Clara was growing up to be the most "American" of us all, a quiet, shy undemanding little girl, whom everyone liked but to whom I had never paid much attention and whom I didn't really know very well. Now that I was going to leave her, I remember feeling a sudden sense of responsibility. It turned out, though I couldn't have known it then, that being the only child at home was actually to make her life easier. My parents were far more lenient with Clara than they had ever been with Sheyna or with me, and my mother even spoiled her sometimes. We weren't a demonstrative family, but that night I stroked her face and kissed her, although she slept through my farewell.

Very early the next morning, I left home as planned and went to the station to board the train for Denver. I had never traveled alone before, and the idea that trains run according to a timetable had never occurred either to me or to my fellow conspirator, so I was still sitting nervously, with a pounding heart, on a bench in the station when my parents opened and read the note I had written for them at home. But as the Yiddish saying goes, I had considerably more luck than brains, and somehow or other, in the confusion, no one looked for me until the train had left and I was on my way to Sheyna, knowing that I had done something that deeply wounded my mother and father, but that was truly essential for me. In the two years that I was to spend in Denver, my father, unforgiving, wrote to me only once. But from time to time my mother and I exchanged letters, and by the time I came back I no longer had to battle for the right to do as I wanted.

In Denver, life really opened up for me, although Sheyna and Shamai proved to be almost as strict as my parents and we all had to work very hard. Shamai was now employed as a part-time janitor at the local telephone company, as well as working in his own dry-cleaning shop, and the arrangement was that when I got through with school in the afternoons, I would take over for him in the shop so that he could go on to his second job. I could do my homework at the shop, and if a customer wanted something pressed, I could do that, too.

In the evenings, after supper, Sheyna badgered me to go on with my schoolwork, but I was fascinated by the people who used to drop into their home and sit around talking till late at night. I found the endless discussions about politics much more interesting than any of my lessons. Sheyna's small apartment had become a kind of center in Denver for the Jewish immigrants from Russia who had come out west for treatment at Denver's famous Jewish Hospital for Consumptives (in which Sheyna herself had spent so much time). Almost all of them were unmarried. Some of them were anarchists, some were socialists, and some were Socialist Zionists. They all had either been ill or were still ill; they all were uprooted; they all were passionately and vitally concerned with the major issues of the day. They talked, argued and even quarreled for hours about what was happening in the world and what ought to happen. They talked about the anarchist philosophy of Emma Goldman and Peter Kropotkin, about President Wilson and the European situation, about pacificism, the role of women in society, the future of the Jewish people—and they drank cup after cup of tea with lemon. I blessed those rounds of tea because although Sheyna so strongly disapproved of the hours I was keeping, I managed to stay up most nights by volunteering to disinfect the cups afterward—an offer which was rarely turned down.

Of course, I was always the youngest person in the room, and my Yiddish wasn't as literary as that of many of the debaters; but I hung on their words as though they would change the fate of mankind and sometimes, after a while, even voiced opinions of my own. Much of that nightly conversation was way over my head. I didn't know what dialectical materialism was or who exactly Hegel, Kant or Schopenhauer were, but I knew that socialism meant democracy, the right of workers to a decent life, an eight-hour workday and no exploitation. And I understood that tyrants had to be overthrown, but dictatorship of any kind—including that of the proletariat—held no appeal for me at all.

I listened raptly to everyone hold forth, but it was to the Socialist Zionists that I found myself listening most attentively, and it was their political philosophy that made the most sense to me. I understood and responded fully to the idea of a national home for the Jews—one place on the face of the earth where Jews could be free and independent—and I took it for granted that in such a place no one would be in want or be exploited or live in fear of other men. I was much more interested in the kind of Jewish national home the Zionists wanted to create in Palestine than I was in the political scene in Denver or in what was then going on in Russia.

The talk at Sheyna's—almost all of it in Yiddish, since very few of the talkers spoke English well enough to express themselves properly on these urgent ideological matters—was very free-ranging. There were evenings in which most of the discussion was about Yiddish literature—Sholom Aleichem, I. L. Peretz, Mendele Mocher Sforim—and other evenings that were devoted to specific questions such as women's suffrage or the future of trade unionism. I was interested in all of it, but when they talked about people like Aaron David Gordon, for instance, who had gone to Palestine in 1905 and helped found Degania (the kibbutz established three years later on the deserted tip of the Sea of Galilee), I was absolutely fascinated and found myself dreaming about joining the pioneers in Palestine.

I can't remember which of the young men it was who first spoke about Gordon at Sheyna's, but I do remember how fascinated I was by what he told us about that middle-aged man with a long white beard that made him look like Father Time, a man who had never done any physical work before and who came to Palestine with his family when he was almost fifty to till its soil with his own hands and write about the "religion of labor," as his credo came to be known by his disciples. The building of Palestine, Gordon believed, was to be *the* great Jewish contribution to humanity. In the Land of Israel the Jews would find their way to the making of a just society through their own physical labor—provided that each and every individual made a massive personal effort in this direction.

Gordon died in 1922—one year after I myself came to Palestine—and I never met him. But I think that of all the world's great thinkers and revolutionaries about whom I heard so much at Sheyna's, he is perhaps the one I would most have wanted to know myself—and would most like my grandchildren to meet.

I was enthralled also by the romantic story of Rachel Bluwstein, a delicate girl from Russia who came to Palestine at about the same time as Gordon and was deeply influenced by him. A remarkably gifted poet, she went to work on the soil in a new settlement near the Sea of Galilee, where some of her most beautiful poems were written. Although she didn't know a word of Hebrew before she came to Palestine, she was to become one of the first modern Hebrew poets, and many of her poems have been set to music and are still sung in Israel. Eventually she became too ill (with the TB that killed her at forty) to work the land she loved so much, but she was still alive and young when I was in Denver and heard her name for the first time from someone who had known her in Russia.

Years later, when it became fashionable for young people to deride my generation for its rigidity, conventionality and loyalty to the Establishment, it was about intellectual rebels such as A. D. Gordon and Rachel and dozens of others like them that I used to think. No modern hippie, in my opinion, has ever revolted as effectively against the Establishment of the day as those pioneers did at the beginning of the century. Many of them came from the homes of merchants and scholars; many even from prosperous assimilated families. If Zionism alone had fired them, they could have come to Palestine, bought orange groves there and hired Arabs to do all the work for them. It would have been easier. But they were radicals at heart and deeply believed that only self-labor could truly liberate the Jews from the ghetto and its mentality and make it possible for them to reclaim the land and earn a moral right to it, in addition to the historic right. Some of them were poets, some were cranks, some had stormy personal lives; but what they all had in common was a fervor to experiment, to build a good society in Palestine, or at least a society that would be better than what had been known in most parts of the world. The communes they founded—the kibbutzim of Israel—have endured, I am sure, only because of the genuinely revolutionary social ideal that underlay and still underlies them.

At all events, to the extent that my own future convictions were shaped and given form, and ideas were discarded or accepted by me while I was growing, those talk-filled nights in Denver played a considerable role. But my stay in Denver had other consequences, too. One of the less articulate young men who came to Sheyna's often was a gentle, soft-spoken friend of theirs, Morris Meyerson, whose sister had met Sheyna in the sanatorium. Morris' family had immigrated to America from Lithuania and, like ours, was very poor. His father had died when he was just a boy, and he had gone to work early in life in order to support his mother and three sisters. At the time we met, he was working as a sign painter.

Although he never raised his voice, even during the stormiest of the nightly sessions, I think I first noticed Morris because although he was almost entirely self-educated, he was so well versed in the kind of things that neither I nor most of Sheyna and Shamai's friends knew anything at all about. He loved poetry, art and music and knew and understood a great deal about them, and he was prepared to talk at length on the merits of a given sonnet or sonata to someone as interested (and as ignorant) as I.

When Morris and I came to know each other better we started to go to free concerts in the park together, and Morris patiently introduced me to the joys of classical music, read Byron, Shelley, Keats and the *Rubáiyát* of Omar Khayyám to me and took me to lectures on literature, history and philosophy. To this day I associate certain pieces of music with the clear, dry mountain air of Denver and the wonderful parks in which Morris and I walked every Sunday in the spring and summer of 1913.

I admired Morris enormously—more than I had ever admired anyone except Sheyna—not only for his encyclopedic knowledge, but for his gentleness, his intelligence and his wonderful sense of humor. He was only five or six years my senior, but he seemed much older, much calmer and much steadier. Without at first being aware of what was happening to me, I fell in love with him and couldn't help realizing that he loved me, too. But for a long time we said nothing to each other about the way we felt.

Sheyna was very fond of Morris, too, and luckily approved of my seeing him so often. Still, that was not, she informed me sternly, why she had helped me run away from home. I had come to Denver to study, she said, not to listen to music or learn poetry. She took her mission of being my guardian very seriously, which meant watching me like a hawk, and after several months I began to feel that I might just as well have stayed in Milwaukee. Shamai put much less pressure on me; but the reins had definitely tightened, and I began to feel very restive. One day, after Sheyna had been particularly bossy, ordering me about and scolding me as though I were still a child, I decided that the time had come for me to try to live alone, without a mother hen and without being nagged all the time, and I marched out of the apartment in the black skirt and white blouse I had been wearing all day without taking anything else with me, not even a nightgown. If I was leaving Sheyna's home and authority, I was not entitled, I thought, to keep anything she had bought for me. I closed the door behind me, and that, I thought, was that: I was on my own at last.

It was something of a comedown to realize ten minutes later that now I had to find somewhere to live until I could support myself. A little crestfallen but very grateful, I accepted the invitation extended by two of Sheyna's friends who had always been especially nice to me and to whom I confided that for the moment I was homeless. Unfortunately, it was not exactly the best choice of a haven. Both my hosts were in a fairly advanced stage of TB, and to this day I can offer no explanation other than what my mother used to call *a na'ar's mazel* (the luck of a fool) for the fact that I remained free of the disease. They lived in rather cramped quarters that consisted of a room (with a niche at one end of it) and a kitchen. The niche was mine for as long as I wanted it, they told me; but since they both were so sick, I felt I had to let them go to bed early, and I didn't dare switch the light on over my couch when it grew dark. In fact, the only place I could read without bothering them—or be disturbed myself by their nightlong coughing—was the bathroom, where wrapped up in a blanket and armed with Morris' current reading list (which was always terrifyingly long) and a pile of books, I spent most of my nights.

At sixteen, of course, one can do without almost everything, including sleep, and I was delighted with my setup—and even more, to be quite honest, with myself. Not only had I found myself somewhere to live, but I had also come to the conclusion that high school would have to wait after all. It was even more important for me to learn to cope with life alone, I told myself, than to acquire the schooling for which I had so longed. The first thing to do now that I had my niche was to find a job. Within a day or two I found work in a shop where my chief responsibility was to take measurements for custom-made skirt linings. It wasn't exactly a stimulating or elevating job, but it kept me going and soon made it possible for me to rent a tiny, but at least germ-free, room of my own. Incidentally, one by-product of that job is that even today I find myself automatically giving a quick glance at skirt hems and can run one up with total confidence.

After I had been on my own for about a year, I got a letter from my father, the only one he wrote to me during this period. It was very short and to the point: if I valued my mother's life, he wrote, I should come back home at once. I understood that for him to write to me at all meant swallowing his pride and he would only have done so if I were really needed at home. So Morris and I talked it over, and I decided that I should go back—to Milwaukee, to my parents and Clara and to high school. To be quite frank, I was not sorry to return, although it meant leaving Morris, who had to stay on in Denver for a while till his sister recovered. One night, before I left, Morris told me shyly that he was in love with me and wanted to marry me. I explained happily and just as shyly that I loved him, too, but that I was still much too young for marriage, and we agreed that we would have to wait. In the meantime, we would keep our relationship a secret and write to each other all the time. So I left for Milwaukee in what I told Regina the next day was a blissful state of mind.

CHAPTER 3

I CHOOSE PALESTINE

I found our home quite changed. My parents had mellowed a lot, their economic situation had improved, and Clara was already a teenager. The family had moved to a new and nicer apartment on Tenth Street, and it bustled with people and activity. My mother and father now took it for granted that I would be going to high school, and even after I had been graduated from high school and registered in October, 1916, at the Milwaukee Normal School (the Teachers' Training College, as it was then called), they made no protest at all. I don't think that they really ever believed I needed any more education; but they let me have my way, and our relationships improved beyond recognition—although my mother and I still fought sometimes. One of those rows was about Morris' letters to me. My mother felt that it was her duty to know all about my romance in Denver (about which someone, perhaps Sheyna, had written to her), and once she even made Clara read a bunch of them and translate them into Yiddish for her (Morris and I wrote to each other in English, which my mother found hard to read). Aware of the fact that she had done something dreadful, Clara told me about it later, swearing that she had left out what she tactfully called "the more personal bits," and from then on Morris sent his letters to Regina's house.

During World War I my mother turned our house into a makeshift depot for the boys who had volunteered for the Jewish Legion and were going to fight under the Jewish flag within the framework of the British army to liberate Palestine from the Turks. Most of the young men from Milwaukee who joined the legion (immigrants exempt from conscription) left our house equipped with little bags embroidered by my mother in which they kept their prayer shawls and phylacteries and much larger bags full of cookies still warm from her oven.

My father, too, had become deeply involved with Jewish life in the city. Most of the people who slept on our famous couch during those years were socialists (Labor Zionists) from the East, Yiddish writers on lecture tours or out-of-town members of the B'nai B'rith (the Jewish fraternal order to which my father belonged). My parents, in short, had become completely integrated, and their home had turned into a kind of institution, as far as the Jewish community in Milwaukee and its visitors were concerned. Of the many people whom I first met or first heard speak in public then, some were to become major influences not only on my life, but, much more important, on the Zionist movement, particularly on

Labor Zionism. And some of them were later to be numbered among the founding fathers of the Jewish state.

The first Palestinians I ever encountered were Yitzhak Ben-Zvi, who was to become Israel's second president; Ya'akov Zerubavel, a well-known Labor Zionist and writer, and David Ben-Gurion. Ben-Zvi and Ben-Gurion came to Milwaukee to recruit soldiers for the Jewish Legion in 1916, soon after they had been expelled from Palestine by the Turks and ordered never to return. Zerubavel, whom the Turks sentenced to prison, had succeeded in escaping but was sentenced *in absentia* to fifteen years of penal servitude.

I had never met people like those Palestinians before or heard stories like those they told about the *yishuv* (the small Jewish community of Palestine, which had by then been reduced from some 85,000 to only 56,000). This was my first clue to how terribly it was suffering from the brutality of the Turkish regime, which had already brought normal life in the country to a virtual standstill. They were in a fever of anxiety about the fate of the Jews of Palestine and convinced that an effective Jewish claim could be made to the Land of Israel after the war only if the Jewish people played a significant and visible military role, *as Jews,* in the fighting. In fact, they spoke about the Jewish Legion with such feeling that I immediately tried to volunteer for it—and was crushed when I learned that girls were not being accepted.

I knew much about Palestine by then, of course, but my knowledge was rather theoretical. These Palestinians, however, talked to us not about the vision or theory of Zionism, but about its reality. They told us in detail about the fifty-odd Jewish agricultural settlements that had already been established there and described Gordon's settlement, Degania, in a way that made it seem real and populated by flesh-and-blood people, not mythical heroes and heroines. They told us also about Tel Aviv, which had just been founded on the sand dunes outside Jaffa, and about Hashomer, the *yishuv's* Jewish self-defense organization, in which both Ben-Zvi and Ben-Gurion were active. But most of all, they talked about their hopes and dreams for an Allied victory over the Turks. They all had worked very closely together in Palestine, and Ben-Zvi often talked about a fourth member of their group, Rachel Yanait, who was later to become his wife. As I listened to him, I began to think of her as typical of the women of the *yishuv,* who were proving that it was possible to function as wives, mothers and comrades-in-arms, enduring constant danger and hardship, not only without complaining, but with a sense of enormous fulfillment, and it seemed to me that she, and women like her, were doing more—without the benefit of publicity—to further the cause of our sex than even the most militant suffragists in the United States or England.

I listened spellbound to the Palestinians, and I took every opportunity to hear them speak, although it was months before I actually dared approach them myself. Ben-Zvi and Zerubavel were much easier to talk to than Ben-Gurion; they were far less dogmatic and warmer. Ben-Zvi came to Milwaukee—and to my parents' house—several times and would sit around, sing Yiddish folk songs with us and patiently answer our questions about Palestine. He was a tall, rather gawky young man with a sweet smile and a kindly, hesitant manner that drew people to him at once.

As for Ben-Gurion, my first recollection is actually of *not* meeting him. He was due to visit Milwaukee, and it had been arranged for him to give a speech on Saturday night and to have lunch at our home on Sunday. But that Saturday night the Chicago Philharmonic was in town. Morris (who had come to Milwaukee by then) had invited me to the concert weeks earlier, and I felt duty-bound to go with him, although I can't say that I enjoyed the music that night. The next morning the Labor Zionists informed me that the lunch was off. It wasn't proper, they said, that a person who couldn't be bothered to hear Ben-Gurion speak—and of course, I was too embarrassed to explain the extremely personal reason for my absence—would have the privilege of entertaining him for lunch. I was heartbroken but thought that they were perfectly right, and I accepted their verdict stoically. Later, of course, I did meet Ben-Gurion, and I remember remaining in awe of him for a very long time. He was one of the least approachable men I ever knew, and there was something about him even then that made it hard for one to get to know him. But more about Ben-Gurion later.

Slowly, Zionism was beginning to fill my mind and my life. I believed absolutely that as a Jew I belonged in Palestine and that as a Labor Zionist I could do my full share within the *yishuv* to help attain the goals of social and economic equality. The time hadn't quite come yet for me to decide to live there. But I knew that I was not going to be a parlor Zionist—advocating settlement in Palestine for others—and I refused to join the Labor Zionist Party until I could make a binding decision.

In the meantime, there was school and Morris. While he was still in Denver, we corresponded regularly, and through those letters—read again after so many years—I see that there were also the small, private tragedies and doubts of every girl's life. Why didn't I have black hair and big, lustrous eyes? Why wasn't I more attractive? How *could* Morris love me? *Did* he really love me? I must have peppered my letters to him with

ill-concealed requests for assurance and the assurance always came—
although it was not always phrased very gallantly. "I have repeatedly
asked you not to contradict me on the question of your beauty," he wrote
once. ". . . You pop up every now and then with these same timid and
self-deprecating remarks which I cannot bear."

In other letters we tried rather awkwardly to plan a joint future and inevitably ended up by writing to each other about Palestine. Morris was
much less sure then about Zionism than I was, and he had a more romantic, more speculative nature. He dreamed of a world in which everyone would live in peace, and national self-determination held little attraction for him. He didn't really think that a sovereign state would help the
Jews much. It would just be one more state with the usual burdens and
penalties of statehood.

By 1915 Jews were suffering in many places, and my father and I started
to work together on a variety of relief activities, which were incidentally
to bring us closer together. As was true in World War II most of the relief
work for the Jews of Europe during World War I was handled by the
newly formed Joint Distribution Committee. But unlike the situation in
the 1940s, this remarkable organization was then being run badly from
New York by a handful of bureaucrats, and it had become the target of
much sharp criticism. One result of this situation was that the Jewish lab-
or groups decided to found their own organization, which they called the
People's Relief Committee, and that was the organization my father and I
joined. We worked very well together and today it fills me with joy to recall our cooperation—although I think it came as somewhat of a shock to
my father that I was now on my way to becoming an adult.

Toward the end of the war another major Jewish movement was born:
the American Jewish Congress, which was to play a leading role in the
formation of the World Jewish Congress in the 1930s. In those days, although the Bund (which had been transplanted to the United States)
didn't object to the formation of the congress, it violently opposed its pro-
Palestine orientation. In 1918, when elections to the congress were held
in all the large Jewish communities of the United States (this was the first
time that the Jews of America held elections of their own), feelings ran
high. The Zionists pulled one way; the Bundists pulled the other. Both
my father and I were actively involved in that election campaign and felt
strongly that the congress must put itself on record as favoring Zionism.

If you wanted to campaign among Jews, I decided, the logical place to
locate yourself was the neighborhood synagogue, particularly around the
time of the Jewish High Holidays, when everyone went to the synagogue.

But since only men were allowed to address the congregation, I put up a box just outside the synagogue, and people walking out on their way home had no alternative other than to hear at least part of what I had to say about the Labor Zionist platform. I suppose I had more than my fair share of self-confidence in this respect, if not in others, and when a great many people actually stopped to listen to me outside the synagogue, I thought I ought to try it again in another place. But this time my father learned about my plans, and we had a terrible row. Moshe Mabovitch's daughter, he stormed, was not going to stand on a box in the street and make a spectacle of herself. It was out of the question, a *shandeh* (a disgrace). I tried to explain that I had committed myself to going, that my friends were waiting for me in the street, that it was a perfectly acceptable thing to do. But my father was so angry that he didn't listen to a word I said. My mother stood between us like a referee at a fight, and we went on arguing at the top of our voices.

In the end neither of us gave in. My father, red in the face with fury, said that if I insisted on going, he would come after me and publicly pull me home by my braid. I had no doubt that he would do so, because he generally kept his promises. But I went anyway. I warned my friends on the street corner that my father was on the war path, got up on my soapbox and made my speech—not without some panic. When I finally got home, I found my mother waiting up for me in the kitchen. Father was already asleep, she told me, but he had been at the street corner meeting and had heard me speak. "I don't know where she gets it from" he said to her wonderingly. He had been so carried away listening to me perched on my soapbox that he had completely forgotten his threat! Neither of us ever referred to the incident again but I consider that to have been the most successful speech I ever made.

Around this time I began to do some real teaching. The Labor Zionists had started a part-time *folkschule,* a Yiddish school in the Jewish Center of Milwaukee. Classes were held on Saturday afternoons, Sunday mornings and one other afternoon during the week. I taught Yiddish: reading, writing and some literature and history. Yiddish, it seemed to me was one of the strongest links that existed between the Jews, and I loved teaching it. It wasn't what the Milwaukee Normal School was preparing me for, but I found it exceedingly satisfying to be able to introduce some of the Jewish children of the city to the great Yiddish writers I so admired. English was certainly a fine language, but Yiddish was the language of the Jewish street, the natural, warm, intimate language that united a scattered nation. In retrospect, I can see that I was a bit of a prig then about

Yiddish; there was no greater crime in my eyes at that stage than, for in- stance, for one of the children to mix Yiddish with English, and I even thought for a while that the Jews should have two languages in Pales- tine—Hebrew and Yiddish. How could one think of doing away with Yid- dish there, of all places? When the Labor Zionists wanted to start an Eng- lish-speaking branch and asked me to take it over, I would have nothing to do with it. If people wanted to belong to the Poalei Zion, they should at least know Yiddish! It turned out, of course, that I would have been bet- ter off applying myself to Hebrew, but who knew it then? Eventually, when we went to Palestine, I learned Hebrew, of course, but my Hebrew has never really been as good as my Yiddish.

I realized I could no longer postpone a final decision about Palestine. However hard it might be for those who were dearest to me, I could no longer put off making up my mind about where I was going to live. The Jews must have a land of their own again—and I must help build it, not by making speeches or raising funds, but by living and working there.

First I formally joined the Labor Zionist (Poalei Zion) Party and thus took what for me was the first step on the road to Palestine. At that time the Labor Zionists didn't have a youth movement. According to the con- stitution of the party, only people over the age of eighteen were accepted. I was only seventeen, but I was already known to the membership, and they let me enter the party ranks. Now I had to persuade Morris to come to Palestine with me, for it was unthinkable to me that we should not be together. I knew that even if he agreed to come, we would still have to wait for a year or two—until we raised enough money for the fare, among other things—but it was imperative that before we got married, Morris should know that I was determined to live there. I didn't present the situa- tion to him as an ultimatum, but I did make my position clear. I wanted very much to marry him, *and* I was set on going to Palestine. "I know that you don't feel as strongly about living in Palestine as I do," I told him, "but I beg you to come with me." He loved me very much, Morris an- swered, but regarding Palestine, he wanted to think things over and arrive at a decision himself. Today I understand that Morris, who was far more perceptive and far less impulsive than I, wanted time not only to weigh the matter of moving to Palestine, but also perhaps to consider whether we were really suited to each other after all.

So we parted for a while. I left school (how strange that it had lost its great importance for me) and went to Chicago, where, on the strength of my having worked briefly as a librarian in Milwaukee, I was taken on by the public library. Sheyna, Shamai and their two children had also moved to Chicago, and Shamai was working on a Jewish newspaper there. Regina came to Chicago, too, and I saw all of them quite often, although I stayed with another friend. But I wasn't at all happy. The idea that I might have to choose between Morris and Palestine made me miserable, and for the most part I kept to myself, working for the Labor Zionists in my free time—making speeches, organizing meetings, raising funds. There was always something that took precedence over my private worries and therefore served to distract me from them—a situation that was not to change much in the course of the next six decades.

Fortunately, though he still had reservations about Palestine, Morris was sufficiently drawn to the idea of living there to agree to go with me. His decision was undoubtedly influenced to some extent by the fact that in November, 1917, the British government announced that it favored "the establishment in Palestine of a National Home for the Jewish People" and that it would use "its best endeavours to facilitate the achievement of this objective." The Balfour Declaration—so named because it was signed by Arthur James Balfour, who was then Britain's foreign secretary—was couched in the form of a letter addressed by Lord Balfour to Lord Rothschild. It came just at the time that British forces, under General Allenby, had begun to conquer Palestine from the Turks, and although in years to come the ambiguous way in which it was worded was to be responsible for virtually endless bloodshed in the Middle East, in those days it was greeted by the Zionists as laying the foundations at last for a Jewish commonwealth in Palestine. It goes without saying that the announcement filled me with elation. The exile of the Jews had ended. Now the ingathering would really begin, and Morris and I together would be among the millions of Jews who would surely stream to Palestine.

It was against the background of this historic event that we were married, on December 24, 1917, at my parents' home. Our marriage was preceded by a familiarly long and emotional argument with my mother. We wanted a civil ceremony, no guests and no fuss. We were socialists, tolerant of tradition, but in no way bound by ritual. We neither wanted nor needed a religious ceremony. But my mother informed me in no uncertain terms that a civil marriage would kill her, that she would have to leave Milwaukee at once, and that I would be shaming the entire family, to say nothing of the Jewish people, if I didn't have a traditional wedding. Besides, would it harm us? So Morris and I gave in; indeed, what damage could fifteen minutes under the *chuppah* (bridal canopy) do to us or to our principles? We invited a few people, my mother prepared refreshments, and Rabbi Schonfeld, one of the true Jewish scholars of Milwaukee, officiated. To her dying day, my mother talked with pride about the fact that Rabbi Schonfeld had come to our house for my wedding, had made a short speech wishing us well and even—though he was known for his strictness in religious matters and as a rule refused to drink, let alone eat anything outside his own home—had tasted a piece of her cake. I have often thought about how much that day meant to her and how I nearly ruined it for her by wanting to be married at city hall.

Once again I was starting out on a new life; Pinsk, Milwaukee, Denver all had been stations of a sort. Now I was nearly twenty, a married woman and on my way to the only place that had any real call on me. But since the war had not ended yet, it was still impossible for us to go. There wasn't any room in my parents' house for us, nor did we particularly want to live with anyone, so we moved to a place of our own for a couple of years. I traveled a lot for the Labor Zionists during those years and seem to have been away from Milwaukee almost as much as I was there. I suppose that I was in demand because I was young, I could speak both English and Yiddish fluently, and I was prepared to travel anywhere and to make speeches without much prior notice.

In the winter of 1918 the American Jewish Congress held its first convention in Philadelphia. The main purpose was the formulation of a program (to be presented at the Peace Conference in Versailles) for the safeguarding of the civil rights of the Jews in Europe. To my astonishment and delight, I was chosen to be one of the delegates from Milwaukee. It was a marvelously stimulating experience for me; I can still remember how proud I was to have been chosen to represent my own community and what it was like sitting with the rest of the delegation in the overheated train on our way to Philadelphia. I was (as always in that period) the youngest in the group and, in a way, everyone pampered me—except when it came to giving me assignments. Today when journalists ask me when my political career actually began, my mind always flashes back to that convention, to the smoke-filled hall in a Philadelphia hotel where I sat for hours listening, completely absorbed, to the details of the program being thrashed out, to the excitement of the debates and of being able to cast my own vote. "I tell you that some moments reached such heights that after them one could have died happy," I scribbled ecstatically to Morris.

From Chicago, Sheyna wrote less ecstatic letters warning me that I was becoming much too involved in matters of public—rather than private— concern. "As far as personal happiness is concerned, grasp it, Goldie, and hold it tight," she wrote in one troubled letter. "The only thing I heartily wish you is that you should not try to be what you *ought* to be but what you are. If everybody would only be what they are, we would have a much finer world. . . ." I was quite sure, however, that I could cope with everything and assured Morris that when we got to Palestine at last, I would no longer be constantly on the move.

By the winter of 1920 it began to look as though we might soon really be able to depart. We rented an apartment in Morningside Heights in New York and started to prepare for the trip. Regina and a Canadian couple called Manson (who didn't go to Palestine in the end) and Yossel Kopelov joined us in the flat. In the early spring, we bought tickets for the SS *Pocahontas* and began to rid ourselves of those of our meager possessions that seemed unsuitable for the life we were now going to lead as pioneers. Despite everything we had heard and read about Palestine, our ideas of life there were somewhat primitive; we expected to live in tents, so I cheerfully sold all our furniture, our curtains, the iron, even the fur collar of my old winter coat (because we rather unrealistically believed that there was no need for winter clothes in Palestine). The only thing we agreed to take with us, in fact, was our record player and our records. The record player was the kind you wound by hand—so it could be played even in a tent— and we would at least have music in the wilderness for which we were headed. For the same reason, I stocked up on blankets, of all things. If we were going to sleep on the ground, better we should be prepared for it.

Then we began a round of farewells. On our way to Milwaukee to say good-bye to my parents and Clara, we stopped off in Chicago to part from Sheyna and Shamai. I felt a little anxious about the visit since I knew that Sheyna didn't really approve of our going to Palestine ("Goldie, don't you think there is a middle road for idealism, right here on the spot?" she had asked in one of her recent letters). I remember how we sat in their tiny living room with their children—ten-year-old Judith and the three-year-old Chaim—and told them all about the ship, what we were taking with us and so forth. Sheyna listened so attentively to all the details that at one point Shamai said with a smile, "Maybe you'd like to go, too?" To my utter astonishment—and probably hers also—Sheyna suddenly replied, "Yes, I would." For a moment, we thought she was joking, but she was absolutely serious. If we were going because we felt that it was necessary for us to go, then by the same token, it was no less necessary for her to go, too. What's more, she said, if Shamai were willing to stay behind in order to earn the money without which she wouldn't be able to keep them in Palestine, she would take the children with her.

In one sense, it cannot be said that Sheyna's abrupt announcement that day was entirely unexpected. She had been a Zionist since she was a young girl, and although she was much more cautious than I in certain respects, she was fundamentally and profoundly committed to the same cause. Of course, I don't really know just what it was that triggered her actual decision, but I would like to make the point that neither Morris nor Sheyna went to Palestine as my escort. Both of them went because both of them had concluded that Palestine was where they should be.

I can think of no greater compliment to Sheyna or to the quality of her marriage than Shamai's loving acceptance of that decision. Not that he didn't try hard to get her to change her mind. He pleaded with her to wait until they could all go together and said that she had chosen the worst possible time for her to take the two children, because on May 1, 1921, following a series of attacks on the Jewish settlements in the north of the country, full-scale Arab riots against the Jews had broken out in Palestine. More than forty people, many of them new immigrants, had been murdered and raped by Arab gangs in the Old City of Jerusalem, and although it was hoped that the British civil administration (which had just taken over from the military) would deal sternly with those responsible for the riots and thus restore calm, violence had just erupted again. Within a few years, Shamai argued, Palestine might be at peace; the Arab nationalists might no longer be able to incite Arab villagers to bloodshed; it might become a reasonably safe country in which to live! But having made her decision, Sheyna was adamant, and even after we learned that a Jew from Milwaukee had been killed in those riots, she serenely continued to pack.

In Milwaukee we parted from my parents and Clara. It wasn't an easy parting, although we took it for granted that eventually, when Clara finished her studies at the University of Wisconsin, they all would follow us to Palestine. Still, I felt terribly sorry for my parents—especially for my father—when I kissed them good-bye at the station. My father was a strong man and able to bear pain, but that morning he just stood there, tears rolling down his cheeks. And my mother—perhaps remembering her own voyage across the ocean—looked so small and withdrawn.

The American chapter of my life was closing. I was to return to the United States often, in good times and bad and even to remain there for many months at a time. But it was never to be my home again. I took a great deal with me from America to Palestine, more perhaps than I can express: an understanding of the meaning of freedom, an awareness of the opportunities offered to the individual in a true democracy and a permanent nostalgia for the great beauty of the American countryside. I loved America and was always glad to come back to it. But never in all the years that followed have I known one moment of homesickness or ever once regretted leaving it for Palestine. Of course, at the station that morning I thought I would never be back, and I parted from the friends of my youth very sorrowfully, promising to write and keep in touch.

About our voyage to Palestine aboard the wretched SS *Pocahontas*, one could write a whole book. It was doomed from the outset; whatever could possibly go wrong did, and the miracle was that we managed to live through it all. Because the vessel was known to be absolutely unseaworthy, the crew went on strike even before we embarked. Finally, on May 23, 1921, we got under way—but not for long. The moment we put out to sea, supposedly repaired, the crew mutinied, expressing resentment of the shipping company by tormenting the poor passengers. Not only did the sailors mix sea water with our drinking water and sprinkle salt on our food, but they managed to damage the engines so severely that the ship listed alarmingly and even had to stop altogether now and then. It took a full week to get from New York to Boston, and then we had to wait for another nine days before we could continue the uneasy journey. In Boston, a delegation of Labor Zionists came to visit us aboard ship; they brought refreshments, made speeches and cheered us up by referring to us as their heroic comrades. Three of our group (it numbered twenty-two at the start) proved, understandably enough, not to be so heroic; one old couple and a young bride left the ship in Boston. Sheyna received a pathetic cable from Shamai, begging her to disembark, too, but of course, she refused to budge.

At last we set off again. The voyage across the Atlantic was a nightmare. The mutiny had only subsided somewhat, not ended, and every day there were power cuts, salty water to drink and indescribably bad food. At Ponta Delgada in the Azores, the *Pocahontas* was discovered to be in such bad shape that it required another week for repairs. Four crew members went ashore boasting that they would sink the ship before it got to Naples, and when the captain found out about their talk, he clapped them into irons. In the meantime, we spent the week trying to relax, which was not easy. I remember touring the pretty port town, enjoying the mild climate and the lovely, unfamiliar scenery. One curious aspect of our enforced stopover was that we discovered a tiny Sephardic Jewish community (some thirty people in all) which was extremely observant. The rabbi had died several years earlier, and the community—like my grandfather—was so worried about the possibility of violating the Jewish dietary laws that it decided to forgo eating meat permanently. By the time we left the Azores we had been en route for one month, but we still had to face the horror of the rest of the voyage. During the last lap of our trip—the semimutiny still in force—the ship's refrigerator was smashed, so we had to make do with rice and salty tea three times a day, but we were kept from being bored by a succession of incredible dramas. First of all, one of the passengers died, and since the *Pocahontas'* cooling facilities no longer functioned, the body was simply thrown overboard. Then the captain's brother, who was also on board, went stark raving mad and had to be chained and locked up in his cabin.

The state of affairs aboard the *Pocahontas* had not escaped attention abroad, and a rumor spread among our friends in New York and Boston that we had all gone down with the ship. But in Naples we were able to write home that we were more or less all right. We stayed in Naples for five days, ironing out the inevitable complications over our passports, buying oil lamps and some food and looking for our baggage, which had disappeared. Finally, we boarded a train for Brindisi.

There we met up with a group of Labor Zionists from Lithuania who had actually reached Palestine twice before but had been turned away. Now they were going to try to enter the country again. We had never met "real" pioneers of our own age before, and we were very impressed by them. They reminded me of people like Ben-Zvi and Ben-Gurion, although they were much younger. Compared to us, they were so experienced and hardy, and they seemed so sure of themselves. In Europe they had worked on training farms established by the Zionist movement, and they obviously regarded themselves, not without reason, as being infinitely superior to us. They made it quite clear that we were "soft," spoiled immigrants from the United States, members of the bourgeoisie, in fact, who would probably run away from Palestine after a few weeks. Although we were all bound for the same destination on the same ship, they were going to travel as deck passengers and wanted nothing to do with us. I could hardly take my eyes off them; they were everything I wanted and hoped to be myself—dedicated, austere, and determined. I admired and envied them enormously and wanted them to accept us as comrades, but they were very aloof.

When we boarded the ship that was to take us to Alexandria, I suggested to my companions that we give up our "luxurious" cabins and join the young Lithuanians on deck. No one was very keen about the idea, particularly since deck passengers were not entitled to any hot meals and by now we were all looking forward to some decent food. "Let's organize our own 'kitchen' on deck," I proposed, adding that we could probably make some sort of arrangements so that the children in the group wouldn't have to sleep in the open. Gradually, despite their reluctance, I succeeded in wearing my friends down, and the Lithuanians thawed out a bit. For a few dollars we got the head waiter in the dining room to agree to let the children eat there—after everyone else was through—and we found them empty cabins for the night (except for Sheyna's daughter; I persuaded the chief steward to let her sleep on a couch in the lounge but she had to vacate it at 5 A.M.!). On deck the barriers between the two groups finally collapsed. We told the Lithuanians about life in America, they told us how they had lived in Eastern Europe, and as the stars came out, we sang Hebrew and Yiddish songs together and danced the hora.

But bad luck still dogged us. In Alexandria Egyptian police boarded the ship looking for a couple called Rapaport—"miserable Communists," they called them. There were a pair of Rapaports traveling in our group, but of course, they were the wrong ones. Nonetheless, they were hauled off the ship and questioned for hours. The incident frightened and depressed us all. When the Rapaports finally came back to the ship, we decided to continue on by rail, so we said good-bye to our Lithuanian friends and set off for the station to take the train to El Qantara. On the way to the station we got our first taste of the Middle East at its worst: crowds of beggars—men, women and children wrapped in filthy rags and covered wth flies. They made me think of the beggars who had so terrified me in Pinsk, and I knew that if one of them actually touched me, I would scream—pioneer or not. Somehow we pushed and shoved our way through them and got to the train. By now we were so resigned to minor disasters that we weren't really surprised to find it unspeakably dirty. The heat was close to unbearable, and there was no water to be had anywhere; but at least we knew that we were nearly at our journey's end. At last the train moved out, and we were on our way again, a bit more travel-stained, but still able to sing, quite rousingly, about our "Return to Zion."

In El Qantara, covered with dust, we changed trains in the middle of the night. The procedure took hours; the immigration officials, when we finally found them, were in no hurry at all to attend to the necessary formalities and seemed unable to understand why we were all so despondent. I remember standing on that dark platform and losing my temper with one of them, to very little avail. But before dawn we climbed wearily on to our last train, the one that was to bring us, jolting and jogging, through a blinding sandstorm, across the Sinai Peninsula to Palestine. Sitting there, on a hard, dirt-encrusted bench, with one of Sheyna's children asleep in my arms, I wondered for the first time since we left Milwaukee whether we would ever really reach Tel Aviv.

CHAPTER 4

THE START OF A NEW LIFE

Although Tel Aviv looked to me like a large and not very attractive village on that scorching July morning when I first saw it through the filthy windows of the train from El Qantara, it was, in fact, already well on its way to becoming the world's youngest city and the pride of the *yishuv*. I don't know what I had expected it to look like, but I certainly was not at all prepared for what I saw.

Actually all that I (or any of us, for that matter) knew about Tel Aviv at that point was that it had been founded in 1909 by sixty optimistic Jewish families. Some of them had even dared predict that one day their new garden suburb (built on the outskirts of Arab Jaffa) might achieve a population of 25,000. But none of them dreamed in their wildest dreams that within only fifty years Tel Aviv would be a major metropolis, with barely enough housing for its more than 400,000 inhabitants, or that in 1948 it would be the first provisional capital of a Jewish state.

During the war Tel Aviv's entire population had been expelled by the Turks. But by the time we arrived 15,000 people were living there again, and a real building boom was on. Some parts of the town, as I was to discover later, were really very pretty; row upon row of neat little houses, each with its own garden, was set out on paved streets lined with casuarina and pepper trees, through which caravans of donkeys and camels passed, laden with bags of course sand that was taken from the seashore for building. But other sections looked—and were—unplanned, unfinished and frightfully untidy. The May Day riots of 1921 had flooded Tel Aviv with Jewish refugees from Jaffa, and when we came, only a few weeks afterward, several hundred of these refugees were still living in ramshackle huts and even in tents.

The population of Tel Aviv in 1921 was made up in part of Jews who had come to Palestine (mostly from Lithuania, Poland and Russia) in what was known as the Third Aliyah (or wave) of Zionist immigration and in part of "old-timers" who had been there from the beginning. Although some of the new immigrants were self-defined "capitalists"—merchants and tradesmen who set up small factories and shops—the vast majority were laborers. Just a year earlier a General Federation of Jewish Labor (the Histadrut) had been established, and within twelve months it already had a membership of more than 4,000.

Although it was only twelve years old, Tel Aviv was rapidly becoming self-governing. It had just been permitted by the British mandatory government to levy its own taxes on buildings and workshops and to run its own water system.

By 1921 Tel Aviv already had a thriving cultural life; a number of writers were settling there, among them the great Jewish philosopher and writer Ahad Ha-Am and the poet Chaim Nachman Bialik. A workers' theatrical group called the Ohel (Tent) was already functioning, and so were a few cafés where lively debates on political and cultural problems went on every afternoon and evening. But none of this activity or any of Tel Aviv's remarkable potential was at all apparent to us as we pulled into the town's tiny railway station. We could hardly have arrived at a worse time; everything—the air, the sand, the white stucco houses—blazed in the midday sun, and as we stood wilting on the empty platform, we realized with sinking hearts that no one was coming to meet us, although we had carefully written to tell friends of ours in Tel Aviv (who had emigrated to Palestine two years before) when we were due. Later on we learned that on that very day they had gone to Jerusalem to complete arrangements for *leaving* the country, news that added to our mood of confusion and uncertainty.

Anyhow, there we were—after that terrible journey—in Tel Aviv at last. Our dream had come true. The railway station, the houses we could see in the distance, even the deep sand that surrounded us all were part of the Jewish national home. But as we waited there in the glaring sun, not knowing where to go or even where to turn, it was hard to remember just why we had come.

Suddenly a man came up to us and introduced himself, in Yiddish, as Mr. Barash, the owner of a nearby hotel. Perhaps he could help us. He hailed a carriage for us, and we gratefully piled our luggage into it. Then, as it led the way, we trudged wearily behind it, wondering how far we could manage to walk in the dreadful heat. Just outside the station I caught sight of a tree. It wasn't a very large tree, by American standards, but it was the first one I had seen that day, and I thought that it was like a symbol of the young town itself, growing miraculously out of the sand.

In the hotel we ate, drank and bathed. The rooms were large and light, and Mr. and Mrs. Barash were very hospitable. We cheered up considerably and decided not to unpack or make any plans until we had rested. Then, to our horror, we discovered that the beds bore traces of bedbugs. Mr. Barash denied the accusation very indignantly; maybe there were fleas, he said, but bedbugs? Never! By the time the linen had been changed Sheyna, Regina and I had lost any desire to sleep, and we spent the remainder of our first day in Tel Aviv assuring each other that problems more serious than bedbugs probably lay ahead of us.

Early the next morning Sheyna volunteered to go to the market to buy some fruit for the children. In a little while she was back, filled with gloom. Everything was covered with flies, she said; no wrapping paper or paper bags were available; it was all so primitive; and the sun was so strong that she could hardly stand it. I don't think I had ever heard Sheyna complain about anything before, and now I began to wonder how she and I would ever get used to our new life. It was all very well to talk in Milwaukee about pioneering, but was it, after all, possible that we weren't up to facing these minor inconveniences and that those Lithuanians on the trip were right when they thought we were too soft for the country? My sense of uneasiness and guilt about my own failings—to say nothing of my nervousness about Morris' reaction to these unfortunate experiences—lasted throughout our first week in Tel Aviv. Perhaps if we had arrived in the autumn, rather than in the middle of the summer, or stayed closer to the sea and its breezes, it would have been easier. But as it was, we were hot, tired and dispirited most of the time.

On top of everything else, our friends came back from Jerusalem and invited us for Saturday dinner. Not only did they go on at great length about all the difficulties we would encounter, but they fed us hamburgers that tasted of soap, and we couldn't make ourselves swallow them. After some embarrassment all around—and telling the children that they must stop choking and crying—it turned out that a piece of soap had fallen into the precious ground meat. But the explanation didn't make the meat more palatable, and we went back to Mr. Barash's hotel feeling sick as well as dejected.

After a few days there seemed no point in staying at Mr. Barash's hotel any longer. Like that tree near the station, we had to strike roots sooner or later, and besides, our money was running out. True, we had come from America, but we nonetheless had only very limited funds—though no one seemed to believe this. That summer I met a woman in Tel Aviv who threw her arms around me, kissed me and said with tears in her eyes, "Thank God you millionaires have come to us from America. *Now* everything will be all right here!"

Our original plan had been to stay in Tel Aviv for a week or two and then to join a kibbutz. In Milwaukee we had even picked out the kibbutz to which we would apply for membership. But when we made inquiries in Tel Aviv, we were told to wait until the summer was over and then submit formal applications. So instead of starting our conquest of the land at once, we embarked on a far less heroic mission: the conquest of landlords. That wasn't a simple matter either. Housing was very scarce, prices were sky high, and we needed room for at least seven beds. We split up into teams and began to house-hunt feverishly. Within a few days we found a two-room apartment at the end of a still-unpaved street in the oldest part of Tel Aviv, Neveh Zedek, a quarter that was actually founded even before Tel Aviv itself. The apartment had no electricity and no bathroom or toilets; these amenities, shared with some forty other people, were located in the yard. But there was a little kitchen, and we were asked to pay only three months' rent in advance, despite the fact that we were from the States.

We moved in—without much enthusiasm but with great relief—and began to get organized. We borrowed sheets, pots and pans and some cutlery, and Sheyna undertook to housekeep for all of us, cooking on a Primus stove (fueled by kerosene), which periodically and noisily exploded. Regina got a job as a typist in an office; Yossel went to work in a barbershop; Morris was taken on as a sort of bookkeeper in a British public works installation at Lydda, and I began to give private English lessons. Actually, I was asked to teach at the high school, but since we were going to join a kibbutz as soon as possible, I thought it would be better not to commit myself to a steady job. Teaching, however, was regarded by most of the people we met in Tel Aviv then as being too intellectual an occupation for a would-be pioneer, and I had to keep explaining that it was only temporary and that I had not come to Palestine to spread American culture.

On the whole, we managed pretty well, although it took a long time for our neighbors to accept the strange American way in which we did things, like putting screens on our windows against flies. Everybody else had big mesh screens to protect them against the stray cats that roamed the city, but against *flies*? What was wrong with flies? Surely they were inevitable in this part of the world? Nonetheless, we persisted in trying to make the apartment livable, and on the whole we succeeded. When our trunks came from Naples, we turned them into sofas and tables. Morris decorated the bare walls for us, and we improvised bedspreads and curtains. Our most cherished possessions, needless to say, were our record player and records, and slowly people began to drop by in the evenings to drink tea and listen to music with us.

I have often been tempted to explain to new immigrants to Israel just how well I understand the difficulties of adjustment and to tell them something of what it was like when I myself first came to Palestine, but I have learned, through bitter experience, that people tend to regard such stories as propaganda or, even worse, as preaching and generally would much rather not listen to them. Still, the fact remains that we had to make our way alone in the land in which we had chosen to live. There was no State of Israel then, no Ministry of Absorption, no Jewish Agency. No one helped us settle or learn Hebrew or find a place to live. We had to do everything ourselves, by ourselves, and it never occurred to us that anyone else was morally obligated to assist us. Not that we were in any way superior to the immigrants who come to Israel today, nor am I in the least sentimental about the greater discomforts (many of them quite unnecessary) that we faced sixty years ago and for which we were so woefully unprepared. But I am quite convinced, in retrospect, that having always to bear in mind the purpose for which we had come to Palestine and knowing that nobody had asked us to come or had promised us anything did, in the end, make our acclimatization fairly rapid. We knew that it was up to each one of us personally to make our life in Palestine easier or better or more meaningful and that we had no alternative other than to settle in and settle down as quickly as we possibly could.

I wrote to Shamai after we had been in Palestine for about six weeks expressing something of our feelings about the great adventure:

Those who talk about returning are the recent arrivals. An old worker is full of inspiration and faith. I say that as long as those who created the little that is here are still here, I cannot leave and you must come. I would not say this if I did not know that you are ready to work hard. True, even hard work is hard to find, but I have no doubt you will find something. Of course, this is no America, and one may have to suffer a lot economically. There may even be riots again. But if one wants one's own land and if one wants it with one's whole heart, one must be ready for this. When you come, I am sure we will be able to plan . . . There is nothing to wait for.

It was, I suppose, natural that I should feel that way; after all, I was in my very early twenties, doing exactly what I wanted to do, physically fit, full of energy and together with the people who meant most to me—my husband, my sister, my best friend. I had no children to worry about, and I didn't really care whether we had an icebox or not, or if the butcher wrapped our meat in pieces of newspaper he picked up off the floor. There were all kinds of compensations for these small hardships, like walking down the street on our first Friday evening in Tel Aviv and feeling that life could hold no greater joy for me than to be where I was—in the only all-Jewish town in the world, where everyone from the bus driver to our landlady shared, in the deepest sense, not only a common past, but also common goals for the future. These people hurrying home for the Sabbath, each one carrying a few flowers for the table, were really brothers and sisters of mine, and I knew we would remain bound to each other for all our lives. Although we had come to Palestine from different countries and from different cultures and often spoke different languages, we were alike in our belief that only here could Jews live as of right, rather than sufferance, and only here Jews could be masters, not victims, of their fate. So it was not surprising that for all the petty irritations and problems, I was profoundly happy.

But when I remember how Sheyna managed to cope with everything and everybody without ever once suggesting that perhaps it was all too much for her—despite the fact that both her small children were sick and Shamai was so far away and the postal service so inefficient that she only got letters from him months after they were written—or how determined Morris was to stick it out—despite his hesitations about coming to Palestine at all or the fact, for instance, that the books which meant so much to him arrived in Palestine torn and waterlogged—I am filled again with admiration for them and can only wonder whether in their place I myself would have been as adamant about staying. Of course, like those friends who were supposed to meet us when we first arrived, there were newcomers in Palestine even then who couldn't take it and who left—just as there are some people who can't take it today and leave. I have always felt sorry for those people because, to my mind, the loss has always been theirs.

In September we applied for membership to Kibbutz Merhavia in the Plain of Jezreel, which we call the Emek. We had chosen this particular kibbutz (as so often happens) for a not very important reason; a friend of Morris' and mine, who had come to Palestine with the Jewish Legion, was already there. We knew very little about Merhavia itself; in fact, we knew very little about kibbutzim in general, other than that they were communal farming settlements in which there was no personal property, no hired labor and no private trading and that the group as such was responsible for all production, all services and the supplying of all individual needs. But we both believed—I with complete faith, Morris less so—that the kibbutz way of life was more likely than any other to offer us a channel for expressing ourselves as Zionists, as Jews and as human beings.

Perhaps at this point, I should say something briefly about the Emek, because the story of the struggle to develop it is so integral a part of the story of the whole Zionist effort. When World War I ended and the mandate over Palestine was awarded by the League of Nations to Great Britain, the new hopes raised by the Balfour Declaration for the establishment of a full-fledged Jewish national home seemed to be on the way toward fulfillment. Years earlier, however, in 1901, the Jewish National

Fund had already been formed by the Zionist movement for the exclusive purpose of buying and developing land in Palestine in the name of the entire Jewish people. And a great deal of the Jewish-owned land in Palestine was bought by the "people"—the bakers, tailors and carpenters of Pinsk, Berlin and Milwaukee. As a matter of fact, ever since I was a little girl, I can remember the small tin blue collection box that stood next to the Sabbath candles in our living room and into which not only we but our guests dropped coins every week, and this blue box was likewise a feature in every Jewish home we visited. The truth is, from 1904 on it was with these coins that the Jewish people began to buy extensive tracts of land in Palestine.

Come to think of it, I am more than a little tired of hearing about how the Jews "stole" land from Arabs in Palestine. The facts are quite different. A lot of good money changed hands, and a lot of Arabs became very rich indeed. Of course, there were other organizations and countless individuals who also bought tracts. But by 1947 the JNF alone—millions of filled blue boxes—owned more than half of all the Jewish holdings in the country. So let that libel, at least, be done with.

About the time that we came to Palestine a number of such purchases were carried out in the Emek—despite the fact that much of the area consisted of the kind of deadly black swamps that inevitably brought malaria and blackwater fever in their wake. Still, what mattered most was that this pestilential land could be bought, though not cheaply; much of it, incidentially, was sold to the Jewish National Fund by a single well-to-do Arab family that lived in Beirut.

Since we were so anxious to join Merhavia, one of the first kibbutzim in the Emek valley, and had applied for membership so quickly, we were very much taken aback when our application was turned down flat, for reasons that seemed to me to be quite inadequate. As a matter of fact, at first no one even wanted to explain to us why we had been rejected; but I insisted on being told the truth, and we were rather reluctantly informed that there were two basic objections to us. One was that the kibbutz didn't want any married people yet; babies were a luxury that the young settlement couldn't afford. The other reason—and this was really unacceptable to me—was that the group, which was made up at that time of about seven women and thirty men, couldn't imagine that an "American" girl either could or would do the extremely tough physical work that was required. Since many of the members had come from the States, they regarded themselves as experts on everything American, including the character and capabilities of an "American" girl like myself. I argued fiercely that no one had the right to make such assumptions and that it was only fair to give us a chance to show what we could do.

We won the battle. We were invited to come to Merhavia for a few days so that the members could look us over and make their minds up about us on the spot. I was sure that in the end they would let us stay—which was, in fact, what happened. Our Tel Aviv "commune" began to disintegrate; Regina left for a new job, and Yossel also moved. Only Sheyna and the children remained in the apartment. I remember happily packing for Merhavia one hot evening in late September and suddenly realizing that in a way Morris and I were walking out on Sheyna, leaving her alone with an apartment she couldn't afford to maintain by herself, with Shamai still thousands of miles away and both the childrn still ill. I asked her if she thought we should stay in Tel Aviv a little longer, but she wouldn't hear of any change in our plans. "I am going to rent one of the two rooms," she said crisply, "and look for work. Don't worry about me," She would try, she said, to get taken on as a volunteer nurse at the Hadassah Hospital, which had just opened in Tel Aviv, and perhaps eventually she would be put on the payroll. As for Shamai, she was sure that he would be able to come to Palestine soon. In the interim she could manage. Human nature being what it is, I pretended to believe her, although in my heart of hearts I knew that however hard life in Merhavia might be for us, it would be easier than whatever faced Sheyna on her own in Tel Aviv.

Today Merhavia is a big, bustling settlement with a regional high school to which children come from all over the Emek. Like many of the other great kibbutzim, it has successfully combined industry with agriculture and now houses a factory for plastic pipes and a printing press. The men and women of modern Merhavia live well, although they still work hard. Their rooms are attractive and comfortable, the collective dining room is spacious and air-conditioned, and the kitchen is fully mechanized, all without having to sacrifice or even radically to change any of the principles on which life in kibbutzim was based back in 1921. Today kibbutz members still work an eight-hour day at whatever jobs are assigned to them by the work committee, although nowadays they are usually able to do the work they do best, have been trained to do and enjoy. Everyone still takes turns with chores—serving in the dining room, working in the kitchen, doing guard duty and so on—and everyone participates in all major decisions affecting the settlement, which are discussed and voted on at the weekly general meeting. As was true in 1921, the kibbutz children are still brought up together; they eat together, sleep in dormitories and study together—although, of course, their parents' room is still home to them, the place reserved for the family, and in some kibbutzim children even sleep in an adjoining room.

I myself have always believed that the kibbutz is the one place in the world where people are judged, accepted and given a chance to participate fully in the community to which they belong not in accordance with the kind of work they do or how well they do it, but for their intrinsic value as human beings. Not that kibbutz life is never flawed by envy, dishonesty or laziness. Kibbutz members are not angels, but they are the only people, as far as I know, who truly share almost everything—problems, rewards, responsibilities and satisfactions. And because of the way in which they live, they have certainly been able to contribute to Israel's development far in excess of their numbers. Today there are only some 230 kibbutzim in Israel, but it is impossible (at least for me) to imagine what the country would be like without them. My daughter, Sarah, has been a member of Kibbutz Revivim in the Negev for the past thirty years, and whenever I visit her and her family there—which in the past was only as often as circumstances permitted and therefore never often enough—I always recall with what mingled hopes and fears her father and I set out for Merhavia so long ago, fully expecting to remain there all our lives—if they would only have us.

For many years I hoped that one day I would be able to return to life on a kibbutz, and one of my great disappointments in myself has been that I never did so. Of course, there were always reasons why this seemed impossible, mostly the accumulating obligations of public life and my involvement with it. But to this day I deeply regret that I failed to find the strength within myself to ignore those pressures and persuasions, and when the time finally came, I was too old to make the change. There are a great many things about which I am unsure, but of this I am certain: had I spent my life as a member of a kibbutz—a real member of a kibbutz, not just a weekend visitor—the inner rewards and satisfactions would have been at least as great as those I derived from public office.

The kibbutz to which we came in the autumn of 1921 consisted of a few houses and a cluster of trees left over from the original settlement. There were no orchards, no meadows, no flowers, nothing, in fact, except wind, rocks and some sun-scorched fields. In the spring the entire Emek would bloom. The mountains that framed the valley, even the black swamps, would be covered with wild flowers, and for a few weeks Merhavia would turn into the most beautiful place I had ever seen. But my first sight of it was before the reviving winter rains fell, and it looked not at all as I had imagined it. The first and most important obstacle to be overcome, however, had nothing to do with scenery. I was determined to prove that I was at least as rugged as many of the older women in the settlement and that I could carry out whatever mission was assigned to me. I can't remember all the jobs that I was given during that crucial "trial period," but I know that I picked almonds for days on end in a grove near the kibbutz and that I helped plant a little forest in the rocks on the road leading to Merhavia. Today it is quite an impressive forest, and whenever I pass it, I remember how we dug endless holes in the soil between the rocks and then carefully planted each sapling, wondering whether it would ever grow to maturity there and thinking how lovely the roadside, the whole country in fact, would be if only those trees of ours managed to survive. I will never forget the first day I worked at that job. When I returned to my room in the evening, I couldn't as much as move a finger, but I knew that if I didn't show up for supper everyone would jeer, "What did we tell you? That's American girls for you!" I would gladly have forgone my supper, for the chick-pea mush we ate wasn't worth the effort of lifting the fork to my mouth, but I went. In the end the trees survived, and so did I. After a few months Morris and I were accepted as members, and Merhavia became our home.

Life on a kibbutz in the twenties was very far from luxurious. To begin with, there was very little to eat, and what was available tasted dreadful. The staples of our diet were sour cereals, unrefined oil (which we bought from the Arabs in goatskin bags, making it as bitter as death), a few vegetables from the kibbutz's own precious vegetable patch, canned bully beef that came from British military supplies left over from the war and an incredible dish made up of herring preserved in tomato sauce, which, ironically enough, was know as "fresh" (I suppose from the misleading "fresh herring" printed on the label). We ate "fresh" every morning for breakfast! When my turn came to work in the kitchen, to everyone's astonishment I was delighted. Now I could do something about the frightful food.

Let me explain that in those days kibbutz women hated kitchen duty, not because it was hard (compared to other work on the settlement, it was rather easy), but because they felt it to be demeaning. Their struggle wasn't for equal "civic" rights, which they had in abundance, but for equal burdens. They wanted to be given whatever work their male comrades were given—paving roads, hoeing fields, building houses or standing guard duty—not to be treated as though they were different and automatically relegated to the kitchen. All this was at least half a century before anyone invented the term "women's lib," but the fact is that kibbutz women were among the world's first fighters for true equality.

I began energetically to reorganize the kitchen. First of all, I did away with the dreadful oil. Then I eliminated "fresh" from the breakfast menu and substituted oatmeal, so that when people came in from work on cold, damp winter mornings, they could at least have something hot and nutritious to eat with their compulsory dose of quinine. No one objected to the disappearance of the oil, but there was an immediate outcry about the oatmeal. "It's food for babies," everyone said. "One of her American ideas." But I persisted, and gradually Merhavia became accustomed to the novelty.

The herring—eliminated for breakfast but now served in the middle of the day—also presented a problem. Not everyone had a knife, fork *and* spoon; mostly each person had one utensil, either a knife, a fork or a spoon. The girls who worked in the kitchen used to wash the herring and cut it into small pieces, but they didn't peel off the skin, so that when the herring was brought to the table, everyone had to peel his own. And since there was nothing on which one could wipe one's hands, they were wiped on our work clothes. When I came to work in the kitchen, I decided to peel the herring. The other girls complained. "You'll see, she'll get them used to that, too." But I had an answer for this as well. "What would you have done in your own home? How would you have served herring at your own family table? This is your home! They are your family!"

Saturday mornings we used to make coffee. Because we couldn't ship our milk to Haifa on the Sabbath, our Saturday menu was based on milk. We had coffee, and we made *leben* (cultured milk similar to yogurt) and *lebeniya* (a slightly enriched version of *leben*). The girl in charge of the cookies, who was on the Saturday-morning kitchen shift, guarded them as if her life depended on it. Because breakfast consisted of coffee and cookies. Friday nights, after supper, some of the young men used to start hunting for the cookies and sometimes managed to lay their hands on them, so that on Saturday mornings there would be a tragedy. When my turn came to work on Saturday morning, I figured as follows: we have no more oil, sugar or eggs (we started off with a few scrawny chickens that laid a solitary egg now and again), so let's add more water and a little flour and make a lot of cookies, enough for Friday night and Saturday breakfast, too. At first this was regarded as being "counterrevolutionary," but after a while everyone liked the idea of cookies twice a week—for the same money.

My most celebrated "bourgeois" contribution, however—about which settlers all over the Emek talked disparagingly for months—was the "tablecloth" (made from a sheet) that I spread on the table for Friday night suppers—with a centerpiece of wild flowers yet! The members of Mer-havia sighed, grumbled and warned me that I was giving the kibbutz a bad name, but they let me have my way.

We had the same arguments about other things—clothes, for instance. The girls all wore the same kind of dresses then, made of a rough material woven by the Arabs into which we cut three holes: one for the head and two for the arms. Then we tied a piece of rope around the waist, and that was that. On Friday evenings it was customary for the kibbutzniks to change: the men put on clean shirts, and the girls wore skirts and blouses instead of work dresses or pants. But I couldn't see the logic of once-a-week neatness. I didn't care what I wore every day, but it *had* to be ironed. Every night, using a heavy iron heated by coal, I religiously pressed my "sack," knowing that the kibbutzniks not only thought I was mad, but also suspected me of not being a true pioneer at heart. There was similar disapproval about the flower designs that Morris painted on the walls of our room so that it would look nicer, to say nothing of the fuss about the crates he painted and turned into cupboards for us. It took quite a while, in fact, for the kibbutz to accept our strange "American" ways and us. It is more than probable that the one most important factor in this acceptance was our famous record player. I had left it behind in Tel Aviv for Sheyna; but after a few months I felt that the kibbutz needed it more than she did, and I ruthlessly hauled it off to the Emek, where it drew almost as many people to the kibbutz as it had done in Tel Aviv. I even wonder sometimes whether it might not have been a relief for Mer-havia to accept the dowry without the bride!

That winter I was assigned to work in the kibbutz poultry yard and was sent to an agricultrual school for a few weeks to study the finer points of poultry breeding. For a while I talked poultry, poultry breeding and poultry feeding morning, noon and night, and when a jackal once raided the coops, I dreamed of the hen-house slaughter for weeks afterward. There was also one significant by-product of the energy and time I invest-ed in the poultry yard. Although God knows we could never afford to be lavish with them, eventually eggs and even chickens and geese appeared on the dining-room table.

The months passed very quickly. We were always short of working hands, and sometimes it seemed as if all the people who weren't down with malaria had dysentery or were sick with pappataci, a very unpleasant local form of sand-fly fever. All winter the kibbutz swam in a sea of mud, through which we waded for meals, to the outhouse and to work. The summers were no easier; they were very long and terribly hot. From spring to autumn we were tormented by clouds of gnats, sand flies and mosquitoes. By 4 A.M. we were usually at work, since one had to come in from the fields by the time the merciless sun was up. Our only defenses against the insects were Vaseline (when it was available)—which we smeared on the exposed parts of our bodies and onto which the gnats and flies resolutely stuck—and the high collars, long skirts, sleeves and kerchiefs—which we wore miserably throughout the summer, despite the great heat. Once or twice I fell ill myself, and to this day I remember how grateful I was when one of the boys brought me a lump of ice and a tiny lemon from a nearby village so I could make myself lemonade. Perhaps if we had been able to boil a cup of hot tea when it was cold or make a cold drink when we were exhausted by the summer heat, it wouldn't have been so physically grueling. But kibbutz discipline included not taking anything unless it was shared by everyone.

I understood and approved of the underlying reason for this seemingly exaggerated attitude, but Morris, for whom kibbutz life was holding less and less charm as time passed, thought it was absurd for the group to be so rigid and for a difficult life to be made more difficult for doctrinaire reasons. He suffered greatly from the lack of privacy and from what he felt to be the intellectual limitations of our way of life. No one in Merhavia at that time was interested in talking about the kinds of things that mattered to Morris—books and music and paintings. Not that the kibbutzniks were uneducated. Far from it. But their priorities were different. They were as concerned with whether the kibbutz could afford to buy a "giant" 500-egg incubator or with thrashing out the ideological implications of something that someone had said at last Tuesday's general meeting as they were with books, music or paintings. Nonetheless, Morris felt that people in Merhavia had one-track minds—and even that track was too narrow. Also, he said, they were much too earnest about everything and seemed to think that a sense of humor was somehow out of place.

He was not entirely wrong, of course. Now I can see that if the kibbutzim of that time had had the means and the ideological flexibility, for instance, to accept two things which today are commonplace—private showers and toilets and private tea-making facilities in members' rooms—thousands of people like Morris who later left the kibbutzim might have stayed. But these were the kinds of things which no kibbutz could possibly afford in the 1920s, and I wasn't especially bothered by their absence.

Naturally there were penalties to be paid for the hard work out of doors all year round and in all kinds of weather and for the primitive conditions in which we lived. The wind and sun battered and burned my skin, and in those days there were no beauty parlors or cosmeticians on kibbutzim, as there are now, so kibbutz women aged much more rapidly than women in the towns. But they weren't any the less feminine, despite their wrinkles. I remember a friend from Merhavia, a girl from New York who had come to the kibbutz about a half a year before we did, telling me that she once went to say good-bye to a young poet who had served in Palestine with the Jewish Legion but was going back to the States. When she held her work-worn hand out to shake his, he said, "In America, it was a pleasure to hold your hand. Now, it is an honor." She was very impressed with this gallantry, but I thought it was nonsense. Men enjoyed holding women's hands on the kibbutz then—and still do—just as much as anywhere else. In those days—and now, too—kibbutz romances and marriages were like romances and marriages everywhere, some better, some worse. Of course, young people then were much more discreet about their love lives and talked about them less openly than they do now, but that was because people were universally more puritanical in 1921, not because people didn't fall in love in Merhavia or Degania.

For all the hardship, though, I was very happy in those years. I liked the kibbutz, and the kibbutz liked me and showed it. To begin with, I was elected to the settlement's "steering" committee—the committee that was responsible for setting overall policy—which was a great honor for a relative newcomer. Then I was elected to be Merhavia's delegate to a convention of the kibbutz movement that took place in 1922, and this was really an accolade. Even now, writing about it, I have a sense of pride in the fact that the kibbutz trusted me enough to let me represent it at such an important gathering and even gave me special permission to make my remarks in Yiddish, since my Hebrew was was still so halting.

The convention was held in Degania, "mother of the kibbutzim," the settlement which Gordon had helped build and where, within the year, he would be buried. The sessions I attended dealt mostly with issues that directly concerned the future of the kibbutz as such.

At Degania that week I met many of the major personalities of the yishuv's labor movement—not only Ben-Gurion and Ben-Zvi, whom I had already met in Milwaukee, but also other remarkable people who were later to become close friends and colleagues of mine, men like Avraham Hartzfeld, Yitzhak Tabenkin, Levi Eshkol, Berl Katznelson, Zalman Rubashov (Shazar) and David Remez, to name just a few. I was to be intimately associated with all of them in the stormy years that lay ahead, but then, in Degania, I just listened to their speeches and drank in their words, hardly daring to talk to any of them. I came back to Merhavia stimulated, inspired and barely able to wait to tell Morris about everything that had been said and done.

But life has a way of becoming complicated just when it seems to be at its smoothest. Morris not only was ill at ease in Merhavia, but was now actually physically ill. The climate, recurrent bouts of malaria, the food, the backbreaking work in the fields all were too hard for him. Although he was making an enormous effort for my sake, it was becoming increasingly clear now that one day we would have to leave the kibbutz, at least until he recovered his strength. That day came much sooner than I had expected. We had been at Merhavia for about two and a half years then, and Morris had been sick for several weeks in a row. One afternoon the doctor informed me gravely that it was absolutely out of the question for us to remain there any longer unless I wanted Morris to be chronically ill. We should leave Merhavia as soon as we could.

I have often wondered in the years that have passed whether Morris would have made a better adjustment to the kibbutz, physically and emotionally, had I been more attentive, spent more time with him and generally been less involved with the group as a whole. If I had ever thought deeply enough about our marriage or worried enough about it, I would have realized, of course, that Morris was struggling all alone to get used to a way of life that was really immensely hard for him.

There was also one important and specific ongoing disagreement between us. I wanted very much to have a baby, but Morris was tremendously opposed to the collective child-rearing methods of the kibbutz. Just as he wanted his wife for himself, so he wanted us to bring up our own children as he and I saw fit, not to subject each and every detail of their lives to the scrutiny and approval (or disapproval) of a committee and eventually of the entire kibbutz. And he refused to have children at all unless we left Merhavia. He might have changed his mind about this in time, but his health was so poor that we obviously had to leave.

So we packed up again—for the third time in three years—and made our farewells. It was a great wrench for me to leave the kibbutz, but I consoled myself tearfully by hoping that we would both be back soon, that Morris would regain his health quickly, that we would have a baby and that the relationship between us—which had so deteriorated in Merhavia—would improve. If all this happened, I told myself, then leaving the kibbutz for a while was a very small price to pay. Unfortunately, it didn't work out that way.

For a few weeks we stayed in Tel Aviv. Shamai had arrived in Palestine by then, and the family had moved to a new house (with a bathroom).

Sheyna was earning a fairly good salary and Shamai eventually joined a not very successful shoe-manufacturing cooperative as its "business manager." Still, they had a home and were making enough money to live on. All in all, their situation was enviable compared to ours. Somehow or other, we couldn't find a place for ourselves in Tel Aviv. I got a job as a cashier in the Histadrut's Public Works and Building Office (later to be renamed Solel Boneh), which had recently been established, and Morris tried to regain his health. But we couldn't settle down properly. I missed the kibbutz even more than I thought I would, and Morris was being bombarded by letters from his mother and sisters imploring him to return to the States and offering to pay for his fare. I knew he wouldn't leave me or the country, but we both were very restless and depressed.

Compared with "God's wide spaces" in the Emek, Tel Aviv seemed unbearably small, noisy and crowded. It took Morris a long time to get back on his feet and to shake off the aftereffects of months of sickness, and I felt lost and directionless away from Merhavia and as though we were now doomed to being transients forever. I missed the warmth of the friendships I had made on the kibbutz and the sense of accomplishment that my work there had given me. I couldn't help wondering whether my usual drive and optimism had gone for good and, if so, what would happen to us. Also, although neither of us ever said anything aloud, I think we probably blamed each other for the situation we were in now. After all, it was because of me that Morris had gone to Merhavia in the first place, and now it was because of Morris' "failure" there that I had to tear myself away from it. Maybe if we had reproached each other openly, it would have been much better for us, but we didn't. Instead, we both felt very much at loose ends and were irritable most of the time.

Under the circumstances it was natural that when I bumped one day into David Remez, whom I had met at Degania, and he asked me if Morris and I would be willing to work in the Jerusalem office of Solel Boneh, we both jumped at the opportunity to leave Tel Aviv. Perhaps, we thought, in the crisp mountain air of Jerusalem we would come alive again and everything would be all right. It seemed like a spectacularly good omen to me when, on the very eve of our departure from Tel Aviv, I learned I was pregnant.

That autumn, in Jerusalem, on November 23, our son, Menachem, was born. He was a lovely, healthy baby, and Morris and I were overcome by being parents. We spent hours looking at the baby we had produced and talking about his future. But I had still not got over my hankering for Merhavia, and when Menachem was six months old, I returned to the kibbutz with him for a while. I thought that if I went back, I could find myself again, but of course, things are never so simple. I couldn't settle down there without Morris, and by now I had no illusions; it was clear that he neither could nor would ever go back to Merhavia. A binding decision one way or the other had to be made, and it was up to me to make it. To put it very bluntly, I had to decide which came first: my duty to my husband, my home and my child or the kind of life I myself really wanted. Not for the frist time—and certainly not for the last—I realized that in a conflict between my duty and my innermost desires, it was my duty that had the prior claim. There was really no alternative other than to stop pining for a way of life that couldn't be mine, so I returned to Jerusalem—not without some forebodings, but determined to make a fresh start.

CHAPTER 5

PIONEERS AND PROBLEMS

All these hopes and good intentions notwithstanding, instead of the placid domestic life that I now told myself I was ready to accept, the four years that we lived in Jerusalem were the most miserable I ever experienced. Almost everything went wrong; sometimes I even felt that I was reliving the worst part of my mother's life, and I used to remember—with a heart like a stone—the stories she told us about the years when she and Father were so terribly poor in Russia. It wasn't that money, as such, really mattered to me then, or has ever mattered since, or that physical comfort was particularly important. Both Morris and I had known poverty before only too well, and we both were used to a very modest standard of living, to say the least. We were also committed to a way of life that was based on wanting and having very little. Enough to eat, a clean place to sleep, a new book or record now and again were all that either of us hoped for in material terms.

But times were not easier, and there were basic needs that had to be filled: our own needs and, above all, those of our children. They had to be decently fed and housed somehow. Freedom from the fear that you may not be able to give even these essentials to your children, however hard you try, is, I believe, the fundamental human right of all parents. I knew this in theory long before I experienced such anxiety myself, but having once experienced it, I never forgot it. One of the great built-in strengths of kibbutz life, of course, is that no one ever has to cope with this kind of anxiety alone. Even if a kibbutz is still very young or has had a poor year and the adults have to tighten their belts, kibbutz children always have enough to eat. I thought often and unhappily about Merhavia during that difficult time in Jerusalem.

But it wasn't only our actual poverty—or even my constant fear that my children would be hungry—that made me so wretched. There was also my loneliness, the sense of isolation to which I was so unaccustomed and the constant feeling that I was being deprived of just those things for which I had come to Palestine in the first place. Instead of actively help-ing build the Jewish national home and working hard and productively for it, I found myself cooped up in a tiny apartment in Jerusalem, all my thoughts and energy concentrated on making do with Morris' wages. To make things worse, his salary was more often than not paid by Solel Bo-neh in credit slips that no one—neither the landlord, milkman nor Mena-chem's nursery-school teacher—wanted to accept in lieu of cash.

On "payday" I used to dash to the little grocery store on the corner to try to talk the grocer into taking a chit worth one pound (100 piasters) for 80 piasters, which I knew was all he would give me for it. But even those 80 piasters were given not, God forbid, in cash, but in a handful of more credit slips. With these I would then run to the woman who sold chick-ens, argue with her for twenty minutes or so and finally, on a good day, persuade her to take my slips (after she had deducted 10 or 15 percent of their value) in exchange for a small piece of chicken with which I could make soup for the children.

Until Sarah was born, in the spring of 1926, we made a little extra money by renting out one of our two rooms, though they lacked gas and electricity. But when Sarah arrived, we decided that we would have to forgo the rent, regardless of how difficult it would be to manage without it, so that the children might have a small room of their own. The only way we could possibly make up the difference would be for me to get some sort of work that I could do without leaving the baby alone. So I suggested to Menachem's nursery-school teacher that I do the laundry for the entire nursery school in exchange for the school fees. So, standing in the yard, for hours, I grimly scrubbed piles of little towels, aprons and bibs, heating pail after pail of water on the Primus stove and wondering what I would do if the washboard broke.

It wasn't the work I minded. In Merhavia I had worked much harder—and liked it. But in Merhavia I had been part of a group, a member of a dynamic society whose success mattered to me more than almost any-thing else in the world. Of course, some days were better than others.

When the sun shone and the sky was blue (and in Jerusalem the summer sky is bluer, I think, than anywhere else), I sat on the steps, watching the children play, and counted my blessings. But when it was windy and cold and the children weren't well (particularly Sarah, who seemed to be sick much of the time), I was filled if not with despair then with a bitter resentment against my lot in life. The worst of it was that I couldn't even tell Morris how I felt. He desperately needed rest, proper food and peace of mind; but none of these were available, and I couldn't see how anything would change in the immediate future.

Solel Boneh was doing very badly, too, and we were terrified that it might close down altogether. Of course, when I wrote to my parents, I painted a very different picture of our life, and I even tried to keep Sheyna from knowing how bad it really was—though I don't think I fooled her.

Strangely enough, when I look back to that time, I realize that I wasn't really aware of any but my most immediate surroundings, even though Jerusalem was the seat of the mandatory government then, the place from which the British high commissioners—first Sir Herbert Samuel, who was replaced in 1925 by Lord Plumer—governed the country. As it has always been throughout history, Jerusalem was a fascinating city. In part it was then, as it still is, a mosaic of shrines and holy places, in part it was the headquarters of a colonial administration. But above all, it was the living symbol of the continuity of Jewish history and the tie that bound, and binds, the Jewish people to this land. Its population was unlike that of any other place in Palestine. Even our neighborhood was exotic, located on the frontier of Mea Shearim, the section of Jerusalem that is still inhabited by ultra-Orthdox Jews, whose bearing, dress and religious practices have been carried over, almost intact, from sixteenth-century Eastern Europe and who thought that Jews like Morris and myself were only a step away from being pagan. But somehow the city's landmarks and landscapes, the colorful procession of people of all faiths and races who walked Jerusalem's streets even on the most ordinary days didn't make much of an impression on me. I was too tired, too dispirited and too concerned with myself and my family to look about me as I should have.

One evening, however, I went to the Western Wall—not for the first time. Morris and I had gone there a week or two after our arrival in Palestine. I had grown up in a Jewish home, a good traditional Jewish home, but I wasn't at all pious, and the truth is that I went to the Wall without much emotion, just as something that I knew I ought to do. Then, all of a sudden, at the end of those narrow, winding alleys in the Old City, I saw it. The Wall itself looked much smaller than it does today, after all the excavations. But for the first time I saw the Jews, men and women, praying and weeping before it and putting *kvitlach*—their scribbled petitions to the Almighty—into its crannies. So this was what was left of a past glory, I thought, all that has remained of Solomon's Temple. But at least it was still there. And in those Orthodox Jews with their *kvitlach*, I saw a nation's refusal to accept that only these stones were left to it and an expression of confidence in what was to come in the future. I left the Wall changed in feeling—uplifted is perhaps the word. And on another evening, years later, the Wall still had a message for me.

In 1971 I was awarded the Freedom of Jerusalem—probably the greatest tribute ever paid me—and at that ceremony I told of yet another memorable visit I had made to the Wall, this time in 1967, after the Six-Day War. For nineteen years, from 1948 to 1967, we were banned by the Arabs from going to the Old City or praying at the Wall. But on the third day of the Six-Day War—Wednesday, June 7—all Israel was electrified by the news that our soldiers had liberated the Old City and that it was open to us again. I had to fly to the United States three days later, but I couldn't bring myself to leave Israel without going to the Wall again. So that Friday morning—although civilians were not yet allowed to enter the Old City because shooting was still going on there—I received permission to go to the Wall, despite the fact that I wasn't in the government then but just an ordinary citizen, like any other.

I went to the Wall together with some soldiers. There in front of it stood a plain wooden table with some submachine guns on it. Uniformed paratroopers wrapped in prayer shawls clung so tightly to the Wall that it seemed impossible to separate them from it. They and the Wall were one. Only a few hours earlier they had fought furiously for the liberation of Jerusalem and had seen their comrades fall for its sake. Now, standing before the Wall, they wrapped themselves in prayer shawls and wept, and I, too, took a sheet of paper, wrote the word "*shalom*" (peace) on it and pushed it into a cranny of the Wall, as I had seen the Jews do so long ago. As I stood there, one of the soldiers (I doubt that he knew who I was) suddenly put his arms around me, laid his head on my shoulder, and we cried together. I suppose he needed the release and the comfort of an old woman's warmth, and for me it was one of the most moving moments of my life. But all that, of course, belongs to a much later era.

The late 1920s were depressing years throughout Jewish Palestine, not just for me. By 1927 there were 7,000 men and woman without work in the *yishuv*—a sobering 5 percent of Palestine's total Jewish population. It was almost as though Zionism, in its great zeal, had overreached itself.

Many more immigrants were entering the country than the *yishuv* could possibly employ. Of the 13,000 Jews who arrived in Palestine in 1926, for instance, more than half left, and in 1927, for the first time, emigration was ominously higher than immigration. Some emigrants went to the United States, others to various parts of the British Empire. There was also a group that included members of the "Labor Battalion" (which had been founded in 1920 to employ immigrants in cooperative road building and quarrying projects financed by the mandatory government) who returned for ideological reasons to Russia, where many of them subsequently were sent to Siberia or executed, also for "ideological" reasons.

There was also another very serious problem: the wages of Jewish workers were very low then; but Arab laborers were willing to work for even less, and many Jewish orange growers yielded to the temptation of hiring the cheaper Arab labor. As for the mandatory government, other than the network of roads it constructed, it did virtually nothing to develop the economy of the country and it had already begun to give way to the anti-Jewish pressure of Arab extremists, such as the mufti of Jerusalem, Haj Amin el-Husseini, and others. Although only a few years had passed since the mandate over Palestine was granted to Britain, the government was already displaying considerable hostility to the Jews. Even worse, it had moved to curb the rate of Jewish immigration into Palestine and in 1930 threatened to stop it altogether for a while. In short, the Jewish national home was not flourishing.

I hardly went to Tel Aviv during the years I lived in Jerusalem, and when I did go it was usually only to see Sheyna and her family or to visit my parents, who had come to Palestine in 1926. My father, now that I come to think of it, was in a way typical of the immigrants of 1926 and 1927, even though he had come from the States and not from Europe. In Milwaukee he had managed to save up a little money, with which he proudly bought two plots of land in Palestine—partly because as a Zionist he wanted to live there, partly because he wanted to reunite the family. Both his plots were in places that were little more than sand. One was in Herzlia, a few miles north of Tel Aviv.

He built that home largely with his own hands, as befitted a good carpenter. It was one of the first real houses in the area, and my parents settled down there as quickly as they had once settled in Milwaukee. My father joined the local synagogue, discovered that it had no cantor and promptly volunteered for the position himself. He also joined a carpenters' cooperative, but since work was scarce, that didn't help much. But my enterprising mother had an idea. She would cook and serve midday meals, and he would help her. There were very few restaurants anywhere in Palestine and none at all in Herzlia, so my mother's idea was very successful. For a few piasters she provided the laborers in the vicinity with cheap, nourishing food.

But even so, for all their determination to make a life for themselves in Palestine—although by now they were both well past their prime—my parents suffered greatly from the economic situation. I remember, for example, that once I took the children to Herzlia a week before Passover so I could help my mother prepare for the holiday. Morris was to join us on the eve of the holiday, and Sheyna and her family were also coming. But we all were so poor that there wasn't anything to prepare. My father walked around looking as though someone had beaten him over the head. Imagine, here he was in Palestine with almost his entire family (Clara was still in college at the Universiy of Wisconsin but planned to come to Palestine as soon as she got her degree), and there wasn't even a package of matzo or a bottle of wine in the house, let alone food for the Seder. I couldn't bear to see him look so miserable, and I even thought that he might be driven to do something desperate. He was so humiliated, although poverty had never crushed him before.

Then a wonderful thing happened. I was bitten by a dog! For someone else it would have been terrible, but for me it was a miracle. I had to go to Tel Aviv for antirabies injections, and while I was there, I could scour the town for someone who would lend me money. I managed to find a bank that was willing to lend me 10 pounds (which was a lot of money in those days), provided I had guarantors. So I ran around town again; but no one I found was good enough for the bank, and whenever the bank suggested a name to me, it was someone who wasn't about to run any risks. At last I found a man who had the necessary capital, a fine reputation and a good Jewish heart, and I came back to Herzlia with 10 whole pounds in my pocket for my father—and a warmer feeling then I had ever had in my life for dogs.

On those rare visits to Tel Aviv I was always depressed and shocked by the sight of unemployed men on the street corners and the desolate look of half-finished buildings all over town. It was as though a huge burst of energy had worn itself out. Of course, outsiders, might have seen it all differently. Despite the economic crisis, thousands of Jews were living in Palestine, creating agricultural and urban settlements and doing all this aided—in the final analysis—only by a Zionist movement abroad, which was in itself a remarkable achievement.

My great good fortune was that the Histadrut (the General Federation of Jewish Labor), that organization in which and for which I was to work for so many years, was interested in the services of someone like myself.

In many ways, the Histadrut was unique. It could model itself on no other existing labor organization because the position of the Jeiwsh worker in Palestine then was totally unlike that of the worker in Britain, France, or America. As elsewhere, the economic rights of the Jewish worker, as well as the Arab worker, in Palestine had to be guarded, including the right to strike, the right to a decent wage, the right to paid annual holidays, to sick leaves, and so forth. But even though its official title was the General Federation of Jewish Labor, it would be an oversimplification to describe the Histadrut only as a trade union, because it was much more than that, in concept as well as practice. First of all, the Histadrut based itself on the unity of *all* the workers in the *yishuv*—whether they were wage earners, members of kibbutzim, blue-or white-collar workers, manual laborers or intellectuals, and from the start it was in the forefront of the struggle to bring Jews to Palestine, even though the burden of increased immigration inevitably fell on its own shoulders.

Secondly, Palestine didn't have a "ready-made" economy that could absorb the steady flow of Jewish immigrants into the country. There was the smattering of small industry, of course, and the agricultural settlements. But these enterprises couldn't sustain a country with a growing population, and we who had come to Palestine to build the Jewish national home knew that we had to create what today is so casually referred to as a "national economy"! If you stop to think about what this involves—industry, transporation, construction, finance, not to speak of tools for dealing with welfare, unemployment and so forth—the job ahead of us was actually the creation of something almost out of nothing.

Because it was so highly motivated from the very beginning by the Zionist ideal, the Histadrut regarded every facet of life in the Jewish national home as of equal importance. There were (and there still are) two standards by which all Histadrut projects were judged: did they answer an urgent national need and were they acceptable (or necessary) from the socialist point of view?

One good example is the Histadrut's determination to develop its own economic enterprises, control of which would be vested in the labor community *as a whole*. As early as 1924 a legal body called Hevrat Ha-Ovdim (its clumsy English name was the General Cooperative Association of Jewish Labor in Palestine), representing every member of the Histadrut, become the "owner" of all the Histadrut's "assets," and when it overexpanded and collapsed in 1927, nobody outside the labor movement imagined that it could ever be reestablished. But the Histadrut knew that there was, and would always be, a great need for a building and public works company that could serve the national requirement in a way that no private company ever could or would. So, eventually, Solel Boneh was reborn. Today—having undergone various processes of reorganization, including its 1958 reconstruction on the basis of three companies (a building company, an overseas and harbor works company and an industrial holding company with its subsidiaries), it is one of the largest and most successful firms in the entire Middle East. When I recall the gloom and tension that existed in Solel Boneh's dingy little office in Jerusalem in 1927, when there wasn't enough cash to pay the bookkeeper even once a month, and then think of the 50,000 men and women employed last year by these three components of the original Solel Boneh, with their combined turnover of about 2.5 billion Israeli pounds, I defy anyone to argue that Zionism is not utterly incompatible with pessimisim—or that socialism is, of necessity, inefficient unless combined with ruthlessness.

To those critics of the Jewish labor movement who said fifty years ago that the Histadrut's concept of its role was romantic, grandiose and doomed to failure, let me point out that Solel Boneh not only weathered five remarkably difficult decades, but lived to play a most decisive role in the building of thousands of homes, roads, schools and hospitals in Israel, as well as to pioneer in extensive Israeli projects carried out in Africa, parts of Asia and the Middle East itself. But Solel Boneh was only one of the Histadrut's creations. There are dozens of others—agricultural, industrial, educational, cultural and even medical—and all of them are rooted in the enduring conviction that the real strength of the workers in Israel expresses itself in the priority given to the upbuilding of what is now the Jewish state.

At all events, I was delighted (and very flattered) when one rainy day, as I stood talking to someone outside the Histadrut offices in Tel Aviv, David Remez (who had suggested four years earlier that Morris and I work for Solel Boneh in Jerusalem) asked me if I was interested in returning to work and whether I would like to become the secretary of the Moetzet Hapoalot (Women's Labor Council) of the Histadrut. On the way back to Jerusalem I made up my mind. It wasn't an easy decision to take. I knew that if I took the job, it would involve considerable traveling both in Palestine and abroad and that we would have to find a place to live in Tel Aviv—which was difficult. But, hardest and most serious of all, I had to face up to the fact that going back to work would spell the end of my attempts to devote myself entirely to the family. Although I wasn't yet prepared to concede total defeat, even to myself, I had already realized in the course of those four years in Jerusalem that my marriage was a failure. Taking on a full-time job, under the circumstances, meant reconciling myself to this, and the thought frightened me. On the other hand, I told myself that perhaps if I were happier and more fulfilled, it would be better for everyone—for Morris, for the children and for me. Perhaps I would be able to cope with everything: save what was left of my marriage from going farther downhill, be a good mother to Sarah and Menachem and even have the kind of purposeful, interesting life for which I so yearned.

It didn't work out quite that way, of course. Nothing ever works out exactly as one expects it to. But I can't honestly say that I have ever regretted that decision or that in retrospect I think I was wrong to have made it. What I do regret—and bitterly so—is that although Morris and I remained married to each other and loving each other until the day he died in my house in 1951 (when symbolically enough, I was away), I was not able to make a success of our marriage after all. The decision I took in 1928 actually marked the start of our separation, although it didn't become final for almost ten years.

The tragedy was not that Morris didn't understand me, but, on the contrary, that he understood me only too well and felt that he couldn't make me over or change me. I had to be what I was, and what I was made it impossible for him to have the sort of wife he wanted and needed. So he didn't discourage me from going back to work, although he knew what it really meant.

He remained part of my life always and, of course, of the children's. The bond between Sarah and Menachem and Morris never weakened. They adored him and saw him very often. He had a great deal to give them, just as he had given a great deal to me, and he was a wonderful father to them even after we began to live apart. He read to them, bought them books and talked to them for hours about music, always with the tenderness and warmth that characterized him. He had always been quiet and reserved. To the outside world he may have appeared ineffectual or unsuccessful; but the truth is that his inner life was very rich—richer than mine, for all my activity and drive—and he shared it generously with his close friends, his family and, particularly, his children.

So in 1928 I left Jerusalem with Sarah and Menachem and returned to Tel Aviv; Morris came home to us only for weekends. The children went to a school—one of several run by the labor movement—and I went back to work.

The Women's Labor Council and its sister organization abroad, the Pioneer Women, were the first and last women's organizations for which I ever worked. I was attracted to them not so much because they concerned women as such, but because I was very interested in the work they were doing, particularly in the agricultural training farms they set up for immigrant girls. Today the Labor Council (which is part of the Histadrut) is occupied mainly with social services and with labor legislation for women (maternity benefits, retirement, and so on), but in the 1930s its emphasis was almost entirely on vocational training for the hundreds of young girls who came to Palestine to work on the land but who had no farming background at all, or any trade. The council's training farms gave those girls a lot more than just vocational know-how. They helped speed up the girls' integration in the country, to teach them Hebrew and to give them a sense of stability in a new land, to which most of them came without families and some even without the consent of their parents. These "workingwomen's farms" were set up at a time when the idea that women should be trained for anything, let alone agriculture, was still considered absurd by most people.

I am not a great admirer of the kind of feminism that gives rise to bra burning, hatred of men or a campaign against motherhood, but I have had very great regard for those energetic hard-working women within the ranks of the labor movement—Ada Maimon, Beba Idelson, Rachel Yanait-Ben-Zvi, to name just a few—who succeeded in equipping dozens of city-bred girls with the sort of theoretical knowledge and sound practical training that made it possible for them to do their share (and often much more than their share) of the work going on in agricultural settlements throughout Palestine. That kind of constructive feminism really does women credit and matters much more than who sweeps the house or who sets the table.

About the position of women generally, of course, there is very much to say (and much, perhaps too much, has already been said), but I can put my own thoughts on the subject into a nutshell. Naturally women should be treated as the equals of men in all respects, but, as is true also of the Jewish people, they shouldn't have to be better than everyone else in order to live like human beings or feel that they must accomplish wonders all the time to be accepted at all. On the other hand, a story—which, as far as I know, is all it was—once went the rounds of Israel to the effect that Ben-Gurion described me as the "only man" in his cabinet. What amused me about it was that obviously he (or whoever invented the story) thought that this was the greatest possible compliment that could be paid to a woman. I very much doubt that any man would have been flattered if

I had said about him that he was the only woman in the government!

The fact is that I have lived and worked with men all my life, but being a woman has never hindered me in any way at all. It has never caused me unease or given me an inferiority complex or made me think that men are better off than women—or that it is a disaster to give birth to children. Not at all. Nor have men ever given me preferential treatment. But what is true, I think, is that women who want and need a life outside as well as inside the home have a much, much harder time than men because they carry such a heavy double burden (with the notable exception of women who live in kibbutzim, where life is organized to enable them to work and rear children at the same time). And the life of a working mother who lives without the constant presence and support of the father of her children is three times harder than that of any man I have ever met.

To some extent my own life in Tel Aviv after we moved from Jerusalem is an illustration of these dilemmas and difficulties. I was always rushing from one place to another—to work, home, to a meeting, to take Menachem to a music lesson, to keep a doctor's appointment with Sarah, to shop, to cook, to work and back home again. They grew up to be healthy, productive, talented and good people, and they both are wonderful parents to their own children and wonderful companions to me. But when they were growing up, I knew that they deeply resented my activities outside our home.

I stayed up at night to cook for them. I mended their clothes. I went to concerts and films with them. We always talked and laughed a lot together. But were Sheyna and my mother right when they charged me for years with depriving the children of their due? I suppose that I shall never be able to answer this question to my own satisfaction and that I shall never stop asking it. Were they proud of me, then or later? I like to think so, of course, but I am not really sure that being proud of one's mother makes up for her frequent absences.

Later on I was abroad often. When I traveled, my guilt was overwhelming. I wrote to them all the time, even made records for them, which seemed more intimate and I never came back without presents; but I was also never free of the feeling that I was injuring them in some way.

Today the head offices of the Histadrut occupy an immense building on one of Tel Aviv's main streets and are like a great beehive that hums with the sound of hundreds of voices, typewriters and telephones, but in those days things were very different. We had just a few rooms, a couple of typists, only one telephone, and everybody knew everybody else. We were, in the most literal sense of the word, *chaverim* (comrades), and although we argued among ourselves all the time about details and techniques, we shared the same basic outlook on life and the same values. Most of the relationships I made then have lasted—in one way or another—till today (although, of course, over the past few years I have had to attend a great many funerals of colleagues who were young when I and the Histadrut were also young).

Of that group, three or four were to become well known outside the *yishuv*. Ben-Gurion, who became—and with good reason—the very personification of Israel throughout the world will most certainly be remembered as one of the truly great Jews of the twentieth century. Of all of us he was the only one of whom it could be said that he was literally indispensable to the Jewish people in its struggle for independence. But I hardly knew him at this point. Among the people I was getting to know well were Shneur Zalman Shazar, who was to become third president of Israel; Levi Eshkol, who became its third prime minister; David Remez and Berl Katznelson.

Unlike some of us who were lent stature by the great challenge of Zionism and who might never have amounted to much under other circumstances and in other situations, Shazar had remarkable personal gifts. He was a true scholar, steeped in Jewish learning—as was only proper for a son of the famous Hasidic family of the Lubavitchers (his first names are those of the first Lubavitcher rabbi)—and a most talented journalist, essayist and editor. He died in 1974 at the age of eighty-five, about a year after he left the presidency of the state. When he was already a very old man, the young people in Israel tended to smile (though I think rather affectionately) at his emotion-charged, long and flowery speeches, which had changed very little in style since the 1920s.

Levi Eshkol (his original name was Shkolnik) was another of the promising young men with whom I became friendly in the 1920s. He was quite different from Shazar, although he also came from a Hasidic family in Russia. But he was much more a man of action and much less a man of words. He had come to Palestine when he was only nineteen, and after working as an agricultural laborer in various parts of the country, he joined the Jewish Legion together with Ben-Gurion and Ben-Zvi (for years, he boasted that he had been made a lance corporal before Ben-Gurion). When the war ended, he became a member of Degania, from which he was co-opted by the Histadrut, although his ties with the Kibbutz remained strong all his life. Eshkol was typical of the practical idealists of that era: his great interests were land, water and defense, though not necessarily in that order, and he was happiest dealing with such down-to-earth and crucial problems. Politics in the abstract didn't particularly attract him, and he hated bureaucratic procedures; but give him a specific challenge, and he met it with an extraordinary combination of doggedness, ingenuity and shrewdness. If you wanted a Jewish national home, you had to settle Jews on the land—never mind how much the land cost or what obstacles the mandatory government put in the way of the Jewish institutions that wanted to buy it. "Not enough room to swing a cat in Palestine," said the British Colonial Office in 1929, by way of trying to excuse its inexcusable policy of limiting Jewish immigration and land purchase. So Eshkol spent the next thirty years looking for places in which new settlements could indeed be established, and as head of the Jewish Agency's land settlement department he supervised the founding of nearly 400 new Jewish villages. You couldn't have settlements without irrigation or irrigate without water, so Eshkol proceeded to organize an intensive search for water. It was a very expensive search, so he also looked for money and managed to find both—though not, needless to say, in quantities that would last forever. If you had land and water and the misfortune of having extremely hostile neighbors, you also had to acquire arms and train an army, and the story of Eshkol's contribution to Israel's armed strength from 1921 (when he joined the Histadrut's first defense committee) all the way through his tenure as prime minister and minister of defense which began in 1963 is a story in its own right.

Another dear friend made in those first years after I went back to work was David Remez, whom I have already mentioned. He had Eshkol's warmth and sense of humor, and like Eshkol, he was drawn to the solving of the practical problems of Zionism, in particular to Solel Boneh and later to Histadrut projects that concerned transportation—roads, shipping and even attempts to encourage local aviation. All his life (he died in 1951) Remez combined a passionate concern for the content of the movement—the unity of the workers and the future of socialism in the Jewish national home—with an equally passionate concern for its form. He was as involved with the revival of the Hebrew language as he was with Jewish shipping, and one of his methods of relaxing was to create useful new Hebrew words from ancient Hebrew roots. Even the words that Remez invented (probably the three most important were the Hebrew for bulldozer, road sign and seniority) had to do characteristically with real life—rather than with ideology—although he was extremely active in the leadership of the labor movement and served for many years as secretary-general of the Histadrut. Incidentally, in 1948 Remez was among the drafters of Israel's Declaration of Independence. When the state was established, he became its first minister of transport and then minister of education. We saw a great deal of each other, and we had much in common in terms of our approach to things. Remez was one of the very few of my comrades with whom I even discussed any personal, non-political matters, and I relied a great deal on his advice and guidance—and miss them to this day.

Above all, there was Berl Katznelson. He died in 1944 and so never saw the State of Israel, though I have often wondered what he would have thought of it—and of us. I have no doubt that many things would have been different—and better—had Berl been with us over the past thirty years. What did he believe in? Like most of us—though we might have forgotten had Berl not reminded us so often—he believed that our kind of socialism had to be different, that we were creating a society, not just a trade union, and that the class struggle had no significance in a community that had no classes. He believed that Zionism was one of the world's greatest revolutionary movements, and he described it as the "plot on which contemporary Jewish history hinges." It meant, he said, "a total rebellion against the bondage of the Diaspora—in any form," and the "creation of a working Jewish population versed in all branches of agriculture and industry." He became the intellectual parent of many of the Histadrut's most important bodies.

This concern with essentials led him also to father first the concept of a large *unselective* immigration of Jews to Palestine (at a time when there was a tendency in the labor movements to advocate the support primarily of pioneers who had already received some prior training in agriculture abroad) and then the so-called illegal immigration of Jews into Palestine. "From now on," he said, "not the pioneer but the refugee will lead us," and what he was talking about was the destiny of the *yishuv* working itself out through heroic acts undertaken in small stages, step by step—as indeed happened, although Berl didn't live long enough to know it.

I shall never forget the dreadful night that Berl died, in Jerusalem, of a stroke. I was in Tel Aviv. I had been to a play given by the Habimah Theater, and on the bus going home I heard people whispering to each other as though something awful had happened. Awful things happened all the time in 1944, and I was a bit worried when I saw a knot of friends standing outside the house I lived in on Hayarkon Street. They were waiting for me. "Berl is dead," they said. There was nothing else to say. I left for Jerusalem at once. After Ben-Gurion heard the news, no one dared to talk to him. He just lay on his bed shivering and crying. He had lost the only man whose opinion he really valued, perhaps his only real friend.

CHAPTER 6

"WE SHALL FIGHT HITLER"

I was away from Palestine often in 1929 and 1930. Once I returned to the United States on behalf of the Women's Labor Council, and twice I visited England, also as a representative of the labor movement. It was very strange to be back in the States after eight years. It was like visiting a foreign country, and it took me some time to get my bearings, to find my way around New York, to cope with railway timetables and day coaches and even to get used to the sound of English all around me again, though, in fact, most of the women with whom I actually worked spoke Yiddish. The organization to which I was sent in the States, the Pioneer Women, had been founded by Rachel Yanait-Ben-Zvi only three or four years earlier by women whose husbands were active in the American Labor Zionist movement. Almost all these women were European born. They spoke Yiddish at home, and to people who didn't know them, I suppose they appeared very much like their own mothers, like typical working-class *yiddishe mamas* whose main concern was feeding the family and maintaining the home. But of course, they were different. These were idealistic, politically committed, liberal young women to whom what was happening in Palestine really mattered. They found time to involve themselves in organizational activities and fund raising for farms that were training girls in agricultural work in Petach Tikva, Nachlat Yehuda and Hadera, places that they had never seen and never expected to see.

I talked about the internal Zionist political scene in Palestine and was amazed by and found heartwarming the interest these women showed in the various shades of political belief that were represented in the labor factories of the *yishuv* at that point. Within the year two major labor parties were to merge: Hapoel Hatzair (the Young Worker), which was greatly influenced by A. D. Gordon, and Achdut Ha Avodah (to which I and they belonged), which was based on socialist ideology and considered itself part of the Socialist International. Despite the difference between them, they united into one party called Mapai (which stood for the Labor Party of the Land of Israel), while Hashomer Hatzair (the Young Guard), made up mostly of members of kibbutzim with a Marxist ideology, was on the rise.

Much later, in the 1940s, a group split off from Mapai and eventually joined up with Hashomer Hatzair to form a new party called Mapam (the United Workers Party). Later again, at the end of the 1960s, there were to be other fateful combinations and changes. But Mapai remained dominant throughout the years. Its history has been that of the country itself, and the State of Israel has never yet had a government without at least a Mapai plurality, however small it has been sometimes. As for myself, Mapai was my party from the start, and I have never wavered in my loyalty to it or in my conviction that the only firm foundation for Labor Zionism is the rule of one unified labor party representing the various shades of opinion. In the years to come, I was lucky enough to be able to put this conviction to work, more than once.

At all events, the Pioneer Women were immensely concerned with whatever was going on in Palestine, and it gave me a great deal of satisfaction to know that I was playing a role in their work, although I was worried about the extent to which they seemed determined to remain a Yiddish-speaking group in a country in which the Jewish immigration from Europe was dwindling yearly. It was all very well for them to assure me that all their children spoke Yiddish and that the Yiddish newspapers and theater were still flourishing in America. I came from a country of immigration, too, and just as I was sure that in Palestine Yiddish would eventually be replaced altogether by Hebrew, so I was sure that if it were to survive the next decade, the Pioneer Women would have to broaden its base and attract younger, more Americanized, English-speaking women.

I also went to Cleveland to see Clara. She was married by then to a young man called Fred Stern and had a bright, handsome little boy, Daniel David. I hadn't seen Clara since she was a teenager, and although we sometimes wrote to each other (and, of course, my parents corresponded regularly with her) it took me a while to get used to her. We seemed—and were—worlds apart. Everything I cared for was in Palestine. Everything that Clara cared for was in the United States. I was totally committed to Zionism and to the extent that I had embarked on a career (though I never thought in those terms) it was obviously within the ranks of the labor movement of the *yishuv*; Clara and Fred were both sociologists. Although she was interested in Palestine, it was an academic interest, while Fred made it clear to me within a few hours that he disapproved of all nationalism and regarded Zionism as an extremely reactionary movement.

In 1930 I was away again. I attended the Conference of Socialist Women in England. There were more than 1,000 other delegates, and I think it was the first time that I understood how interested people outside Palestine, non-Jews, could become in what was already being called the "Palestine problem." I addressed the conference for only a few minutes; but afterward I was asked to speak to smaller groups in various parts of England. The socialist women who bombarded me with questions about the Histadrut, the kibbutz, the Women's Labor Council, the way we lived and how we treated the Arabs were quite different from the one or two British women I had met in Palestine itself. There the British regarded us as a singularly complicated breed of native, less charming than the humble and picturesque Arabs and much more pretentious and demanding. But in England itself, in London, Manchester and Hull, I talked to women who were genuinely fascinated by the Zionist "experiment" and who, if not always sympatheitc, were at least eager to learn the facts.

I didn't think that Zionist rhetoric would impress them much, and I decided that a few home truths would be more useful. There had been another wave of Arab riots in 1929, directed by the Mufti of Jerusalem, Haj Amin el-Husseini (who was to become notorious for his pro-Fascist and Nazi agitation among the Arabs during World War II), and although the British had eventually restored peace, they did so in a manner calculated to impress on the Arabs that no one would be punished very severely for murdering Jews or for looting Jewish property. I was only too glad, therefore, to have a chance to explain the real sequence of events to my socialist sisters in England.

On that same visit I met—also for the first time—women members of British cooperative societies and heard their glowing reports about the wonders of Soviet Russia. I remember thinking that perhaps if we brought them to Palestine and showed them what we had accomplished there, they might talk about us in that same breathless way. I have never changed my mind about that either, and to this day I believe that one visit to Israel is worth a hundred speeches.

I returned to London again that year for a week or two as a delegate to the Imperial Labour Conference. Ramsay MacDonald was then prime minister. Although he himself was sympathetic to, even concerned with, the *yishuv's* progress, it was his government that issued the notorious White Paper of 1930 (known as the Passfield Paper) whittling down Jewish immigration and settlement in Palestine. Thirteen years after the Balfour Declaration, the British seemed to be more concerned with appeasing the Arabs than fulfilling their promise to the Jews. Someone in London said to me cynically, "You Jews wanted to own a national home, but all you are getting is a rented flat!"

Perhaps it was because I had lived in America for so long that I didn't fall quite as thoroughly under the spell of the British as many of my colleagues did. I admired and liked the British people, including the leadership of the Labour Party, but I can't honestly say that I was really taken by surprise when we were let down so badly by them, then or later. Many, if not most, Palestinian Jews were afflicted in those years by what turned out to be the pathetic belief—all evidence to the contrary notwithstanding—that Britain would keep faith with us after all, regardless of increasing Arab pressure and the traditionally pro-Arab stand of the Colonial Office. I think that much of this reluctance to face up to the fact that the British government was in the process of changing its mind about its responsibility to the Zionists stemmed from the tremendous respect in which British democracy was held by Jews who had been brought up in nineteenth-century Eastern Europe. Incidentally, it is remarkable that despite the long, stormy and often terrible conflict between us and the British and the way in which that conflict ended in 1948, we Israelis still hold the British people in great and truly affectionate esteem and are more hurt by being let down by the British than by any other nation. There are various reasons for this. One is, of course, that it was Britain that gave us the Balfour Declaration. Another is that the Jews have never forgotten the lonely British stand against the Nazis, and yet another may be, I think, the inborn Jewish respect for tradition.

I probably would have been sent back to the States sooner or later in any case; but in 1932 Sarah became very ill indeed, and it was I who suggested that I return to America with the children so that she could get expert medical treatment there—although the doctors at home weren't even sure that she would survive the trip. One night, while Menachem and Sarah were asleep, Morris and I sat up on the balcony till morning trying to decide what should be done, and by the morning we had made up our minds. I went to the Women's Labor Council and asked if I could be sent as a *shlichah* (an emissary) to the Pioneer women. Morris was going to stay and work in Haifa, and I was going to travel alone with the children, first by train to Port Said, then on a French liner to Marseilles, then by train to Cherbourg and finally on the SS *Bremen* to New York. It would take at least two weeks, and who knew what would happen to Sarah during those two weeks? But I felt there was no alternative, and we set out on our dangerous voyage.

I don't think I relaxed for one minute during those two weeks. Menachem was very good and kept himself busy, and Sarah—considering that she was only six and extremely ill—was amazing. It was almost as though she knew how frightened I was and felt that she had to reassure me.

Fanny and Jacob Goodman, dear and old friends, put us up in their apartment in Brooklyn, and I began at once to arrange for Sarah to be admitted to the Beth Israel Hospital on Manhattan's Lower East Side. It didn't take the Beth Israel doctors long to arrive at a diagnosis. Sarah was indeed suffering from a kidney disease, but not the one for which she had been treated in Palestine. There was no need for a strict diet, no need for her to stay in bed. As soon as she regained her strength, she could go to school, roller-skate and swim, walk down stairs and run up them. She was given treatment, fattened up and, after six weeks, released from the hospital "in perfect health," as I wrote to Morris, tears of relief streaming down my face.

As for myself, I worked very hard indeed during those two years. What I recall most vividly of those months of touring (once I traveled for nearly eight weeks at a stretch, talking about Palestine and trying to raise money and bring in recruits for the organization) was the smell of railway stations and the sound of my own voice.

In the summer of 1934 we got ready to return home. I had arrived in New York in 1932 with two small children, neither of whom spoke one word of English. I arrived back in Palestine in 1934 with two small children who now spoke both English and Hebrew—and who were beside themselves with joy at seeing Morris again. There were many disappointments in Morris' life, but it was a source of constant delight to him that Menachem was profoundly interested in music and obviously talented.

But I had come back to Palestine to face an even greater challenge than serving as national secretary for the Pioneer Women in the United States. Within a few weeks, of our homecoming I was asked to join the Va'ad Hapoel (the Executive Committee of the Histadrut).

To the extent that the Histadrut represented what was, on the whole, an extremely advanced form of Jewish self-government in Palestine, the Va'ad Hapoel was its "cabinet"—within which, for the next very stormy fourteen years, I was assigned various portfolios and responsibilities. None of these, as I look back, were either easy to carry out or likely to make me particularly popular inside the Histadrut itself. But they did have one great asset. They all had to do with what in fact most concerned and interested me—the translation of socialist principles into the down-to-earth terminology of everyday life.

Socialism in practice involved much more than my calling a janitor Shmuel and then his calling me Golda. It meant also that his obligations to the other members of the Histadrut were the same as mine, and the economic situation in Palestine, as well as everywhere else, being as difficult as it was then, this aspect of trade unionism became the focal point of most of my battles within the Histadrut.

Payment of Histadrut dues was fixed according to a sliding scale, like income tax. It was paid every month in a lump sum that covered trade union funds, pension funds and the Kupat Holim (the Workers' Sick Fund) and was know as the single tax. I was convinced that this single tax should be assessed not according to basic wages or average earnings or some theoretical sum, but on the full pay that each worker actually received. Otherwise, where was the "equality" we talked about so much? Was sharing to be the sole property of the kibbutzim, or could give-and-take be made the way of life among the workers of Tel Aviv, too? And what about the Histadrut membership's collective responsibility for comrades who were unemployed? Was it conceivable that the Histadrut should make its voice heard (and its presence felt) on each and every issue that vitally concerned the *yishuv*—immigration, settlement, self-defense—but avert its gaze from the men and women who were without jobs and whose children were barely getting enough to eat? If nothing else, mutual aid—one of the bases of the Histadrut—was certainly a prerequisite of socialism, however hard up an *employed* member of the Histadrut might be and regardless of how painful it was to turn over a day's salary each month to a special unemployment fund. But I felt very strongly about these fundamental matters and persisted in setting up an unemployment fund, despite the very vocal opposition to it.

There were more serious issues at stake. Both in Palestine and abroad, storm clouds had gathered. Hitler had come to power in 1933, and however absurd his loudly proclaimed program for world domination by the Aryan race had seemed at first, the violent anti-Semitism which he had preached from the start was obviously not just a rhetorical device. One of Hitler's very first acts, in fact, was the passage of savage anti-Jewish legislation that stripped Germany's Jews of all usual civil and human rights. Of course, no one, myself included, dreamed then that Hitler's vow to destroy the Jews would ever be carried out. It wasn't that we were gullible. It was simply that we couldn't conceive of what was then still inconceivable. Today, however, no horror is inconceivable to me anymore.

But even before Hitler's "Final Solution," the first results of Nazi persecution—legally enacted—were terrible enough, and I again felt that there was only one place on the face of the globe to which the Jews could come as a right, no matter what restrictions the British sought to impose on their immigration to Palestine. By 1934 thousands of uprooted homeless refugees from Nazism were making their way to Palestine. Some of them brought with them what few possessions they could rescue, but most of them came with nothing at all. They were highly educated, industrious, energetic people, and their contributions to the *yishuv* was immense. But it meant that 60,000 men, women and children had to be absorbed at once by a population of fewer than 400,000 that was barely able to make ends meet in any case, and they all had somehow to survive not only growing Arab terror, but also the indifference—not to say hostility—of the mandatory government.

Absorbing immigrants, particularly if they are refugees, is quite different from merely welcoming them. The thousands of men, women and children who came to us then from Germany and Austria had to be housed, given jobs, taught Hebrew and helped acclimatize. The lawyer from Berlin, the musician from Frankfurt, the research chemist from Vienna had to be turned, overnight, into a chicken farmer, a waiter and a bricklayer; otherwise they wouldn't have work at all.

Today I often think of how it was in Palestine in the 1930s and the 1940s and derive considerable encouragement from these memories, although certainly not all of them are pleasant. But when people say to me in 1975, "How can Israel possibly cope with everything—with the Arab determination to liquidate the state, with the overwhelming Arab superiority of money, men and arms, with the influx of thousands of immigrants from Russia, with the relative indifference, at best, of most of the world to these problems and with a critical economic situation that seems impossible to remedy?" I can only answer, and with perfect honesty, "It was all much more difficult forty years ago, and we did manage somehow—though the price was always very high." Sometimes, in fact, I think that only those of us who were active forty years ago can really understand how much was accomplished since then or how great our victories have really been, and maybe that is why the greatest optimists in Israel today tend to be the old people like myself, who take it for granted that nothing as tremendous as the rebirth of a ntion can be accomplished rapidly, painlessly or effortlessly!

At the same time we had to formulate and implement a series of major decisions about the overall situation of the *yishuv*. The first question that required an immediate reply was what were we going to do about the constant outbreaks of Arab terror? In 1936 alone they had resulted in the wanton destruction of hundreds of thousands of trees planted by the Jews with so much love, care and hope; the derailing of countless trains and buses; the burning of hundreds of fields; and, most dreadful of all, in some 2,000 armed attacks on Jews—eighty of whom were killed (and many more gravely wounded).

The riots started in April, 1936. By the summer it was no longer safe for Jews to travel from one city to another. Whenever I had to go from Tel Aviv to Jerusalem for a meeting—which was frequently—I kissed the children good-bye in the morning knowing that I might well never come home again, that my bus might be ambushed, that I might be shot by an Arab sniper at the entrance to Jerusalem or stoned to death by an Arab mob on the outskirts of Tel Aviv. The Haganah (the underground Jewish self-defense organization) was much better equipped and larger than it had been at the time of the Arab riots of 1929, but we had no intention either of turning it into an instrument of counterterror against the Arabs just because they were Arabs or of providing the British with any excuse for further clamping down on Jewish immigration and settlement, as they tended to do whenever we visibly played too active a role in our own defense. Although it is always much harder to exercise self-restraint than it is to hit back, we had one paramount consideration: nothing must be done—even in the face of constant danger and harassment—that might provoke the British into slashing the number of Jews allowed to enter Palestine. The policy of self-restraint (*havlagah* in Hebrew) was rigidly enforced. Whenever and wherever possible, Jews defended themselves from attack, but there were virtually no acts of retaliation by the Haganah throughout the three years of what the British, with splendid understatement, chose to call "the disturbances."

This determination of ours to defend ourselves but not to retaliate was not, however, universally applauded in the *yishuv*. A minority clamored for counterterror and denounced the policy of *havlagah* as cowardly. I was always among the majority that was absolutely convinced that *havlagah* was the one and only ethical course we could follow.

Let me at this juncture deal also—even if very briefly—with the ridiculous accusation that I have heard for so many years to the effect that we ignored the Arabs of Palestine and set about developing the country as though it had no Arab population at all. When the instigators of the Arab disturbances of the late 1930s claimed, as they did, that the Arabs were attacking us because they had been "disposed," I did not have to look up British census figures to know that the Arab population of Palestine had doubled since the start of Jewish settlements there. I had seen for myself the rate of growth of the Arab population ever since I had first come to Palestine. Not only did the living standard of the Arabs of Palestine far exceed that of the Arabs anywhere else in the Middle East, but attracted by the new opportunities, hordes of Arabs were emigrating to Palestine from Syria and other neighboring countries all though those years. Whenever some kindly representative of the British government sought to shut off Jewish immigration by declaring that there was not enough room in Palestine, I remember making speeches about Palestine's larger absorptive capacity, complete with statistical references which I dutifully took from British sources, but which were based on what I had actually witnessed with my own eyes.

We decided to step into the economic vacuum that was created when the Arab Higher Committee, headed by the mufti, declared a general strike in the hope of paralyzing the *yishuv* altogether. No Arab anywhere in Palestine was to go to work, the mufti ordered, until all Jewish immigration ended and all land purchases by Jews came to a stop. To this we had a simple reply. If the port of Jaffa no longer operated, we would open a port of our own in Tel Aviv. If Arab farmers no longer marketed their crops, then Jewish farmers would double and triple their efforts. If all Arab transport ceased on the roads to Palestine, then Jewish trucks and bus drivers would work extra shifts and armor-plate their vehicles. Whatever the Arabs refused to do, we would get done—somehow or other.

There were, of course, many people whose judgment, opinions and personalities affected these decisions—including, to a very small extent, my own—but there was one man, above all others, on whose remarkable qualities of leadership and stunning political intuition we all relied and were to continue to rely in the years that lay ahead. That man was David Ben-Gurion, the only one among us whose name, I profoundly believe, will be known to Jews and non-Jews alike even in a hundred years. I am sure that the names Israel and Ben-Gurion will be linked in men's minds for a very long time, maybe forever. No one, of course, can tell what or who the future may bring, but I doubt that the Jewish people will ever produce a greater leader or a more astute and courageous statesman.

What was he like as a person? The first thing that occurs to me about Ben-Gurion when I sit down to write about him now is that he was not a man to whom one could be close. Not only to whom I was never really close, but to whom I don't think anyone was ever close, except perhaps his wife, Paula, and maybe this daughter, Renana. The rest of us—Berl, Shazar, Remez, Eshkol—not only were comrades-in-arms, but also liked each other's company, and we used to drop in on one another and talk about all sorts of things—not just the big political or economic issues, but about people, about ourselves and our families. But not Ben-Gurion. It never entered my mind, for instance, to call up Ben-Gurion and say, "Look, suppose I come over tonight?" Either you had something specific to talk about, some business to conduct with him, or you didn't go to him. He had no small talk at all.

Whatever interested him or mattered to him he did with complete and total concentration—something that not everyone always appreciated or understood. Once—I think it was in 1946—he asked for a few months' leave from the Jewish Agency, which he headed at that time, so that he could learn exactly what the Haganah had at its disposal and what it was likely to need for the struggle he was so sure lay ahead. Everyone laughed at the idea of what they called Ben-Gurion's "seminar." Who took time off, in those days of incessant crisis "to study"? The answer, of course, is that Ben-Gurion did, and when he came back to work, he knew more about the real strength of the Haganah than all of us put together. "I tell you," he said to me, "I feel as though I were going mad. What's going to happen to us? I'm sure the Arabs will attack us, and we're not prepared for it. We have nothing. What's going to happen to us?" He was literally beside himself with anxiety. Then we sat down and talked, and I told him how frightened of the future one of our colleagues in the labor movement was, a man who had always been opposed to Ben-Gurion's activism and now, in the dark years of what we called the *ma'avak* (our full-fledged struggle) against the British, was all the more so. Ben-Gurion listened to me very attentively. Then he said, "You know, it takes a lot of courage to be afraid—and still more courage to say so. But even Y. doesn't know how much there is to be afraid of." Fortunately, Ben-Gurion knew. He combined his fantastic intuition with as much information as he could acquire, and then he did something about it. He went to the Jews of the United States—almost three years before the War of Independence broke out in 1948—and enlisted their help in what he called the "probable eventuality" of war with the Arabs. He wasn't always right, but he was more often right than wrong—and he was absolutely right about that.

Was he dictatorial? Not really. It is a vulgarization to say that people were frightened of him, but he was certainly not a man with whom anyone disagreed lightly. Among the people who fell out of favor with Ben-Gurion—and for whom he made life difficult—were two of the prime ministers of Israel, Moshe Sharett and Levi Eshkol.

The really uncanny thing about him for most of his political life was that even when in theory he was quite wrong, he would usually be proved right in practice, and that, after all, is the difference between a statesman and a politician. Although I never forgave him the wounds he inflicted upon us over the Lavon Affair, the abuse he heaped on his former comrades or the damage he did to the labor movement in the last ten years or so of his life, I still feel the way I felt once when I sent him a cable on his birthday from one of my missions abroad. "Dear Ben-Gurion," I wrote. "We have had many arguments in the past and doubtless will have many more, but no one, regardless of what the future may hold, will ever be able to take away from me my sense of the enormous privilege I have had in working side by side, for tens of years, with the one man who, more than any other single person, was responsible for the establishment of the Jewish state." I believed it then, and I still believe it.

In 1937 I was sent back to the United States, this time to raise funds for a Histadrut project that held tremendous appeal for me. It was a campaign to launch a shipping enterprise called Nachshon (after the first of the Children of Israel to obey Moses' command and jump into the Red Sea during the Exodus from Egypt), and I liked everything about it. It was a brainchild of David Remez's, born in the wake of the Arab general strike. The ancient Jews in Palestine had been a seafaring people, of course; but the art was lost in the course of the 2,000 years of landlocked exile, and it was only just being revived. Then the strike of the Jaffa port workers in 1936 served as the starting signal for a major effort on the part of the *yishuv* to train people, as I told audiences throughout the States, "to work on the sea as we had trained them for so many years to work on the soil." This meant opening a port of our own, buying ships, training seamen and generally becoming a seafaring nation again.

The day the port of Tel Aviv opened for business was, in every sense of the words, a national holiday for the Jews of Palestine. It still moves me to remember how the waiting crowds on the shore rushed into the sea to help the longshoremen—all of them Jews from Salonika—to unload the sacks of cement from the Yugoslav ship that was the first to anchor.

Of course, there were skeptics who couldn't understand what difference it made that almost all of Palestine's seaborne traffic was in non-Jewish hands; but I saw Nachshon as one more stage toward Jewish independence, and for a while I ate, drank, slept and talked shipping and fishing—and made yet another fund-raising trip to the United States on their behalf. I knew all the time that for us the real meaning of the sea was much grimmer, for it was only by sea that Jewish refugees from Nazi Europe could make their way to Palestine, provided that the British would let them in. And by 1939, with a world war looming, it was clear that the British Colonial Office was going to give way completely to Arab pressure and virtually stop all immigration of Jews to Palestine.

The Peel Commission, which had toured Palestine in 1936, had recommended that the country be partitioned into two states, a Jewish state to occupy all of 2,000 square miles and an Arab state occupying the rest of the country, with the exception of an international enclave for Jerusalem and a corridor from it to the coast. The proposed Jewish state was not my idea of a viable national home for the Jewish people. It was far too small and far too cramped. I thought it was a grotesque proposal, and I said so, although most of my colleagues, led by Ben-Gurion, reluctantly decided to accept it in the end. "Someday my son will ask me by what right I gave up most of the country, and I won't know how to answer him," I said at one of the many party meetings at which the Peel proposal was debated. I was not entirely alone in my party, of course. Berl, as I have already mentioned, and a few other ranking members of the labor movement agreed with me. But we were wrong, and Ben-Gurion, in his greater wisdom, arguing that any state was better than none, was right.

Thank God it was not because of me that we didn't get that state in 1937, but because of the Arabs, who flatly turned down the partition plan—although had they accepted, they could have had a "Palestinian" state forty years ago. The guiding principle behind the attitude of the Arabs in 1936 and 1937, however, was exactly what it has been ever since: decisions are made not on the basis of what is good for them, but on the basis of what is bad for us. And in retrospect, it is clear that the British themselves never intended to implement the Peel plan. At all events, I certainly couldn't have lived with myself all these years if I had thought—in the light of what happened afterward—that it was I who was to blame for its collapse. If we had had even a tiny little mockery of a state only a year before the war broke out, hundreds of thousands of Jews—perhaps many more—might have been saved from the ovens and gas chambers of the Nazis.

Although the question of immigration was quickly turning into a matter of life or death for the Jews of Europe, we seemed to be the only people in the world who understood this—and who was going to listen to us? It was the British who held the keys to the gates of the Jewish homeland, and they were clearly about to lock them—regardless of what was already happening.

But if Palestine was to be out of bounds for the Jews of Europe, then what about other countries? In the summer of 1938 I was sent to the International Conference on Refugees that was called by Franklin Delano Roosevelt in Évian-les Bains. I was there in the ludicrous capacity of the "Jewish observer from Palestine," not even seated with the delegates but with the audience, although the refugees under discussion were my own people, members of my own family, not just inconvenient numbers to be squeezed into official quotas, if at all possible. Sitting there in that magnificent hall, listening to the delegates of thirty-two countries rise, each in turn, to explain how much they would have liked to take in substantial numbers of refugees and how unfortunate it was that they were not able to do so, was a terrible experience. I don't think that anyone who didn't live through it can understand what I felt at Évian—a mixture of sorrow, rage, frustration and horror. I wanted to get up and scream at them all, "Don't you know that these 'numbers' are human beings, people who may spend the rest of their lives in concentration camps, or wandering around the world like lepers, if you don't let them in?" Of course, I didn't know then that not concentration camps but death camps awaited the refugees whom no one wanted. If I had known that, I couldn't have gone on sitting there silently hour after hour being disciplined and polite.

Nothing was accomplished at Évian except phraseology, but before I left, I held a press conference. At least the journalists wanted to hear what I had to say, and through them we could reach the rest of the world and try again to get its attention. "There is only one thing I hope to see before I die," I told the press, "and that is that my people should not need expressions of sympathy anymore."

But in May, 1939, despite the escalating persecution and murder of Jews in Austria and Germany, the British decided that the time was ripe, after all, for finally slamming Palestine's gates shut. The Chamberlain government gave way to Arab blackmail in much the same fashion that it was giving way to the Nazis. If appeasement was the solution to the "problem" of Czechoslovakia, then it could certainly serve the same purpose in Palestine—about which no one seemed to care very much in any case. The 1939 White Paper on Palestine, in effect, ended the British mandate, although the death throes were to go on for another nine years. A Palestinian state was to be created within a decade based on a constitution that guaranteed the "rights of minorities" and a canton system. Jewish land purchases in Palestine were to end altogether—except in some 5 percent of the country—and Jewish immigration into Palestine was first to be restricted to a maximum of 75,000 Jews over the forthcoming five years and then stopped forever "unless the Arabs of Palestine are prepared to acquiesce in it."

Obviously, the White Paper was unacceptable. We held protest meetings and strikes and signed manifestos. But also decisions had to be taken. It was not enough to bemoan our betrayal at the hands of the British or to march, sick at heart and with bowed heads, down the main streets of Tel Aviv, Jerusalem and Haifa. What were we going to do? Were we going to defy the British, and if so, how? Toward what goal was the Zionist movement going to direct its activities now that the British had chosen—in the hour of our greatest need—to wipe their hands of the national aspirations of the Jews?

In August I wearily explained to the children that I had to go abroad again, this time to the Zionist congress in Geneva, where monumental issues that concerned the life of the *yishuv* were going to be thrashed out. They were terribly disappointed, I could see, but although sometimes they argued and asked if it was really necessary, this time they didn't argue at all. Actually, by the time I left for Geneva, Mapai policy had already been formulated. Whatever position Zionist delegates from abroad would take, we were clear about our own. Immigration would go on, even if it came to armed clashes with the British, and we would also continue to settle and defend the land. This meant, in fact, that we were committing ourselves to waging war against the British—if we had to. We, who were not even important enough to be represented fully and formally at an International Conference on Refugees? But there seemed to be no alternative, unless we, too, adopted a quota system and thus joined the society of nations that "deeply regretted" their inability to participate in the rescue of Jews.

By the time war broke out in September, 1939, Ben-Gurion had defined our position, tersely but very lucidly: "We shall fight Hitler as if there were no White Paper, and fight the White Paper as if there were no Hitler."

CHAPTER 7

THE STRUGGLE AGAINST THE BRITISH

I suppose I must have tried a thousand times since 1939 to explain to myself—let alone to others—just how and why it happened that during the very years that the British stood with so much courage and determination against the Nazis, they were also able (and willing) to find the time, energy and resources to fight so long and as bitter a war against the admittance of Jewish refugees from the Nazis to Palestine. But I have still not found any rational explanation—and perhaps there is none. All I know is that the State of Israel might not have come into being for many years if that British war within a war had not been waged so ferociously and with such insane persistence.

As a matter of fact, it was only when the British government decided—in the face of all reason or humanity—to place itself like an iron wall between us and whatever chance we had of rescuing Jews from the hands of the Nazis that we realized that political independence was not something that we could go on regarding as a distant aim: the need to control immigration because human lives depended on such control was the one thing that pushed us into making the sort of decision which might otherwise have waited for much better (if not ideal) conditions. But the 1939 White Paper—those rules and regulations laid down for us by strangers to whom the lives of Jews were obviously of secondary importance—turned the entire subject of the right of the *yishuv* to govern itself into the most pressing and immediate need that any of us had ever known. And it was out of the depth of this need, essentially, that the State of Israel was founded, only three years after the end of the war.

What was it that we demanded of the British and that they so stubbornly refused to give us? Today the answer seems incredible, even to me. The truth is that all that the *yishuv* wanted from 1939 to 1945 was to take in as many Jews as could be saved from the Nazis. That was all. Just to be allowed to share the little that we had with men, women and children who were fortunate enough not to have been shot, gassed or buried alive yet by the very people to whose downfall the entire British Empire was in any case totally committed.

We didn't ask for anything else: not for privileges of any kind, not for power, not for promises relating to the future. We just begged—in view of the death sentence that had been passed on millions of European Jews by Hitler and was being carried out—to be permitted to try to rescue as many of them as possible before they all perished and bring them to the one place where they were wanted. When the British first turned a deaf ear to this request and then answered that they couldn't "cope" with it, for all sorts of technical and absolutely invalid reasons (for instance, a "lack of ships," although ships were produced in abundance when, in 1940, it became "necessary" to haul "illegal" immigrants from Palestine to Mauritius), we stopped making requests and began to insist.

But nothing—no pleas, no tears, no demonstrations, no intervention by friends, however influential—did any good. The British White Paper remained in force, and the gates of Palestine opened only long enough and wide enough to let in the exact number of Jews stipulated in that shameful document, and not one more. It was then that we all knew what many of us had always suspected : no foreign government could or would ever feel our agonies as we felt them, and no foreign government would ever put the same value on Jewish lives that we did. It wasn't a very complicated lesson to learn, but once it was learned, it wasn't likely that any of us would forget it, although, just as incredibly, the rest of the world, with very few exceptions, seems by now to have done so. It was not, mind you, as though any real choices were involved or as though a long line of other nations were queuing up in front of the British Colonial Office and clamoring to receive refugees, and shelter, feed and rehabilitate them. A few countries were prepared—to their eternal credit—to take in some of the Jews if and when they managed to escape the Holocaust. But nowhere on the face of the earth except in Palestine was there a single country that was anxious to receive the Jews, prepared to pay any price for them, to do anything and take any risks required to save them.

The British remained adamant. They went on fighting like lions against the Germans, the Italians and the Japanese, but they couldn't or wouldn't stand up to the Arabs at all—although much of the Arab world was openly pro-Nazi. For the life of me, I cannot understand to this day, in the light of what was happening to the Jewish people, why the British found it impossible to say to the Arabs, "You have nothing at all to worry about. Once the war is over, we will see to it that each and every clause of the White Paper is fully enforced, and if they defy us, we will send the British army, navy and air force to subdue the Jews of Palestine. But right now what is at stake is not the future of the Middle East or of the mandate or of national aspirations of any kind. It is the lives of millions of human beings, and we, the British, will not stand in the way of the rescue of Hitler's victims. The White Paper will have to wait until after the war."

After all, what would have happened if the British had issued a declaration of this sort? A few Arab leaders might have made threatening speeches. Perhaps there would have been a protest march or two. Maybe there would even have been an additional act of pro-Nazi sabotage somewhere in the Middle East. And maybe it would have been too late to save most of the Jews of Europe anyway. But thousands more of the 6,000,000 might have survived. Thousands more of the ghetto fighters and Jewish partisans might have been armed. And the civilized world might then have been freed of the terrible accusation that not a finger was lifted to help the Jews in their torment.

As it was, in all those long, tragic years of the war and its immediate aftermath, I did not once encounter—or even hear of—a single Palestinian Jew who hesitated for one moment to offer whatever personal or national sacrifices might be needed in order to reach out to the Jews of Europe and bring them into safety. Not that there was always unanimity among us as to how this could be be done, but to the best of my knowledge, the question of whether it should be done or not never once arose. If no one else was going to help us, then we were going to have to try to go it alone— which is just what we did.

"We shall fight Hitler as if there were no White Paper and fight the

White Paper as if there were no Hitler" was a ringing slogan, but not simple to implement. Actually, not one but three closely linked (though still separate) struggles were under way in Palestine during the first years of the war, and as a member of the Va'ad Hapoel I participated in each of them. There was the desperate struggle to get as many Jews as possible into Palestine, the humiliating and inexplicable battle we were forced to fight in order to persuade the British to let us take part in military action against the Nazis, and finally the struggle—in the face of almost total British indifference—to preserve the *yishuv*'s economy so that we could emerge from the war strong enough and healthy enough to absorb a large immigration—provided there were any Jews left to immigrate.

I remember distinctly the day that those first awful reports reached us about the gas chambers and the soap and lamp shades that were being made from Jewish bodies. We held an emergency meeting in the offices of the Histadrut and decided on the spot to send someone to Ankara to try to make contact with the Jews from there. The curious and terrible thing was that none of us questioned the information we received. We all believed the reports immediately and in their entirety. The next day I had an appointment on some minor, routine matter with a British official whom I had always liked, and naturally I told him what we had just learned about the Nazi atrocities. After a few minutes he looked at me with an odd expression and said, "But, Mrs. Meyerson, surely you don't believe all that, do you?" Then he went on to explain to me about the atrocity propaganda of World War I and how utterly outlandish it had been. I couldn't explain to him how or why I knew that this was different, but I could see in his worried, rather kind blue eyes that he thought I had gone quite mad. "You mustn't believe everything you hear," he said to me gently before I left.

Anyhow, we did our regular jobs during the day, and in between and at night we did whatever we could about the war against the Jews. Since I had worked in the field of labor negotiations before, I went on with this work, although now I dealt almost exclusively with the British military authorities. The British, as I have mentioned, were dead set against letting the Jews of Palestine volunteer for the army (although 130,000 did so) and invented a series of complicated schemes (most of which failed) for keeping enlistment in the *yishuv* down to the bare minimum, including insistence on equal numbers of Jewish and Arab recruits. But when the war spread to the Middle East, the Allies found themselves increasingly dependent on the one source of highly skilled (and, of course, politically completely reliable) manpower in the area. Tens of thousands of young

Palestinian Jews who were barred from serving in British combat units worked thoughout the war as army drivers, in the ordnance service corps and with the medical corps. They were known, needless to say, as "Palestinians," not as Jews, and they were treated as "natives," but at least they were part of the army. The *yishuv*'s civilian labor force, however—both skilled and unskilled—was not only treated as "natives" but also paid at Egyptian rates of pay.

The man we had sent to Ankara (Mellech Neustadt, today Noy) came back to the Va'ad Hapoel one day with news that made us tremble. He had found people in Turkey who could establish contact with the Jewish underground in Poland. In addition to asking a great deal of money for their services, he thought they would probably take for themselves huge cuts out of anything they undertook to deliver to the ghettos, and some of them were almost certainly Nazis. But we weren't hiring office workers. We were looking for emissaries who could move more or less freely in Nazi-occupied Europe, and their *curricula vitae* didn't matter. That very day we began to organize a secret fund. We set what was then a staggering goal for ourselves—75,000 pounds sterling—although we already knew that only a fraction of this sum—if we ever raised it—would get to its destination. But with that fraction Jews might be able to secure arms and food, not much of either under any circumstances, but enough perhaps, to keep the Jewish resistance movements going, however briefly.

That was the real beginning of our desperate attempts to batter our way into Nazi-occupied Europe and throw a lifeline to the Jews. By the time the war ended there was no route we hadn't explored, no opening we hadn't pursued, no possibility we hadn't investigated at once.

Interviewers have sometimes asked me what I feel about the Germans. Postwar Germany was something with which the State of Israel had to deal, make contact, and work. That was one of the facts of life after World War II, and facts of life have to be faced, however painful they are. It should go without saying that nothing will ever diminish the impact of the Holocaust. Six million murdered Jews are also a fact of life, a fact that must never be erased from the memory of man and certainly that no Jew—or German—should ever forget. But although it took years before I forced myself—in 1967—to set foot on German soil again, I was always in favor of reparations, of taking money from the Germans so that we could build up the State of Israel, for I believe that they owed us at least that much, so that we could absorb the surviving Jews. I also believe that Israel itself is the strongest guarantee against another Holocaust.

And when the time was ripe, I was also in favor of diplomatic relations with Germany's government, although I violently opposed that government's choice of an ambassador and was outraged when I learned that Rolf Pauls had fought and even been wounded (he lost an arm) in the war. "Never mind that he is a brilliant career diplomat," I said, "and never mind that he was not a member of the Nazi Party. Let the Germans at least send an ambassador who has no war record at all." But the German government refused to change its mind. Rolf Pauls came to Israel, and there were demonstrations against him, and I was sure he would have to be recalled. Fortunately, I was wrong. Today he is Bonn's ambassador to Peking, but he is still one of Israel's staunchest and best friends.

When Pauls first presented his credentials in Jerusalem, I was Israel's foreign minister. Since I assumed that he had been told and thus knew exactly how I felt about his appointment, it was not an easy moment, but at least, I thought, it was a moment for truth. "You have a most difficult task before you," I said to him. "This is a country made up, to a large extent, of the victims of the Holocaust. There is hardly a family that does not live with nightmare recollections of the crematoria, of babies used as targets for Nazi bullets, of Nazi 'scientific' experiments. You cannot expect a warm reception. Even the women who will wait at table, if you ever come to me for a meal, have Nazi numbers tatooed on their arms."

"I know," Pauls answered. "I have come to you now from Yad Vashem [Israel's memorial to the 6,000,000], and there is already one thing I can promise you. For as long as I serve here, I shall make it my business to see that any German who comes to this country goes first—as I did today—to that memorial." And he kept his word.

Although nothing ever can or will bring the slaughtered back to life, the trial of Adolf Eichmann in Jerusalem in 1961 was, I believe, a great, necessary act of historic justice. It took place two decades after those desperate years in which we tried in every way possible to deny him his prey, but it is part of the record of the Holocaust nonetheless. I was (and I am) absolutely convinced that only the Israelis were entitled to try Eichmann on behalf of world Jewry, and I am deeply proud that we did so. It was not, in any sense, a question of revenge. As the Hebrew poet Bialik once wrote, not even the devil himself could dream up an adequate revenge for the death of a single child, but those who remained alive—and generations still unborn—deserve, if nothing else, that the world know, in all its dreadful detail, what was done to the Jews of Europe and by whom.

For as long as I live, I shall never forget sitting huddled in that courtroom with Sheyna, hearing the evidence of the survivors. Many of my friends had the strength to attend the trial day after day, but I must confess that I went only twice. There are not many things in life that I have knowingly dodged; but those living testimonies of torture, degradation and death—given in the chill presence of Eichmann himself—were literally unbearable for me, and instead, I listened to the trial on the radio, as did most people in Israel. But that, too, made it impossible to go on normally with life.

In 1960, standing before the Security Council to answer the charges of illegality brought against Israel by the government of Argentina (from which country Eichmann had been plucked by Israeli volunteers), I tried to explain at least what the trial meant to the Jews. Of all the public addresses I have made, that was the one that most drained me because I felt I was speaking for millions who could no longer speak for themselves and I wanted each word to have meaning—not just to be moving or horrifying for a minute or two. It is always much easier, I have discovered, to make people cry or gasp than to make them think.

It wasn't a long statement, but I shall quote part of it here. I do so because to my sorrow there are still people who do not understand that we are committed to live and act so that those Jews who were killed in the gas chambers will have been the last Jews ever to die without defending themselves. And because they do not or cannot understand *this,* such people have also never understood what is called our "obstinacy."

Hitler did not solve the Jewish question according to his plans. But he annihilated six million Jews—Jews of Germany, France, Belgium, Holland, Luxembourg, Poland, the USSR, Hungary, Yugoslavia, Greece, Italy, Czechoslovakia, Austria, Rumania, Bulgaria. With these Jews were destroyed over thirty thousand Jewish communities which for centuries had been the center of Jewish faith, learning and scholarship. From this Jewry stemmed some of the giants in the field of arts, literature and science. Was it only this generation of Jews of Europe that was gassed? One million children—the future generation—were annihilated. Who can encompass this picture in all its horror and its consequences for the Jewish people for many generations to come and for Israel? Here was destroyed the natural reservoir for all that is needed for a new country—learning, skill, devotion, idealism, a pioneering spirit.

I spoke also of Eichmann himself and of his direct personal responsibility and went on:

I am convinced that many in the world were anxious to bring Eichmann to trial, but the fact remains that for fifteen years nobody found him. And he could break laws of who knows how many countries, by entering them under a false name and forged passport and abuse the hospitality of countries which, I am sure, recoil in horror from his deeds. But Jews, some of whom personally were the victims of his brutality, found no rest until they located him and brought him to Israel—to the country to whose shores hundreds of thousands of the survivors of the Eichmann horror have come home; to the country that existed in the heart and minds of the six million, as on the way to the crematoria they chanted the great article of our faith: *Ani ma'amin be'emuna shlema beviate ha-Mashiah* (I believe with perfect faith in the coming of the Messiah).

And then, I ended with a question:

Is this a problem for the Security Council to deal with? This is a body that deals with threats to the peace. Is this a threat to peace—Eichmann brought to trial by the very people to whose total physical annihilation he dedicated all his energies, even if the manner of his apprehension violated the laws of Argentina? Or did the threat to peace lie in Eichmann at large, Eichmann unpunished, Eichmann free to spread the poison of his twisted soul to a new generation?

That was fifteen years after the Holocaust ended. But in the early 1940s no one knew how or when it would end—or even whether it would end at all. Despite the tightening of the British blockade, one Haganah ship after another (there were more than sixty in all) was purchased, filled with Jews and sent on its way to Palestine. Each time the British patrols were more alert, and the voyage in those barely seaworthy, crowded, filthy ships became more dangerous. It was not, however, only Jews escaping the European camps that the British hunted down so obsessively. It was also the Haganah and whatever arms it managed to accumulate.

It seemed probable to most of us that when the war ended in an Allied victory, as it obviously would, the British would re-think their catastrophic Palestine policy. At the very least we were sure in 1945 that whatever Jews had stayed alive in Europe would be let into Palestine. In the dawn of a new postwar era the White Paper would certainly be abrogated, particularly since there was now a Labour government in Britain. For thirty years the British Labourites had condemned the restrictions on Jewish immigration to Palestine and issued one pro-Zionist statement after another. It may have been extremely naive of us to have believed that now everything would change, but it was certainly not unreasonable—especially in the light of the horrifying spectacle of hundreds of thousands of emaciated survivors tottering out of the death camps into the arms of the liberating British forces.

Of course, we were wrong. British policy certainly did change but it changed for the worse. Not only did Mr. Atlee's government not revoke the White Paper, but it announced that it saw no need to honor any of the pledges it had made about Palestine—pledges made, even worse, not only to us, but to millions of British workers and soldiers. Ernest Bevin, the new British foreign secretary, had a "Final Solution" of his own for the problem of the Jews of Europe, who were now becoming known conveniently as displaced persons. If they pulled themselves together and made a real effort, they could settle down quietly in Europe again. Never mind that the Continent was one great cemetery for millions of murdered Jews or that there was only one place in the whole world to which the wretched DPs wanted to go—Palestine.

It was hard, almost impossible for me to believe that instead of helping us—as it had solemnly promised to do for so long—lay the foundations for Jewish independence in Palestine, a British Labour government, come to power in the wake of a world war, was now prepared to send British soldiers to wage war against innocent people who asked only one thing: that they be allowed to live out their days among other Jews in Palestine. Even today I cannot account—for the blind fury with which the British government pursued those Jews—and us. But it was that fury which left us with no alternative at all other than to take up the challenge, although we certainly weren't equipped to do so. Between the summer of 1945 and the winter of 1947 we transported some 70,000 Jews from the DP camps of Europe on those thoroughly inadequate ships of ours and got them through a blockade ferociously maintained by a government made up of men to whose stirring proclamations of Zionism I myself had listened at countless Labour Party conferences.

The real struggle—the *ma'avak* itself—should be dated from 1945, but 1946 was, I think, the year of decision. The immediate background was the British government's astonishing refusal to agree to an appeal made by no less a person than President Truman, who asked that 100,000 Jewish refugees from Germany and Austria be allowed to enter Palestine—exclusive of the White Paper—in a one time gesture of mercy and humanity. But Mr. Attlee and Mr. Bevin, who apparently thought that the "problem" of European Jews was created only in order to embarrass the British government, said no to President Truman, too.

By now Palestine was in a state of great unrest. Ship after ship brought refugees to its shores only to have the British subtract the number of "illegal" immigrants from that month's quota of certificates of entry, and when the Haganah refused to halt this immigration, the British issued emergency regulations that amounted to martial law.

In April, while the committee was preparing its report, the British took one more step in their war against the refugees. It wasn't enough that the Royal Navy, the Royal Air Force and thousands of British soldiers were engaged in patrolling the coast of Palestine and trying to trap the "dangerous political offenders" who were helping bring the DPs out of Europe. Now the battle spread to another country. Two Haganah ships (one, the *Fede,* renamed the *Dov Hos,* and the second named the *Eliahu Golomb*) were caught at La Spezia, on the Italian Riviera, just before they were due to leave for Palestine with 1,014 refugees on board. Under British pressure the Italians refused to let the ships sail, while the refugees, for their part, refused to disembark. They declared a hunger strike and said that if force were used against them, they would kill themselves and sink the ships.

I had no doubt at all that they were desperate enough to do it, and I couldn't bear the thought of those poor, exhausted people, jammed together like sardines, depriving themselves of even the little food we managed to give them. If we couldn't bring the boats in ourselves, at least we could show the immigrants—and the rest of the world—how profoundly outraged we were. I went first to the Va'ad Hapoel and then to the Va'ad Le'umi (the Jewish National Council, which represented the entire *yishuv* and of which Remez was then chairman) and suggested that we declare a hunger strike to relieve the refugees in La Spezia. We made two conditions: that each major group in the *yishuv* send not more than one representative to the Va'ad Le'umi in Jerusalem, where the strike was to take place, and that only fifteen persons in good health would be allowed to participate.

I was on rather shaky ground here because I had just been rather ill, and I wasn't really surprised when my doctors told me that it was out of the question for me to join the strikers. "OK," I said to him. "You can choose. Either I sit with them in the Va'ad Le'umi or I'll sit at home and fast. You can't expect me not to be in on the strike at all." He wasn't pleased, but he eventually gave in and handed me the precious medical certificate. I wasn't the only person to have trouble with doctors. Shazar had been ill too, but he went to a gynecologist friend of his in Rehovot and got a certificate from him without any trouble (although after the strike, by the way, he was taken straight to hospital, where he stayed for nearly a month).

We set up beds in the Va'ad Le'umi offices, drank tea without sugar when we were parched but ate nothing for 101 hours, though I had decided, thank God, that smoking was permissible. One difficulty that presented itself was that the third day of the hunger strike coincided with the beginning of Passover, and Chief Rabbi Herzog informed us that we must end our strike since, according to Jewish law, all Jews must eat at the Seder. So we had a consultation, the experts among us said that we need not eat more than a piece of matzo (no larger than an olive), and we went on with the strike. The Seder that night was very moving. Then, for the duration of our hunger strike, Jews filled the courtyard below us, praying and chanting and delegations came from all over the country to wish us well. One day, to my delight, Menachem and Sarah appeared, and Ben-Gurion was with us often, although he had been against the strike for some reason. In theory people were only allowed to visit us once a day between 12 and 1 P.M. , but in fact we were very rarely alone.

I remember that a few minutes before we began the strike, we decided to visit the chief secretary of the Palestine government and make one last plea that the people at La Spezia be allowed in. He listened; then he turned to me and said, "Mrs. Meyerson, do you think for a moment that His Majesty's government will change its policy because *you* are not going to eat?" I said, "No, I have no such illusions. If the death of six million didn't change government policy, I don't expect that my not eating will do so. But it will at least be a mark of solidarity."

Nonetheless, the hunger strike *did* make an impression. On May 8 the *Dov Hos* and the *Eliahu Golomb* under heavy British escort, sailed for Palestine—1,014 certificates having been duly deducted from the May quota. That month the Anglo-American Committee published its report. It proposed that 100,000 immigrants be admitted to Palestine at once and the land-sale regulations of the White Paper be abolished. There was also a long-term suggestion that the mandate be extended into a UN trusteeship. But Mr. Bevin said no again. If 100,000 refugees entered in the face of Arab opposition, it would take an entire British division to restore order in Palestine, he said. "In that case," I told a party conference in Haifa that week, "we shall prove to Mr. Bevin that unless his policy is altered, he will have to send an army division to fight *us*." Mr. Bevin was, in fact, quite anxious to do just that—and did.

On Saturday, June 29, 1946, the British government in effect declared war on the *yishuv*. One hundred thousand British soldiers and nearly 2,000 policemen broke into dozens of kibbutzim and villages; raided the national institutions, such as the Jewish Agency, the Va'ad Le'umi and the Va'ad Hapoel; slapped a curfew on all the cities in the country that had a Jewish population; and imprisoned more than 3,000 Jews, including most of the *yishuv*'s leaders. The purpose of this was at least threefold: It was intended to demoralize and punish the *yishuv*, to destroy the Haganah and to put a stop—once and for all—to "illegal" immigration by jailing the people who were responsible. It failed on all three counts, but from that "Black Saturday" (as it is known today in Israel) on, Palestine became literally a police state.

Luckily, we had been tipped off that an operation of this kind was in the making. Dozens of Haganah commanders went into hiding, arms were moved to new caches, and new codes were invented. Ben-Gurion was abroad in any case, but Remez, Sharett and virtually all the members of the Jewish Agency and the Va'ad Le'umi were rounded up and sent to a detention camp in Latrun. I wasn't arrested, however, although there were people who said unkindly that this was the worst thing the mandatory government ever did to me! Perhaps I really wasn't important enough—or perhaps they couldn't accommodate women in Latrun. At all events, it was considered by many to be a mark of honor to have been rounded up that day, and one of my colleagues was so anxious to be jailed with everyone else that instead of hiding, he walked around the streets all day until a policeman finally told him to go home. I remember Paula Ben-Gurion (a woman not known for her tact) phoning me every few hours: "Golda, you are still at home? They didn't come to take you?" I'd say no and hang up. Then she'd call again: "Golda, they haven't come yet?" All this on the phone as though nobody else could listen in.

The British didn't only arrest people and search for arms and documents, but caused enormous wanton damage. One of the big kibbutzim, Yagur, was occupied for a whole week. The British had found a Haganah arsenal there, and they tore the kibbutz apart. The settlers, assumed by the British to be members of the Haganah, refused to identify themselves by name, only as "Jews in Palestine," and the men were all dragged off to detention camps so that only the women and children were left in Yagur when the troops took over. As soon as the soldiers left, I went there to see the damage, and I shall never forget picking up snapshots of kibbutz children with the eyes poked out of the photographs.

Since Sharett was in Latrun, I became acting head of the Jewish Agency's Political Department, and in that capacity I suggested that the yishuv's response to the mass arrest of thousands of people could only be civil resistance. Not only was it impossible to take what had happened lying down, but unless we did something effective, I knew the Irgun Zvai Le'umi and the Stern Group would take matters into their own hands.

There is a time and place for everything, and this book is not the place, nor this the time, for going into the full, detailed and on the whole tragic story of the two dissident underground organizations that existed in the yishuv then or of their relationship with the Haganah. I leave that to others and the future. But I feel that it would be dishonest for me not to make crystal clear my own attitude to the methods (and philosophy) of the Irgun Zvai Le'umi and the Sternists. I was and always have been unalterably opposed—both on moral grounds and tactically—to terror of any kind, whether waged against Arabs because they are Arabs or against the British because they were British. It was, and has remained, my firm conviction that although many individual members of these dissident groups were certainly extremely brave and extremely dedicated, they were wrong (and thus dangerous to the *yishuv*) from start to finish. And I was positive in the summer of 1946 that if we did not react effectively to the events of "Black Saturday," they would do so and bring even greater disasters upon us. As soon as I could, I went to see Dr. Chaim Weizmann in Rehovot in the hope of persuading him to call for this kind of massive demonstration. At that time, Dr. Weizmann was president of the World Zionist Organization and chairman of the Jewish Agency. He was, without question, the leader and the premier spokesman of world Jewry.

A noted scientist, Weizmann was Russian-born, but had lived and worked in England for years and had played a major role in securing the Balfour Declaration. He was a majestic man, tall, good-looking and regal in bearing. Jews throughout the world thought and spoke of him as "king of the Jews," and although he belonged to no one political party, he was always deeply involved with the kibbutz movement in particular and close to the labor movement in general—although inevitably there was friction between Weizmann the gradualist and Ben-Gurion the activist. Their relationship worsened during the war, when Ben-Gurion felt that Dr. Weizmann was not doing enough to press for the creation of a Jewish Brigade and even proposed to the party that we ask Weizmann to resign from office. We didn't go along with Ben-Gurion, of course, but later, at the Zionist Congress of 1946 in Basel, Weizmann received a vote of no-confidence.

Despite stories that are told in Israel today regarding the real relationship between these two men, so entirely different from each other in temperament and approach, Ben-Gurion, like the rest of us, admired and loved Weizmann, although he never shared Weizmann's trusting and optimistic attitude toward the British. Weizmann believed—even after 1946—that the British would come to their senses one day, and he found it impossible to accept the extent of their betrayal of us. But whether in or out of office, he was, for the thirty years of the mandate, the one man who embodied Zionism for the world outside Palestine, and his influence was immense.

It was only Weizmann who could have persuaded President Truman, at zero hour in 1948, to recognize a Jewish state of which the Negev was a part. He was old and frail then and nearly blind, but when Truman did authorize the recognition of Israel by the United States on the afternoon of May 14, 1948, it was of Dr. Weizmann that he thought and spoke. "The old doctor will believe me now," he said. And there was never any doubt in Ben-Gurion's mind that when we had a state of our own, Chaim Weizmann would be its first president.

CHAPTER 8

WE HAVE OUR STATE

If 1946 was difficult, then I can only describe 1947 as the year in which the situation in Palestine got completely out of hand as far as the British were concerned. In the course of that year the battle against Jewish immigration turned into open warfare, not only against the entire *yishuv* as such, but also against the refugees themselves. It was as though Ernest Bevin had nothing else whatsoever on his mind except how to keep Jewish refugees out of the Jewish homeland.

I don't know (nor does it really matter anymore) whether Bevin was a little insane, or just anti-Semitic, or both. What I do know is that he insisted on pitting the strength of the British Empire against the will of the Jews to live and that by so doing he not only brought great suffering to people who had already suffered enormously, but also forced upon thousands of British soldiers and sailors a role that must have filled them with horror. I remember staring at some of the young Englishmen who guarded the DP detention camps on Cyprus—when I went there myself in 1947—and wondering how on earth they managed to reconcile themselves to the fact that not so long ago they were liberating from Nazi camps the very same people whom they now kept penned behind barbed wire on Cyprus only because these people found it impossible to go on living anywhere except Palestine.

At the Zionist Congress in Basel in 1946 it had been decided that Moshe Sharett should head the Political Department of the Jewish Agency from Washington and that I should remain its head in Jerusalem. But by 1947 living in Jerusalem was like living in a city occupied by an extremely hostile foreign power. The British shut themselves up in what was actually an improvised fortress—a heavily guarded compound (we called it Bevingrad) right in the middle of town—sent their tanks rumbling through the streets at the slightest provocation and forbade their troops to have anything to do with the Jews. Whenever the Irgun Zvai Le'umi and the Stern Group took the law into their own hands—which, most unfortunately, they did fairly regularly—the British responded with retaliatory actions that were aimed at the entire *yishuv*, particularly at the Haganah, and hardly a week went by without some sort of crisis—arms searches, mass arrests, curfews that lasted for days and paralyzed everyday life and, finally, the deportation of Jews without even a charge, let alone a trial. When the British began flogging members of the Irgun or Sternists whom they caught, the two dissident organizations responded by kidnapping and even executing two British soldiers—and all this while our battle for free immigration and land settlement was in full force.

Looking back at that period, I can see, of course, that almost any other colonial power imposing itself on a rebellious native population (which is how the British saw us) would probably have behaved in an even harsher manner. But the British were harsh enough. It wasn't only their often very cruel punitive measures that made the situation so intolerable; it was also our knowledge that whenever possible, they aided and abetted the Arabs, not to speak of inciting them against us. On the other hand, the idea of a perpetual bloodbath in Palestine was also not very appealing to Britain—least of all in its postwar mood—and in February, 1947, Mr. Bevin himself decided that his government was tired of the whole thing and said so in the House of Commons. Let the United Nations deal with the Palestine problem. The British had had enough. I can't imagine that the United Nations was overjoyed at having this responsibility dumped on it, but it couldn't very well refuse to accept it.

The UN Special Committee on Palestine (UNSCOP) arrived in the country in June. According to its terms of reference, it was to report back to the UN General Assembly by September 1, 1947, with some sort of concrete proposal for a solution. The Palestinian Arabs, as usual, refused to cooperate with it in any way, but everyone else did, though a little wearily: the leaders of the *yishuv*, the Palestine government and later even the leaders of some of the Arab states. I spent a lot of time with the eleven members of the committee and was horrified to discover how little they knew of the history of Palestine or of Zionism, for that matter. But since it was essential that they learn—and as quickly as possible—we began to explain and expound as we had done so often before, and eventually they started to grasp what all the fuss was about and why we were not prepared to give up our right to bring the survivors of the Holocaust to Palestine.

Then, for reasons which will never be understood by me—nor, I suspect, by anyone else—just before UNSCOP was scheduled to leave Palestine, the British chose to demonstrate in the most unmistakable way just how brutally and tyrannically they were dealing with us and with the question of Jewish immigration. Before the shocked eyes of the members of UNSCOP they forcibly caged and returned to Germany the 4,500 refugees who had come to Palestine aboard the Haganah ship *Exodus 1947*, and I think that by so doing, they actually contributed considerably to UNSCOP's final recommendations. If I live to be a hundred, I shall never erase from my mind the gruesome pictures of hundreds of British soldiers in full combat dress, bearing and using clubs, pistols and grenades against the wretched refugees on the *Exodus,* 400 of whom were pregnant women determined to give birth to their babies in Palestine. Nor will I ever be able to forget the revulsion with which I heard that these people were going to be shipped back, like animals in their cages, to DP camps in the one country that symbolized the graveyard of European Jewry.

The summer of 1947 dragged on and on. Despite the fact that the Tel Aviv-Jerusalem road was increasingly coming under the control of armed Arab bands, who shot at all Jewish transport from the hills above it, there was no alternative other than for me to ferry back and forth between the two cities and rely on the young Haganah guards who accompanied me. What was really at stake was not whether I would be killed or wounded traveling to Tel Aviv and back, but whether the Arabs would succeed in their proclaimed intention of cutting the road altogether and thus starving out the Jews of Jerusalem. And I was certainly not about to help them achieve this aim by refraining from using the one road that connected Jerusalem to the Jewish centers of the country. Once or twice a bullet whizzed through the window of the Jewish Agency car in which I used to travel, and once we took a wrong turn and arrived in an Arab village that I knew to be a nest of cutthroats; but we escaped without a scratch.

The death toll on the roads rose weekly, and by November, 1947, the Arabs—in full view of the British—had begun to lay seige to Jerusalem.

On August 31—only a minute or two before their deadline expired—the eleven gentlemen of UNSCOP, convened in Geneva, turned in their report on Palestine. Eight members of the committee recommended—as the Peel Commission had—that the country be partitioned into an Arab state and a Jewish state, plus an international enclave that would take in Jerusalem and its immediate vicinity. The minority (consisting, among others, of the respresentatives of India, Iran and Yugoslavia—all of which had large Moslem populations) suggested a federal Arab-Jewish state. It was now up to the UN General Assembly to decide. In the meantime, all the parties concerned made their responses known, and I can't say that any surprises awaited the United Nations in this respect. We accepted the plan, of course—without much elation but with great relief—and demanded that the mandate come to an end at once. All the Arabs said that they would have nothing to do with either set of recommendations and threatened war unless all Palestine was made an Arab state. The British made clear that they would not cooperate with the implementation of any partition plan unless both the Jews and the Arabs were enthusiastic about it, and we all knew what that meant. And the Americans and the Russians each published statements in favor of the majority recommendation.

The next day I held a press conference in Jerusalem. In addition to thanking the committee for having worked so rapidly, I stressed that "we could hardly imagine a Jewish state without Jerusalem" and that "we still hoped that this wrong would be rectified by the UN Assembly." We were also very unhappy, I said, about the exclusion of western Galilee from the Jewish state and assumed that this would be taken up at the Assembly, too. But the most important point I wanted to make was that we were extremely anxious to establish a new and different relationship with the Arabs—of whom, I thought, there would be some 500,000 in the Jewish state. "A Jewish state in this part of the world," I told the press, "is not only a solution for us. It should and can be a great aid for everyone in the Middle East." It is heart-rending now to think that we were using those words—to no avail—as long ago as 1947!

The voting took place at Lake Success in New York on November 29. Like everyone else in the *yishuv*, I was glued to the radio, with pencil and paper, writing down the votes as they came through. Finally, at about midnight our time, the results were announced: thirty-three nations (including the United States and the Soviet Union) were in favor of the partition plan; thirteen, including all the Arab states, opposed it; ten, including Great Britain, abstained. I immediately went to the compound of the Jewish Agency building, which was already jammed with people. It was an incredible sight: hundreds of people, British soldiers among them, holding hands, singing and dancing, with truckloads of more people arriving at the compound all the time. I remember walking up to my office alone, unable to share in the general festivity. The Arabs had turned the plan down and talked only of war. The crowd, drunk with happiness, wanted a speech, and I thought it would be wicked to dampen the mood by refusing. So from the balcony of my office I spoke for a few minutes. But it was not really to the mass of people below me that I talked; it was, once again, to the Arabs.

"You have fought your battle against us in the United Nations," I said. "The United Nations—the majority of countries in the world—have had their say. The partition plan is a compromise: not what you wanted, not what we wanted. But let us now live in friendship and peace together." That speech was hardly the solution for our situation. Arab riots broke out all over Palestine the next day (seven Jews were killed in an Arab ambush on a bus) and on December 2 an Arab mob set the Jewish commercial center in Jerusalem on fire, while British police stood by, interfering only when the Haganah tried to take action.

We were of course, totally unprepared for war. That we had managed for so long to hold the local Arabs at bay, more or less, didn't mean that we could cope with regular armies. We needed weapons urgently, if we could find anyone willing to sell them to us; but before we could buy anything, we needed money—not the sort of money which had helped us to afforest the country or bring in refugees, but millions of dollars. And there was only one group of people in the whole world that we had any chance of getting these dollars from: the Jews of America. There was simply nowhere else to go and no one else to go to. So I flew to the United States without any luggage, with only the dress I had on with a winter coat over it.

The first appearance I made in 1948 before American Jewry was unscheduled, unrehearsed and, of course, unannounced. Also, I was quite unknown to the people I addressed. It was in Chicago on January 21, at the General Assembly of the Council of Jewish Federations and Welfare Funds, which were non-Zionist organizations. Palestine, in fact, was not on the agenda at all. But this was a meeting of professional fund raisers, of the tough experienced men who controlled the Jewish fund-raising machinery in the United States and I knew that if I could get through to them, there was some chance of getting the money that was the key to our ability to defend ourselves. I didn't speak for long, but I said everything that was in my heart. I described the situation as it had been the day I left Palestine.

They listened, and they wept, and they pledged money in amounts that no community had ever given before. I stayed in the United States for as long as I could bear to be away from home, for about six weeks, and the Jews all over the country listened, wept and gave money—and, when they had to, took loans from banks in order to cover their pledges. By the time I came back to Palestine in March I had raised $50,000,000, which was turned over at once for the Haganah's secret purchase of arms in Europe. But I never deceived myself—not even when upon my return Ben-

Gurion said to me, "Someday when history will be written, it will be said that there was a Jewish woman who got the money which made the state possible." I always knew that these dollars were given not to me, but to the state of Israel.

That journey to the States, however, was only one of the journeys I made that year. In the six months that preceded the establishment of the state, I met twice with King Abdullah of Transjordan, who was King Hussein's grandfather. Although both those talks remained closely guarded secrets for many years—long after Abdullah's assassination by his Arab enemies (probably the mufti's henchmen) in Jerusalem in 1951—no one knows to this day to what extent rumors about them were responsible for his death. Assassination is an endemic disease in the Arab world, and one of the first lessons that most Arab rulers learn is the connection between secrecy and longevity. Abdullah's murder made a lasting impression on all subsequent Arab leaders, and I remember that Nasser once said to an intermediary whom we dispatched to Cairo, "If Ben-Gurion came to Egypt to talk to me, he would return home as a conquering hero. But if I went to him, I would be shot when I came back." And I am afraid that is still the situation.

The first time I met King Abdullah was early in November, 1947. He had agreed to meet me—in my capacity as head of the Political Department of the Jewish Agency—in a house at Naharayim (on the Jordan), where the Palestine Electric Corporation ran a hydroelectric power station. I came to Naharayim with one of our Arab experts—Eliahu Sasson. We drank the usual ceremonial cups of coffee, and then we began to talk. Abdullah was a small, very poised man with great charm. He soon made the heart of the matter clear: he would not join in any Arab attack on us. He would always remain our friend, he said, and like us, he wanted peace more than anything else. After all, we had a common foe, the mufti of Jerusalem. Not only that, but he suggested that we meet again, after the United Nations vote.

Throughout January and February we maintained contact with Abdullah, as a rule through the good offices of a mutual friend, through whom I was able to send direct messages to the king. As the weeks passed, my messages became more worried. The air was thick with conjecture, and there were reports that despite his promise to me, Abdullah was about to join the Arab League. Was this indeed so? I asked. The reply from Amman was prompt and negative. King Abdullah was astonished and hurt by my question. He asked me to remember three things: that he was a Bedouin and therefore a man of honor; that he was a king and therefore doubly an honorable man; and finally, that he would never break a promise made to a woman. So there could be no justification for my concern.

But we knew differently. By the first week of May there was no doubt that for all his assurances, Abdullah had, in fact, thrown his lot in with the Arab League. We debated the pros and cons of requesting another meeting before it was too late. Perhaps he could be persuaded to change his mind at the last minute. If not, perhaps we could at least find out from him just how deeply he had committed himself and his British-trained and officered Arab Legion to the war against us. A great deal hung in the balance: not only was the legion by far the best Arab army in the area, but there was also another vital consideration. If, by some miracle, Transjordan stayed out of the war, it would be much harder for the Iraqi army to cross over into Palestine and join in the attack on us. Ben-Gurion was of the opinion that we could lose nothing by trying again, so I requested a second meeting, and asked Ezra Danin to accompany me.

This time, however, Abdullah refused to come to Naharayim. It was too dangerous, he told us through his emissary. If I wanted to see him, I would have to come to Amman, and the risk would have to be entirely mine. He could not be expected, he informed us, to alert the legion to the fact that he awaited Jewish guests from Palestine, and he would take no responsibility for anything that might happen to us en route. The first problem was to get to Tel Aviv, which at that point was almost as difficult as getting to Amman itself. I waited in Jerusalem from early in the morning until 7 P.M. for a plane to arrive from Tel Aviv, and when it finally turned up, it was so windy that we could hardly take off. Under normal conditions I would have tried to postpone the trip for another day, but there were no days left. It was already May 10 and the Jewish state would be proclaimed on May 14. This was our very last chance to talk to Abdullah. So I insisted that we try to reach Tel Aviv—even in that Piper Cub, which looked as though it would collapse even in a strong breeze, let alone a gale. After we left, a message arrived at the airstrip in Jerusalem to say that the weather was far too bad for us to attempt the flight, but we were already on our way by then.

The next morning I set out by car for Haifa, where Ezra and I were to meet. It had already been decided that he would not disguise himself other than by wearing traditional Arab headgear. He spoke fluent Arabic, was familiar with Arab customs and could easily be taken for an Arab. As for me, I would travel in the traditional dark and voluminous robes of an Arab woman. I spoke no Arabic at all, but as a Moslem wife accompanying her husband, it was most unlikely that I would be called on to say anything to anyone. The Arab dress and veils I needed had already been ordered and Ezra explained the route to me. We would change several times, he said, in order to be sure that we were not followed, and at a given point that night someone would turn up not far from the king's palace to lead us to Abdullah. The major problem was to avoid arousing the suspicions of the Arab legionnaires at the various checkposts we had to pass before we got to the place where our guide was to meet us.

It was a long, long series of rides through the night. First into one car, then out of it, and into another for a few more miles and then, at Naharayim into a third car. We didn't talk to each other at all during the journey. I had perfect faith in Ezra's ability to get us through the enemy lines safely, and I was much too concerned with the outcome of our mission to think about what would happen if, God forbid, we were caught. Luckily, although we had to identify ourselves several times, we got to our appointed meeting place on time and undetected. The man who was to take us to Abdullah was one of his most trusted associates, a Bedouin whom the king had adopted and reared since childhood and who was used to running perilous errands for his master.

In his car, its windows covered with heavy black material, he drove Ezra and myself to his house. Abdullah was very pale and seemed under great strain. Ezra interpreted for us, and we talked for about an hour. I started the conversation by coming to the point at once. "Have you broken your promise to me, after all?" I asked him.

He didn't answer my question directly. Instead he said, "When I made that promise, I thought I was in control of my own destiny and could do what I thought right, but since then I have learned otherwise." Then he went on to say that before he had been alone, but now, "I am one of five," the other four, we gathered, being Egypt, Syria, Lebanon and Iraq. Still, he thought war could be averted.

"Why are you in such a hurry to proclaim your state?" he asked me. "What is the rush? You are so impatient!" I told him that I didn't think that a people who had waited 2,000 years should be described as being "in a hurry," and he seemed to accept that.

"Don't you understand," I said, "that we are your only allies in this region? The others are all your enemies."

"Yes," he said. "I know that. But what can I do? It is not up to me."

So then I said to him, "You must know that if war is forced upon us, we will fight and we will win."

He sighed and again said, "Yes. I know that. It is your duty to fight. But why don't you wait a few years? Drop your demands for free immigration.

I will take over the whole country and you will be represented in my parliament. I will treat you very well, and there will be no war."

I tried to explain to him that this plan was impossible. "You know all that we have done and how hard we have worked," I said. "Do you think we did that just to be represented in a foreign parliament? You know what we want and to what we aspire. If you can offer us nothing more than you have just done, then there will be a war and we will win it. But perhaps we can meet again—after the war and after there is a Jewish state."

"You place much too much reliance on your tanks," Danin said. "You have no real friends in the Arab world, and we will smash your tanks as the Maginot Line was smashed." They were very brave words, particularly since Danin knew exactly what the state of our armor was. But Abdullah looked even graver and said again he knew we had to do our duty. He also added, unhappily I thought, that events would have to run their course. All of us would know eventually what fate had in store for us.

"I hope we will stay in touch even after the war starts," Danin said. Then Danin chided him for not taking adequate precautions. "You worship at the mosque," he said to Abdullah, "and permit your subjects to kiss the hem of your garments. One day some evildoer will harm you. The time has come for you to forbid the custom, for safety's sake."

Abdullah was visibly shocked. "I shall never become the prisoner of my own guards," he said very sternly to Danin. "I was born a Bedouin, a free man, and I shall remain free. Let those who wish to kill me try to do so. I will not put myself in chains." Then he bid us farewell and left.

I never saw Abdullah again, although after the War of Independence there were prolonged negotiations with him. Later I was told that he said about me, "If any one person was responsible for the war, it was she, because she was too proud to accept the offer I made her." I must say that when I think of what would have befallen us as a "protected" minority in the kingdom of an Arab ruler who was himself murdered by Arabs within just over two years, I can't bring myself to regret the fact that I disappointed Abdullah so much that night. But I wish that he had been brave enough to stay out of the war. It would have been so much better for him—and for us—if he had been a little prouder.

I was driven back to Tel Aviv. The next morning there was to be a meeting at the headquarters of the Mapai—almost incessant rounds of meetings were going on, of course, all that week—and I knew that Ben-Gurion would be there. When I entered the room, he lifted his head, looked at me and said, "*Nu?*" I sat down and scribbled a note. "It didn't work," I wrote. "There will be war. From Mafraq, Ezra and I saw the troop concentrations and the lights." I could hardly bear to watch Ben-Gurion's face as he read the note, but thank God, he didn't change his mind—or ours.

Within two days the final decision had to be taken: should a Jewish state be proclaimed or not? After I had reported on my conversation with Abdullah, a number of people on the Minhelet Ha'am (literally the People's Administration), made up of members of the Jewish Agency, the Va'ad Le'umi and various small parties and groups which later became the provisional government of Israel, pressed Ben-Gurion for one last evaluation of the situation. They wanted to know what the Haganah's assessment was at zero hour. So Ben-Gurion called in two men: Yigael Yadin, who was the Haganah's chief of operations, and Yisrael Galili, who was its *de facto* commander in chief. Their answers were virtually identical—and terrifying. We could be sure of only two things, they said: the British would pull out, and the Arabs would invade. And then? They were both silent. But after a minute Yadin said, "The best we can tell you is that we have a fifty-fifty chance. We are as likely to win as we are to be defeated."

So it was on that bright note that the final decision was made. On Friday, May 14, 1948 (the fifth of Iyar, 5708, according to the Hebrew calendar), the Jewish state would come into being, its population numbering 650,000, its chance of surviving its birth depending on whether or not the *yishuv* could possibly meet the assault of five regular Arab armies actively aided by Palestine's 1,000,000 Arabs.

On the morning of May 14, I participated in a meeting of the People's Council at which we were to decide on the name of the state and on the final formulation of the declaration. We were all deeply aware of the fact that the proclamation not only spelled the formal end to 2,000 years of Jewish homelessness, but also gave expression to the most fundamental principles of the state. For this reason, each and every word mattered greatly. Incidentally, my good friend Zeev Sharef, the first secretary of the government-to-be (who laid the foundation for the machinery of government), even found time to see to it that the scroll we were about to sign that afternoon should be rushed to the vaults of the Anglo-Palestine Bank after the ceremony, so that it could at least be preserved for posterity—even if the state and we ourselves did not survive for long.

It had been decided to hold the ceremony at the Tel Aviv museum on Rothschild Boulevard because it was small enough to be easily guarded. Although supposedly only the 200-odd people who had been invited to participate knew the details, a large crowd was already waiting outside the museum by the time I arrived there.

A few minutes later, at exactly 4 P.M., the ceremony began. Ben-Gurion, wearing a dark suit and tie, stood up and rapped a gavel. According to the plan, this was to be the signal for the orchestra, tucked away in a second floor gallery, to play "Hatikvah." But something went wrong, and there was no music. Spontaneously, we rose to our feet and sang our national anthem. Then Ben-Gurion cleared his throat and said quietly, "I shall now read the Scroll of Independence." It took him only a quarter of an hour to read the entire proclamation. He read it slowly and very clearly, and I remember his voice changing and rising a little as he came to the eleventh paragraph:

Accordingly we, the members of the National Council, representing the Jewish people in the Land of Israel and the Zionist movement, have assembled on the day of the termination of the British mandate for Palestine, and, by virtue of our natural and historic right and of the resolution of the General Assembly of the United Nations, do hereby proclaim the establishment of a Jewish state in the Land of Israel—the State of Israel.

The State of Israel! My eyes filled with tears, and my hands shook. We had done it. We had brought the Jewish state into existence—and I, Golda Mabovitch Meyerson, had lived to see the day. Whatever happened now, whatever price any of us would have to pay for it, we had recreated the Jewish national home. The long exile was over. From this day on we would no longer live on sufferance in the land of our forefathers. Now we were a nation like other nations, master—for the first time in twenty centuries—of our own destiny. The dream had come true—too late to save those who had perished in the Holocaust, but not too late for the generations to come. Almost exactly fifty years ago, at the close of the First Zionist Congress in Basel, Theodor Herzl had written in his diary: "At Basel, I founded the Jewish state. If I were to say this today, I would be greeted with laughter. In five years perhaps, and certainly in fifty, everyone will see it." And so it had come to pass.

As Ben-Gurion read, I thought again about my children and the children that they would have, how different their lives would be from mine and how different my own life would be from what it had been in the past, and I thought about my colleagues in besieged Jerusalem, gathered in the offices of the Jewish Agency, listening to the ceremony through static on the radio. It seemed to me that no Jew on earth had ever been more privileged than I was that Friday afternoon.

Then, as though a signal had been given, we rose to our feet, crying and clapping, while Ben-Gurion, his voice breaking for the only time, read : "The State of Israel will be open to Jewish immigration and the in-gathering of exiles." This was the very heart of the proclamation, the reason for the state and the point of it all. I remember sobbing out loud when I heard those words spoken in that hot, packed little hall. But Ben-Gurion just rapped his gavel again for order and went on reading:

"Even amidst the violent attacks launched against us for months past, we call upon the sons of the Arab people dwelling in Israel to keep the peace and to play their part in building the state on the basis of full and equal citizenship and due representation in all its institutions, provisional and permanent."

And: "We extend the hand of peace and good neighborliness to all the states around us and to their peoples, and we call upon them to cooperate in mutual helpfulness with the independent Jewish nation in its land. The State of Israel is prepared to make its contribution in a concerted effort for the advancement of the entire Middle East."

When he finished reading the 979 Hebrew words of the proclamation, he asked us to stand and "adopt the scroll establishing the Jewish state," so once again we rose to our feet. Then, something quite unscheduled and very moving happened. All of a sudden Rabbi Fishman-Maimon stood up and, in a trembling voice, pronounced the traditional Hebrew prayer of thanksgiving. "Blessed be Thou, O Lord our God, King of the Universe, who has kept us alive and made us endure and brought us to this day. Amen." It was a prayer that I had heard often, but it had never held such meaning for me as it did that day.

Before we came up, each in turn, in alphabetical order, to sign the proclamation, there was one other point of "business" that required our attention. Ben-Gurion read the first decrees of the new state. The White Paper was declared null and void, while, to avoid a legal vacuum, all the other mandatory rules and regulations were declared valid and in temporary effect. Then the signing began. I walked straight to the middle of the table, where Ben-Gurion and Sharett sat with the scroll between them. All I recall about my actual signing of the proclamation is that I was crying openly, not able even to wipe the tears from my face, and I remember that as Sharett held the scroll in place for me, a man called David Zvi Pincus, who belonged to the religious Mizrachi Party, came over to try and calm me. "Why do you weep so much, Golda?" he asked me.

"Because it breaks my heart to think of all those who should have been here today and are not," I replied, but I still couldn't stop crying.

Only twenty-five members of the Council signed the proclamation on May 14. Eleven others were in Jerusalem, and one was in the States.

After the Palestine Philharmonic Orchestra played "Hatikvah," Ben-Gurion rapped his gavel for the third time. "The State of Israel is established. This meeting is ended." We all shook hands and embraced each other. The ceremony was over. Israel was a reality.

Not unexpectedly, the evening was filled with suspense. I stayed in the hotel, talking to friends. Someone opened a bottle of wine, and we drank a toast to the state. A few of the guests and their young Haganah escorts sang and danced, and we heard people laughing and singing in the street. But we knew that at midnight the mandate would terminate, the British high commissioner would sail away, the last British soldier would leave Palestine, and we were certain that the Arab armies would march across the borders of the state we had just founded. We were independent now, but in a few hours we would be at war. Not only was I not gay, but I was very frightened—and with good reason. Still, there is a great difference between being frightened and lacking faith, and although the entire Jewish population of the reborn state numbered only 650,000, I knew for certain that night that we had dug in and that no one would be able to disperse or displace us ever again.

But I think it was only on the following day that I really grasped what had happened in the Tel Aviv Museum. Three separate but very closely linked events brought the truth home to me as nothing else could have done, and I realized, perhaps for the first time, that nothing would ever be the same again. Not for me, not for the Jewish people, not for the Middle East. To begin with, just before dawn on Saturday, I saw for myself through the windows of my room what might be called the formal start of the War of Independence: four Egyptian Spitfires zooming across the city on their way to bomb Tel Aviv's power station and airport in what was the first air raid of the war. Then, a little later, I watched the first boatload of Jewish immigrants—no longer "illegals"—enter the port of Tel Aviv, freely and proudly. No one hunted them down anymore or chased them or punished them for coming home. The shameful era of the "certificates" and the human arithmetic had ended, and as I stood there in the sun, my eyes fixed on that ship (an old Greek vessel called the SS *Teti*), I felt that no price demanded of us for this gift could possibly be too high. The first legal immigrant to land in the State of Israel was a tired, shabby old man called Samuel Brand, a survivor of Buchenwald. In his hand he clutched a crumpled slip of paper. It said only, "The right to settle in Israel is hereby given"; but it was signed by the "Immigration Department" of the state, and it was the first visa we ever issued.

And then, of course, there was the wonderful moment of our formal entry into the family of nations. A few minutes after midnight on the night of May 14, my phone rang. It had been ringing all evening, and as I ran to answer it, I wondered what bad news I would hear now. But the voice at the other end of the phone sounded jubilant. "Golda? Are you listening? Truman has recognized us!" I can't remember what I said or did, but I remember how I felt. It was like a miracle coming at the time of our greatest vulnerability, on the eve of the invasion, and I was filled with joy and relief. In a way, although all Israel rejoiced and gave thanks, I think that what President Truman did that night may have meant more to me than to most of my colleagues because I was the "American" among us, the one who knew most about the United States, its history and its people, the only one who had grown up in that great democracy. And although I was astonished as everyone else by the speed of the recognition, I was not at all surprised by the generous and good impulse that had brought it about.

As for the Soviet recognition of Israel, which followed the American recognition, that had other roots. There is now no doubt in my mind that the primary Soviet consideration was to get the British out of the Middle East. But all through the debates that had taken place at the United Nations in the autumn of 1947, it had seemed to me that the Soviet bloc was supporting us also because of the terrible toll that the Russians themselves had paid in the world war and their resultantly deep feeling that the Jews, who had also suffered so bitterly at the hands of the Nazis, deserved to have their state. However radically the Soviet attitude has changed in the intervening two and a half decades, I cannot now falsify the picture as I saw it then. Had it not been for the arms and ammunition that we were able to buy in Czechoslovakia and transport through Yugoslavia and other Balkan countries in those dark days at the start of the war, I do not know whether we actually could have held out until the tide changed, as it did by June, 1948. For the first six weeks of the War of Independence, we relied largely (though not, of course, entirely) on the shells, machine guns, bullets—and even planes—that the Haganah had been able to purchase in Eastern Europe at a time when even the United States had declared an embargo on the sale or shipment of arms to the Middle East. One cannot and must not try to erase the past merely because it does not fit the present, and the fact remains that although the Soviet Union was to turn so savagely against us in the years to come, the Soviet recognition of the State of Israel on May 18 was of immense significance for us.

By the morning of May 15 Israel was already under armed attack by the Egyptians from the south, the Syrians and Lebanese from the north and the northeast, the Jordanians and the Iraqis from the east. On paper it seemed that week as though there might be some grounds for the Arab boast that within ten days Israel would be crushed.

The most relentless advance was that of the Egyptians—though of all the invading armies, the Egyptians certainly had least to gain. Abdullah had a reason. It was a bad one; but it was there, and he was able to define it: he wanted the whole country and especially Jerusalem. Lebanon and Syria also had a reason: they hoped to be able to divide up the Galilee between themselves. Iraq wanted to participate in the bloodletting and—as a fringe benefit—acquire an outlet to the Mediterranean, through Jordan if necessary. But Egypt had no real war aim at all—except to loot and destroy whatever the Jews had built. As a matter of fact, it has never ceased to astonish me that the Arab states have been so eager to go to war against us. Almost from the very beginning of Zionist settlement until today they have been consumed by hatred for us. The only possible explanation—and it is a ridiculous one—is that they simply cannot bear our presence or forgive us for existing, and I find it hard to believe that the leaders of *all* the Arab states have always been so hopelessly primitive in their thinking.

On the other hand, what have we ever done to threaten the Arab states? True, we have not stood in line to return territory we won in wars they started, but territory, after all, has never ever been what Arab aggression is all about—and in 1948 it was certainly not a need for more land that drove the Egyptians northward in the hope of reaching and destroying Tel Aviv and Jewish Jerusalem. So what was it? An overpowering irrational urge to eliminate us physically? Fear of the progress we might introduce in the Middle East? A distaste for Western Civilization? Who knows? Whatever it was, it has lasted—but then so have we—and the solution will probably not be found for many years, although I have no doubt at all that the time will come when the Arab states will accept us. Almost from the very beginning of Zionist settlement until today they been—dependent entirely on only one thing: the Arab leaders must acquiesce in our being here.

In 1948, however, it was understandable that the Arab states—given in any case to chronic flights of fancy—saw themselves as racing through what was now Israel in a matter of days. To begin with, they had begun the war, which gave them great tactical superiority. Secondly, they had easy, not to say effortless, overland access to Palestine, with its Arab population, which had been incited against the Jews for years. Thirdly, the Arabs could move without any problems from one part of the country to the other. Fourthly, the Arabs controlled most of the hilly regions of

Palestine from which our lowland settlements could be attacked without much difficulty. Finally, the Arabs had an absolute superiority of manpower and arms and had been given considerable help by the British in various ways, both direct and indirect.

And what did we have? Not much of anything—and even that is an exaggeration. A few thousand rifles, a few hundred machine guns, an assortment of other firearms, but on May 14, 1948, not a single cannon or tank, although we had all of nine planes (never mind that only one had both engines!). The machinery for making arms had been bought abroad—thanks to Ben-Gurion's amazing foresight—but couldn't be brought into Israel until the British had left, and then it had to be assembled and run in. Our trained manpower situation was also very unimpressive, as far as statistics were concerned. There were about 45,000 men, women and teenagers in the Haganah, a few thousand members of the two dissident underground organizations and a few hundred recent arrivals who had been given some training—with wooden rifles and dummy bullets—in the DP camps of Germany and the detention camps of Cyprus and after independence, another few thousand Jewish and non-Jewish volunteers from abroad. That was all. But we couldn't afford the luxury of pessimism either, so we made an altogether different kind of calculation based on the fact that the 650,000 of us were more highly motivated to stay alive then anyone outside Israel could be expected to understand and that the only option available to us, if we didn't want to be pushed into the sea, was to win the war. So we won it. But it wasn't easy, it wasn't quick, and it wasn't cheap. From the day that the UN resolution to partition Palestine was passed (November 29, 1947) until the day that the first armistice agreement was signed by Israel and Egypt (February 24, 1949) 6,000 young Israelis were killed, 1 percent of our entire population, and although we couldn't have know it then, we hadn't even bought peace with all those lives.

For me to have to leave Israel the moment the state was established was more difficult than I can say. The very last thing I wanted to do was to go abroad, but on Sunday, May 16, a cable came from Henry Montor, vice-president of the United Jewish Appeal. American Jewry had been profoundly moved by what had happened. There were no limits to its excitement or its pride. If I came back, even for a short tour, he thought we might raise another $50,000,000. No one knew better than I what that kind of money would mean to Israel, how desperately we needed the arms it would buy or how much it would cost to move and settle the 30,000 Jews penned up in Cyprus, who had waited so long to come to Israel. After discussing the matter with Ben-Gurion, I cabled back at once that I would leave on the first plane. My clothes, such as they were, were all in Jerusalem, as out of reach as though they were on the moon, so all I had to "pack" was a hairbursh, a toothbrush and a clean blouse.

In the States I was greeted as though I were the personification of Israel. I spoke in city after city throughout the States, at UJA lunches, dinners and teas and at parlor meetings in people's homes. Whenever I felt overwhelmed by fatigue—which was often—all I had to do was to remind myself that I was now talking as an emissary of a Jewish state, and my tiredness simply drained away. It even took me weeks to accustom myself to the sound of the word "Israel" and to the fact that I now had a new nationality. The State of Israel, I told Jews all over America, could not survive on applause. The war would not be won by speeches or declarations or even tears of happiness.

"We cannot go on without your help," I said in dozens of public and private appearances. "What we ask of you is that you share in our responsibility, with everything that this implies—difficulties, problems, hardships and joys."

They answered with unprecedented generosity and speed, with their whole hearts and souls. Nothing was too much or too good, and by their response they reaffirmed their sense of partnership with us, as I had hoped they would. Although there was as yet no separate drive for Israel, and although less than 50 percent of the $150,000,000 raised for the UJA in 1948 actually went to Israel (the rest was turned over to the Joint Distribution Committee for aid to Jews in European countries), that 50 percent unquestionably helped us win the war.

I waited anxiously for the moment when I could return home, although I already knew that the newly created Foreign Office, particularly the new foreign minister, Moshe Sharett, had other plans for me. The day before I left for the States, Sharett and I had met in my hotel, and he has spoken to me of the problems of manning the embassies and consulates that Israel would have to establish in those countries that had either already recognized it or were likely to do so within a few weeks.

"I have no one for Moscow," he said in a very worried voice.

"Well, thank God, you can't offer it to me," I replied. "My Russian is almost nonexistent."

"As a matter of fact, that isn't what matters," he answered. But he didn't pursue the topic and I tried to dismiss it as a good joke.

One day, a cable came from Tel Aviv. I glanced at the signature before I read the text to make sure that it wasn't about Sarah or Menachem (already with his brigade and in combat). But when I saw the name Moshe, I knew that it was about Moscow, and I had to steel myself to read the message. Of all my comrades, I thought, I was surely the least suited to diplomatic life. But I also knew that Sharett must have secured Ben-Gurion's consent to the appointment.

I answered Sharett's cable, not very enthusiastically but affirmatively. "When I get back to Israel, I will try to persuade Moshe and Ben-Gurion that they have made a mistake," I promised myself. At the end of the first week of June, however, my appointment as Israel's minister to Moscow was made public.

While I was in New York I got a cable from Tel Aviv: DO YOU HAVE ANY OBJECTION TO APPOINTMENT OF SARAH AND ZECHARIAH AS RADIO OPERATORS IN MOSCOW EMBASSY? I was very touched—and grateful. To have Sarah and Zechariah, her future husband, with me in Russia was almost worth the exile from Israel. When I came back to Tel Aviv I asked Sheyna if Sarah and Zechariah could be married in the small house which Shamai and she had bought years ago. We decided it would be a real family wedding, with only a few "outside" guests. My father had died in 1946—another of the people who were most dear to me and who had not lived to see the state—and my mother, poor soul, had been incapacitated for several years, her memory gone, her eyesight bad, her personality quite faded away, leaving almost no trace of the critical, energetic, peppery woman she had been. But Morris was there, as gentle as ever and beaming with pride, and so were Zechariah's parents. His father had come to Palestine from Yemen when the Turks still ruled the country. He was very poor, very religious and not formally educated, except in the Torah, but he had brought up a wonderful and loving family—though Zechariah himself by now was quite removed from Yemenite customs and traditions.

I settled in again at the hotel on the seashore. Sarah flew from Revivim to Tel Aviv and moved in with me for a few days, and Zechariah, who had been very ill and in a hospital near Tel Aviv for weeks, was finally discharged. Of our immediate family, only Clara and Menachem were missing at the wedding in Sheyna's garden. I couldn't help thinking how different my own wedding had been—under what different circumstances it had taken place and how differently Morris and I had started out in life together. There was no point to wondering now who had been to blame or why our marriage had fallen apart, but I felt (and rightly it turned out) that Sarah and Zechariah, although they were the same age that we had been when we stood under that bridal canopy in Milwaukee, were more mature and better suited to each other and that they would succeed where Morris and I had failed.

The legation in Moscow would be run in the most typically Israeli style I knew: like a kibbutz. We would work together, eat together, get the same amount of pocket money and take turns doing whatever chores had to be done. As in Merhavia or Revivim, people would do the work that they were trained for and suited to in the opinion of our Foreign Office but the spirit of the legation, its atmosphere and flavor would be that of a collective settlement—which, apart from any other consideration, ought, I believed, to be especially attractive to the Russians (not that their own brand of collectivism was or is anything to write home about). We were to be twenty-six people in all, including Sarah, Zechariah and myself, and the legation's counselor, Mordechai Namir, a widower who brought his fifteen-year-old daughter, Yael, with him. (Namir afterward served as Israel's ambassador to the USSR, then as minister of labor and, for ten years, as mayor of Tel Aviv.) As my personal assistant I chose a most charming woman, Eiga Shapiro, who not only spoke Russian, but also knew much more about the niceties of life than I did and who could be entrusted with such (to me terrifying) missions as deciding what furniture and clothing legation personnel and the minister would need.

I stayed in Israel long enough that summer to welcome the first U.S. ambassador to Israel, that delightfully frank and warm gentleman James G. McDonald, whom I had met before, and to meet the Russian minister, Pavel I. Yershov. It was typical of the newness of the state—and of its lack of proper housing—that the American and Soviet missions in Tel Aviv made their first home in the same hotel, not far from mine, and I never quite got used to seeing the stars and stripes fly from one end of the hotel roof and the hammer and sickle from the other.

A second truce began on July 19, signaling the start of a long, painful round of negotiations over the Negev, which Count Folke Bernadotte, the Swedish UN mediator, recommended be handed over to the Arabs. Considering the fact that he was really a referee, his position was amazingly lacking in neutrality, and he became extremely unpopular—particularly when he added insult to injury by advocating also that Jerusalem be torn away from the Jewish state and that the UN supervise Israel's air and seaports. God knows that these recommendations were unacceptable and that they proved only that Bernadotte really never understood what the State of Israel was all about. But it is certainly no crime to be obtuse, and I was horrified when, on September 17, only two weeks after I arrived in Moscow, I learned that Bernadotte had been shot to death on a quiet street in Jerusalem. Although his assailants were never identified, we knew it would be assumed that they were Jews. I thought the end of the world had come, and I would have given anything to have been able to fly home and be there during the ensuing crisis, but by then I was already deeply involved in a totally new and very demanding way of life.

CHAPTER 9

MINISTER TO MOSCOW

We arrived in Moscow (via Prague) on the gray rainy afternoon of September 3, 1948. The first thing I was told by the officials of the Soviet Ministry of Foreign Affairs who welcomed me at the airport was that we might have some difficulty getting to the hotel because at that very moment, the funeral of Andrei Zhdanov, one of Stalin's closest associates, was taking place in the city. My first impressions of the Soviet Union, therefore, were the length and solemnity of that funeral and the hundreds of thousands—perhaps millions—of people whom we saw in the streets on our way to the Hotel Metropole.

By the time we had been in the hotel for a week I realized that we would have to start our kibbutz style of life as soon as possible or else we would run out of money. The cost of living was unbelievably high, and the first hotel bill we got staggered me. "There is only one way we can manage on our very modest budget," I told my staff, "and that is if we all eat only one meal a day in the hotel dining room. I will provide food for breakfasts and suppers, and on Fridays we'll have our main meal together in the evening." The very next day we went out to buy electric plates, which I then distributed to each of our rooms, together with crockery and cutlery that I borrowed from the hotel—since there was still none to be had in any shop in postwar Moscow.

I was charmed by the politeness, sincerity and warmth of the ordinary Russian although, of course, as a socialist I was constantly shocked by what I saw of the supposedly classless Soviet society. I couldn't believe my eyes when I used to drive through the streets of Moscow and see middle-aged women digging ditches and sweeping the roads with only rags bound around their feet when it was 40 degrees below zero, while other women in furs and high heels stepped into enormous shiny cars.

My first official job was to write a formal letter of condolence to Mr. Molotov, the Soviet foreign minister, on Zhdanov's death and then to present my credentials. The president of the USSR, Nikolai Shvernik, was away, so the ceremony took place in the presence of the deputy president. After my credentials were read, I delivered a little speech in Hebrew (we had sent it earlier to the Soviet chief of protocol so he could prepare a translation), and then there was a modest, rather pleasant reception in my honor.

Now that the major formality was over, I desperately wanted to make contact with the Jews. I had already told my staff that just as soon as I presented my credentials, we all would visit the synagogue. There, if nowhere else, I was sure we would meet the Jews of Russia, from whom we had been separated for thirty years since the Revolution—and about whom we knew almost nothing. What were they like? What had remained of their Jewishness after so many years of life under a regime that had proclaimed war not only against all religions as much, but also specifically against Judaism and that regarded Zionism as a crime for which the only appropriate punishments were penal servitude in a forced-labor camp or exile to Soviet Asia. By the time we arrived in the USSR there was not only overt repression, but also a vicious brand of government-directed anti-Semitism, which was to "blossom" within a few years into the wholesale and ruthless persecution of Jews and the imprisonment of Jewish intellectuals—actors, doctors, writers—accused of "cosmopolitanism" and "Zionist imperialism."

On the first Saturday following the presentation of credentials, we set off on foot for the Great Synagogue (Moscow's other two synagogues were only small wooden structures), each of the legation's men carrying a prayer shawl and a siddur (prayer book). In the synagogue we found only about 100 or perhaps 150 elderly Jews, who, of course, had no idea that we were coming, although we had notified Rabbi Schliefer that we hoped to attend the Sabbath services. As was customary, toward the end of the service, a blessing was recited for the good health of the heads of the state—and then, to my surprise, a blessing for me. I was sitting in the women's gallery (in Orthodox synagogues men and women are separated), and when my name was mentioned, the whole congregation turned to stare at me as though it were memorizing my face. No one said anything. They just looked and looked at me.

A few weeks later it was Rosh Hashanah, the Jewish New Year. I had been told that on the High Holidays many more people came to the synagogue than on Saturdays, and I decided, once again, that the entire legation would attend the Rosh Hashanah service. Then, a day or two before the holiday, a long article appeared in *Pravda*, written by Ilya Ehrenburg, the well-known Soviet journalist and apologist who himself was a Jew. Were it not for Stalin, Ehrenburg wrote piously, there would be no such thing as a Jewish state. "Nonetheless, let there be no mistake about it," he explained, "the State of Israel had nothing to do with the Jews of the Soviet Union, where there is no Jewish problem and therefore no need for Israel. That is for the Jews of the capitalist countries, in which, inevitably, anti-Semitism flourishes. And in any case there is no such entity as the Jewish people. That is as ridiculous a concept as if one claimed that everybody who had red hair or a certain shape of nose belongs to one people." Not only I but the Jews of Moscow read this article. And like me, because they were used to reading between the lines, they understood what it was all about and knew that they were being warned to keep away from us! The response which thousands upon thousands of these Jews deliberately and courageously chose to make to that sinister warning was something which shattered and overwhelmed me at the time I witnessed it and which has inspired me ever since. There is not a detail about what happened on that New Year's Day that I do not remember as vividly—and with as much emotion—as if it had taken place only a few hours ago.

As we had planned, we went to the synagogue on Rosh Hashanah. All of us—the men, women and children of the legation—dressed in our best clothes, as befitted Jews on a Jewish holiday. But the streets in front of the synagogue had changed. Now it was filled with people, packed together like sardines, hundreds and hundreds of them, of all ages, including Red Army officers, soldiers, teenagers and babies carried in their parents' arms. Instead of the 2,000-odd Jews who usually came to the synagogue on the holidays, a crowd of close to 50,000 people was waiting for us. For a minute I couldn't grasp what had happened—or even who they were. And then it dawned on me. They had come—those good, brave Jews—in order to be with us, to demonstrate their sense of kinship and to celebrate the establishment of the State of Israel. Within seconds they had surrounded me, almost lifting me bodily, almost crushing me, saying my name over and over again. Eventually, they parted ranks and let me enter the synagogue, but there, too, the demonstration went on. Every now and then, in the women's gallery, someone would come to me, touch my hand, stroke or even kiss my dress. Without speeches or parades, without any words at all really, the Jews of Moscow were proving their profound desire—and their need—to participate in the miracle of the establishment of the Jewish state, and I was the symbol of the state for them.

I couldn't talk, or smile, or wave my hand. I sat in that gallery like a stone, without moving, with those thousands of eyes fixed on me. No such entity as the Jewish people, Ehrenburg had written. The State of Israel meant nothing to the Jews of the USSR! But his warning had fallen on deaf ears. For thirty years we and they had been separated. Now we were together again, and as I watched them, I knew that no threats, however awful, could possibly have stopped the ecstatic people I saw in the synagogue that day from telling us, in their own way, what Israel meant to them. The service ended, and I got up to leave; but I could hardly walk. I felt as though I had been caught up in a torrent of love so strong that it had literally taken my breath away and slowed down my heart. I was on the verge of fainting, I think. But the crowd still surged around me, stretching out its hands and saying *Nasha Golda* (our Golda) and *Shalom, shalom,* and crying.

Out of that ocean of people, I can still see two figures clearly: a little man who kept popping up in front of me and saying, *"Goldele, leben zolst du. Shana Tova!"* (Goldele, a long life to you and a Happy New Year), and a women who just kept repeating, "Goldele! Goldele!" and smiling and blowing kisses at me.

It was impossible for me to walk back to the hotel, so although there is an injunction against riding on the Sabbath or on Jewish holidays, someone pushed me into a cab. But the cab couldn't move either because the crowd of cheering, laughing, weeping Jews had engulfed it. I wanted to say something, anything, to those people, to let them know that I begged their forgiveness for not having wanted to come to Moscow and for not having known the strength of their ties to us. For having wondered, in fact, whether there was still a link between them and us. But I couldn't find the words. All I could say, clumsily, and in a voice that didn't even sound like my own, was one sentence in Yiddish. I stuck my head out of the window of the cab and said, *"A dank eich vos ihr seit geblieben Yidden"* (Thank you for having remained Jews), and I heard that miserable, inadequate sentence being passed on through the enormous crowd as though it were some wonderful prophetic saying.

Finally, after a few more minutes, they let the cab move forward and leave. In the hotel everyone gathered in my room. We had been shaken to our very depths. Nobody talked. We just sat there. It had been far too great a revelation for us to discuss it, but we needed to be together. I just sat, my face drained of color, staring in front of me. And that was how we stayed, for hours, flooded with emotions so powerful that we couldn't even communicate them to each other. I can't pretend that I knew for certain then that within twenty years I would see many of those Jews in Israel. But I did know one thing: I knew that the Soviet Union had not succeeded in breaking their spirit, that Russia, with all its power, had failed. The Jews had remained Jews.

On Yom Kippur (the Day of Atonement), which comes ten days after the Jewish New Year, thousands of Jews once again crowded the synagogue, and this time I stayed there with them all day. I remember that when the rabbi recited the closing sentence of the service, *"Leshanah haba'ah b'yerushalayim"* (Next year in Jerusalem), a tremor went through the entire synagogue, and I said a little prayer of my own: "God, let it happen. If not next year, then let the Jews of Russia come to us soon." But even then I didn't really expect that it would happen within my lifetime.

Not long afterward I was also given the privilege of meeting Mr. Ehrenburg. One of the foreign correspondents stationed in Moscow, an Englishman, who used to drop in on Friday nights, asked me once if I wanted to meet Ehrenburg. "As a matter of fact, I do," I said. "There are one or two things I'd very much like to talk to him about."

"I'll arrange it," promised the Englishman, but he never did. Then, a few weeks later, there was an Independence Day party in the Czech embassy, and the same journalist came up to me. "Mr. Ehrenburg is here," he said. "Shall I bring him over to you?" Ehrenburg was quite drunk—not an unusual condition for him, I was told—and, from the start, very aggressive. He began speaking to me in Russian.

"I'm sorry, but I can't speak Russian," I said. "Do you speak English?"

He looked at me nastily and replied, "I hate Russian-born Jews who speak English."

"And I am sorry for Jews who don't speak Hebrew or at least Yiddish!" I answered. Lots of people milling around overheard this exchange, and I don't think it increased anyone's respect for Mr. Ehrenburg.

By January, 1949, it was apparent that Russian Jewry was going to pay a heavy price for the welcome it had given us, for the "treachery" to communist ideals that was—in the eyes of the Soviet government—implicit in the joy with which we had been greeted. The Yiddish theater in Moscow was closed. The Yiddish newspaper *Enigkeit* was closed. The Yiddish publishing house Emes was closed. It didn't matter that all these had faithfully followed the communist line. The fact remained that Russian Jewry had shown far too great an interest in Israel to please the Kremlin. Within five months there was practically no single Jewish organization left in Russia, and the Jews kept their distance from us.

I went back to Israel twice during my seven months in Moscow. On the first of those two visits—which was after our elections in January, 1949—Ben-Gurion asked me if I would join the cabinet he was forming. "I want you to serve as minister of labor," he said. Mapai, the Labor Party, had won an overwhelming victory at the polls by receiving 35 percent of the total vote (20 percent more than Mapam, its nearest rival) in an election in which 87 percent of all the eligible voters in Israel had voted.

I was overjoyed by Ben-Gurion's offer. At last I would be where I wanted to be, doing what I most wanted to do and what, for a change, I felt completely qualified to do. I said yes to Ben-Gurion at once, without a moment's hesitation, and I never regretted it. My seven years in the Ministry of Labor were, without doubt, the most satisfying and the happiest of my entire life.

But before I could plunge into my new job, I had to return to Moscow for another few weeks. Most of all, of course, I wanted to say not good-bye but *au revoir* to the Jews; but almost none of them dared come to the legation anymore, and there were no more crowds at the synagogue.

On April 20, 1949, I returned to Israel. At this point, I think it is important to describe what was happening there because in the course of 1949 and 1950 Israel underwent a process that no other country has ever undergone in quite the same way and that was to result in the doubling of our population within only two years. The War of Independence ended (to the extent that it ever ended) in the spring of 1949, and armistice agreements—though not peace treaties—had been signed with Egypt, Lebanon, Jordan and Syria, through the good offices of Dr. Ralph Bunche (who had taken Count Bernadotte's place as UN mediator). Unfortunately, however, their signatures didn't mean that the Arab states were now reconciled to our existence. On the contrary, it meant that the war which they were so anxious to wage against us and which they had lost on the battlefield would now be fought differently and in a manner less likely to result in their defeat but just as likely, they hoped, to destroy the Jewish state. Having been trounced in battle, the Arabs now switched from military weapons to economic ones. They boycotted any companies or individuals that traded with us. They closed the Suez Canal to Israeli shipping, in the face of the international convention which stipulated that the Canal must be open to all nations at all times.

But they didn't stop killing Jews altogether. For years there was a steady infiltration across our borders of armed Arab gangs that murdered and robbed Israelis, set fields and orchards on fire, stole cattle and generally made life a misery in our border settlements.

It may be difficult today to imagine what that flood of human beings was like. These were not immigrants of the kind that had come when Sheyna and I did—sturdy young idealists in good physical condition who couldn't wait to settle on the land and who regarded the discomforts of pioneering as part of the great Zionist experiment in which they had so eagerly involved themselves. Nor were they the professionals, tradesmen or artisans who came in the 1930s with some means of their own and whose contribution to the *yishuv's* economy began as soon as they reached Palestine. The hundreds of thousands of Jews who streamed into Israel in those early years of statehood were utterly destitute. They had nothing at all except the will to live and the desire to get away from their past. Most of them were broken in body, if not in spirit, and many thousands were broken in both. All the Jews of Europe had suffered crippling tragedies; as for the Jews from the Arab lands of the Middle East and North Africa, they had lived, for the most part, uneducated, poverty-stricken and terrorized in the ghettos and casbahs of some of the most repressive countries on earth, and they knew little or nothing about twentieth-century life. It was, in short, a flood of Jews from opposite ends of the earth who spoke different languages, came from widely contrasted backgrounds, ate different foods and were frequently quite ignorant of each other's traditions and customs. The one thing they had in common was that they were all Jews, but that was a great deal—everything, in fact.

I am still amazed by the sheer number of the immigrants we absorbed. But we weren't dealing with abstract numbers then. It wasn't the arithmetic of the Law of the Return—the bill passed by the Knesset in July, 1950, giving the right of immigration to all Jews and automatic Israeli citizenship to all Jewish immigrants—that most concerned us. What worried us was how were we ever going to feed, clothe, house, educate and generally care for those thousands of immigrants. How and with what? By the time I arrived back in Israel there were 200,000 people living (if that's the word) in tents all over the country, more often than not two families to a tent—and not necessarily families from the same country or even the same continent. Apart from the fact that none of the services we improvised in such a rush really worked well or was geared for so many thousands of people, there were also a great many sick, undernourished and handicapped people who might have managed better had they been housed differently but who just couldn't cope at all under the circumstances. The man who had lived through years of Nazi slave labor, survived the DP camps and braved the trip to Israel and who was, at best, in poor health and, at worst, badly damaged physically and entitled to the best possible conditions found himself and his family (if he still had one) living in unbearable proximity with people with whom he didn't even have a common language. Nine times out of ten, he even regarded his

At left, the young Golda in a wedding portrait with her husband, Morris Meyerson; the couple were married in Milwaukee on December 24, 1917.

Only a few days before the outbreak of the Yom Kippur War, Mrs. Meir was in Strasbourg, addressing the Council of Europe (above). Below, the outgoing Prime Minister and Defense Minister Moshe Dayan (left) join in a toast to Israel.

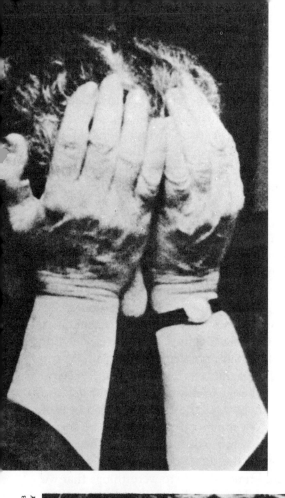

Left, overwhelmed with emotion at being named Prime Minister, Mrs. Meir hides her face in her hands. Below, the busy stateswoman—then Foreign Minister—takes a stroll with one of her grandchildren.

new neighbors as primitive because they had never seen a flush toilet.

In theory, none of this should have mattered. In theory, no over-crowding, no misery, no cultural or intellectual differences should have been at all important for people who had experienced the Holocaust or for those who had literally walked out of Yemen through the robber-infested, scorching desert. But theory is for theoreticians. People are peo-ple, and the tensions and discomforts of those hideous tent cities that I saw everywhere in 1949 were really unbearable. Something had to be done at once about housing, and jobs had to be created for those unhap-py people as soon as possible. Their health and their nutrition were taken care of more or less adequately: the TB, trachoma, ringworm, malaria, ty-phoid, dysentery, measles and pellagra that the immigrants brought with them were all being coped with, although I don't know how our over-worked and exhausted doctors and nurses did it. And all the tent cities had schools of some sort where Hebrew was being taught intensively. But in 1949 housing seemed an insurmountable problem.

As for our resources, despite the magnificent response of world Jewry, there was never enough money. Thanks to our neighbors, our defense budget had to stay sky-high, and anyhow, all the other essential needs of the state had to be met somehow. We couldn't close down our schools or our hospitals or our transportation or our industries (such as they were) or put too tight a rein in any way on the state's development. So every-thing had to be done at the same time. But there were things that we could do without, after all—so we did without them. We rationed almost everything—food, clothing and shoes—and got used to the idea of an aus-terity that lasted for years. Recently I came across one of my own ration books, a drab little booklet issued by the Ministry of Commerce and In-dustry, and I recalled the hours I stood in line for a few potatoes or eggs or the frozen fish on which we feasted so gratefully—when we got it.

Most Israelis had a very hard time indeed. Their standard of living dropped drastically. Whatever had been sufficient for one family in 1948 now had to be shared with two or three other families. Old-timers, who had just emerged from a terrible war, might have been forgiven for rebel-ling against the new demands made on them. But no one rebelled.

A few weeks after I returned from Moscow, I went to the Knesset with a plan for building an initial 30,000 housing units and got it through, de-spite the objections. But we couldn't make houses out of milk and honey (not that those commodities were available either), so I took myself off to the States in search of the necessary funds and once again asked the Jews of America for help—this time "not to win a war but to maintain life."

I got the money, and we began to build those units. Of course, at first we made all kinds of mistakes—some of them serious—both in planning and in execution. We miscalculated, sited badly, fell behind the flow of immigration. In the end we couldn't build quickly enough or well enough, and by October, 1950, we had constructed only a third of the units we had undertaken to build because an unusually severe winter forced us to divert funds earmarked for building to the emergency purchase of thousands of metal huts, which were better than tents in the winter but like roasting ovens all through Israel's long, hot summer.

By the end of 1950, however, we knew that we couldn't go on thinking of those "temporary camps" as reception centers that could be neatly folded away within a few months. They were obviously going to have to do for several years, and that being the case their entire character would have to change. They would have to be turned into work villages and moved to the outskirts of towns and cities, so that the new immigrants could live near places where labor was in demand. They would have to be so organized that the people in them could become more or less self-sufficient, cooking for themselves, rather than eating in public food kitchens, and participating in the upkeep of public services. We couldn't levy rates and taxes on penniless men and women, but we could prevent them from feeling that they were the objects of charity.

The new camps were called *ma'abarot,* the plural of the Hebrew word *ma'abara* (place of transit), and by November, 1951, we had set up 112 *ma'abarot,* housing a total population of 227,000 new immigrants. But if we were not to create two classes of Israelis—the relatively well-established old-timers, on the one hand, and the new immigrants in their crowded ugly *ma'abarot,* on the other—we would have to supply a lot more than just housing. We would have to see to it that the new immigrants worked and got paid for their work, and I believed that there was only one way of doing this: a public works program.

In 1952, when the immigration began to taper off at last—to 1,000 a day—we started to direct newcomers away from the *ma'abarot* into regular quarters in new development areas and border villages all over Israel and to stress agriculture, rather than public works. We gave each immigrant family not only a tiny house, but also a plot of land, livestock and lessons in farming. We made mistakes about that, too. We tried, probably too soon, to turn the pressure cooker into a melting pot. We created villages populated by combinations of people. They had nothing much in common with each other and found it difficult (sometimes impossible) to live together in a totally isolated part of the country, and they usually had neither any experience nor any taste for farming. Many of them rebelled and drifted away to the towns, where they settled into slums. But most of them stayed and became first-rate farmers, whose children today grow the Israeli fruit, flowers and vegetables that are bought around the world.

Though I begrudged every minute that I was away from Israel, I went on with my fund-raising speeches abroad, traveling often to Europe, the United States and South America. But fund raising, too, had to be suited to our new circumstances. The United Jewish Appeal had become a magnificent instrument for the raising of money; but it was still an appeal, and the money was still "gift" money. I had been troubled for years by the picture of a Jewish state that relied on charitable funds, which, apart from everything else, could never begin to meet our growing needs for development capital. It seemed to me that a continued dependence on philanthropy violated the most elementary concepts of Zionism, of self-reliance and self-labor, to say nothing of national independence, and I began to think of other possible sources of funds, sources that would make world Jewry fuller partners in the Zionist enterprise and in the "ingathering of the exiles." After my 1948 visits to the United States I had corresponded steadily on this subject in dozens of letters and cables with Henry Montor, and whenever he and I and Eliezer Kaplan (Israel's first minister of finance) met, we talked in depth about the feasibility of entering into a new economic activity that would express itself in the floating of an Israel bond issue.

The first time that the bond idea surfaced in public was September, 1950, at a special three-day conference convened in Jerusalem by Ben-Gurion and attended by the leaders of the major Jewish communities in the United States. At the beginning there was very little enthusiasm for the idea. What if the sale of bonds undermined the efforts of the UJA? And who wanted either to make money out of Israel or, as seemed more likely and worse, lose it? Philanthropic contributions were tax-deductible, but the bonds would not be. And what if the U.S. government did not look with favor on a bond issue? Underlying all these reservations and anxieties, I felt, was a general unease about an altered relationship with Israel. No one came out and bluntly said that Israel wasn't a good financial risk but I couldn't help sensing a feeling that the whole notion of an assumption of indebtedness by us at this time was more undesirable. The bonds, however, found one very powerful champion—far more influential than Ben-Gurion, Kaplan, Montor and myself put together. Henry J. Morgenthau, the former U.S. Secretary of the Treasury, with whom I had traveled to so many communities in 1948 and who had served as general chairman of the UJA, understood at once and immediately approved. He did more than that. He went to see President Truman at the White House and we discovered that the president also understood and approved. So another conference was convened—this time in Washington, D.C.—and I was handed the "choice" assignment of trying to convert the nonbelievers and turn their skepticism and resistance into support and cooperation.

From the time that the first Israel bond campaign was launched in May, 1951, up to the present, close to $3 billion worth of bonds have been sold, of which $1 billion has already been repaid. Flowing into Israel's economy by way of a development budget, the bonds helped substantially and dramatically to establish the new state's economic viability.

But work was not everything for me during that period. There were also the private joys and sorrows of every life. One day in 1951, when I was away from home on one of those interminable trips to raise money, a cable arrived informing me that Morris was dead. I flew back to Israel at once to attend his funeral, my head filled with thoughts about the life we might have lived together if I had only been different. It was not a bereavement that I either could or wanted to talk about with other people, even my own family. Nor am I prepared to write about it now, except to say that although we had been apart for so long, standing by his graveside, I realized once again what a heavy price I had paid—and made Morris pay—for whatever I had experienced and achieved.

I can't help reflecting on how lucky I was to have been in on the beginnings of so many things—not that I influenced the course of events, but that I was so much a part of what was happening all around me, and sometimes my ministry and I were even able to play a decisive role in the upbuilding of the state. I suppose that if I were to limit myself—as I must—to singling out the two or three developments that were the most rewarding during those seven years that I was minister of labor I would have to start with the legislation for which the Ministry of Labor was responsible. For me, that, more than anything else, symbolized the kind of social equality and justice without which I couldn't even imagine the state functioning at all. Old age pensions, widows' and orphans' benefits, maternity leaves and grants, industrial accident insurance, disability and unemployment insurance were essentials in any self-respecting society.

Whenever I read or hear about the Arabs whom we allegedly dealt with so brutally, my blood boils. In April, 1948, I myself stood on the beach in Haifa for hours and literally beseeched the Arabs of that city not to leave. Moreover, it was a scene that I am not likely to forget. The Haganah had just taken over Haifa, and the Arabs were starting to run away—because their leadership had so eloquently assured them that this was the wisest course for them to take and the British had so generously put dozens of trucks at their disposal. Nothing that the Haganah said or tried did any good—neither the pleas made via loudspeakers mounted on vans nor the leaflets we rained down on the Arab sections of the town ("Do not fear!" they read in Arabic and Hebrew. "By moving out, you will bring poverty and humiliation upon yourselves. Remain in the city which is both yours and ours"). They were signed by the Jewish Workers' Council of Haifa. To quote the British general, Sir Hugh Stockwell, who was in command of the troops then, "The Arab leaders left first, and no one did anything to halt what began as a rush and then became a panic." They were determined to go. Hundreds drove across the border, but some went to the seashore to wait for boats. Ben-Gurion called me in and said, "I want you to go to Haifa at once and see to it that the Arabs who remain in Haifa are treated properly. I also want you to try to persuade those Arabs on the beach to come back. You must get it into their heads that they have nothing to fear." So I went immediately. I sat there on the beach, and I begged them to return to their homes. But they had only one answer: "We know that there is nothing to fear, but we have to go. We'll be back." I was sure that they went, not because they were frightened of us, but because they were terrified of being considered traitors to the Arab "cause." At all events, I talked myself blue in the face, and it didn't help.

Why did we want them to stay? There were two very good reasons: first of all, we wanted to prove to the world that Jews and Arabs could live together—regardless of what the Arab leadership was trumpeting—and secondly, we knew perfectly well that if half a million Arabs left Palestine at that point, it would create a major economic upheaval in the country. This brings me to another issue with which I might just as well deal now. I should very much like, once and for all, to reply to the question of how many Palestinian Arabs did, in fact, leave their homes in 1947 and 1948. The answer is: at the very utmost, about 590,000. Of these, some 30,000 left right after the November, 1947, UN partition resolution; another 200,000 left in the course of that winter and the spring of 1948 (including the vast majority of the 62,000 Arabs of Haifa); and after the establishment of the state in May, 1948, and the Arab invasion of Israel, yet another 300,000 Arabs fled. It was very tragic indeed, and it had very tragic consequences; but at least let everyone be clear about the facts as they were—and still are. The Arab assertion that there are "millions" of "Palestinian refugees" is as dishonest as the claim that we made the Arabs leave their homes. The "Palestinian refugees" were created as a *result* of the Arab desire (and attempt) to destroy Israel. They were not the *cause* of it. Of course, there were some Jews in the *yishuv* who said, even in 1948, that the Arab exodus was the best thing that could have happened to Israel, but I know of no serious Israeli who ever felt that way.

Those Arabs who stayed in Israel, however, had an easier life than those who left. There was hardly an Arab village with electricity or running water in all Palestine before 1948, and within twenty years there was hardly an Arab village in Israel that wasn't connected to the national electric grid or a home without running water. I spent a lot of time in those villages when I was minister of labor, and I felt as delighted with what we were doing for them as I was when the *ma'abarot* disappeared. Hearsay and propaganda are one thing; facts are another. It was I—and not members of the New Left—who as minister of labor opened roads and visited new housing units in Arab villages all over Israel. One of my favorite recollections of that era, by the way, is of the village in Lower Galilee that needed a road because it was on a hill, while the village well was below, and carrying water uphill was no joke. So we built the road, and when it was done, there was a celebration with refreshments, speeches and flags. Then, all of a sudden, a young woman got up to speak—which is not customary among Arabs. She looked very pretty, in a long purple dress, and made a very charming speech. "We want to thank the Ministry of Labor and the minister for easing the burden of the feet of our men," she said. "But now we would like to ask the minister if she could ease the burden also of the heads of our women." She put it poetically, but what she meant was that she wanted running water so that she needn't carry those heavy jars on her head anymore, even on the new road. So, a year later, I went to another celebration there, and this time I turned on tens of taps!

CHAPTER 10

THE RIGHT TO EXIST

It was while I was minister of labor that Ben-Gurion—physically and spiritually worn out—decided to resign as prime minister and minister of defense. The past twenty years had utterly exhausted him, and he asked for a two-year leave of absence. He needed a change of scene, and he was going off to a small Negev kibbutz, Sdeh Boker, not far from Beersheba. There, he told us, he would live as a member of a collective settlement. It was like a thunderclap. We begged him not to go. It was far too soon; the state was only five years old; the ingathering of the exiles was far from completed; Israel's neighbors were still at war with her. It was no time for Ben-Gurion to desert the country that had looked to him for guidance and inspiration for so many years—or us. It was inconceivable that he should leave. But he was determined to go, and nothing we said had any affect on him. Moshe Sharett, retaining the portfolio of foreign affairs, became Israel's prime minister, and in January, 1954, Ben-Gurion went off to Sdeh Boker (where he stayed until 1955, when he returned to public life first as minister of defense and then as prime minister, while Sharett went back to being a full-time foreign minister).

As prime minister Sharett was the same intelligent, cautious man he had been before. I must admit that although the leadership of Mapai had tremendous respect and affection for him—most of us were fonder of Sharett than of Ben-Gurion—whenever there was a really difficult problem to be solved, it was to Ben-Gurion that people still turned for advice—and that included Sharett himself. There was a steady stream of visits and correspondence to Sdeh Boker—which became one of the most famous places in Israel overnight—and although Ben-Gurion liked to think of himself as a simple philosopher-shepherd who tended the kibbutz sheep for half the day and spent the other half reading and writing, he still kept his hand very near, if not actually on, the helm of the ship of state. That, I think, was inevitable under the circumstances, but what made for trouble was that Ben-Gurion and Sharett never really got together, despite all the years of their partnership. They were too different in their basic personalities, although they were both ardent socialists and ardent Zionists.

Ben-Gurion was an activist, a man who believed in doing rather than explaining and who was convinced that what really mattered in the end— and what would always really matter—was what the Israelis did and how they did it, not what the world outside Israel thought or said about them. The first question he asked himself—and us—about almost any issue that came up in those days was: "Is it good for the state?" And what he meant was: *"In the long run,* is it good for the state?" Ultimately, history would judge Israel on the record of its deeds, not its statements or its diplomacy and certainly not on the number of favorable editorials that appeared in the international press. Being liked or not—or even being approved of or not—was not the kind of thing that interested Ben-Gurion. He thought in terms of sovereignty, security, consolidation and real progress, and he regarded world opinion as relatively unimportant compared to these.

Sharett, on the other hand, was immensely concerned with the way in which policymakers elsewhere reacted to Israel and what was likely to make the Jewish state look "good" in the eyes of other foreign ministers or the United Nations. Israel's image and the verdict of his own contemporaries—rather than history or future historians—were the criteria he tended to use most often. And what he really wanted most for Israel, I think, was for it to be viewed as a progressive, moderate, civilized European country of whose behavior no Israeli ever need be ashamed.

Luckily, for many years, until the 1950s in fact, the two worked together very well. Sharett was a born diplomat and negotiator. Ben-Gurion was a born national leader and fighter. And the Zionist movement in general, as well as the labor movements in particular, benefitted tremendously from their combined talents and even, I would say, from their very different temperaments and attitudes. They weren't similar, and they weren't really friends; but they did complement each other, and of course, they did share the same fundamental aims. But after the establishment of the state their basic incompatibility grew—or maybe it simply became more obvious and more significant. When Ben-Gurion came back from Sdeh Boker in 1955, the tension and disagreements grew to such a point that they became intolerable.

One major area of conflict between them then was the question of Israeli retaliation for terrorist activities. Sharett was just as convinced as Ben-Gurion that the incessant incursions across our frontiers by gangs of Arab infiltrators had to end, but they disagreed sharply on the method that should be used. Sharett did not rule out retaliation. But he believed more strongly than most of us did that the most effective way of dealing with this very acute situation was by continuing to put maximum pressure on the Arab states to stop aiding and abetting the infiltrators. Well-worded protests to the United Nations, skillful and informed diplomatic notes and clear, repeated presentation of our case to the world would, he was sure, eventually succeed, whereas armed reprisals by Israel could only result in a storm of criticism and make our international position even less comfortable than it was. He was 100 percent right about the criticism. It was more than just a storm; it was a tornado. Whenever the Israel Defense Forces retaliated against the infiltrators—and sometimes, unavoidably, innocent Arabs were wounded or killed along with the guilty—Israel was promptly and very severely censured for "atrocities."

But Ben-Gurion still saw his primary responsibility, not to the statesmen of the West or to the world tribunal, but to the ordinary citizens who lived in the Israeli settlements that were under constant Arab attack. The duty of the government of any state, he believed, was first and foremost to defend itself and to protect its citizens—regardless of how negative the reaction abroad might be to this protection. There was also another consideration of great importance to Ben-Gurion: the citizens of Israel—that conglomeration of people, languages and cultures—had to be taught that the government, and *only* the government, was responsible for their security. It would obviously have been much simpler to have permitted the formation of a number of antiterrorist vigilante groups, shut an official eye to private acts of retaliation and vengeance and then loudly disclaim all responsibility for the resultant "incidents." But that was not our way. The hand extended in peace to the Arabs would remain extended, but at the same time the children of Israeli farmers in border villages were entitled to sleep safely in their beds at night. And if the only way of accomplishing this was to hit back mercilessly at the camps of the Arab gangs, then that would have to be done.

By 1955 dozens of such Israeli punitive raids had been carried out, all of them in answer to our growing death toll, the mining of our roads and the ambushing of our traffic. They didn't end the terror; but they did put a very high price on the lives of our settlers, and they did teach the Israelis that they could rely on their own forces. In fact, they underlined, at least for the new half of the population, the real difference between living in a country on sufferance and living in a country that belonged to one. But unfortunately, they also served to widen the breach between Ben-Gurion and Sharett, who continued to disapprove of some of the reprisals.

After a while Ben-Gurion stopped calling Sharett by his first name and began to talk to him as though he were a stranger. Sharett was terribly hurt by Ben-Gurion's coldness. He never said anything about it in public, although he would sit at home at night and fill the pages of his diary with furious analyses of Ben-Gurion's character and maltreatment of him. In 1956 it so happened that Mapai was looking for a new secretary-general. Ben-Gurion decided that this would be an ideal job for me, and he asked me what I thought about it, suggesting that we meet with some of our colleagues at his Jerusalem home to talk about the idea. Not everybody was equally enthusiastic; but although it meant that I would have to part from the cabinet and the labor ministry, I was prepared to leave the decision up to the party, and I listened with great interest to the ensuing discussion. I certainly didn't want to turn my ministry over to anyone else, but on the other hand, I was extremely concerned about the future of Mapai (which had suffered in the July, 1955 elections). I thought that its membership should—and, what's more, could—be substantially broadened, and that the threat to Mapai—both from the extreme left and the extreme right—could be overcome, provided that an intensified effort was made on the part of the Mapai leadership which tended, not unnaturally I suppose, to rely on Ben-Gurion to do much of its work for it. All of a sudden I heard Sharett say, jokingly, "Well, maybe *I* should become the secretary-general of the party." Everyone laughed—except Ben-Gurion, who jumped at Sharett's little joke. I don't think he would ever have brought himself to ask Sharett to leave the cabinet. But the opportunity had unexpectedly presented itself, and Ben-Gurion was never one to ignore opportunities.

"Marvelous," he said at once. "A wonderful idea! It will save Mapai." The rest of us were a bit taken aback and embarrassed, but on second thought, it did seem like a very good idea to the party, too. Cabinet meetings were increasingly turning into open disputes on policy between Ben-Gurion and Sharett, and although it wasn't an elegant solution, it was—or at least it looked like—a way of lessening the growing strain, on all of us, created by the perpetual wrangling between the two men. "Don't *you* think it is a good idea for Moshe to become secretary of the party?" Ben-Gurion asked me a day or two later.

"But who will be foreign minister?" I wanted to know.

"You," he said calmly.

I couldn't believe my ears. It had never occurred to me, even as the remotest possibility, and I wasn't at all sure that I could or wanted to cope with it. In fact, I was only sure of one thing: I didn't want to leave the Ministry of Labor, and I told this to Ben-Gurion. I also told him that I didn't want to step into Sharett's shoes in this manner. But Ben-Gurion wouldn't listen to my objections. "That's that," he said—and it was.

Sharett was very bitter. I think he always imagined that had I refused to take over his beloved Foreign Ministry, Ben-Gurion would have acquiesced in his staying on indefinitely. But he was wrong. The tension between Ben-Gurion and Sharett would have never merely blown over; it was far too late for that, although Sharett didn't seem to realize this for a long time. It was only when two very close friends of his, Zalman Aranne and Pinchas Sapir, told him in so many words that unless he resigned from the cabinet, Ben-Gurion might bid us all farewell once more that Sharett gave in. The story of their relationship didn't end then. Sharett removed himself from public life for a while and later became the chairman of the Jewish Agency. In 1960, when the so-called Lavon Affair exploded, Sharett—already stricken by the illness that was to kill him in 1965—became one of the most outspoken critics of Ben-Gurion's refusal to let the "affair" die a natural death.

Since I've raised the subject of the Lavon Affair, I might as well go into it now, although I hardly intend to write an exhaustive tract on it. The original issue dated back to a security blunder related to an espionage mission in Egypt in 1954 (disastrous in its very conception, to say nothing of its execution). That was at the time when Sharett was prime minister and foreign minister. The new minister of defense, who had been hand-picked by Ben-Gurion himself, was Pinchas Lavon, one of the most capable, if least stable, members of Mapai, a handsome, complicated intellectual who had always been a great dove, but who turned into the most ferocious sort of hawk as soon as he began to concern himself with military matters. Many of us thought that he was extremely unsuitable for that very sensitive ministry. He had neither the necessary experience nor, we thought, the necessary powers of judgment. Not only I but various other colleagues had tried—in vain—to argue Ben-Gurion out of his choice of successor. As usual, he wouldn't change his mind. He went off to Sdeh Boker, and Lavon took over the defense ministry. But he couldn't get along with the bright young men who had been Ben-Gurion's most devoted disciples—among them Moshe Dayan, who was Israel's chief of staff then, and Shimon Peres, who was director general of the Defense Ministry. They neither liked nor trusted Lavon, and they made this quite clear to him, while he, for his part, made it equally clear that he was not going to live in Ben-Gurion's shadow and that he was going to make his own mark. So the seeds of trouble were already sown.

When the security blunder, which was the start of the whole affair, occurred, a committee was appointed to look into its whys and wherefores. I am not free to go into any details about the actual mishap, nor do I want to. It is enough, I think, to say that Lavon claimed to have known nothing at all about the operation and accused the head of intelligence of having planned it behind his back. The committee didn't come up with any really conclusive findings one way or the other, but it also did not fully absolve Lavon of responsibility for what had happened. At all events, the public was unaware of the entire top-secret episode, and the few people who did know about it assumed that it was now a closed chapter. Nonetheless—and regardless of who was to blame—a terrible mistake had been made. Lavon had no alternative other than to resign, and Ben-Gurion was summoned back to the Defense Ministry from Sdeh Boker.

Then, six years later, the whole thing flared up again—and this time it turned into a major political scandal with the most tragic aftereffects inside Mapai itself. It upset and confused the Israeli public for months, and it led, indirectly, to my own break with Ben-Gurion and to his second and final resignation as prime minister. In 1960 Lavon claimed that false evidence had been given at the initial inquiry and even that documents had been forged. Lavon therefore demanded that Ben-Gurion publicly clear his name. Ben-Gurion refused; he had not accused Lavon of anything, he said, and therefore he couldn't acquit him. That would have to be done by a court of law. A committee was formed at once to inquire into the conduct of the army officers whom Lavon had charged with conspiring against him. But before it could complete its work, Lavon had brought the entire matter to the attention of an important Knesset committee, and it eventually reached the press.

The rest of the Lavon-Ben-Gurion battle was fought out largely in public. Levi Eshkol, characteristically, undertook to try to calm everyone concerned, but Ben-Gurion was adamant about the need for a juridical inquiry. He was evidently quite prepared to injure his closest colleagues and the party he led in order to solve the problem in the only way he believed was right—and to prevent anyone from casting any aspersions either on the army or on the Defense Ministry. He went on demanding legal procedures, while Eshkol, Sapir and I tried to get the conflict resolved at the cabinet level—decently and discreetly. Seven ministers were appointed to a special committee of investigation, and we all were thankful that Ben-Gurion raised no objection to this. But in due course the ministerial committee, which Ben-Gurion hoped would back him in his demand for legal proceedings, announced that nothing further need be done: Lavon had not been responsible for giving the order that led to the blunder, and there was no need to go on pursuing the matter. Ben-Gurion was furious and argued that if the committee was sure that Lavon had not given the order, then the blame could only fall on the head of military intelligence. Since, however, there was no proof of this, only a judicial committee could decide who had been responsible. Furthermore, he said the ministerial committee had behaved most improperly. It had not done what it was supposed to do, it had covered up for Lavon, and generally, it was a disgrace. In January, 1961, Ben-Gurion resigned again, Levi Eshkol became prime minister at Ben-Gurion's suggestion, and Ben-Gurion started up his campaign for a judicial inquiry all over again. But Eshkol had had enough of the Lavon Affair. He rejected the idea. Ben-Gurion was like a man possessed. He had counted on Eshkol to obey him, and Eshkol had refused. So now poor Eshkol and all his supporters within the party became the prime targets of Ben-Gurion.

I couldn't forgive Ben-Gurion either for the ruthless way in which he was pursuing Eshkol or for the way in which he treated and spoke about the rest of us, myself included. It was as though all the years that we had worked together counted for nothing. In Ben-Gurion's eyes we had turned into personal enemies, and that was how he behaved toward us. We didn't see each other for years after that. I even thought that feeling as I did, it wouldn't be right for me to attend Ben-Gurion's eightieth birthday party in 1969 (from which Eshkol had been excluded), though Ben-Gurion had sent a special emissary to invite me. I knew that it would hurt him very much if I refused, but I just couldn't say yes. He had injured all of us too badly, and I couldn't get over it. If we were really as stupid as he had said we were, well, when people are born stupid, not much can be done about it, and it isn't anyone's fault. But no one is born corrupt, and that is a terrible accusation! If other party leaders were willing to overlook the fact that Ben-Gurion thought, or at any rate said, that they were corrupt, well and good. Eshkol wasn't and neither was I. I couldn't pretend that it never happened. I couldn't rewrite history, and I wouldn't lie to myself. I didn't go to that birthday party.

In 1969, when I presented my first cabinet to the Knesset, Ben-Gurion—who in the meantime had broken away from Mapai to form Rafi (the Israel Workers List) together with Dayan and Peres—abstained from voting. But he did make a statement. "There is no doubt at all," he told the Knesset, "that Golda Meir is capable of being a prime minister. But it must never be forgotten that she lent her hand to something immoral." And he went on and on again about the Lavon Affair. Toward the end of his life, however, we made up. I went down to Sdeh Boker on his eighty-fifth birthday, and though we didn't have a formal reconciliation, we were friends again. He, in turn, made a point of coming to Revivim when Sarah's kibbutz gave me a seventy-fifth birthday party in 1973. Of course, by then Ben-Gurion wasn't really Ben-Gurion anymore. Still, we had at least repaired that awful and unnecessary breach—for which I have no adequate explanation to this day. That, in a very small nutshell indeed, was the Lavon Affair, the first installment of which was already behind us in 1956, when I became Israel's second foreign minister.

My first few months as foreign minister were not much happier. It wasn't only that I was a novice among experts. It was also that Sharett's style was so different from mine, and the kind of people he had chosen to work with him—though they were all remarkably competent and genuinely dedicated—were not necessarily the kind of people with whom I was accustomed to work. Many of the more senior ambassadors and officials had been educated at British universities, and their particular brand of intellectual sophistication, which Sharett admired so much, was not always my cup of tea. Nor, to be honest, could I have any illusions about the fact that some of them obviously didn't think I was the right person for the job. I was certainly not known either for my subtle phraseology or for my great concern with protocol, and seven years at the Ministry of Labor wasn't their idea of the most suitable background for a foreign minister. But after a while we all got used to each other, and I must say that on the whole we worked very well together, perhaps because there was always so much at stake.

I had entered the Foreign Ministry in the summer of 1956, when the activities of the Arab terrorists—especially of the fedayeen (the bands of armed raiders supported and trained by Egypt)—had reached an intolerable peak. The fedayeen operated mainly from the Gaza Strip; but they also had bases in Jordan, Syria and Lebanon, and Jews were being killed by them right in the center of Israel, in such places as Rehovot, Lydda, Ramle and Jaffa. The Arab states had long ago explained their position. "We are exercising a right of war," an Egyptian representative had said in 1951 in defense of Egypt's refusal to let Israel ships go through the Suez Canal. "An armistice does not put an end to a state of war. It does not prohibit a country from exercising certain rights of war." That these "rights" were still being fully upheld in 1956 we knew all too well.

Colonel Gamal Abdel Nasser, who had to come to power in Egypt in 1952 and was now the most powerful figure in the Arab world, openly applauded the fedayeen. "You have proven," he told them, "that you are heroes upon whom our entire country can depend. The spirit with which you enter the land of the enemy must be spread." Cairo Radio also praised the murderers endlessly in crystal clear language. "Weep, oh Israel," was one refrain, "the day of extermination draws near."

The United Nations did nothing effective to put a halt to the fedayeen outrages. The UN secretary-general, Dag Hammarskjold, did succeed in arranging a cease-fire that lasted for a few days in the spring of 1956, but when the fedayeen went back to crossing the border, he let it go at that and didn't return to the Middle East. I know that today a small cult has grown up around the personality and fine perceptions of Mr. Hammarskjold, but I am not a party to it. I used to meet with him often, after he had seen Ben-Gurion and talked to him for an hour or two about Buddhism and other philosophical topics, in which they had a common interest. Then he and I would discuss such commonplace subjects as a clause in the armistice agreement with Jordan that was being contravened or some complaint we had against the United Nations. No wonder Hammarskjold thought that Ben-Gurion was an angel and that I was impossible to get along with. I never considered him a friend of Israel, and although I tried hard not to show it, I expect he sensed my feeling that he was less than neutral as far as the situation in the Middle East was concerned. If the Arabs said no to something—which they did all the time—Hammarskjold never went any further. Not that U Thant (the Burmese statesman who followed him at the United Nations) was a great improvement. Despite all the years of Burmese-Israeli friendship and his own really warm personal relationship with the country and with us, the moment that U Thant became secretary-general we were in for a very hard time. He also found it absolutely impossible, apparently, to be firm either with the Russians or with the Arabs, though he had no trouble at all being exceedingly firm with Israel.

But that is all by the way. Certainly it was not the UN secretary-general who was responsible for the almost daily murder, robbery and sabotage carried out by the fedayeen. The real responsibility lay—not for the last time—with the Russians.

In 1955 an agreement was concluded between Czechoslovakia (read the Soviet Union) and Egypt as a result of which Egypt was receiving an almost unending supply of arms, ranging from submarines and destroyers to tanks and troop carriers. It may well be asked how it happened that the Soviet Union suddenly decided to arm a state that was making no bones whatsoever about its intention of "reconquering Palestine," as Colonel Nasser put it. The answer is that it was not really sudden at all. In the global struggle of the 1950s, known (not very accurately as far as we were concerned) as the cold war, both the United States and the Soviet Union were busy outbidding each other for the favors of the Arab states, especially those of Egypt. The United States and Britain may have felt a little uneasy about their courtship of Nasser's Egypt, but the Soviet Union had no qualms at all. The fact that the USSR was making possible the fulfillment of the Egyptian dream of a second round of war against Israel was justified—to the extent that the Russians ever feel that they had to justify themselves—on the grounds that Zionism, which was such an evil thing, had to be suppressed everywhere. And to prove how evil it was, the so-called Doctors' Plot was invented in Moscow in 1953. The Russian people were informed that nine doctors (no less than six of whom were Jewish) had tried to murder Stalin, as well as a number of other Soviet leaders, and an infamous trial was staged as part of an anti-Jewish campaign set in motion throughout the Soviet Union.

Then, one night, a small bomb exploded in the garden of the Soviet legation in Tel Aviv. The Russians at once accused the government of Israel of having engineered the incident and broke off diplomatic relations. But even when diplomatic relations were renewed a few months later, the anti-Semitic propaganda campaign in the USSR, with its constant references to Zionism, went on, and the chant about the "Zionist stooges of imperialist warmongers" was taken up in Czechoslovakia, which mounted its own despicable campaign against the Jews.

Despite all this—and the unconcealed Soviet-Arab preparations for another war—the United States and Britain refused to sell us arms. It didn't matter how often or how loudly we knocked on their doors. The answer was always negative, although at the very beginning of 1956 the United States—still refusing to sell us arms—indicated to France and Canada that it didn't mind if *they* did so. But France hadn't waited for U.S. permission. For its own reasons, it had decided to come to Israel's aid, and while there was no possibility of matching the boundless Soviet "generosity" to Egypt, we were no longer totally defenseless nor alone.

In the summer of 1956, just as I was settling into my new office and getting used, among other things, to being called Mrs. Meir—the closest I could get to a Hebrew version of Meyerson and still obey Ben-Gurion's order that I take a Hebrew name (Meir means illuminate in Hebrew)—the noose tightened a bit more around our necks. Nasser made his most dramatic gesture. In July he nationalized the Suez Canal! No Arab leader had ever done anything so spectacular before, and the Arab world was profoundly impressed. There was, indeed, only one more thing that Nasser needed to do in order for the Egypt he ruled to be acclaimed as the supreme Moslem power, and that was to annihilate us. Elsewhere in the world, the nationalization of the Canal was anxiously discussed in terms of big-power politics, but we in Israel were more worried about the increase in the military strength of Egypt and Syria, which had signed a pact to unite their high commands. There was no longer any doubt that war was inevitable and that the Egyptians had once again fallen prey to a fantasy of victory over Israel—a self-glorifying fantasy, incidentally, which Nasser himself had developed in his *Philosophy of a Revolution.*

There is already so much literature (some of it fact and some of it fiction) about the Sinai Campaign that I think my own contribution can be quite modest. But I must stress one fact: regardless of the abortive French and British attempt to seize the Suez Canal, Israel's own strike against the Egyptians in 1956 had one goal and one goal only—to prevent the destruction of the Jewish state. The threat was unmistakable. As I later said at the UN General Assembly, "Even if no one else chose to do so, *we* recognized the symptoms." We knew that dictatorships—including those given disarmingly to informing the world of their plans—usually keep their promises, and no one in Israel had forgotten the lesson of the crematoria or what total extermination really meant. Unless we were prepared to be killed off, either piecemeal or in one sudden attack, we had to take the initiative, although God knows, it was not an easy decision to make. Nonetheless, it was made. We began secretly to plan the Sinai Campaign (known in Israel as Operation Kadesh).

The French offered us arms and began making their own secret plans for the joint Anglo-French assault on the Suez Canal. In September they invited Ben-Gurion to send a delegation to France for talks with Guy Mollet (who headed the French socialist government), Christian Pineau, (the French foreign minister) and Maurice Bourges-Manoury (the French minister of defense), and he asked me, as Israel's foreign minister, to join the group. It included Moshe Dayan, Shimon Peres and Moshe Carmel (our minister of transport, who had served with great distinction as a brigadier general during the War of Independence).

We flew to France from a secret airfield in a rickety old French army plane that was very badly lit. We were all very silent and, of course, tense. And no one's frame of mind was helped much when Moshe Carmel, while walking through the plane, almost fell out of the bomb bay, which was not properly closed. Fortunately, he managed to pull himself back into the plane, breaking three ribs in the process!

Our first stop was in North Africa, where we were put up at a very pleasant French guesthouse and given a marvelous meal. Our hosts had no idea of our identity, and I remember how astonished they were when they discovered that the mysterious mission included a woman. Anyhow, we flew on from there to a military airfield outside Paris and to our meetings with the French. I didn't even venture into Paris, and I remember being furious with Dayan, who did—although luckily, no one recognized him. The main point of those talks was to work out various details of the military aid the French had promised us, especially the essential French undertaking to protect our skies, should we request it. But this was only the first of a series of such conferences, one of which was attended by Ben-Gurion himself.

The Sinai Campaign began as scheduled after sunset on October 29 and ended as scheduled on November 5. It took the Israel Defense Forces, made up mainly of reservists traveling in a crazy assortment of military and civilian vehicles, less than 100 hours to cross and capture from the Egyptians the whole of the Gaza Strip and the Sinai Peninsula— an area two and a half times larger than Israel itself. We had counted on surprise, speed, and utterly confusing the Egyptian army, but it was only when I myself flew to visit Sharm el-Sheikh at the southernmost tip of the Sinai and toured the Gaza Strip by car afterward that I really understood the extent of our victory—the sheer size and desolation of the territory through which those tanks, half-tracks, ice-cream trucks, private cars and taxis had raced in under seven days. The Egyptian defeat was absolute. The nests of the fedayeen were cleaned out. The elaborate Egyptian system to defend the Sinai—the fortresses and the battalions concealed in the desert—was put totally out of commission. The hundreds of thousands of weapons and the millions upon millions of rounds of ammunition—mostly Russian—stockpiled for use against us were worthless now. A third of the Egyptian army was broken. Of the 30,000 Egyptian soldiers whom we found pathetically wandering in the sand, 5,000 were taken as prisoners to save them from dying of thirst (and eventually exchanged for the one Israeli the Egyptians had managed to capture).

But we hadn't fought the Sinai Campaign for territory, booty or prisoners, and as far as we were concerned, we had won the only thing we wanted: peace, or at least the promise of peace for a few years, perhaps even for longer. Although our casualties were "light," we desperately hoped that the 172 Israelis who were killed and 800 wounded would be the last battle casualties we would ever have to mourn. Now we would insist that our neighbors come to terms with us—and with our existence.

Of course things didn't turn out that way. Although we had won our war against Egypt, the French and British had lost theirs—to some extent owing to their ineptness, but mostly to the overwhelmingly negative public reaction in France and Great Britain to what was viewed as an imperialist assault on an innocent third party. I have always thought that had the Anglo-French attack on Suez been more swift and efficient, the storm of protest in those countries would have died down in the face of a *fait accompli*. But as it was, the combined assault failed, and the French and British backed down as soon as the United Nations, under intense U.S. and Soviet pressure, demanded that they withdraw their troops from the Suez Canal zone. It also demanded Israel's withdrawal from the Sinai Peninsula and the Gaza Strip.

That was the beginning of the four and a half heartbreaking months of diplomatic battle that we waged—and lost—at the UN in our attempt to persuade the nations of the world that if we retreated to the armistice lines of 1949, war would again break out in the Middle East one day. Those people, those millions of people who even today have still not quite grasped the realities of Israel's struggle to stay alive and who are so quick to condemn us for not being "more flexible" and for not retreating pleasantly to our former borders each time we were forced to go to war might do well to ponder the course of events following 1956 and ask themselves what was gained by the fact that we did reluctantly withdraw then from the Sinai and the Gaza Strip. The answer is: nothing, only more wars, each one bloodier and far more costly than the Sinai Campaign had been. Had we been allowed to stay where we were until the Egyptians agreed to negotiate with us, the recent history of the Middle East would certainly have been very different. But the pressure was intense, and in the end we gave in. President Eisenhower, who had been kept totally in the dark by his European allies, was furious and said that unless Israel withdrew at once, the United States would support sanctions against it at the United Nations.

The source of the greatest pressure, however, was the Soviet Union, which not only had witnessed a complete Egyptian defeat—all the Soviet support notwithstanding—but was also now able to becloud the issue of the recent Soviet invasion of Hungary by screaming to high heaven about the terrible colonialist conspiracy against Egypt and, most of all, about Israel's "unrestrained oppression." In retrospect, it is unlikely that Soviet Prime Minister Nikolai Bulganin's threat of direct Soviet intervention in the Middle East would have resulted in a third world war, but at the time that was what was being read into his grim warnings. It looked as though virtually the whole world was against us, but I didn't believe that we should give in without a fight.

In December, 1956, I left for the United Nations, filled with forebodings. But before I went, I wanted to see the Sinai and the Gaza Strip for myself, and I am glad that I did, because otherwise I would never have really comprehended the full gravity of the situation we had been in prior to the Sinai Campaign. I shall never forget my first sight of the elaborate Egyptian military installations—built in defiance of the United Nations itself—at Sharm el-Sheikh for the sole purpose of maintaining an illegal blockade against our shipping. The area of Sharm el-Sheikh is incredibly lovely; the waters of the Red Sea must be the bluest and the clearest in the world, and they are framed by mountains that range in color from deep red to violet and purple. There, in that beautiful tranquil setting, on an empty shore, stood the grotesque battery of huge naval guns that had paralyzed Eilat for so long. For me, it was a picture that symbolized everything. Then I toured the Gaza Strip, from which the fedayeen had gone out on their murderous assignments for so many months and in which the Egyptians had kept a quarter of a million men, women and children (of whom nearly 60 percent were Arab refugees) in the most shameful poverty and destitution. I was appalled by what I saw there and by the fact that those miserable people had been maintained in such a degrading condition for more than five years only so that the Arab leaders could show the refugee camps to visitors and make political capital out of them. Those refugees could, and should, have been resettled at once in any of the Arab countries of the Middle East—countries, incidentally, whose language, traditions and religion they share. The Arabs would still have been able to continue their quarrel with us, but at least the refugees would not have been kept in a state of semistarvation or lived in such abject terror of their Egyptian masters.

I couldn't help comparing what I saw in the Gaza Strip to what we had done—even with all the mistakes we had made—for the Jews who had come to Israel in those same eight years, and I suppose that is why I began my statement to the UN General Assembly on December 5, 1956, by talking not about the war we had won, but about the Jewish refugees we had settled. Then I went on to those celebrated "rights of war," to that discredited excuse of a "belligerent status" against Israel, the screen behind which Colonel Nasser had trained and unleashed the fedayeen.

The real point of the address, however, was not to make the familiar accusations—however justified they were—or even to try to bring home again to the so-called family of nations the immediate background to the Sinai Campaign. It was not even to put on the record what we knew to have been the very well-laid Egyptian plans for the annihilation of Israel. It was something else, something far more important: to try once again, and in public, to explore the source of the hatred the Arab leaders bore toward Israel and to make some concrete proposals for a possible peace. I want to emphasize the fact that I made this speech at the end of 1956, twenty years ago. If it is in any way familiar, that is only because we have gone on saying the same thing ever since, with about as much success as we had in 1956!

I had spoken to the United Nations, and one would have thought from the expression on the faces of most of the delegates that I had asked for the moon, when in fact all I had done—all that Israel had ever done at the United Nations—was to suggest that the Arabs, fellow members of that organization, recognize our existence and work together with us toward peace. That no one jumped up to seize the opportunity, to say, "All right, let's talk. Let's argue it all out. Let's make an effort to find a solution," was like a physical blow to me—not that I had many illusions left about the kind of family that family of nations was. Anyhow, I promised myself then that before the session was over, whatever else happened, I would try once again to reach the Arabs, to make a person-to-person appeal to them because unless something was done soon, the future, as I saw it, looked pretty grim.

Those were terrible months. Our phased-out withdrawal from the Gaza Strip and Sinai was going on all the time, but nothing was being said or done to force the Egyptians to agree to enter into negotiations with us, to guarantee the lifting of the blockade of the Strait of Tiran or to solve the problem of the Gaza Strip. I couldn't get through to the Americans—least of all to the U.S. secretary of state, that cold, gray man John Foster Dulles—that our very life depended on adequate guarantees, real guarantees with teeth in them, and that we couldn't return to the situation which had existed before the Sinai Campaign. But nothing helped. None of the arguments, none of the appeals, none of the logic, not even the eloquence of Abba Eban, our ambassador to Washington. We just didn't talk the same language, and we didn't have the same priorities. Dulles was obsessed by his own "brinkmanship," by his fear of a looming world war, and he told me, more than once, that Israel would be responsible for that war, if it broke out, because we were so "unreasonable."

There were many days during that period when I wanted to run away, to run back to Israel and let someone else go on hammering away at Dulles and Henry Cabot Lodge, the head of the U.S. delegation at the United Nations. I would have done anything just not to have to face another exhausting round of talks that always seemed to end in recriminations. But I stayed where I was, and tried to swallow my bitterness and a sense of betrayal, and at the end of February we arrived at a compromise of sorts. The last of our troops would leave the Gaza Strip and Sharm el-Sheikh in return for the "assumption" that the United Nations would guarantee free passage for Israeli shipping through the Strait of Tiran and that Egyptian soldiers would not be allowed back in the Gaza Strip. It wasn't much, and it certainly wasn't what we had been fighting for; but it was the best we could get—and it was better than nothing.

On March 3, 1957, having first had each last comma of it checked and cleared by Mr. Dulles in Washington, I made our final statement:

The government of Israel is now in a position to announce its plans for full and prompt withdrawal from the Sharm el-Sheikh area and the Gaza Strip. In compliance with Resolution 1 of February 2, 1957, our sole purpose has been to ensure that on the withdrawal of Israeli forces, continued freedom of navigation will exist for Israel and international shipping in the Gulf of Aqaba and the Strait of Tiran.

But no sooner had I taken my seat than Henry Cabot Lodge got up. To my astonishment, I heard him reassure the United Nations that while the rights of free passage for all nations through the Strait of Tiran would indeed be safeguarded, the future of the Gaza Strip would have to be worked out within the context of the armistice agreements. Perhaps not everyone at the United Nations that day understood what Cabot Lodge was saying, but *we* understood all too well. The U.S. State Department had won its battle against us, and the Egyptian military government, with its garrison, was going to return to Gaza. There was nothing I could do or say. I just sat there, biting my lip, not even able to look at the handsome Mr. Cabot Lodge while he pacified all those who had been so worried lest we refuse to withdraw unconditionally. It was not one of the finest moments of my life.

But reality had to be faced, and we had not lost everything. For the time being, the fedayeen terror was over; the principle of freedom of navigation through the Strait of Tiran had been upheld; the UN Emergency Force moved into Gaza and the Sharm el-Sheikh area; and we had won a victory that had made military history, proving again our ability—if need be—to take up arms in our own defense.

During my term of office as foreign minister, I visited the United Nations often. I was there at least once a year as head of Israel's delegation to the General Assembly, and there wasn't a single time that I didn't make an attempt to contact the Arabs somehow—or, to my sorrow, a single time that I succeeded. I remember once, in 1957, seeing Nasser there from a distance and wondering what would happen if I just went over to him and began to chat. But he was surrounded by his bodyguards, and I had my bodyguards, and it obviously wouldn't work. But Tito was at the same session, and I thought perhaps I could talk to him and he would arrange something. So I asked someone in our delegation to talk to a member of the Yugoslav delegation and try to set up a meeting between Tito and me. I waited and waited and waited. I even postponed my return to Israel, but there was no reply. Then, the day after I had left New York, we got an answer: Tito would meet me in New York. But I was already back home. We tried again. There was silence again.

But there were brighter moments during those years, and some very memorable meetings. The most interesting and most memorable, perhaps, were those with John F. Kennedy, Lyndon Johnson and Charles de Gaulle. I met Kennedy twice. The first time was right after the Sinai Campaign, when he was a senator from Massachusetts. The Zionists of Boston had organized a tremendous demonstration and a gala dinner in support of Israel, which was attended by the entire consular corps, the state's two senators—and the Israeli foreign minister. I was seated next to Kennedy, who was one of the speakers, and I remember being tremendously impressed by him, by how young he was and how well he spoke, although he was not really easy to talk to. I had a feeling that he was very shy, and we exchanged only a few words. The next time I met him was shortly before he was assassinated. I went down to Florida, where he was vacationing, and we talked for a very long time—and very informally. We sat on the porch of the big house in which he was staying, and I can still see him, in his rocking chair, without a tie, with his sleeves rolled up, listening very attentively as I tried to explain to him why we so desperately needed arms from the United States. He looked so handsome and still so boyish that it was hard for me to remember that I was talking to the president of the United States—although I suppose he didn't think I looked much like a foreign minister either! Anyhow, it was a strange setting for such an important talk.

At first, I went into the current situation in the Middle East. Then, suddenly, it occurred to me that this bright young man might not understand very much about the Jews and what Israel actually meant to them, and I decided that I ought to explain that to him before I went on talking about why we had to have arms. So I said, "Mr. President, let me tell you in what way Israel is different from other countries." To do so, I had to go back a long way because the Jews are such an ancient people. I said: "The Jews came into being more than four thousand years ago and lived alongside nations that have long since disappeared—the Ammonites, the Moabites, the Assyrians, the Babylonians and others. In ancient times, they were all subject to oppression from foreign powers at one time or another, and in the end they all accepted their fate and became part of whatever the dominant culture was. All of them, that is, except the Jews. Like these other people," I said, "the Jews had their land occupied by foreign powers. But the fate of the Jews was very different, because, of all these nations, only the people of Israel were determined to remain what they were. The people of other nations stayed in their lands but abandoned their identity, while the Jews, who were dispersed among the nations of the world and lost their land, never let go of their determination to remain Jewish—or of their hope of returning to Zion. Well, now we are back there, and that places a very special burden on the leadership of Israel. In many ways, the government of Israel is no different from any other decent government. It cares for the welfare of the people, for the development of the state and so on. But, in addition, there is one other great responsibility, and that is for the future. If we should lose our sovereignty again, those of us who would remain alive—and there wouldn't be very many—would be dispersed once more. But we no longer have the great reservoir we once had of our religion, our culture and our faith. We lost much of that when six million Jews perished in the Holocaust."

Kennedy didn't take his eyes off me, and I went on: "There are five and a half or six million Jews in the United States. They are wonderful, generous, good Jews, but I think that they themselves would be the first to agree with me if I say that I doubt very much whether they would have the tenacity which those lost six million had. And if I am right, then what is written on the wall for us is: 'Beware of losing your sovereignty again, for this time you may lose it forever.' If *that* should happen, then my generation would go down in history as the generation that made Israel sovereign again, but didn't know how to hold onto that independence."

When I finished, Kennedy leaned over to me. He took my hand, looked into my eyes and said very solemnly, "I understand, Mrs. Meir. Don't worry. *Nothing* will happen to Israel." I think he did truly understand.

I saw Kennedy again at a formal UN reception where he was greeting the heads of delegations; but we only said hello to each other then, and I never met him again. But I did go to his funeral, and afterward—with all the other heads of delegations—I went to shake Mrs. Kennedy's hand. I never saw her again either, but I can't forget how she stood there, pale and with tears in her eyes, but still finding something special to say to each of us. It was also at Kennedy's funeral—or, more accurately, at the state dinner given that evening by the new president—that I met Lyndon B. Johnson. I had met him before, during the General Assembly of 1956-57, when he was the Democratic majority leader of the Senate and came out, strongly and publicly, against President Eisenhower's threat of sanctions against us, so I already knew how he felt about Israel. But when I came up to him that night in the receiving line, he put his arm around me, held it there for a minute and said, "I know that you have lost a friend, but I hope you understand that I, too, am a friend"—which he certainly proved himself to be.

Often, throughout the period of the Six-Day War, when President Johnson backed our refusal to return to the pre-1967 lines unless we could do so within the framework of a peace settlement—and helped us achieve the military and economic means to maintain that position—I used to think back to the night of Kennedy's funeral and to the words that he said to me then, when he had so much else to think and worry about. I never saw him again either, although I wasn't at all surprised that he got along so well with Levi Eshkol when he was prime minister. They were very similar in many ways—open, warm and easy to establish contact with. I know how unpopular Johnson eventually became in the United States; but he was a very staunch friend indeed, and Israel owes a lot to him. I think he was one of the very few leaders abroad who understood what a mistake had been made by the Eisenhower administration after the Sinai Campaign, when we were forced to retreat before any negotiations with the Arabs got under way.

Another of the personalities who were to have such a decisive effect on Israel's future was General de Gaulle, whom I met for the first time in 1958. I must say that I was very nervous about meeting De Gaulle. Everything I had heard about him—including the fact that he expected everyone to know French perfectly, while I didn't know it at all—scared me. First, I met with the then French foreign minister, Maurice Couve de Murville, the most British Frenchman I ever encountered. He had served in various Arab countries. He was very correct, very cold and, on the whole, unfriendly—none of which helped me look forward to meeting De Gaulle the next day. I was received at the Élysée palace with all the standard pomp and circumstance. Walking up the steps, I felt as though I were reviewing the entire French army, and I wondered what those splendid French guards in their red cloaks thought of me as I trudged up to the general's office, feeling very ill at ease. And there he was, in all his height and glory, the legendary Charles de Gaulle. Walter Eytan, who was the director general of our Foreign Ministry then and who afterward served as our ambassador to France, had come with me, and between De Gaulle's interpreter and Eytan, the general and I managed to converse. He was remarkably cordial and very kind. It only took a few minutes for me to feel quite relaxed, and we had a most satisfactory talk about the problems of the Middle East, with his assuring me of his undying friendship for Israel.

Then at Kennedy's funeral I saw him again, first at the cathedral (the only people who were not kneeling, I believe, were De Gaulle, Zalman Shazar—who was president of Israel—and myself) and later at the dinner which I've already mentioned. Before we went into dinner, I spotted De Gaulle (not a great feat, considering how he towered over everyone) at the other end of the room. I was just considering whether I ought to go over to him or not when he moved in my direction. There was a great flurry all around. Who was De Gaulle going to? "He never goes over to anyone himself; people are always summoned to him," someone standing next to me explained. "He must be going to talk to a very important person." It was like the Red Sea parting so that the Children of Israel could get through; De Gaulle walked straight ahead, and everyone scuttled out of his way. I almost fell over when he stopped in front of me and did something that was really unprecedented for him: he spoke to me in English. "I am enchanted to see you again, even on this so tragic occasion," he said, and bowed. It made an enormous impression on everyone, but most of all on me. In the course of time, I even became very good friends with Couve de Murville, who used to tell me that De Gaulle had a soft spot in his heart for me. I only wish it had stayed that way, but we didn't do what he told us to do (which was to do nothing) in 1967, and he never forgave us for that disobedience. In those dreadful days before the Six-Day War he told Abba Eban that there were two things Israel should know: "If you are in real danger, you can depend upon me; but if you move first, you will be destroyed, and you will bring a catastrophe on the entire world." Well, De Gaulle was wrong. We weren't destroyed, and there wasn't a world war; but our relationship with him—and with the French government—was not the same from that day on. The same De Gaulle who, in 1961, toasted "Israel, our friend and ally" summed up his attitude toward the Jews after the Six-Day War by describing us as "an elitist, self-confident and domineering people."

In 1964, 1965 and 1966 I was in orbit again. I traveled to Europe, Africa and to Latin America, and I was frequently ill. I had begun to feel the strain of perpetual travel; I seemed always to be either en route to somewhere or from somewhere or sick. Besides, I was no longer as young as I had been. In 1963 I had celebrated my sixty-fifth birthday. I didn't feel at all old or depleted of energy, but I was beginning to think how nice it would be to have a day to myself or to visit old friends again without having a bodyguard following me around, and the children and my doctor kept telling me that the time had come for me to take it easy. I tried, but I never succeeded in learning how to do so. There was always a pressing commitment—either abroad or in Israel—and however early I began my workday, it never ended until the early hours of the next morning.

One such occasion was the party I gave in July, 1961, to the friends with whom I had come to Palestine aboard the *Pocahontas* forty years earlier. I can't remember now how or when I got the idea of an anniversary celebration, but I was very curious to meet the group again, to find out who had settled in Israel and who had gone back to the States, and I wanted to see their children. One of the topics of conversation and debate between myself and my colleagues in Mapai in those days was why there was such a relatively small emigration of Jews from the West. "They have it too good," was one explanation. "They will come to us only when they face real anti-Semitism elsewhere." But I felt this to be a very unjust oversimplification, and I used to have long arguments with Ben-Gurion about the unimpressive rate of emigration from such countries as the United States, Canada and Britain. "They will come, one day, if we are patient," I used to tell him. "It is not as simple to transplant oneself and one's family as it used to be. Also people are not as idealistic, as romantic or as dedicated anymore. It takes a tremendous amount of determination and guts for a Zionist from Pittsburgh, Toronto or Leeds to decide one day to settle permanently in Israel. It means much more than merely moving to another country. It involves learning a new language, accepting a different standard and way of life, and getting used to the sort of tensions and insecurities that we take for granted."

But the nineteen men and women who had taken that trip on the *Pocahontas* with Morris and me in 1921 had made that great decision, and I had a sudden urge to see them again. I didn't have their addresses, so I put an advertisement in the paper: "The foreign minister invites the *Pocahontas* contingent to an evening at her home; not only the original group but husbands, wives, children and grandchildren."

Most of the people who had made that dreadful journey with me in 1921 did not come. They were either dead or too infirm, and one had gone back to the United States for good. But seven or eight of the original group loyally turned up and, what's more, brought their children and grandchildren with them. We had a wonderful party, reminiscing, singing and eating cake and fruit in my garden. There weren't any formal speeches, and I refused to let the press attend—although the journalists implored me to let them come "only for a few minutes." But it was a personal marking of a personal anniversary, and I wanted it to be private.

I suppose that some of the songs we sang (which were the same songs with which we had tried to boost our morale on that miserable ship) must have sounded very sentimental and naïve, maybe even banal to our children. They were all about building the land and pioneering. Nonetheless, they reminded us of the days when we believed we could do anything and everything, and we sang for hours. Afterward, when the party was over and the guests had gone, I sat on for a while in the dark garden, thinking about those forty years and wishing that Morris could have been with us.

By the end of 1965 even I began to realize that I needed a change. The election campaign in the summer of that year had exhausted me. I have never felt really well in the heat, and now the migraine headaches from which I had suffered off and on for years were getting worse. I couldn't avoid coming to the conclusion that the responsibilities I had shouldered for more than thirty years were starting to weigh on me too heavily. I didn't want to live forever, but also I didn't want to turn into a semi-invalid. However, it wasn't only my health that bothered me; it was also the need to recharge my emotional batteries, which seemed to be running down slightly because I was tired. And the internal situation in Israel was not good. There was a severe economic depression, emigration—which we call *yerida* (descent) as opposed to the "ascent" of immigration—and the aftermath of the Lavon Affair, which was demoralizing the public and wreaking havoc in the ranks of the labor movement. My own battles with Ben-Gurion were, of course, not the least of my headaches. Nothing catastrophic would happen if I left public life: the party would heal its own wounds, and I couldn't do much to solve Israel's economic plight, which was largely caused by the ending of German reparations while neither our defense budget nor the Arab boycott was reduced at all.

To add to my dispiritedness, Sheyna was not at all well. She, too, was growing old and, like our mother before her, was aging in both body and mind. Eshkol, who became prime minister in 1963, and Pinchas Sapir, who was minister of finance, tried valiantly to keep me from resigning; but I knew that Abba Eban was waiting in the wings to become foreign minister, and I could see no reason for my clinging to the ministry. Eshkol offered me the deputy prime ministership, but it held no appeal for me at all. Better, I thought, to be a full-time grandmother than a part-time minister, and I told Eshkol that I really wanted to retire. "I won't go into a political nunnery," I assured him, "but I do want to be able to read a book without feeling guilty or to go to a concert on the spur of the moment, and I don't want to see another airport for several years."

CHAPTER 11

WE ARE ALONE

It took me some time, several months in fact, to "organize" my retirement. To begin with, there was the move from Jerusalem to the small, semidetached house on a quiet street of a Tel Aviv suburb, right next door to Menachem and his wife, Aya. It wasn't just a matter of moving from one city to another; it involved hours and hours of sorting things out, deciding what was mine and what belonged to the government, what I wanted to take with me and what I was going to give away.

My new home—which is where I still live—was probably a quarter of the size of the foreign minister's residence that I had occupied for nine years; but it was exactly what I wanted and needed, and I felt comfortable in it from the very first day.

Even my immediate family, I suspect, didn't really believe that I would enjoy the transition to life as an ordinary citizen, but I was as happy as I had known I would be. For the first time in years I was free—to do my own shopping, to use public transportation instead of being driven everywhere and being concerned about the fact that a driver was forever waiting for me outside and, most of all, to call my time my own. I really felt like a prisoner released from jail. I made long lists of the books I wanted to read, called up old friends whom I hadn't seen for years. What's more, I cooked, ironed and cleaned house with enormous pleasure. I had stepped out of office at exactly the right time, of my own accord and before anyone could say, "For God's sake, when is that old woman going to realize that it's time for her to quit?" and I felt as though I had taken on a new lease on life.

I should have guessed, I suppose, that this newfound tranquillity with which I was so pleased wouldn't last long. There was a succession of interruptions, of which by far the most pressing was the appeal made by my colleagues in the party that I return on a full-time basis—at least for a while—to help bring about the unification of all or most of the various sectors of the labor movement, which had recently been so seriously shaken by the Lavon Affair. If ever there was a time for unification, this was certainly it. There was, said my colleagues (who took to coming to talk to me in relays), only one person who had all the necessary qualifications—and time. If I were unwilling to take the job, for purely selfish reasons, it would never be done. All that they were asking of me was that I become secretary-general of Mapai until the unification was achieved—and assured. Then I could go back into my retirement.

It was the one appeal that I couldn't turn down. Not because I was so sure that I would succeed or because I so yearned to be in the middle of a crucial struggle all over again—and not because I was bored, as many probably thought—but for a simpler and more important reason: I truly believed that the future of the labor movement was at stake.

In the meantime, a number of events had occurred in the Middle East which were to place Isreal's future in far greater jeopardy than labor disunity at home could ever have done. In 1966 preparations were already being made by the Arabs for another round of war. The symptoms were all familiar. As a matter of fact, in a way the prelude to the Six-Day War of 1967 was identical to the prelude to the Sinai Campaign: terrorist gangs—as actively encouraged and supported by President Nasser as the fedayeen had been in the fifties—were operating against Israel from both the Gaza Strip and Jordan. They included a new organization, founded in 1965, known as the El Fatah, which, under Yasir Arafat's leadership, subsequently became the most powerful and well-publicized element in the Palestine Liberation Organization. Also a united Egyptian-Syrian high command had been established, and vast sums of money were allocated at an Arab summit conference for the express purpose of stockpiling weapons to be used against Israel—and, of course, the Soviet Union was still pumping both arms and money into the Arab states. The Syrians seemed bent on an escalation of the conflict; they kept up an endless bombardment of the Israeli settlements below the Golan Heights, and Israeli fishermen and farmers faced what was sometimes virtually daily attack by snipers. I used to visit those settlements occasionally and watch the settlers go about their work as though there were nothing at all unusual in plowing with a military escort or putting children to sleep—every single night—in underground air-raid shelters. But I never believed them when they said that they had got quite used to living under perpetual fire.

Then, in the autumn of 1966, the Soviet Union suddenly began to accuse Israel of readying its forces for a full-scale attack against Syria. It was an absurd charge, but it was duly investigated by the United Nations and, naturally, found to be without any basis. The Russians, however, kept on making the same accusations and talking about the Israeli "aggression" that was bound to cause a third round of the Arab-Israeli war, while the Syrians, receiving arms and financial aid from the Soviet Union, kept up their raids on our border settlements. Whenever the Syrian terror reached an intolerable point, Israel's air force would go into action against the terrorists, and for a few weeks the border settlements could relax. But by the early spring of 1967 these periods of relative relaxation were becoming fewer and shorter. In April, 1967, the air force was sent up in an action that turned into an air battle and resulted in the downing by Israeli planes of six Syrian MIGs. When this happened, the Syrians, egged on as always by the Soviet Union, once again screamed that Israel was making preparations for a major offensive against Syria, and an official complaint to this effect was even made on Syria's behalf to Prime Minister Eshkol by the Soviet ambassador to Israel, Mr. Chuvakhin. Not only was this one of the most grotesque incidents of the period, but it actually helped trigger the war that broke out in June.

"We understand," Chuvakhin said very unpleasantly to Eshkol, "that in spite of all your official statements, there are, in fact, extremely heavy concentrations of Israeli troops all along the Syrian border." This time Eshkol did more than merely deny the allegation. He asked Chuvakhin to go up north and look at the situation along the border for himself, and he even offered to accompany the ambassador on the trip. But Chuvakhin promptly said he had other things to do and refused the invitation, although all that was involved was only a few hours' drive.

At the beginning of May, responding to what he termed the "desperate plight" of the Syrians, Nasser ordered Egyptian troops and armor to mass in the Sinai, and just in case anyone misunderstood his intentions, Cairo Radio shrilly announced that "Egypt, with all its resources . . . is ready to plunge into a total war that will be the end of Israel."

On May 16 Nasser moved again—only now he gave orders not to his own army but to the United Nations. He demanded that the UN Emergency Force that had been stationed both at Sharm el-Sheikh and in the Gaza Strip since 1956, get out at once. Legally, he had a right to evict the UNEF because it was only with Egypt's consent that the international police force had been stationed on Egyptian soil, but I don't for a minute believe that Nasser actually expected the United Nations to do his bidding meekly. It was against all rhyme or reason for a force that had come into existence for the sole purpose of supervising the cease-fire between Egypt and Israel to be removed at the request of one of the combatants the very moment that the cease-fire was seriously threatened, and I am sure that Nasser anticipated a long round of discussions, arguments and haggling. If nothing else, he almost certainly reckoned that the United Nations would insist on some kind of phasing-out operation. However, for reasons which have never been understood by anyone—least of all by me—the UN secretary-general, U Thant, gave in to Nasser at once. He didn't refer that matter to anyone else. He didn't ask the Security Council for an opinion. He didn't even suggest a delay of a few days. Entirely of his own accord, U Thant instantly agreed to the immediate withdrawal of the UNEF. It started to move out of Sharm el-Sheikh and the Gaza Strip the very next day, and by May 19, to the tune of wild Egyptian applause, the last unit of the UNEF had pulled out, leaving the Egyptians in full control of their border with Israel.

I don't think that anyone could have felt more bitter than I did about U Thant's ludicrous surrender to Nasser. Not, God forbid, because I was the only person to understand what was happening. Far from it. But because it brought back to me, in an almost intolerable rush of pain and anxiety, the memory of those frightful months in New York after the Sinai Campaign, when the entire world seemed bent on forcing us to withdraw our troops from the Sinai and the Gaza Strip, regardless of what we knew, and said, would inevitably happen as a result. The more I thought about those months in 1956 and 1957, the more apparent it became to me now that nothing at all had changed since then and that the Arabs were once again being permitted to delude themselves that they could wipe us off the face of the earth.

That delusion was further strengthened on May 22, when Nasser, intoxicated by the success of his dismissal of the UNEF, made another test of the world's reaction to his stated intention of entering an all-out war with Israel. He announced that Egypt was reimposing its blockage of the Strait of Tiran, despite the fact that a score of nations (including the United States, Britain, Canada and France) had guaranteed Israel's right of navigation through the Gulf of Aqaba. It was without any question another deliberate challenge, and Nasser waited to see how it would be met. He didn't have to wait very long. No one was going to do much about that either. Of course, there were protests and angry reactions. President Johnson described the blockade as "illegal" and "potentially disastrous to the cause of peace" and suggested that an international convoy, including an Israeli vessel, sail through the strait to call Nasser's bluff. But even he couldn't persuade the French or British to join him. The Security Council met in an emergency session, but the Russians saw to it that no conclusions were reached. The British prime minister, my good friend Harold Wilson, flew to the States and to Canada to suggest that an international naval task force be organized to police the Strait of Tiran, but he also got nowhere with his suggestion. Even U Thant—realizing at last what a terrible mistake he had made—bestirred himself sufficiently to go to Cairo and try to reason with Nasser, but it was too late.

Nasser had drawn his own conclusions: if the so-called guarantees that had been given to Israel after the Sinai Campaign by the maritime powers were as worthless as they now appeared to be, then what and who were to stop the Egyptians from winning that final, glorious and total victory over the Jewish state that would make Nasser the supreme figure of the Arab world? To the extent that he had any remaining doubts regarding the adventure into which he was about to plunge himself and his nation, they were swept away by the Russians. The Soviet minister of defense brought Nasser a last-minute message of encouragement from Kosygin: the Soviet Union would stand by Egypt in the battle that lay ahead. So the stage was set. As for war aims, to the extent that Nasser felt obliged to explain anything to the Egyptian people—who were already in the first throes of war hysteria—it was enough to go on repeating the clause "We aim at the destruction of the State of Israel" and to tell the Egyptian National Assembly, as he did in the last week of May, "The issue is *not* the question of Aqaba, the Strait of Tiran or the UNEF . . . . The issue is the aggression against Palestine that took place in 1948." In other words, the war that was now in the making was to be the *ultimate* Arab war against us, and on the face of it, Nasser had every reason to think he would win.

By June 1 there were 100,000 Egyptian soldiers and more than 900 Egyptian tanks in the Sinai, plus six Syrian brigades and nearly 300 Syrian tanks straining at the leash in the north. Also—after having hesitated for a few weeks—Jordan's King Hussein had finally decided to take the risk of joining Nasser in the great exploit. Although we had sent him constant messages promising that if he kept out of the war nothing would happen to him (the last of these messages was sent to Hussein by Eshkol through the good offices of the UN Truce Supervison Organization on the very morning that the war broke out), the temptation of participating in the victory—as well as his fear of defying Nasser—finally got the better of Hussein, and he, too, threw his lot in with the Egyptians—which provided the Arab war effort with seven more brigades, about 270 more tanks and a small but competent air force. The last to join in the coalition against Israel was Iraq, which signed a mutual defense pact with Egypt a day before the war began. It was certainly a most formidable array of military might, and since the West seemed to be either paralyzed or totally indifferent, while the Russians were backing the Arabs to the hilt, one can't really blame Nasser very much for having assumed that at last he was in a position to deal a deathblow to Israel.

Well, so much for the Arab mood and the Arab dream. What was happening to us? I neither want nor do I think it is necessary to retell in detail the story of the Six-Day War, about which so much has already been written. But no one who lived in Israel during the weeks that preceded it will ever, I believe, forget the way in which we faced the terrible danger that confronted us. And no one can possibly understand Israel's reaction to its current situation without first understanding what we learned about ourselves, about the Arab states and about the rest of the world in the course of those three weeks in the spring of 1967 that came to be known in Hebrew as the period of *konnenut* (preparedness). Of course, I was not a member of the cabinet any longer, but it was only natural that in the developing crisis I should be called on to help arrive at some of the life-or-death decisions that faced the cabinet, and it was taken for granted, I think, by everyone that I had to make myself available.

From the beginning there was no question in anyone's mind that war had to be averted—at almost any cost. There was no question that if we had to fight, we would do so—and win—but first, every possible avenue had to be explored. Eshkol, his face gray with weariness and tension, set in motion a search for some kind of diplomatic intervention. That was the sum total of his requests; needless to say, we never asked for military personnel. Eban was sent on a round of missions to Paris, London and Washington, and at the same time Eshkol quietly gave the signal for the nation to ready itself for the third time in nineteen years to defend its right to exist. Eban came back with nothing except the worst possible news. Our gravest fears had been confirmed. London and Washington were sympathetic and worried, but still not prepared to take any action. It was too bad, but maybe the Arab frenzy would wear itself out. At all events, they recommended patience and self-control. There was no alternative other than for Israel to wait and see. De Gaulle had been more direct: whatever happened he told Eban, Israel must not make the first move until and unless the Arab attack actually began. When that happened, France would step in to save the situation. To Eban's question "But what if we are no longer there to be saved?" De Gaulle chose not to reply, but he made clear to Eban that France's continued friendship with us depended entirely on whether or not we obeyed him.

Within a matter of a few days our survival was suddenly at stake. In the most literal sense of these dreadful words, we were alone. The Western world, of which we had always considered ourselves to be a part, had heard what we had to say, had listened to our assessment of the extreme danger confronting us, and had done nothing. So we began to get ready for the inevitable war. The army turned to its contingency plans. Eshkol ordered a general mobilization. The overage men and the women and children of Israel buckled down to clean out basements and cellars for use as makeshift air-raid shelters, to fill thousands of sandbags with which to line the pathetic homemade trenches that fathers and grandfathers dug in every garden and schoolyard throughout the country and to take over the essential chores of civilian life, while the troops waited, under camouflage nets in the sands of the Negev—waited, trained and went on waiting. It was as though some gigantic clock were ticking away for all of us, although no one except Nasser knew when the zero hour would be. The clock ticked on, and we waited and waited.

There were also the grim preparations that had to be kept secret: the parks in each city that had been consecrated for possible use as mass cemeteries; the hotels cleared of guests so that they could be turned into huge emergency first-aid stations; the iron rations stockpiled against the time when the population might have to be fed from some central source, the bandages, drugs and stretchers that were obtained and distributed. And of course, above all, there were the military preparations, because even though we had by now absorbed the fact that we were entirely on our own, there wasn't a single person in Israel, as far as I know, who had any illusions about the fact that there was no alternative whatsoever to winning the war that was being thrust on us. When I think back on those days, what stands out in my mind is the miraculous sense of unity and purpose that transformed us within only a week or two from a small, rather claustrophobic community, coping—and not always well—with all sorts of economic, political and social discontent into 2,500,000 Jews, each and every one of whom felt personally responsible for the survival of the State of Israel and each and every one of whom knew that the enemy we faced was committed to our annihilation.

So the issue was not, as it is perhaps for other countries, how best to remain intact and least damaged by the inevitable war, but rather how to survive as a people. The answer to that question was never in doubt. We could survive only by being victorious, and everything else—all the complaints, pettinesses and dissensions—fell away from us; we became, to put it very simply, one family, determined not to budge. Not one Jew left Israel during those awful weeks of waiting. Not one of the mothers in the settlements below the Golan Heights or in the Negev took her children and ran. Not one survivor of the Nazi death camps, many of whom had lost their children in the gas chambers, said, "I cannot bear to suffer again." And hundreds upon hundreds of Israelis who had gone abroad returned, although no one had called them back. They returned because they just could not stay away.

The war began early in the morning of Monday, June 5. As soon as we heard the whine of the air-raid sirens, we knew that the waiting was over, although it was not until very late that night that the dimensions of Israel's strike were revealed to the nation. All day, while wave after wave of our planes flew over the Mediterranean to blast the Egyptian airfields and demolish the aircraft poised to attack us, we waited for news, ears glued to the transistor radios that we all carried around with us but on which there was nothing to hear except music, Hebrew songs and the passwords that were used to call up reservists who had still not been mobilized. It was only after midnight that the official and almost incredible story of the first of those six days was unfolded to the civilian population by the chief of the air force and that, sitting in their blacked-out rooms, the people of Israel learned that they had been delivered from destruction within the six hours that it had taken the air force to put out of action more than 400 enemy planes, including those parked on Syrian and Jordanian airfields, and to gain full command of the air from Sinai to the Syrian border. I had been kept informed all day of the general situation, but even I had not quite grasped the implications of what had happened until after the broadcast. I stood alone for a few minutes at the door of my house, looked up at the cloudless and undisturbed sky and realized that we had been rescued from the terrible fear of air raids that had haunted us all for so many days. True, the war had only started; there would still be death and mourning and misery. But the planes that had been readied to bomb us were all mortally crippled, and the airfields from which they had been about to take off were now in ruins. I stood there and breathed in the night air as though I had not drawn a really deep breath for weeks.

It was not only in the air that we had won a conclusive victory, however. That same day, racing along the three routes they had taken in 1956, our ground forces, backed by the air force, had pushed their way deep into the Sinai, were already gaining the upperhand in tank battles that involved even more armor than had clashed in the Western Desert in World War II, and were already well on their way to the Suez Canal. Israel's hand, held out in peace for so long, turned into a fist, and there was no stopping the forward advance of the Israeli Defense Forces. But Nasser was not the only Arab ruler whose plans were shattered on June 5.

There was also Hussein, who had measured Eshkol's promise that nothing would happen to Jordan if he kept out of the war against the message he had received from Nasser that very morning informing him that Tel Aviv was being bombed by the Egyptians—never mind that Nasser didn't have a single bomber to his name by then. Like his grandfather before him, Hussein had carefully weighed the odds and made a mistake. On June 5 he ordered his troops to start shelling Jerusalem and the Jewish settlements on the Jordan-Israeli border. His army was to serve as the eastern arm of the pincer movement that was to do us in, but failed in its mission. As soon as the Jordanian shelling began, the Israeli Defense Forces struck at Hussein also, and although the fighting on the Jerusalem front cost the lives of very many young Israelis—who fought hand to hand and street by narrow street, rather than resort to the mortars and tanks that might have damaged the city and the Christian and Moslem holy places—it was already clear that night that Hussein's greed was going to lose him his hold on eastern Jerusalem, at the very least. At the risk of repeating myself, I must emphasize, at this point, that just as in 1948 the

Arabs had hammered at Jerusalém without the slightest regard for the safety of its churches and holy places, so in 1967 Jordanian troops didn't hesitate to use churches and even the minarets of their own mosques for emplacements. This may explain why we resent the fears that are sometimes expressed for the sanctity of Jerusalem under Israeli administration, to say nothing of what we discovered when we finally entered East Jerusalem: Jewish cemeteries had been desecrated, the ancient synagogues of the Jewish Quarter of the Old City had been razed to the ground, and Jewish tombstones from the Mount of Olives had been used to pave Jordanian roads and Jordanian army latrines. So let no one ever try to convince me that Jerusalem is better off in Arab hands or that we cannot be trusted to take care of it.

It took all of three days for the Egyptians to be beaten and two days for Hussein to pay for his error of judgment. By Thursday, June 8, the governor of the Gaza Strip had surrendered, Israeli forces were settled in on the east bank of the Suez Canal, the Strait of Tiran was back under Israel's control and 80 percent, if not more, of Egypt's military equipment had been destroyed. Even Nasser, not the most accurate of men, admitted that 10,000 Egyptian soldiers and 1,500 Egyptian officers had been lost, and we had nearly 6,000 Egyptian prisoners. The whole of the Sinai and the Gaza Strip had fallen to Israel again. So had East Jerusalem, the Old City and virtually half of the kingdom of Jordan. But we had still not learned how many of our boys had died in the fighting, and there was still one more aggressor to deal with. On Friday, June 9, the Israel Defense Force turned their attention to Syria and to rectifying the Syrian mistake in believing that the guns on tops of the Golan Heights that had been pounding away relentlessly at the Jewish villages in the valley below were really invincible. I must confess that there was some justification for the Syrian self-confidence. After the war, when I visited the Golan Heights and saw for myself the miles upon miles of reinforced concrete bunkers bristling with barbed wire and filled with antitank guns and artillery, I understood why the Syrians had been so sure of themselves and why it took two bloody days and one terrible night for the Israeli Defense Force to scale the Golan Heights, inch by inch, and then force their way into those bunkers. But it was done—by the army, the air force, the paratroopers and brave engineers in bulldozers—and by June 10 the Syrians were begging the United Nations to arrange a cease-fire. General David Elazar was then the commander of the northern front. When the fighting was over, he sent a message to those Israeli settlements in the valley: "Only from these heights can I see how really great you are."

It was all over. The Arab states and their Soviet patrons had lost their war. But this time, the price for our withdrawal was going to be very high, higher than it had been in 1956. This time the price would be peace, permanent peace, peace by treaty based on agreed and secure borders. It had been a lightning war, but it had also been a cruel one. All over Israel there were military funerals again, many of them the funerals of boys whose fathers or older brothers had fallen in the War of Independence or the fighting that had plagued us ever since. We were not going to go through that anguish again if we could possibly help it. We were not going to be told what a wonderful people the Israelis are. They win wars every ten years, and they have done it again. Fantastic! Now that they have won this round, they can go back where they came from, so that Syrian gunners on the Golan Heights can again shoot into the kibbutzim, so that Jordanian legionnaires on the towers of the Old City can again shell at will, so that the Gaza Strip can again be a nest for terrorists and the Sinai Desert can again become the staging ground for Nasser's divisions.

We had fought alone for our existence and our security and paid for them, and it seemed to most of us that a new day was really about to dawn, that the Arabs—trounced on the battlefield—might agree at last to sit down and thrash out the differences between us, none of which ever was, or is, insoluble.

There was no sense of triumph, only an enormous surge of hopefulness. And in the sheer relief of the victory, in the delight of finding ourselves alive and relatively unscathed and dazed momentarily by the prospect of peace, the whole of Israel went on a sort of holiday that lasted most of the summer. I don't think that there was a single family, including my own, that didn't take off a few days right after the Six-Day War to indulge in what looked to strangers like mass sightseeing, but was really a kind of pilgrimage to those parts of the Holy Land from which we had been excluded for nearly twenty years. In the first place, of course, the Jews streamed to Jerusalem; thousands and thousands of people daily crowded the Old City, praying in front of the Western Wall and picking their way through the ruins of what had been the Jewish Quarter. But we also went to Bethlehem, Jericho, Hebron and Gaza and Sharm el-Sheikh. Offices, factories, kibbutzim and schools—all participated in the endless excursions, and hundreds of cars, buses, trucks and even taxis, packed to the brim, criss-crossed the country for months en route to Mount Hermon in the north or Mount Sinai in the south. Everywhere we went during that elated, almost carefree summer, we met the Arabs of the territories that we now administered, smiled at them, bought their produce and talked to them, sharing with them—even if not always in words—the vision of peace that suddenly seemed about to become a reality and trying to convey to them our joy that now we would all be able to live together normally.

Everyone was on wheels in those days because the Arabs in the administered territories were traveling around almost as much as we were. They flocked to Tel Aviv, to the seashore and to the zoo, stared at the shopwindows in West Jerusalem and sat in the cafés of all the main streets. Most of them were as excited and as curious as we were and, like us, were absorbed in looking at landscapes which the adults had forgotten and the children had never seen. All this may sound too good to be true, and I certainly don't want to convey the impression that the Arabs turned to Mecca five times a day to thank Allah for their good fortune in having been defeated or that there were not Jews who preferred to stay home rather than participate in what they felt to be an indecent celebration of peace before the scars of war had had time to heal. But anyone who visited Israel in the summer of 1967 will testify to the extraordinary euphoria that gripped the Jews and appeared also to affect the Arabs. It was, in short, as though a death sentence had been lifted.

If I have to choose one particular aspect of that immediate post war period as an illustration of the general atmosphere, I would certainly point to the tearing down of the concrete barricade and barbed-wire fences that had separated the two halves of the city of Jerusalem ever since 1948. More than anything else, those hideous barricades had signified the abnormality of our life, and when they were bulldozed away and Jerusalem overnight became one city, it was like a sign and symbol of a new era. As someone who came to Jerusalem then for the very first time said to me, "There is light from within the city," and I understood exactly what he meant. "Very soon," I told my grandchildren, "the soldiers will come home; there will be peace; we will be able to travel to Jordan and to Egypt; and all will be well." I honestly believed it, but it wasn't to be.

In August, 1967, at a summit conference in Khartoum, the Arab leaders reviewed the situation and came to an altogether different conclusion. They issued their notorious three noes: there would be no peace with Israel, no recognition of the Jewish state and no negotiations. No, no, no! Israel must withdraw, totally and unconditionally, from the territories taken in the Six-Day War, and the Arab terrorists who were invited to the conference added a fourth helpful statement of their own: Israel must be destroyed, even within the pre-1967 boundaries. This was their answer to the Israeli government's appeal: "Let us meet not as conqueror and conquered, but as equals to negotiate peace—with no preconditions." Never mind who started the war, and never mind who won it. As far as the Arabs were concerned, nothing had changed. So the so-called fruits of the victory turned into ashes before they could ripen, and the lovely dream of immediate peace faded away. But if the Arabs had learned nothing, we had learned something. We were not prepared to repeat the exercise of 1956. Discuss, negotiate, compromise, concede—all these, yes! But not go back to where we had been on June 4, 1967. That accommodating we couldn't afford to be, even to save Nasser's face or to make the Syrians feel better about not having destroyed us! It was a great pity that the Arab states felt so humiliated by losing the war which they had started that they just couldn't bring themselves to talk to us, but on the other hand, we couldn't be expected to reward them for having tried to throw us into the sea. We were bitterly disappointed, but there was only one possible reply: Israel would not withdraw from any of the territories until the Arab states once and for all put an end to the conflict. We decided—and, believe me, it was not a painless decision, that whatever it cost us in terms of public opinion, money or energy, and regardless of the pressures that might be brought to bear on us, we would stand fast on the cease-fire lines. We waited for the Arabs to accept the fact that the only alternative to war was peace and that the only road to peace was negotiation.

In the meantime, the close to 1,000,000 Arabs living in the territories on our side of the cease-fire lines—about 600,000 on the West Bank of the Jordan and some 365,000 in the Gaza Strip and the Sinai, plus the Druze villagers who had opted to stay on the Golan Heights after the Syrian army had gone—would live pretty much as they had lived before the Six-Day War. It is never a great pleasure to be accountable to a military government, and none of the Arabs in the territories enjoyed having Israeli patrols move around in their midst. But the army kept a very low profile indeed, and the military government—thanks largely to Dayan's concept of its role, interfered with daily life as little as possible. Local laws were retained, and so were local leaders. The bridges over the Jordan were open, and the Arabs on the West Bank went on trading with the Arab states, studying in the Arab states and visiting their relatives there, while their relatives were free to visit them—which they did by the thousands. It was only going to be an interim arrangement anyhow; no sane Israeli ever assumed that all the territories were going to remain under Israeli rule. Jerusalem, of course, would stay united, but an arrangement could be made regarding Moslem control over the Moslem holy places. New borders would have to be drawn up between Jordan and Israel; it was unlikely that the Golan Heights would be handed back, lock, stock and barrel, to the Syrians or that all of Sinai would be returned at once to the Egyptians, and the Gaza Strip was certainly a problem. But there was no point whatsoever in drawing maps of what the Middle East would look like or even to arguing among ourselves what territory would be returned to whom until these matters could be taken up with the only other people to whom they were of real concern—our neighbors. After all, you can't return territory by parcel post. So, we went on waiting for a response to our repeated call for talks.

In the meantime, the Security Council passed a resolution—the celebrated Resolution 242, sponsored by the British—which outlined a framework for the peaceful settlement of "the Arab-Israeli dispute" and appointed a special representative, Dr. Gunnar V. Jarring, who was charged with supervising a "peaceful and accepted settlement." So much has been written and said about Resolution 242, and it has been so thoroughly distorted by the Arabs and the Russians, that I think it might be useful for me to quote it, particularly since it isn't very long:

The Security Council,

Expressing its continuing concern with the grave situation in the Middle East.

Emphasizing the inadmissibility of the acquisition of territory by war and the need to work for a just and lasting peace in which every State in the area can live in security.

Emphasizing further that all Member States in their acceptance of the Charter of the United Nations have undertaken a commitment to act in accordance with Article 2 of the Charter.

1. Affirms that the fulfillment of Charter principles requires the establishment of a just and lasting peace in the Middle East, which should include the application of both the following principles:

(i) Withdrawal of Israeli armed forces from territories occupied in the recent conflict;

(ii) Termination of all claims of states of belligerency and respect for and acknowledgment of the sovereignty, territorial integrity and political independence of every State in the area and their right to live in peace within secure and recognized boundaries free from threats or acts of force; and

2. Affirms further the necessity

(i) For guaranteeing freedom of navigation through international waterways in the area;

(ii) For achieving a just settlement of the refugee problem;

(iii) For guaranteeing the territorial inviolability and political independence of every State in the area, through measures including the establishment of demilitarized zones.

It will be noted that it does *not* say that Israel must withdraw from all territories, nor does it say that Israel must withdraw from *the* territories; but it *does* say that every state in the area has a right to live in peace within "secure and recognized boundaries" and it *does* specify the termination of belligerency. Furthermore, it does *not* speak of a Palestinian state, while it *does* speak of a refugee problem. But it wasn't only Resolution 242 that was misinterpreted, but also our attitude that was being misinterpreted. After the Six-Day-War, Israel's leading satirical writer, Ephraim Kishon, together with the Israeli cartoonist Dosh, published a book called *So Sorry We Won*. It was a bitter title, but not in the least ambiguous to its Israeli readers. In fact, it summed up rather succinctly the way we were beginning to feel, by 1968, which was that the only recipe for improving Israel's rapidly deteriorating image was to forget all about peace. Our crime appeared to be that we kept saying to the Arabs, "Let's negotiate." Not, as we were entitled to do, "This is the new map; sign on the dotted line," but "Let's negotiate."

In some mysterious way, this made us the villains. I couldn't for the life of me ever grasp, for instance, why Willy Brandt when he recognized the Oder-Neisse border because the time had come to put right the wrong that Germany had done to Poland in World War II, got (and richly deserved) the Nobel Prize for it and was hailed as a great statesman and a man of peace, while Eshkol and later I were branded as expansionists for wanting exactly the same kind of border adjustments between Israel and its neighbors. And not only were we called expansionists by our critics, but we were constantly being asked by our friends whether we weren't worried about Israel's turning into a militarisitic nation ("a little Sparta" was the phrase most often used) that had to rely on its "brutal" occupation forces to preserve law and order in the administered territories. And, of course, "intransigent" was to become my middle name. But neither Eshkol nor I nor the overwhelming majority of other Israelis could make a secret of the fact that we weren't at all interested in a fine, liberal, antimilitaristic, *dead* Jewish state or in a "settlement" that would win us compliments about being reasonable and intelligent but that would endanger our lives. Dr. Weizmann used to say that he had become the president of a country where everybody is a president; Israeli democracy is so lively that there were, and are, almost as many doves as hawks, but I have yet to come across any Israeli who thinks that we should turn ourselves, permanently, into clay pigeons—not even for the sake of a better image.

Now I was seventy. It is not a sin to be seventy but it is also no joke. I had been ill again in 1967, and the Six-Day War was not exactly what the doctor had ordered. I felt that I owed myself some peace and quiet, and this time nothing and no one would change my mind. I went to the States for an Israel bond drive and visited Menachem, Aya and the children in Connecticut, where Aya was working on a university research grant and Menachem was teaching cello. I even spent a few weeks in Switzerland on what I think, was the first complete holiday I had ever taken, and I came back home feeling as fit as a fiddle.

The situation at home, however, hadn't progressed much. Despite the cease-fire, there was still a war of sorts going on at the Suez Canal. The Egyptians, secure in the knowledge that the Russians had already replaced all the guns, tanks and planes that they had lost in the Six-Day War, were keeping up a constant barrage of bombardments again just as soon as they dared. "When the time comes, we will strike," Nasser roared, and he repeated what he called "the principles of Egyptian policy": no negotiations with Israel, no peace with Israel, no recognition of Israel. And in the spring of 1969 he launched his war of attrition.

I suppose that from a distance, that continuous shelling of the Israel Defense Forces positions on the Canal might have seemed merely like another one of the protracted "incidents" that had been going on in the Middle East since anyone could remember, another demonstration of the supposed inability of Jews and Arabs to get along together, and I imagine that at first no one abroad took the reports about the endless Egyptian violations of the cease-fire very seriously. But we did, because we knew what those violations foretold, and we began to build a fortified defense line—the Bar-Lev line—to protect our troops on the Canal.

At the same time, when the Arab terrorist organizations found they were unable to persuade or provoke the population of the administered territories into taking any major action against the Israelis—other than an occasional, though certainly deeply felt, protest march in Hebron or strike in Jenin—they decided to go in for terrorism thousands of miles away from Israel. It was obviously much safer for them and a great deal more effective, and there was a wide choice of potential targets, including civilian aircraft and innocent passengers in foreign air terminals. Besides, the terrorists would then not have to restrict their terror to Jews. The Saudi Arabians saw to it that El Fatah didn't lack money; Nasser again bestowed his official blessings on them ("El Fatah," he proclaimed, "fulfills a vital task in drawing the enemy's blood"); and King Hussein took another stroll on his tightrope. Although the terrorists were soon to fight him, tooth and nail, for control of Jordan and to endanger him more than they had ever endangered us, Hussein—with the same lack of foresight that he had shown in the Six-Day War, gave them his enthusiastic support. In 1970, when he found himself in such trouble with the so-called Palestinian terrorists organizations and began looking around everywhere for aid, I couldn't help thinking that he was like a man who murders his mother and father and then begs for mercy on the grounds that he is an orphan!

In the north there was also no peace. Southern Lebanon was gradually being turned into a playground for the terrorists; Israeli towns, villages and farms—even school buses filled with children—were regularly being shelled and fired upon from what was now nicknamed Fatahland, while the Lebanese government wept crocodile tears and said it could do "nothing" about the activity of the terrorists or even the fact that they were trained and operating from Lebanese territory.

But we had decided that we were going to defend the cease-fire lines regardless of Nasser or El Fatah and, what's more, press on with our search for peace, however disheartening that search had become.

Then, on February 26, 1969, my dear friend Levi Eshkol, with whom I had worked for so many years and whom I had loved and admired so much, had a heart attack and died. I was at home alone when the news reached me, and I was stunned. I sat by the phone for several minutes in a state of shock, unable to pull myself together enough to find someone to drive me to Jerusalem. It seemed impossible that Eshkol was gone. I had talked to him only the night before, and we were to meet the next day. I couldn't imagine what would happen now or who would take his place as prime minister. In Jerusalem I immediately went to Eshkol's home. While the cabinet met in an emergency session, I sat in someone's office and waited for it to end so that I would know what had been decided about the funeral arrangements. As I sat there, an Israeli newspaperman came in.

"I know how you must feel," he said to me. "But I have just come from the Knesset. Everyone says there is only one solution. Golda must come back."

"I don't know what you are talking about," I answered furiously. "Please don't bother me now. This is no time to talk politics. Please, please, go away."

"Well," he said, "my editor wants to know where you'll be tonight. He wants to talk to you."

"Look," I said, "I don't want to see anyone now. I don't know anything, and I don't want to know anything. I just want you to leave me alone."

The cabinet meeting ended. Yigal Allon, who was deputy prime minister, took over as acting prime minister. I went with a group of cabinet ministers to see Miriam Eshkol again. Then, toward evening, I returned to Tel Aviv. At about 10 P.M. the editor rang my doorbell. "I come to tell you," he said, "that everybody has decided that you must take Eshkol's place. You are the only person with enough authority, experience and credit within the party to be acceptable to almost everyone."

If I had been in a different mood, I might have reminded him then and there that in a recent poll, when the public was asked about its choice of the next prime minister, I had won exactly 3 percent of the votes, which was all right by me, but not what one would call a landslide. The greatest number of votes had been received by Moshe Dayan, and Yigal Allon had not done so badly either. But I was in no frame of mind to discuss the matter. "Eshkol isn't even buried yet," I said to the editor. "How can you talk to me about these things?" and I sent him away.

But within a few days the party began to press me. "National elections are scheduled to take place in October; an interim prime minister will have to be appointed; it is only a question of a few months! And there is no one else." Even Allon himself beseeched me, for the sake of the party, so recently unified, and for the sake of the country, which was still in such peril, to perform this last service. Not that the entire Labor Party was so keen on me. The ex-Rafi faction, headed by Dayan and Peres, was less than anxious to have me as prime minister, and I could certainly understand the reservations of those other people in the country who thought that a seventy-year-old grandmother was hardly the perfect candidate to head a twenty-year-old state.

As for me, I couldn't make up my mind. On the one hand, I realized that unless I agreed, there would inevitably be a tremendous tug-of-war between Dayan and Allon, which was one thing that Israel didn't need then. It was enough that we had a war with the Arabs on our hands; we could wait for that to end before we embarked on a war of the Jews. On the other hand, I honestly didn't want the responsibility, the awful stress and strain of being prime minister. I wanted to talk to the family, so I telephoned Menachem and Aya in Connecticut; and then I called up Sarah and Zechariah in Revivim and told them that I had to see them but was much too tired to go to the Negev. Could they possibly come to me? They managed to get in by truck at midnight, and we sat up all through the night, talking, smoking and drinking coffee. In the morning, Sarah told me that Zechariah and she had made up their minds. They agreed with Menachem and Aya; I had no choice. "Ima, we know it will be terribly hard for you, harder than anyone will ever guess. But there is simply no way out—you must say yes." So I did. On March 7 the Central Committee of the Labor Party voted, none against, and the Rafi faction abstained. I have often been asked how I felt at that moment, and I wish that I had a poetic answer to the question. I know that tears rolled down my cheeks and that I held my head in my hands when the voting was over, but all that I recall about my feelings is that I was dazed. I had never planned to be prime minister; I had never planned any position, in fact. I had planned to come to Palestine, to go to Merhavia, to be active in the labor movement. But the position I would occupy? That never. I only knew that now I would have to make decisions every day that would affect the lives of millions of people, and I think perhaps that is why I cried. But there wasn't much time for reflection, and any thoughts I had about the path that had begun in Kiev and led me to the prime minister's office in Jerusalem had to wait. Today, when I can take time for those reflections, I find I have no appetite for them. I became prime minister because that was how it was, in the same way that my milkman became an officer in command of an outpost on Mount Hermon. Neither of us had any particular relish for the job, but we both did it as well as we could.

CHAPTER 12

THE PRIME MINISTER

So I moved again, this time to the large, not especially attractive prime minister's residence in Jerusalem—in which Ben-Gurion, Sharett and Eshkol had lived before me—and began to accustom myself to the permanent presence of police and bodyguards, to a workday of at least sixteen hours and to the minimum of privacy. Obviously some days were easier, shorter and less tense than others, and I have no intention of pretending that I spent the five years that I was prime minister of Israel in a state of martyrdom or that I never enjoyed myself at all. But my term of office began with one war and ended with another.

The Egyptian War of Attrition had started at the beginning of March, 1968, and went on, with increasing ferocity, till the summer of 1970. Not only did the Soviet Union refrain from pressuring Nasser to end the violence and the killing, but it rushed to Egypt thousands of Soviet instructors, to help retrain the battered Egyptian army and lend it a helping hand in combat against us and a flood of military equipment, conservatively valued at some $3.5 billion. Egypt was not the sole beneficiary of this Soviet largess; it went to Syria and Iraq also. But Nasser was certainly the main beneficiary. Two-thirds of all the hundreds of tanks and fighter aircraft that Russia poured into the area immediately following the Six-Day War were earmarked for Egyptian use in the hope that in the face of the incessant fire and our own mounting losses, we would be unable to maintain our position along the Canal and that broken in spirit as well as in body, we would finally agree to withdraw from the Canal zone without achieving peace or any kind of end to the conflict.

We weren't very eager to go on fighting anyone—not the Egyptians and even less the Russians—but we had absolutely no alternative. The only way we could possibly prevent that total war which Nasser himself proclaimed day and night to be the ultimate goal of his War of Attrition was by striking back, and striking hard, at the Egyptian military installations, by bombing Egyptian military targets, not only at the cease-fire line but inside Egypt itself, and, if and when necessary, even by bringing our message to the very doorstep of the Egyptians by raiding deep into Egyptian territory. It wasn't an easy decision to make, particularly since we knew that the Soviets might extend their involvement in Egypt even further. (Incidentally, this was the first actual Soviet intervention anywhere outside the accepted Soviet sphere of influence since World War II.) So we reluctantly began our strategic "in-depth" retaliatory bombardments, using our planes as flying artillery and trusting that the Egyptian people, hearing those planes over Cairo's military airfield, would understand they couldn't have it both ways: war for us and peace for themselves.

So much has happened since then that reading about the War of Attrition today may not be very vivid for most people. Even the terrible story of the Soviet ships that sailed secretly to Egypt laden with the SA-3 ground-to-air missiles that were to be installed, manned and operated by Soviet specialists throughout the Canal zone is probably not of any great interest now, though, we all know how those missiles were used against Israel in the autumn of 1973. But for us the War of Attrition was a real war, and it took all the determination, courage, strength and skill of our soldiers and pilots to hold the cease-fire lines and to try, regardless of the cost, to stop the forward movement of the missile pads that the Egyptians and their Russians were so busy setting up adjacent to the cease-fire lines. Still, there was a limit to our ability to go it alone. We had to have support and help, aircraft and arms, and we had to have them soon.

There was only one world power to whom we could turn: the United States, our traditional and great friend, which was selling us planes but did not, at that point, seem fully to understand our situation and might, we feared, cut that aid at any moment. President Nixon was more than just friendly. But neither he nor his secretary of state, William Rogers, was sympathetic to our refusal to accept any solution for the Middle East that would be imposed upon us by others nor to my strong opposition to Mr. Rogers' idea that the Russians, the Americans, the French and the British should sit down comfortably somewhere to work out a "feasible" compromise for the Arabs and for us.

Let me say at the outset that personally I always liked William Rogers. He is a very nice, very courteous and extremely patient man, and in the end it was he who proposed and brought about the cease-fire in August, 1970. But (and I hope he will forgive me for writing this) I suspect that he never really understood the background to the Arab wars against Israel or ever realized that the verbal reliability of the Arab leaders was not, in any way, similar to his own. I remember how enthusiastically he told me about his first visits to the Arab states and how immensely impressed he was by Faisal's "thirst for peace." As is true of many other gentlemen I have known, Rogers assumed—wrongly, unfortunately—that the whole world was made up solely of other gentlemen.

All my attempts to establish direct contact with the Arab leaders had failed miserably—including the appeal I made on the first day I assumed office, when I had declared that "we are prepared to discuss peace with our neighbors, any day and on all matters," only to read, within seventy-two hours, Nasser's reply that "there is no voice transcending the sounds of war . . . and no call holier than the call to war." Nor were the responses from Damascus, Amman or Beirut any more encouraging. To quote just one example of the reaction of the Arab world to my plea that we enter into negotiations at once, here is an excerpt from an article published in a leading Jordanian newspaper in June, 1969:

. . . Mrs. Meir is prepared to go to Cairo to hold discusssions with President Nasser but, to her sorrow, has not been invited. She believes that one fine day a world without guns will emerge in the Middle East. Golda Meir is behaving like a grandmother telling bedtime stories to her grandchildren. . . .

I felt as if we were caught in a vise. All the time the war was going on, people abroad were asking whether our real intention was not to bring Nasser down—as though we had set him up and were now preoccupied with plans to replace him. What enraged me, though, was that we were also being questioned whether our bombing in depth was "really" necessary and a matter of self-defense, as though one must wait till a murderer actually reaches one's home before it is morally permissible to stop him from trying to kill one, particularly when—as in Nasser's case—we were being left in no doubt whatsoever as to his intentions.

It was, in short, a difficult period, and one not made any easier for me by having inherited from Eshkol the National Unity Government which included the antisocialist bloc known as Gahal (made up of the extreme right-wing Herut Party and the far more moderate but smaller Liberal Party) and led by Menachem Begin. Quite apart from the deep-seated and very basic differences in ideology that had obviously always existed between the left and the right wings of Israel's political spectrum, there was a serious immediate difference in our approaches to the situation in which Israel now found itself. In June, Secretary of State Rogers proposed that Israel hold discussions with Egypt and Jordan, under the auspices of Dr. Jarring, with the aim of arriving at a just and lasting peace. These discussions were to be based upon "mutual acknowledgment of each other's sovereignty, territorial integrity and political independence" and on "Israeli withdrawal from territories occupied in the 1967 conflict," in accordance with Resolution 242. He also proposed that the cease-fire with Egypt, which had been shattered by the War of Attrition, be renewed for at least ninety days. Gahal, however, stood firm on the fact that the policy of the government of Israel since 1967 had been—and still was, as far as Gahal was concerned—that the Israel Defense Forces would remain on the cease-fire lines until peace was attained. Formally, of course, Gahal had a point. I knew that I would have to go to the Knesset to get its consent for this change in policy. But it didn't matter how hard I argued that the situation had changed. Though it accepted the cease-fire proposal, Gahal refused to agree to any negotiations on the subject of withdrawal from the territories until there was peace.

"But we won't have any cease-fire unless we also accept some of the less favorable conditions," I tried to explain repeatedly to Mr. Begin. "And what's more, we won't get any arms from America." "What do you mean, we won't get arms?" he used to say. "We'll *demand* them from the Americans." I couldn't get it through to him that although the American commitment to Israel's survival was certainly great, we needed Mr. Nixon and Mr. Rogers much more than they needed us, and Israel's policies couldn't be based entirely on the assumption that American Jewry either would or could force Mr. Nixon to adopt a position against his will or better judgment. But Gahal, intoxicated by its own rhetoric, had convinced itself that all we had to do was to go on telling the United States that we wouldn't give in to any pressure whatsoever, and if we did this long enough and loud enough, one day that pressure would just vanish. I can only describe this belief as mystical because it certainly wasn't based on reality as I knew it, and today I shudder to think what would have happened in October, 1973, if we had behaved in 1969 and 1970 as defiantly and self-destructively as Gahal wanted us to. There might well have been no U.S. military aid at all from 1970 on, and the Yom Kippur War would have ended very differently.

And in August, 1970, when the four Gahal ministers resigned from the cabinet on the absurd grounds that the Israeli government's acceptance of the cease-fire was the beginning of a major unconditional retreat from the cease-fire lines, I wasn't particularly taken aback. For the sake of avoiding additional problems, we asked them to stay. But they were adamant and left.

The other (though minor) bane of my life during all the time that I was prime minister—and one that it took me months to accustom myself to, even partially—was the freedom with which various ministers confided in the press, to put it very politely. The constant leaks from cabinet meetings infuriated me, and although I had my own suspicions all along as to the source of the sensational revelations by so-called diplomatic correspondents which greeted me so often in the morning papers, I could never prove them—which meant that I couldn't do much about them. But my staff very quickly got used to seeing me turn up at the office on the day after a cabinet meeting looking as black as thunder because over breakfast I had read something garbled in the paper that shouldn't have been there at all, garbled or otherwise. But these, need I say, were not my major anxieties. The real problems, as they had been for so long, were survival and peace, in that order.

A number of months after I had taken office, I made a decision. I would go to Washington myself—if it could be arranged—to speak with President Nixon, to talk to congressmen and senators and to find out just what the American people thought and felt about us and what they were willing to do to help us. It wasn't that I deluded myself for a moment that I had any magical powers of persuasion. After all, I hadn't succeeded in changing Mr. Rogers' mind about the need for the Russians to participate in the Middle Eastern settlement—though I had certainly tried my best to do so. Nor did I expect to accomplish more than gifted men like our foreign minister, Abba Eban, or our new ambassador to Washington, General Yitzhak Rabin, had been able to accomplish. But I felt a deep need to establish, for and by myself, just where we stood as far as our relationship with the United States was concerned, and the cabinet thought it was a very good idea for me to go. As soon as the official invitation arrived from the White House, I began to prepare for the trip.

I certainly had doubts about its prospects for success. I had never met Richard Nixon, and I didn't even know most of the men around him. I had no idea what the president was being told about me; for all I knew, he might regard me (understandably enough) as a stopgap premier who didn't carry much weight in her own country and would probably not be reelected. But I was sure of one thing: whatever impression I might make on him, I had to lay before the president all our problems and difficulties, quite candidly, and try to convince him, beyond a shadow of doubt, that there was a great deal that could be asked of us by way of compromise and concessions, but that we could not be expected to give up our dream of peace or to withdraw a single soldier from one inch of land until an agreement could be reached between the Arabs and ourselves. And that was not all. We desperately needed arms, and I felt that I should ask him for them myself. On the face of it, they weren't very complicated messages, but I think that I would have been less than human and a fool if I hadn't been extremely nervous about delivering them.

My personal preparations were very simple. I bought two evening dresses (including the beige lace and velvet one that I wore to the White House dinner), a knitted suit, a couple of hats (that I never wore at all) and some gloves (to hold in my hand). With the consideration that was to typify his entire relationship with me, President Nixon saw to it that Clara and Menachem and his family were also invited to the White House dinner that was to be held on my first evening in Washington, and we arranged to meet on September 24 in Philadelphia (which, for some reason—perhaps because of its historic importance—is a customary first stop for guests from abroad). From Philadelphia we were flown by helicopter to the lawn of the White House. With all the arrangements made, I was free to spend the weeks before my departure working overtime with my advisers, in particular with Dayan and the chief of staff, Chaim Bar-Lev, on the "shopping list" that I was going to take to Washington with me. In addition to a specific request for twenty-five Phantoms and eighty Skyhawk jets, I planned to ask the president for low-interest loans of $200,000,000 a year for five years to help us pay for the planes we hoped to be able to buy. I must explain here that the first U.S. president to authorize the sale of Phantoms and Skyhawks to Israel was President Johnson, whom Eshkol had visited in Texas and who had promised to give "sympathetic consideration" to the request. But it had taken some time before those first Skyhawks had actually been delivered to us, and I was sure that even if President Nixon agreed to sell us Phantoms, we would not be able to get them quickly unless I was able to convey to him the urgency of our situation and of the imbalance in the flow of arms to the Middle East. As for the money, I thought we would probably get that (though money is also something one can never be sure about) if for no other reason than that our credit was excellent. As a matter of fact, Israel had never fallen down on a single payment due anyone.

Anyhow, on the plane going to the States, I was immersed in my thoughts, trying to guess what my visit to Nixon would be like and whether we would get along together. I wasn't even sure any more of the reception I would get in the United States as a whole. After the Six-Day War, I had been greeted with warmth, love and pride by American Jewry; but more than two years had passed since then, and it seemed possible that the enthusiasm for Israel's cause might have waned somewhat. But I needn't have worried so much, on either score.

At the Philadelphia airport a crowd of thousands was waiting for me; hundreds and hundreds of schoolchildren, singing "Hevenu Shalom Aleichem" were waving and carrying banners. I remember one of these banners read WE DIG YOU, GOLDA, and I thought it was the most charming expression of support for Israel—and perhaps for me—that I had ever seen. But I had no idea, other than smiling and waving at them, how to make clear to those youngsters that I certainly "dug" them, too. So I just smiled and waved and was delighted when I spotted my own family. At Independence Square an even larger crowd greeted me—30,000 American Jews, many of whom had been standing there for several hours to see me. I couldn't get over the sight of all those people pressing against the police barricades and applauding. I spoke to them only very briefly, but as someone said to me, "You could have read a page from the telephone book, and that crowd would still have cheered."

We stayed overnight in Philadelphia and then flew on to Washington in the morning. It had rained all night, and the sky was still cloudy and gray, as if it were going to go on raining. But (as though that, too, had been arranged by the White House) the sun came out just after my two-minute ride in a limousine from the helicopter to the bright-green White House lawn. President Nixon put me at ease at once. He helped me out of the car, and Mrs. Nixon handed me a huge bunch of red roses. There was something about the way the Nixons received me that made me feel at home with them from the start, and I was very grateful to both of them.

The formal ceremony was very formal indeed, full of spit and polish. The president and I stood on a raised platform covered by a red carpet, while a marine band played the two national anthems. I listened to "Hatikvah," and although I made an effort to look perfectly calm, my eyes filled with tears. There I was, the prime minister of the Jewish state, which had come into existence and survived against such odds, standing to attention with the president of the United States while my country was accorded full military honors.

My meetings with the president were as warm as his initial welcome. We were together for a couple of hours, and we talked about everything as bluntly and frankly as I had hoped we would. We were in complete agreement that Israel should stay put until some kind of acceptable agreement with the Arabs was reached and that a big power which promises assistance to a small country when it is in trouble must keep its word. We also talked about the Palestinians and I spoke my mind as openly on that topic as I did on others. "Between the Mediterranean and the borders of Iraq," I said, "in what was once Palestine, there are now two countries, one Jewish and one Arab, and there is no room for a third. The Palestinians must find the solution to their problem together with that Arab country, Jordan, because a 'Palestinian state' between us and Jordan can only become a base from which it will be even more convenient to attack and destroy Israel."

That night President and Mrs. Nixon gave a state dinner in my honor. People in Washington later said that it was one of the finest White House parties of the Nixon administration—though no one could explain just what made it such a success. For me it was, from start to finish, one of the most wonderful evenings of my life, partly, I expect, because I had met with such understanding from President Nixon, and partly because I now felt sure that the United States would stand by us and I really relaxed for the first time in months. Also, everything had been superbly planned to give me pleasure—from the presence of my family to the "Charlotte Revivim" dessert that so tactfully indicated that Sarah and Zechariah were also included in the celebration. Among the 120 guests were many old friends from both political parties, including the former U.S. ambassador to the United Nations Arthur Goldberg, Senator Jacob Javits, and of course, Mr. Rogers, Dr. Kissinger, Eban and Rabin, as well as various high-ranking members of the Nixon administration. Throughout the dinner Israeli music was played, and then—as a special treat—Leonard Bernstein and Isaac Stern performed, giving us one encore after another. I could see and hear how tremendously moved they both were, and I was so enraptured by their music and their presence that when they stopped playing, I forgot where I was and I jumped up to hug them both.

At about 11 P.M., the president, Mrs. Nixon and I left the party, and at my car Mrs. Nixon and I kissed each other good-night, as though we had been friends for years. The rest of the guests went on dancing until long after midnight.

In all, I spent four days in Washington. Walking in step with the bemedaled adjutant general of the United States army (not the easiest thing I have ever done), I placed a wreath of blue and white flowers on the Tomb of the Unknown Soldier at Arlington National Cemetery, preceded by a nineteen-gun salute and color-bearers carrying Israeli flags. I visited Mr. Rogers at the State Department and was entertained at lunch by him, saw Mr. Melvin Laird at the Department of Defense, met with members of the House Foreign Affairs Committee and "appeared" at the National Press Club, where I met the toughest and most experienced journalists in the United States and felt at first as if I were in a boxing ring with them. But they were very nice to me, too, and seemed to like the fact that I answered their questions as briefly and as simply as I could—though I can't say that they asked me anything that I hadn't been asked a dozen times before.

There were only two queries that were at all new. One newspaperman asked: "Would Israel employ nuclear weapons if her survival were in jeopardy?" to which I could only reply, truthfully, that I thought we hadn't done so badly with conventional weapons—an answer that was greeted by laughter and applause. The second was a request from the president of the Press Club that made me laugh. "Your grandson Gideon says that you make the best gefilte fish [stuffed fish] in Israel," he said. "Would you reveal your recipe to us?"

"I'll do better than that," I answered. "When I come here again, I promise to arrive three days in advance and make gefilte fish for lunch for all of you." Months later, incidentally, I was once interviewed in Los Angeles and asked if I made good chicken soup. "Of course, I do," I replied. Would I send the recipe? "Gladly," I said, never imagining that within the week the interviewer would get 40,000 requests for it. I only hope it resulted in 40,000 pots of good Jewish soup.

When I got back to Israel, although I could not yet make any announcement about the Phantoms, I knew we were going to get them, and my heart was much lighter than it had been when I took off. But the War of Attrition was still being waged; the terrorists were still active; the number of Soviet military personnel in Egypt was increasing by leaps and bounds, including combat pilots and the crews of the ground-to-air missiles. In a word, peace was as remote as ever. In fact, nothing at all had changed substantially since I had assumed office. Whatever reasons existed then for my becoming prime minister were, unfortunately, still valid on the eve of our national elections—the seventh since the state was established. In the months that had passed, however, my so-called rating had improved, and although I wasn't out to win any popularity contests, it certainly feels a lot better to have a rating of seventy-five or eighty than of three! Now I was prime minister in my own right, so to speak.

I very much hoped that I would be able to do something to help solve those of Israel's growing social and economic problems that were beginning to cause a real rift between various sections of the population. For years, both in the Histadrut and in the party, I had pleaded that since we unfortunately couldn't do anything about having to maintain our enormous defense budget, we should at least pull together and try to do away with the widening gap between the people who had everything they needed—if not everything they wanted—and those tens of thousands who were still ill housed, ill clothed, undereducated and sometimes even ill fed. For the most part this segment of our population belonged to what was bitterly called "the second Israel," Jews who had come to us in 1948, 1950 and 1951 from Yemen, the Middle East and North Africa and whose standard of living in the late 1960s and early 1970s still left a great deal to be desired. Of course, we could go on congratulating ourselves on the fact that between 1949 and 1970 we had built more than 400,000 units of public housing and that there wasn't a single place in the country—however isolated—that didn't have a school, a kindergarten and, in most cases, also a nursery school. But no amount of justified pride in what we had managed to achieve could possibly eliminate the other less pleasant facts. There was poverty in Israel, and there was also wealth. Neither the poverty nor the wealth was great, but they both existed.

There were, and still are, Israelis who live ten to a two-room house, whose children are dropouts (even though they would probably be totally exempt from paying secondary-school fees) and delinquents (largely because of their disadvantaged background) and who, because they believe that they are in danger of turning into permanently underprivileged second-class citizens, regard all other newer immigrants as inevitably making their own situation worse. There are also Israelis, though not many, who live in relative luxury, who drive large cars, entertain lavishly, dress in the height of fashion and have adopted a life-style that is imported from abroad and has nothing whatsoever to do either with our real national economic capacity or with the real circumstances of our national life. In between these two groups are the masses of skilled laborers and white-collar workers who have a hard time making ends meet, who can't maintain their standard of living (which is in no way immodest) on one salary, who for decades have proved themselves capable of the most remarkable self-discipline, patriotism and sacrifice, but who were nonetheless responsible, I believe, for the strikes that plagued us and guilty of insisting that each time the low-wage earners got an increase, everyone—right up the ladder—also had to get a pay raise.

It was with this strata that I tried, though not very successfully, to reason. Something was happening to the rank and file of the Histadrut, to the good sense of the Israeli worker, that frightened me, and I couldn't and didn't keep quiet about it. No one believed more strongly than I that a trade union was not only entitled but obliged to safeguard the rights of workers and to call for strikes when negotiations dragged on for too long or when agreements weren't being met. But agreements that were signed had to be honored without new claims being submitted at once, and those who were not at the bottom of the nation's economic scale had to understand and accept the fact that whatever increases could be given had to be given to those whose need was greatest. There is nothing sacred about the principle of differentials. I had fought it in the Histadrut years ago, and I was prepared to fight it again. The line had to be held somewhere. God knows that Israel's doctors, nurses and teachers didn't have an easy time economically, but they could keep going while other lower-paid groups who were becoming submerged in the rising inflation and high cost of living had to be given salary increases or they couldn't have survived. It was just that simple.

I was also extremely unsympathetic to the idea of strikes in essential services, especially in a country in a state of war. I don't think that I need to explain to anyone what it meant to me personally to have to decide on issuing restraining orders when the staffs of hospitals went on strike. But there was no other way to ensure that there wouldn't be a resultant loss of life, so I grit my teeth and did it.

"The government," I told the nation repeatedly, "cannot do everything at once. It can't wave a magic wand and meet everyone's demands simultaneously: eradicate poverty without imposing taxes, win wars, go on absorbing immigration, develop the economy and still give everyone his due. No government can do all this at one and the same time." But it wasn't only a question of money. Social equality isn't attained merely with material resources. To wipe out poverty and its aftermath, you need two partners who are equally willing to make an effort, and I didn't mince any words about this either.

"In the first place," I said, "those among us who are poor mustn't permit themselves to be turned into the passive objects of other people's concern. They must be active on their own behalf. And the more settled more affluent sections of the population will have to join in a great volunteer movement aimed at achieving social integration. The gap between those who have education and training and those who don't is at least as great and as tragic as the gap between those who can cope economically and those who can't."

Some progress was made, but nowhere near enough. I formed a prime minister's committee for tackling the problems of underprivileged youngsters. It included distinguished educators, psychologists, doctors, probation officers and so forth, all of whom worked voluntarily. Although it took two years, instead of what I hoped would be just a few months, for it to come up with recommendations, we implemented many of its recommendations even before they were published. When we had to raise the price of staple foods, we gave tax benefits to lower-income groups, and we went on building as much low-income housing as we possibly could, while I waged a ceaseless war of my own for the building of rental housing that would be subsidized, if necessary. And of course, whatever we tried to do had to be done either in the midst of actual warfare or during periods of terrorism, and there was never enough time or money to concentrate even on our most urgent domestic problems—for which, apart from everything else, I found it impossible to forgive our neighbors. Given peace, I knew that while we might never be able to build an ideal society, we could certainly build a better one. But where was that peace?

In August, 1970, Mr. Rogers' cease-fire materialized. Nasser said that as far as he was concerned, it would only last for three months, but—as though the timing were symbolic—he died in September, and Anwar el-Sadat became the president of Egypt. Not only did Sadat seem, at first glance, to be a more reasonable man who might soberly consider the benefits of an end to the war to his own people but there were also indications that he wasn't getting along too well with the Russians. And in Jordan, King Hussein, having happily sheltered the Palestinian terrorists for months, suddenly found himself so threatened by them that in September he turned on them and crushed them. So though it may have been a Black September for El Fatah, to me it looked, at long last, as if the U.S. peace initiative and Dr. Jarring might have some slim chance of success. The Arab leaders didn't modify their statements about Israel in any way or alter their demands for a total withdrawal of our troops, but there was talk about reopening the Suez Canal and rebuilding the ruined Egyptian towns along its banks, so that normal life could be restored in them—all of which gave rise to some optimism in Israel. Well, the cease-fire held, we stayed where we were, the Arabs continued to refuse to meet us or deal with us in any way, and the optimism in Israel slowly died down—but it didn't vanish altogether, and war didn't break out in 1971 or 1972! But neither did peace, and Arab terrorism mounted both in its ferocity and its inhumanity.

Certainly no one in the civilized world approved of the gunning down, at Lydda Airport, of Catholic pilgrims from Puerto Rico and one of Israel's most distinguished scientists, of the horrifying public kidnapping and murder of Israeli athletes at the Munich Olympic Games or of the slaughter of Israeli children trapped in the school building in the development town of Ma'alot. No one approved, and each outrage brought me its flood of official condolences and expressions of shock and sympathy. Nonetheless, we were expected (and still are expected by many) to come to terms with the murderers in the way that other governments had, as if these suicidal fanatics should have been allowed to blackmail us and bring us to our knees. It has certainly been proved time and again that giving in to terror only leads to more terror. No one will ever know, however, what it cost the government of Israel to say no to the demands of the terrorists or what it was like to feel that no Israeli official working abroad was entirely safe from death by letter bomb, to say nothing of the fact that any quiet border town in Israel could be turned (as several were) into the scene of massacres caused by a few demented men who had been reared on hatred and the belief that they could drain Israel of its ability to stand firm in the face of grief and pain.

But we learned to hold out against the terror, to protect our aircraft and passengers, to turn our embassies into small fortresses and to patrol our schoolyards and city streets. I walked behind the coffins and visited the bereaved families of the victims of Arab terrorism, and I was filled with pride that I belonged to a nation that was able to take these blows—these cowardly, evil blows—without saying, "Enough. We have had enough. Give the terrorists whatever they want because we have taken all that we can take." Other governments surrendered to the demands of the terrorists, put planes at their disposal and released them from jail, while the foreign press and the New Left called them "guerrillas" and "freedom fighters." For us, however, they remained criminals, not heroes, and though each funeral was a torment for me, I remained unimpressed by the "glory" of hiding mines in supermarkets and buses or the "glamour" of a holy war that required killing seven old Jews in a home for the aged in Munich. And I was literally physically sickened when the Arabs who had murdered the eleven Israeli athletes at the Olympic Games in 1972 were set free in a blaze of publicity and flown to Libya only six weeks later. The Arab states went on giving the terrorists money, arms and backing and then screaming to high heaven whenever we made clear, by raiding the terrorist bases in Syria and Lebanon, that we held the governments of those states responsible for what was happening.

The only solution, the only possible solution, was peace—not only peace with honor, but a lasting peace. And the only way of achieving it was to go on trying to convince our friends that our stand was right—since our enemies wouldn't talk to us—and to examine every single possibility that might lead to negotiations.

Many of the trips I took and talks I held must remain secret, but I think that today I can write about one of them. At the beginning of 1972 the deputy foreign minister of Rumania came to Israel on a visit, ostensibly just to meet with people in our Foreign Office. But he made one special request: he asked to see me, and he stressed that he wanted to see me alone; no one else should be present at our conversation. We had very good relations with Rumania. It was the only East European country that hadn't severed diplomatic relations with us after the Six-Day War and that consistently refused to take part in the Soviet Union's vicious anti-Israel propaganda campaign or join in the Soviet bloc's denunciations of our "aggression." We had entered into mutually profitable trade agreements with the Rumanians, exchanged art exhibitions, musicians, choirs and theatrical groups, and there was some immigration from Rumania. I had met (and liked) the attractive and energetic president of Rumania, Nicolae Ceauşescu, in 1970 and I admired him for not giving way to Arab pressure and for managing to retain diplomatic links with us as well as with the Arab states. I knew that Ceauşescu was anxious to promote a Middle Eastern peace settlement, and I wasn't really surprised when his deputy foreign minister announced to me as soon as we were alone that actually he had come to Israel only in order to tell me the following: "I have been sent by my president," he said, "to inform you that when he visited Egypt recently, he saw President Sadat and that, as a result of their meeting, my president has a most important message for you. He would like to bring it to you himself, but since he can't [he was going to China], he suggests that you come to Bucharest. You can come either incognito or, if you prefer, we will gladly issue you a formal invitation." I didn't accept that going to China automatically ruled out a visit to Israel, but I said that of course, I would come to Bucharest as soon as possible. Not incognito—that didn't appeal to me as a way for the prime minister of Israel to travel (unless it was absolutely essential)—but just as soon as I got an official invitation. Ceauşescu's invitation arrived shortly afterwards, and I flew to Rumania.

I spent fourteen hours (in two long sessions) with Ceauşescu, who told me that he understood from Sadat himself that the Egyptian leader was ready to meet with an Israeli, maybe with me, maybe not; maybe the meeting would be on a slightly lower level than the heads of state. But a meeting of some sort could take place. I said, "Mr. President, this is the best news I have heard for many years"—as indeed it was. We talked for hours about it, and Ceauşescu was almost as excited as I was. There was no question in his mind that he was delivering a historic and absolutely genuine message. He even talked to me about details. "We won't work through ambassadors or foreign officers," he said, "not mine and not yours." He suggested that his deputy foreign minister maintain personal contact with me through Simcha Dinitz, then my political secretary, who had come with me to Bucharest.

After so many years it really looked as though the ice were about to break. But it didn't. When I came back to Israel, we waited and waited— in vain. There was no follow-up at all. Whatever Sadat had told Ceauşescu—and he had certainly told him something—was totally meaningless, and I suspect that the reason I never heard anything more from Ceauşescu about the meeting with Sadat was that he couldn't bring himself to confess, even to me, that Sadat had fooled him.

As far as the public and press—both in Israel and Rumania—were concerned, this had just been a standard visit; Ceauşescu gave me a luncheon, the prime minister gave me a dinner, and I gave him a dinner. But the only meaningful result of my visit to Bucharest—on which I had pinned such high hopes—was that I was able to attend the Friday night services at the Chorale Synagogue in Bucharest and meet many hundreds of Rumanian Jews—infinitely freer than the Jews of Moscow had been, or are, but almost as overwhelmed by my presence among them. They greeted me with such a torrent of love for Israel that I felt bodily buffeted by it, and I don't think I have ever heard Hebrew songs sung more beautifully or with greater tenderness than on that Friday night. As I walked to my car, I saw a vast crowd waiting for me in complete silence; ten thousand Jews had come from all over Rumania to see me. I turned, crossed over to them and said, *"Shabbat shalom,"* and I heard 10,000 voices call back, *"Shabbat shalom."* That encounter in itself was more than worth the trip for me.

There were also other journeys to other places and once even an adventure abroad that taught me that nothing I did was ever going to go unnoticed again. In the spring of 1971 I made a ten-day trip to Denmark, Finland, Sweden and Norway. Between my visit to Helsinki and to Stockholm there was a weekend and a rare chance, if I planned it properly, to be out of reach of the telephone, the telex, cables and reporters. But it isn't so simple to find a secluded place for a rest and still conform to the security regulations that increasingly governed where and how I traveled. My office in Jerusalem asked the Israeli ambassador in Stockholm to look around for some suitable spot not too far from the Swedish capital and to let us know in good time. Just before I left Israel, there was a phone call; one of the ministers wanted to say how sorry he was that he wouldn't be able to see me off, but there *was* something interesting he wanted to tell me. We chatted for a couple of minutes, and then I left for the airport.

In Helsinki, I got word from our embassy in Stockholm that nothing had been found and that the best thing for me to do with those two free days was to go to Stockholm and take it easy in my hotel there until my official visit began. All of a sudden I remembered that last-minute phone call I had received just before my departure, and I asked Lou Kaddar—to her amazement—whether she fancied a weekend in Lapland. "Lapland?" She couldn't believe that I was serious.

"Well," I explained, "I forgot all about it till just now, but we have been invited to stay at a marvelous lodge in the wilds of Finnish Lapland that belongs to a devoted friend of Israel. He has promised to give us a very good time there, and I, for one, would like to go."

There were all kinds of objections: my bodyguards said it was much too isolated and much too far away; Lou said that we didn't have the right clothes and that we'd freeze to death; the Finnish and Swedish security people were appalled at the idea of my taking off for a place that was only about 100 miles from the Soviet border; and everyone decided that it was mad to travel a total of 1,200 miles for a two-day vacation. But I wanted to go—and go we did.

Our trip was veiled in the utmost secrecy, of course. We went to Stockholm and flew on to Lapland in a small plane, arriving at Rovaniemi, the capital of Finnish Lapland, in the brilliant sunshine of the early afternoon. At the airport, which was the size of a small tennis court, there were some taxis waiting for us, and the mayor of Rovaniemi with his wife. He had only been told that some important guests were coming, but he hadn't even been told who they were. There was also, it turned out, one newspaperman who just happened to be there and just happened to notice that the mayor's wife was holding a rose. Who sees roses in Lapland? He took another look at the people who were getting off the plane, stared at the short woman in a heavy coat who was obviously the VIP traveler for whom that precious rose was intended, told himself it was impossible and then, when we were already on our way through the snow to the lodge, suddenly realized that it was really me and immediately sent a cable off to his editor.

I had a wonderful time in Rovaniemi, rested and came back to Stockholm in great shape only to discover that the whole world wanted to know about my clandestine meeting with the Russians. Why else would Golda Meir have gone to Finnish Lapland? What had we talked about? With whom had I met? No one in Scandinavia or anywhere else, for that matter, believed the truth until Mr. Tsarapkin, the Soviet deputy foreign minister, arrived in Oslo the day before I left it—without seeing me. The press then finally resigned itself to the undramatic fact that all I had done in Lapland for forty-eight hours was eat, sleep, buy souvenirs made of reindeer fur for my grandchildren and drive around the lovely, silent, frozen lakes.

There were times during those five years as prime minister when I would have gladly run away from it all if I had felt free to do so, not because my strength was giving out or because the pace was too much for me, but primarily because I was so tired of repeating myself so often, saying the same things over and over again and getting nowhere. I was also tired of hearing about my supposed complexes from people who thought we should act in a way that would result in handing Israel over either to President Sadat or, better yet, to Mr. Arafat. This meant, I gathered, that I should stop remembering the lessons of the past and try to persuade the population of Israel that because our national home had been broken into once, twice, three times, we should now move out and go elsewhere, instead of putting up iron bars on the windows and extra strong locks on the doors. Yes, I had complexes. They had started, if not in Kiev, then at the Évian Conference, in 1938, and nothing that had happened to us since was conducive to lessening them. Even in Israel itself, there were people who thought—and said loudly—that the government wasn't doing "enough" to find common ground with the Arabs, though they never managed to suggest anything that we hadn't tried ourselves.

There was also a constant uproar from a numerically small but exceedingly vocal segment of the population about such things as the government's decision, after the Six-Day War, to allow a number of Jews to settle in Hebron, a town on the West Bank of the Jordan River (some thirty-five kilometers south of Jerusalem) in which, according to Jewish tradition, the Biblical Patriarchs are buried and which was King David's capital before he moved it to Jerusalem. The Crusaders had expelled the Jews from Hebron, but during Ottoman rule in Palestine some Jews had returned there, and the town had had a Jewish community right up to the time when a terrible Arab massacre finally drove the surviving Jews out of the town in 1929. After 1948 the Jordanians wouldn't even let the Jews visit the holy Cave of Machpelah to pray at the Tomb of the Patriarchs. But Hebron remained holy to the Jews, and on Passover eve, 1968, after it had come under Israeli administration, a group of young and militant Orthodox Jews, defying the military ban on settlement in the West Bank, moved into the Hebron police compound and remained there without permission. There was no question but that they were behaving most improperly and in a manner that was very damaging to Israel's "image." The Arabs at once set up a great hue and cry about the "Jewish annexation" of Hebron, and Israeli public opinion was very divided on the subject. On the one hand, the would-be settlers were obviously trying to create a *fait accompli* and force the Israeli government to make up its mind prematurely about the future of the West Bank and Jewish settlement there. On the other hand, although I deplored the way in which they had taken the law into their own hands, as though they were in the Wild West, I thought that the real issue was not really what they had done or even how they had done it, but something far more serious.

Was it logical, I asked myself and my colleagues, for the world (including our own superpious doves) to demand of a Jewish government that it pass legislation expressly forbidding Jews to settle anywhere on earth?

I didn't know any more than anyone else did exactly what would happen to Hebron eventually. But let's suppose, I said, that one day, please God, we will sign a peace treaty with Jordan and "return" Hebron. Would that mean that we would agree that no Jews would ever be allowed to live there again? Obviously, no Israeli government could ever obligate itself to a permanent banning of Jews from any part of the Holy Land. And Hebron was not an ordinary market town; it meant a lot to believing Jews.

We debated and argued and examined the pros and cons for months, and then, in 1970, we permitted the building of a limited number of housing units for Jews in an area on the outskirts of Hebron that the settlers named Kiryat Arba (The Town of the Four, Hebron's other Hebrew name)—and that particular storm died down. But other subsequent attempts at illegal settlements were more firmly dealt with—however painful it was for the government to have to order Israeli soldiers to drag Jews away from places in the West Bank in which they wanted to settle. We did allow Jews to settle in certain spots in the administered territories, but only when such settlement was fully in accordance with our political and military interests.

Another constant focus of international attention was the Christian holy places both in the West Bank and in Jerusalem. So, needless to say, I was very glad to be able to go to the Vatican in January, 1973, when I was received by Pope Paul VI in an eighty-minute audience. It was the first time that a prime minister of Israel had been given an audience by the pope, though, on his one-day visit to Israel in 1964, when he came to the Holy Land as a pilgrim, the pontiff had met President Shazar, Eshkol and virtually the entire Israeli cabinet. It had not been the happiest of meetings. The pope had made it clear that his visit in no way constituted full recognition by the Vatican of the State of Israel; he had made Jordan, rather than Israel, his headquarters for three days, and the parting message he had sent us from his plane was carefully addressed to Tel Aviv, not Jerusalem.

The relation between the Vatican and the Zionist movement had always been delicate, ever since Theodor Herzl, who had been granted an audience by Pius X in 1904, had been told by the pope, "We cannot prevent Jews from going to Jerusalem, but we could never sanction it . . . the Jews have not recognized our Lord; we cannot recognize the Jews." Other popes had been friendlier. Sharett was received twice (once as Israel's foreign minister) by Pius XII. Pope John XXIII had been sympathetic and even warm to Israel, and we were invited to send a representative both to his funeral and to Paul VI's coronation. In 1969 Paul had received Abba Eban in an official audience, and our ambassadors to Rome always had good and fairly close contacts with various high-ranking Vatican personalities. Although the Vatican has recognized all the Arab states, recognition is still withheld from Israel, and the exact stand of the Vatican on the question of Jerusalem has still to be clarified. But it seems to me that the Vatican has indeed reconciled itself after all, to the reality of the Jewish state.

Then, in January, 1973, I was informed that the pope would receive me in audience. I was immensely impressed—it is impossible not to be—not only by the Vatican, but by the pope himself, by the simplicity and graciousness of his manner and the penetrating gaze of his deepset dark eyes. I think I would have been much more nervous about our talk if he hadn't started it by telling me that he found it hard to accept the fact that the Jews—who, of all people, should have been capable of mercy toward others because they had suffered so terribly themselves—had behaved so harshly in their own country. Well, that is the kind of talk that I can't bear and particularly since it is simply not true that we have mistreated the Arabs in the territories. There is still no death penalty in Israel, and the most we have ever done is to jail terrorists, blow up the houses of Arabs who have gone on sheltering terrorists, despite repeated warnings, and sometimes, when we have had no alternative, even expelled Arabs who have openly incited and encouraged the terrorists. I was very tempted to ask the pope what his sources of information were since they were obviously so different from mine, but I didn't. Instead, I said, and I could hear my own voice trembling a little with anger: "Your Holiness, do you know what my own very earliest memory is? It is waiting for a pogrom in Kiev. Let me assure you that my people know all about real 'harshness' and also that we learned all about real mercy when we were being led to the gas chambers of the Nazis."

It may not have been a conventional way of talking to the pope, but I felt that I was speaking for all Jews everywhere, for those who were alive and for those who had perished while the Vatican maintained its neutrality in World War II. I had a sense of participating in a truly historic confrontation, and the pope and I stared at each other for a second. I think he was quite surprised by my words, but he didn't say anything. He just looked at me, right into my eyes, and I looked back at him in the same way. Then I went on to tell him, very respectfully, but very firmly and at some length, that now that we had a state of our own, we were through forever with being "at the mercy" of others. "This is truly a historic moment," he said, as though he had read my mind.

Then we went on to talk about other matters, the status of Jerusalem and the Middle East in general. There would have to be special provisions for the holy places, and that, I gathered, could be taken up in the "continuing dialogue" between the church and ourselves, to which he enthusiastically referred. He also went out of his way to express his deep appreciation for the care that Israel had taken of the Christian holy places. For my part, I assured the pope that we would make whatever arrangements would be required of us for the administration not only of the Christian but also of the Moslem holy places in Israel, but that Jerusalem itself would remain the capital of Israel. I also asked the pope to use his influence to try to bring about a settlement in the Middle East and to do whatever he could to secure the return to Israel of the Israeli prisoners who had been in Egyptian and Syrian jails ever since the War of Attrition and whom the Arab states had refused to release.

After the first difficult minute or two the atmosphere was very relaxed and cordial. We sat in the pope's private library on the second floor of the

Apostolic Palace and conversed without any strain—all of which made the unpleasant episode that immediately followed my visit very hard to understand. Along with the customary statement that had been initially agreed upon, the pope's spokesman, Professor Alessandrini, issued an unusual "verbal note" to the press. It was an obvious attempt to appease the Arab states about the implications of my meeting with the pope. Announcing that "it was not a gesture of preference or exclusive treatment," Professor Alessandrini went on to say, "The pope met with Mrs. Meir because he considers it his duty not to let slip any opportunity to act in favor of peace, in defense of all religious interests, particularly of the weakest and most defenseless, and most of all of the Palestinian refugees."

Najjar telephoned to the Vatican at once and protested most strongly about the utterly misleading statement. And I didn't mince words either. I hadn't broken into the Vatican, and I told that to the journalists at the press conference I held that afternoon at the Israeli embassy in Rome. Regardless of whether or not the Vatican tried to play down the importance of my audience with Paul VI, "it was greatly appreciated," I said, "by me and by my people. . . . In the quest for peace and goodwill all over the world, there is a complete identity of views between the pope and the Jews."

The next day I got lovely gifts from the Vatican: a magnificent silver dove of peace with an inscription to the prime minister of Israel from the pope, a beautiful Bible and—as a gesture, I suspect, to make up for Professor Alessandrini's inaccurate "note"—a catalogue of all the Hebrew publications in the Vatican Library. All in all, it was an intensely interesting and intensely meaningful experience for me, and I hope that, in a small way, it brought the Vatican closer to understanding Israel, Zionism and the feeling of Jews like me about themselves.

When I think back on the spring and summer of 1973, I must say that I do so with very little pleasure. There were days when I fell into bed at two in the morning and lay there, telling myself that I was crazy. At seventy-five I was working longer hours than I had ever worked before and traveling more, both inside Israel and abroad, than was good for anyone. Although I really did my best to cut down on appointments and delegate more work, it was much too late for me to turn myself into another person. Regardless of all the good advice I was given by the people closest to me—the children, Clara (who was now coming fairly regularly from Bridgeport to stay with me for a few weeks at a time), Galili, Simcha and Lou—there was only one way I could be prime minister, if that was what I had to be, and that was by talking to the people who wanted to talk to me and listening to the people who had something to tell me.

I couldn't just go to the opening of a symposium being held by the teacher's union, for instance, without preparing myself for it ahead of time, and reading memos wasn't my idea of doing my homework properly. Memos always left unanswered questions in my mind that often turned out to be the most crucial questions. I was very worried about the rate of dropouts from schools in the development towns and thought that might be a topic for the speech that the teachers had asked me to give. But I couldn't get the *exact* number of dropouts from anyone—not from the chairman of the teachers' union, not from the Ministry of Education—and that bothered me. How come no one knew exactly how many children had dropped out of school in each town? If teachers reported nonattendance to principals and principals reported to the Ministry of Education, then why were the specific figures unavailable? The more questions I asked, the more I understood about the dropout situation, about the way that schools and the ministry operated, and, most of all, about life in the new towns and the standards of teaching in them. And when I went to that symposium, I had something to say, more questions to ask and a chance of getting more answers that would eventually help me to suggest ways of doing something about a problem that vitally concerned Israel's future.

I also wasn't about to make myself unavailable to anyone. When I invited Jews who had just immigrated from the Soviet Union after months, often years, of persecution and suffering and who wanted and deserved to talk to the prime minister, I tried to spend as much time as possible with them. And when party leaders came to talk to me in the evening about urgent local political matters, I also didn't want to cut these sessions short. Either I was the head of the Labor Party or I was not, but if I was, then I wasn't going to be a figurehead. Nor was I going to limit the amount of time I spent with delegations of "Oriental" Jews or students or landlords or anyone else who wanted to tell me how badly (or sometimes even how well) I was conducting the affairs of the nation. There were also the constant visitors from abroad who felt themselves entitled—and rightly so—to spend half an hour with me. Some were American Jews who had given Israel the staunchest moral and financial support for years; some were European would-be investors whom we needed like lifeblood; others were people sent to me by other people whom I had met and who had helped us in the States, or in Africa, or in Latin America.

I liked seeing people, and I felt that it was my duty to do so, but the more people I saw in my office or at home, the more papers and mail I had to plow through at night. I tried to get home for lunch whenever I could; sometimes there were official lunches, but sometimes I would just drive back home with Lou around two o'clock, eat quickly and be back at the office by three for another round of meetings and phone calls. If I was lucky, and no evening functions were planned, I would leave the office by seven or eight, go home, shower, change and have some supper. I had a maid, of course. She left as soon as she had done the lunch dishes (unless there was an official luncheon, in which case we got outside help), but she usually left something in the refrigerator for my evening meal. Occasionally I could stay home in the evenings and someone from the office would come over with piles of correspondence that had to be attended to. And sometimes, but very rarely indeed, I could just sit in an armchair and look at an old movie on television or fiddle around with little things, like tidying up my shelves, which always relaxed me.

Now and then different members of the cabinet dropped in so that we could talk about specific problems in a relaxed and informal way. These were not official meetings, and no decisions were ever taken at them, of course. But I am convinced that they helped make the process of government more efficient just because we could talk things out over a cup of coffee or a bite to eat around my kitchen table. Every two or three weeks Pinchas Sapir, my minister of finance (and now chairman of the Jewish Agency), came over so that we could discuss in depth suggestions that he wanted to bring before the cabinet. Sapir is a man with an immense capacity for work, and he is also Israel's most successful fund raiser. When Sapir meets a Jew abroad, he says "How much money have you got?" And the funny thing is the man tells him! One of his great preoccupations is the bettering of life—and in particular of education—in the development towns, for which he has done a great deal more than most people know. We always worked very well together, despite the fact that we were poles apart on a number of policy questions, and I personally couldn't have imagined heading a cabinet without him.

Another indispensable member of my cabinet was Yisrael Galili, a minister without portfolio, upon whom I relied very heavily for advice. Galili is not only a wise and unusually modest man, but also someone with a unique talent for getting to the heart of complicated issues and formulating things in the most lucid way possible. I suspect I shall go on asking Galili for his opinions on important matters for a long time.

Generally speaking, I was very fortunate in having good people around me: the director general of my ministry, the late Ya'akov Herzog, was among the most intellectually sophisticated men I have met. And no one could have asked for more devoted aides that Mordechai Gazit (who took over after Herzog's untimely death); Yisrael Lior, Eli Mizachi and, of course, Simcha Dinitz and Lou.

One nice thing that happened in 1973 was that Sarah decided to take a year's leave of absence from the kibbutz and study English literature at the Hebrew University, which meant that I wasn't alone at night anymore. But the penalty for that was that she and I would sit up until all hours talking, mostly about whether I should head the party list again and run for office (to the extent that one can "run" for anything at seventy-five!) in the elections that were scheduled to take place that autumn. I thought a great deal about retiring, but wherever I turned, I heard the same arguments that I had heard in 1969: the problem of my so-called succession was no less acute than the problem of Eshkol's succession had been; the three elements that made up the Labor Party were still very uneasy partners; the military situation—though it was fairly quiescent since the War of Attrition—was certainly liable to worsen at any time; my relationship with President Nixon was one of great rapport and not likely to be established quickly by anyone else; and so on and so forth. I loathed being the subject of endless speculation—will she or won't she?—but I couldn't honestly counter any of those arguments with effective arguments of my own, other than the fact that I felt I owed it to myself to retire. All through the spring the conversations went on with my colleagues in the party, followed avidly by the press, as though Israel had no other worries. In the end, I said, "All right. There is no point to dragging the decision out any longer, and there are other things to think about." Later I often thought to myself bitterly that even if I had then refused to head the party list again, I would still have been prime minister in October, 1973, because the elections were due to take place only in November.

In March, 1973, I visited Washington again. There had just been a most unfortunate incident that might have cast something of a cloud over my visit: the Israeli air force had shot down a Libyan Boeing 727 that had strayed over the Sinai Peninsula, and the lives of 106 people had been lost. It was one of those tragedies that can't be avoided when a nation has to stay on the alert, night and day, against terrorism. We had been warned that a possible suicide attack was being readied against us somewhere in Israel by terrorists who would try to land a plane loaded with explosives, and we were in no mood to take chances—though we would have done so if we had had even the slightest inkling that there were any passengers aboard that plane. But the pilot had ignored all our attempts to identify him, as was proved later when the "black box" was found. Both

President Nixon and the House Foreign Affairs Committee listened sympathetically to my explanation of what had happened and why, and in the ninety minutes that I spent with the president, he again assured me warmly that U.S. aid to Israel would continue and that we would go on getting U.S. backing for our demand for negotiations with our neighbors. But I was no less eager to explain our position to the nations of Europe, and when the president of the Council of Europe invited me to attend the meeting of the council's Consultative Assembly in Strasbourg, I said I would be glad to come. This time, however, I would not go to Paris. I asked our ambassador only to notify the French Foreign Office that I would be visiting France and not in any way to give the impression that I wanted to be invited to Paris. So I went directly to Strasbourg.

But just before I left Israel, I got some devastating news. Arab terrorists had succeeded in "convincing" the Austrian government to shut down the Jewish Agency transit camp at Schonau Castle, near Vienna, which had served for a number of years as the indispensable halfway station for Jews leaving the Soviet Union en route to Israel. Before I go into the story of this surrender to blackmail and what I tried to do about it, let me say something about the function of Schonau. As most people probably know by now, those courageous Soviet Jews who have dared to apply for an exit permit in order to emigrate to Israel are usually forced to wait for it for years. And when it is granted, there is no prior notice whatsoever—only the curt stipulation that its recipient must leave the USSR within a week or, at most, ten days. There have been exceptions, of course; some Jews have even been told that if they want to go, they must clear out within a matter of hours. But most of the time prospective emigrants are given a few days to put all their personal affairs in order; arrange for those possessions that they are allowed to send to Israel to be packed, cleared by customs and dispatched; organize their own passage; give up their Soviet citizenship; and go through a whole host of other formalities, while finding time to say their good-byes to people whom they will probably never see again as long as they live. It is not the way that most emigrants leave their countries; it is neither humane nor decent, but it is the only way that Jews can leave the Soviet Union, as though they are criminals who are being deported.

The first stop for the trains that bring them into freedom, generally via Prague, is a little railway crossing on the Czechoslovak-Austrian frontier; where the Austrian authorities issue on the spot the vital transit visas that make it possible for the emigrants to enter the free world and for the Jewish Agency officials in Austria, who welcome them into it, to learn the number and names of the Jews aboard a particular train. From the frontier, the trains—with their special compartment for Jewish immigrants—continue on to Vienna, where buses stand ready to take the emigrants to the transit camp. Schonau, a large white stucco *Schloss* rented to the Jewish Agency by an Austrian countess, was much more, however, than just a place for the immigrants to rest and realize that they were at last on their way to the Jewish state. It was a place where the immigrants—confused and exhausted—could be given information about Israel, be classified according to their professions and prepared, if only very minimally, for the new life they were going to lead in a new land.

No one stayed long in Schonau. The average emigrant family spent only two or three days there before being bused to the airport and to the El Al planes that brought them, still weary but ecstatic, to us. I had visited Schonau the year before and seen for myself the state of mind and body in which those people had come from the Soviet Union, and I knew the importance of that gateway to freedom. I also knew that there was virtually no other way for the Jews to leave the Soviet Union except through Austria, and I knew that for millions of Russian Jews who were still there, Schonau was a symbol of liberty and hope.

But the Arab terrorists knew all this, too, and at the end of September, 1973, two gunmen broke into one of those trains just as it crossed into Austria, kidnapped seven Russian Jews (including a seventy-one year-old man, an ailing woman and a three-year-old child) and brazenly informed the Austrian government that unless it instantly put an end to the assistance it had given the Soviet Jewish immigrants and closed down Schonau, not only would the hostages be killed, but there would be violent retaliation against Austria. To our astonishment and horror, the Austrian cabinet, led by Chancellor Bruno Kreisky, gave in at once, to the tunes of loud rejoicing both from the gunmen (who were immediately whisked away to Libya) and from the entire Arab press, which could hardly contain its glee at what it called "the successful commando blow to the movement of Russian Jews emigrating to Israel."

I had known Kreisky for quite a long time and fairly well. He served for several years as the foreign minister of Austria, and we used to meet at the United Nations. He was also a socialist, and I had, in fact, seen him last at the Socialist International in Vienna two years before. As a Jew, Mr. Kreisky had not displayed any interest in Israel, although in 1974 he was to visit us as the head of a delegation of socialists.

There were many socialists in Austria, some Jews, some not, with whom we had a much closer relationship. But I wanted to talk to Kreisky himself and explain to him the full implications of closing Schonau and what it would do not only to Austria, but to the Jews of Russia. I told our ambassador in Vienna to ask Kreisky whether he would see me on my way to Strasbourg.

To be quite fair, I must note that although I don't believe there is ever a good enough excuse for knuckling under to terrorism, the Austrian decision was not altogether unreasonable. To begin with, Schonau had become far too well known, although we had all tried very hard to discourage visitors from going there and the press from writing about it too often, and there were rumors all the time that the terrorists would attack it. The Austrian security was very good indeed; the trains were met; the emigrants were escorted to Schonau; the castle itself was well guarded. The Austrians were extremely helpful in this regard and very efficient. But if Schonau were closed, then whatever other place was made available would also be held to ransom. I felt that if I could discuss it all with Kreisky, I might get him to change his mind. I waited very tensely for a reply; when it came, I learned that Kreisky couldn't see me on my way to Strasbourg but would see me on my way back.

I had prepared an address for presentation at the Council of Europe meeting, in which I thanked the council and individual European parliaments and political parties for having raised their voices in the demand that Soviet Jewry be permitted to emigrate and touched upon a variety of other subjects, including the refusal of the Arab states to deal with us and the prospects, as we saw them, of Arab-Jewish coexistence.

I stayed in Strasbourg for two days and attended the necessary luncheons and dinners; but my mind was fixed on Schonau all the time, and when I got to Vienna, I went straight to Kreisky's office. The prime minister listed for me all the reasons for his government's capitulation to the Arabs and asked why Austria should be the only country to have the problem of the Russian Jews. Why not the Dutch? They could let emigrants through also. I told him that I thought the Dutch were surely prepared to share this burden with him. But it didn't depend on them; it depended on the Russians. And the Russians had agreed to let the Jews out via Austria. Then Kreisky said something I really couldn't accept. "We belong to two different worlds," he told me. Under normal circumstances, there wouldn't have been more for me to say; but I wasn't there for my own sake, and I had to continue the conversation.

Kreisky was adamant about closing Schonau. "I will never be responsible for any bloodshed on the soil of Austria," he repeated. "Other arrangements must be made."

"But if you close Schonau," I pleaded, "you will be handing the Russians the perfect excuse for not letting the Jews go, because they will certainly say if there is no possibility of transit, then they won't allow any emigrants to leave Russia."

"Well," Kreisky said, "there isn't anything I can do about that. Let the Jews be picked up by your people just as soon as the trains arrive."

"That is impossible," I said, "since we never know how many Jews are on each train. Anyhow, I don't think it is safer to have dozens of people waiting at the airport for an El Al plane to collect them." But I could see that it was no use. Nothing I said would make any difference. Above all, Kreisky wanted to avoid more trouble with the Arabs. I thanked him for having received me, and I left.

I felt as though my mouth were filled with ashes. *We* belonged to different worlds! The things that Kreisky had said to me just went around and around in my head. Of course, I had no idea what awaited me in Israel.

CHAPTER   13

THE YOM KIPPUR WAR

Of all the events upon which I have touched in this book, none is so hard for me to write about as the war of October, 1973, the Yom Kippur War. But it happened, and so it belongs here—not as a military account, because that I leave to others, but as a near disaster, a nightmare that I myself experienced and which will always be with me.

Even as a personal story, there is still a great deal that cannot be told, and what I write is far from being definitive. But it is the truth as I felt and knew it in the course of that war, which was the fifth to be forced on Israel in the twenty-seven years that have passed since the state was founded.

There are two points I should like to make at once. The first is that we won the Yom Kippur War, and I am convinced that in their heart of hearts the political and military leaders of both Syria and Egypt know that they were defeated again, despite their initial gains. The other is that the world in general and Israel's enemies in particular should know that the circumstances which took the lives of the more than 2,500 Israelis who were killed in the Yom Kippur War will never ever recur.

The war began on October 6, but when I think about it now, my mind goes back to May, when we received information about the reinforcement of Syrian and Egyptian troops on the borders. Our intelligence people thought that it was most unlikely that war would break out; nonetheless, we decided to treat the matter seriously. At that time I went to general headquarters myself. Both the minister of defense and the chief of staff, David Elazar (who is known throughout the country by his nickname, Dado) briefed me thoroughly on the armed forces' state of preparedness, and I was convinced that the army was ready for any contingency—even for full-scale war. Also, my mind was put at rest about the question of a sufficiently early warning. Then, for whatever reason, the tension relaxed.

In September we started to receive information about a buildup of Syrian troops on the Golan Heights, and on the thirteenth of that month an air battle took place with the Syrians, which ended in the downing of thirteen Syrian MIGs. Despite this, our intelligence people were very reassuring: it was most unlikely they said, that there would be any major Syrian reaction. But this time, the tension remained, and what's more, it had spread to the Egyptians. Still our intelligence assessment remained the same. The continued Syrian reinforcement of troops was, they explained, caused by the Syrians' fear that *we* would attack, and throughout the month, including on the eve of my departure to Europe, this explanation for the Syrian move was repeated again and again.

On Monday, October 1, Yisrael Galili called me in Strasbourg. Among other things, he told me that he had talked to Dayan and that they both felt that as soon as I got back, we should have a serious discussion about the situation on the Golan Heights. I told him that I would definitely return the next day and that we should meet the day after.

Late on Wednesday morning I met with Dayan, Allon, Galili, the commander of the air force, the chief of staff and, because the head of intelligence was sick that day, the head of military intelligence research. Dayan opened the meeting, and the chief of staff and the head of intelligence research described the situation on both fronts in great detail. There were things that disturbed them, but the military evaluation was still that we were in no danger of facing a joint Syrian-Egyptian attack. The buildup and movement of Egyptian forces in the south was probably due to the maneuvers that were always held around this time of year, and in the north the bolstering and new deployment of forces were still explained as they had been before. The fact that several Syrian army units had been transferred only a week before from the Syrian-Jordanian border was interpreted as part of a recent détente between the two countries and as a Syrian gesture of goodwill toward Jordan. Nobody at the meeting thought that it was necessary to call up the reserves, and nobody thought that war was imminent. But it was decided to put a further discussion of the situation on the agenda for Sunday's cabinet meeting.

On Thursday, as usual, I went to Tel Aviv. For years I had been spending Thursdays and Fridays in my Tel Aviv office, Saturdays at my house in Ramat Aviv and returning to Jerusalem either late Saturday evening or early Sunday morning, and there seemed to be no reason for changing the pattern that week. In fact, it was a short week in any case, because Yom Kippur (the Day of Atonement) was to begin on Friday evening, and most people in Israel were taking a long weekend.

I suppose that by now, thanks in part to the war, even non-Jews who had never heard of Yom Kippur before know that this is the most solemn and the most sacred of all the days in the Jewish calendar. It is the one day in the year that Jews throughout the world—even if they are not very pious—unite in some sort of observance. Believing Jews, totally abstaining from food, drink and work, spend Yom Kippur (which, like all Jewish holidays and the Sabbath itself, begins in the evening of one day and ends in the evening of the next) in the synagogue, praying and atoning for sins that they may have committed in the course of the past year. Other Jews, including those who do not actually fast, usually find their own individual way of marking Yom Kippur, by not going to work, by not eating in public and by going to the synagogue, even if for only an hour or two, to hear the great opening prayer, Kol Nidrei, on the eve of Yom Kippur or to listen to the ritual blowing of the shofar, the ram's horn, that closes the fast. But for most Jews everywhere, regardless of how they observe it, Yom Kippur is a day unlike any other.

In Israel it is a day on which the country comes to a virtual standstill. For Jews, there are no newspapers, no television or radio broadcasts, no public transportation, and all schools, shops, restaurants, cafes and offices are closed for twenty-four hours. Since nothing, however, not even Yom Kippur, is as important to Jews as life itself, danger to life overrides everything, and all essential public services function, though many make do for those twenty-four hours with skeleton staffs. The most essential public service for all in Israel, unfortunately, is the army, but as many soldiers as possible are always given leave so that they can be at home with their families on this day.

On Friday, October 5, we received a report that worried me. The families of the Russian advisers in Syria were packing up and leaving in a hurry. It reminded me of what happened prior to the Six-Day War, and I didn't like it at all. Why the haste? What did those Russian families know that we didn't know?

I asked the minister of defense, the chief of staff and the head of intelligence whether they thought this piece of information was very important. No, it hadn't in any way changed their assessment of the situation. I was assured that we would get adequate warning of any real trouble, and anyway, sufficient reinforcements were being sent to the fronts to carry out any holding operation that might be required. Everything that was necessary had been done, and the army was placed on high alert, particularly the air force and the armored corps. At any rate, I wanted a meeting at least of those cabinet ministers who would be spending the Yom Kippur weekend in Tel Aviv. It turned out that very few of them were around. I was reluctant to ask the two National Religious Party ministers who lived in Jerusalem to come to a meeting in Tel Aviv on the eve of Yom Kippur, and several other ministers had already left for their kibbutzim, which were all fairly far away. Still, nine ministers were in town, and I scheduled an emergency meeting for Friday noon.

We gathered in my Tel Aviv office. In addition to the cabinet members, the meeting was attended by the chief of staff and the head of intelligence. I decided to speak my mind. "Look," I said, "I have a terrible feeling that this has all happened before. It reminds me of 1967, when we were accused of massing troops against Syria, which is exactly what the Arab press is saying now. And I think that it all means something." As a result, although as a rule a cabinet decision is required for a full-scale call-up, that Friday we passed a resolution that if necessary, the minister of defense and I could do so by ourselves. I also said that we should get in touch with the Americans so that they could get in touch with the Russians and tell them in no uncertain terms that the United States was not in the mood for trouble. The meeting broke up, but I stayed on at the office for a while, thinking.

How could it be that I was still so terrified of war breaking out when the present chief of staff, two former chiefs of staff (Dayan and Chaim Bar-Lev, who was my minister of commerce and industry) and the head of intelligence were far from sure that it would? After all, they weren't just ordinary soldiers. They were all highly experienced generals, men who had fought and led other men in spectacularly victorious battles. Each one of them had an outstanding military record, and as for our intelligence services, they were known to be among the best in the world. Not only that, but foreign sources with whom we were in constant touch agreed absolutely with the assessment of our experts. So why was it that I was still so ill at ease? Was I perhaps talking myself into something? I couldn't answer my own questions.

Today I know what I should have done. I should have overcome my hesitations. I knew as well as anyone else what full-scale mobilization meant and how much money it would cost, and I also knew that only a few months before, in May, we had an alert and the reserves had been called up; but nothing had happened. But I also understood that perhaps there had been no war in May exactly because the reserves had been called up. That Friday morning I should have listened to the warnings of my own heart and ordered a call-up. For me, that fact cannot and never will be erased, and there can be no consolation in anything that anyone else has to say or in all of the commonsense rationalizations with which my colleagues have tried to comfort me.

It doesn't matter what logic dictated. It matters only that I, who was so accustomed to making decisions—and who did make them throughout the war—failed to make that one decision. It isn't a question of feeling guilty. I, too can rationalize and tell myself that in the face of such total certainty on the part of our military intelligence—and the almost equally total acceptance of its evaluations on the part of our foremost military men—it would have been unreasonable of me to have insisted on a call-up. But I know that I should have done so, and I shall live with that terrible knowledge for the rest of my life. I will never again be the person I was before the Yom Kippur War.

Then, however, I sat in the office, thinking and agonizing until I just couldn't sit there anymore and I went home. Menachem and Aya had invited a few friends to drop in after dinner. Jews eat dinner early on the eve of Yom Kippur because traditionally it is their last meal for twenty-four hours, and by the time the stars are out the fast has begun. We sat down to eat; and I was very restless and had no appetite at all, and although they wanted me to stay on with their friends, I excused myself and went to bed. But I couldn't sleep.

It was a still, hot night, and through the open window I could hear the voices of Menachem and Aya's friends talking quietly in the garden below. Once or twice the children's dog barked, but otherwise it was a typically silent Yom Kippur night. I lay awake for hours, unable to sleep. Eventually I must have dozed off. Then, at about 4 A.M., the phone next to my bed rang. It was my military secretary. Information had been received that the Egyptians and the Syrians would launch a joint attack on Israel "late in the afternoon." There was no doubt anymore. The intelligence source was authoritative. I told Lior to ask Dayan, Dado, Allon and Galili to be in my office before 7 A.M. On the way there, I caught sight of an old man going to a synagogue, his prayer shawl over his shoulders, holding the hand of a small child. They looked like symbols of Judaism itself, and I remember thinking sorrowfully that all over Israel, young men were fasting in synagogues today and that it was from their prayers that they would soon be called to arms.

By eight o'clock the meeting had begun. Dayan and Dado differed as to the scale of the call-up. The chief of staff recommended the mobilization of the entire air force and four divisions and said that if they were called up at once, they could go into action the next day—that is, Sunday. Dayan, on the other hand, was in favor of calling up the air force and only two divisions (one for the north and one for the south), and he argued that if we had a full mobilization before a single shot was fired, the world would have an excuse for calling us "aggressors." Besides, he thought that the air force plus two divisions could handle the situation, and if toward evening the situation worsened, we could always call up more within a few hours. "That's my suggestion," he said, "but I won't resign if you decide against me." "My God," I thought, "*I* have to decide which of them is right?" But what I said was that I had only one criterion: if there really was a war, then we had to be in the best position possible. "The call-up should be as Dado suggested." But, of course, it was the one day of the year that even our legendary ability to mobilize rapidly partly failed us.

Dado was in favor of a preemptive strike since it was clear that war was inevitable in any case. "I want you to know," he said, "that our air force can be ready to strike at noon, but you must give me the green light now. If we can make that first strike, it will be greatly to our advantage." But I had already made up my mind. "Dado," I said, "I know all the arguments in favor of a preemptive strike, but I am against it. We don't know now, any of us, what the future will hold, but there is always the possibility that we will need help, and if we strike first, we will get nothing from anyone. I would like to say yes because I know what it would mean, but with a heavy heart I am going to say no." Then Dayan and Dado went to their offices and I told Simcha Dinitz (then our ambassador to Washington, who happened to be in Israel that week) to fly back to the States immediately and I called in Menachem Begin to tell him what was happening. I also asked for a cabinet meeting for noon and called the then U.S. ambassador, Kenneth Keating, and asked him to come and see me. I told him two things: that according to our intelligence, the attacks would start late in the afternoon and that we would not strike first. Maybe something could still be done to avert the war by U.S. intervention with the Russians or maybe even directly with the Syrians and the Egyptians. At all events, we would not make a preemptive strike. I wanted him to know that and to relay that information as soon as possible to Washington. Ambassador Keating had been a very good friend to Israel for many years, both in the U.S. Senate and in Israel itself. He was a man I liked and trusted and on that dreadful morning I was grateful to him for his understanding.

When the cabinet met at noon, it heard a full description of the situation, including the decision to mobilize the reserves and also my decision regarding a preemptive strike. Nobody raised any objections whatsoever. Then, while we were meeting, my military secretary burst into the room with the news that the shooting had started, and almost at once we heard the wailing of the first air-raid sirens in Tel Aviv. The war had begun.

Not only had we not been warned in time, but we were fighting on two fronts simultaneously and fighting enemies who had been preparing themselves for years to attack us. We were overwhelmingly outnumbered—in guns, tanks, planes and men—and were at a severe psychological disadvantage. The shock wasn't only over the way in which the war started, but also the fact that a number of our basic assumptions were proved wrong: the low probability of an attack in October, the certainty that we would get sufficient warning before any attack took place and the belief that we would be able to prevent the Egyptians from crossing the Suez Canal. The circumstances could not possibly have been worse. In the first two or three days of the war, only a thin line of brave young men stood between us and disaster. And no words of mine can ever express the indebtedness of the people of Israel to those boys on the Canal and on the Golan Heights. They fought, and fell, like lions, but at the start they had no chance.

What those days were like for me I shall not even try to describe. It is enough, I think, to say that I couldn't even cry when I was alone. But I was very rarely alone. I stayed in the office most of the time, although now and then I went to the war room. There were meetings all through the day and all through the night, incessantly interrupted by phone calls from Washington and bad news from the front. Plans were presented, analyzed and debated. I couldn't bear to be away from the office for more than an hour at a time because Dayan, Dado, Foreign Office people and various ministers were constantly coming in either to report to me on the most recent developments or to ask my advice on various matters.

But even on the worst of those early days, when we already knew what losses we were sustaining, I had complete faith in our soldiers and officers, in the spirit of the Israel Defense Forces and their ability to face any challenge, and I never lost faith in our ultimate victory. I knew we would win sooner or later; but each report of the price we were paying in human lives was like a knife being turned in my heart, and I shall never forget the day when I listened to the most pessimistic prediction I had yet heard.

On the afternoon of October 7, Dayan returned from one of his tours at the front and asked to see me at once. He told me that in his opinion the situation in the south was so bad that we should pull back substantially and establish a new defensive line. I listened to him in horror. Allon, Galili and my military secretary were in the room. Then I asked Dado to come in too. He had another suggestion—that we should go on with the offensive in the south. He asked if he could go to the southern front to supervise things himself and for permission to make whatever decisions might have to be made on the spot. Dayan agreed and Dado left. That night I called a cabinet meeting and got the ministers' approval for us to launch a counterattack against the Egyptians on October 8. When I was alone in the room, I closed my eyes and sat perfectly still for a minute. I think that if I hadn't learned, during all those years, how to be strong, I would have gone to pieces then. But I didn't dare.

The Canal had been crossed by the Egyptians, and our forces in the Sinai had been battered. The Syrians had penetrated in depth on the Golan Heights. On both fronts the casualties were already very high. One burning question was whether at this point we should tell the nation how bad the situation really was, and I felt very strongly that we should wait for a while. The very least we could do for our soldiers, and for their families, was to keep the truth to ourselves for a few more days. Nonetheless, some kind of statement had to be made at once, so on that first day of the war I addressed the citizens of Israel. It was one of the most difficult assignments of my life because I knew that, for everyone's sake, I could not tell all the facts.

Talking to a nation that had no idea yet of the terrible toll being taken in the north and in the south or of the peril that Israel faced until the reserves were fully mobilized and in action, I said, "We are in no doubt that we shall prevail. But we are also convinced that this renewal of Egyptian and Syrian aggression is an act of madness. We did our best to prevent the outbreak. We appealed to quarters with political influence to use it in order to frustrate this infamous move of the Egyptian and Syrian leaders. While there was still time, we informed friendly countries of the confirmed information that we had of the plans for an offensive against Israel. We called on them to do their utmost to prevent war but the Egyptian and Syrian attack had started."

On Sunday Dayan came in to my office. He closed the door and stood in front of me. "Do you want me to resign?" he asked. "I am prepared to

do so if you think I should. Unless I have your confidence, I can't go on."
I told him—and I have never regretted this—that he had to stay on as
minister of defense. We decided to send Bar-Lev to the north for a personal assessment of the situation. Then we began our negotiations to get
military aid from the United States. Decisions had to be taken very quickly—and they had to be the right ones. There was no time nor any margin
for mistakes.

By Wednesday, the fifth day of the war, we had pushed the Syrians
back across the 1967 cease-fire line and begun our attack into Syria, while
in Sinai the situation was sufficiently static for the cabinet to consider our
crossing of the Canal. But what if our troops crossed and then were
trapped? I also had to consider the possibility that the war would not be a
short one and that we might find ourselves without the planes, tanks and
ammunition we needed. We needed arms desperately, and, in the beginning they were slow in coming.

I talked to Dinitz in Washington at all hours of the day and the night.
Where was the airlift? Why wasn't it under way yet? I remember calling
him once at 3 A.M., Washington time, and he said, "I can't speak to anyone now, Golda. It is much too early." But I couldn't listen to reason. I
knew that President Nixon had promised to help us, and I knew from my
past experience with him that he would not let us down. Let me, at this
point, repeat something that I have said often before (usually to the extreme annoyance of many of my American friends). However history
judges Richard Nixon—and it is probable that the verdict will be very
harsh—it must also be put on the record forever that he did not break a
single one of the promises he made to us. So why was there a delay? "I
don't care what time it is," I raged at Dinitz. "Call Kissinger now. In the
middle of the night. We need the help today because tomorrow it may be
too late."

The story has already been published of that delay, of the U.S. Defense
Department's initial reluctance to send military supplies to us in U.S.
planes and of the problems that arose when we feverishly shopped around
for other planes—when all the time huge transports of Soviet aid were being brought by sea and air to Egypt and Syria and we were losing aircraft
at a disturbing rate (not in air battles but to the Soviet missiles on both
fronts). Each hour of waiting that passed was like a century for me, but
there was no alternative other than to hold on tight and hope that the
next hour would bring better news. I phoned Dinitz and told him that I
was ready to fly to Washington incognito to meet with Nixon if he
thought it could be arranged. "Find out immediately," I said, "I want to

go as soon as possible." But it wasn't necessary. At last Nixon himself ordered the giant C-5 Galaxies to be sent, and the first flight arrived on the ninth day of the war, on October 14. The airlift was invaluable. It not only lifted our spirits, but also served to make the American position clear to the Soviet Union, and it undoubtedly served to make our victory possible. When I heard that the planes had touched down in Lydda, I cried for the first time since the war had begun, though not for the last. That was also the day on which we published the first casualty list—656 Israelis had already died in battle.

But even the Galaxies that brought us tanks, ammunition, clothing, medical supplies and air-to-air rockets couldn't bring all that was required. What about the planes? The Phantoms and Skyhawks had to be refueled en route, so they were refueled in the air. But they came—and so did the Galaxies that landed in Lydda, sometimes at the rate of one every fifteen minutes.

When it was all over, in the spring, the U.S. colonel who had been in charge of the airlift came back to visit Israel with his wife, and they came to see me. They were lovely young people, filled with enthusiasm for the country and with admiration for our ground crews, who had learned, almost overnight, to use the special equipment for unloading those giants. I remember going out to Lydda once to watch the Galaxies come in. They looked like some kind of immense prehistoric flying monsters, and I thought to myself "Thank God I was right to reject the idea of a preemptive strike! It might have saved lives in the beginning, but I am sure that we would not have had that airlift, which is now saving so many lives."

In the meantime, Dado shuttled from one front to the other. Bar-Lev returned from the north, and we sent him to the south to straighten out the confusion that had arisen there because the generals on the spot had such critical differences of opinion about the tactics to be employed. He was asked to stay there as long as necessary. On Wednesday he phoned me from the Sinai. It was right after a colossal tank battle in which our forces had smashed the Egyptian armored advance. Dado has a slow, very deliberate way of speaking, and when I heard him say, "G-o-l-d-a, it will be all right. We are back to being ourselves and they are back to being themselves," I knew that the tide had turned, although there were still bloody battles ahead in which hundreds of young men, and older ones too, lost their lives. It was not for nothing that people bitterly suggested later that this war should be known, not as the Yom Kippur War, but as the War of the Fathers and Sons, for all too often they fought side by side on both fronts.

For days I was tormented by the fear that a third front would be opened and that Jordan would join in the attack on us. But apparently King Hussein had learned his lesson in the Six-Day War, and luckily his contribution to the Yom Kippur War was only one Jordanian armored brigade sent to help the Syrians. But by then we were already attacking strategic targets deep in Syria, and our artillery had come well within range of the suburbs of Damascus, so Hussein's tanks were not much use after all.

On October 15, the tenth day of the war, the Israel Defense Forces began their crossing of the Canal in order to establish a bridgehead on the other side. I spent that night in my office and thought that it would never end. The paratroops had crossed on time, but the crossing by the infantry, artillery and tanks was held up by fierce fighting.

The next day I addressed the Knesset. I was very tired, but I spoke for forty minutes because I had a lot to say, although most of it didn't make pleasant hearing. But at least I could tell the Knesset that, as I was speaking, a task force was already operating on the west bank of the Canal. I wanted also to make public our gratitude to the president and the people of America, and, equally clear, our rage at those governments, notably the French and British, that had chosen to impose an embargo on the shipments of arms to us when we were fighting for our very lives. And most of all, I wanted the world to know what would have happened to us had we withdrawn before the war to pre-Six-Day War lines of 1967—the very same lines, incidentally, that had not prevented the Six-Day War itself from breaking out, although no one seems to remember that.

I have never doubted for an instant, that the true aim of the Arab states has always been, and still is, the total destruction of the State of Israel or that even if we had gone back far beyond the 1967 lines to some miniature enclave, they would not still have tried to eradicate it and us.

One of the most terrible aspects of the Yom Kippur War was that for days we could not determine the fate of soldiers who had failed to communicate in any way with their families since the attacks began. Israel is a very small country, and its army, as everyone knows, is a citizens' army, made up of a limited standing force and of reserves. We have never fought far from our own borders, and contact between our soldiers and their homes is always closely maintained. But this war was already lasting longer than any other war we had ever had to fight—with the exception of the War of Independence—and we had been taken by surprise.

Reservists throughout the country had been called away from the synagogue and their homes. In the rush, some had not even taken time to look for dog tags or been able to find their units. Reservists in the armored corps had joined improvised tank crews, jumped from one burning tank to another and then from that, when it exploded, into a third. And, the antitank missiles supplied to the Egyptians and Syrians by the Russians left tanks in flames and their crews so badly burned that often identification was almost impossible. One of the proudest traditions of the Israel Defense Forces is that our dead and wounded are never left to the enemy; but in the first days of the Yom Kippur War, there was often no alternative, and hundreds of parents were now beside themselves with worry. "Is he dead? If so, where is his body? Is he a prisoner of war? If so, why doesn't anyone know?"

I had been through this torment with the parents of boys taken prisoner in the War of Attrition, and there were days in the winter of 1973 when I could hardly bring myself to face yet another group of parents, knowing that I had nothing to tell them and that the Egyptians and Syrians had not only refused to give the Red Cross lists of captured Israelis months after the cease-fire, but even to let our army chaplains search the battlefields for our dead.

But how could I say no to parents and wives who thought that if they reached me, I would, magically, have some sort of answer for them, although I knew that in their hearts some of them blamed me for the war and for our lack of preparedness. So I saw them all and for the most part they were very brave indeed. All they wanted from me was some scrap of information, a fact or two, however bitter, that they could cling to, something concrete to ease their pain. But there was nothing I could say.

I don't think I ever wanted anything as desperately as I wanted those POW lists that were dangled in front of us so long and so cruelly. There is much for which I personally shall never forgive the Egyptians or the Syrians, but above all, I shall never forgive them for withholding that information for so many days, out of sheer malice, and for trying to use the anguish of Israeli parents as a political trump card against us.

After the cease-fire and after the months of negotiations that led at last to the disengagement of troops on both fronts, when our prisoners finally returned from Syria and Egypt, the world at last learned for itself what we had already known for years: that amenities such as the Geneva Convention go by the board when Jews fall into the hands of Arabs—particularly into the hands of the Syrians—and perhaps our anxiety about our POWs was better understood. Often when I sat with those frantic parents, wives and sisters, listening to their plans for yet another petition or demonstration, and when all that I could tell them for weeks on end was that we were doing everything possible to get the lists, I thought to myself that torture by our enemies is worse than death.

By October 19, the thirteenth day of the war, although the fighting had certainly not ended, Mr. Kosygin had already made a rushed visit to Cairo. His "clients" were obviously losing the war they had begun with his assistance, and it was, therefore, not only Egyptian "face" that needed saving, but also that of the Soviet Union itself. It was bad enough that the Egyptians hadn't managed to destroy the Israeli bridgehead on the west bank of the Canal, but worse than that they now had to admit to their patron that the Israel Defense Forces were entrenched west of the Canal, some 60 miles away from Cairo, in an area that soon became known in Israel as Africa. As for the situation of the Soviet Union's other protégé, Syria, it was even graver. That being the case, the Russians did what they have always done: they began a full-scale campaign for a quick cease-fire. Never mind who started the war, and never mind who lost it. The important thing was to get the Arabs out of the mess they had got themselves into and to resuce the Egyptian and Syrian forces from total defeat.

I remember driving back from the office through Tel Aviv's blacked-out streets on one of those nights when the Brezhnev-Kissinger talks about a cease-fire were going on in Moscow and taking a silent oath that, to the extent that it depended in any way at all on me, this war would end in a peace treaty obliterating, for all time, the famous three "noes" of the Arabs declared in Khartoum after the Six-Day War, when their response to our plea that we sit down with them and negotiate was no recognition, no negotiation, no peace! I looked at the dark windows of the houses I passed and wondered behind which of them families were sitting *shiva* (the traditional first week of mourning) and behind which other families were trying to carry on as usual, although there was still no answer to the question "Where is he?" Dead somewhere in the Sinai, dead on the Golan Heights or a prisoner of war? That night I swore that I would do whatever lay in my power to bring about the peace which the Arab people needed no less than we did and which could be secured only in one way—by negotiation.

Now that we were about to be placed under extreme pressure regarding a cease-fire, I felt more strongly than ever that we must make no substantive concession of any sort that did not include direct negotiations—at any time or in any place that the Arabs chose. Not that I made light of the oil embargo with which Saudi Arabia, and other enlightened Arab states were holding the West, including the United States, to ransom, but a limit had to be set as to how accommodating we were going to be.

In the final analysis, to put it bluntly, the fate of small countries always rests with the superpowers, and they always have their own interests to guard. We would have liked the call for a cease-fire to have been postponed for a few more days so that the defeat of the Egyptian and Syrian armies would be even more conclusive than it was, and on October 21 there was every reason to believe that, given just a little more time, this would have happened. North of Ismailia we were pressing hard on the Egyptian Second Army. South of Suez we were completing the encirclement of the Egyptian Third Army. On the Golan Heights the Syrian positions on Mount Hermon had fallen to our forces. We had complete air supremacy on both fronts and thousands of prisoners. But Sadat, of course, was in a far stronger position than we were diplomatically, and the bait he held out to the United States was very tempting: its reentry into the Middle East, plus the removal of the oil embargo. Nor was the Soviet Union without its own means of persuasion. The stakes in Moscow were very high indeed. So I was not at all surprised when, early on the morning of October 22, the Security Council, meeting in an emergency session, predictably enough passed a resolution calling for a cease-fire to go into effect within twelve hours.

There was no question but that Resolution 338, passed with such indecent speed, was intended to avert the total destruction of the Egyptian and Syrian forces by us, though the pill was sugar-coated, to some extent. The resolution called for "negotiations to start between the parties concerned under appropriate auspices aimed at establishing a just and durable peace in the Middle East," but it did not spell out how this would be done. The U.S. secretary of state flew from Moscow to Jerusalem to convince me that we ought to accept the cease-fire, and we announced that we would do so. But the Syrians did not accept it at all, and although the Egyptians declared their acceptance, they did not stop shooting on October 22. The fighting went on, and we completed the encirclement of the Third Army and gained control of parts of the city of Suez.

On October 23 I made a statement in the Knesset about the cease-fire. I wanted the people of Israel to know that we had not accepted it out of military weakness, nor had we asked for it. If the Egyptians did not conform to it, I said, we would certainly not remain silent. Our position on both fronts was better than it had been when the war broke out. True, Egypt held a narrow strip on the east bank of the Suez Canal, but the Israel Defense Forces sat firmly on a large section of the Canal's west bank, and in the north, on the Golan Heights, we had occupied all the territory that had been under our control before the war and moved into a salient in Syria. Nonetheless, I said, and I meant every word with all my heart,

"Israel wants peace negotiations to start immediately and concurrently with the cease-fire. It can display the inner strength necessary to bring about an honorable peace within secure borders." But unless and until the Egyptians and Syrians felt the same way and acted accordingly, these would, of course, remain just words.

The war entered its nineteenth day with a new crisis. Knowing that the request had no chance of being accepted by us, Sadat asked that a Soviet-U.S. force be entrusted with supervising the cease-fire, and the Russians themselves made active preparations to step into that area. The story of the subsequent U.S. alert is not for me to tell. There is only one thing that I wish to say about it. I know that in the United States at that time many people assumed that the alert was "invented" by President Nixon in order to divert attention from the Watergate problem, but I didn't believe that then, and I do not believe it now. I have never claimed to be unusually perceptive about people, but I think that at this stage of my life I can probably tell when someone speaks with true conviction. I am sure that President Nixon ordered the U.S. alert on October 24, 1973, because, détente or no détente, he was not about to give in to Soviet blackmail. It was, I think, a dangerous decision, a courageous decision and a correct decision.

But it brought about an escalation of the crisis, and someone had to pay to bring about a relaxation of tension. The price demanded, needless to say from Israel, included our agreeing to permit supplies to reach the encircled Egyptian Third Army and to accept a second cease-fire that was to go into effect under the supervision of a UN force. The demand that we feed the Third Army, give it water and generally help its 20,000 soldiers recover from their defeat was not, in any way, a matter of humanitarianism. We would gladly have given them all this had the Egyptians been willing to lay down their arms and go home. But this was exactly what President Sadat wanted to avoid. He was desperately anxious not to make public within Egypt the fact that Israel had prevailed in yet another attack upon it—the more so since for a few days in October the Egyptians were intoxicated by their apparent victory over us. So once again there was the standard concern for those tender feelings of the Arab aggressor, rather than for those of the victims of Arab aggression, and we were urged to compromise in the name of "world peace."

"At least," I told the cabinet that week, "let's call things by their right name. Black is black and white is white. There is only one country to which we can turn and sometimes we have to give in to it—even when we know we shouldn't. But it is the only real friend we have, and a very powerful one. We don't have to say yes to everything, but let's call things by their proper name. There is nothing to be ashamed of when a small country like Israel, in this situation, has to give in sometimes to the United States. And when we do say yes, let's for God's sake, not pretend that it is otherwise and that black is white."

At this point the outstanding personality in the Middle East became not President Sadat, or Syrian President Assad, or Faisal or even Mrs. Meir. It was the U.S. Secretary of State, Henry Kissinger, whose efforts on behalf of peace in the area can only be termed superhuman. My own relationship with Henry Kissinger had its ups and downs. At times it became very complicated, and at times I know I annoyed and perhaps even angered him—and vice versa. But I admired his intellectual gifts, his patience and his perseverance were always limitless, and in the end we became good friends. I met and spent time in Israel with his wife, too, and liked and admired her immensely. I think that possibly one of the most impressive of Kissinger's many impressive qualities is his fantastic capacity for dealing with the minutest details of whatever problems he undertakes to solve.

When he first started on the long and rocky road that was to lead to the disengagement of forces on the Golan Heights, and we said that we could not give up certain positions on the hills near Kuneitra because to do so would mean endangering the Israeli settlements below, he was very skeptical. "You talk about those hills as though they were the Alps or the Himalayas," he said to me. "I've been to the Golan Heights and I couldn't see any Alps there." But, as he always did, he listened very attentively, learned every detail of the topography for himself, and when he was quite satisfied that we were making sense, he was prepared to spend days upon days persuading Assad that on such and such a point the Syrians must give way. And in the end they did. But all the time Kissinger went back and forth as though he had never heard of the word "fatigue."

I had one or two very difficult conversations with Kissinger regarding the Soviet and Egyptian allegations that we had violated the cease-fire. Kissinger apparently was inclined to believe this, and at one point Dinitz called from Washington to implore me to give Kissinger my personal assurance that we had done no such thing. All that week, there had been an exchange of messages between us in which President Nixon and Kissinger had asked us to yield—first on one thing, then another, then on a third—and while I understood the U.S. position in regard to the Soviet Union only too well, I found this stream of requests very disturbing. I wrote a letter to Kissinger asking him to tell us everything he wanted all at once, so that we could meet and make some decisions ourselves, rather than get a new request every few hours. So when Dinitz called in such a state, I decided to pick up the phone and talk to Kissinger, rather than send yet another letter. I said, "You can say anything you want about us and do anything you want, but we are *not* liars. The allegations are *not* true."

On October 31 I flew to Washington to try to straighten out the rather strained relationship that had come into being with Washington and to explain, in person, exactly why some of the demands being made of us were not only unfair, but unacceptable. The day before, I had gone to "Africa" myself with Dayan and Dado to visit the commanders there, get their explanations about the terrain and spend some time with the troops. We made three stops at the front, and I must say that the soldiers were all rather surprised to see me in the middle of the desert, and I myself had certainly never expected to be answering questions showered at me by Israeli boys on Egyptian territory. I spoke to large gatherings of soldiers once deep underground, once in the sand outside a tent and once in a battered Egyptian customshouse at Suez. Most of the boys' questions had to do, naturally, with the cease-fire. Why had we allowed supplies to be brought to the Third Army? Why had we agreed to a premature cease-fire? Where were our prisoners of war? I did my best to explain the facts of political life to them, and later I flew to the Golan Heights, and had the same conversation there.

I also had questions that weren't answered to my satisfaction. I was still enraged over the refusal of my socialist comrades in Europe to let the Phantoms and Skyhawks land for refueling as part of the airlift operation. One day, weeks after the war, I phoned Willy Brandt, who is much respected in the Socialist International, and said, "I have no demands to make of anyone, but I want to talk to my friends. For my own good, I need to know what possible meaning socialsim can have when not a single socialist country in all of Europe was prepared to come to the aid of the only democratic nation in the Middle East. Is it possible that democracy and fraternity do not apply in our case?"

In Washington, I spent an hour and a half with President Nixon. Afterward the press wanted to know whether Israel was being pressured to make further concessions to the Arabs. I assured them that there had been no pressure. "If so, Madame Prime Minister," said one of the reporters, "then why did you come to Washington?"

"Just to find out that there is no pressure," I said. "That in itself was worthwhile!"

The focal point of my talks with Kissinger had to do with the cease-fire lines in the south, and they were not easy or pleasant talks; but then we were not discussing easy matters. I had brought a six-point proposal, and I remember that Kissinger and I sat up practically all of one night at Blair House, where I was staying. At one stage I said to him, "You know, all we have, really, is our spirit. What you are asking me to do is to go home and help destroy that spirit, and then no aid will be necessary at all."

The text of the agreement between Israel and Egypt was signed on November 11, 1973, at Kilometer 101 of the Cairo-Suez road. It read:

1. Egypt and Israel agree to observe scrupulously the cease-fire called for by the UN Security Council.
2. Both sides agree that discussions between them will begin immediately to settle the question of the return to the October 22 positions in the framework of agreement on the disengagement and separation of forces under the auspices of the United Nations.
3. The town of Suez will receive daily supplies of food, water and medicine. All wounded civilians in the town of Suez will be evacuated.
4. There shall be no impediment to the movement of nonmilitary supplies to the east bank.
5. The Israeli checkpoints on the Cairo-Suez road will be replaced by UN checkpoints. At the Suez end of the road, Israeli officers can participate with the UN to supervise the nonmilitary nature of the cargo at the bank of the canal.
6. As soon as the UN checkpoints are established on the Cairo-Suez road, there will be an exchange of all POWs, including wounded.

For the first time in a quarter of a century there was direct, simple, personal contact between Israelis and Egyptians. They sat in tents together, hammered out details of the disengagement and shook hands. And our prisoners of war came back from Egypt, those who had been captured in the War of Attrition and those taken in the Yom Kippur War. Miraculously, they returned without a scratch on their spirits, despite everything they had gone through, although some of them wept like babies when we met. They even brought presents with them, things they made in jail, including a blue-and-white Star of David which they had knitted themselves and which had served as their flag during the long imprisonment. "Now that our 'unit' has been disbanded," a group of young officers told me, "we would like you to have it."

But we still knew nothing about our POWs in Syria, and almost every day there were military funerals for boys killed in the Sinai whose charred bodies had only now been found in the sand, identified and brought to burial. Worst of all, despite the growing feeling that perhaps this time the disengagement would grow into a real peace, the general mood in Israel was very black. From all sections of the population there came demands that the government resign, accusations that the army's poor state of preparedness was the result of faulty leadership, of complacency and of a total lack of communication between the government and the people.

A number of protest movements arose. They were different in emphasis, and they had different programs; but they shared a demand for change. And they included reservists who often expressed themselves hastily and sometimes even in a way that was painful for me. I disagreed with much of what they had to say about the past, but some of their criticism was justified. At all events, I had to hear what they had to say, and I met with many of the young people from these movements. I tried to make it easy for them to talk to me, and I came away with the feeling that they were often surprised by the difference between the woman who listened to them so attentively and the image they had of me. In that atmosphere charged by suspicion and accusation, I think they were often equally surprised by what I had to say to them.

Much of the outcry was genuine. Most of it, in fact, was a natural expression of outrage over the fatal series of mishaps that had taken place. It was not just my resignation or Dayan's that was being called for in that storm of protests; it was a call to eliminate from the scene everyone who could possibly be held responsible for what had happened and to start all over again with new people, younger people, people who were not tainted by the charge of having led the nation astray. It was an extreme reaction to the extreme situation we were in, and therefore, though it was very painful, it was understandable. But part of the outburst was vicious, and some of it was demagoguery, pure and simple, and the making of political capital by the opposition over a national tragedy.

The center of the storm was Moshe Dayan. Dayan came to my office and once again asked, "Do you want me to resign? I am prepared to do so." Once again I said no. I knew that an official commission of inquiry would have to be formed soon—as it was under the chairmanship of Supreme Court President Shimon Agranat on November 18—and certainly until it had completed its work and submitted its findings, the principle of collective cabinet responsibility was still held and was at least as important as that of ministerial responsibility. The one thing that Israel did not need at that point was a cabinet crisis. Anyhow, we had rescheduled the elections from their original October 31 date to December 31, and the nation would be able to give adequate and effective vent to its feelings then. So although I myself was tremendously tempted to resign, I thought I ought to hold on for a little longer—and so should Dayan.

Of all the members of the cabinet, Dayan was, of course, the most controversial and probably the most complicated. He is, and always has been, a man who elicits very strong responses from the public. Naturally, he has his faults, and like his virtues, they are not small ones. One of the things of which I am most proud, to be quite frank, is that for more than five years I kept together a cabinet that included not only Dayan, but also a number of men who greatly disliked and resented him. But from the start I had a good idea of the problems I was likely to face in this respect. I had known Dayan for years, and I knew that he had opposed my becoming prime minister when Eshkol died.

To his credit, I must say that when I did not support Dayan in something, he always took it very well, although he doesn't work easily with people and is used to getting his own way. In the end we became good friends, and there was not a single occasion when I could complain of any disloyalty on his part. Not once. Even on military matters, he would always come—with the chief of staff—to talk to me first. Sometimes I said to him, "I won't vote in favor of this, but you are free to take your proposal to the cabinet." But if I didn't go along with one of his ideas, he never took it any further.

It is also not true that he is a hard man. I saw him come back shattered from those agonizing funerals following the war, when children were pushed at him by mothers who shrieked, "You killed their father," and mourners shook their fists at him and called him a murderer. I know how I felt—and I know how Dayan felt. In the first days of the Yom Kippur War, he was very pessimistic and wanted to prepare the nation for the worst. He called a meeting of newspaper editors to describe to them the situation as he saw it—which was certainly not easy for him.

I kept him from resigning during the war, but I think perhaps he should have done so immediately after the Agranat Commission of Inquiry published its first preliminary report on April 2, 1974. That report cleared Dayan (and myself) of any "direct responsibility" for Israel's unpreparedness on Yom Kippur, but it dealt so harshly with the chief of staff and the head of military intelligence that Dado resigned at once. I have always suspected that Dayan might have retained his "charismatic" image—or at least some of it—had he then, publicly, stuck by his comrades-in-arms. He read that preliminary (and only partial) report in my office and, for the third time, asked me whether he should resign. "This time," I said, "it must be the decision of the party." But he was following a logic of his own, and I didn't feel that on such a weighty matter I should give him advice. Now I am sorry that I didn't, though he may not have taken it.

As for me, the commission said that on Yom Kippur morning "she decided wisely, with common sense and speedily, in favor of the full mobilization of the reserves, as recommended by the chief of staff despite
weighty political considerations, thereby performing a most important
service for the defense of the state."

CHAPTER 14

THE END OF THE ROAD

The weeks passed. The reserves were still mobilized in the south and
in the now-icy north. Even the shooting hadn't come to an end, and
the mood in Israel remained black, restive and very anxious. Kissinger
continued his efforts to secure a separation of forces between Syria and to
bring about the Geneva talks between the Egyptians, the Jordanians and
ourselves—the Syrians having announced in December that they would
not participate. Although, on the surface, we seemed to be closer to
peace than we had ever been before, the truth is that neither I nor most
other Israelis really believed, in our heart of hearts, that we would leave
Geneva with peace treaties in our hands, and we didn't go there with
many illusions or in a state of euphoria. Still, the Egyptians and Jordanians had agreed to sit in the same room with us, and that, in itself, was
something that they had never consented to do before.

The Geneva talks opened on December 21 and, as I had feared, led almost nowhere. There was no real dialogue between the Egyptians and us.
On the contrary, from the very first moment it was all too clear that nothing much had changed. The Egyptian delegation literally refused to permit its table to be placed next to ours, and the atmosphere was far from
friendly. A military agreement was obviously a necessity for the Egyptians, but peace, we realized once again, was not what they were driving
at. Still, even though no political solution came of that meeting, within a
few days, at Kilometer 101, the disengagement treaty was signed, and we
went on hoping that somehow or other a political solution could be
found.

On December 31 we held our elections. The ballots showed that the
country was not keen on changing horses in midstream, and although we
lost some votes—as did the National Religious Party—the Ma'arach still
came out as the leading bloc. But the opposition to the Ma'arach had become more forceful because the entire right wing had now combined into

a bloc of its own. A coalition would have to be formed again, and it would clearly be a backbreaking job to form it, since the religious bloc, which was a traditional coalition partner of ours, was itself deeply divided on the question of who should lead it and what its policy should be at this tremendously difficult time.

I was beginning to feel the physical and psychological effects of the draining past few months. I was dead tired and not at all sure that, in this kind of situation, I could ever succeed in forming a government—or even whether I should go on trying to do so. Not only were there problems from without, but there were also difficulties within the party. At the beginning of March I felt I couldn't go on, and I told the party that I had had enough. But I was bombarded by delegations imploring me to change my mind. It was still quite likely that war would break out again since there was still no disengagement of forces with Syria and the Syrians were continually violating the cease-fire. And again I was told that the Ma'arach would disintegrate unless I stayed on.

Sometimes it seemed to me that everything that had happened since the afternoon of October 6 had happened on one endless day—and I wanted that day to end. I was deeply distressed by the breaking down of solidarity within the inner circle of the party. People who had been ministers in my government, colleagues with whom I had worked closely throughout my years in office and who had been full partners in the formation of government policy now appeared unwilling to stand up to the barrage of unjust criticism, even slander, that was being hurled against Dayan, Galili and myself on the grounds that the three of us—without consulting others—had presumed to make crucial decisions that had allegedly led to the war. I also resented the irresponsible talk of my so-called kitchen cabinet that had supposedly replaced the government to some extent by acting as a decision-making body. This accusation was utterly without foundation. It was only natural on my part to seek the advice of people whose judgment I valued. At no time, however, did these informal consultations ever take the place of government decisions.

Nonetheless, throughout March I went on with the struggle to form a government, though, increasingly, it began to look like an impossible task, particularly in the face of growing demands for a "wall-to-wall" coalition, something to which both I and most of the party were more opposed than ever. The more I talked with my colleagues about the ongoing conflict in the party and the more I analyzed it for myself, the more I began to feel that I couldn't go on any longer. I had reached a point where I felt that without the support of the entire party (the majority was with me all

477

the time) I couldn't function as its head anymore. And the moment came when I said to myself, "This is it. I am going to resign, and other people will have to see what they can do about forming a coalition. There is a limit to what I can take, and I have now reached that limit."

During all those weeks of interminable talk, argument and bitterness, I had been getting the most moving letters of encouragement and support from people all over Israel whom I had never met but who seemed to understand what I was going through. Some of these were wounded soldiers, still in the hospital; others were parents of boys who had fallen. "Be well. Be strong. Everything will be all right," they wrote to me. I truly didn't want to fail them, but on April 10 I told the party leadership that I had had enough.

"Five years are sufficient," I said. "It is beyond my strength to continue carrying this burden. I don't belong to any circle or faction within the party. I have only a circle of one to consult—myself. And this time my decision is final, irrevocable. I beg of you not to try to persuade me to change my mind for any reason at all. It will not help." Of course, attempts were made all the same to talk me out of my decision, but they were to no avail. I was about to conclude fifty years of public service, and I knew with absolute certainty that I was doing the right thing. I had wanted to do it much earlier, but now *nothing* was going to stop me, and nothing did. My political career was over.

Still, I had to stay on as head of a caretaker government until a new cabinet could be formed. Before I left office on June 4, I was able, thank God, to tell the Knesset that a disengagement agreement with Syria had been concluded through the good offices of Dr. Kissinger. On June 5 that agreement was signed in Geneva, and our POWs returned. It meant more to me than I can ever say to have been able to welcome them back—though fewer returned from their imprisonment than we had hoped.

And then I myself went home, this time for good. The new prime minister of Israel is a sabra—Yitzhak Rabin—born in Jerusalem the year that Morris and I had come to Merhavia. There are many differences between his generation and mine—differences of style, of approach and of experience. And that is how it should be, because Israel is a country of growth in which everything moves forward. But these differences are not as significant as the similarities.

Like my generation, this generation of sabras will strive, struggle, make mistakes and achieve. Like us, they are totally committed to the development and security of the State of Israel and to the dream of a just society here. Like us, they know that for the Jewish people to remain a people, it is essential that there be a Jewish state where Jews can live as Jews, not on sufferance and not as a minority. I am certain that they will bring at least as much credit to the Jewish people everywhere as we tried to bring. And at this point I would like to add something about being Jewish. It is not only a matter, I believe, of religious observance and practice. To me, being Jewish means and has always meant being proud to be part of a people that has maintained its distinct identity for more than 2,000 years, with all the pain and torment that have been inflicted upon it. Those who have been unable to endure and who have tried to opt out of their Jewishness have done so, I believe, at the expense of their own basic identity. They have pitifully impoverished themselves.

I don't know what forms the practice of Judaism will assume in the future or how Jews, in Israel and elsewhere, will express their Jewishness 1,000 years hence. But I do know that Israel is not just some small beleaguered country in which 3,000,000 people are trying hard to survive; Israel is a Jewish state that has come into existence as the result of the longing, the faith and the determination of an ancient people. We in Israel are only one part of the Jewish nation, and not even its largest part; but because Israel exists Jewish history has been changed forever, and it is my deepest conviction that few Israelis today do not understand and accept the responsibility history has placed on their shoulders as Jews.

As for me, my life has been greatly blessed. Not only have I lived to see the State of Israel born, but I have also seen it take in and successfully absorb masses of Jews from all parts of the world. When I came to this country in 1921, its Jewish population amounted to 80,000, and the entry of each Jew depended on permission granted by the mandatory government. We are now a population of over 3,000,000 of whom more than 1,000,000 are Jews who have arrived since the establishment of the state under Israel's Law of Return, a law that guarantees the right of every Jew to settle here. I am also grateful that I live in a country whose people have learned how to go on living in a sea of hatred without hating those who want to destroy them and without abandoning their own vision of peace. To have learned this is a great art, the prescription for which is not written down anywhere. It is part of our way of life in Israel.

Finally, I wish to say that from the time I came to Palestine as a young woman, we have been forced to choose between what is more dangerous and what is less dangerous for us. At times we have all been tempted to give in to various pressures and to accept proposals that might guarantee us a little quiet for a few months, or maybe even for a few years, but that could only lead us eventually into even greater peril. We have always been faced by the question "Which is the greater danger?" And we are still in that situation or perhaps in an even graver one. The world is harsh, selfish and materialistic. It is insensitive to the sufferings of small nations. Even the most enlightened of governments, democracies that are led by decent leaders who represent fine, decent people, are not much inclined today to concern themselves with problems of justice in international relations. At a time when great nations are capable of knuckling under to blackmail and decisions are being made on the basis of big-power politics, we cannot always be expected to take their advice, and therefore, we must have the capacity and the courage to go on seeing things as they really are and to act on our own most fundamental instincts for self-preservation. So to those who ask, "What of the future?" I still have only one answer: I believe that we will have peace with our neighbors, but I am sure that no one will make peace with a weak Israel. If Israel is not strong, there will be no peace.

My vision of the future? A Jewish state in which masses of Jews from all over the world will continue to settle and to build; an Israel bound in a collaborative effort with its neighbors on behalf of all the people of this region; an Israel that remains a flourishing democracy and a society resting firmly on social justic and equality.

And now I have only one desire left: never to lose the feeling that it is I who am indebted for what has been given to me from the time that I first learned about Zionism in a small room in czarist Russia all the way through to my half century here, where I have seen my five grandchildren grow up as free Jews in a country that is their own. Let no one anywhere have any doubts about this: our children and our children's children will never settle for anything less.